A HANDLIST TO
JAMES JOYCE'S *ULYSSES*

GARLAND REFERENCE LIBRARY
OF THE HUMANITIES
(VOL. 582)

A HANDLIST TO
JAMES JOYCE'S *ULYSSES*
A Complete Alphabetical Index to the
Critical Reading Text

Prepared by Wolfhard Steppe
with Hans Walter Gabler

GARLAND PUBLISHING, INC. • NEW YORK & LONDON
1986

This volume was electronically typeset by pagina GmbH, Tübingen.

Library of Congress Cataloging in Publication Data

Steppe, Wolfhard.
A handlist to James Joyce's Ulysses.

(Garland reference library of the humanities ;
vol. 582)
Includes index.
1. Joyce, James, 1882–1941. Ulysses—Indexes.
I. Gabler, Hans Walter, 1938–   .   II. Joyce, James,
1882–1941. Ulysses.   III. Title.   IV. Series: Garland
reference library of the humanities ; v. 582.
PR6019.O9U725   1985   823'.912   84-48862
ISBN 0-8240-4749-4 (alk. paper)

Cover Design by Jonathan Billing

Printed on acid-free, 250-year-life paper

Manufactured in the United States of America

CONTENTS

INTRODUCTION

> ... words. They are not in my dictionary.
> (15.3279)

WHAT THIS BOOK IS, AND IS NOT

This book provides a handlist to James Joyce's *Ulysses*, or a complete alphabetical index to the critical reading text, that is, the text on the right-hand pages in the critical edition of 1984 and all its future reprintings.[1] The list is an unedited compilation to meet immediate needs of orientation for the new original text of *Ulysses*. Established directly from the output files generated in the computer-controlled typesetting of the critical edition, it leaves every differentiating or controlling feature of the printing intact, save for suppressing marks of punctuation, dialogue dashes, and positioning codes for paragraph indentations or insets. Specifically, it distinguishes upper and lower case, preserves accents and super- or subscripts, and gives separate entries to capitalized and noncapitalized forms as well as to distinct occurrences of the same forms in the edition's respective typefaces of roman, sloped roman, italics, full caps, and small caps. In reproducing without editorial interference what the superior text-sorting routines of the Tübingen text-processing system TUSTEP are capable of providing, it may be deemed a thoroughly unintelligent compilation. This is for the present unashamedly acknowledged, and no pretense to achievement is made for what is a mere automatized derivation from the text of *Ulysses* in computer storage.

No forms are excluded from the complete index. Although the listings of those with the highest frequency fill several columns each, they do not proportionally swell the compilation unduly. This is partly due to the circumstance that the critical edition's reference system serves to economize on space. It is also a function of the high total of entries resulting from the richness and variety of the language in *Ulysses*. Besides, the division by upper- and lower-case initials and the distinction of forms according to typeface breaks up somewhat the highest-frequency entries as, more usefully at times, it breaks up those of lower frequency. Possible uses of the typographic distinctions preserved may be found to lie in the easier recognition of certain forms or usages in specific contexts or sections of the text indexed. Owing to the manner of division adopted, only the absolute frequency of each listed form is given and no relative frequencies are indicated. The references are by episodes and line numbers within episodes, according to the reference system devised for the reading text of the critical edition and every subsequent edition that, regardless of its individual pagination, opts for the lineation of the critical edition's right-hand pages. The multiple occurrence of a form within a line is covered by a single line-reference.

Strictly, and in accordance with our epigraph, the index entries in the *Handlist* are graphic units or language tokens,

not words. From 25.545 lines of text our programs extracted 264.485 graphic units that were arranged under 39.806 entries. In their vast majority, it is true, these entries take the form of words that may directly, or indirectly by lemmatized reduction, be matched against standard dictionary listings. But lemmatization, i.e. reduction to standard base forms, or dictionary matchings are operations that from the materials provided in this *Handlist* must as yet be left to its users. For if the index is not properly a word list, it is even less a concordance, let alone a dictionary of the language of *Ulysses*. Working our listings into a concordance properly speaking – leaving aside its savage cousin the KWIC (Key Word in Context) Index bred and promoted by computer specialists – or into a *Ulysses* dictionary worthy the name would require the comprehensive and long-term application of a philologist's skills, intelligence, and sense of purpose. Unprovided with either a concordance or a dictionary, however, the user of this *Handlist* may gain both excitement and insight from exploring on his own the paths of the philologist that often enough lead to discoveries of some moment in the language universe of *Ulysses*.

GLIMPSES OF CONCORDING

1. Two objections are commonly raised against 'word' lists sorted by the computer in a purely mechanical way: they lump together different words if they are spelled alike (homographs), and they do not assemble occurrences of the same word so as to form one entry if they are spelled differently. If 'ditto', under Joyce's hands, comes out as 'do' (16.1700) and 'number' as 'no' (16.1301, 16.1249, 17.1791, 17.1869, 18.573), they will inevitably add to, and get lost within, the large entries provided mainly for other kinds of 'do' and 'no', and they will leave incomplete the entries for 'ditto' and 'number', invalidating at the same time the frequency counts for all entries concerned. A dictionary would put them in their right places and insert cross-references at the alphabetical positions defined by their actual spellings. The roman numeral 'I' (1.0) that signifies the first part of *Ulysses* is drowned among several thousand personal pronouns spelled in the same way: 'I'. These are, to be sure, separated from the pronoun 'i' adopted by H. Rumbold, Master Barber (12.419–428), which appears in a batch with Irish 'í' and Italian 'i' (12.265, 16.314). A dictionary would not only have to rearrange matters – breaking up entries, and joining others – it would moreover have to define meanings and to subdivide entries in order to specify special meanings and connotations. The 'gods' that come to Bloom's mind (8.924) are after all not quite the same as the 'gods and little fishes' appealed to by his daughter (6.88), and still less are they to be confused with those in the theatre (11.624): 'In the gods of the old Royal with little Peake.' The '*gods*' appearing in the lines taken from *Cymbeline* (9.1223), on the other hand, should be marked as part of a quotation, as belonging to a passage that is artistic language of an earlier date turned to an artistic use in a modern context. All these 'gods' are not a plural of the one 'God' so often invoked by the Dubliners in *Ulysses*. He undergoes transformations that a dictionary would have to unite with his normal name: 'Goooooooooood' is an instance (15.4716); 'Dooooooooooog' (15.4711) is another. A dictionary would separate 'ram' = 'male sheep' from 'to ram' = 'to push' and distinguish further between literal (15.30) and

1 James Joyce, *Ulysses. A Critical and Synoptic Edition*, prepared by Hans Walter Gabler with Wolfhard Steppe and Claus Melchior, vols. 1–3, New York & London: Garland Publishing, Inc., 1984.

figurative, and moreover idiomatic, uses of the verb: 'he wanted to ram it down my neck' (18.173). It would also have to account for the fact that the 'rams' marching with the lambs (12.103) have more affinity with the 'bellwethers' (12.102) marching at the opposite end of the alphabet than with the 'ram' that holds his station in the zodiac (12.360). A dictionary would go on to composite expressions and make sure, largely by means of cross-references, that rams' horns can be associated and contrasted with 'inkhorns' (12.1715). It would point out that the 'ram's horn' used as an example of crookedness (13.952) is something different from the shophar of Jewish rite – '*The rams' horns sound for silence*' (15.1619) – and different as well from the '*ramshorns*' prominent on the forehead of sir Frederick Falkiner (15.1165), an excellent occasion, by the way, to comment on the theoretical borderland between genitive group and compound. It would finally put Cissy Caffrey's 'jaspberry ram' (13.272) on its proper shelf in the larder of *Ulysses*, next to Molly Bloom's 'black currant jam' (18.940).

2. When dealing with hyphenated compounds or compounds spelled in one word ('publichouse', 'musichall'), compilers of word indexes have usually thought it desirable to have special entries or cross-references accounting for the second elements.[2] They seem to consider the compound as something to be cut up. Quite to the contrary, a dictionary would take care to bring together the elements that make up a compound that is not spelled as one graphic unit: 'black currant jam', 'burned cork moustache' (13.276f.),[3] 'bread and butter' (8.40), 'half and half' (12.1052-55), 'beef to the heels' (4.403, 8.617f.). 'Fair day and all the beef to the heels were in', writes Milly Bloom (4.402f.), and some readers seem to have taken this to imply that the Irish peasants, unmindful of their crops, just wait for fair weather to drive to the nearest town in order to have themselves photographed: 'Quel beau temps', reads the French translation; 'Ganz phantastischer Tag', a more recent German one, while the Italian version makes it 'una bella giornata'. They have overlooked that there is another compound involved, and thus they have picked the wrong meaning for its first element – the wrong entry in the dictionary, so to speak – for 'Fair'; it is of course the *fair-day* (*OED s.v.* Fair *sb.*[1] 2.) that attracts the farmers.

3. That a dictionary has to provide explanations or definitions for rare words and expressions will seem quite natural to the reader who looks them up because he does not know them. He will be glad to find 'beef to the heels' and 'cessile air' (14.1409) explained, and quoted from *Ulysses*, in the *Supplement* to the *OED*.[4] A dictionary dealing with *Ulysses*,

however, will also have to cope with words for which it might fail to find a satisfactory explanation or any other evidence at all; 'kinnatt' (13.601) might be such a word. While the *Supplement* can afford to ignore it altogether, a dictionary to *Ulysses* would have to state its failure, thereby still giving an important piece of information, and a challenge, to the student of English. But it is not only the rare and obscure words that deserve attention. The student will also like to learn how everyday words are used, and whether they are used in a particular sense. A 'finger' can be a measure, something like the breadth of a finger (*OED s.v.* Finger *sb.* 5.a.), and the reader has a right to be told that this particular use of 'finger' is present in *Ulysses* (13.160). Bloom slams the carriage door 'twice' (6.10), but the sailor, demonstrating the marksmanship of Simon Dedalus' namesake, does not shout twice when the text seems to say so; having just shouted 'once' (16.398), he now shouts only once more, for the second time: 'Pom! he shouted twice.' (16.401; cf. *OED s.v.* Twice 1.c. See also 17.834). 'Stately', the first word in the book, is commonly known to be an adjective. Anthony Burgess remarks on it: "Sometimes . . . one wonders if Joyce meant it adverbially."[5] The *OED* (*s.v.* Stately B.) does indeed record the form 'stately' in adverbial senses, though it has no quotations from modern texts. Joyce definitely wanted to have an adverb when he made William Brayden pass 'statelily up the staircase' (7.45). The adverb here was at once misprinted, and the corrupt form 'stately', in the position of an adverb, was swallowed by English-speaking readers ever since. This might be interpreted as evidence that English usage would after all admit of an adverb 'stately', and the question raised by Burgess would be open again.

4. Usually the maker of a word list or concordance has to deal with a certain amount of *types*, i.e. different words as defined by their meanings, while his text contains a much larger number of *tokens*, i.e. individual occurrences of these different words. In *Ulysses*, however, and this might go for many other texts written or spoken, there are *tokens* that belong to more than one *type*. 'Humour wet and dry', is Stephen's mental comment on his having stood drinks to some pressmen; bottles and jokes have been cracked. A dictionary of the English language, intending to document the different meanings of 'humour', would simply reject such a quotation as it cannot be filed under any one particular meaning. The meaning of the phrase depends on the condition that two different meanings of the word, or rather two different words, are understood. There are other cases in which one meaning is clearly felt to predominate, so as to be the 'literal' meaning appropriate to the narrative context, while a secondary meaning provides a humorous connotation: 'pressgang' (7.625), 'to show her understandings' (13.917), 'The unfair sex' (8.269), perhaps also 'nautical chest' (16.726). In Mulligan's remark on Bannon's acquaintance with Milly Bloom ('Photo girl he calls her') a bawdy meaning is camouflaged by a perfectly harmless one (1.686): 'Snapshot, eh? Brief exposure.' Short-time exposure of a film, exhibition of briefs: the meanings evoked, if taken apart, would exclude each other, but the joke works only if both are understood and felt to be present.

---

2 Miles L. Hanley, *Word Index to James Joyce's Ulysses* (Madison, 1937), p. xii, proposes cross-references. Leslie Hancock, *Word Index to James Joyce's Portrait of the Artist* (Carbondale & Edwardsville, 1967), pp. 141-145, has a section listing second elements only. Wilhelm Füger, *Concordance to James Joyce's 'Dubliners'* (Hildesheim & New York, 1980), pp. 843-856, supplies a Reverse Index, which groups compounds containing the same second elements together.

3 *The Oxford English Dictionary* (Reissue of *A New English Dictionary on Historical Principles*, 1882-1928; Oxford, 1933) lists all kinds of moustaches in men and women, and in cats, seals, fish, birds, and monkeys. Curiously enough no instance is cited of a 'figurative' moustache painted on an otherwise beardless face. One may wonder whether 'burned cork' should signify a pigment (cf. 'burnt sienna', 'burnt umber') or whether Cissy Caffrey simply held a cork stopper into the flame until it was scorched and fit to be used as a crayon.

4 *A Supplement to the Oxford English Dictionary*, ed. R. W. Burch-field, vols. I-III (A-Scz; Oxford, 1972-82). The *Supplement* takes its quotations "from the Random House edition" (vol. I, p. xviii); the references given show this to mean the edition of 1934, which is the most corrupt of all authorized editions ever published.

5 Anthony Burgess, *Joysprick* (London, 1973), p. 70.

5. People in *Ulysses* use the staircase (7.45ff., 10.1019ff.), as there do not appear to be any lifts in the book. There is a 'foodlift' in the Burton (8.690), but no lift or elevator to carry people is to be found in the whole of Dublin. Patrick Dignam, however, has departed to a place where they have such a machine, but that is likely to go undetected as it is spelled Sanskrit fashion: 'ālāvātār' (12.354). A dictionary would try to reduce words of this kind to normalized forms and, while leaving behind cross-references, enter and describe them under such headings as might make them accessible to those students too who do not know them beforehand. Thus 'Plamtroo' and 'Trumplee' (17.640f.) could meet under the sign of 'Plumtree', and the entry for 'bottom' would be enriched by a 'beeoteetom' (13.263). Miss Douce's disappointed 'hopk' (11.712), made up from 'cork' and 'hope', could be claimed by both its constituents. Molly Bloom, even in her silent thoughts, is a bad speller, and this is why the present *Handlist* has no entries for 'carat' and for 'viaticum' (cf. *OED s.v.* Viaticum 1.); the student relying on it will come to the conclusion that these words are not attested at all in *Ulysses*. Molly has disfigured them: 'and when the priest was going by with the bell bringing the vatican to the dying ... still it must have been pure 18 carrot gold' (18.760f., 18.869f.; cf. 'vaunted' for 'vaulted', 'place' for 'plaice', 18.899 and 18.939). If the user of this *Handlist* wants to know whether the phrase 'off with you!' is contained somewhere in the text, he may work this out by starting simultaneously from the various entries for 'off' ('Off', *off*), 'with', and 'you', and by trying to match the references there given. A dictionary would devote a special entry, or subentry, to just this phrase (cf. *OED s.v.* Off A.9.b.), and there would be found also its grammatical transformation (13.250): 'Edy told him no, no and to be off now with him ...'

6. A tramdriver who has a 'pugnose' (5.132) is a 'pugnosed' man (8.349; cf. 15.192, 15.4347), and a Jewish businessman said to belong to 'the bottlenosed fraternity' (12.1086) may be assumed to have a *bottle-nose* which can be found in the *OED*, though not in *Ulysses*. The *OED*, on the other hand, lists an adjective *button-nosed* with the possible meaning "(*b*) having a small roundish nose" (old "Supplement" *s.v.* Button *sb.* 12.), while a noun that might go with the adjective is not attested. It may at last be supplied from *Ulysses*: Mrs Dignam is said to have just such a *button-nose*. The word, it is true, does not appear in its own shape; it has to be inferred from the context (13.114f.): 'you have a beautiful face but your nose? That would suit Mrs Dignam because she had a button one.' — In the *Supplement* to the *OED*, which discards a taboo that had restricted the editors of the original volumes, four-letter words are no longer ignored, and *Ulysses* has furnished quotations. One of them concerns 'cunt' used in a transferred sense that rather ennobles it: 'the grey sunken cunt of the world' (see 4.227f.). According to this *Handlist*, this should be the word's unique occurrence in *Ulysses*. And yet it is there at least once more, in transparent disguise: 'See you in tea' (15.1895), runs a line sung by the Prison Gate Girls. The word in question is here neither spelled out, nor misspelled, nor otherwise transmuted, but still it is incorporated in the text and makes itself understood.[6] A dictionary to *Ulysses* aspiring to be complete

and exhaustive would certainly try to find out and to register such cases in which a word makes what could be called an undercover appearance.

7. While this *Handlist* draws on the critically established reading text alone, a dictionary devoted to *Ulysses* would also have to make use of some of the information provided by the synoptic text in the critical edition (which documents the growth of the text) and by the apparatus. Readings that were canceled or superseded in the course of the textual development — in the genetic display of the synoptic text this would mean: text enclosed between square, pointed, or wavy brackets — might still be interesting for the student. Where we now read, e.g., 'What compensated in the false balance of her intelligence for these and such deficiencies ...' (17.688f.), Joyce had started by writing 'outweighed' instead of 'compensated'; 'outweighed' was deleted *currente calamo*, and it never fitted with what was to follow. Still, a dictionary should have a record of the word, which does not occur anywhere else in the final text. The student might furthermore like to learn which readings in the critically established text are editorial emendations of authorial readings judged to be mistakes. Joyce wrote, e.g., 'MXMIV' for 'MCMIV' (17.99), 'Premonstratesians' for 'Premonstratensians' (12.1681). A reader depending on this *Handlist* alone might like to make a point of the fact that 'agnathia' and *prognathic*', otherwise probably not very common in fictional literature, do indeed occur in *Ulysses* (14.963, 15.2151); a dictionary would have to tell him that Joyce, perhaps influenced by Italian orthography, misspelled them 'agnatia' and *prognatic*'. Less attention would be paid to corruptions that went into the hitherto received text; the 'phila' and the 'sidevalue' listed in Hanley's *Word Index*, e.g., are simply misprints for 'Phial' and 'side. Value' (11.691, 16.1277). The case is different for the word 'Neopoetic', which was miscopied, probably misread, by an amanuensis from Joyce's own word 'Uropoetic' (15.4388). A meaning, maybe a modernistic meaning, can be attached to it, and for more than sixty years 'Neopoetic' has held a place in a highly influential book. In the play *La Leçon* by Eugène Ionesco[7] the professor asks his pupil to answer in several real or imaginary languages (it is easy, for they are all exactly like French), and ever and again he hits upon *néo-espagnol*. Who is to rule out that this might go back, directly or indirectly, to a neologism created inadvertently by a scribe who could not make out what a great author had written?

H. W. G.   W. St.

The present *Handlist* was processed at the Zentrum für Datenverarbeitung of the University of Tübingen by routines of the program system TUSTEP, designed and maintained by Wilhelm Ott and his team. Wilhelm Ott, Kuno Schälkle, and Harald Fuchs helped me in every respect. With Harald Beck I discussed some of the points touched on in the preceding paragraphs. To Hans Walter Gabler I owe the privilege of having been in the team that worked on the critical edition of *Ulysses*, to which this *Handlist* is a kind of an appendix; I thank him for it.

Lustheim   W. St.
October 1984

---

6 An unfinished limerick of Mulligan's that has not gone into the final version of the book breaks off with 'blunt' (448.13 in the critical edition). The rhyme-word insinuated is easily guessed.

7 Eugène Ionesco, *Théâtre*, 1 (Paris, 1954).

NOTE

The second impression of the Critical and Synoptic Edition of *Ulysses* issued in 1986 incorporates some modifications and corrections. In the reading text, consequently, it differs in a few places from the reading-text version from which this *Handlist* was processed. The following survey should help the user of the *Handlist* to adjust the information given to the slightly altered circumstances.

Several entries are easily remedied by simply adopting the changed forms of the new text: 'bee's' for 'bees'' (15.4045), 'beurla' for 'beurla' (9.367), 'Hurhausdirektorpresident' for 'Hurhausdirektorpräsident' (12.566), 'irreducible' for 'irreductible' (17.762), 'Ueberallgemein' for 'Überallgemein' (12.569). The emended spelling 'ferrule' for 'ferule' (1.628), however, requires the entry also to be moved up in the alphabetical sequence.

In further instances, the changed matter needs to be shifted from one entry to another existing one. To account for the new readings 'and' for 'atolls' (17.201), 'there' for 'them' (10.175), 'there' for 'then' (11.541), and 'what's' for 'what' (12.1163), their reference indications should be transferred from their former entries to their actual ones, and at the same time the frequency counts given should be adjusted; thus, the frequencies of 'and', 'there', and 'what's' increase by one or, in the case of 'there', by two, while those for 'atolls', 'them', 'then', and 'what' decrease correspondingly.

Some new readings, while detracting matter (and frequency) from existing entries, themselves go to form new entries: 'Bueñas' for 'Buenas' (15.216), 'gobbles' for 'gabbles' (15.2433). Elsewhere entries become eliminated. Thus, 'breeches'' (15.2859) and 'Mecklenburg' (15.109) disappear, as the amended word forms merge with the adjacent entries for 'breeches' and 'Mecklenburgh' (raising their frequencies). Further invalid entries are those for 'broodmare' (8.345), 'dragonscaly' (2.74), and 'Saltgreen' (10.877), since these compounds have been separated in the new text. The constituents set free should go to the existing entries for 'brood', 'dragon', 'green', 'mare' and 'Salt', while 'scaly' forms a new entry of its own. The entries for 'im' and 'barr' are no longer valid as the new text redivides the Irish words in question as 'i mbarr' (15.1771); while 'mbarr' becomes an entry by itself, the Irish 'i' goes to an already existing one. Finally, the change 'nux' for 'mix.' (15.1652) requires eliminating the entry 'mix' and creating a new entry 'nux'.

From the phrase that originally read 'but as in a glass darkly' (12.349), the new text has dropped the word 'but'; as there is another instance of 'but' in the same line, the reference 12.349 still remains with the entry for 'but'; only its frequency count is to be corrected. The space caused by the deletion of this 'but' in line 12.349 was adjusted by moving down the word 'that' from the end of the preceding line 12.348; the old reference 12.348 must therefore be canceled from the entry 'that'. There is, however, no need to add the new reference 12.349: it is already present, due to a second occurrence of the word in the same line.

The lines 11.843–846 have been reordered and thus redivided in the new text; some of the references to them are therefore inaccurate within the range of these four lines. The first of Don Emile Pope Hennessy's speeches in "Circe" has been canceled from the reading text (39 words); hence, all references to the lines 15.1914–1917 are obsolete, and the fre-

quencies of the following entries should be reduced by one each: 'all', 'and', 'appears', 'big', 'Bloom', 'covered', 'Don', 'down', 'Emile', 'eyes', 'footboden', 'Franz', 'geese', 'grand', 'gravy', 'hauberk', 'helm', 'Hennessy', 'his', 'in', 'indignation', 'medieval', 'noble', 'of', 'on', 'Patrizio', 'pig', 'Pope', 'Put', 'Rupert', 'to', 'two', 'volant', 'wild', 'with', 'with', 'your'. The entries for 'disowns' and for 'Jude' (the German word for 'jew') should be canceled altogether.

Finally, the remarks on statistics made above (p. vii) require correction. The new reading text, running to 25.541 lines, provides 264.448 graphic units arranged under 39.801 entries.

February 1986   W. St.

ARRANGEMENT

Capitals precede lower-case letters, accented letters precede unaccented ones. Roman, italics, sloped roman and small caps are arranged in this order.

Clusters of initials or of one-letter abbreviations are listed as units. (Full stops are suppressed.)

Symbols and arabic numerals precede the alphabet. Arabic numerals connected with symbols or abbreviations are listed as units, as are composite expressions denoting weights, measures, amounts of money, or the time of the day.

Frequencies are indicated within parentheses. References are to episode (large numerals) and line numbers (small numerals).

The episodes of *Ulysses*:

1	Telemachus
2	Nestor
3	Proteus
4	Calypso
5	Lotus Eaters
6	Hades
7	Aeolus
8	Lestrygonians
9	Scylla and Charybdis
10	Wandering Rocks
11	Sirens
12	Cyclops
13	Nausicaa
14	Oxen of the Sun
15	Circe
16	Eumaeus
17	Ithaca
18	Penelope

Symbols and Numerals

* * * (18) 10 206 227 257 298 337 367 397 464 584 642 717 799 881 955 1042 1100 1121 1175

— (35) 1 599 7 871 1006 1050 1071 8 964 977 9 444 445 1014 12 14 15 595 1461 13 188 511 579 659 770 14 796 975 1012 1071 1075 1229 1230 1249 1306 1430 15 952 16 955 1261 1838

. (1) 17 2332

£ (1) 17 1939

£-s-d (2) 17 1457

£1 (2) 17 1545 18 1523

£1-7-0 (1) 17 958

£2 (1) 17 1545

£5 (2) 17 166 2001

£18-14-6 (1) 17 1863

£42 (1) 17 1501

£60 (1) 17 1660

£64 (1) 17 1666

£100 (1) 16 950

£133-10-0 (1) 17 1860

£200 (1) 16 1240

£299-10-0 (1) 17 1859

£300 (1) 16 1135

£430 (1) 17 1858

£462-10-0 (1) 17 1858

£500 (2) 17 1856 1858

£800 (1) 17 1663

£900 (1) 17 1864

£1200 (1) 17 1661

£10000 (1) 18 229

£1000000 (1) 17 1697

£5000000 stg (1) 17 1690

£ 2-19-3 (2) 17 1478

£ s d (3) 8 38 16 88 1076

+ (1) 16 1242

+ (1) 17 1782

0 (1) 17 450

0-0-1 (4) 17 1459 1461 1463 1469

0-0-2 (1) 17 1466

0-0-3 (2) 17 1458 1471

0-0-4 (3) 17 1470 1473 1474

0-0-7 (1) 17 1464

0-1-0 (2) 17 1465 1472

0-1-6 (1) 17 1460

0-2-0 (1) 17 1467

0-2-8 (1) 17 1468

0-4-9 (1) 17 1458

0-5-0 (1) 17 1462

0-16-6 (1) 17 1476

1 (57) 15 1632 16 1279 1280 1281 17 193 270 480 590 625 740 909 911 983 1203 1453 1458 1459 1460 1462 1464 1465 1466 1467 1468 1470 1471 1472 1473 1474 1514 1520 1521 1604 1675 1676 1682 1778 1806 1819 2275 2289 18 60 190 371 551 554 579 967 1232 1357 1403 1492 1529 1545

1-7-0 (2) 17 1460 1475

1-7-6 (1) 17 1459

1/8 (1) 16 1257

½ (1) 18 1354

½d (1) 17 1694

⅓ (1) 17 1662

¼ (1) 18 344

¼d (3) 17 1693 1694 1939

⅙ (1) 17 1660

1 C P (1) 17 111

1½ (1) 17 374

1d (4) 17 578 580 1694 1814

1s (1) 18 1007

1s 4d (1) 17 1694

1st (3) 17 1876 18 479 1192

1st (5) 17 1119 18 367 1360 1450 1501

2 (46) 14 1540 15 1770 16 1280 17 98 625 909 913 1385 1447 1448 1463 1505 1520 1521 1568 1604 1654 1694 1777 1778 1808 1809 1816 1981 2076 18 249 258 344 372 539 631 636 730 925 1016 1032 1070 1232 1320 1365 1404 1430 1492 1529 1545 1595

2/- (2) 17 308 981

2/6 (2) 17 394 18 63

⅔ (1) 17 1761

2.59 p m (1) 17 1678

2 lb (1) 18 941

2½ (1) 16 1284

2½% (1) 17 1663

2d (3) 16 1700 17 580 1694

2nd (4) 17 1854 1873 1877 18 586

2nd (3) 17 1123 18 389 1396

2s 8d (1) 17 1694

3 (20) 16 1280 17 193 740 1449 1778 1796 1799 1807 18 143 344 471 609 760 774 943 1109 1151 1231 1318 1545

3.15 p m (1) 17 628

3.33 a m (1) 17 656

3 hr 8 m p m (1) 17 1677

3rd (1) 18 362

4 (17) 11 517 16 1280 1281 17 632 740 1377 1521 1681 18 143 474 756 895 927 1109 1179 1219 1545

4.46 a m (1) 17 1336

4 a m (1) 6 788

4 oz (1) 17 601

4% (1) 17 1864

4d (2) 17 1694 18 6

4th (2) 17 71 1841

5 (24) 15 1652 16 1280 1281 17 98 469 472 485 1391 1431 1511 1777 1981 2076 2171 2280 2282 18 587 895 1109 1179 1280 1327 1511 1545

5/- (3) 17 394 18 946 1289

5 ft 9½ inches (1) 17 2003

5 yrs (1) 16 1278

5⁵⁄₁₁ (1) 17 918

5% (2) 17 1661 1689

6 (10) 17 179 448 861 967 1511 1750 1906 1912 18 1327 1512

6/- (1) 18 466

6½d (1) 17 579

6d (1) 17 1791

6th (1) 17 2304

7 (7) 10 543 17 71 1581 1680 2001 18 552 1522

7 (1) 12 415

7/6 (1) 17 1829

7/6 (1) 15 1579

7½d (1) 18 1555

7s (1) 18 1430

7th (1) 18 1317

7th (1) 17 1106

8 (8) 12 1729 17 329 861 2253 2275 2276 18 329 1319

8/6 (2) 17 1582 18 1497

8.29 p m (1) 17 656

8.35 a m (1) 15 4738

8 87 (1) 17 321

8½ in (1) 17 1818

8d (1) 17 1694

8s (1) 18 1320

8th (2) 18 330 389

9 (9) 12 1729 17 98 329 1074 1429 2253 2281 2289 18 269

9 (1) 16 1249

9.15 (1) 4 521

9.20 (1) 4 522

9.23 (1) 4 522

9.24 (1) 4 523

9 in (2) 17 1818

9 st 4 lbs (1) 16 1279

9th (2) 17 1074

10 (13) 12 1729 17 329 968 1047 1116 1564 2254 2278 2282 18 269 284 1183 1317

10/- (3) 17 394 1535 1723

10.20 a m (1) 17 626

10 in (2) 17 1818

10th (1) 17 1404

10th (1) 18 401

11 (7) 15 1658 17 339 393 586 2282 18 1307

11/- (1) 17 586

11/- (1) 8 91

11/6 (1) 18 448

11 in (1) 17 1819

11 p m (1) 6 788

11d (1) 18 1555

12 (1) 12 235

12 (1) 12 420

12.25 (1) 15 2191

12 in (2) 17 1819

12½ (1) 17 171

13 (3) 12 33 17 98 1377

13½ (1) 17 450

14 (5) 10 1063 17 130 330 411 948

14 A (2) 12 802 1493

14 C P (1) 17 110

14 h (1) 17 1578

15 (12) 4 199 16 1301 17 140 178 865 1516 2277 2288 18 400 887 1064 1327

15/- (1) 17 1817

15th (1) 17 881

16 (10) 10 376 16 675 17 145 447 448 450 1176 1455 18 1216 1575

17 (4) 7 652 17 627 1431 1454

17½ (1) 17 450

18 (3) 17 591 2282 18 870

18/6 (1) 18 1497

18th (2) 16 1391 17 2275

19 (3) 17 93 602 1087

20 (14) 15 1651 16 1280 1281 17 1662 1665 1761 18 231 424 823 992 1236 1328 1408 1462

20/- (1) 17 1817

21 (4) 17 655 1336 1376 2105

22 (4) 17 168 453 2105 18 1051

23 (5) 17 600 1449 1559 2105 18 1328

24 (1) 18 1328

25 (1) 17 1857

26 (3) 17 168 423 952

27 (6) 15 731 1231 17 623 626 629 2280

27th (1) 17 921

27th (1) 18 350

28 (1) 18 573

28 in (1) 17 1818

29 (6) 10 946 12 36 14 1301 17 480 969 2280

29½ in (1) 17 1818
30 (7) 14 1301 15 1653 17 422 579 969 1546 2067
30/- (1) 18 1523
31 (3) 14 1302 17 969 1862
32 (5) 15 1605 17 1691 1694 1805 1813
33 (2) 17 1075 18 475
34 (1) 4 199
35 (3) 12 235 17 2258 18 475
36 (1) 17 2258
37 (1) 17 2258
38 (1) 17 454
40 (3) 17 2002 18 825 1127
40 (1) 15 1574
42 (1) 17 578
43 (1) 17 1730
45 (2) 17 1730 18 484
45° (1) 17 2304
'46 (1) 2 269
46 (3) 17 420 2080 2257
'47 (1) 12 1366
47 (3) 17 420 2080 2257
48 (3) 17 420 2080 2257
49 (3) 17 420 2080 2257
50 (3) 17 1676 18 494 887
50 (1) 15 1579
50° (1) 17 271
52 (1) 17 1869
53rd (1) 17 2303
54 (3) 17 449 482
57 C (1) 10 217
60 (1) 17 1858
62 (1) 17 142
65 (2) 17 1546 1858
65 C (1) 15 4336
66 C (1) 15 4336
70 (3) 17 449 456 1760
72 (1) 17 270
77 (1) 12 1890
78 (1) 12 1890
79 (1) 12 1890
80 (2) 12 1890 18 753
80 lbs (1) 17 1706
82 (1) 17 2055
85 (1) 8 142
88 (4) 6 162 18 1326 1327
88 6 (1) 17 321
89 (2) 17 1785 18 1327
90 (1) 17 1785
90% (1) 17 226
91 (1) 17 1785
'92 (1) 16 1243
93 (1) 18 555
100 (5) 17 740 1050 1689 1791 18 753
106 (1) 17 1376
IIO (1) 8 101
113th (1) 17 1030
120 (1) 17 1655
159 (1) 12 1889
164 (1) 16 1255
179 (1) 12 228
210 (1) 17 1196
212° (1) 17 271
221 (1) 17 457
242 (1) 17 749
250 (1) 17 1659
260 (1) 17 34
266 A D (1) 17 35
279 (1) 2 11

374 (1) 17 454
432 (1) 17 34
646 (1) 17 455
714 (1) 17 457
900 (1) 17 1047
969 (1) 17 458
999 (1) 17 1519
1000 (4) 16 1277 1286 17 442 1075
1190 (1) 17 456
1534 (2) 10 409 12 1861
1763 (1) 7 739
1820 (1) 17 429
1822 (1) 17 1404
1837 (1) 17 429
1849 (1) 10 1281
1852 (1) 17 1876
1855 (1) 17 1682
1860 (1) 10 831
1865 (1) 17 1638
1866 (2) 2 303 17 1681
1870 (1) 17 2276
1874 (1) 17 1659
1877 (1) 17 393
1878 (1) 17 1683
1880 (2) 17 1195 1635
1882 (1) 17 1641
1883 (1) 17 452
1884 (2) 17 48 60
1885 (3) 17 51 60 1645
1886 (10) 15 2400 17 53 61 623 627 629 1071 1362 1788 1790
1887 (2) 17 468 1260
1888 (7) 17 55 61 411 447 480 1640 1654
1889 (2) 17 865 2277
1891 (1) 17 480
1892 (6) 17 57 61 423 471 481 1781
1893 (8) 17 58 61 177 422 481 483 2280 2281
1894 (3) 17 481 483 2281
1896 (1) 17 1336
1898 (2) 17 144 980
1899 (1) 17 1804
1900 (1) 12 420
1901 (3) 17 794 1051 1708
1903 (7) 9 599 17 948 952 1454 1862 2170 2288
1904 (8) 3 181 10 376 17 61 453 1377 1449 1455
1914–1921 (1) 18 1611
1920 (2) 17 448 454
1936 (1) 17 449
1952 (1) 17 455
2000 (1) 17 1655
2004 (1) 17 1791
2400 (1) 17 165
3000 (2) 16 1277 1287
3072 A D (1) 17 459
5000 ft (1) 17 1045
5427 (1) 15 1785
6617 (1) 17 99
8000 (1) 17 187
20000 (2) 17 179 1655
81396 B C (1) 17 461
83300 (1) 17 460
500000 W H P (1) 17 1714
4386035 (1) 17 1707
57000000000000 (1) 17 1047
??? (1) 7 512
&c (3) 10 56 600 1239
† (2) 17 35 794
———— (2) 17 1477

A

À (1) 14 1545
à (9) 3 170 234 8 883 15 4090 4103 4576 16 44 342 1889
A (549) 1 2 22 33 51 59 73 95 108 170 172 185 200 227 245 248 256 267 291 312 319 396 404 453 518 629 640 656 675 680 741 742 2 8 15 22 24 32 41 43 55 61 86 98 100 118 147 205 217 227 242 249 286 359 370 378 386 390 392 394 403 443 3 11 36 48 74 82 109 114 116 124 152 153 219 227 276 286 294 303 311 320 328 331 378 390 393 472 476 482 4 56 93 94 97 145 158 186 218 219 222 224 251 308 392 429 447 465 477 523 544 549 5 6 75 93 131 233 239 274 307 343 475 6 25 70 126 129 133 175 180 240 243 252 282 288 289 308 314 322 325 326 385 411 421 429 439 470 481 507 540 541 565 589 674 703 708 773 790 807 902 907 949 970 981 7 64 69 78 84 142 161 195 232 270 303 369 414 443 536 549 558 560 646 648 657 759 766 781 860 874 882 955 965 968 969 983 8 1 5 37 123 235 295 368 379 406 411 621 637 656 658 659 663 689 759 764 789 890 894 910 934 1008 1027 1075 9 2 3 7 130 164 211 228 232 269 310 347 361 374 406 464 485 503 509 541 548 597 768 818 828 876 928 944 974 1034 1121 1157 1203 1208 1214 10 7 25 36 65 76 98 125 164 183 199 228 238 250 251 252 277 288 294 315 327 391 520 542 604 652 725 726 794 808 809 816 826 829 858 890 1166 1220 11 5 8 21 31 47 85 97 153 314 321 323 384 470 502 590 591 612 630 631 642 663 822 823 878 917 943 945 959 1016 1043 1082 1098 1104 1203 1234 1237 1252 1273 12 20 70 163 199 208 531 534 652 658 897 1055 1058 1068 1104 1109 1163 1219 1325 1332 1338 1422 1489 1514 1557 1619 1666 1774 1814 13 28 35 150 188 325 360 526 578 746 774 793 933 1076 1166 1264 1286 14 61 74 214 253 309 408 764 782 784 806 835 930 1037 1043 1080 1136 1150 1203 1302 1359 1362 1371 1394 1419 1427 1446 15 167 234 293 428 495 518 699 712 775 790 822 846 985 999 1093 1095 1153 1156 1227 1234 1262 1278 1313 1455 1458 1461 1463 1465 1467 1468 1535 1645 1758 1833 1870 1875 1877 1922 1967 1974 2144 2254 2331 2562 2575 2615 2651 2784 2786 2944 3084 3092 3093 3097 3105 3110 3141 3149 3174 3193 3319 3358 3465 3484 3545 3563 3748 4272 4281 4471 4521 4594 4600 4758 4779 4808 4950 16 78 112 185 260 325 345 406 471 536 699 940 959 1085 1101 1109 1235 1298 1349 1388 1625 1820 17 84 273 278 375 424 577 603 865 866 888 951 1211 1281 1303 1335 1375 1568 1617 1674 1687 1690 1694 1696 1710 1714 1718 1720 1724 1726 1775 1841 2010 2074 2092 2102 2245
A (10) 7 1057 8 1051 9 726 1173 11 590 12 917 14 650 16 489 17 640 1391
A (81) 15 14 15 25 26 29 33 35 37 50 100 139 145 156 212 222 247 248 289 299 300 312 314 335 365 683 726 748 903 929 931 934 1005 1038 1139 1173 1178 1268 1296 1328 1329 1399 1407 1469 1554 1558 1565 1584 1587 1811 1953 2034 2035 2040 2053 2076 2150 2167 2174 2263 2277 2570 2677 2697 2727 2734 3414 3620 3726 3952 3974 3990 4111 4161 4220 4328 4457 4548 4672 4945 4967
a (5321) 1 1 2 20 24 32 41 50 52 57 59 61 62 67 69 70 77 97 102 105 106 107 112 117 130 136 143

146 154 155 156 163 182 206 210 233 249 256 257
268 270 272 284 291 296 299 312 316 322 331 333
338 339 340 363 368 375 378 380 390 398 399 401
405 413 415 418 426 434 436 442 443 444 446 450
451 475 477 478 480 482 483 498 504 515 548 561
572 575 577 579 582 583 588 594 605 610 611 612
615 617 619 623 625 638 641 652 661 662 666 676
679 680 684 688 703 716 724 732 739 742 **2** 4 16
26 28 31 32 39 41 44 46 47 48 54 61 67 70 71 73 75
85 87 94 111 115 116 118 126 127 129 130 139 141
145 148 154 160 163 164 169 176 191 202 208 224
258 263 266 272 277 289 290 291 295 303 312 313
314 318 321 329 335 348 352 375 377 378 379 390
395 402 416 425 430 443 **3** 6 8 11 14 36 42 46 52
53 59 64 71 77 79 82 93 96 97 106 115 120 121 122
128 130 132 143 144 147 151 154 155 164 175 184
188 190 197 212 221 222 236 240 242 245 248 255
256 275 277 284 286 287 289 301 304 307 315 316
318 321 324 331 332 333 334 336 337 342 346 347
349 354 355 356 357 362 363 371 394 399 406 411
412 415 418 422 429 430 438 446 450 456 468 469
471 473 476 479 484 495 500 503 504 505 **4** 2 4
9 15 18 29 31 37 44 45 51 53 58 62 63 76 78 80 85
86 88 90 91 93 99 101 109 110 115 118 130 131 132
137 147 150 153 154 161 162 166 168 177 181 195
197 203 210 212 215 223 224 232 237 241 243 251
262 271 291 296 302 305 317 318 321 322 331 333
352 376 380 384 385 386 387 389 390 391 394 403
404 405 406 425 426 433 435 451 452 453 457 460
469 475 476 489 490 498 502 503 504 518 529 544
5 5 6 8 14 15 20 25 32 38 41 49 52 56 60 67 74 77
79 101 109 110 124 136 151 162 163 170 179 185
187 196 213 218 225 231 232 233 234 235 239 250
251 255 262 263 269 272 274 285 287 296 297 299
302 303 304 305 307 308 309 311 315 316 321 333
335 345 348 352 354 360 362 364 370 376 377 382
392 396 400 406 408 410 419 453 454 458 460 470
475 478 480 485 500 502 503 507 512 513 520 524
532 543 547 550 552 556 560 561 565 567 571
6 14 19 36 39 40 41 57 58 63 66 67 70 77 80 88 89
92 98 130 137 138 162 172 173 175 178 180 188
199 203 204 213 225 226 229 231 235 240 243 247
252 253 269 275 282 286 289 294 295 297 298 300
303 307 311 322 323 327 328 333 340 341 345 347
349 352 353 369 372 373 383 395 400 409 422 429
432 435 440 443 445 447 450 479 499 500 508 511
517 518 519 533 550 551 552 557 564 565 569 573
581 583 589 590 591 594 595 598 599 605 610 612
614 623 630 638 639 647 650 651 657 670 681 696
697 704 708 710 713 721 723 726 735 737 744 751
752 754 755 758 763 766 778 779 783 785 795 806
812 816 817 819 837 839 843 847 851 853 855 868
869 873 886 887 899 908 909 912 918 932 939 940
944 949 950 952 955 963 964 971 980 983 988 989
990 996 998 1000 1006 1012 1015 1018 1028 1029
7 10 29 30 34 36 42 46 65 70 74 81 85 89 96 104
108 109 128 135 146 155 156 160 161 167 168 169
184 188 200 204 213 223 233 241 260 261 293 309
329 334 343 344 345 351 356 361 371 372 376 379
388 399 418 419 421 425 432 445 453 455 461 462
465 466 469 475 482 484 508 510 514 538 539 545
546 556 558 569 574 585 588 593 594 611 612 615
616 621 628 630 635 653 663 664 676 682 693 702
706 714 728 735 742 772 777 784 788 792 793 802
804 807 811 814 816 817 818 853 870 875 887 917
932 934 941 949 950 951 963 967 969 973 977 978
983 985 989 997 999 1000 1023 1028 1035 1037
1038 1064 **8** 2 6 12 21 36 44 46 48 53 55 57 58
69 72 75 84 85 88 94 95 98 100 101 111 117 118

120 127 128 131 135 138 143 144 146 154 163 167
168 171 188 206 209 214 216 229 239 240 245 251
255 258 267 268 284 295 296 297 301 321 322 333
334 337 343 345 346 351 355 356 360 364 373 379
384 386 387 393 394 397 401 408 409 415 420 424
426 436 445 446 447 458 462 468 470 475 479 480
497 498 502 503 504 508 511 513 521 525 530 531
533 535 537 546 547 553 556 560 567 570 576 584
588 598 601 602 618 622 625 634 673 682 684 686
690 697 698 710 712 715 720 732 733 740 743 744
747 756 758 759 761 771 784 790 799 800 806 807
814 815 825 832 836 837 846 850 852 857 858 864
871 879 881 882 887 888 893 894 898 911 926 933
935 947 951 963 964 965 966 967 971 973 976 980
982 984 986 990 997 1003 1006 1007 1010 1025
1031 1037 1047 1066 1067 1086 1093 1097 1098
1100 1102 1106 1110 1111 1112 1113 1116 1117
1124 1125 1127 1132 1133 1135 1141 1144 1145
1148 1152 1155 1158 1159 1160 1165 1177 1183
9 3 5 6 7 31 43 49 50 59 73 75 88 105 115 116 131
134 141 147 154 165 166 169 171 174 175 181 226
232 237 245 246 252 255 257 259 260 276 289 290
295 302 310 329 334 337 339 340 353 357 362 363
371 382 392 393 397 402 406 407 421 425 432 444
446 450 452 453 454 456 457 462 464 466 467 478
480 485 489 519 524 531 535 536 539 542 546 549
556 560 565 566 578 580 585 586 592 602 620 623
624 629 639 640 651 654 658 660 665 666 667 669
680 710 711 712 714 742 745 746 751 752 753 754
761 763 764 773 774 779 788 801 804 805 812 815
819 821 822 828 830 838 844 850 855 860 865 868
873 895 897 898 901 903 921 922 925 927 928 942
948 981 985 986 991 994 1007 1022 1027 1031 1032
1034 1052 1054 1057 1061 1064 1065 1068 1077
1085 1107 1108 1110 1111 1117 1130 1136 1154
1159 1167 1177 1181 1182 1186 1190 1211 1214
1219 **10** 9 25 37 44 46 51 66 67 70 74 89 97 101
102 103 115 116 120 122 135 147 148 151 176 177
179 180 181 184 199 200 202 203 208 218 221 222
237 238 247 249 252 253 261 275 285 294 301 312
319 328 331 336 353 357 363 369 373 383 384 400
403 406 409 425 438 440 442 451 459 460 469 474
479 482 492 494 496 499 503 511 512 514 518 526
530 535 536 544 552 554 557 559 561 565 566 571
581 582 587 597 636 641 654 678 683 697 699 700
706 707 713 724 729 730 732 735 738 743 747 753
759 769 770 771 772 783 785 797 801 808 809 811
812 814 819 820 831 847 860 863 885 891 893 894
895 898 908 910 915 921 922 932 935 937 939 940
948 977 987 1013 1018 1046 1047 1050 1053 1054
1074 1087 1088 1091 1093 1104 1116 1117 1123
1134 1135 1137 1150 1151 1161 1170 1189 1197
1230 1236 1240 1243 1244 1261 1264 1270 1271
1275 1282 **11** 12 38 50 75 81 82 83 105 108 111
119 124 126 140 145 158 163 169 171 208 211 215
220 225 237 238 247 253 254 279 282 286 293 297
298 300 302 313 325 328 346 348 350 354 359 360
371 374 375 376 391 392 397 410 414 422 428 434
438 440 442 446 456 457 462 467 471 482 486 506
511 514 518 543 554 555 563 567 576 581 590 616
620 621 626 627 637 659 661 664 670 674 679 683
698 702 712 715 733 745 757 773 781 782 784 793
798 799 806 822 833 840 844 849 853 854 855 859
867 868 879 880 882 884 915 916 921 934 936 937
938 946 957 959 973 976 979 980 986 987 1001
1005 1009 1017 1021 1025 1057 1061 1070 1076
1089 1101 1104 1116 1118 1140 1144 1161 1176
1192 1193 1196 1197 1201 1207 1209 1219 1220
1234 1235 1236 1238 1240 1241 1247 1248 1249

1259 1271 1273 1274 **12** 2 13 15 16 21 25 26 52
60 67 68 69 87 90 108 119 124 125 126 127 128 136
141 142 143 151 152 157 161 162 168 169 173 201
202 204 207 226 236 243 244 245 247 255 257 258
260 264 269 270 271 274 280 291 293 297 305 311
323 339 347 349 356 365 381 388 392 394 399 401
405 426 432 437 439 440 445 448 453 455 461 464
472 474 477 483 484 487 494 495 497 503 505 507
508 509 511 512 517 527 544 545 549 551 555 558
580 597 599 602 610 613 616 618 621 627 635 639
645 657 658 663 664 668 671 673 675 676 681 686
688 689 691 699 702 706 708 709 713 718 722 726
729 730 738 749 756 757 760 765 767 772 776 783
785 788 802 803 804 811 812 814 821 834 835 837
845 857 866 884 886 887 891 892 893 903 904 912
914 915 942 955 956 960 963 968 969 970 976 979
980 982 988 991 992 994 1008 1023 1024 1032 1037
1047 1048 1052 1065 1069 1071 1082 1088 1089
1097 1098 1116 1139 1140 1145 1160 1167 1176
1178 1179 1192 1194 1198 1204 1205 1207 1208
1212 1215 1216 1222 1223 1224 1260 1263 1280
1281 1282 1286 1290 1292 1295 1303 1305 1309
1312 1319 1322 1324 1325 1326 1335 1336 1342
1343 1348 1355 1359 1374 1377 1386 1400 1419
1424 1433 1444 1445 1446 1467 1476 1477 1478
1479 1480 1486 1487 1492 1495 1498 1500 1519
1525 1526 1531 1540 1543 1550 1552 1556 1558
1567 1568 1569 1570 1578 1585 1586 1589 1602
1604 1611 1614 1615 1616 1619 1620 1623 1628
1631 1635 1638 1647 1648 1651 1654 1658 1659
1660 1661 1663 1668 1676 1716 1719 1726 1752
1755 1760 1761 1765 1766 1779 1781 1787 1793
1794 1799 1800 1801 1804 1805 1808 1810 1822
1823 1824 1826 1834 1836 1838 1845 1853 1860
1864 1867 1870 1872 1880 1881 1884 1901 1910
1914 1915 1918 **13** 7 10 11 23 26 28 33 34 36 37
40 42 44 55 57 80 83 85 88 91 92 97 99 100 105
106 114 115 116 118 120 121 126 127 129 134 141
145 147 148 149 151 153 154 155 156 157 160 166
177 180 187 191 193 195 198 200 203 205 207 209
210 213 214 223 224 226 231 236 239 242 249 256
266 267 268 274 277 285 293 299 301 307 308 309
311 316 318 320 323 325 326 334 335 337 338 339
340 358 362 365 368 389 408 410 416 419 420 422
433 435 439 444 450 451 460 461 462 464 469 473
475 479 480 481 482 486 487 493 494 501 506 507
508 509 510 511 512 517 518 519 527 530 541 548
549 560 565 570 586 587 593 595 596 600 616 625
626 628 629 635 656 657 659 660 663 665 666 690
694 695 706 719 723 727 728 735 736 738 739 742
743 745 748 750 755 757 762 763 764 765 769 773
774 776 777 778 789 796 801 802 806 807 815 820
823 825 827 829 831 839 842 845 859 863 865 873
874 880 895 901 908 909 911 915 917 920 942 944
946 952 953 964 972 975 982 994 998 1005 1011
1015 1019 1024 1032 1034 1051 1055 1056 1069
1071 1078 1083 1091 1098 1104 1112 1117 1119
1128 1130 1131 1133 1137 1141 1150 1151 1153
1156 1160 1163 1167 1172 1173 1175 1179 1208
1211 1219 1222 1234 1235 1239 1246 1250 1257
1260 1271 1276 1278 1286 1288 1299 1301
14 13 19 41 99 114 115 120 121 124 125 129 130
133 134 138 139 141 144 147 149 154 155 157 159
160 169 172 181 188 192 193 204 205 220 231 232
245 248 250 256 259 260 261 269 274 280 287 291
301 309 310 314 315 322 326 327 328 330 339 346
348 350 357 361 365 368 373 377 378 380 383 390
394 395 402 404 410 414 417 418 421 426 427 430
436 439 440 448 452 457 465 471 475 476 482 483

487 489 491 495 496 497 499 501 502 504 506 507
508 509 510 513 514 516 517 518 519 520 521 523
524 526 530 533 534 538 539 540 541 542 543 545
547 548 552 553 554 555 557 559 562 563 565 571
574 577 579 584 585 586 590 592 594 597 600 602
608 611 612 614 615 616 624 626 627 630 633 634
636 637 638 639 641 647 652 653 654 655 656 658
659 668 670 674 675 678 680 683 684 689 693 695
696 697 698 700 703 706 713 717 720 723 725 730
733 734 738 739 740 741 742 743 746 748 749 753
754 756 758 759 763 774 775 776 777 778 780 781
785 787 791 793 796 797 799 801 802 803 806 808
813 814 815 817 821 822 826 828 831 832 837 839
840 843 844 854 855 857 861 862 866 867 870 874
876 877 882 887 889 895 900 904 906 909 911 913
915 916 921 922 927 929 932 936 939 942 950 952
963 975 979 980 981 985 988 1000 1013 1015 1021
1025 1031 1042 1044 1046 1048 1049 1050 1051
1052 1054 1057 1058 1060 1061 1063 1065 1066
1071 1073 1082 1083 1084 1086 1102 1104 1107
1108 1116 1119 1122 1127 1135 1139 1140 1141
1147 1155 1156 1157 1158 1163 1165 1166 1167
1168 1174 1175 1176 1182 1183 1195 1196 1203
1214 1236 1237 1239 1255 1256 1272 1274 1292
1299 1304 1311 1317 1318 1322 1323 1333 1340
1348 1350 1356 1358 1360 1366 1369 1374 1375
1377 1383 1387 1391 1393 1397 1398 1401 1404
1410 1413 1415 1420 1421 1424 1440 1452 1457
1466 1471 1472 1473 1474 1475 1478 1482 1492
1498 1501 1503 1508 1510 1511 1513 1514 1515
1516 1517 1519 1525 1526 1528 1531 1532 1543
1549 1550 1551 1554 1558 1577 1586 1590

15 94 95 105 112 116 170 202 231 277 329 338
343 359 369 371 404 429 433 434 437 439 442 448
458 493 519 523 524 539 546 548 549 551 558 559
564 571 572 596 602 611 638 639 657 661 710 739
743 745 747 762 775 776 777 778 793 794 797 802
803 819 821 823 824 827 837 842 844 853 857 867
868 873 878 880 886 887 897 941 942 943 944 952
953 967 968 978 998 999 1019 1020 1023 1032 1033
1034 1035 1045 1050 1064 1067 1069 1072 1100
1117 1153 1158 1159 1183 1192 1195 1199 1201
1301 1304 1323 1344 1347 1350 1353 1357 1358
1359 1367 1384 1394 1468 1527 1530 1538 1540
1542 1543 1561 1564 1640 1663 1674 1679 1681
1687 1693 1695 1720 1724 1731 1736 1739 1741
1754 1756 1781 1782 1784 1798 1800 1801 1802
1803 1804 1805 1807 1808 1810 1817 1838 1871
1886 1964 1977 1980 1985 2057 2068 2081 2087
2118 2119 2124 2144 2192 2194 2198 2199 2200
2201 2226 2228 2233 2259 2284 2289 2297 2315
2321 2325 2331 2356 2371 2374 2375 2380 2384
2389 2402 2409 2415 2417 2446 2469 2471 2472
2489 2497 2498 2508 2516 2517 2525 2541 2542
2558 2561 2572 2573 2575 2579 2649 2673 2750
2780 2781 2782 2783 2790 2795 2796 2805 2807
2814 2882 2883 2884 2886 2896 2899 2934 2947
2948 2949 2965 2981 2986 2999 3006 3009 3015
3024 3025 3028 3032 3038 3039 3053 3067 3074
3083 3086 3090 3105 3106 3116 3131 3132 3136
3138 3142 3165 3198 3205 3206 3209 3251 3268
3276 3295 3319 3322 3334 3355 3365 3392 3397
3398 3418 3424 3458 3476 3487 3493 3511 3513
3515 3520 3528 3557 3559 3560 3586 3588 3615
3625 3634 3676 3692 3721 3743 3746 3763 3764
3771 3778 3780 3789 3792 3804 3833 3887 3922
3924 3926 3931 3949 4002 4027 4074 4115 4130
4276 4281 4297 4299 4310 4383 4390 4392 4394
4439 4461 4462 4484 4486 4488 4493 4495 4497

4526 4534 4539 4540 4555 4563 4597 4600 4602
4609 4628 4645 4757 4762 4788 4796 4797 4801
4813 4832 4840 4841 4858 4863 4875 4883 4897
4901 4953 16 4 9 10 15 18 25 26 28 29 30 31 32
42 48 49 60 62 64 65 67 68 72 75 76 78 79 88 90 91
92 96 100 101 102 109 110 118 122 125 126 132
133 134 138 145 146 147 148 153 157 158 160 161
165 166 167 168 170 173 174 178 180 181 183 188
189 197 198 199 200 202 203 205 208 209 213 214
217 218 219 221 222 224 225 226 234 236 237 243
248 254 261 274 275 276 281 285 287 290 291 295
302 310 311 322 326 331 333 336 338 340 341 350
354 355 356 357 362 364 375 380 400 407 409 410
411 424 427 428 433 438 441 443 444 445 454 456
458 462 464 466 472 473 475 477 481 482 485 494
499 502 503 505 508 511 516 517 518 522 526 529
531 539 541 543 545 547 549 551 559 566 570 572
573 576 578 580 581 585 595 597 598 601 602 610
612 616 617 625 627 629 630 643 649 653 654 655
658 661 662 664 671 675 679 685 696 698 704 712
718 721 722 723 724 729 736 738 739 740 742 743
744 745 746 748 754 756 762 763 765 769 770 771
778 785 787 790 793 794 797 799 800 802 807 810
811 814 818 826 832 833 834 842 846 848 850 859
861 863 869 871 894 896 897 898 900 902 903 905
908 910 919 921 922 927 928 929 930 931 937 938
940 948 950 953 954 955 966 976 978 986 993 994
997 1000 1005 1008 1012 1025 1029 1034 1035
1037 1047 1050 1051 1052 1058 1059 1060 1064
1073 1075 1082 1084 1086 1088 1089 1090 1091
1098 1101 1113 1114 1120 1134 1138 1141 1145
1160 1163 1173 1174 1176 1179 1188 1189 1191
1192 1195 1196 1202 1203 1207 1209 1212 1222
1225 1232 1234 1238 1247 1254 1262 1272 1275
1281 1284 1286 1289 1290 1300 1302 1306 1308
1310 1311 1316 1317 1318 1325 1326 1327 1329
1335 1339 1340 1345 1354 1355 1356 1357 1358
1360 1365 1367 1373 1375 1377 1378 1380 1381
1382 1387 1389 1395 1398 1401 1404 1405 1408
1421 1425 1426 1427 1430 1432 1438 1442 1444
1445 1448 1455 1457 1459 1461 1462 1463 1464
1471 1481 1488 1494 1499 1501 1505 1507 1508
1510 1511 1513 1514 1518 1523 1525 1526 1530
1532 1534 1535 1537 1543 1545 1548 1553 1555
1557 1558 1563 1579 1582 1584 1587 1590 1592
1593 1594 1601 1602 1604 1606 1607 1614 1621
1622 1623 1630 1638 1639 1640 1641 1656 1657
1664 1669 1672 1676 1677 1679 1684 1689 1691
1695 1696 1700 1707 1711 1715 1717 1718 1719
1723 1724 1729 1733 1734 1736 1740 1744 1745
1750 1751 1753 1754 1758 1759 1760 1771 1772
1775 1778 1781 1783 1784 1785 1786 1787 1789
1790 1791 1795 1796 1803 1811 1814 1824 1826
1827 1829 1832 1833 1834 1836 1837 1839 1843
1846 1848 1849 1851 1852 1853 1854 1855 1856
1857 1859 1863 1864 1865 1866 1869 1870 1872
1875 1877 1881 1885 1890 17 21 22 39 40 42 64
87 105 106 107 110 111 112 114 121 124 127 129
148 150 158 159 164 165 168 169 179 180 231 234
235 242 257 264 269 278 279 281 282 283 284 285
286 299 301 302 303 305 307 308 311 312 316 317
331 346 352 354 363 374 376 379 390 395 417 433
442 463 470 477 479 483 484 492 498 499 502 510
516 517 521 530 544 550 563 603 609 625 629 639
651 667 676 679 687 694 699 715 718 720 730 731
733 736 739 768 777 780 795 799 810 830 836 839
855 863 868 869 870 872 876 882 883 884 890 891
900 902 904 905 909 921 925 927 928 935 940 941
942 946 957 962 963 964 969 970 971 975 977 981

989 1008 1012 1013 1014 1019 1034 1035 1037
1045 1055 1063 1070 1072 1073 1084 1085 1086
1088 1092 1093 1119 1120 1123 1139 1140 1143
1144 1173 1174 1178 1216 1217 1244 1258 1259
1260 1262 1265 1276 1277 1285 1287 1292 1294
1295 1298 1304 1305 1312 1313 1314 1321 1322
1324 1326 1329 1331 1336 1337 1344 1350 1410
1412 1414 1419 1427 1436 1447 1448 1449 1453
1480 1487 1500 1502 1503 1504 1509 1512 1513
1514 1515 1532 1552 1553 1554 1560 1568 1569
1571 1572 1575 1577 1584 1603 1605 1610 1618
1626 1640 1641 1652 1653 1654 1659 1665 1667
1675 1687 1688 1695 1706 1745 1746 1750 1753
1756 1758 1760 1761 1763 1771 1777 1780 1781
1783 1785 1786 1787 1790 1794 1795 1801 1803
1808 1809 1813 1814 1815 1829 1830 1831 1832
1838 1839 1846 1847 1851 1853 1860 1866 1878
1880 1883 1887 1891 1893 1906 1913 1926 1934
1954 1996 1998 2003 2004 2021 2050 2051 2052
2061 2062 2071 2074 2092 2093 2095 2097 2103
2109 2110 2112 2118 2123 2124 2128 2129 2130
2135 2140 2145 2146 2157 2159 2160 2163 2168
2170 2178 2181 2182 2191 2207 2210 2238 2239
2245 2246 2256 2259 2260 2261 2265 2274 2282
2284 2288 2289 2300 2313 2316 2328 18 1 2 3 5
8 12 13 19 20 21 22 23 28 30 33 37 40 43 44 47 50
51 58 65 69 74 78 81 83 85 90 92 96 102 106 108
114 117 118 120 121 123 132 133 136 144 147 148
150 151 152 154 158 160 161 162 163 167 171 174
176 179 183 195 200 206 210 215 219 220 224 229
231 236 244 253 254 261 262 264 278 284 295 298
307 312 315 318 321 325 326 328 329 338 340 342
343 347 348 353 355 360 364 366 367 375 378 382
387 390 397 404 405 407 412 413 414 423 434 435
437 444 448 450 451 453 455 464 465 468 469 477
483 484 486 487 489 490 494 495 498 500 503 505
506 508 509 512 517 519 522 535 542 544 548 556
557 558 559 560 563 567 570 572 580 582 583 590
593 603 608 613 614 615 623 624 628 629 634 636
638 640 648 649 650 651 657 658 666 674 694 698
703 705 707 711 714 715 717 720 721 723 726 728
729 731 734 739 740 743 744 746 750 753 758 768
770 772 773 775 776 782 784 786 790 800 802 805
807 808 811 813 815 816 818 819 823 827 830 832
842 845 847 854 855 861 865 866 871 872 883 884
887 892 893 894 896 905 906 907 909 912 919 920
933 935 938 939 943 946 952 953 954 959 966 968
975 976 978 979 981 985 988 990 994 996 997 998
1000 1001 1007 1013 1020 1031 1033 1037 1039
1044 1056 1057 1059 1061 1066 1067 1068 1073
1079 1080 1081 1084 1087 1088 1089 1092 1104
1107 1111 1116 1118 1120 1126 1127 1134 1136
1142 1143 1144 1146 1147 1161 1164 1167 1177
1179 1180 1186 1188 1191 1192 1196 1197 1199
1202 1203 1208 1210 1215 1232 1248 1253 1254
1256 1262 1267 1270 1274 1275 1280 1287 1288
1294 1297 1298 1300 1301 1304 1310 1311 1312
1315 1316 1317 1318 1319 1322 1324 1332 1333
1338 1339 1341 1344 1347 1349 1354 1359 1362
1370 1374 1376 1377 1380 1381 1383 1385 1388
1389 1396 1399 1402 1404 1406 1407 1408 1411
1412 1413 1415 1417 1418 1423 1429 1432 1438
1440 1441 1444 1455 1459 1461 1466 1467 1470
1473 1477 1478 1479 1481 1486 1493 1494 1495
1496 1503 1507 1509 1515 1519 1525 1526 1530
1531 1534 1535 1538 1540 1553 1554 1555 1556
1564 1576 1577 1579 1594 1595 1602 1603
a (74) 1 300 304 383 585 2 253 3 161 201
383 4 289 6 164 730 7 494 578 829 830 839

846 849 850 855 8 68 417 748 1040 9 25 32 288 304 551 716 726 919 1127 1144 1174 10 205 350 358 573 611 614 1242 1251 1254 12 29 148 427 751 895 1801 13 927 1149 14 306 406 649 650 792 15 77 2583 3894 16 1231 1250 1251 1252 1681 17 820 823 825

a (435) 15 9 20 25 26 28 29 30 33 36 38 39 40 41 42 50 61 75 78 101 125 131 134 135 143 144 151 158 159 160 183 184 190 196 197 212 213 218 249 285 286 288 289 296 297 313 314 320 329 353 365 404 416 428 451 465 468 471 492 501 509 516 536 538 578 579 580 605 606 649 650 659 666 667 689 693 704 705 708 715 728 738 748 752 806 807 809 816 862 863 898 899 901 902 903 906 907 914 921 934 935 936 939 958 960 989 992 1014 1015 1081 1122 1129 1136 1143 1174 1177 1178 1179 1191 1205 1207 1210 1237 1238 1239 1241 1255 1257 1262 1263 1265 1268 1279 1280 1309 1316 1326 1340 1343 1346 1412 1440 1442 1444 1487 1490 1509 1510 1519 1520 1548 1549 1554 1558 1579 1600 1603 1606 1608 1609 1610 1613 1614 1617 1622 1704 1798 1812 1822 1841 1876 1908 1909 1927 1928 1935 1961 1962 1964 1993 2005 2006 2033 2037 2039 2041 2045 2046 2047 2049 2050 2051 2057 2071 2074 2079 2123 2137 2145 2146 2148 2177 2181 2184 2185 2249 2250 2252 2253 2257 2265 2266 2268 2269 2271 2286 2291 2292 2306 2307 2334 2337 2339 2399 2412 2420 2432 2461 2479 2480 2481 2482 2486 2489 2501 2537 2571 2587 2588 2600 2606 2620 2624 2627 2628 2631 2636 2657 2659 2660 2668 2705 2709 2714 2715 2723 2728 2742 2743 2744 2746 2762 2810 2835 2852 2923 2924 2931 2932 2942 2943 2962 3028 3045 3067 3091 3102 3160 3195 3211 3233 3254 3297 3318 3328 3360 3367 3377 3383 3402 3420 3421 3457 3460 3469 3475 3524 3531 3540 3562 3565 3583 3595 3597 3619 3622 3667 3707 3726 3739 3740 3751 3764 3773 3828 3840 3842 3844 3845 3877 3911 3916 3957 3974 3975 3979 3980 3982 3990 4018 4031 4032 4033 4034 4035 4038 4039 4054 4091 4095 4100 4145 4158 4161 4166 4168 4189 4284 4290 4293 4298 4312 4317 4322 4326 4329 4360 4366 4367 4449 4449 4454 4456 4477 4481 4502 4508 4524 4579 4611 4672 4675 4692 4693 4695 4703 4706 4737 4805 4915 4956 4957 4958 4965 4966

a' (1) 3 20

a' (1) 14 650

.a–e (1) 18 490

a/c (1) 17 1862

A 1 (1) 6 684

A B S (1) 16 452

A D C (3) 10 1179 1223 1235

A E (8) 7 784 785 8 332 527 9 54 65 412 13 930

A E I O U (1) 9 213

A E's (1) 7 787

A J (1) 15 2205

Aaron (1) 11 149

Aaron (1) 15 4357

aback (1) 14 1395

Abaft (1) 14 1452

abandon (1) 16 1410

abandoned (6) 3 275 13 380 15 2778 17 513 683 834

abandoned (1) 10 16

abandoning (1) 15 4255

abandonment (1) 17 253

abasement (2) 17 1148 2245

abatement (1) 17 1133

abattoir (1) 14 1294

Abba (1) 12 1915

Abbas (2) 3 108 112

abbess (1) 14 595

Abbey (9) 7 916 8 425 9 554 1131 12 1452 16 709 17 757 967 2259

abbey (4) 10 408 434 929 16 515

abbot (2) 10 850 15 3466

abbot's (1) 10 851

abbots (1) 12 1678

abbreviation (1) 17 410

abdomen (2) 16 876 17 1439

abdominal (2) 14 1257 17 523

Abe (1) 15 2190

Abeakuta (2) 12 1515 1522

Abeakutic (1) 12 1531

aberration (2) 15 945 17 1766

abetting (1) 12 1900

abhorrence (1) 15 3562

abhors (2) 8 498 9 871

abide (2) 9 361 14 1346

abigail (1) 14 951

abilities (2) 15 4044 16 307

ability (3) 12 1289 17 2146 2148

abject (1) 17 1812

abjectly (1) 15 3397

abjured (1) 17 1639

ablation (1) 14 391

Able (1) 7 683

able (11) 1 636 5 73 170 9 305 14 50 236 1303 16 1123 1823 18 364 1445

ableeding (1) 9 460

abluted (1) 17 1451

ablutions (1) 16 7

Abnegation (1) 17 2169

abnegation (3) 12 632 17 2155 2195

abnormal (2) 15 1776 17 2190

abnormalities (2) 14 984 17 912

abnormally (1) 17 523

Aboard (1) 6 441

abode (5) 8 749 15 733 1158 17 599 2115

abode (1) 5 147

abodes (1) 12 353

abodes (1) 7 856

abominable (2) 14 1566 15 1717

abomination (1) 14 372

abortion (2) 14 329 1261

abortions (1) 14 242

abound (1) 14 146

abounding (1) 16 1744

About (10) 3 166 218 374 5 311 485 6 61 266 9 1197 14 277 16 190

About (1) 15 932 2264

about (512) 1 10 23 31 57 61 231 314 366 402 438 478 483 499 595 674 675 2 21 71 196 218 321 353 366 369 3 49 117 134 135 159 311 332 432 4 6 101 118 393 409 423 435 5 30 32 70 105 112 201 216 250 293 294 310 332 356 383 413 415 424 526 6 16 235 244 264 343 354 393 418 433 479 484 574 596 641 717 724 742 749 781 787 793 827 853 897 990 993 7 152 172 183 208 247 308 346 376 378 430 493 502 603 698 782 786 789 790 906 993 1011 8 30 109 112 131 185 226 381 463 479 514 558 564 568 574 581 582 769 852 863 1058 1060 1064 1138 1164 9 49 76 94 113 307 429 635 1082 1158 10 133 162 307 410 423 438 444 528 530 578 582 925 1007 1194 11 186 463 546 619 626 749 866 867 904 1161 1195 12 15 54 62 63 128 169 303 330 395 400 435 450 453 466 480 482 484 493 498 500 609 638 679 683 684 687 690 709 761 770 781 831 836 851 858 889 890 892 895 939 945 952 1000 1052 1097 1122 1144 1181 1192 1227 1235 1329 1330 1331 1333 1349 1393 1397 1401 1416 1473 1474 1507 1510 1567 1576 1587 1611 1623 1777 1794 1798 1910 13 18 97 118 124 130 186 205 220 260 323 330 342 343 400 453 463 480 531 575 577 647 700 702 713 811 826 862 943 983 985 998 999 1065 1094 1117 1125 1151 1216 1221 1238 1295 1301 14 58 271 314 492 507 530 531 536 546 581 723 875 1062 1104 1111 1174 1188 1197 1310 1328 1366 1383 1540 15 355 523 640 829 1542 1634 1701 1810 2093 2135 2197 2395 2416 2508 2523 2526 2553 2935 2958 3001 3118 3178 3204 3885 4052 4447 4566 16 75 124 131 170 205 211 248 304 421 428 443 517 518 563 583 618 626 637 657 663 665 699 778 819 820 837 844 846 847 864 883 895 900 913 946 1004 1099 1113 1132 1144 1201 1239 1246 1258 1271 1412 1415 1434 1438 1472 1481 1482 1484 1512 1544 1545 1559 1635 1638 1657 1733 1755 1762 1799 1813 1889 17 337 528 529 1114 1116 1121 1125 1128 1423 1442 2002 2059 18 8 13 49 75 81 90 92 100 102 121 135 138 169 175 177 180 212 221 228 246 277 279 282 306 336 359 371 383 392 466 485 489 494 496 507 509 519 524 559 564 565 566 587 592 601 658 686 690 738 752 776 784 825 830 838 846 850 879 880 886 891 898 915 916 920 928 957 970 1078 1112 1115 1118 1151 1159 1163 1183 1187 1190 1218 1242 1321 1323 1326 1327 1334 1342 1364 1366 1395 1451 1506 1517 1532 1549 1561 1597

about (2) 5 115 9 1013

about (8) 15 126 591 958 1270 2186 3904 4048 4319

Above (2) 10 1197 17 2004

above (38) 2 16 3 280 4 512 5 313 6 69 765 7 860 8 1135 10 103 901 963 11 181 410 557 1072 12 611 13 729 14 169 751 1177 1293 1319 1386 15 877 1082 3082 3263 4517 4525 16 559 841 17 933 1212 1513 2019 2298 18 1122

above (1) 6 165

above (2) 15 2185 4678

aboveboard (1) 16 1484

abovementioned (1) 12 419

abraded (1) 2 199

Abraham (4) 5 201 10 971 12 1736 15 262

Abraham (1) 15 3326

Abram (1) 17 128

Abramovitz (1) 15 3224

abreast (2) 6 413 7 1001

abreast (1) 15 2240

abridged (1) 14 838

Abrines (1) 18 1482

Abroad (1) 17 1979

abroad (5) 1 130 15 3924 16 121 843 17 1969

abrupt (1) 11 452

abruptly (5) 1 86 10 201 487 17 880

abruptly (2) 15 2117 3692

abscission (1) 17 1208

absconded (1) 16 1304

Absence (2) 15 646 1606

absence (11) 9 148 174 1031 12 997 14 951 16 1265 17 250 288 738 951 2077

absences (1) 17 2296

AEROLITHS (1) **7** 1022
aeronautic (1) **17** 566
aeronautical (1) **17** 2264
Afar (1) **9** 654
afar (14) **9** 136 **10** 1184 **11** 59 112 113 302 338 455 855 937 1008 1269 **12** 69 83
afar (1) **15** 2687
afasting (1) **12** 1609
afeard (1) **14** 284
affair (9) **5** 151 371 468 **10** 537 725 **14** 219 **16** 305 597 **18** 1196
affairs (2) **14** 947 **16** 1867
affect (2) **14** 999 **15** 2738
affected (3) **12** 654 **15** 1790 **17** 2154
affecting (3) **12** 525 1820 **14** 757
affection (5) **4** 432 **9** 855 **14** 764 **16** 1387 **17** 1180
affectionate (1) **16** 1363
affectionate (1) **15** 908
affections (4) **6** 673 **9** 786 **16** 432 1549
affianced (1) **13** 215
affidavits (2) **6** 1008 **15** 1231
affiliated (1) **17** 1914
affinities (1) **17** 1157
affinity (1) **17** 1063
affirm (4) **14** 12 596 **15** 1804 **16** 1152
affirmation (4) **1** 654 **17** 30 180 1016
affirmations (1) **17** 1179
affirmative (1) **12** 868
affirmatively (1) **18** 745
affirmed (7) **6** 289 **9** 1018 **14** 210 **16** 382 1002 1297 **17** 1012
affirming (2) **14** 28 839
affixed (2) **17** 1521 1571
afflatus (1) **7** 774
afflict (2) **17** 884 **18** 1105
afflicted (3) **13** 442 445 **15** 4170
affliction (1) **11** 588
affluence (1) **16** 180
affly (1) **18** 623
afford (4) **15** 3276 **16** 1493 1618 **17** 1214
afforded (2) **12** 356 1517
affording (1) **12** 550
affray (1) **12** 587
aflame (1) **11** 747
afloat (1) **12** 1308
aforesaid (4) **16** 944 **17** 631 2265
Afraid (5) **4** 30 **8** 511 **12** 701 **13** 1218
afraid (22) **1** 668 **3** 367 **5** 273 **6** 958 **7** 944 1010 **9** 271 **10** 721 **13** 471 1069 **15** 3761 4428 **16** 916 **18** 6 32 526 558 630 803 889 1039 1568
afraid (1) **9** 1151
afresh (1) **6** 352
Africa (5) **15** 4606 **16** 1299 **18** 794 867 871
African (6) **1** 659 **5** 323 **9** 862 **10** 144 **14** 1331 **17** 1839
After (49) **1** 633 636 **2** 60 111 **3** 365 **6** 5 108 466 581 620 724 964 **7** 973 **8** 109 408 710 720 1152 1178 **9** 1028 1108 **10** 510 548 1130 **11** 153 271 726 **12** 903 979 1434 1905 **13** 891 1055 1195 **14** 629 696 **15** 461 2027 2625 2706 4259 **16** 356 544 586 983 1155 **17** 114 682
After (1) **12** 747
After (4) **15** 1256 1426 1436 4335
after (369) **1** 103 189 339 610 629 **2** 311 433 443 **3** 58 143 192 **4** 41 75 187 209 345 352 362 424 523 525 **5** 69 136 191 270 313 375 409 410 472 474 559 **6** 2 10 20 162 168 204 255 301 350 373 485 504 525 549 590 606 674 730 742 764 809 856 967 1000 1001 1002 1031 **7** 137 214 334 351 440 586 660 956 1025 **8** 42 115 129 169 182 185 199 306 340 356 365 393 402 419 422 425 477 489 610 675 721 755 975 1025 1047 **9** 87 217 380 457 513 634 987 1030 1044 1158 1208 1210 **10** 199 364 389 390 391 396 444 455 552 553 968 1051 1092 1118 1177 1250 **11** 116 174 175 176 299 421 509 511 793 1230 1232 **12** 29 255 315 323 445 461 516 517 802 1061 1064 1112 1161 1174 1186 1230 1292 1327 1437 1529 1582 1628 1672 1689 1856 1902 1907 **13** 27 56 139 255 286 363 467 470 506 547 597 646 722 862 935 939 1055 1057 1074 **14** 94 121 139 199 291 417 456 475 484 486 493 523 588 609 624 686 845 878 893 1020 1057 1107 1187 1194 1275 1331 1334 1392 1483 **15** 266 540 585 1066 1727 1784 1963 2030 2366 2550 2786 2895 2914 3036 3294 3560 3836 4203 4302 4881 **16** 18 20 40 177 204 250 273 336 362 423 496 545 691 807 906 930 937 941 952 969 976 1062 1092 1155 1190 1191 1273 1288 1301 1316 1328 1462 1508 1515 1526 1527 1576 1643 1805 1850 1877 **17** 191 282 357 448 628 629 749 1130 1131 1260 1422 1546 1747 1816 1851 2020 2275 **18** 101 131 146 151 177 182 212 217 219 254 258 263 274 300 313 319 320 337 344 346 355 360 388 399 404 423 427 428 443 461 465 496 532 553 556 588 606 647 676 704 719 742 803 830 840 843 847 862 900 904 910 954 1044 1062 1065 1082 1120 1137 1141 1165 1184 1216 1222 1279 1305 1317 1402 1423 1424 1425 1441 1456 1540 1575
after (2) **16** 1251 1894
after (3) **15** 34 101 3472
afterbirth (1) **14** 946
afterclang (1) **11** 767
aftercourse (1) **7** 765
Aftereffect (1) **13** 852
afterlife (1) **9** 77
Afternoon (2) **8** 1187 **11** 564
afternoon (13) **5** 198 **6** 190 359 **10** 29 430 **11** 563 **12** 1266 **13** 158 **15** 1010 **16** 451 712 1450 **17** 629
afterwards (4) **17** 474 **18** 211 655 1056
Afterwit (1) **9** 1137
Afterwits (1) **11** 403
Again (10) **2** 110 314 **8** 1136 **11** 165 303 947 **13** 1127 **15** 1085 3334 **17** 901
Again (1) **12** 917
again (206) **1** 75 95 111 141 152 233 282 381 398 426 441 564 572 622 642 695 730 742 **2** 34 82 131 187 226 353 354 388 408 426 446 **3** 102 147 270 343 344 358 362 **4** 18 234 427 510 549 **5** 28 66 149 189 195 263 319 416 521 543 **6** 134 139 140 343 616 633 636 662 908 924 926 995 1023 **7** 28 254 415 467 562 960 1061 **8** 49 74 315 317 580 610 801 846 870 1083 1105 **9** 60 545 1004 1204 **10** 3 24 31 333 579 618 644 667 750 812 1033 1051 1155 1169 **11** 137 163 164 314 407 479 565 573 650 651 717 958 1034 **12** 377 381 407 699 758 891 952 1078 1299 1300 1301 1306 1357 1374 1613 1671 1755 **13** 96 173 355 359 381 466 533 553 563 595 746 760 1093 1102 1154 1272 1278 **14** 38 416 433 564 631 766 888 1098 1307 1326 1470 1480 1533 **15** 200 798 975 1364 1768 2367 2425 3331 4467 **16** 113 279 697 783 856 947 1073 1128 1233 1301 1888 **17** 1066 1486 **18** 29 187 460 515 585 874 878 904 926 954 996 1075 1080 1102 1218 1251 1268 1276 1338 1388 1425 1548 1605
again (6) **1** 592 **7** 243 295 313 **12** 28 **17** 816
again (22) **15** 28 165 196 1267 2079 2301 2500 3006 3459 3545 3594 3737 4128 4556 4869 4891 4917 4925 4926 4928 4936 4944
Against (3) **5** 187 **7** 927 **8** 1066
Against (1) **15** 4956
against (102) **1** 101 162 180 **2** 250 361 **3** 6 357 368 455 **4** 113 276 329 383 525 532 **5** 50 58 400 444 **6** 13 175 490 591 909 984 **7** 416 433 459 1036 1037 **8** 187 446 604 831 **9** 3 10 576 732 828 **10** 89 93 212 465 517 559 597 831 875 1216 **11** 75 178 414 975 **12** 25 1042 1139 1361 1364 1380 **13** 180 432 561 744 1073 **14** 21 125 226 320 370 493 497 911 982 992 1371 1576 **15** 200 1783 1952 3026 4597 4645 **16** 84 893 964 1042 1341 1342 1687 1833 **17** 51 109 345 844 1196 1560 1628 2210 **18** 292 935 1011 1418
against (22) **15** 26 133 135 161 212 237 659 2212 2337 2476 2764 2768 4508 4683 4684 4685 4686 4687 4861
agallop (1) **3** 24
agapo (1) **15** 2524
agate (1) **12** 117
Agatha (1) **15** 3435
Agatha's (1) **10** 111
Age (1) **9** 1011
age (42) **4** 232 **5** 474 **8** 489 **9** 803 810 894 **11** 1007 **13** 379 389 836 1086 1189 **14** 502 847 1038 1040 **15** 855 1145 4470 **16** 66 660 1236 1442 1567 1581 1629 **17** 393 403 447 448 456 458 459 469 1000 **18** 51 97 641 1036 1327 1359
age (2) **7** 831
age (1) **15** 4019
Aged (1) **6** 162
aged (8) **10** 80 **12** 235 655 **14** 392 **17** 1906 1912 1947 2282
aged (1) **15** 905
agelong (1) **7** 850
Agenbite (6) **1** 481 **9** 196 809 **10** 875 879
agenbite (1) **10** 879
Agenbuyer (2) **9** 494 **14** 295
agencies (1) **17** 1764
agency (2) **17** 256 2207
agenda (1) **7** 885
Agendath (14) **4** 191 492 **8** 635 1184 1186 **11** 884 **13** 1284 **14** 1086 **15** 982 1857 1900 **17** 1325 1700
agent (10) **10** 1193 **14** 1042 **15** 834 **16** 1239 **17** 180 1980 2075 2163 2207 2222
agents (4) **6** 316 **17** 1558 1738 2164
ages (16) **1** 33 **3** 48 **8** 205 **9** 811 **12** 912 **13** 736 **14** 252 1019 1222 **15** 399 2499 **16** 776 **17** 446 450 861 **18** 697
agglutinated (1) **17** 279
aggrandising (1) **17** 1382
aggravating (2) **11** 104 **18** 237
aggrieved (1) **16** 1540
agility (3) **12** 945 **17** 518 519
aging (2) **15** 2811 3453
agitated (3) **2** 270 **11** 391 **15** 2394
agitation (2) **15** 2464 **17** 1649
agitation (1) **15** 310
agitations (1) **14** 735
aglitter (1) **3** 302

aglow (1) 9 284
agnathia (1) 14 963
agnostic (1) 15 1712
Agnus (1) 15 289
ago (49) 3 322 4 364 5 485 6 173 300 697 1009 7 744 8 156 158 179 265 274 940 11 779 12 323 1450 13 201 1072 1137 14 1151 1383 1501 15 539 1525 2472 2541 3275 3289 3629 3714 3718 3719 3720 16 409 18 375 636 666 698 726 734 940 977 1079 1116 1307 1497 1557 1575
ago (1) 9 799
agog (1) 11 69
agog (1) 15 526
agone (2) 14 103 205
agonies (1) 17 998
Agonising (1) 7 241
agonising (1) 15 2574
agony (5) 1 274 6 527 15 2643 2679 4240
agony (2) 15 932 4238
agrarian (1) 17 1648
agree (2) 12 736 15 1235
agree (1) 1 586
agree (1) 15 1703
agreeable (6) 14 391 674 1252 17 673 1510 1598
agreeableness' (1) 16 406
agreeably (1) 10 1236
agreed (8) 6 542 7 55 364 9 189 11 213 12 49 16 994 1106
agreeing (1) 14 256
agreement (1) 15 1380
agriculture (1) 2 329
agrin (1) 10 1274
agueshaken (1) 15 2598
agus (2) 12 1825 17 727
Ah (68) 1 79 112 391 697 3 351 419 4 62 469 510 5 38 463 6 22 297 524 878 7 226 313 708 844 8 455 579 731 979 1189 1192 11 26 162 248 252 584 599 611 734 930 12 238 242 390 991 13 741 793 821 850 1043 1049 14 756 1024 15 154 170 334 516 720 1610 2455 2522 2787 2808 3230 3231 3753 3809 3849 4830 4896 16 160 614 1576 1800
Ah (3) 3 221 11 735 15 4227
ah (15) 11 162 248 249 12 1571 13 385 739 955 14 1049 18 38 751 1207 1208 1568 1570
Aha (10) 3 177 7 412 413 10 41 11 307 858 12 1619 15 2524 3024 4582
Aham (2) 10 748 761
Ahasuerus (1) 12 1667
Ahbeesee (1) 4 137
ahead (9) 3 347 6 565 707 8 315 12 1797 1806 14 1452 16 202 1855
ahead (1) 15 649
aheah (1) 18 701
aheating (1) 14 1059
Ahem (1) 7 612
Aherlow (1) 12 1456
Ahhkkk (1) 15 2214
Aho (1) 13 869
aholt (1) 14 1493
ahome (1) 14 1522
ahorizontal (1) 17 208
ahoy (1) 1 280
ahumming (1) 11 387
ahunger (1) 11 387
aid (13) 8 327 531 1163 10 1269 12 558

13 835 14 156 16 293 915 1214 17 564 682 1165
aided (1) 17 389
aiding (1) 12 1900
Aids (1) 8 922
Ailesbury (1) 8 708
ailments (1) 18 7
ails (1) 15 2066
aim (4) 6 917 11 391 13 362 1193
aimed (1) 13 353
Aimless (1) 11 391
aimlessly (1) 16 1236
Aims (1) 16 394
aims (1) 17 1623
aint (6) 12 676 14 817 1526 1586 15 616 2223
Air (2) 6 606 15 4756
air (103) 1 4 12 130 168 283 328 595 2 199 301 345 440 445 3 102 210 266 362 401 504 4 7 136 306 458 540 544 549 5 34 36 50 302 401 6 489 635 839 858 989 7 396 459 612 682 8 45 403 702 789 958 1126 9 107 117 346 1128 1218 10 404 443 564 632 933 1031 1232 11 220 407 610 628 638 642 674 695 767 794 1081 1153 1182 12 1004 13 10 281 383 719 741 782 1191 14 147 703 1146 1407 1409 15 1630 3344 4313 16 825 1180 1716 1718 1756 1810 17 133 211 1144 1265 1684 18 292 1335 1456
air (10) 15 310 1118 1265 1447 2467 3377 3649 3945 4048 4679
airbladders (1) 17 571
aired (1) 13 176
airhole (1) 6 869
airing (2) 6 196 16 986
Airs (1) 3 55
airs (4) 3 55 96 14 1205 16 1769
airslits (1) 7 946
aisle (3) 5 353 457 12 812
ait (1) 9 954
aitch (1) 17 1793
Aitcha (1) 8 894
Aiulella (1) 15 4708
ajar (6) 1 328 4 496 6 27 7 424 9 581 11 670
Ajax (1) 15 709
Ak (1) 15 2268
Akasic (2) 7 882 928
akeled (1) 14 270
akimbo (2) 15 2670 2768
akin (1) 12 289
Al (1) 15 3113
Al (1) 15 4325
al (1) 3 366
alabaster (5) 5 476 12 1213 13 89 640 17 1525
alack (1) 14 408
Alacrity (1) 11 217
alacrity (3) 11 213 214 288
Alaki (2) 12 1515 1526
Alameda (4) 12 1005 18 644 884 1599
alanna (1) 15 4586
alarm (3) 1 707 8 248 17 2151
alarm (2) 15 286 1304
alarmclock (1) 18 1543
Alarmed (1) 9 332
alarmed (1) 15 4651
alarms (1) 14 1583
Alas (3) 2 281 11 24 693

alas (2) 13 48 14 1052
alas (1) 11 694
ālāvātār (1) 12 354
Alba (2) 14 191 233
Albany (1) 5 498
albatross (1) 8 120
albatrosses (1) 15 4669
albeit (1) 9 9
Albert (7) 2 266 6 550 8 528 12 1683 14 1329 16 910 17 975
Albert (1) 15 271
Alberta (1) 15 3084
ALBERTA (1) 15 3099
albino (1) 15 988
Albion (2) 12 1388 18 1194
Albion (1) 12 1209
Albion's (1) 12 666
albs (1) 3 118
album (2) 13 465 636
albuminoid (1) 15 1793
alchemists (1) 5 474
Alcibiades (1) 14 1111
alcohol (1) 12 511
alcoholic (1) 17 38
Aldborough (1) 10 83
Aldebaran (1) 15 1656
Alderman (5) 8 160 10 971 17 1339 1344 2139
alderman (3) 6 950 8 162 15 1383
alderman's (1) 15 1366
Ale (1) 5 193
ale (9) 5 389 11 373 377 422 12 281 1211 1298 14 218 580
ale (1) 9 726
Alec (2) 14 497 653
alemates (1) 8 1005
Aleph (3) 3 39 5 11 15 1623
aleph (1) 17 738
alert (1) 14 1366
alert (2) 15 1296 4955
Alessandro (1) 12 198
alevats (1) 12 282
Alexander (9) 7 25 143 8 13 17 12 1816 14 1584 17 587 791 2046
Alexander (2) 15 1422 4337
ALEXANDER (2) 15 1682 1752
Alexander's (1) 16 1278
Alexandra (2) 16 959 17 1779
Alexandria (1) 3 143
Alf (59) 8 320 11 437 12 249 252 256 267 273 274 279 303 308 313 314 317 319 321 323 327 331 334 336 382 387 390 434 439 455 457 459 487 491 823 824 826 887 939 942 947 953 955 988 1012 1031 1036 1038 1040 1045 1050 1079 1096 1100 1165 1321 1406 1484 1626 1786 1797 1844
Alf (1) 15 481
ALF (1) 15 484
Alfred (2) 12 228 1694
algate (1) 14 98
Algebra (1) 16 1636
algebra (2) 1 555 2 152
Algeciras (2) 18 399 1597
Algy (2) 1 77 3 31
Ali (1) 12 562
alias (3) 12 1087 17 686
alias (2) 16 596 859
aliases (1) 16 1322
alibi (3) 3 180 7 667 15 736
Alice (7) 12 1496 14 1329 15 437 2980 2981 16 425

Alice (1) 16 1321
Alice (1) 15 3846
alicui (1) 9 430
alien (1) 14 906
alienated (1) 12 45
alienation (1) 17 2208
Alighieri (1) 12 182
alight (1) 10 134
alight (1) 15 1275
alighted (2) 10 153 12 1593
aligned (1) 17 1583
aliment (1) 17 36
alimentary (1) 17 997
aliments (1) 14 1289
alimony (1) 15 3477
aliorelative (2) 17 1350 1354
aliquantulum (1) 15 84
aliquid (1) 9 430
aliquot (1) 12 634
alive (19) 1 144 5 88 6 202 284 865 975
    8 886 9 16 751 10 722 11 504 1089
    12 1869 13 792 15 1083 16 696
    17 456 460 18 1454
alkali (1) 14 1297
All (164) 1 476 632 2 27 36 380 3 316 452
    490 4 60 76 222 294 477 5 224 318 414 448
    476 6 21 24 37 61 100 401 525 551 578 626 634
    739 766 816 908 933 960 7 47 208 338 605 620
    890 983 8 10 16 39 95 211 338 394 432 513 617
    634 642 704 714 744 856 915 923 1146 9 46 53
    505 598 674 748 777 1020 10 76 390 588 666
    875 894 1033 11 22 44 154 178 474 634 635 727
    728 754 802 825 830 1063 1113 1192 1196 1242
    1248 12 569 712 1311 1761 1865 13 158 779
    828 842 843 868 949 1097 1099 1115 1129 1198
    1248 1261 1267 14 97 252 481 893 1119 1120
    1124 1129 1133 1312 1440 1444 1481 1521
    15 86 264 478 701 1061 1095 1361 1464 1485
    1527 1631 1688 1964 2208 2341 2516 2635 2645
    2792 2794 3202 3891 4182 4834 16 383 384 475
    889 957 1111 1307 1652
All (5) 1 456 4 437 9 733 10 608
    11 629
All (8) 15 1266 1400 1460 1581 1703 1823 1902
    4122
ALL (4) 15 1474 2154 4707 4712
all (1096) 1 23 57 98 132 138 210 235 275 285
    287 307 380 420 505 506 524 581 633 635 636 662
    2 9 45 75 91 96 131 196 203 224 225 279 280 325
    347 370 424 3 2 25 27 37 105 122 142 188 189
    190 191 279 292 326 333 344 350 391 435 452 480
    482 491 4 3 27 48 91 125 211 225 266 349 356
    363 373 402 455 480 5 33 45 57 104 174 198 215
    217 219 224 254 266 267 285 299 302 311 316 349
    362 363 367 377 382 399 405 414 416 424 426 452
    476 505 514 564 6 8 20 59 64 65 108 169 221
    254 259 261 314 335 394 395 407 425 426 498 514
    558 585 604 617 622 627 674 678 681 711 714 735
    749 752 753 756 786 808 809 816 834 836 847 848
    865 879 900 923 926 937 1024 7 88 92 97 214
    218 222 311 380 381 513 586 621 623 689 701 732
    883 902 903 956 1015 1047 8 23 50 76 79 97 115
    122 151 173 192 210 215 324 365 383 393 397 422
    444 483 488 511 531 536 537 538 541 543 607 625
    633 638 667 674 713 714 716 718 720 755 824 904
    926 945 969 1038 1046 1049 1096 1115 1121 1126
    1188 9 13 65 89 158 167 205 253 265 291 342
    359 361 379 430 433 453 499 506 522 524 528 602
    619 648 653 663 677 783 851 862 868 965 988 998

1014 1018 1019 1021 1028 1036 1049 1050 1059
1065 1094 1110 10 151 169 385 409 448 501 552
562 567 570 588 683 697 698 703 720 729 783 805
845 851 872 873 946 956 999 1002 1061 1073 1092
1126 1139 1149 1152 1160 1161 1274 11 69 179
182 199 301 310 324 361 378 470 474 488 496 515
517 557 626 631 634 641 643 646 687 736 739 749
758 780 790 792 834 839 876 908 966 1027 1060
1063 1082 1089 1102 1108 1144 1152 1156 1157
1199 1201 1235 1236 1245 1270 12 26 80 89 130
214 241 257 357 390 402 436 441 451 452 454 482
485 493 497 518 526 572 582 583 605 641 649 680
685 693 710 770 809 829 833 841 881 891 915 948
958 981 1070 1090 1123 1130 1146 1152 1163 1166
1184 1222 1257 1259 1404 1406 1417 1461 1479
1481 1547 1569 1575 1576 1587 1628 1636 1639
1673 1689 1712 1738 1745 1751 1767 1769 1774
1778 1796 1856 1859 1868 1882 1885 1897 1908
1910 13 2 17 82 127 161 189 213 215 226 300
308 311 376 400 407 408 437 455 476 483 489 494
555 558 560 575 585 611 665 671 672 680 683 698
707 717 720 741 747 776 779 783 784 796 797
799 816 855 878 885 897 910 912 937 939 940 944
963 990 997 1005 1019 1026 1039 1063 1074 1077
1086 1089 1100 1101 1122 1159 1205 1211 1279
14 30 45 51 52 55 65 83 117 161 193 194 207 214
219 222 234 236 237 248 252 254 274 277 287 289
293 300 305 309 320 324 326 337 340 366 388 398
403 413 422 427 446 455 457 467 470 478 479 487
503 517 522 526 546 567 577 583 591 599 601 609
610 617 619 631 641 642 656 699 703 762 766 771
800 815 836 862 864 868 912 975 1014 1019 1065
1085 1095 1132 1157 1177 1241 1242 1247 1251
1254 1265 1268 1278 1295 1306 1347 1392 1399
1404 1415 1416 1420 1428 1498 1536 1545 1551
1557 1561 15 206 290 370 375 384 461 540 657
743 797 820 878 955 1126 1289 1359 1452 1481
1613 1686 1687 1688 1691 1727 1737 1900 1917
1950 1963 2100 2191 2199 2350 2393 2422 2580
2647 2750 2769 2868 2994 3035 3042 3082 3086
3115 3121 3139 3153 3335 3450 3473 3487 3535
3629 3907 3945 4106 4117 4193 4227 4228 4235
4286 4488 4780 4813 4817 4821 4845 16 37 47
57 61 88 93 95 96 97 146 149 154 183 185 214 223
282 287 302 380 479 524 544 556 560 590 622 623
635 637 638 673 725 758 781 804 823 828 845 848
899 901 903 915 931 934 936 945 950 958 991 994
998 1010 1037 1045 1048 1084 1090 1092 1096
1098 1133 1143 1144 1150 1155 1178 1188 1197
1207 1224 1273 1286 1302 1312 1354 1369 1401
1433 1452 1460 1502 1517 1530 1589 1613 1620
1651 1658 1687 1699 1724 1726 1729 1755 1760
1794 1818 1828 1853 1865 17 69 189 194 197
355 391 690 699 831 833 1099 1161 1497 1625 1628
1629 1630 1631 1632 1771 1871 1884 1934 2097
2165 2190 2230 2329 18 5 7 9 28 34 43 51 55 61
100 104 130 146 148 149 152 157 191 212 215 239
246 252 267 276 298 315 316 318 333 334 337 354
372 378 386 399 410 415 439 457 461 465 466 467
470 474 475 483 485 491 495 506 538 568 572 583
585 588 589 591 597 598 599 604 610 611 612 628
633 634 636 637 646 661 680 681 701 710 721 727
733 739 745 753 755 756 758 765 778 784 785 793
803 806 808 814 816 827 832 849 861 868 887 890
913 917 928 946 948 957 958 960 962 963 971 972
974 977 983 984 989 995 997 1007 1013 1035 1036
1065 1090 1096 1106 1116 1120 1126 1134 1155
1157 1159 1161 1162 1168 1170 1175 1186 1187
1198 1200 1202 1204 1212 1216 1221 1225 1228

1236 1249 1261 1268 1270 1271 1275 1279 1287
1297 1305 1313 1319 1331 1333 1338 1348 1350
1352 1361 1363 1364 1365 1380 1388 1392 1398
1404 1439 1441 1452 1459 1468 1472 1475 1483
1484 1490 1499 1500 1516 1517 1524 1528 1537
1560 1561 1562 1564 1570 1577 1580 1584 1588
1589 1593 1600 1608
all (11) 1 596 7 848 9 798 1152 11 685
    12 222 16 1252 17 802 807 814 818
all (32) 15 139 388 526 917 1147 1151 1205
    1208 1421 1423 1494 1521 1546 1553 1576 1880
    2017 2044 2045 2158 2175 2654 2668 2852 3341
    3604 3757 3990 4152 4245 4315 4361
Allah (1) 14 1563
Allah (1) 12 601
allayed (3) 14 1126 17 342 1434
allbeplastered (1) 14 1480
Allbright (1) 3 486
alle (1) 15 3653
alle (1) 16 1884
Allee (1) 14 1448
allegations (1) 12 1626
allege (1) 12 1625
alleged (5) 14 985 1245 15 946 1046
    16 701
alleging (1) 16 1483
alleled (1) 7 167
Alleluia (3) 7 267 15 1954 4713
Alleluia (1) 15 77
alleluia (1) 7 209
Allelujurum (1) 14 888
allembracing (1) 16 1237
Allen (1) 12 1461
All'erta (1) 3 99
alles (1) 14 1378
alleviated (2) 14 877 17 1757
alley (2) 15 2341 16 1105
Alleyne's (1) 6 159
Allfather (1) 9 61
Allfather's (1) 14 1409
Allfours (3) 12 865 872 876
allhardest (1) 14 46
allhorse (1) 9 85
allied (1) 17 796
alligator (2) 12 1627 16 1795
Allimportant (1) 2 335
allimportant (1) 13 656
allimportant (1) 2 306
allincluding (1) 14 1412
Allingham (1) 17 1388
alliterative (1) 12 734
allmoist (1) 15 2550
allocution (1) 14 998
allotted (3) 14 859 17 1055 1762
Allow (3) 13 971 15 729 3584
allow (8) 7 489 9 600 10 418 504 695
    15 3534 3557 16 1619
allow (1) 15 4914
allowance (2) 16 1553 17 1546
allowed (9) 4 150 507 6 652 9 949
    10 730 14 90 16 305 17 88 278
allowing (5) 12 1672 16 1023 17 132 798
    1137
allpowerful (1) 15 4197
Allpox (1) 14 464
allround (1) 16 288
allroundman (1) 10 581
Allruthful (1) 14 103
all's (1) 11 1242

Allsop (2) 8 927 12 1320
alltimesticking (1) 10 1215
Allude (1) 4 530
allude (1) 17 525
alluded (3) 14 1293 16 605 1270
Alluding (1) 16 231
alluding (1) 17 695
Alluring (1) 11 26
alluring (1) 11 734
allusion (6) 2 329 8 686 12 733
    14 1305 16 1773 17 883
allusions (2) 17 441 1179
alluvial (1) 17 200
allwisest (1) 15 112
allwombing (1) 3 402
allwool (1) 17 1582
Ally (1) 15 2152
ally's (1) 7 896
Alma (1) 16 1139
almanac (3) 12 1476 13 334 14 524
Almany (2) 9 759 14 315
Almidano (8) 10 338 344 355 358 362 363
    1101 1281
Almidano (1) 15 2501
almightiness (2) 14 298 15 2093
Almighty (4) 8 978 14 166 1589 15 2999
almighty (2) 12 1354 18 42
Almighty's (1) 17 1074
almond (2) 5 490 12 1004
Almonds (1) 13 1043
almonds (1) 4 196
Almost (4) 7 175 8 741 1171 13 1131
almost (25) 1 74 5 260 324 477 6 351
    8 31 563 1128 13 87 233 450 511 513 707 722
    14 992 15 1051 3268 16 1394 17 1112
    18 106 676 859 1142 1408
almost (2) 15 998 4308
almosting (1) 3 366
alms (1) 10 9
alnight (1) 18 1196
Aloft (1) 15 2147
aloft (3) 1 4 7 1067 11 343
aloft (1) 15 3847
Alone (3) 11 742 17 1242 1245
alone (46) 1 250 274 565 654 2 123 3 133
    435 5 233 6 50 204 554 9 224 929
    10 164 601 11 54 733 935 956 1164 1198 1221
    12 1788 13 202 441 692 751 1219 14 284
    379 15 380 1594 3873 16 7 1526 1863
    17 542 547 2129 2130 18 67 86 118 311 370
    978
alone (1) 15 3386
Along (1) 3 356
Along (2) 15 1401 2176
along (111) 1 454 499 629 735 3 18 206
    4 86 91 109 191 231 241 5 1 155 317 344 392
    450 467 6 8 30 366 436 639 928 973 7 70 71
    877 909 916 959 1043 8 27 124 129 175 295 363
    428 523 643 9 160 10 54 63 73 85 514 532
    635 674 703 719 794 819 934 936 1104 1107 1124
    1154 1181 1247 11 1246 1253 12 2 4 1343
    1764 1829 1857 13 5 254 307 505 507 570 630
    815 1149 1231 14 188 546 773 965 15 547
    3849 4732 4896 4901 16 21 41 473 512 569 1369
    17 120 379 1437 1440 2048 2086 2087 18 78
    285 300 697 763 848 1228
along (1) 17 822
along (1) 15 3983
alongside (1) 16 238

aloof (1) 13 602
alors (1) 16 1453
alors (1) 15 3940
aloud (1) 9 549
Aloysius (6) 10 534 1122 1265 12 1704 1707
    17 656
alpaca (1) 7 131
alpaca (1) 15 3386
alpenstocks (1) 14 1394
Alpha (2) 14 1108 1171
alpha (5) 3 39 17 1046 1993 1995
alphabet (1) 3 427
alphabetic (1) 17 1799
alphabetical (1) 17 1194
alphabets (1) 17 771
Alphonsus (2) 8 529 15 3467
Alpine (1) 15 270
alpine (1) 15 2859
already (21) 2 350 6 348 8 162 844
    9 499 983 12 531 821 865 923 13 249
    14 50 1050 1207 15 3143 16 328 1003 1218
    1575 17 558 18 113
alright (2) 18 191 522
alrightness (1) 15 2093
Also (21) 5 290 503 6 449 838 8 59 1124
    12 1467 13 969 987 1023 1070 1087 1239
    14 134 178 15 1028 1060 16 531 715 1153
    1287
also (63) 1 740 2 83 263 4 536 5 435
    493 6 425 1020 7 68 500 9 789 957
    10 82 128 927 1223 1267 11 695 718
    12 343 1428 1840 13 144 226 797 968
    14 47 56 154 240 247 256 275 281 331 704 1195
    15 1780 1789 2089 2388 3065 3908 16 86 135
    220 392 551 646 864 929 1089 1408 1440 1524 1718
    1743 1830 17 481 484 576 18 623 1352
also (3) 15 1706 1745 2656
altar (12) 5 413 417 431 8 37 9 64 1222
    13 449 621 1038 15 2092 3405 18 837
altar (1) 7 491
altare (2) 1 5 15 4699
altarlist (1) 6 603
altarrails (2) 5 344 10 131
altar's (1) 3 117
altars (1) 8 13
altars (1) 9 1225
altarstone (2) 15 4691
alter (1) 15 3373
alteration (3) 15 1911 17 1282 2218
alterations (2) 17 1279 1433
altercation (5) 12 572 13 40 16 310
    17 2050 2252
altered (3) 16 934 1505 17 2191
alternately (4) 16 1631 17 25 960 2163
alternating (1) 17 2152
alternative (1) 16 1065
alternatives (2) 16 1612 17 80
alther (1) 14 168
Although (1) 14 1261
altitude (3) 9 329 17 1088 1195
altius (1) 15 84
altogether (13) 7 817 13 706 14 1187
    16 189 226 1050 1606 1610 18 71 519 982
    1305 1447
altruism (1) 17 2174
alumno (1) 10 841
Always (18) 4 209 483 5 133 563 6 345
    583 807 8 198 199 618 11 832 1194
    13 807 829 972 1054 1218 15 2444

always (155) 1 139 562 2 163 5 119 201
    277 383 558 6 1013 7 50 224 342 463 553 573
    8 30 94 177 245 299 445 574 582 729 9 10 67
    472 959 999 1032 1046 10 138 724 737 822 823
    897 993 1070 11 149 690 722 842 1047 1057
    12 508 1388 1794 13 36 131 153 208 227 235
    261 324 366 401 419 477 523 651 956 984 1020
    1143 1207 1251 14 542 841 844 15 448 645
    1115 2323 4952 16 17 117 543 992 1052 1072
    1074 1206 1403 1544 1624 17 1885 2128
    18 15 17 83 112 114 161 181 203 205 213 226 227
    238 252 277 289 322 357 416 435 468 549 620 659
    668 678 722 725 728 730 738 782 836 891 902 936
    938 943 966 1017 1041 1052 1063 1100 1108 1125
    1159 1167 1179 1205 1212 1221 1222 1242 1273
    1281 1290 1293 1295 1324 1342 1381 1391 1475
    1579
always (1) 3 203
AM (1) 13 1264
Am (10) 3 18 61 158 8 662 9 860
    11 114 15 2325 2769 16 969 1086
am (142) 1 63 218 311 416 430 638 677
    2 279 314 341 343 377 389 395 402 425 3 2 11
    15 26 127 267 324 366 391 425 434 435 442 452
    4 232 233 399 400 413 5 242 243 311 380 522
    6 21 36 203 712 880 7 218 8 141 142 145
    608 1188 9 63 64 179 205 208 271 382 390 526
    875 963 974 981 10 1068 1069 1120 11 198
    206 533 655 863 874 1069 13 833 929 1098
    14 826 1017 1115 1134 15 402 519 639 658
    682 762 775 776 777 803 804 873 998 1218 1231
    1634 1769 1966 1980 2091 2191 2204 2219 2258
    2275 2455 2508 2519 2546 2778 3655 3718 4174
    4575 16 242 728 766 17 1793 18 123 125
    450 475 503 737 882 914 1079 1107 1180 1366 1469
    1470 1516
am (4) 1 260 6 670 8 67 9 170
ama (1) 13 1209
amalgamated (1) 12 625
amalgamation (1) 17 1121
Amant (1) 8 832
amare (1) 9 941
amassed (1) 17 1750
amateur (1) 16 1734
amatory (2) 14 353 17 1590
amawf (1) 6 966
amawfullyglad (1) 6 965
amazing (1) 16 948
amazingly (1) 14 1464
amazon (1) 15 1058
amber (1) 1 256
amber (2) 15 465 4057
amberoid (1) 4 285
Ambidexterity (1) 15 1780
ambition (2) 17 1497 2173
ambition (1) 17 396
ambitions (1) 17 1497
ambitious (1) 17 1496
amble (1) 10 903
ambled (3) 3 332 347 11 450
ambles (1) 15 315
Ambrose (1) 3 465
ambrosial (2) 8 926 15 1108
ambulance (1) 10 504
ambush (2) 16 1068 17 2118
ambushed (1) 6 708
Amby (1) 14 1537
ameliorating (1) 17 1586
Amen (12) 9 482 11 46 1120 12 1674
    14 367 1527 15 1242 2442 3460

1138 1145 1160 1165 1168 1206 1208 1219 1221
1235 1241 1242 1256 1296 1299 1300 1306 1311
1324 1341 1352 1373 1382 1390 1402 1407 1467
1478 1482 1488 1500 1505 1536 1540 1580 1586
1600 1628 1647 1657 1675 1676 1689 1712 1719
1726 1728 1737 1744 1751 1753 1766 1768 1781
1789 1796 1803 1805 1848 1901 1904 1906 1911
1914 1915   **13** 20 27 38 51 55 119 163 188 218
257 281 303 304 320 327 374 386 388 399 411 470
525 531 596 607 627 680 683 715 719 736 788 797
809 814 844 871 873 895 897 920 934 962 988 1000
1040 1061 1067 1094 1108 1111 1122 1123 1124
1146 1157 1172 1180 1187 1189 1275   **14** 123
124 126 131 133 138 141 143 146 148 149 152 154
157 160 161 165 172 177 182 197 202 207 211 268
285 309 366 378 387 396 410 412 431 440 568 599
613 830 1017 1087 1097 1099 1153 1319 1336 1337
1366 1478 1498 1509 1537   **15** 91 95 546 564 570
584 631 657 857 887 1156 1338 1456 1466 1876
1878 1898 1900 1990 2529 2578 2590 2647 2690
2718 2759 2897 2935 2968 2990 3019 3035 3068
3105 3163 3188 3265 3279 3295 3322 3323 3346
3402 3476 3485 3528 3572 3620 3778 3861 3868
3935 4131 4306 4390 4445 4519 4656 4775 4863
4933   **16** 98 195 249 370 434 470 576 633 636
683 686 695 700 785 845 952 1017 1043 1048 1107
1189 1306 1331 1341 1401 1412 1462 1480 1671
1728 1755 1859 1866 1878   **17** 1101
And (28) 1 239 264 597 599   2 398   3 202
382 445   6 355   7 750 835 838   9 1148 1224
10 571 1252   11 344   12 742 746   13 948
16 980   17 804 806 814 816 822 826 827
And (1) 15 2587
and (6031) 1 2 4 6 9 10 12 13 14 15 16 17 21
22 24 25 30 32 35 37 38 39 42 44 53 60 61 65 67 70
75 80 82 83 93 95 99 101 104 107 112 123 125 131
135 136 145 147 148 155 157 163 168 186 191 192
194 195 200 205 206 207 210 211 212 224 225 230
232 243 251 258 271 273 279 283 287 289 298 311
314 316 317 320 327 328 329 331 332 335 337 342
344 349 360 366 368 370 378 385 389 392 397 399
403 405 412 413 414 420 431 433 438 443 444 445
446 447 449 452 461 465 466 467 472 481 485 491
495 499 500 502 508 513 514 516 520 525 529 541
547 554 556 559 567 573 575 578 582 593 595 604
612 616 618 619 620 634 638 640 643 644 652 654
655 656 657 658 659 662 664 666 689 690 692 693
694 696 704 709 710 714 731 741   2 9 10 12 23
29 37 43 44 50 61 68 71 72 82 84 87 96 116 118
121 122 124 125 126 127 129 130 131 139 140 146
147 148 150 154 156 158 165 166 170 176 178 184
186 190 202 205 209 211 213 214 217 221 224 227
228 229 233 247 268 273 274 275 282 292 297 304
308 310 311 313 317 322 332 338 340 345 353 359
368 369 370 371 372 375 387 389 393 413 427 428
436   3 2 6 9 10 13 26 27 30 41 43 46 47 48 49 53
55 64 66 68 70 74 76 79 81 82 86 105 106 117 118
125 126 155 157 159 193 213 225 239 240 248 249
254 255 265 277 278 284 288 290 306 315 316 317
331 341 342 343 344 347 354 357 358 360 361 373
386 401 406 429 431 438 462 463 464 465 487
4 1 7 11 13 18 34 37 40 43 50 59 64 67 114 118
127 131 133 141 143 147 160 163 166 171 174 181
182 183 193 194 195 198 208 223 243 247 251 253
257 261 266 272 274 275 277 280 296 298 300 304
314 327 328 333 338 350 371 373 382 386 387 389
390 393 394 395 400 401 402 404 405 408 424 425
453 456 468 489 497 501 504 505 506 512 514 516
517 518 535 537 538 539 541 544   5 4 14 17 18

21 22 26 28 37 47 50 57 61 65 67 70 76 77 80 89
104 105 107 110 132 143 155 156 163 171 181 185
190 193 201 204 205 210 213 217 221 229 231 242
251 255 261 263 267 298 301 309 314 315 319 323
330 339 346 347 349 354 355 356 365 369 376 377
381 389 405 413 414 415 416 418 419 420 423 431
437 439 444 445 446 448 457 459 464 468 477 488
489 490 497 499 507 509 513 519 529 535 543 553
568 569 570   **6** 2 6 9 10 11 17 19 26 27 29 31 37
43 45 46 52 56 65 73 88 91 100 102 111 122 129
140 159 162 209 222 225 255 264 269 272 278 279
282 283 291 300 314 319 326 336 350 354 361 373
379 387 405 407 409 416 417 422 433 462 465 488
491 492 495 498 500 503 504 517 519 520 521 523
544 550 554 560 562 575 578 584 585 586 588 593
610 611 612 615 616 627 631 632 633 634 638 652
655 675 677 679 680 715 719 720 724 732 733 747
750 767 774 775 777 791 798 800 801 820 834 847
850 858 863 864 868 869 873 875 898 907 910 930
932 938 944 945 953 955 957 982 985 1003 1008
1013 1021   **7** 4 5 6 8 10 15 18 19 22 26 32 40 42
44 57 65 70 73 89 91 93 94 102 103 109 116 123
130 135 138 143 147 156 188 201 209 211 212 218
228 255 258 293 299 301 304 309 311 318 329 331
344 346 360 369 371 372 379 391 394 395 397 399
408 415 417 421 424 437 447 448 459 465 466 467
481 490 494 516 527 532 533 534 535 554 563 565
566 598 599 619 622 639 644 653 660 664 680 685
690 702 705 706 731 732 733 734 738 746 762 772
776 778 794 797 805 810 817 820 826 870 877 880
881 883 890 902 904 912 923 932 933 934 935 939
941 943 945 948 951 964 972 993 999 1000 1001
1002 1011 1012 1023 1024 1026 1028 1029 1037
1039 1045 1046 1061 1064 1067   **8** 3 17 19 33 34
35 36 40 42 53 74 75 77 85 88 118 128 129 130 152
168 171 186 190 192 194 198 215 227 232 237 264
298 310 312 335 337 339 340 344 350 359 364 385
386 391 404 409 421 430 438 464 468 470 488 490
495 498 499 503 507 513 516 518 523 533 535 551
552 557 559 564 577 597 605 615 635 657 663 668
673 675 678 681 689 699 701 702 705 707 715 717
718 719 722 725 726 728 733 740 742 745 750 751
752 753 754 785 790 795 799 811 813 826 834 838
839 845 850 861 865 870 874 907 924 927 929 934
950 962 963 970 976 988 989 1001 1007 1014 1018
1025 1032 1037 1046 1070 1083 1104 1141 1143
1146 1147 1153   **9** 5 13 61 77 85 105 107 129 131
139 159 166 172 174 187 188 210 212 218 219 226
227 229 231 235 239 245 249 251 254 258 269 290
296 301 307 308 329 330 338 340 342 345 360 376
377 378 382 402 413 433 446 448 454 455 457 458
464 469 472 493 494 495 497 498 504 528 536 556
558 559 560 561 564 585 606 623 624 631 632 634
636 638 639 651 654 663 664 667 674 675 676 677
710 711 714 716 720 721 723 724 729 732 739 742
743 746 747 749 751 754 755 780 802 803 805 806
808 813 834 836 839 841 842 843 851 868 884 896
898 925 930 934 938 951 953 959 971 973 986 991
995 1002 1007 1008 1011 1014 1018 1021 1032
1034 1036 1039 1047 1048 1050 1054 1076 1086
1089 1090 1095 1100 1130 1138 1141 1156 1160
1162 1184 1188 1190 1191 1219   **10** 9 13 14 17
27 30 33 34 37 47 49 52 54 58 63 68 73 80 85 87 88
89 94 98 100 103 104 105 106 117 121 123 127 133
135 136 137 143 144 145 146 154 155 157 158 162
167 170 172 174 175 177 183 186 189 193 195 199
201 203 207 209 210 211 215 229 233 234 238 240
242 247 251 252 254 258 262 268 270 283 296 297
300 305 307 308 313 319 321 333 357 369 372 373

377 379 381 382 385 390 391 400 404 411 424 425
432 434 451 453 455 460 472 474 480 482 484 499
501 502 507 520 525 527 532 535 538 539 546 547
548 549 553 555 556 562 565 567 568 569 575 578
579 591 598 600 626 630 633 635 644 646 649 652
661 664 665 667 683 686 699 702 707 708 727 729
742 752 761 764 767 773 780 790 801 803 804 807
809 810 813 816 821 823 825 826 828 836 844 845
850 855 865 870 876 884 895 899 900 901 913 921
929 930 935 937 940 960 965 971 999 1002 1010
1015 1018 1022 1035 1040 1047 1050 1052 1055
1056 1069 1074 1087 1089 1097 1098 1104 1107
1116 1123 1125 1126 1129 1132 1140 1145 1149
1151 1152 1155 1160 1161 1163 1165 1166 1169
1171 1176 1179 1181 1184 1185 1190 1191 1194
1199 1201 1204 1206 1208 1209 1213 1215 1217
1219 1221 1222 1224 1228 1235 1237 1238 1240
1241 1243 1244 1246 1249 1260 1266 1272 1275
1276 1277 1281   **11** 12 34 35 56 67 111 113 119
123 126 144 163 165 167 177 201 211 214 217 244
246 249 253 264 266 268 271 278 283 286 297 302
315 317 318 330 331 335 338 339 341 348 350 353
363 366 375 377 383 384 394 398 399 408 422 454
467 479 486 491 493 495 499 521 570 571 600 609
620 634 652 655 660 661 683 698 727 760 768 772
795 796 815 821 822 840 842 861 868 878 881 883
896 920 923 940 950 952 960 972 992 1002 1003
1008 1009 1015 1031 1038 1042 1065 1081 1114
1115 1135 1143 1149 1152 1181 1198 1226 1230
1238 1241 1270 1272   **12** 2 3 10 15 21 24 26 35
38 39 41 43 44 45 46 47 50 51 57 62 64 70 73 75 77
82 84 85 86 89 94 95 96 97 98 101 102 103 104 105
106 107 108 110 111 112 113 114 115 116 118 119
120 122 129 132 134 137 150 155 158 161 166 167
169 170 175 176 192 193 196 203 206 213 222 223
226 227 228 231 245 246 247 249 252 254 267 268
270 280 282 283 284 285 288 295 297 299 300 305
326 338 342 343 344 354 356 359 361 368 371 372
376 379 381 393 402 405 410 436 437 442 444 445
447 450 451 452 454 466 467 470 477 480 481 482
483 484 485 486 491 492 493 494 496 497 498 499
500 501 505 507 508 509 511 513 515 519 524 526
529 536 539 542 545 547 549 551 577 579 582 589
590 593 605 611 621 622 623 625 627 628 630 633
634 635 637 648 652 653 655 657 660 662 663 664
665 673 679 680 681 683 687 688 689 690 691 693
698 699 705 709 710 713 716 718 721 728 729 735
738 748 754 755 763 771 772 773 776 778 781 782
785 788 792 800 803 805 807 808 809 812 813 830
831 832 833 834 836 843 844 848 850 886 889 890
891 894 896 899 900 902 904 906 907 909 910 911
912 914 920 925 942 945 948 952 955 956 957 958
960 966 967 971 974 975 976 977 978 981 983 985
986 997 1000 1002 1004 1005 1010 1023 1025 1028
1037 1038 1052 1054 1055 1068 1069 1074 1081
1087 1090 1098 1109 1112 1115 1117 1118 1119
1120 1123 1124 1126 1127 1128 1129 1130 1131
1132 1133 1134 1138 1139 1143 1145 1146 1150
1157 1161 1162 1172 1173 1178 1184 1186 1191
1193 1194 1195 1196 1199 1210 1211 1216 1223
1227 1235 1242 1243 1244 1245 1246 1250 1251
1255 1256 1257 1262 1263 1275 1277 1282 1283
1284 1286 1289 1290 1294 1297 1304 1309 1311
1313 1319 1320 1325 1326 1327 1333 1334 1335
1336 1338 1344 1348 1349 1350 1355 1356 1357
1359 1365 1366 1367 1371 1374 1378 1380 1381
1382 1383 1388 1390 1392 1395 1396 1397 1402
1404 1414 1415 1426 1432 1436 1438 1439 1441
1446 1447 1448 1449 1452 1454 1463 1467 1482

1304 1305 1307 1314 1317 1318 1332 1338 1340
1347 1358 1399 1402 1404 1410 1412 1421 1431
1432 1435 1437 1440 1441 1442 1449 1451 1452
1460 1466 1467 1468 1474 1481 1484 1486 1488
1490 1494 1496 1497 1501 1502 1506 1508 1509
1511 1513 1522 1523 1524 1527 1528 1530 1531
1533 1536 1538 1539 1540 1541 1542 1543 1544
1546 1547 1548 1552 1555 1558 1559 1565 1568
1569 1572 1582 1583 1590 1593 1594 1596 1598
1600 1602 1603 1604 1606 1607 1609 1610 1611
1613 1614 1617 1619 1622 1627 1628 1629 1638
1640 1641 1644 1645 1646 1648 1650 1651 1656
1657 1662 1668 1674 1676 1677 1686 1701 1704
1705 1706 1710 1715 1716 1719 1720 1722 1723
1725 1727 1729 1730 1733 1734 1735 1736 1737
1738 1739 1740 1741 1745 1746 1750 1758 1772
1779 1780 1785 1798 1806 1808 1810 1816 1818
1819 1826 1828 1829 1832 1845 1858 1859 1863
1871 1875 1877 1890 1895 1897 1902 1904 1907
1913 1917 1918 1919 1934 1937 1938 1963 1964
1965 1969 1971 1975 1981 1982 1994 1995 2006
2010 2014 2015 2017 2020 2025 2026 2033 2040
2041 2044 2046 2048 2056 2057 2076 2083 2094
2104 2106 2107 2111 2113 2117 2118 2119 2120
2129 2131 2141 2142 2143 2148 2153 2157 2158
2159 2160 2163 2164 2165 2166 2171 2172 2173
2174 2178 2180 2183 2190 2192 2213 2214 2221
2227 2229 2230 2232 2233 2252 2253 2254 2258
2263 2265 2266 2270 2271 2272 2273 2276 2278
2281 2282 2285 2286 2288 2289 2291 2298 2300
2301 2302 2304 2307 2308 2313 2315 2322 2323
2324 2325 2326   18 5 6 8 10 13 14 15 16 20 23
24 31 37 38 39 40 43 48 52 63 72 74 75 77 81 82 84
86 89 92 93 98 99 100 101 102 105 106 108 111 112
119 128 132 133 136 137 138 147 155 159 164 169
170 172 173 178 180 182 184 185 188 190 193 194
195 197 200 204 205 210 219 221 226 227 228 234
236 238 244 248 249 250 251 255 256 258 262 264
265 266 269 271 275 280 286 291 296 298 302 308
310 312 316 317 323 325 334 336 337 341 347 348
351 352 360 361 376 377 378 383 384 388 390 393
394 395 408 410 411 418 419 421 422 424 425 431
433 439 440 442 444 445 446 453 460 463 466 467
469 471 472 473 480 481 485 486 490 492 493 498
500 504 511 513 516 517 519 523 525 527 532 534
537 539 543 552 553 554 561 562 565 566 567 577
580 581 585 592 593 597 599 601 602 604 606 608
610 615 617 621 622 631 635 639 644 645 649 651
654 656 659 661 664 665 667 668 669 670 672 675
679 680 683 684 685 687 688 689 690 691 700 705
712 714 715 717 721 729 730 735 738 739 748 750
751 752 755 757 759 760 766 768 774 779 784 786
791 792 795 804 807 813 815 816 821 822 824 826
831 832 833 839 840 842 849 850 852 854 858 860
863 865 868 871 878 882 886 888 889 890 893 894
898 901 904 917 922 923 929 930 932 933 934 936
938 941 942 945 946 947 950 957 958 959 962 963
971 972 973 976 977 982 983 985 986 991 993 995
1000 1001 1008 1009 1014 1018 1020 1022 1028
1031 1034 1043 1046 1047 1049 1050 1052 1055
1062 1069 1072 1074 1075 1083 1085 1089 1090
1098 1101 1106 1110 1111 1114 1115 1119 1125
1130 1139 1147 1153 1155 1157 1163 1166 1169
1176 1178 1179 1186 1188 1190 1194 1204 1213
1217 1219 1220 1223 1224 1225 1230 1241 1243
1244 1247 1249 1251 1254 1259 1260 1264 1266
1268 1270 1271 1274 1278 1279 1280 1282 1285
1286 1287 1290 1299 1301 1302 1305 1306 1311
1312 1318 1319 1320 1323 1325 1330 1336 1342

1343 1347 1350 1351 1354 1361 1363 1365 1372
1373 1378 1381 1382 1385 1386 1387 1388 1394
1395 1397 1411 1412 1415 1416 1418 1422 1423
1427 1431 1434 1436 1438 1440 1443 1445 1454
1466 1467 1468 1469 1476 1478 1481 1489 1490
1491 1495 1500 1501 1502 1505 1507 1509 1511
1514 1515 1521 1526 1531 1533 1535 1547 1548
1552 1555 1559 1560 1561 1562 1563 1565 1566
1567 1573 1574 1577 1579 1580 1581 1582 1583
1584 1585 1586 1587 1588 1589 1590 1591 1592
1593 1594 1595 1596 1597 1598 1599 1600 1601
1603 1604 1605 1606 1607 1608

and (95) 1 239 264 301 587 591 597 2 14
3 384 445 4 290 348 437 6 166 670 7 43
44 253 322 327 428 471 523 768 769 771 828 832
839 845 847 848 850 855 856 857 858 862 863 868
8 783 9 137 190 249 252 401 416 455 807
10 235 248 609 616 838 11 459 553 685 780
785 787 1074 1289 12 27 100 420 423 1527
13 313 14 660 16 420 1251 1255 1261 1348
1743 1894 17 419 513 802 817 1352 1397 1783
and (504) 15 2 3 5 6 8 9 20 27 28 29 31 48 49
60 62 67 100 124 131 135 141 143 149 151 161 164
193 196 229 241 249 256 257 271 283 284 286 288
289 296 299 301 322 336 365 373 412 413 416 451
465 481 482 500 501 502 503 538 543 590 607 650
668 672 673 705 729 741 758 759 808 816 863 896
898 901 903 904 906 913 914 919 921 928 929 935
939 957 958 959 974 989 992 993 994 995 1000
1014 1015 1026 1027 1038 1059 1103 1129 1143
1176 1177 1179 1206 1208 1213 1238 1246 1259
1265 1281 1309 1310 1333 1341 1346 1355 1366
1376 1377 1379 1382 1398 1399 1403 1406 1407
1409 1413 1416 1417 1420 1425 1426 1429 1432
1434 1435 1440 1443 1448 1477 1480 1490 1491
1493 1496 1501 1550 1553 1569 1576 1578 1584
1587 1588 1602 1604 1610 1614 1622 1706 1710
1741 1745 1764 1811 1812 1815 1821 1824 1825
1826 1854 1898 1903 1904 1915 1927 1928 1939
2005 2006 2007 2019 2020 2021 2023 2031 2033
2035 2036 2041 2043 2047 2052 2058 2063 2072
2123 2142 2147 2152 2157 2160 2164 2169 2174
2175 2178 2183 2239 2245 2249 2252 2257 2264
2265 2281 2303 2305 2306 2340 2420 2435 2460
2461 2465 2479 2481 2482 2484 2486 2512 2571
2575 2586 2606 2611 2612 2624 2627 2628 2630
2636 2656 2658 2661 2670 2678 2682 2683 2697
2698 2699 2700 2709 2714 2721 2724 2727 2744
2745 2747 2753 2800 2809 2810 2811 2812 2831
2858 2860 2871 2885 2924 2925 2929 2942 2943
2945 2985 2986 3009 3089 3124 3127 3169 3195
3221 3233 3235 3317 3318 3325 3326 3328 3341
3342 3372 3382 3402 3420 3421 3434 3453 3460
3502 3524 3530 3535 3542 3545 3546 3550 3556
3565 3575 3583 3589 3595 3597 3622 3641 3649
3695 3708 3710 3722 3726 3728 3730 3733 3740
3757 3760 3821 3837 3838 3839 3840 3841 3842
3857 3858 3875 3876 3905 3916 3951 3956 3961
3962 3990 3995 4013 4016 4021 4028 4034 4037
4040 4049 4061 4063 4075 4077 4082 4083 4095
4101 4110 4118 4122 4128 4141 4143 4149 4158
4159 4160 4161 4162 4167 4186 4217 4223 4243
4244 4245 4251 4255 4256 4260 4275 4288 4312
4323 4324 4326 4329 4335 4355 4361 4367 4370
4387 4388 4396 4447 4451 4452 4453 4454 4455
4463 4476 4490 4498 4524 4543 4550 4556 4557
4560 4585 4613 4614 4622 4630 4670 4671 4672
4673 4674 4675 4682 4689 4694 4696 4703 4717
4718 4747 4749 4764 4869 4890 4902 4908 4909

4910 4913 4919 4921 4922 4926 4930 4936 4938
4944 4945 4946 4947 4958 4964 4965
AND (11) 15 419 925 1039 1458 1470 1592 1906
2536 3754 4001 4362
Andalusian (2) 18 441 1603
Anderson (2) 6 219 12 1893
Anderson's (2) 10 988 1214
André (1) 9 577
Andrew (4) 14 320 501 15 1488 17 2139
Andrew's (1) 15 537
Andrews (3) 4 203 12 1116 15 2741
androgynous (1) 9 1052
Andromeda (1) 17 1128
Andy (1) 15 2824
anear (9) 11 59 112 338 855 937 1269
18 304 787
anearby (1) 11 424
anecdotes (1) 16 1632
Anemic (1) 4 433
anemone (1) 5 266
anemones (1) 14 1134
anent (4) 16 323 431 986 1797
anesthesia (1) 14 966
angel (8) 1 655 7 212 9 989 1052
13 326 14 76 924 15 854
angel's (1) 15 1001
Angels (1) 15 3901
angels (8) 1 663 5 360 6 928 12 1737
1916 13 489 14 1383 15 2198
angels (2) 9 33 16 1868
angelus (1) 18 1542
anger (3) 9 784 12 1553 14 409
anger (1) 15 4275
angered (1) 14 411
angerly (1) 14 318
anglais (1) 12 1209
angle (11) 10 1116 1244 12 360 1917
14 1560 15 2781 17 917 1223 1276 1285
2304
angles (3) 17 1223 1441 1537
Anglia (1) 12 1255
Anglican (1) 17 789
angriling (1) 15 317
angrily (3) 7 649 10 242 273
angrily (3) 15 2937 4302 4788
Angry (1) 5 264
angry (9) 2 188 4 385 5 244 6 72
8 663 11 1200 12 532 14 156
15 2555
anguish (2) 14 771 15 4239
Angus (2) 12 106 194
ani (1) 15 1333
animadversions (1) 14 715
animae (1) 12 1749
animal (17) 4 376 6 951 971 8 722
11 1026 12 201 844 14 621 711 852
15 1234 2784 3358 16 870 17 1012 1706
1741
animal (1) 15 903
animality (1) 17 2236
animal's (2) 12 997 16 1792
Animals (1) 13 1030
animals (15) 4 349 6 401 8 652
11 1094 12 713 843 863 870 1062 13 904
14 1248 15 697 17 911 1134 2183
animated (2) 12 572 16 312
animation (2) 14 978 1178
animato (1) 17 1310
animosities (1) 17 1632

animosity (2) 16 1600 17 992
aniseed (1) 15 4327
anker (1) 14 1479
ankle (2) 8 165 13 168
ankles (3) 8 542 10 185 265
ankles (1) 15 313
Ann (9) 1 376 9 180 240 257 668 675 795 986
  18 952
Ann (1) 1 382
Anna (2) 8 80 12 647
annals (2) 8 1153 9 850
ANNE (1) 7 1070
Anne (4) 7 90 948 17 308
Anne's (1) 12 225
Annesley (1) 10 133
annex (1) 14 1458
annihilation (3) 16 758 17 464 2181
anniversaries (1) 17 602
Anniversary (1) 6 531
anniversary (5) 17 881 921 952 2275
  18 350
anno (1) 7 422
annos (1) 16 1763
annotations (1) 17 1381
ANNOUNCE (1) 7 78
announce (1) 15 1505
announced (8) 6 427 7 590 891 10 1110
  12 201 594 14 944 17 272
announcement (1) 16 1665
announces (1) 15 1898
announcing (1) 7 682
annoy (1) 15 4497
Annoyed (1) 5 455
annoyed (2) 5 240 18 178
annoying (1) 18 972
Ann's (1) 13 225
annual (8) 8 595 10 537 17 422 1115
  1545 1663 1664 1666
annually (1) 17 1705
annuals (1) 8 362
annular (1) 17 1107
annum (2) 16 1135 17 1660
annuntio (1) 15 1487
anointed (1) 15 1489
anon (4) 12 651 14 164 891 15 2467
anon (1) 15 917
Anonymous (1) 12 1696
anonymous (3) 15 1016 16 1534
  17 2260
Another (13) 4 11 185 5 136 7 919
  13 1196 14 599 15 865 1153 1808 2906
  16 82 516 1040
Another (1) 2 14
another (109) 1 166 311 2 56 3 121 122
  4 177 187 357 358 362 395 5 113 392 6 178
  405 548 667 712 818 914 1001 7 51 268 311 1025
  8 469 476 861 9 395 403 428 439 812 866 885
  1003 1009 10 372 485 711 11 540 1226
  12 65 750 753 756 785 810 1120 1193 1324 1409
  1778 13 103 602 715 798 819 846 864 874 967
  1050 14 55 609 784 886 892 894 1141 1367
  15 1360 2093 2105 2419 3085 3254 16 191 572
  602 603 770 1103 1206 1266 1385 1493 1550 1877
  17 182 372 1098 18 79 164 166 213 232 266
  970 1183 1198 1239 1242 1271 1436 1450 1605
another's (4) 3 447 16 1536 17 637
ans (1) 9 1135
answ (1) 11 866
Answer (3) 2 231 8 591 15 3052

ANSWER (1) 15 12
answer (44) 2 94 421 3 278 4 18 462
  5 58 439 7 658 8 88 324 613 1001 1078 1095
  1132 10 277 11 13 208 323 635 12 706
  867 872 1613 13 870 1242 14 254 730 1117
  1229 15 493 2437 3607 16 16 253 1085 1123
  17 946 18 89 333 728 739 744 1581
answer (5) 15 9 3942 4925 4926 4928
Answered (1) 5 65
answered (65) 1 26 114 184 198 220 229 416
  430 523 608 643 2 114 135 175 260 386 4 56
  320 5 94 177 418 537 6 111 536 562 713
  7 270 530 8 815 995 1088 9 235 516 636 974
  997 10 431 675 741 883 892 1041 11 235 237
  334 436 957 12 1739 1915 13 576 747
  14 95 102 113 336 1168 16 197 258 373 458
  664 1414 1668 1671 1676
Answering (1) 11 886
answering (7) 7 108 12 1834 13 513
  16 621 17 2002 18 1067 1071
Answers (1) 11 1023
answers (5) 6 619 8 323 11 690
  17 391 18 1529
Ant (1) 15 2457
antagonistic (2) 17 2154 2227
antarctic (1) 17 192
antecedent (3) 14 991 17 1278 1317
antechamber (2) 14 737 1380
antediluvian (2) 16 356 17 458
antelucan (1) 14 1103
anteponunt (1) 14 710
anterior (1) 17 2232
antesatisfaction (1) 17 2237
anthem (4) 12 921 13 282 14 347
  17 761
Anthony (1) 16 1666
anthropoid (1) 15 2590
antiBloomites (1) 15 1753
Antichrist (2) 15 2135 2141
Antichrist (1) 15 2145
anticipated (3) 14 1015 16 25 17 429
anticipating (3) 9 964 16 399 17 925
anticipation (6) 14 57 1279 15 2869
  17 761 771 2032
anticipatorily (1) 17 2277
antics (1) 15 1607
antidote (1) 14 869
Antient (2) 6 180 11 139
antifat (1) 18 456
antimacassar (1) 12 893
antiphoned (1) 9 792
antipodes (1) 16 635
antiquated (1) 15 3293
antique (5) 11 1261 16 819 892 17 1392
  1683
antiques (1) 11 87
Antiquity (2) 9 718 720
antiquity (3) 12 176 17 748 1159
Antisthenes (4) 7 1035 9 621 10 816
  15 2642
Antithesis (1) 7 952
Antitreating (1) 12 684
antitreating (1) 12 683
antlered (3) 15 2032 3764 3823
Antoinette (1) 17 1308
Antonio (5) 6 375 16 679 683 839 1197
Antonio (1) 16 702
Antonio (1) 15 150
Antonio's (1) 16 686

Antony (1) 9 252
Antrim (2) 9 818 12 1244
ants (1) 6 810
anvils (1) 12 1717
anxiety (2) 1 187 16 118
anxious (1) 16 766
Anxiously (1) 9 292
anxiously (3) 9 291 10 939 16 1288
Any (11) 2 17 7 992 10 647 11 494
  1255 12 1200 1583 14 1166 1442 15 364
  3671
any (180) 1 151 162 490 2 17 46 3 250 319
  4 61 429 5 55 90 211 271 390 394 6 747
  7 257 8 83 131 190 217 767 1116 9 423 644
  844 845 1134 10 668 851 864 11 98 437 494
  12 15 357 361 763 826 1052 1088 1542 1845
  13 101 229 308 379 984 995 1038 14 121 173
  237 284 418 422 519 596 687 721 782 786 811 874
  920 1179 1197 1250 1561 1574 15 968 1066
  1111 1295 2207 2738 3204 3206 4427 4597 4644
  4839 4952 16 83 84 85 99 120 182 226 501 584
  650 730 739 741 750 808 813 844 863 995 1024
  1056 1060 1069 1074 1092 1095 1100 1125 1221
  1288 1326 1418 1539 1566 1624 1625 1627 1802
  1843 1865 1892 17 9 68 343 487 519 657 850
  858 1081 1222 1413 1762 2008 2178 2200 2206
  18 52 83 98 156 171 187 201 224 299 319 351 396
  437 456 472 490 507 530 693 714 1037 1043 1244
  1247 1269 1401 1403 1451 1471 1473 1499 1537
Anybody (1) 15 4024
anybody (14) 6 373 810 900 931 14 1179
  16 426 18 492 1092 1094 1233 1419 1434 1570
anybody's (2) 16 1282 1633
Anycock (1) 9 646
Anyhow (9) 12 850 13 785 1226 16 153
  209 804 976 1603 1725
anyhow (39) 4 76 5 65 274 6 789
  7 193 340 999 8 228 628 949 995 10 447 500
  566 915 11 909 12 206 333 885 1178 1573
  1656 1844 13 506 15 171 4891 4939
  16 182 195 667 18 72 100 225 284 536 891 925
  952 1123
anyone (14) 6 597 741 7 711 9 80
  11 1045 12 1762 1765 14 20 28 16 1195
  18 149 312 454 955
anyone (1) 1 589
anyone's (1) 14 1185
Anything (3) 12 59 13 256 15 593
anything (85) 1 89 184 192 2 21 80 3 62
  4 55 58 380 512 5 216 410 6 201 757 956
  7 319 8 276 321 448 493 581 815 824 859 1035
  1068 10 263 679 715 1085 11 832 12 53
  758 867 1036 1230 13 951 1021 1301 14 17
  40 15 977 4892 16 1 29 85 149 183 216 1047
  1051 1100 1101 1228 1247 1369 1519 1741 1782
  1862 18 18 28 279 298 304 356 432 589 616 659
  671 865 880 911 937 1021 1023 1050 1136 1149
  1174 1191 1339 1343 1403
anythingarian (1) 15 1712
Anyway (1) 15 116
anyway (14) 6 762 13 928 14 50
  16 203 941 1247 1867 18 35 99 462 905 944
  1207 1395
anywhere (10) 3 414 485 7 883 12 1204
  13 143 16 26 997 1651 1768 18 327
anywise (1) 14 901
aorist (2) 17 2218 2220
apache (1) 15 1356
Apart (1) 6 130

archbishop's (1) **7** 181
archbishops (1) **8** 708
archconspirator (1) **15** 855
archdiocese (1) **7** 1016
archduke (1) **8** 871
arched (3) **4** 379 **10** 621 **16** 30
archery (1) **15** 1434
arches (3) **10** 402 **12** 1734 **16** 112
arches (4) **15** 1398 2371 2460 3393
Archimedes (1) **13** 1142
arching (1) **10** 221
arching (1) **15** 4100
archipelago (1) **10** 1097
archipelagos (1) **17** 219
architect (1) **18** 721
architecturally (1) **13** 44
architecture (1) **8** 1181
Archjoker (1) **12** 559
archly (2) **10** 333 **11** 955
archons (1) **9** 239
archway (1) **3** 376
archway (2) **15** 578 4449
arclamp (1) **15** 151
arctic (1) **17** 192
Arcturus (1) **17** 1048
Arden (2) **9** 880 **16** 426
ardent (3) **14** 1371 **15** 2610 **17** 1149
ardent (2) **11** 530 551
ardentbold (1) **11** 526
ardenti (1) **7** 722
ardently (1) **14** 982
Ardilaun (1) **5** 306
Ardilauns (1) **14** 1476
ardour (1) **12** 642
ardri (1) **12** 177
Ards (1) **2** 283
Are (53) **1** 228 415 428 522 712 717 **5** 55 246
6 8 85 215 977 **7** 419 504 527 692 **8** 10 242
451 612 **9** 273 322 849 1068 **10** 657 1004
11 296 810 1126 **12** 52 148 307 758 852 1319
1473 **13** 1105 **15** 260 261 355 600 865 1283
1344 1990 2194 2199 2533 2953 3946 4303 4647
16 1674
are (426) **1** 113 120 161 210 425 505 611 636
2 49 50 190 219 263 279 347 349 350 362 380 389
418 **3** 11 17 50 55 272 288 312 322 409 432 464
485 494 **4** 17 47 68 138 202 249 313 400 403 407
479 480 **5** 84 87 135 254 325 346 388 496 510
6 57 61 118 128 170 239 367 501 546 556 558 644
656 657 662 675 677 754 759 770 780 849 857 871
947 951 961 1004 1014 1033 **7** 47 82 288 453 481
565 730 739 842 890 900 902 911 948 1010 1011
1023 **8** 10 86 96 125 130 140 156 209 366 389
445 454 483 539 542 543 544 569 640 868 920 982
1116 1118 **9** 11 46 105 132 178 229 255 289 291
312 323 328 356 388 400 408 429 467 516 654 666
709 744 754 775 776 783 784 794 846 850 883 884
898 903 928 947 954 999 1007 1011 1048 1051 1059
1060 1064 1081 1130 1156 **10** 407 480 595 666
682 722 724 740 834 854 857 873 882 949 989 1119
11 156 566 582 599 814 831 872 949 970 971 979
1064 1069 **12** 6 12 24 136 278 303 310 331 523
712 722 723 732 797 836 850 865 1141 1240 1248
1260 1296 1301 1377 1436 1449 1462 1560 1645
1882 **13** 192 382 807 816 822 828 888 913 929
984 1037 1065 1073 1075 1078 1116 1128 **14** 8
44 64 75 78 144 146 152 227 300 497 527 546 771
785 816 1043 1069 1083 1090 1161 1233 1241 1262
1278 1293 1314 1328 1344 1345 1373 1380 1398

1459 1505 1559 **15** 120 195 329 338 400 428 438
623 635 655 702 736 741 794 802 825 827 836 941
1043 1066 1195 1291 1301 1395 1538 1642 1760
1779 1834 1980 2106 2195 2200 2258 2315 2330
2359 2361 2425 2434 2447 2680 2726 2775 2800
2848 2933 2965 2973 3025 3066 3127 3137 3175
3199 3279 3289 3393 3458 3485 3535 3558 3604
3835 3885 3888 3903 4176 4308 4370 4401 4478
4566 4648 4784 4817 **16** 194 362 471 655 821
822 849 851 874 889 1088 1119 1124 1125 1126
1156 1645 1780 **17** 1004 1761 1793 **18** 94 184
205 245 260 275 281 300 456 538 541 678 882 950
1057 1145 1180 1207 1215 1280 1363 1425 1459
1481 1502 1545 1571 1576
are (15) **2** 14 **3** 257 **4** 287 288 **7** 427 846
847 856 857 858 859 **10** 614 **12** 362
17 416
are (39) **15** 6 125 251 312 313 367 501 1136
1179 1208 1324 1400 1405 1413 1501 1520 1550
1551 1552 1553 1568 1588 1704 1815 1823 1828
2021 2043 2046 2485 2513 2658 2727 2745 2746
3340 4077 4082
area (11) **8** 882 **10** 253 1063 **16** 119
17 84 87 102 109 126 **18** 1085 1233
area (2) **15** 36 695
areas (1) **12** 641
arecanut (1) **10** 32
arena (1) **9** 107
arenary (1) **17** 1699
Aren't (2) **11** 79 **12** 1386
aren't (4) **11** 416 **13** 855 **15** 819 1660
arent (6) **18** 570 706 1081 1236 1340 1348
aresouns (1) **14** 202
Argal (1) **9** 298
argent (2) **9** 925 **15** 3949
Argive (2) **7** 1039 **9** 622
argol (1) **12** 1580
Argos (1) **2** 48
argue (1) **7** 1011
arguing (2) **12** 435 1235
argument (5) **12** 498 575 **14** 216 1000
16 1547
Argumentum (1) **15** 2371
Argus (1) **17** 2140
aria (1) **3** 100
arid (1) **17** 1169
Aries (1) **17** 573
aright (2) **10** 942 **16** 1773
arise (2) **14** 1102 **15** 2496
arise (3) **15** 139 1164 4671
arisen (1) **14** 1001
arises (1) **15** 336
Arising (1) **12** 860
aristocracy (2) **15** 3256 **16** 1809
Aristocrat (1) **18** 1240
aristocrat (1) **13** 339
aristocratic (1) **5** 387
Aristocrats (1) **18** 1238
aristocrats (1) **8** 873
Aristotle (5) **9** 57 80 996 **14** 976 **17** 716
Aristotle's (3) **2** 68 **9** 297 **10** 586
Arith (1) **14** 1268
arithmetical (4) **17** 574 739 919 1089
Arius (3) **1** 657 **3** 50 **15** 2643
ark (2) **14** 788 **15** 3868
arks (1) **13** 869
Arm (1) **7** 983
arm (35) **1** 147 159 182 502 **3** 451 **6** 10 491
519 648 **7** 40 434 959 982 983 **8** 297 519 590

9 59 **10** 222 251 551 **11** 203 360 813
13 64 202 915 **14** 472 1149 **16** 1721 1735
18 885
arm (17) **15** 20 27 218 538 562 863 1316 1909
2083 2636 2724 2901 2925 3089 3090 4218 4472
Armada (1) **3** 149
armada (1) **9** 752
Armageddon (1) **17** 2056
Armagh (2) **2** 274 **12** 85
Armagh (2) **15** 1421 1423
ARMAGH (2) **15** 1479 1486
armchair (3) **11** 1230 **12** 585 **15** 3174
Armed (1) **15** 4680
armed (2) **2** 275 **17** 2188
armfolded (1) **15** 4142
armful (2) **4** 266 **6** 697
arming (1) **15** 4029
armless (1) **15** 581
armlet (1) **6** 181
armorial (1) **15** 1049
armour (3) **12** 215 1183 **15** 4402
armour (1) **15** 4611
armpit (4) **4** 468 **5** 517 519 **7** 131
armpit (1) **15** 3124
armpits (2) **13** 1026 **15** 2974
armpits (3) **15** 2015 2290 2658
Armpits' (1) **10** 622
armplates (1) **15** 1853
armrests (1) **17** 1542
arm's (1) **8** 565
Arms (13) **2** 416 **4** 406 **8** 716 848
12 60 504 **13** 964 1136 **17** 481 **18** 2 711
965 1220
Arms (1) **15** 1413
arms (50) **1** 13 **2** 140 445 **3** 462 **4** 150
5 57 204 367 540 **7** 487 **8** 450 **9** 3 406 710
934 937 1163 **10** 158 341 **11** 256 589
12 1343 1873 **13** 212 341 734 810 **14** 1321
15 786 3949 **16** 30 947 1027 1536 1727
17 220 340 690 1118 1222 1292 1611 2111
18 105 200 497 642 895 1263 1607
arms (2) **7** 858 868
arms (24) **15** 1164 1601 1886 2158 2217 2612
2670 2678 2721 3063 3168 3224 3453 3503 3930
4021 4031 4047 4058 4063 4100 4121 4255 4944
armstrap (1) **6** 11
Armstrong (4) **2** 18 21 27 32
armstrong (1) **14** 1440
Armstrong's (1) **2** 22
Army (1) **15** 730
army (10) **1** 696 **3** 106 **5** 72 432 **8** 439
15 614 750 **16** 1016 **17** 869 **18** 377
Arnold (1) **16** 1765
Arnold's (1) **1** 173
Arnold's (1) **15** 2514
Arnott's (1) **8** 159
Aroma (1) **15** 1325
aroma (1) **11** 537
Aromatic (1) **5** 193
aromatic (3) **5** 390 **17** 302 1332
Aroon (1) **15** 4591
arose (4) **12** 1357 **14** 836 **17** 714 2196
Around (1) **3** 224
around (55) **2** 300 **3** 275 **5** 167 450 559
571 **6** 676 680 763 846 893 **8** 346 583
9 352 **10** 296 827 876 888 **11** 592 749
12 3 58 64 213 526 695 698 752 780 842 1479
1591 1754 **13** 1051 1066 **15** 1674 2666
16 33 517 550 1545 1714 **17** 1721 **18** 380

468 879 922 965 1102 1159 1410 1431 1437 1453 1607

around (2) 15 3408 4152
aroused (1) 16 1361
Arrah (4) 12 141 193 491 1792
arrah (1) 18 1462
Arran (4) 10 1186 1187 12 36 15 1366
Arranged (1) 17 1608
arranged (7) 12 618 13 195 990
    15 4043 17 1358 1444 1554
arrangement (8) 10 783 11 798
    12 1290 14 1044 1282 15 443 16 1401
    17 1907
arrangement (1) 6 150
arrangements (3) 12 366 16 518 1314
arrears (1) 12 1097
Arrest (1) 15 1016
arrest (3) 14 990 17 583 1961
arrested (6) 3 180 9 628 17 765 1274
    1286 2081
arresting (1) 14 1369
arrises (1) 12 1733
arrival (5) 12 596 15 2141 16 437
    17 61 70
arrive (5) 10 1188 15 1669 3891 16 766
    1295
arrived (2) 6 789 16 983
Arrivederla (1) 10 360
arrives (2) 15 4317 4673
arriving (1) 16 1381
arrogant (1) 7 864
arrows (1) 12 1715
arruginated (1) 17 1215
Ars (1) 10 839
ars (1) 7 167
Arse (1) 15 1149
arse (8) 7 241 981 991 10 900 12 1792
    14 639 15 53 848
arse (1) 16 980
Arsenic (1) 18 240
arsenic (1) 15 4541
arsenic (1) 15 1746
Arsewipe (1) 15 812
Arsing (1) 12 752
arson (1) 17 2186
Art (4) 9 48 183 12 177 14 1416
Art (1) 13 645
art (42) 1 73 146 152 290 484 4 370 5 405
    6 597 7 608 9 49 132 425 625 626 1131 1211
    10 291 12 175 1199 1442 13 57 14 35
    255 267 901 1411 1415 1456 15 840 2497 3186
    4042 4413 4952 16 598 1451 1455 1733 1794
    17 581 18 1296
art (1) 16 1322
art' (1) 15 3186
Artane (2) 6 537 10 3
Artane (1) 15 1887
ARTANE (1) 15 1889
artcolours (1) 15 3234
artery (1) 6 434
Artesian (1) 17 205
Arthur (7) 3 227 4 101 8 462 528
    9 881 12 196 1453
Arthur (1) 12 422
Arthur (1) 15 4685
artichokes (1) 13 1090
article (9) 9 322 1082 12 1445 1871
    16 818 1653 17 1151 2107 18 830
articles (13) 9 440 12 586 1725 14 896

15 3250 3761 17 439 440 1279 1432 2072 2109
2110
articulation (1) 15 4720
articulo (1) 12 478
artifice (1) 17 2202
artificer (1) 9 952
artificial (6) 4 196 8 863 14 969
    16 293 17 1763 2069
Artifoni (7) 10 338 344 355 358 362 363 1101
Artifoni (1) 15 2501
ARTIFONI (1) 15 2503
Artifoni's (1) 10 1282
Artillery (1) 15 4663
artillery (1) 12 530
artillery (1) 15 4453
artilleryman (1) 12 966
artisans' (1) 8 709
artist (7) 3 62 9 377 10 582 13 583
    15 2508 16 1436 1448
artistic (7) 12 1450 13 323 14 1254
    16 1835 17 20 560 1542
artists (2) 6 220 12 1821
ARTIUM (1) 7 754
artless (2) 14 759 15 1190
Arts (1) 9 577
arts (6) 1 32 9 1061 15 4952 17 553
arts (1) 15 1826
arun (1) 17 727
Arval (1) 9 65
As (76) 1 136 2 200 349 409 3 452
    4 267 5 48 6 189 303 347 372 616 687 936
    961 7 885 8 44 166 352 9 186 376 660 696
    757 879 10 851 904 1043 1115 1246 1265
    11 519 623 641 1245 12 614 760 1258 1312
    1362 13 129 171 593 976 14 93 810 1038
    15 880 2087 2973 3198 3472 4555 16 42 385
    1359 1444 1509 1888 17 66 895 911 1552 1562
    1658 1760 1761 1763 1896 2178 2180 2182 2190
    2194
As (5) 7 320 580 9 304 1013 16 702
as (1073) 1 37 92 106 152 185 333 357 374 381
    476 491 506 529 549 566 573 622 666 704 730
    2 8 67 111 127 170 174 178 193 214 237 272 298
    331 332 349 352 424 425 429 446 3 38 195 217
    228 242 255 272 345 390 408 440 4 6 31 39 59
    63 81 108 128 198 216 297 303 394 466 508
    5 74 76 214 225 250 272 6 67 138 172 189 233
    257 303 327 374 375 427 450 510 733 821 870 871
    1028 7 42 69 173 219 223 280 395 401 415 460
    463 497 506 602 628 729 755 778 824 919 1028
    1031 8 48 119 128 218 296 313 345 475 495 511
    537 598 662 682 715 759 769 883 894 967 1151
    9 4 45 78 149 227 241 246 259 317 341 350 370
    378 384 418 419 485 489 531 620 626 648 665 708
    766 785 801 870 922 924 932 975 1041 1042 1048
    1060 1077 1193 10 2 30 59 79 137 169 286 363
    379 747 750 758 851 852 859 941 953 956 995 999
    1038 1056 1106 1118 11 100 101 187 366 421
    555 569 623 661 757 763 789 799 800 849 853 859
    982 1052 1146 1161 12 49 69 80 156 207 244
    245 270 282 287 323 345 348 349 351 354 369 395
    463 474 475 510 511 554 573 580 635 642 645 697
    707 726 752 776 778 787 788 813 852 863 885 900
    905 910 921 925 962 1082 1097 1179 1213 1239
    1258 1312 1362 1368 1390 1449 1466 1479 1522
    1535 1613 1664 1719 1723 1736 1761 1768 1776
    1789 1838 1840 1845 1850 1901 1913 13 4 19 20
    34 80 81 82 90 120 178 186 260 269 293 302 346
    347 382 412 461 468 484 499 516 517 532 588 589

594 595 599 600 611 691 697 709 721 742 772 806
833 855 913 950 952 1021 1054 1058 1141 1197
1224 1227 1301 14 8 20 33 42 52 62 108 110
116 124 125 131 180 196 200 203 212 244 253 254
255 256 266 273 278 281 288 289 319 331 339 344
382 384 387 396 411 412 415 420 432 433 439 442
446 447 451 479 483 485 490 548 551 563 564 565
607 615 638 639 640 652 656 661 662 666 670 700
705 717 729 739 745 757 758 763 777 788 795 815
818 819 840 843 846 848 857 872 873 879 887 890
912 914 917 924 925 927 928 958 965 968 978 979
983 985 992 994 997 999 1007 1040 1041 1044 1067
1127 1139 1153 1154 1165 1166 1174 1179 1186
1190 1191 1228 1230 1234 1235 1241 1253 1265
1268 1273 1289 1292 1294 1302 1304 1307 1315
1316 1319 1344 1347 1353 1357 1358 1360 1361
1364 1367 1374 1381 1383 1429 1435 1500 1515
    15 95 266 325 521 556 571 788 794 823 873 887
943 945 973 980 1019 1033 1045 1047 1062 1066
1067 1071 1082 1151 1385 1390 1762 1769 2090
2091 2221 2284 2372 2410 2673 2733 2786 2818
2826 2941 3001 3130 3131 3256 3392 3425 3483
3485 3486 3588 3827 4519 4527 4822 16 9 12 14
15 18 21 24 39 54 64 68 77 90 93 107 117 139 142
145 176 178 187 193 203 216 234 266 269 281 284
290 302 358 364 392 435 443 444 467 488 490 516
526 539 549 553 556 564 587 603 605 612 627 633
645 654 670 721 744 748 749 751 753 769 774 783
794 813 817 836 851 856 864 871 874 934 958 988
1005 1023 1027 1030 1036 1037 1042 1045 1046
1048 1051 1061 1064 1070 1078 1079 1086 1095
1118 1126 1132 1138 1149 1157 1158 1173 1192
1202 1204 1218 1221 1225 1228 1230 1233 1262
1268 1291 1321 1323 1325 1336 1339 1345 1346
1349 1366 1389 1394 1395 1400 1403 1404 1405
1408 1420 1428 1442 1449 1451 1469 1471 1492
1493 1506 1514 1518 1530 1542 1551 1554 1561
1580 1589 1593 1598 1601 1603 1605 1606 1609
1612 1618 1623 1635 1636 1644 1660 1678 1687
1692 1693 1694 1701 1727 1729 1734 1739 1742
1755 1775 1778 1787 1802 1804 1805 1807 1808
1822 1831 1832 1838 1843 1849 1860 1863 1892
    17 5 7 67 68 69 92 177 216 226 269 344 369 385
450 451 454 490 516 521 557 585 588 596 640 647
651 657 666 678 730 739 784 835 896 909 995 996
1012 1019 1051 1089 1092 1098 1117 1144 1151
1153 1154 1155 1205 1208 1329 1503 1512 1758
1857 1891 1969 2006 2035 2059 2115 2118 2178
2181 2201 2218 2221 2269 2274 2285 18 1 22 46
48 52 55 133 136 161 204 239 241 242 283 288 297
333 349 369 393 419 431 432 437 440 451 454 480
490 503 512 517 525 528 551 572 608 632 655 676
702 727 746 747 752 788 836 868 880 935 938 942
951 965 1001 1002 1011 1020 1027 1060 1076 1093
1099 1116 1123 1165 1183 1191 1204 1216 1239
1246 1255 1269 1340 1353 1376 1409 1449 1461
1479 1491 1516 1521 1522 1548 1563 1571 1602
1604
as (14) 7 243 317 9 33 1144 10 15 617
    16 702 979 980 1252 1680 1886
as (19) 15 49 192 353 468 901 903 912 1349
    1830 1844 1853 2184 2482 2699 3227 3988 4454
    4796 4915
ascend (2) 12 1911 1916
ascendancy (2) 14 684 861
ascendant (1) 17 750
ascendants (1) 15 1779
ascended (2) 7 46 9 1219
ascending (4) 7 835 10 971 1027
    17 1608

230 235 244 245 318 325 338 345 347 358 373 390
426 437 452 471   4   45 46 62 63 84 140 146 151
154 163 201 212 244 250 257 340 344 349 394 405
419 421 432 456 458 465 498 503   5   20 50 56 61
71 98 103 135 151 164 169 171 192 207 233 274
297 342 344 345 347 359 381 416 428 431 494 555
567   6   11 39 78 79 86 137 204 235 239 310 313
349 398 446 481 509 510 518 519 543 544 575 576
577 582 583 597 614 636 643 683 697 701 714 715
716 726 728 730 753 762 786 794 812 844 853 913
918 923 933 951 986 998 1012 1019   7   99 127 132
163 239 292 338 361 432 440 444 447 470 503 566
568 635 642 650 671 706 729 773 793 819 820 836
870 880 912 939 941 943 946 1017 1067   8   29 88
114 121 134 135 146 159 166 191 270 284 322 341
344 347 363 368 384 397 472 507 534 551 553 560
565 571 654 664 688 723 768 824 830 867 925 945
979 993 1006 1069 1115 1126 1154 1178 1180
9   19 60 63 215 216 271 274 386 513 619 636 711
787 803 846 929 933 965 1035 1061 1088 1154 1166
10   6 20 30 40 42 47 59 68 103 129 131 142 176
187 208 240 245 261 283 313 321 322 330 339 380
383 395 442 488 508 536 578 580 588 591 601 647
666 667 694 732 734 738 755 784 813 858 903 960
973 992 993 1052 1063 1109 1110 1126 1131 1187
1188 1192 1231 1244 1262 1279   11   70 186 198
220 232 266 284 291 362 377 569 608 609 686 689
725 771 808 822 893 902 921 934 968 1016 1041
1045 1047 1063 1199 1205 1219 1229 1247 1250
12   1 14 30 38 39 47 60 151 163 174 186 200 219
220 229 230 231 235 257 278 304 310 346 358 368
401 407 426 514 520 533 581 730 732 763 800 809
827 882 939 1019 1022 1046 1069 1123 1132 1162
1167 1181 1219 1250 1267 1288 1291 1324 1325
1329 1332 1343 1362 1370 1378 1387 1393 1426
1457 1458 1518 1573 1591 1598 1639 1671 1676
1756 1769 1798 1840 1866 1880 1917   13   6 38 54
60 93 103 105 119 142 143 157 159 162 210 253
264 269 270 295 305 331 340 346 368 397 412 415
449 478 479 497 502 518 521 539 564 573 588 590
625 653 687 690 742 764 783 792 809 816 819 829
847 914 915 917 941 952 957 963 970 986 1000
1028 1030 1038 1054 1061 1074 1086 1122 1127
1133 1151 1152 1171 1172 1181 1188 1190 1193
1202 1218 1219 1224 1229 1256 1302   14   52 71
109 124 167 192 218 247 257 327 338 395 421 424
446 452 455 458 481 485 486 531 539 540 556 602
618 659 678 717 730 740 742 757 785 797 831 864
865 885 911 914 930 937 946 951 990 1019 1027
1039 1056 1110 1117 1152 1159 1177 1178 1182
1195 1204 1208 1213 1223 1230 1282 1316 1348
1351 1363 1367 1376 1393 1417 1444 1455 1466
1495 1511 1547 1554 1576   15   203 232 234 290
381 410 458 496 636 650 796 853 940 941 948 975
978 981 982 1003 1010 1012 1020 1021 1055 1061
1160 1171 1201 1361 1383 1525 1543 1613 1631
1807 2331 2717 2741 2780 2795 2933 2936 2978
2981 2991 2994 3029 3030 3084 3086 3102 3116
3125 3162 3183 3355 3357 3484 3632 3949 4109
4195 4227 4445 4618 4817 4847   16   22 47 49 51
59 61 71 84 94 104 122 125 149 152 158 162 164
183 215 216 227 245 250 256 263 273 293 295 296
301 302 351 358 375 378 380 389 430 433 475 502
508 537 546 627 629 630 632 637 644 650 654 667
673 685 710 766 795 798 807 808 816 824 828 871
882 889 892 900 933 938 950 952 959 1005 1048
1074 1081 1089 1094 1114 1130 1132 1136 1142
1149 1206 1211 1230 1244 1272 1273 1276 1290
1295 1302 1307 1318 1326 1340 1362 1434 1440

1442 1460 1479 1488 1503 1517 1520 1521 1535
1542 1567 1578 1586 1588 1589 1592 1595 1616
1622 1663 1669 1707 1709 1714 1729 1730 1736
1762 1781 1803 1821 1841 1846 1863 1865 1866
1888   17   2 4 6 7 36 42 48 61 70 85 102 103 128
130 137 140 142 155 160 166 168 170 210 273 280
308 326 378 393 484 578 579 589 623 626 627 628
630 631 669 678 694 765 861 873 917 923 947 975
990 1000 1032 1045 1186 1194 1221 1222 1236
1265 1309 1335 1363 1371 1384 1400 1423 1441
1488 1509 1512 1513 1514 1535 1537 1585 1609
1635 1640 1661 1662 1676 1677 1678 1689 1692
1695 1712 1713 1715 1760 1761 1857 1858 1860
1869 1871 1897 1986 1992 1994 2079 2085 2086
2088 2110 2135 2141 2165 2229 2252 2257 2258
2295 2304   18   11 25 27 28 40 51 61 87 97 176
209 234 247 290 291 294 298 308 330 333 337 343
351 358 369 374 391 398 401 428 429 438 439 450
453 470 471 473 475 476 485 497 529 533 543 581
582 589 625 626 628 634 639 643 645 647 649 665
691 705 708 733 750 766 787 803 851 852 853 855
862 887 888 893 898 903 919 923 927 937 950 955
977 978 990 1007 1013 1018 1026 1036 1038 1041
1045 1047 1064 1069 1089 1090 1112 1114 1148
1179 1183 1195 1198 1199 1205 1216 1233 1234
1257 1259 1260 1261 1272 1284 1293 1299 1302
1312 1320 1323 1327 1337 1350 1359 1382 1402
1433 1439 1442 1443 1490 1537 1539 1544 1554
1596 1597
at (5)   1 464   7 859   12 894   16 1253
17 400
at (68)   15 145 168 173 185 250 477 485 632 758
907 914 1492 1559 1717 1739 1763 1902 1905 2027
2038 2053 2055 2066 2072 2085 2095 2123 2158
2216 2223 2292 2299 2405 2460 2491 2668 2678
2751 2853 2926 2951 2953 3461 3542 3562 3621
3692 3701 3831 3982 3989 4168 4225 4256 4318
4331 4332 4543 4597 4673 4764 4782 4888 4910
4955
atavism (1)   15 950
atavistic (1)   17 847
ataxy (1)   15 2592
Ate (2)   16 691 699
ate (21)   1 374   4 1 424   6 502   7 258
8 818 908   11 520 521 522 523 569   12 126
497 959   15 208 3357   17 1923   18 1074
ate (1)   8. 748
atelier (2)   8 174   17 1876
Athanatos (1)   12 561
atheists (1)   18 1566
Athena (1)   9 876
Athenian (1)   7 567
Athens (1)   1 43
athirst (1)   14 477
athlete's (1)   17 1817
athlete's (1)   15 4673
Athlone (1)   6 444
Athlone (1)   15 1413
Athos (5)   6 125   15 2786   17 1885 1890
athwart (1)   17 151
atitudes (1)   14 1459
Atkinson (2)   9 1141   15 2525
Atkinson (1)   9 1146
Atlantic (1)   18 754
Atlas (1)   18 860
atmic (1)   12 350
atmosphere (9)   5 393   12 1880   13 1064
14 1215   16 22 977 1077   17 40 1088
atmospheric (2)   12 1870   17 1087

atmospherics (1)   14 715
atolls (2)   17 201 219
atom (2)   18 293 1403
atoms (1)   7 81
atoned (1)   1 578
atonement (1)   17 2058
atop (1)   12 492
atque (1)   14 709
atrocious (1)   14 1261
atrocities (1)   14 384
Atrot (1)   11 763
atrot (1)   11 525
attached (7)   15 3033 3520   16 1177 1802
17 1099 1299 1576
attached (1)   15 271
attachment (3)   16 1365 1485   17 1148
attack (6)   3 295   8 410   11 528   14 316
18 998 1418
attacked (1)   1 115
attacks (1)   14 1427
attain (1)   17 459
attainder (1)   12 1194
attained (2)   17 455 856
attaining (1)   17 1195
attempt (5)   7 569   11 1196   14 922
15 948 3457
attempted (3)   17 693 698 1110
attempts (1)   9 435
atten (1)   9 600
attend (1)   13 835
attendance (8)   8 399   10 1179   12 608 625
902   15 835 3076   18 1048
attendant (8)   9 7 581 585 966   17 1021 1132
1948 2192
attendant's (1)   9 13
attended (7)   10 929   12 372 1266 1727
14 62   16 1831   17 277
attending (3)   9 827   11 391   12 1322
attends (1)   15 75
attention (29)   1 25   7 157 176 974
10 566 1247   11 658   13 49 364 614
14 795 917 1565   15 518 2332 2343   16 339
368 475 1006 1536   17 319 368 584 699 1313
1349   18 33 1433
attention (1)   15 1404
attentions (3)   13 129   14 1255   16 1548
attentive (1)   17 924
attentiveness (1)   14 1196
Attic (1)   10 1073
attire (2)   17 857 862
attire (1)   15 2247
attired (1)   16 216
attires (1)   1 571
attitude (3)   13 338   17 2313 2316
attitude (2)   15 2854 4956
attitudes (1)   15 4675
attorney (1)   11 1227
Attract (1)   13 923
attract (4)   14 1184   15 518 2417   18 1269
Attracta (1)   12 1710
attracted (6)   16 103 1568   17 319 1171 1348
attraction (8)   15 3083 3355   16 482
17 1170 2164 2167 2174
attractions (2)   16 549   17 1551
attractive (6)   13 572   16 1550   17 1177
1969   18 648 1520
attractive (1)   15 1745
attributable (1)   17 1154
attribute (1)   17 633

ay (13) 7 890 11 56 496 1277 12 521 1090 15 4822 16 612 690 691 697 18 280 882
Ayes (1) 14 1454
Azazel (1) 15 1899
Azotes (1) 5 34
Aztec (1) 9 281
Aztecs (1) 16 851
azure (1) 11 394
azure (1) 15 2043
azured (1) 9 652

B

B (14) 7 659 9 28 12 931 993 16 594 618 714 1049 1094 1177 1495 1765 18 613 858
B (1) 15 4337
b (2) 17 1811 2171
B A (4) 10 69 16 1264 1266 1827
B A (1) 16 1259
B C (1) 2 11
B C T (1) 17 2099
b h (1) 16 1278
B L (2) 10 1186 12 1895
B R (1) 12 936
Ba (9) 2 249 13 1117 1119 1127 1143 15 114 2097 2098 2103
baaaa (1) 13 398
baaaahabaaa (1) 13 398
Baba (1) 12 562
babbles (1) 7 243
Babby (1) 15 2003
babby (1) 13 530
babby (1) 15 424
babbyface (1) 18 39
babe (6) 14 60 215 224 1074 1190 1319
babemaries (1) 7 853
Babes (1) 13 1190
Babes (1) 15 1588
BABES (1) 15 1592
babes (1) 12 1716
babies (5) 4 418 8 394 13 904 14 1254 18 1238
baboon's (1) 15 2602
Baby (1) 6 328
Baby (2) 15 1578 1595
BABY (1) 15 1597
baby (26) 8 1027 12 577 13 13 21 26 27 33 246 253 383 387 388 400 404 523 605 608 609 610 684 767 954 1082 14 1317 15 1810
baby (1) 15 3846
babyclothes (1) 18 548
babyish (1) 13 23
babylinen (1) 15 2005
Babylon (4) 8 490 9 339 14 1091 16 514
Bacc (2) 14 1257 1268
baccy (1) 9 101
bachelor (3) 9 1061 11 524 15 857
Bachelor's (6) 7 430 8 27 11 524 15 731 1231 17 1429
bachelor's (1) 15 2341
bachelors (4) 6 323 14 252 1249 15 3887
Bacibaci (1) 12 556
Bacilikil (1) 17 592
bacilli (1) 17 1061
Back (7) 1 19 6 995 7 436 8 458 13 987 14 1072 1482
Back (1) 12 1828
back (307) 1 145 392 467 602 618 695 2 34 82 177 193 226 261 353 379 426 435 444 3 37 74 84 116 123 189 196 269 279 283 299 310 334 336 354 356 373 406 413 419 437 467 4 53 76 191 215 261 374 386 445 456 458 485 515 539 5 38 60 110 267 372 394 417 472 515 540 548 6 47 48 61 91 129 175 243 256 337 430 491 553 616 692 716 732 824 989 7 46 47 103 180 227 280 301 383 459 593 638 653 664 763 904 967 997 8 167 261 270 478 518 569 610 611 628 633 654 659 702

875 881 1046 1060 1105 1135 1186 9 152 197 253 275 422 474 573 629 817 897 953 1109 1137 1214 10 35 369 379 391 455 518 661 783 891 986 1026 1107 1233 11 77 108 159 194 478 492 556 564 640 798 929 1160 12 64 384 503 646 1069 1195 1487 1554 1561 1573 1810 1908 13 142 162 342 357 470 496 508 550 559 576 582 587 653 674 696 697 716 718 722 724 728 744 759 766 876 905 924 941 979 999 1006 1045 1051 1054 1114 1145 1147 1204 1216 1217 1254 1276 14 408 479 564 844 1011 1020 1026 1519 1591 15 332 438 442 1967 2070 2201 2848 3206 3406 3509 3515 3566 3751 3780 3873 4768 4809 16 36 45 68 101 197 208 262 296 429 509 568 576 582 609 865 1078 1114 1181 1303 1332 1340 1400 1402 1452 1760 1796 17 72 120 126 880 1292 1342 1343 18 40 79 80 258 318 373 423 427 443 449 478 616 639 667 785 816 821 832 854 897 904 920 974 1120 1258 1277 1336 1338 1416 1489 1530
back (5) 17 419 815 817
back (42) 15 32 125 256 323 417 516 616 663 666 668 758 934 1139 1343 1404 1850 2049 2051 2083 2085 2460 2465 2712 3439 3503 3504 3589 3900 3911 4151 4255 4271 4288 4333 4429 4481 4628 4694 4696 4768 4909
Backache (1) 11 615
backache (3) 3 98 6 60 11 1001
Backbone (1) 15 2322
backbone (2) 4 447 16 1022
backdoor (4) 4 472 5 318 8 447 16 48
backdoors (1) 3 155
backed (2) 8 697 12 1552
Backers (1) 15 4663
backers (1) 10 832
backerup (1) 16 1856
backgammon (1) 17 663
backgate (1) 15 3000
background (1) 15 3305
backhand (1) 15 1017
backhand (1) 15 3723
backhands (1) 17 619
backing (3) 2 303 7 106 12 1230
backmost (1) 11 74
backs (4) 7 752 9 469 10 688 15 3632
Backsheesh (1) 12 562
backside (3) 12 1344 18 523 880
backslapping (1) 11 1143
backstairs (1) 2 343
backtothelander (1) 16 1593
backview (1) 15 2314
backward (7) 1 714 4 256 7 114 9 6 472 10 966 14 399
backwards (2) 7 205 207
backwards (1) 15 2436
bacleis (1) 12 884
Bacon (3) 9 410 16 170 783
bacon (7) 8 498 955 11 499 614 12 1615 16 997 17 250
baconflitches (1) 10 88
baconhogs (1) 12 105
Bacon's (1) 9 410
bacteria (2) 14 1245 17 1061
Bad (15) 5 271 8 3 537 839 10 269 767 916 11 561 13 862 966 1048 1081 15 700 840 2826
bad (71) 3 494 4 233 413 421 5 250 255 285 286 482 552 6 374 607 611 982 8 216 245 282 292 508 588 983 9 70 1040 10 733 797 905 1058 11 1052 12 24 855 893 1543

13 778 825 1014 1142 1220   14 568 618 815
1494 1548   15 867 1715 1762 2616 4586 4822
16 517 738 790 1111 1218 1567 1674 1729 1885
17 1937   18 57 239 397 632 702 869 935 1216
1480 1524 1568
bad (2)   9 366   16 702
bad (2)   15 931 1918
Baddybad (1)   14 1487
bade (9)   2 305   9 633 818   10 1274
11 925 1016   14 410 890   16 289
badge (3)   5 93   12 689   13 639
badge (3)   15 451 728 3318
badger (1)   15 3953
badgered (1)   15 968
badges (1)   15 1570
badhachs (1)   12 1090
badly (10)   8 854   9 256 1047   14 1225
15 2463   16 3 303   18 733 1478 1496
badtempered (2)   10 82   18 1073
Bag (3)   3 476   13 1028   15 3086
bag (21)   1 347   2 22   3 32 36   5 376
6 56   7 785 1024   8 264 559   10 820 1275
11 343 359 390   14 521 616 1304 1556
17 308   18 831
bag (3)   15 500 1928 4537
baggage (1)   14 1583
bagged (2)   5 12 15
Baggot (1)   14 490
baggy (1)   16 375
bagman (1)   12 1581
bagnio (1)   14 538
bagpipes (2)   12 693   18 689
Bags (1)   16 205
bags (5)   3 343 370   9 746   10 421
18 542
bagslops (1)   15 2607
bagstrousers (1)   11 578
bagweighted (1)   15 2789
bail (2)   12 1139   14 1538
Bailer (1)   17 2324
Bailey (3)   13 409 1068   18 1282
Bailey (1)   15 3382
bailiff (2)   8 688   10 935
bailiff's (1)   17 1941
Baird's (1)   16 53
bairns (2)   14 75 527
bairns (1)   15 915
baisemoins (1)   14 1055
bait (2)   8 858 1074
baited (1)   2 318
Bak (1)   15 189
bak (1)   15 4462
baked (2)   5 73   15 2900
baker's (2)   8 211   16 59
Bakery (1)   8 464
bakery (2)   7 339   16 56
baking (2)   8 616   15 2900
Balancé (1)   15 4060
Balance (1)   17 1476
balance (11)   4 198   10 1062 1066
13 1056   14 670 744   15 2893   17 681 688
1663 1862
balances (1)   17 690
balancing (1)   6 591
Balbriggan (1)   12 171
balconies (1)   15 1446
balcony (1)   17 1510
balcony (1)   15 4418
Bald (10)   3 6   5 372   9 12   11 444 453
478 571 822 847 915

Bald (1)   15 506
bald (13)   3 82   6 563   9 231 720   11 30
287 318 391 464 670 1029   15 1780   18 649
bald (1)   15 2036 3668
balderdash (1)   16 1030
Baldhead (1)   4 111
baldheaded (2)   6 625   7 311
baldness (1)   16 832
baldpink (1)   9 243
baldpoll (1)   3 116
baldynoddle (1)   10 852
bale (1)   14 637
balejwaw (1)   17 763
Balfe's (1)   8 418
balked (1)   15 205
balks (1)   5 230
Ball (2)   15 1011   17 1373
ball (29)   2 154   4 469   5 156   8 57 58 571
10 304 587   13 20 246 247 248 252 254 347 350
353 357 362 424 467 505 606 950   16 494 1863
17 661   18 496
ball (6)   17 803 804 806 816 820 827
ballad (7)   1 608   5 185   10 791   11 1148
14 1578   16 1433 1883
ballad (1)   6 147
ballagh (1)   13 1149
ballalley (1)   12 504
Ballast (1)   12 1839
ballastoffice (2)   8 109 114
balldress (1)   15 1014
Balldresses (1)   11 493
ballets (1)   17 426
Ballina (1)   7 93
ballocknaked (1)   16 481
ballocks (3)   12 8   15 3663   18 1288
Ballocky (1)   9 1176
balloon (1)   7 98
balloons (1)   15 2164
ballrooms (1)   13 1090
Ball's (1)   8 110
balls (3)   7 620   15 4043   17 575
Ballsbridge (3)   6 742   7 193   8 1165
ballstop (1)   15 1031
bally (2)   15 836   16 266
Ballybough (2)   12 1245   15 1876
Ballyhooly (1)   12 689
Ballykinlar (1)   12 1671
Ballymote (2)   14 404   17 755
Ballymun (1)   12 1707
balm (2)   14 931 939
balmy (6)   5 522   12 1045   13 214
15 616 2690   18 1288
Balor (1)   12 197
balusters (1)   17 1538
balustrade (1)   9 1124
Bam (1)   6 853
bamboo (1)   15 2481
bamboozled (1)   16 303
Banana (1)   18 803
banana (1)   10 512
Banba (1)   12 375
Banbury (3)   8 74   15 2944   17 1463
Banbury (1)   15 684
band (13)   4 441 526   8 162 438 471   10 76
353 384   11 682 1229 1231   12 536   18 644
band (2)   15 1407 1960
bandaged (1)   8 755
bandaging (1)   18 31
bandanna (1)   15 1239

banderilleros (1)   18 631
Bandez (1)   16 1454
Bandmann (5)   5 195   6 185   15 496
17 2079 2256
bandnight (1)   18 885
bandog (1)   14 1415
bandolier (1)   15 538
bandolierwise (1)   14 1047
bands (2)   6 802   10 821
bands (1)   15 4630
bandy (1)   15 33
bane (1)   9 373
Bang (4)   10 651 693   15 189
Bang (1)   15 4140
bang (6)   3 188 291   13 737   16 964
18 559 832
bang (1)   15 4140
bangbang (1)   7 374
banged (3)   7 408   10 712   11 90
banging (1)   3 185
bangle (1)   15 3063
bangs (2)   15 187 3502
banished (1)   9 82
banishment (3)   9 999 1000
banisters (1)   15 286
banjo (1)   15 423
banjo (1)   15 414
Bank (4)   6 198   8 866   12 186   17 1861
bank (21)   3 332   4 102 452   5 305   8 561
866   10 342 411 746   12 1433   13 1056 1180
14 1324   15 798   16 1659   17 1695 1860
1931   18 108 505 952
bankbook (1)   12 660
banking (1)   17 1688
banknote (1)   15 3531
banknotes (1)   3 404
banknotes (1)   15 1813
bankrupt (1)   17 1939
banks (3)   12 647 1454   18 951
banks (1)   7 245
banks (1)   15 1830
bankside (2)   9 155 640
banner (1)   17 1531
banner (1)   15 2186
banners (1)   13 447
banners (1)   15 1409
Bannon (5)   1 684   4 407   14 497 654 1211
Bannon (1)   15 2239
Bannons (1)   1 683
banquet (2)   8 516   11 1247
banshee (1)   11 630
banshee (1)   15 4587
Bantam (18)   5 108 519 523 526 532 535 539
8 989 997 1016 1023   10 517   12 400 1554
14 1508 1522   16 1287   17 334
BANTAM (1)   15 1839
Bantam's (1)   14 1511
Bantry (1)   12 237
banzai (1)   12 600
baptise (1)   5 334
baptised (1)   17 540
baptism (1)   10 146
baptist (1)   15 1424
Bapty (1)   11 927
Bar (1)   15 1624
bar (37)   3 163 471   4 106   7 292 706
8 654 688 822   10 249 512 1136   11 65 89
192 286 421 463 478 670 671 723 923 1151
12 925 1133   14 1503   15 1003 3102 3968
3970 3973   16 988 1629   17 791 1712

Bath (4) 3 236 8 851 15 1942 17 1460
Bath (1) 4 369
bath (19) 3 235 4 490 5 502 504 565
  6 105 169 522 13 786 1214 14 246 796
  15 1031 3767 17 238 2045 18 562 615 905
bathchair (2) 8 710 17 489
Bathe (1) 7 318
bathe (1) 7 316
bathers (1) 7 97
Bathing (1) 3 87
bathing (4) 15 1701 16 519 17 245 1718
bathing (1) 15 2607
bathingplace (1) 18 1346
bathingsuits (1) 18 10
bathroom (1) 17 1539
Baths (1) 17 338
baths (1) 5 549
bathslippers (1) 12 254
bathtowel (1) 1 535
bathtub (1) 12 1716
Bathwater (1) 13 1025
bathwater (1) 8 172
bating (1) 15 1964
batiste (1) 17 2096
baton (9) 5 49 58 143 517 523 10 363
  11 47 856 1116
batonroll (1) 15 2501
bats (1) 13 752
batten (1) 14 393
battened (1) 17 2098
Batter (1) 12 4
battered (4) 5 7 11 88 1263 14 1441
battered (2) 15 605 2657
batteringram (1) 12 1367
Battersby (1) 4 236
battery (2) 12 1899 17 317
battle (8) 2 4 7 572 12 960 13 1192
  16 343 1104 1240 17 1419
battledog (1) 15 2242
BATTLES (1) 7 358
battles (5) 2 317 9 136 12 177 15 780
  18 400
battleship (1) 12 1307
battleships (1) 14 1460
Battling (1) 12 982
battling (2) 2 314 9 828
bauble (1) 9 490
baubles (1) 12 1582
baulk (1) 14 1266
Baum (1) 15 2275
Bawd (1) 10 826
BAWD (8) 15 80 85 358 368 379 533 4518 4761
bawd (3) 9 1021 1050 15 1159
bawd (3) 15 78 356 531
bawdy (1) 14 314
Bawdyhouse (1) 14 1573
bawdyhouse (1) 16 1629
bawl (2) 12 1765 15 3948
bawl (1) 15 4664
bawled (3) 5 279 7 7 14 408
bawler (1) 13 1215
bawling (4) 8 483 10 1168 12 1797
  18 164
bawling (1) 15 4145
bawls (2) 2 308 12 1790
bawls (1) 15 3961
Bawn (1) 12 194
bawn (3) 14 1512 18 656
bawns (1) 12 690

bawways (1) 12 382
Bay (2) 12 1302 17 1253
bay (22) 1 75 107 248 574 672 675 2 246
  3 107 8 311 900 901 9 452 12 1329 1878
  13 4 1053 16 965 1284 17 1990 18 399
  860 974
bay (1) 15 3382
bayed (2) 3 311 10 247
baying (2) 15 1258 4331
bayleaves (1) 12 1293
Bays (1) 12 1270
bays (1) 17 218
bays (1) 15 1213
baywindow (1) 17 1520
bazaar (11) 4 525 8 1162 10 1269
  12 777 13 686 1166 15 2717 2826 4109
  17 578 1790
bazaar (1) 15 1494
Bazan (1) 16 493
Bbbbbllllllblblblblobschb (1) 15 3381
Be (21) 4 53 78 238 5 443 6 125 744 1031
  8 46 322 9 979 11 61 392 12 125
  13 813 14 284 1561 15 2197 2198 2792
  3043 3604
be (845) 1 116 170 279 318 390 391 422 578 627
  673 2 49 67 87 172 202 232 263 316 322 330 338
  339 391 402 406 3 27 38 128 142 295 320 328
  400 413 474 491 4 117 129 210 347 367 376 405
  420 494 511 5 9 30 69 92 170 174 177 189 219
  220 305 341 376 394 409 434 437 450 480 505
  6 77 88 126 227 301 369 371 401 409 412 420 435
  475 481 484 512 602 607 619 621 645 687 695 739
  751 767 768 776 783 818 844 866 872 906 933 941
  954 955 991 1008 7 55 106 165 177 181 292 297
  299 380 462 485 543 565 586 702 715 809 844 890
  902 930 947 8 21 28 71 96 116 190 229 245 267
  304 323 356 361 403 415 448 504 527 544 547 558
  566 570 575 584 623 633 703 705 718 747 754 853
  874 972 996 1018 1029 1037 1057 1097 1113 1121
  1127 1139 9 103 127 241 298 305 309 316 322
  383 385 388 393 397 444 450 457 499 504 505 510
  519 539 564 566 595 619 722 723 783 787 811 813
  843 844 864 865 938 954 1011 1037 1050 1099 1102
  1118 1156 10 22 27 71 75 105 139 151 162 383
  395 418 501 677 707 721 822 916 956 1069 1070
  1074 1095 1135 1142 1170 11 154 219 255 257
  358 459 545 560 699 838 905 914 970 1073 1121
  1126 1210 1232 1256 1268 1287 12 2 42 44 45
  46 59 74 221 238 242 290 311 335 367 369 371 372
  400 464 471 515 557 634 638 674 692 737 738 790
  793 839 863 884 918 924 994 1016 1041 1071 1075
  1123 1152 1160 1174 1188 1241 1258 1301 1347
  1359 1361 1368 1445 1487 1543 1571 1607 1646
  1649 1661 1669 1755 1769 1793 1849 1868 1884
  13 30 33 41 44 58 61 99 113 125 149 151 183 190
  197 199 207 208 209 214 215 220 221 235 245 247
  250 265 280 292 302 320 390 405 408 427 444 455
  458 471 494 523 533 547 562 566 593 603 629 653
  654 655 659 665 673 710 837 870 895 896 944
  945 1036 1037 1039 1063 1084 1095 1119 1122
  1139 1144 1147 1212 1213 1218 1237 1245 1274
  14 9 15 19 24 28 41 51 52 55 58 100 114 115 128
  151 166 171 175 178 187 232 240 291 327 332 334
  345 351 371 397 412 431 432 445 479 485 510 514
  519 546 559 591 665 685 690 700 763 767 775 800
  807 811 828 877 883 886 891 899 905 915 918 1019
  1039 1058 1062 1072 1076 1124 1165 1166 1167
  1183 1223 1226 1228 1229 1237 1251 1264 1281
  1286 1297 1316 1334 1339 1347 1372 1454 1473

1479 1555 15 11 105 171 205 370 523 662 772
852 854 976 983 1001 1111 1168 1170 1350 1383
1384 1386 1481 1488 1544 1783 1785 1790 1817
1819 1962 1965 1995 2088 2192 2236 2351 2360
2396 2409 2410 2437 2463 2679 2739 2814 2869
2877 2880 2904 2920 2973 2975 2978 2981 3001
3009 3067 3078 3081 3100 3187 3204 3208 3388
3450 3799 3935 3985 4410 4569 4738 4821 4832
4870 16 18 26 43 121 124 157 195 207 225 226
255 272 283 296 303 323 326 341 353 360 365 370
411 435 441 464 473 496 510 528 532 556 557 565
608 612 618 645 658 665 668 714 730 740 757 793
841 890 897 953 954 1000 1003 1031 1036 1044
1060 1113 1120 1125 1136 1160 1164 1191 1193
1238 1258 1271 1324 1385 1392 1434 1534 1540
1547 1596 1604 1623 1625 1626 1630 1660 1688
1708 1757 1788 1791 1794 1830 1840 1846 1849
17 69 242 252 287 376 421 448 449 450 453 454
455 515 609 839 840 941 1009 1050 1073 1076 1093
1405 1519 1567 1579 1606 1623 1626 1662 1693
1707 1710 1742 1841 1872 1883 1885 1954 2004
2006 2127 2129 2133 2214 18 3 12 35 49 67 83
118 134 165 168 183 192 197 202 237 289 325 339
350 368 369 393 406 420 436 437 475 487 489 503
509 511 525 532 546 562 591 599 616 622 662 682
732 737 774 776 789 790 810 841 855 864 893 909
921 927 988 990 997 999 1042 1056 1082 1113 1118
1127 1140 1152 1174 1189 1224 1225 1232 1248
1263 1268 1273 1301 1307 1332 1341 1348 1356
1358 1374 1376 1387 1390 1391 1408 1409 1412
1431 1434 1435 1439 1440 1441 1488 1501 1504
1519 1524 1529 1533 1536
be (10) 1 464 2 66 398 7 490 494 9 417
  11 1291 12 428 16 1743 1887
be (2) 15 3955 4914
Beach (1) 13 1060
beach (6) 3 33 155 300 11 310 12 1878
  14 1585
beach (1) 15 4360
beacon (1) 13 7
beaconjars (1) 5 464
Beaconsfield (1) 15 1845
beaded (1) 3 53
beadle (1) 14 558
beads (2) 1 256 10 31
beagle (1) 15 1204
beaglebaying (1) 15 3955
beagle's (1) 15 3950
beak (1) 15 807
beaked (1) 7 344
beaker (1) 10 809
beaks (1) 15 684
beam (5) 12 406 1238 13 1005 1161
  15 2355
beam (1) 10 557
beamend (1) 12 1358
Beaming (1) 11 711
beaming (3) 8 589 10 913 18 80
beamy (1) 12 375
bean (1) 15 3200
beanfeast (1) 8 1146
beans (2) 3 218 12 93
Bear (2) 8 1160 9 372
bear (17) 4 227 9 156 912 932 10 568
  14 115 250 867 1073 1139 15 867 3121 4534
  16 31 439 480 18 1482
bearbaiters (1) 15 3959
Beard (1) 8 523
beard (22) 6 73 110 141 260 745 7 817

8 313 533 9 242 10 425 813 964 1014 1047
11 170 535 1032 12 1063 16 1676
17 278 2003 18 30
beard (4) 15 480 2037 2484 2627
bearded (5) 9 30 60 269 11 538 15 3779
bearded (5) 15 248 993 2262 3161 3854
beardframed (2) 7 46 52
beardless (1) 9 832
beardless (2) 15 3822 3855
beards (3) 6 625 8 847 12 1717
beards (1) 15 1905
Beare (1) 12 199
bearer (1) 12 665
beargarden (1) 15 941
bearing (20) 1 1 5 317 6 589 7 17
 11 86 87 381 12 246 1713 14 659
 15 1233 2779 16 1828 17 4 6 340 391 1377
 1655 1780
bearing (1) 7 868
bearing (4) 15 1399 1417 1443 1918
bearings (2) 15 1050 16 924
bearish (1) 3 345
bearpit (1) 14 560
Bear's (1) 15 2418
Bears (1) 13 1185
bears (2) 12 722 16 1411
bears (3) 15 1163 1821 2148
bearsgrease (1) 13 834
bearskin (1) 5 67
bearskin (1) 15 4613
Beast (1) 12 1324
beast (12) 7 752 9 469 12 173 755
 13 837 14 233 15 209 476 845 1717 3631
 17 609
beastly (6) 1 206 210 7 583 14 250
 15 833 4170
beastly (1) 1 198
beasts (6) 4 1 159 9 862 12 1445
 14 569 1088
beat (11) 2 345 3 448 8 515 10 98 217
 11 1033 1255 14 870 15 4402 16 356
 18 269
beaten (2) 18 538 868
beaters (1) 15 1408
Beati (1) 10 196
beating (7) 1 225 2 72 8 914 1180
 12 956 14 1130 15 1283
beating (2) 15 4013 4047
Beatitudes (1) 14 1454
BEATITUDES (1) 15 2241
beatitudes (1) 15 2237
beatitudes (1) 15 2238
beats (5) 3 149 8 410 10 645 16 728
 18 1101
beats (3) 15 2049 4021 4256
Beau (1) 14 356
beau (3) 11 96 13 209 18 1189
•Beaufort's (1) 2 302
Beaufort's (1) 15 3978
Beaufoy (9) 4 503 516 8 276 278 13 959
 15 640 825 16 1229 17 650
Beaufoy (1) 15 814
BEAUFOY (4) 15 818 831 841 851
Beaumont (1) 14 350
Beauties (1) 17 1369
beauties (4) 3 213 13 35 16 1629
 18 881
Beautiful (4) 6 239 10 23 13 110
 15 3015

beautiful (32) 3 233 5 248 9 9 37 62 251
 1164 11 543 610 642 12 1449 1462 13 82
 106 114 642 1163 14 804 1327 1456 15 1802
 3013 3267 3885 4173 16 345 520 1820
 18 210 542 1340 1560
beautiful (2) 10 615 618
beautifulinsadness (1) 9 735
beautifully (4) 13 231 583 698 18 1336
beautify (3) 6 945 14 1272 15 1667
beautifying (1) 15 2253
Beauty (5) 3 107 8 920 9 1011 11 1060
 13 837
beauty (42) 2 227 6 254 7 1038 8 920
 9 621 735 740 854 959 10 935 11 679 1105
 12 289 1004 1442 13 647 774 1222 14 935
 15 206 453 476 1108 2254 3268 3656 16 139
 896 1458 17 1165 1780 1852 2011 18 347 392
 484 540 559 606 964 1178 1351
beauty (4) 7 322 10 235 248 16 420
beautys (1) 18 477
beautyspot (1) 15 2293
Beaver (3) 15 585 16 21 17 2056
Beaver (2) 15 930 4365
beaver (2) 9 478 14 162
becalmed (3) 7 1047 14 199 16 678
became (9) 6 901 12 340 971 13 451 519
 16 994 1366 1490 18 635
Because (43) 1 53 208 2 236 442 5 39
 8 95 9 997 11 875 981 1103 12 835 843
 1147 13 529 790 883 990 1018 1026 1209
 15 45 556 1029 1060 16 563 1124 1129 1641
 1658 17 78 289 498 557 943 990 1008 1071 1493
 1894 2149 2163 2164 2166
Because (1) 12 31
because (175) 1 213 5 245 261 461 6 958
 1011 8 137 165 328 851 9 208 451 476 841
 956 10 1058 1078 1173 1209 11 843 1093
 1196 12 465 508 681 1065 1500 13 115 128
 146 150 154 178 181 182 183 192 196 221 226 294
 309 342 418 429 431 445 455 456 464 470 477 480
 482 493 495 504 521 533 547 562 569 579 590 601
 607 619 620 628 668 676 700 701 706 707 731 770
 808 880 952 985 1036 1153 1159 1226 1263 1299
 1300 14 117 153 208 298 320 1241 15 550
 570 2097 2105 2706 3020 16 187 751 842 853
 1102 1125 1149 1161 1165 1198 1309 1402 1449
 1454 1471 1522 1625 1723 1784 1893 17 78 890
 891 1422 18 1 11 22 44 50 75 76 81 90 132 141
 142 143 152 183 208 214 220 239 259 270 329 343
 424 473 489 499 754 756 757 804 808 811 870 973
 1054 1073 1075 1215 1277 1369 1378 1385 1438
 1568 1578
Becche (1) 16 489
beck (5) 3 220 9 8 13 687 14 741 1519
beckoned (3) 6 584 7 1029 16 1648
Become (1) 6 900
become (10) 4 155 14 22 791 913
 15 1498 2121 16 918 17 1603 1670 1745
becomes (12) 3 478 7 137 11 1087
 14 291 293 928 15 2119 2201 18 1366
becomes (1) 1 592
becomes (2) 15 1207 1956
becoming (4) 9 313 12 1285 13 112
 18 1284
Bective (1) 15 767
Bed (2) 5 74 9 699
bed (99) 1 252 713 2 127 140 3 76 211 396
 4 234 266 322 328 369 372 469 5 8 6 17 363
 380 555 754 8 198 373 479 867 9 195 634 713

800 801 804 11 557 12 809 1358 1396
13 91 706 912 1024 1280 14 366 394 1341
15 1055 1971 2234 2786 3001 3038 3085 3199
 3273 16 1472 17 196 1238 1239 1240 1241
 1889 2032 2036 2110 2113 2119 2144 2203 2328
 2329 18 2 30 44 134 222 224 352 641 740 748
 905 914 920 998 1126 1131 1199 1205 1212 1215
 1238 1376 1479 1489 1491 1499
bed (2) 14 351
bed (1) 15 1136
bedad (2) 8 889
bedchamber (2) 9 250 14 915
bedchamber (1) 15 1437
bedded (2) 10 299 17 305
beddyhouse (1) 8 200
bedesman (1) 14 220
Bedford (2) 10 830 17 2048
bedhead (1) 4 301
bedight (1) 12 215
Bedlam (1) 18 1468
bedlinen (2) 17 2113 2123
bedlock (1) 15 1777
bedpal (1) 3 88
bedpost (1) 15 382
bedraggled (1) 3 350
bedridden (1) 15 905
bedrock (1) 15 2205
bedroom (8) 4 50 247 5 154 8 196
 16 1373 18 28 287 1193
bedrooms (1) 17 1521
beds (10) 6 443 1004 1005 8 644 9 714 718
 12 1256 14 74 15 3073 18 948
bedside (3) 1 252 14 809 1329
bedsmiling (1) 9 718
bedsores (1) 14 1426
bedsores (1) 15 1608
bedspread (2) 4 253 309
bedstead (1) 4 59
bedthanes (1) 14 78
bedvow (1) 9 666
bedwarmed (1) 4 239
Bee (2) 12 1274 15 2429
bee (5) 4 483 6 381 13 1143 17 1449
 18 953
Beech (1) 12 1272
beechleaf (1) 17 1363
beechmast (1) 12 1293
beechmast (1) 15 3421
Beef (1) 13 931
beef (12) 4 403 8 121 617 668 12 1176
 14 503 548 1459 1460 15 565 2242 18 945
beef (1) 16 980
Beefeaters (1) 15 1440
beefsteak (1) 8 535
beefsteaks (3) 6 608 760 14 1424
beeftea (2) 15 3851 18 462
beehive (1) 17 1554
beehives (1) 12 1717
Beekeeper (1) 15 838
beeline (2) 8 1112 16 100
Beelzebub (1) 15 3931
Been (2) 7 986 11 938
been (200) 1 320 328 603 2 35 49 51 147
 4 504 5 294 470 6 77 98 259 958 7 258
 744 785 787 997 8 495 983 9 54 176 215 334
 349 379 397 445 456 466 611 685 1032 10 13
 139 150 1124 1280 11 208 272 1249 12 48
 339 365 367 476 540 571 584 587 606 617 628 731
 736 869 965 1725 1862 1868 1875 1883 1887 1889

1899 **13** 84 104 195 206 432 443 476 487 541 746 747 816 885 **14** 23 35 39 59 381 531 552 554 563 570 657 664 668 699 760 811 821 833 837 845 884 895 918 924 945 997 1110 1160 1181 1311 1347 1509 **15** 646 837 950 952 972 1121 1778 1810 2218 2221 2271 2331 2380 2453 3397 4557 **16** 71 72 107 135 322 477 751 772 777 798 830 878 1044 1056 1178 1351 1404 1582 1610 **17** 179 327 337 349 456 460 461 483 519 520 540 558 660 718 748 787 800 853 904 923 925 1075 1195 1259 1281 1284 1286 1288 1637 1763 1839 1845 2198 2274 2277 2283 2292 **18** 219 242 301 343 387 397 510 652 869 896 1061 1087 1096 1288

been (1) **7** 830
been (2) **15** 904 905
beent (1) **14** 1541
beeoteetom (1) **13** 263
Beer (3) **14** 1459 1460 **15** 2242
beer (7) **8** 671 826 **12** 947 1389 1731 **14** 1197 **15** 4564
beer (1) **1** 301
Beerbohm (1) **18** 1042
beerchops (1) **15** 3884
beerfroth (1) **11** 1111
Beerpull (1) **11** 1183
beerpull (3) **11** 516 1044 1112
beery (1) **8** 671
bees (2) **15** 2418 **16** 1795
bees' (1) **15** 4045
beest (1) **14** 1482
beeswaxed (1) **10** 176
Beethoven (1) **12** 194
beetle (1) **11** 911
beetle (1) **15** 506
beetlebrowed (1) **14** 1582
beetles (1) **3** 14
beetles (1) **1** 567
beeves (1) **12** 108
befall (1) **14** 831
befallen (2) **12** 1185 **14** 718
befit (1) **14** 53
befitting (1) **14** 1382
Before (12) **3** 286 **4** 497 **6** 170 **7** 3 **8** 24 401 675 **11** 985 **12** 366 **14** 60 **15** 3833 **17** 1343
Before (1) **9** 1145
Before (1) **15** 1129
before (193) **1** 600 609 640 645 726 **2** 271 299 345 417 **3** 5 47 471 **4** 140 363 364 370 378 457 **5** 17 98 199 254 370 456 459 **6** 46 464 510 527 582 617 748 885 992 **7** 231 353 435 633 699 778 **8** 161 395 470 526 551 600 674 806 832 949 1011 1012 1083 **9** 16 169 216 371 466 1214 **10** 8 191 310 412 413 459 460 554 742 846 965 1036 1103 1148 **11** 450 519 569 690 761 763 1122 1270 **12** 213 524 686 866 1037 1109 1297 1580 1650 1652 **13** 192 241 287 501 508 512 709 732 745 926 997 1013 1053 1108 **14** 206 372 413 492 570 589 788 1011 1060 1110 1210 1314 1356 1383 1491 **15** 370 1360 2525 2708 2768 2779 2807 2861 2941 2951 3082 3254 3604 3609 4732 **16** 73 108 209 322 339 587 620 693 755 768 946 947 1079 1203 1318 1320 1419 1577 **17** 8 61 80 447 506 1131 1145 1757 1816 2042 2043 **18** 1 46 54 201 210 242 247 272 294 406 481 557 607 684 781 828 962 1015 1035 1074 1152 1315 1372 1399 1404 1569
before (4) **7** 864 **9** 637 **12** 28 543
before (6) **15** 1 298 1268 1349 3479 4082

before's (1) **14** 1188
Beg (4) **12** 1763 **15** 2941 3107 **16** 408
beg (9) **1** 160 407 **7** 284 **12** 387 **15** 225 228 2455 **16** 780 **18** 882
beg (1) **12** 419
begad (2) **7** 364 **11** 508
began (50) **1** 46 65 248 447 583 633 **2** 297 400 409 **4** 218 334 507 **5** 419 **6** 25 95 262 269 593 647 654 898 906 **7** 131 161 301 307 401 450 549 827 **8** 433 **9** 181 772 1057 **10** 85 **11** 971 **12** 263 **13** 466 498 568 1001 **14** 1010 1016 1191 **16** 106 1025 **18** 175 630 862 876
begat (29) **15** 1855 1856 1857 1858 1859 1860 1861 1862 1863 1864 1865 1866 1867 1868
begetter (1) **9** 839
begetting (1) **9** 837
Beggar (3) **6** 328 **8** 606 **12** 1491
beggar (7) **9** 125 **13** 1120 **15** 3594 **17** 662 1836 **18** 377 990
beggar (1) **15** 1613
beggaring (1) **16** 599
beggarly (1) **16** 953
Beggar's (1) **15** 171
beggar's (1) **17** 1837
beggars (1) **18** 17
begged (7) **10** 27 **11** 428 993 **14** 167 819 **16** 714 1818
begging (5) **1** 93 **9** 154 **11** 648 **16** 1538 **18** 284
begging (1) **15** 664
Begin (4) **6** 872 **11** 63 839 **15** 2887
begin (9) **2** 56 **4** 234 **6** 779 **7** 943 **9** 619 **10** 487 **13** 1086 1200 **15** 1985
begin (1) **9** 1145
beginneth (1) **12** 1722
Beginning (1) **6** 60
beginning (18) **1** 558 **2** 201 441 **3** 268 **8** 168 611 **12** 631 **13** 23 538 879 **14** 208 **15** 2236 **16** 1002 **18** 218 342 394 464 789
beginning (1) **15** 1121
Begins (2) **4** 514 **13** 852
begins (4) **3** 23 **6** 81 **9** 164 **12** 679
begins (6) **15** 291 899 961 2115 2524 4030
beglamoured (1) **12** 603
Begob (3) **12** 337 1060 1853
Begob (1) **1** 361
begob (11) **12** 134 137 206 253 381 996 1080 1562 1783 1789 1899
Begone (2) **7** 435 **11** 449
begot (1) **9** 493
begotten (2) **3** 45 **9** 839
beguiled (1) **14** 450
begun (3) **13** 1 **14** 59 **17** 373
behalf (4) **12** 1822 **14** 853 **15** 1773 **16** 1398
Behan (1) **15** 4881
Behan's (1) **15** 4864
behave (1) **15** 3024
behaving (1) **13** 732
beheld (8) **10** 470 637 **12** 69 1911 1915 **14** 757 1201
behest (1) **14** 375
Behind (5) **1** 534 **3** 374 502 **8** 1100 **10** 1102
behind (119) **1** 3 283 654 710 **2** 165 **3** 325 409 **4** 102 171 172 200 349 **5** 25 320 360 372 376 449 454 459 **6** 26 111 208 533 569 575 585 690 699 841 1028 **7** 34 48 85 447 458

506 821 876 908 **8** 127 186 270 523 557 929 1106 **9** 344 650 1197 **10** 523 598 604 688 786 903 968 1043 1104 1237 **11** 82 83 703 913 1127 1289 **12** 245 249 1161 **13** 76 218 337 347 384 475 744 860 1029 1190 **14** 420 563 1089 **15** 13 438 638 1049 1064 1873 2293 2886 2991 3131 3142 3395 3476 4053 4382 4420 **16** 581 855 **17** 1413 **18** 109 122 254 293 408 417 545 546 586 824 1085 1264 1276 1369 1390 1447 1528
behind (1) **9** 247
behind (21) **15** 105 256 284 372 408 616 765 769 2057 2085 2261 2629 2686 2958 3666 3729 4063 4325 4327 4502 4705
Behold (1) **3** 395
Behold (1) **14** 405
behold (5) **1** 625 **4** 128 **14** 1141 1319 **15** 3743
behold (1) **6** 853
Beholden (1) **12** 1412
beholden (1) **14** 365
beholdeth (1) **14** 1045
beholding (1) **14** 53
behoof (1) **9** 142
behoved (1) **16** 1613
behoves (2) **14** 21 445
behung (1) **2** 274
Being (2) **14** 879 **16** 218
Being (1) **9** 1151
being (170) **1** 483 **2** 146 437 **4** 226 **5** 436 **6** 746 989 **8** 392 421 887 1145 **9** 425 750 793 868 913 1052 **10** 1161 1210 1248 1266 **11** 169 **12** 172 341 457 607 613 654 801 970 984 1061 1113 1130 1283 1286 1826 1882 **13** 531 664 687 709 726 728 988 1189 **14** 8 12 43 48 56 57 139 319 392 423 501 654 694 713 828 846 860 913 994 1175 1287 1297 1404 **15** 776 946 1315 2772 4427 4540 **16** 6 17 35 74 81 94 140 165 204 269 277 312 352 392 400 531 542 563 610 720 760 790 801 807 812 829 856 975 1045 1052 1194 1207 1218 1317 1320 1380 1436 1448 1459 1484 1495 1518 1532 1543 1549 1638 1639 1647 1693 1716 1739 1748 1823 1829 1837 1860 **17** 9 176 246 266 456 469 472 484 743 797 1081 1140 1297 1298 1518 1626 1660 1677 1705 1963 1988 2097 2116 2262 2307 **18** 176 243 377 532 648 746 978 996 1146 1184 1461
being (1) **15** 127
Beingless (1) **10** 822
beings (6) **6** 1003 **10** 822 **12** 352 **17** 1094 1096 1136
belauded (1) **16** 1731
belch (1) **7** 860
belches (1) **15** 2897
belching (1) **3** 178
belching (1) **15** 609
beldam's (1) **2** 48
Belfast (9) **5** 17 152 188 **10** 390 **13** 1275 **16** 47 **17** 1978 **18** 349 404
belfries (1) **12** 525
Belfry (1) **13** 1120
belfry (1) **13** 626
Belgian (1) **10** 147
Belgians (1) **12** 1542
Belgium (1) **17** 1739
Belial (1) **15** 1907
belie (1) **14** 914
belied (1) **2** 368
BELIEF (1) **7** 1022
Belief (1) **9** 455

belief (4) 9 370 10 i077 16 780
  17 1151
beliefs (4) 14 979 17 1895 1902 1904
Believe (2) 7 306 11 872
believe (70) 1 622 4 362 376 5 127 365
  6 19 68 536 844 7 310 815 8 106 220 250
  585 9 520 685 696 1065 1072 1078 1079
  10 938 953 11 38 152 815 818 819 820 872
  12 732 736 788 1352 1353 1354 1647 13 200
  808 14 447 568 15 1028 1099 1561 1736 1783
  2218 4886 16 258 748 750 767 770 800 880 1129
  18 159 277 354 356 531 673 721 736 1058 1187
  1237 1514
Believe-on-Me (2) 14 444 459
believed (11) 9 349 11 1170 13 1118
  14 213 1479 15 2784 16 117 1543
  17 993 1763 18 774
believer (5) 1 606 611 16 92 491
believers (1) 10 851
Believers' (1) 9 807
Believes (2) 11 627 16 434
believes (4) 9 226 1072 1074 1077
belike (1) 14 257
Bell (1) 13 1121
bell (23) 3 70 126 7 415 10 281 645 651
  688 691 11 286 757 12 974 1676 1785
  13 620 1286 14 797 799 18 359 409 635
  712 761
bell (3) 15 3220 4140 4167
Bella (1) 17 2055
Bella (2) 16 346 1343
Bella (10) 15 2742 2770 2809 2829 3479 3540
  3548 3583 4028 4320
BELLA (25) 15 2749 3480 3488 3495 3499 3527
  3541 3555 3585 3697 3774 3785 3817 3870 3910
  3917 4253 4258 4267 4274 4280 4287 4294 4301
  4307
Belladonna (1) 16 347
belladonna (1) 18 576
bellchime (1) 17 1249
Belle (1) 12 1171
belle (2) 4 399 12 1170
belle (2) 10 362 15 122
Belleisle (1) 13 15
Bellew (1) 16 1346
BELLHANGER (1) 15 1467
bellhorses (1) 15 4143
Bellicosus (1) 12 1708
bellies (1) 8 391
Bellingham (1) 15 1050
Bellingham (1) 15 4550
BELLINGHAM (5) 15 1025 1044 1074 1090 1102
Bello (2) 15 2877 2880
Bello (2) 15 2884 2951
BELLO (37) 15 2834 2838 2842 2846 2856 2865
  2881 2890 2905 2909 2915 2930 2940 2956 2963
  2972 2989 2998 3014 3021 3041 3051 3058 3064
  3072 3101 3114 3126 3135 3148 3152 3164 3172
  3182 3197 3203 3217
bellow (1) 14 608
bellowing (1) 12 109
bellows (4) 7 969 11 973 1200 12 1717
bellows (2) 15 387 921
Bells (1) 9 501
Bells (1) 15 4663
BELLS (2) 15 180 1185
bells (11) 1 651 3 127 4 544 9 501
  12 1718 13 625 15 3335 3578 17 1226
  18 1231

bells (1) 2 104
bells (3) 15 179 1184 4083
bellshade (1) 17 1337
bellstrap (1) 10 135
Belluomo (1) 3 211
Belly (1) 3 42
belly (22) 6 591 598 8 374 479 1137 1142
  10 811 11 806 12 1547 14 310 511 607
  733 15 57 710 2495 3140 3909 18 450 904
  1514
belly (3) 15 3911 4556 4693
bellyband (1) 10 558
bellycrab (1) 14 102
bellyful (1) 8 53
bellying (1) 12 1773
belong (4) 12 1467 1871 16 1159 1161
belonged (5) 13 343 14 534 633 16 266
  18 1247
belonging (2) 15 1482 16 1234
belongings (4) 11 557 1027 1056 13 910
belongs (6) 12 1470 15 3903 16 419 1165
  1166 1174
beloved (5) 1 21 15 1542 16 1396 1628
  18 828
below (15) 6 880 8 900 9 1154 12 443
  695 14 731 15 487 1259 3518 17 172 195
  1246 1448 18 814 1012
below (1) 15 2054
belt (4) 12 696 13 1171 15 2549
  17 1049
belt (4) 15 959 1179 4597 4644
belts (1) 8 408
Belturbet (1) 15 55
Belvedere (5) 10 21 41 163 165 167
bemired (1) 9 822
bemoiled (1) 14 1416
bemused (1) 1 577
Ben (64) 6 145 8 117 119 839 911 9 45
  10 791 893 897 901 906 907 911 915 916 921 925
  932 940 945 950 11 39 436 442 449 459 472 480
  481 490 533 541 554 582 586 599 758 772 800 849
  851 853 959 990 991 992 997 1011 1070 1146 1151
  1157 1160 1163 1183 1214 1272 1277 1282
  12 195 15 2614 16 425 18 1285
Ben (2) 15 2604 3367
BEN (4) 15 1664 1668 2608 2617
ben (5) 12 1916 15 1834 1864
Benaben (2) 11 53 1154
Benady (1) 18 831
Benamor (2) 15 1865
Benben (3) 11 53 1154
bench (13) 2 35 177 5 354 417 7 744
  8 1153 10 473 626 12 771 875 1099
  13 911 17 1943
bench (1) 15 1163
bencher (1) 15 4452
benches (2) 2 120 5 343
Bend (2) 8 931 13 1260
bend (9) 1 273 5 413 8 595 9 925
  10 1166 11 406 13 839 14 393
  15 3120
bend (1) 15 1130
Bending (2) 10 333 11 410
bending (9) 1 559 2 81 4 163 11 164
  411 1085 12 1183 16 1166 17 1314
bending (3) 15 160 1595 2420
bends (3) 2 169 5 107 9 258
bends (14) 15 2038 2060 2082 2811 2945 3124
  3291 3549 3589 4890 4922 4925 4926 4936

bene (1) 16 1139
Beneath (2) 2 129 12 170
Beneath (1) 15 3840
beneath (17) 1 115 249 2 148 3 412 474
  5 111 10 261 12 1726 1868 13 169 802
  15 825 3935 16 1145 17 1060 1413 2110
beneath (1) 2 66
beneath (2) 15 3995 4365
Benedetto (1) 15 2087
Benedicat (1) 14 1445
Benedict (1) 12 1679
Benedictine (1) 5 407
benediction (4) 13 284 619 622 676
benedictionem (1) 12 1746
benefaction (1) 14 17
Beneficent (1) 14 766
beneficent (1) 12 626
beneficial (1) 14 1284
benefit (7) 12 771 13 100 15 1004 3485
  16 510 590 18 1003
benefits (3) 14 913 966 16 557
Beni (1) 15 1624
Beni (1) 16 474
benign (1) 9 436
benign (1) 15 3673
benignant (2) 10 1203 17 1480
benignly (1) 10 77
Beninobenone (2) 12 556 584
Benjamin (4) 10 539 918 12 187
  17 2138
Benjamin (1) 15 4341
Bennett (8) 6 370 419 10 1134 15 627
  3004 4796 16 1241
Bennett'll (1) 15 4793
Bennett's (3) 12 969 982 984
benoith (1) 15 1333
Ben's (2) 11 1032 1160
Benson's (1) 10 1098
Bensoulbenjamin (1) 11 531
Bent (1) 6 935
bent (35) 1 11 105 135 272 494 2 426
  3 406 408 4 23 224 475 5 348 6 198 252
  588 719 911 7 820 821 9 568 573 10 201
  597 636 1071 11 312 405 637 1057 1059
  13 24 264 728 742 15 519
bent (3) 15 578 2574 4019
bentwood (1) 17 1534
benzoin (1) 5 490
bequest (1) 17 1747
Bequests (1) 5 435
Berchmans (1) 12 1705
bere (1) 12 96
bereavement (1) 18 730
Berenice (1) 17 1213
Beresford (4) 12 1339 16 52 1735 17 2
Bergan (7) 8 320 11 438 12 249 273 278
  954
Bergan (1) 15 481
BERGAN (1) 15 484
Bergin's (2) 10 93 16 24
Berkeley (2) 4 240 6 372
Berlin (4) 4 199 9 1074 15 991
  17 1700
Bermudas (1) 9 755
Bernagh (1) 12 1833
Bernard (12) 5 398 9 440 10 24 34
  12 1695 1729 13 378 17 329 1240 2051
  2135 2253
Bernard (1) 16 1256

Bernardus (1) 14 297
berries (2) 8 859 12 283
Bert (1) 15 3003
berth (1) 16 938
Bertha (4) 13 92 221 635 701
Bertha (1) 15 88
beryl (1) 15 2748
beseeched (1) 18 308
beseeching (1) 13 288
beseeming (1) 14 323
beset (1) 1 265
besetting (1) 15 734
beshrew (1) 14 774
Beside (2) 6 662 16 1440
Beside (3) 15 297 313 1237
beside (39) 1 107 108 330 603 2 169
  3 411 6 76 524 646 902 1016 8 986 9 44
  10 497 913 1021 1142 11 600 854 12 1081
  13 12 101 286 662 681 890 14 195 483 1011
  1144 16 1179 1233 1351 1474 17 151 1287
  18 91 351 1548
beside (1) 15 472
Besides (9) 6 962 13 708 827 837 1262
  15 3359 16 895 1478 1847
besides (16) 13 145 713 15 3908 16 86
  18 31 120 244 357 414 661 978 1158 1316 1345
  1356 1527
besmirched (1) 14 339
bespeaks (1) 15 3826
bespoke (1) 11 349
Bess (1) 9 758
Best (34) 4 479 481 8 334 410 9 74 90 111
  263 275 362 387 425 512 522 527 715 725 735 768
  793 955 960 1059 1068 11 357 571 618
  13 919 1074 15 505 2789 4106 4951
Best (1) 15 2247
BEST (3) 9 902 915 15 2251
best (89) 1 55 4 112 409 5 137 208 496 520
  6 222 312 462 770 7 176 935 8 151 234 266
  457 465 471 9 227 315 713 714 959 960
  10 224 724 886 1145 1147 11 888 1011 1046
  1051 12 471 844 882 911 976 1381 1520 1601
  13 388 577 786 888 14 33 230 358 603 780 843
  937 1186 1228 1557 15 490 640 1007 1972 2438
  2718 2910 4106 4461 4636 16 305 348 392 462
  546 756 993 1016 1017 1344 1446 1546 1630 1647
  1650 1825 17 128 309 1553 18 798 1116 1509
Bestabed (1) 9 704
Besteglinton (1) 9 728
bester (1) 17 2146
bestest (1) 14 1541
besthearted (1) 7 680
bestia (1) 10 345
bestial (1) 15 3908
bestialities (1) 9 851
Bestir (1) 12 1600
bestknown (1) 16 773
bestow (1) 15 291
bestowed (2) 10 305 15 1506
bestquoted (1) 14 576
bestride (1) 15 1072
bestrode (1) 2 144
Best's (4) 9 142 189 240 618
bestselling (1) 15 824
Bet (4) 3 430 12 1555 14 1466 1499
bet (12) 3 331 5 359 7 223 8 133 321
  14 1472 15 1739 2867 16 1298 18 501
  1121 1144
beta (1) 17 1993

betaken (1) 14 945
Beth (2) 5 11 15 1623
Bethany (1) 12 1709
Bethel (1) 5 11
Bethlehem (1) 14 1383
bethought (1) 7 825
betide (2) 6 597 15 406
betokened (1) 14 728
betrayal (1) 17 2184
betrayed (3) 3 243 9 1036 12 1380
betrayer (1) 1 405
Better (38) 1 702 3 456 499 4 45 366 451
  494 543 5 450 462 529 6 22 330 455 474 946
  7 144 153 219 8 370 844 1092 10 771
  11 821 889 1148 1191 13 980 1071 1129 1211
  1247 1248 15 174 381 660 763 2741
better (92) 1 440 2 178 330 391 3 97
  4 26 48 187 367 5 456 6 106 295 425 435
  558 613 620 649 744 792 984 8 640 769 851 952
  1042 9 960 10 1172 11 650 721 723 814
  826 12 148 708 796 886 13 85 86 128 584
  725 792 1071 1195 14 356 508 591 933 999 1005
  1223 15 1350 1367 3020 3118 3601 3625 3903
  4519 16 173 431 784 1049 1130 1469 1831
  18 18 71 155 356 408 412 417 660 662 843 903
  907 913 953 967 999 1121 1144 1195 1211 1273
  1377 1435 1536 1547
better (2) 11 781 12 1568
better (1) 15 914
bettered (1) 9 716
Betting (2) 5 544 16 1280
betting (1) 17 320 1678
Betty's (1) 13 1065
Between (5) 9 139 10 824 1184 11 341
  16 51
Between (1) 9 266
Between (1) 15 4032
between (117) 1 571 2 23 388 3 226 239
  4 304 5 131 218 6 208 209 440 562 7 43
  274 372 601 1024 1027 8 51 564 1140 9 494
  631 673 1009 1202 1203 10 297 335 377 823 935
  1246 11 467 577 12 49 53 326 707 1132 1522
  13 40 944 974 985 14 358 539 557 618 644 993
  1001 1238 15 953 4648 16 312 468 495 580
  990 1043 1062 1105 1137 1209 1210 1329 1338
  1363 1365 1381 1386 1485 1550 17 18 49 52 151
  258 402 428 434 446 478 745 931 940 942 956 971
  1014 1090 1157 1340 1414 1447 1617 1722 1729
  1809 1907 2025 2040 2164 2192 2213 2251 2286
  2290 18 215 395 593 967 1130 1146 1430
between (9) 15 6 26 492 694 806 3195 3382
  3583 4706
betweenmaid (1) 17 1544
betweenwhiles (1) 16 1634
beurla (1) 9 367
bevelling (1) 16 33
beverage (5) 5 388 12 288 15 2233
  16 5 810
beverages (4) 12 690 1738 17 798 2193
bevy (2) 7 955 13 1107
bevy (1) 15 1122
bewail (1) 9 286
Beware (7) 9 451 15 245 2340 4217 4219
  16 1780 17 604
beware (3) 3 483 15 2271 2642
bewept (2) 9 1036 12 405
bewitching (1) 15 715
Bewley (1) 16 718
bewray (1) 14 239

beyant (1) 9 203
Beyond (3) 6 500 10 37 1211
beyond (33) 3 425 4 96 7 135 984
  9 169 10 743 930 1097 1183 12 13 295 348
  499 1365 13 667 908 935 15 455 3118 3701
  4535 16 92 793 1381 1771 1794 1844 1852
  17 520 521 1212 2014 18 578
beyond (2) 15 140 604
beyondre (1) 18 875
bézique (1) 12 507
bezique (2) 17 504 662
Bheag (1) 12 898
Bi (1) 12 265
bi (1) 16 1563
bias (2) 6 1012 16 1543
bib (4) 13 34 393 612 613
bib (1) 15 2924
bibendum (1) 14 1439
biberimus (1) 14 1533
bible (7) 2 275 12 1335 1508 1509 1523 1535
  14 518
bible (1) 15 1440
bibles (2) 14 1459 1461
bibulous (1) 16 337
biceps (1) 17 1818
biche (1) 14 781
bickering (1) 15 91
bicycle (8) 8 524 533 12 1494 13 130 135
  143 18 839 1026
bicycle (2) 15 2265 2273
bicyclers (1) 15 4147
bicycles (2) 17 493 18 290
Bid (1) 16 1742
bid (5) 12 1815 14 318 402 15 2733
  16 1394
bidden (1) 14 532
BIDDER (1) 15 3092
bidder's (1) 15 3091
biddeth (1) 14 473
Bidding (1) 11 123
bidding (6) 1 410 8 795 9 171 10 352
  12 1070 17 1236
BIDDY (4) 15 4438 4442 4514 4635
bide (1) 12 446
bids (3) 1 422 3 395 9 723
bids (1) 15 1850
bien (1) 18 1472
bien (1) 14 746
biennial (1) 17 1544
bier (4) 6 582 593 817 11 1220
Biff (2) 15 4392 4399
bifurcated (1) 17 1194
Big (20) 6 186 376 7 342 8 490 11 53
  808 959 1012 1070 1154 12 655 13 983 1148
  15 171 1273 2217 2614
big (102) 1 367 2 264 3 42 4 87 89 405
  407 509 5 30 298 360 553 6 82 361 395 752
  7 398 8 48 115 119 159 337 375 382 715 771
  839 849 9 875 10 269 290 895 1166 1206
  1209 11 800 1152 1228 1272 12 13 96 254
  957 1097 1834 13 19 26 55 389 399 665 666
  1082 1198 1267 14 482 502 635 1515 1525
  15 404 1916 2552 3901 4509 16 782 955 1789
  1857 17 2314 18 39 43 144 146 151 155 307
  329 415 429 450 498 582 597 608 707 901 917 978
  997 1089 1092 1123 1206 1223 1287 1426 1503
  1554 1591
big (1) 15 2005
bigamist (1) 15 1159

bigdrumming (1) 3 103
bigger (7) 2 111 13 494 14 785
  16 1033 17 42 18 1203 1506
bigger (3) 8 783
biggest (1) 7 98
biggish (1) 14 484
bigheaded (1) 15 2005
bights (1) 17 218
bigness (2) 14 242 311
bigsplash (1) 14 1556
bijou (1) 16 521
bilbos (1) 14 1393
bile (1) 1 109
bile (1) 15 4189
bilgewater (1) 16 939
biliary (1) 8 1048
bilious (2) 8 790 14 1426
bilks (1) 14 1503
Bill (2) 1 442 18 1282
Bill (1) 16 404
bill (11) 1 440 7 997 8 884 9 712
  11 248 12 1194 13 1051 15 2988
  16 1693 17 1790 18 713
bill (2) 15 1798 1909
billet (1) 13 951
billets (1) 15 1572
billhook (1) 17 1565
billiardmarking (1) 7 629
billies (1) 8 437
billing (1) 16 1654
Billington (1) 12 425
billions (2) 17 1061 1079
billows (1) 11 591
billowy (1) 15 3016
Bills (1) 15 2633
bills (6) 3 80 4 237 6 187 14 1417
  17 681 18 127
bills (2) 15 1814 2147
BILLS (1) 8 101
billsticker (3) 16 199 234 17 2145
Billy (3) 1 543 8 1059 18 1342
billy (1) 13 608
billycock (1) 15 539
Billyo (1) 14 1441
Billy's (1) 10 1232
Binbad (1) 17 2323
Binding (1) 10 844
binding (3) 11 1180 17 1367 1377
binds (1) 12 1778
Bing (1) 15 2475
bing (1) 3 375
Bingbang (1) 7 374
Bingham (1) 17 1308
binocular (1) 17 492
binomial (1) 17 2006
Bip (1) 15 3441
birching (1) 15 1096
birchwood (1) 14 141
Bird (1) 11 1024
bird (9) 3 164 6 949 952 11 745 13 872
  1129 15 557 2511 18 813
bird (1) 1 585
bird (1) 15 1427
Bird-in-the-Hand (2) 14 450 457
birdcage (1) 1 256
birdchief (1) 15 3420
birdgod (1) 9 353
birdlime (1) 11 1034
birdnotes (1) 11 323

Birds (2) 13 1128 1145
Birds (1) 15 4665
birds (14) 6 957 987 8 73 481 9 1093 1184
  1206 1218 13 903 1118 14 904 15 1452
  18 1584
Birds' (1) 8 1071
birdseye (1) 15 652
birdsnies (1) 9 638
birdsweet (2) 1 602 11 631
birdy (1) 15 3130
Birmingham (1) 8 18
Birth (2) 8 11 31
birth (29) 8 284 9 929 10 1074 12 574
  14 114 117 203 258 310 390 446 822 1233 1380
  1485 16 1007 17 882 921 998 1115 1122 1126
  1129 1130 1131 1855 2119 2275 2280
birthaiding (1) 9 878
birthday (7) 4 284 398 416 8 628 1119
  13 316 18 680
birthmark (1) 9 393
birthplace (1) 17 1984
birthplaces (1) 12 1460
birthright (1) 13 200
births (3) 12 222 14 116 974
Bis (1) 15 4135
biscuit (6) 7 258 259 12 495 1227 1229
  17 2041
biscuitbox (1) 12 1812
biscuitboxes (1) 15 4334
biscuitfully (1) 7 237
biscuitmush (1) 4 107
biscuits (4) 16 185 190 17 575 18 831
biscuits (1) 16 979
bisected (1) 17 310
bisection (1) 17 971
bisexually (1) 15 1775
Bishop (2) 15 444 18 837
BISHOP (1) 15 1470
bishop (8) 3 416 10 1050 12 1683
  15 2227 2243 2559 18 90
bishop (2) 15 1420 1477
Biſhop's (1) 17 1400
Bishops (1) 14 1462
bishops (3) 9 1008 12 1402 14 1460
Bisley (1) 16 407
bison (1) 14 1431
bispherical (1) 17 1996
bissextile (1) 17 95
Bit (6) 6 819 7 519 11 512 1023
  13 1252 15 209
bit (134) 3 64 4 9 99 215 435 502 5 187
  274 304 364 408 479 480 6 19 57 204 853 996
  1000 7 200 213 969 983 8 21 58 386 447 513
  836 10 331 383 1088 11 170 375 446 840
  1249 12 20 311 507 1208 13 147 180 311 360
  508 594 990 1145 1150 14 516 557 807 1473
  15 309 551 657 829 2057 2541 2910 3800 4808
  4813 16 5 178 428 459 469 529 585 694 762 787
  859 864 869 976 1012 1157 1238 1272 1365 1448
  1604 1677 1717 1736 1814 18 8 30 51 69 171
  184 207 215 284 312 343 413 435 450 464 503 535
  593 623 830 892 904 907 919 939 953 979 1033
  1044 1061 1146 1265 1274 1298 1362 1470 1479
  1507 1574 1594
bit (1) 6 730
bitch (7) 12 398 1392 15 371 16 1352
  18 45 564 1256
bitchbody (1) 15 4179
bitched (1) 16 1263

bitches (3) 10 682 18 1159 1459
bitch's (4) 10 1120 11 285 1041 1098
bite (12) 3 96 6 381 7 616 621 8 852
  11 521 522 12 701 1162 16 466 1640
  18 569
bites (1) 15 2554
bites (3) 15 1339 2714 3202
Biting (1) 4 520
biting (2) 18 555 1029
biting (1) 15 4332
Bits (2) 3 189 18 601
Bits (2) 4 370 15 3261
bits (16) 3 188 5 352 6 953 7 933 943
  11 586 12 445 495 1321 1397 13 768
  15 928 16 781 18 699 1468
bitted (1) 15 112
Bitten (1) 8 661
bitten (1) 16 1639
bitter (9) 1 249 253 3 330 11 350
  12 97 233 14 378 16 1176
bitter (2) 1 240 15 4190
bitterer (1) 7 1036
bitterly (1) 15 1974
Bitterness (1) 14 430
bitterness (4) 1 145 9 387 12 794
  14 379
bittern's (1) 15 4111
bitters (1) 5 389
bituminous (1) 17 260
bivalve (1) 15 2444
bivalves (1) 15 2438
bivouac (1) 14 407
biweekly (1) 17 665
biz (2) 4 402 15 642
Bla (1) 15 189
Black (13) 4 79 6 323 11 39 342
  12 846 1295 15 401 2997 3029 4930
  16 461 678 18 400
Black (2) 12 1324 1527
Black (4) 15 1437 1509 3707 4689
BLACK (1) 15 3709
black (103) 1 57 62 101 340 518 690 2 275
  3 26 485 4 21 79 141 534 536 542 5 89 156
  218 376 458 6 122 587 779 841 7 811 8 35
  138 213 350 403 567 988 1129 1130 9 882 911
  1156 10 100 143 145 474 764 1267 11 110
  244 446 726 998 1252 12 440 441 848 1366
  13 93 349 600 1013 1281 14 408 1025 1033
  1556 1575 15 203 409 1116 1156 1295 1958
  2738 2805 2993 3476 16 671 704 879 1886
  17 159 303 1321 1377 1383 1394 1435 1438 2004
  2092 2103 18 163 251 265 483 608 759 780 826
  900 940 963 1053 1264
black (23) 15 61 424 451 500 664 901 1168
  1173 1280 1310 1325 1355 1938 1961 2037 2216
  2570 2607 2744 3317 3828 4498 4671
blackbearded (1) 6 252
blackbearded (1) 15 1918
blackbeetles (1) 18 1252
blackberry (1) 18 1128
Blackbird (1) 11 633
blackbottom (1) 18 1034
Blackburn (1) 12 1590
blackbuttocker (1) 16 1784
blackdraped (1) 12 537
blacked (1) 6 544
Blackedged (1) 6 603
Blackened (1) 5 155
blackened (1) 15 4218

blacker (1) 8 1109
blackgrouse (1) 15 4668
blackguard (3) 12 385 15 1069
    16 1805
blackguardism (1) 10 684
blackguardlooking (1) 18 1417
blackguards (1) 18 492
Blacking (1) 17 593
blackmail (1) 17 2186
blackmasked (1) 15 4537
blacknailed (1) 5 523
Blackpitts (2) 3 377 7 926
blackrimmed (1) 7 440
Blackrock (2) 7 4 1045
blacks (2) 5 334 18 227
Blacksmith (1) 12 182
BLACKSMITH (1) 15 1455
Blacksod (1) 12 1302
blackspectacled (1) 7 335
blackthumbed (1) 14 626
Blackwood (4) 2 279 334 340 12 1277
bladder (2) 8 933 15 1649
Bladderbags (1) 7 260
bladderwrack (1) 3 286
blade (10) 6 913 7 934 10 97 210 216
    11 1237 14 695 885 894 16 587
blades (1) 6 911
blades (1) 3 258
blague (1) 14 783
Blake (2) 17 2136 18 726
Blake's (3) 2 8 7 94 9 88
BLAME (1) 7 1071
blame (11) 1 649 2 247 3 452 8 422
    9 257 13 173 14 1016 15 4372
    16 540 1185 18 1469
Blameless (1) 15 3177
blames (1) 14 1243
Blanc (1) 3 197
Blanca (1) 15 216
Blanche (1) 12 1272
blancmange (1) 18 940
blandiloquence (1) 16 231
blandishments (1) 14 326
blandly (2) 1 472 5 21
Blank (1) 11 1086
blank (11) 1 675 2 6 3 405 6 922
    8 65 9 1133 11 1025 13 737 17 733
    2051
blank (1) 15 1813
blanket (3) 4 334 13 395 18 660
blanketcloth (1) 5 102
blanketed (1) 3 76
blankets (1) 9 637
blare (2) 15 2115 4630
blared (1) 10 1249
blares (1) 15 2169
blarney (2) 7 984 16 1635
blasé (1) 15 3118
blases (1) 14 148
blasphemous (1) 1 605
Blast (2) 9 847 10 457
blast (5) 3 404 10 459 11 514 586
    14 1446
blasted (3) 7 900 12 220 15 4721
blasts (1) 14 290
blatant (4) 5 432 7 555 10 690
    16 1529
blather (1) 18 1187
Blavatsky (1) 7 784

blay (1) 15 288
Blaze (1) 14 1569
blaze (2) 13 578 15 171
blazer (1) 15 4396
Blazes (32) 4 281 408 6 196 8 787 807
    10 300 304 307 318 321 324 327 334 984 1241
    1242 11 337 345 364 370 385 388 399 430 498
    524 761 12 943 947 997 15 3750 17 2141
Blazes (4) 15 3728 3738 3740 4147
blazes (6) 11 290 430 766 14 1108
    18 424 951
blazes (1) 15 807
Blazing (1) 6 307
blazing (1) 3 403
Blazure's (1) 11 394
bleaching (2) 2 197 8 265
bleachworks (1) 17 222
bleak (2) 1 542 6 183
blear (1) 15 2461
bleared (1) 10 640
bleating (2) 6 387 12 109
bleats (2) 15 2864 3370
bleed (1) 6 432
Bleeding (1) 16 198
bleeding (15) 1 703 5 366 12 584 676 677
    14 1424 1447 1451 15 1977 4573 4628 4645
    4721 4776 4778
bleeds (1) 18 24
Bleibtreu (1) 9 1073
Bleibtreustrasse (4) 4 199 8 863
    15 991 17 1700
Blemblem (1) 15 2058
blemish (2) 3 42 14 310
blemishes (1) 16 1019
blend (3) 5 19 29 14 1078
blended (2) 1 654 11 158
blender's (1) 12 516
Blending (1) 11 852
Blephen (1) 17 551
Bless (2) 1 335 14 814
Bless (2) 11 1074
bless (8) 5 414 10 559 959 12 1609 1673
    1736 14 764 15 1618
bless (1) 10 139
bless'd (1) 9 1225
Blessed (18) 3 129 5 443 7 318 946
    9 646 10 81 12 1711 13 139 284 458 492
    497 553 622 674 15 2236 4590 18 497
BLESSED (1) 15 4712
blessed (27) 1 10 15 6 65 10 10 203 850
    11 151 12 1678 1714 1732 1735 1736 1738
    1744 13 448 14 251 1160 15 287
    16 1553 1829 17 2231 18 135 305 521 629
    759
blessedness (1) 16 1556
blesses (2) 15 1222 2682
blessing (10) 12 1292 1504 1664 1726
    14 592 594 791 1320 15 3538 18 761
blessings (2) 1 346 14 766
Blessington (1) 6 366
Blew (2) 8 192 11 6
blew (11) 6 839 7 480 8 186 442 688
    10 565 1013 11 5 217 1236 18 830
blight (1) 8 1073
blight (1) 15 4580
blighted (2) 9 337 14 1387
blighter (1) 15 4392
Blimey (1) 12 676
blimey (1) 12 676

Blind (3) 5 367 11 1212 12 802
blind (46) 2 130 3 277 4 111 255 256
    5 201 353 6 318 361 8 1075 1078 1104
    9 859 10 250 342 1105 1117 1126 1270
    11 280 1190 1234 1236 12 251 622 700 1194
    1239 1394 1550 1664 1725 13 737 946 1118
    14 468 1476 15 3716 4479 16 424 1192
    17 1174 1175 1941 18 340 695
blind (3) 15 1600 3045 4147
blinder (1) 10 1119
blindfold (1) 15 445
blindly (1) 8 376
blinds (5) 6 12 26 15 1967 2991 18 146
Blingee (1) 15 963
blinked (3) 4 33 6 728 14 1228
blinking (9) 1 379 581 5 234 6 581 726
    730 12 1193 16 476 18 206
blinking (1) 15 321
bliss (3) 8 749 14 60 17 599
bliss (2) 5 147 16 594
blissful (1) 12 647
blissfully (1) 16 70
blister (1) 14 385
blisters (1) 15 4680
blithe (3) 1 579 9 486 14 1151
blithering (1) 16 1050
blizzard (1) 8 191
Blmstup (1) 11 1126
bloated (2) 3 286 8 48
bloated (1) 15 2662
bloater (1) 8 538
blob (1) 13 1133
blobs (2) 8 782 14 480
Block (1) 15 710
block (5) 6 509 7 899 9 1005 12 612
    18 822
block (1) 15 1178
blocking (1) 6 403
Blockwell (1) 15 3002
Bloemfontein (2) 15 796 18 388
bloke (1) 14 1510
blond (11) 9 265 531 10 299 303 319 326
    330 14 739 17 868 896
blond (2) 15 62 2074
Bloo (6) 8 8 11 19 309 860 14 1535
    15 189
Blood (2) 8 9 729
blood (48) 1 22 269 2 142 166 278 3 306
    394 4 144 149 232 6 674 771 7 743 776
    8 11 483 622 729 929 9 80 87 434 669 782
    10 765 11 945 12 448 475 624 953 980
    1381 13 924 969 14 618 812 1269 1580
    16 672 889 1112 1412 1638 17 294
    18 1122
blood (2) 15 996 1330
bloodbeaked (1) 3 301
bloodboltered (1) 9 133
bloodbright (1) 15 61
bloodcoloured (1) 15 1177
blooddripping (1) 15 4703
blooded (1) 15 3956
bloodflows (1) 14 122
bloodgouts (1) 4 145
bloodhounds (1) 15 4328
bloodhued (1) 8 622
bloodied (1) 2 318
bloodied (1) 15 373
bloodiest (1) 7 533
Bloodless (1) 8 1112

bloodless (2) 2 126 6 520
bloodmaking (1) 16 91
bloodoath (1) 15 3649
bloodpoisoning (1) 18 32
bloodred (1) 10 587
bloodshot (2) 6 661 12 710
bloodshot (1) 15 1207
bloodsmeared (1) 4 277
bloodthirstily (1) 16 403
bloodthirsty (1) 12 347
bloodvessel (1) 6 511
Bloody (2) 10 1183 12 1849
bloody (100) 1 52 157 3 188 292 6 64 271
7 350 474 676 680 708 8 726 1008 10 499
518 558 690 12 2 6 13 25 66 101 119 124 126
141 149 253 254 263 270 275 300 392 397 432 488
491 492 494 497 518 775 784 808 886 893 956 1031
1062 1089 1100 1190 1198 1312 1321 1323 1344
1357 1400 1558 1571 1578 1579 1662 1760 1766
1770 1794 1795 1800 1811 1843 1845 1855 1856
1904 1906 1907 1908 13 1150 15 609 1346
2674 2681 3053 3209 3863 4215 16 147 165 462
1104 18 1534
bloody (2) 6 730 10 445
bloodying (1) 3 398
bloodypapered (1) 8 727
bloodz (1) 3 293
Bloohimwhom (1) 11 309
Bloohoom (1) 15 157
BLOOM (2) 7 429 962
Bloom (540) 4 1 17 21 139 171 244 518 5 1
84 91 94 98 123 136 142 150 154 162 168 174 177
183 192 210 394 414 421 486 490 509 512 516 520
531 534 537 543 6 5 8 9 39 50 54 72 105 111 114
119 154 200 212 213 216 221 225 262 269 272 276
285 290 312 343 401 405 412 527 535 540 542 574
585 635 655 661 667 671 693 739 824 841 865 875
882 894 898 902 928 1016 1018 1027 7 26 33 36
42 54 67 85 112 116 121 124 126 132 134 149 155
162 187 217 269 273 277 280 283 375 411 419 423
430 436 608 609 671 963 971 988 993 8 6 108
114 202 206 214 219 249 254 257 260 276 283 286
293 299 303 308 315 523 593 694 737 777 818 843
984 1020 1028 1033 1069 1077 1080 1086 1089
1106 1167 9 607 10 546 555 567 572 581 583
585 601 618 637 974 11 49 52 133 180 228 229
230 296 299 341 358 390 445 457 476 496 522 523
553 569 608 614 628 637 642 646 669 681 682 704
705 768 776 784 786 787 795 802 824 829 860 863
886 887 888 934 1000 1028 1071 1076 1127 1130
1136 1137 1142 1221 1224 1253 1262 1274
12 379 407 410 434 435 450 464 498 501 506 514
520 522 682 760 767 769 780 833 852 855 888 891
894 912 944 952 991 994 1051 1054 1060 1143 1147
1152 1155 1160 1195 1235 1237 1360 1376 1414
1420 1422 1426 1431 1467 1474 1485 1550 1555
1574 1580 1581 1621 1624 1638 1650 1833 1916
13 744 772 851 1042 1060 1181 1246 1256 1266
1287 14 424 504 507 845 952 1004 1230 1300
1393 1401 1535 15 338 395 677 721 740 813 859
976 1158 1218 1386 1456 1459 1513 1542 1543
1677 1720 1727 1734 1753 1775 1798 1834 1868
1871 1913 1941 2196 3153 3230 3757 3758 4363
16 1 6 28 35 61 78 111 116 211 229 236 245 254
260 279 320 331 340 351 357 365 371 380 385 406
409 414 422 487 603 611 614 706 728 761 790 817
821 884 889 924 929 1029 1092 1106 1163 1166
1172 1270 1295 1307 1349 1359 1418 1437 1510
1514 1524 1575 1578 1691 1711 1718 1734 1736

1772 1778 1781 1814 1817 1821 1867 1880 17 1
18 29 30 37 46 61 70 123 157 160 183 241 275 297
354 378 405 447 449 453 454 455 456 459 473 483
528 534 535 540 542 549 550 555 561 621 622 715
729 734 737 761 787 929 953 973 978 979 980 1016
1033 1040 1126 1130 1178 1187 1201 1232 1235
1242 1245 1311 1341 1345 1346 1494 1580 1581
1612 1614 1637 1776 1788 1795 1796 1816 1822
1840 1855 1857 1872 1873 1881 1888 1893 1905
1906 1912 1933 2002 2043 2059 2063 2068 2071
2081 18 256 513 531 841 842
Bloom (4) 4 287 10 524 12 894
17 401
Bloom (98) 15 142 147 150 190 196 238 242
260 291 322 384 487 531 597 632 772 898 929 930
935 973 983 1079 1267 1310 1377 1442 1490 1499
1508 1559 1565 1595 1702 1717 1763 1787 1812
1821 1841 1885 1902 1905 1916 1927 1931 1956
2021 2033 2038 2123 2142 2300 2301 2405 2491
2698 2751 2811 2829 2871 2883 2901 2929 3167
3195 3219 3225 3236 3329 3377 3439 3506 3535
3554 3589 3641 3722 3788 3821 3827 4030 4261
4318 4323 4351 4365 4463 4726 4749 4888 4912
4915 4918 4920 4944 4946
BLOOM (278) 15 153 162 166 169 182 198 215
219 224 227 230 239 244 255 263 268 276 280 282
295 303 308 324 331 344 348 354 377 391 397 407
427 432 440 449 456 464 475 489 494 517 522 527
535 545 555 563 569 592 634 656 681 687 698 719
727 737 757 768 774 784 792 801 828 839 849 856
874 889 956 984 1006 1084 1094 1106 1120 1187
1200 1215 1219 1277 1284 1292 1300 1305 1312
1322 1335 1342 1348 1354 1365 1389 1476 1483
1503 1515 1524 1541 1563 1599 1621 1635 1641
1650 1657 1661 1666 1670 1676 1680 1684 1698
1721 1730 1738 1767 1816 1835 1879 1912 1934
1959 1973 1979 1987 1992 2000 2004 2026 2317
2326 2336 2347 2352 2368 2378 2387 2407 2428
2443 2454 2563 2567 2704 2720 2730 2735 2756
2761 2765 2771 2776 2793 2799 2804 2813 2821
2825 2832 2836 2840 2844 2850 2863 2874 2888
2903 2907 2913 2938 2954 2961 2969 2984 2996
3008 3018 3048 3056 3061 3070 3123 3133 3145
3150 3159 3180 3190 3201 3214 3241 3253 3260
3266 3271 3280 3287 3292 3310 3315 3332 3352
3364 3371 3389 3396 3404 3423 3448 3462 3471
3482 3491 3497 3508 3512 3519 3555 3582 3591
3596 3600 3605 3612 3616 3643 3694 3703 3712
3759 3766 3790 3814 3830 3834 3932 3937 4007
4209 4224 4248 4270 4277 4283 4289 4296 4305
4311 4422 4430 4485 4510 4599 4605 4646 4723
4731 4743 4767 4781 4787 4800 4807 4837 4848
4857 4865 4872 4885 4893 4900 4906 4924 4935
4948 4961 17 1025
bloom (11) 11 6 54 230 1178 14 91 676
1145 1317 15 1032 3354 16 1429
bloom (2) 15 3342 4077
Bloombella (1) 15 4122
bloomers (3) 12 1172 13 1235 18 839
bloometh (2) 15 2490 18 775
Bloomfield (3) 17 50 52 18 1414
Bloomfield (1) 17 1388
blooming (7) 10 1125 1129 1139 1156
11 32 18 843
Bloomite (1) 15 1736
Bloom's (43) 5 540 6 157 176 260 494
7 40 356 445 968 8 234 789 1082 10 1115
11 151 720 856 1203 12 513 784 15 1383
16 973 1871 17 28 59 83 122 236 315 448 527

529 779 781 786 985 987 1137 1171 1173 1186 1189
1193 2108
Bloom's (21) 15 678 726 1447 1469 1487 1568
1585 1908 2427 2728 2931 2937 3089 3108 3128
3698 3701 3764 4268 4911 4964
BLOOM'S (1) 15 1450
Blooms (1) 18 981
Bloomusalem (1) 15 1544
Bloomusalem (1) 15 1548
Bloomville (1) 17 1613
Bloowho (1) 11 86
Bloowhose (1) 11 149
blossom (2) 4 128 15 1034
blossomed (1) 16 1370
blossoming (1) 14 1271
blossoming (1) 15 3342
blossomtime (1) 14 1372
Blot (1) 11 901
blot (2) 2 130 11 823
blotch (1) 13 1133
blotches (1) 15 994
Blotchy (1) 4 235
blotchy (1) 4 153
blotted (3) 8 566 11 895 13 408
blottingpad (1) 11 902
blottingpaper (4) 2 176 6 703 8 133
18 49
blouse (12) 8 914 10 327 334 13 150 507
799 18 189 788 798 850 1033 1139
blouse (1) 15 284
blouses (1) 11 110
Blow (1) 11 1089
blow (12) 1 499 6 541 10 825 11 1088
1237 13 1151 14 258 418 15 2964 4763
16 1366 18 899
blow (1) 8 183
blow (4) 15 296 1440 4290 4321
blowbags (1) 11 1263
Blowing (1) 2 205
blowing (13) 1 688 2 298 7 331 400 438
10 796 11 576 1200 12 6 693 1784
18 291 672
blowing (1) 15 157
Blown (2) 8 311 13 1053
blown (7) 7 600 701 9 1220 12 671
13 1017 14 1043 18 855
blowout (2) 7 342 8 877
blows (5) 7 311 12 204 577 16 1028
18 335
blows (3) 15 2263 2427 4858
blowy (1) 18 972
blub (2) 5 336 10 1273
blubber (1) 15 2365
blubbery (1) 3 306
blubble (1) 14 1556
Blud (1) 15 189
bludgeon (1) 15 1179
Bludso (1) 15 797
Blue (5) 3 273 8 838 11 6 230 15 3655
Blue (1) 17 650
Blue (1) 15 2301
blue (62) 2 275 352 3 197 239 274 425
4 435 5 481 6 122 611 7 345 355 396 1011
8 265 310 870 9 249 10 115 553 901
11 1126 12 127 242 689 1309 1764 13 59
108 150 151 175 179 180 199 220 447 586 670 681
716 815 1076 1188 15 1116 2579 16 668 765
1244 17 158 1283 1289 1368 1373 1556 1681
2096 18 420 674 963 1335 1600

blue (2) 2 103 7 245
blue (11) 15 9 269 450 471 988 1604 3167 3325 3988 4055 4126
Bluebags (1) 15 813
Bluebeard (1) 15 1040
bluebottle (2) 4 484 15 2429
bluecircled (1) 9 473
bluecircled (1) 15 4160
BLUECOAT (1) 15 1535
bluecoat (1) 8 1153
blued (2) 3 370 13 176
blueeyed (1) 15 3003
blueglancing (1) 6 913
bluehued (1) 11 458
Blueribboned (1) 9 1123
Bluerobed (1) 11 151
blues (1) 8 1043
bluesilver (1) 3 3
bluest (1) 13 108
bluestreaked (1) 15 3420
bluey (4) 5 334 8 22 25 13 1132
bluffing (1) 16 842
bluggy (1) 14 1528
Blum (2) 15 721 17 1748
Blumenbach (1) 14 1236
Blumenduft (1) 12 468
Blumenfeld (1) 7 688
Blumenlied (1) 11 844
blunder (1) 11 535
blunderbusses (1) 12 575
blunders (1) 15 191
blunt (4) 1 181 3 354 6 638 16 818
bluntungulated (1) 15 3750
blurred (3) 4 157 158 201
blurred (1) 15 986
blurry (1) 14 1513
Blurt (1) 8 116
blurt (1) 8 577
blush (7) 8 810 12 1207 13 723 15 1190 16 828 18 815 1386
blushed (2) 7 776 11 483
blushes (3) 5 432 14 91 1521
blushes (2) 15 1880 3402
Blushing (1) 9 326
blushing (8) 7 530 10 331 333 12 636 667 13 113 978 14 789
blushing (3) 15 1609 3124 4638
Bn (1) 18 389
Bo (1) 15 4610
boa (2) 8 193 10 562
boa (1) 15 2082
boar (2) 9 460 15 3038
Board (2) 13 703 17 1737
board (15) 2 136 259 3 275 8 89 13 1183 14 141 143 149 189 192 313 611 1214 16 1347 18 858
boarded (1) 16 368
boardinghouses (1) 17 1718
Boardman (22) 13 13 20 33 38 66 69 71 76 92 146 165 218 243 253 266 359 383 521 605 607 684 767
Boardman (2) 15 88 1595
BOARDMAN (2) 15 90 1597
boards (5) 7 71 8 124 16 860 17 1383 1394
boarhound (1) 15 706
boar's (1) 12 1615
boast (4) 2 251 12 1349 1355 16 1098
boaster (2) 14 418 17 2146

Boasthard (1) 14 469
Boasthard's (1) 14 429
boasts (1) 15 2100
boat (13) 1 311 3 287 320 5 186 6 272 279 663 10 730 13 1274 16 959 18 795 954 1597
boatbearers (1) 12 1677
boatclub (1) 10 385
boater (1) 17 629
boater (1) 15 3738
boating (1) 17 1595
boatman (6) 1 670 672 6 266 282 286 18 955
boatpole (1) 15 2148
boatrace (1) 14 624
boatraces (1) 15 4302
boat's (1) 16 1344
boats (5) 6 402 14 568 16 619 622 18 669
boatswain (1) 14 647
Bob (32) 2 257 5 107 180 8 595 9 826 10 741 883 938 11 437 449 482 774 929 958 998 1272 1282 12 251 273 278 310 325 330 384 388 391 394 486 487 780 1229 15 1012
Bob (4) 15 689 694 3360 4352
BOB (2) 15 691 3362
bob (27) 1 676 4 131 6 565 7 119 8 128 724 1016 10 526 11 805 1076 1264 1267 12 16 445 1088 1216 1550 13 840 1073 14 497 1292 1298 15 3109 16 170 183 209 17 914
bobbed (1) 8 58
bobbed (1) 15 2857
bobbies (1) 15 4914
bobbing (1) 3 473
bobbing (2) 15 315 4022
Bobbob (1) 8 161
bobby (2) 5 75 12 802
Bobrikoff (1) 7 602
Bob's (1) 12 311
Bobs (2) 14 1332 15 3005
Bobsy (1) 14 1331
bobtail (1) 14 1392
Boccaccio's (1) 9 836
bockedy (1) 10 897
Bode (1) 17 1111
Bodega (1) 10 937
bodice (1) 18 765
bodies (14) 2 314 3 45 277 5 45 8 642 9 376 15 2782 17 1064 1065 1066 1067 1118 1142
bodies (1) 15 4676
bodily (5) 9 850 14 664 17 2157 2160 2192
bodiment (1) 14 283
Body (4) 6 204 11 1088 13 1137 18 1177
body (64) 1 21 103 270 659 729 2 144 3 347 352 4 306 362 5 40 86 172 350 566 567 6 327 481 7 85 8 1048 9 152 172 340 379 653 10 565 757 1066 1117 11 241 908 1131 12 157 343 970 1396 13 440 1040 1064 14 272 282 310 511 724 814 15 646 788 2908 4541 4706 16 395 737 748 17 86 88 227 855 1267 18 180 567 1108 1380 1577
body (1) 12 362
body (3) 15 2045 3394 4944
bodycoats (1) 15 1883
bodyguard (1) 15 1568

body's (2) 3 375 17 91
Boer (1) 16 1305
Boers (6) 8 434 12 999 15 791 4760 16 1002 18 867
bog (4) 2 202 12 1257 1460 14 629
bogeyman's (1) 15 4176
boggled (1) 16 1814
boggles (1) 16 486
bogoak (2) 3 82 12 1444
bogoak (1) 15 1961
Bograghs (1) 12 1832
bogs (2) 6 451 10 105
bogswamp (1) 1 413
bogus (3) 15 897 2340 16 1045
Bohee (1) 15 411
Bohee (1) 15 412
Bohemia (1) 9 995
boia (1) 9 1049
boil (3) 4 271 9 80 14 1491
Boiled (1) 10 537
boiled (7) 8 886 926 12 511 15 4202 16 1571 17 275 18 43
boiler (1) 16 597
boiling (7) 4 46 264 15 1760 16 354 17 269 18 337 358
boilingcook's (1) 14 540
bois (1) 15 4098
boisterous (1) 14 1138
boisterously (1) 16 978
Boland's (1) 4 82
Bold (5) 4 244 311 12 193 13 843 14 1494
bold (9) 4 113 7 345 624 10 1246 11 952 13 63 346 15 4407 16 382
boldfaced (1) 9 259
boldly (8) 4 168 7 861 9 670 10 673 719 952 11 382 16 1883
boldly (2) 15 2291 4075
boldness (2) 1 216 12 790
bole (1) 12 1263
boleros (1) 11 495
boles (1) 15 3341
Bolivia (1) 16 474
Bollopedoom (1) 17 408
bolster (2) 17 2110 18 1199
bolster (1) 15 2076
Bolt (2) 8 514 16 425
bolt (3) 3 74 15 3140 17 1217
bolt (1) 15 3987
bolted (2) 18 995 1010
Bolting (1) 8 661
Bolton's (1) 8 371
bolts (1) 15 3974
bolus (1) 14 577
Bom (1) 6 421
bom (3) 8 624
bomb (1) 15 1197
bombarding (1) 11 529
Bombast (1) 7 315
Bomboost (1) 12 561
bona (3) 3 440 7 996 16 498
Bonafide (1) 15 1530
bonafide (1) 15 1902
Bonafides (1) 14 1440
Bonaparte (1) 12 187
bond (2) 14 768 954
bondage (5) 7 209 9 1016 12 1373 13 1159 17 1022
bondage (1) 7 865

bonded (1) 14 1064
bonds (1) 15 1813
bondslave (1) 15 2861
bondwoman (1) 7 1037
Bone (1) 4 351
bone (9) 5 422 6 172 8 129 663 11 249
   13 918 16 1075 1339 1520
bone (1) 1 598
bonedry (1) 14 492
boneless (1) 2 142
bones (19) 3 292 6 333 358 776 981 8 726
   9 722 1011 12 1396 13 1131 15 234 410
   4215 4896 16 276 1544 1633 1783 18 942
bones (4) 15 29 674 1341 2609
bonesetter (1) 1 419
bonfire (1) 12 1326
bonfires (1) 12 1829
bonham (1) 15 148
Boniface (1) 14 1533
Bonifacius (1) 12 1705
Bonjour (2) 3 440 15 4501
bonne (1) 3 234
bonnet (4) 6 518 551 8 602 18 1258
bonnet (1) 15 3839
bonnets (1) 7 935
bonny (1) 15 1739
bonnyclaber (1) 14 1438
bono (2) 12 708 15 1369
Bonsoir (1) 14 1536
bonum (1) 9 430
bonus (1) 17 1545
bonuses (1) 15 1691
bony (2) 6 387 8 295
bony (3) 15 2050 2598 3161
bonzes (1) 14 674
boo (1) 18 1121
boodle (1) 16 125
Boody (11) 10 233 258 260 266 268 273 283
   286 290 293 16 274
booed (1) 15 791
Boof (1) 13 1033
Boohoo (1) 7 574
Book (6) 12 1440 14 1340 15 2193
   17 754 755
Book (1) 17 442
book (76) 1 365 2 13 30 56 61 90 133
   4 198 213 324 329 360 382 5 38 155 471
   6 154 591 592 593 631 7 206 1038 8 110 333
   834 938 957 9 93 263 279 365 955 1002 1115
   1164 10 147 161 162 438 526 844 856 867 1060
   11 1058 12 836 1134 1530 1785 13 633
   14 443 1155 1456 15 953 1001 2365 2393 2423
   2424 2538 16 202 1421 1422 1472 1679
   17 694 733 1403 1405 1414 1465 1878 18 580
   968 1178
book (1) 9 115
book (1) 15 4958
bookcart (1) 10 836
bookcase (1) 17 1523
booked (2) 10 673 719
bookhunt (1) 17 2048
bookies (2) 2 308 14 537
bookies (1) 15 3962
booking (1) 16 1855
bookkeeper (1) 16 207
booklet (1) 9 96
bookloving (1) 12 726
bookmark (4) 10 190 17 1363 1371 1384
Books (1) 3 139

Books (1) 15 1578
books (16) 2 95 3 136 427 10 260 315 521
   591 597 873 12 254 1080 15 825 17 1361
   18 488 657 1443
booksatchel (1) 14 1047
bookseller (1) 15 4354
bookshelves (1) 17 1360
bookshop (1) 10 632
bookstore (1) 8 1070
booktalk (1) 9 1117
booky's (1) 10 500
Booloohoom (2) 15 146 3045
Boom (4) 16 1262 1265 1274 18 1264
Boom (1) 16 1260
boom (1) 15 4662
boomblebee (1) 14 1473
Boomed (1) 11 20
boomed (3) 1 237 7 88 10 943
boomhammer (1) 15 4125
booming (3) 11 528 12 528 18 680
boon (4) 14 21 15 232 16 280 746
boons (1) 16 1820
boose (7) 8 807 10 1169 12 238 1398
   13 965 14 1535 16 376
boosebox (1) 14 1463
Boosed (1) 12 800
boosed (2) 10 1167 15 4741
booseguzzling (1) 14 1581
booser (1) 5 391
booser's (1) 8 661
boosingshed (1) 7 892
Boot (1) 17 593
boot (12) 3 3 4 524 6 466 8 689
   10 635 12 367 837 13 1266 1287 16 371
   1006 1686
boot (2) 15 1717 1763
bootblack (1) 17 2141
Booted (1) 9 413
booted (1) 15 366
Booterstown (2) 12 579 16 909
booth (2) 14 1148 15 2189
booths (1) 17 1717
bootjack (1) 15 1431
bootlace (1) 15 202
bootlace (1) 15 2800
Bootlaces (1) 15 3045
bootlaces (1) 6 231
Bootle (1) 12 420
bootless (1) 3 354
bootmakers (1) 18 882
Boots (1) 6 361
Boots (1) 15 3732
boots (50) 1 516 687 2 122 3 10 17 147
   266 446 4 49 160 5 117 6 131 544 638
   7 63 985 8 937 9 946 947 10 58 215 859
   1168 11 89 94 1142 1143 1144 12 496 813
   1028 1718 13 771 1225 14 1499 15 926
   16 823 1316 17 111 590 1484 1583 1814
   18 223 227 230 267 672 793
boots (3) 15 816 3729 3841
bootsboy (1) 11 1142
bootsole (1) 5 370
bootssnout (1) 11 100
bootstraps (1) 16 1214
booty (1) 3 196
booty (1) 15 31
Bopeep (1) 15 1602
borax (1) 11 116

Bordeaux (1) 14 553
bordel (1) 15 3536
border (3) 12 440 17 1527 2096
bordered (1) 15 3317
Borderers (1) 15 1403
Bore (2) 5 468 11 863
bore (25) 1 602 4 215 223 6 521 579 610
   801 9 74 218 350 10 175 598 756 11 923
   1068 12 296 14 198 733 1206 15 3263
   16 661 924 1408 17 1776 18 230
borealis (1) 15 170
borealis (1) 15 1373
Bored (1) 11 863
bored (1) 18 699
boreens (1) 15 919
bores (1) 11 810
Born (5) 8 356 684 686 10 805 15 1777
born (71) 2 402 4 226 417 5 199 7 633
   8 25 384 480 482 685 1146 9 68 105 180 216
   217 379 854 870 1031 1135 10 589 11 1102
   12 287 1207 1356 1431 1646 1651 1656 1897
   13 99 784 14 60 108 855 945 988 1166 1242
   1558 15 820 1384 1984 3683 16 261 502 878
   1325 1518 17 429 457 461 534 536 537 539 868
   952 953 1795 1796 1846 1873 2277 18 489 501
   781 1187 1253 1268
borne (6) 2 140 14 266 822 846 17 1024
   1027
borne (1) 15 1510
Borneo (1) 13 1223
Boroimhe (1) 6 453
borough (2) 17 173 1499
Borris-in-Ossory (1) 7 620
borrow (2) 9 681 11 554
borrowed (2) 3 411 18 1285
borrowed (1) 2 253
borrowers (1) 9 744
borrows (1) 12 1169
Boru (1) 17 433
Boru (1) 17 419
Borus (1) 12 566
Bos (1) 14 628
Bosh (1) 9 228
bosh (1) 15 2522
bosky (1) 7 322
Bosom (1) 11 731
bosom (20) 8 381 877 11 348 748 1134
   12 638 13 858 14 242 430 754 765 1337
   15 1002 2356 3265 16 892 1056 1411 1430
   18 778
bosom (2) 7 247 253
bosom (1) 15 909
bosom's (1) 11 1106
bosoms (1) 12 1007
Boss (1) 12 196
boss (7) 4 133 7 412 732 14 629 1485
   16 609 1012
bossed (1) 17 499
Bosses (1) 6 596
bosses (1) 12 1346
bosthoon (1) 10 777
bot (1) 15 3077
Botanic (2) 5 35 6 770
botanical (3) 15 1033 17 1553 1568
botch (1) 14 1411
botched (1) 10 586
botchup (1) 18 264
Both (11) 6 577 760 7 444 9 935
   14 224 15 2942 17 20 21 22 25 1182

Both (2) 15 2513 4623
both (83) 1 447 2 171 4 176 6 33 270
272 840 7 765 9 878 10 203 591 825 926
11 110 129 678 731 843 970 12 581 649 964
13 15 145 240 467 469 602 14 105 174 503 666
668 695 698 992 1191 1236 1268 1311 15 1295
4461 16 16 20 90 152 308 594 760 775 1026
1039 1094 1158 1580 1673 1844 1886 17 2 8 41
58 273 463 686 731 741 748 965 966 971 1183 1186
1210 1228 1441 1517 2209 2308 18 248 1204
1244
both (8) 15 35 125 1208 1587 2303 4243 4532
4838
bother (4) 8 326 18 352 728 1513
botheration (1) 12 1195
Bothered (1) 11 453
bothered (5) 11 287 318 444 915 1003
bothered (1) 15 506
bothers (1) 15 2418
both's (1) 14 181
Bottle (2) 13 1249 15 509
bottle (24) 4 224 5 508 6 359 7 951
8 595 927 1155 10 300 11 317 318 447
12 1320 14 434 435 744 780 15 611 1233
1974 2896 16 927 17 305 18 453 461
bottle (1) 15 30
bottled (1) 14 1182
bottleful (1) 7 950
bottleneck (1) 15 40
bottlenosed (1) 12 1086
bottlers (1) 15 1433
Bottles (1) 16 393
bottles (8) 6 444 7 1049 13 1045 1141
15 3562 16 389 393 18 714
bottles (1) 15 1573
bottleshouldered (1) 15 3316
bottlewasher (1) 10 546
bottleworks (1) 6 55
bottom (27) 6 138 9 1121 12 495
14 526 15 384 3186 16 791 1268 18 27
53 56 77 110 234 568 663 747 844 845 951 959
1030 1133 1369 1402 1520 1531
botty (1) 18 1288
Boucicault (1) 8 601
Boudin (1) 16 1235
Boudin (1) 16 489
boudoir (1) 15 2258
bough (1) 18 1292
boughs (2) 15 3242 3302
Bought (3) 4 62 8 339 13 838
bought (26) 6 862 8 74 172 10 526 863
11 296 844 882 12 33 1371 13 507 642 799
14 633 15 2736 3183 17 232 707 2104
18 125 458 515 618 939 1214 1349
Boulangère (1) 15 4098
boulder (1) 12 151
boulders (4) 3 206 207 279 292
Boulevard (1) 15 1386
boulevards (1) 15 1066
boul'Mich' (1) 3 179
boumboum (1) 14 1454
bounce (1) 16 529
bouncing (2) 12 1173 14 823
Bound (1) 8 412
Bound (1) 9 96
bound (15) 2 208 7 1044 9 504 593 786
10 109 110 113 779 12 169 14 501 1455
15 1642 16 294 763
boundary (2) 17 170 2015

bounded (2) 3 336 459
bounden (1) 15 4849
bounder (1) 17 2145
bounding (3) 3 334 11 498 525
bounds (5) 4 469 12 669 16 827 1324
18 1027
bountiful (1) 12 1006
bounty (4) 14 21 176 879 961
bouquet (1) 5 262
bouquet (1) 15 4103
Bournemouth (1) 16 521
Bous (1) 14 1115
Bous (1) 9 939
boustrophedonic (1) 17 1800
Bout (1) 14 1570
bout (2) 12 963 972
Bouverist (2) 17 427 440
Bouverist's (2) 17 437 438
Bovril (1) 14 1547
Bovum (1) 14 629
Bow (2) 15 2861 16 438
bow (15) 2 157 4 292 5 23 120 8 396
11 394 12 1599 13 88 157 14 89 720 802
16 844 1443 17 1216
bow (2) 15 451 2023
bowed (12) 3 137 5 343 357 6 655
7 196 682 10 62 11 562 659 12 1006
1613 13 745
bowed (3) 7 863
bowed (1) 15 2854
Bowel (1) 15 930
bowels (3) 4 460 508 14 97
bowels (2) 15 4127 4532
bowend (1) 11 575
Bower (1) 18 898
bowers (1) 15 1269
Bowery (1) 7 733
bowieknife (1) 15 3195
bowing (6) 2 426 4 495 9 602 1203
10 1248 16 340
bowing (2) 15 3858 4062
bowknot (2) 15 4022 4967
bowknots (1) 7 446
bowknotted (1) 15 4018
bowl (13) 1 2 4 18 38 108 249 5 25 458
10 285 292 11 223 14 513 17 1525
bowl (1) 15 2481
bowlegged (1) 16 852
bowlinggreen (1) 6 1011
Bowls (1) 10 739
bowls (2) 6 701 14 1373
bows (3) 1 418 11 1017 16 920
bows (4) 15 1262 2312 3062 4040
Bowsing (1) 14 1508
bowsy (1) 1 117
Box (2) 17 1805 1813
box (16) 4 400 5 53 6 327 815 10 48
11 576 616 1050 13 628 15 1019 2779
16 947 17 1321 1785 18 116 1111
box (1) 15 3597
boxed (1) 16 496
boxes (1) 12 1718
boxes (1) 15 1553
boxing (2) 10 832 18 1421
boxingmatch (1) 8 801
Boy (1) 12 193
Boy (2) 6 145 11 991
Boy (2) 15 4531 4546
boy (72) 2 61 5 5 245 247 252 273 6 505

523 567 575 576 584 620 634 772 840 908 957 958
7 64 408 8 364 601 612 648 1144 9 142 255
258 1020 1032 11 268 290 612 715 850 853 1043
1092 1098 1141 1144 12 279 644 985 1494 1905
13 130 577 902 1175 1263 14 823 1528
15 3131 3319 3671 3676 3908 3946 3950 4407
16 1535 1562 17 868 18 84 85 770 1015
1311 1461
boy (2) 1 260 17 815
boy (1) 15 4957
boyaboy (3) 14 5
boyconnell (1) 14 39
Boycott (1) 12 182
boycott (1) 18 387
Boyd (1) 10 967
Boyd's (2) 11 125 16 507
Boyes (1) 16 1239
boyhood (1) 14 1188
boyish (2) 13 305 18 1354
Boyl (1) 8 130
Boylan (53) 4 312 529 6 196 8 787
10 300 304 307 318 321 324 327 334 394 486 984
1241 1243 11 234 236 289 345 349 364 375 385
417 419 426 430 524 526 765 766 952 953 977
12 1000 1001 1222 16 199 234 17 2141
18 78 170 246 736 846 895 949 1008 1254 1262
Boylan (2) 15 3728 3738
BOYLAN (7) 15 3745 3749 3756 3762 3772 3782
3787
Boylan's (8) 4 282 408 11 337 382 388 399
761
Boylan's (1) 15 3741
BOYLAN'S (1) 15 3808
Boyle (7) 8 302 9 1115 10 919 1102 1106
1261 12 86
Boyle (1) 15 2308
Boylo (1) 11 1124
Boyne (2) 8 665 9 203
boyo (1) 12 1401
boy's (8) 2 6 24 30 179 3 241 6 614
10 3 15 2081
boy's (2) 15 4499 4544
Boys (4) 4 138 13 41 15 2191 4832
Boys (1) 17 1370
Boys (1) 15 1404
Boys (1) 15 1450
boys (28) 2 378 3 66 5 545 7 253
10 20 42 49 78 11 1064 12 1402 1764
13 14 41 754 14 519 1446 1459 15 623 785
1615 3081 3090 3246 3971 4460 4832 18 87
boys (2) 3 257 7 427
boys (3) 15 1447 1602 3325
boys' (3) 2 313 10 187 16 157
boysof (1) 3 261
boyson's (1) 9 881
boywomen (1) 9 254
brace (3) 14 487 1369 17 1541
braced (2) 4 538 17 1444
Bracegirdle (1) 13 857
bracegirdle (1) 13 1279
bracelet (3) 4 423 10 861 18 262
BRACELETS (1) 15 4085
bracelets (1) 2 37
bracelets (3) 15 1815 3063 4083
braceletted (1) 15 3079
braces (2) 4 497 8 1139
braces (1) 15 2037
bracing (2) 16 510 549
brack (1) 13 501

bronze (4) 15 1280 1327 2006 4958
bronzed (1) 15 1757
Bronzedouce (1) 11 398
bronzefoil (1) 6 946
bronzegold (1) 11 175
bronzelid (1) 11 1213
bronzelidded (1) 9 222
Bronzelydia (1) 11 48
bronze's (1) 11 266
Broo (1) 16 437
brooch (3) 12 664 17 1795 18 378
brooch (1) 15 285
Brood (1) 9 492
brood (2) 1 657 14 569
brood (3) 1 239 264 3 445
brood (2) 15 3840 3843
brooddam (1) 9 622
brooded (1) 3 446
brooder's (1) 9 242
brooding (3) 1 236 266 9 346
broodmare (1) 8 345
broods (1) 15 2262
brook (1) 12 290
brooms (1) 12 10
broomsticks (1) 15 4679
Brophy (2) 15 3466 16 133
Bros (2) 6 54 18 831
Broth (1) 8 601
broth (1) 8 885
broth (1) 15 3991
brothel (1) 15 4281
brothel (1) 15 2923
brothels (1) 17 668
Brother (7) 5 450 10 4 12 1707 1708
  15 1600 2217 17 136
BROTHER (2) 15 1837 1926
brother (48) 1 370 682 3 62 66 237 314 349
  450 5 100 306 6 471 568 8 2 502 509 511
  963 9 3 668 913 956 959 962 975 977 987 998
  10 78 169 170 758 1045 1049 12 785 1688
  13 39 134 197 665 1127 14 499 1032
  15 766 1514 1769 16 97
brother-in-law (6) 6 524 634 909 914
  7 691 10 985
brother-in-law (1) 16 1256
brotherhood (1) 15 1692
brotherly (1) 13 345
brother's (2) 8 243 509
Brothers (1) 9 67
Brothers (1) 17 1352
brothers (14) 7 210 9 677 894 957 960 963
  11 1064 12 281 286 499 1688 14 956
  15 411 16 162
Brothers-in-law (1) 11 789
brothers-in-love (1) 9 1046
brougham (1) 15 1027
broughams (1) 7 1048
brought (79) 1 141 451 2 208 390 392 394
  3 196 354 4 293 5 507 6 989 7 161 208
  492 536 8 622 9 221 559 732 748 880 1065
  10 150 770 1127 1201 11 30 217 847 864 922
  1157 1167 12 206 280 356 510 646 817 913 980
  1157 1336 13 181 182 1012 1158 1247
  14 153 606 926 1056 1135 1310 15 945 1356
  1359 1360 16 645 1183 1304 1560 1607
  17 352 18 140 443 493 658 749 778 869 968
  979 1125 1239 1262 1452 1478
brought (1) 7 864
brought (2) 15 904 4860

broughtedst (1) 14 368
brow (17) 1 101 186 594 693 5 22 27
  6 192 7 469 10 262 12 211 375
  13 102 519 735 14 1090 17 322 18 275
brow (7) 15 74 472 477 1775 2420 4088 4436
browbeating (1) 5 438
Brown (4) 4 176 488 8 620 16 538
Brown (1) 13 947
brown (47) 1 104 267 742 3 156 376 482
  4 235 286 387 5 117 6 422 451 906 8 902
  10 143 145 1271 11 116 940 1250 1257
  12 96 236 1498 1684 13 32 116 293 1062 1135
  14 480 15 2227 16 276 714 809 1189
  17 312 1298 1366 1374 1379 1385 1391
  18 276 296 470 1522
brown (7) 15 270 1207 1255 1558 1854 2290
  2306
Browne (2) 6 609 12 1383
browned (1) 18 431
brownsocked (1) 15 2036
brows (6) 1 369 2 296 9 374 10 807
  13 108 109
brows (1) 15 2023
Brrfoo (1) 8 192
Bruce's (1) 3 313
brud (1) 9 896
brücken (1) 16 1884
Bruin (1) 15 2417
bruise (1) 12 284
bruiser (2) 10 1134 12 983
bruited (1) 16 75
Brummagem (1) 16 1002
brunette (1) 16 879
Brunetto (1) 9 375
Brunny (3) 10 44 46 52
Brunswick (5) 5 183 6 34 11 883
  12 293 1890
brush (10) 1 38 44 310 6 95 12 7
  13 950 16 1876 17 278 1565
brush (1) 15 3952
brushed (4) 10 885 1116 12 673 16 1
brushes (1) 17 507
brushes (3) 15 196 1617 4937
brushing (5) 8 1028 13 962 15 3743
  16 19 1772
brushtray (1) 17 2106
brushup (2) 4 489 16 656
brusquely (1) 15 4110
Brusselette (1) 15 3183
Brutal (1) 5 273
brutal (2) 10 727 12 1190
brute (10) 6 127 12 485 13 745
  15 409 660 16 1787 18 144 594 635 997
BRUTES (1) 15 2018
brutes (8) 5 219 8 723 13 1148 14 993
  16 1797 18 244 631 1405
brutes (1) 15 2017
brutish (1) 15 4569
Brutus (1) 5 105
B's (1) 16 1652
bub (1) 4 532
bub (1) 15 1343
Bubble (1) 8 724
bubbled (1) 11 373
bubbles (2) 14 148 18 1143
bubbling (1) 10 261
Bubbly (2) 15 2434
bubblyjocular (1) 15 2449
bubs (4) 4 305 13 1282 15 3141
  18 901

bucaneering (1) 15 1369
buccal (1) 17 1809
Buccinator (1) 11 512
Buck (101) 1 1 17 40 50 64 71 85 92 111 115
  121 127 138 147 179 184 191 197 201 219 221 229
  281 287 293 296 313 318 323 330 338 342 346 355
  360 373 377 408 416 427 431 435 446 451 461 471
  485 494 499 502 523 531 534 539 543 546 554 559
  564 569 579 678 687 692 697 703 717 721 722 726
  733 3 112 9 485 507 515 545 568 573 605 645
  655 716 726 731 792 794 1053 1086 1100 1119 1155
  1170 1204 1209 10 1043 1055 1065 1071 1080
  1087 1224
Buck (1) 15 4166
BUCK (2) 15 4169 4177
buck (10) 1 42 706 3 254 337 5 214
  9 165 14 712 1537 15 2200 3184
buckbasket (1) 9 760
bucked (1) 16 2
bucket (13) 4 114 5 5 6 589 615 616 937
  8 482 13 296 15 586 3131 4179 4460 4752
bucket (8) 15 863 929 930 931 933 4456 4464
  4560
bucketdredger (1) 16 237
buckets (3) 8 725 13 19 606
buckets (1) 15 3990
bucking (1) 15 709
bucking (1) 15 3976
Buckingham (1) 8 461
buckle (1) 13 167
Buckled (1) 14 1474
buckled (2) 2 96 13 515
buckler (1) 3 42
BUCKLES (1) 15 2008
buckles (1) 13 424
buckles (2) 15 1280 2006
Buckley's (1) 4 45
Buckleys (1) 18 944
BUCKMULLIGAN (1) 9 906
bucko (2) 12 1001 14 892
buck's (2) 3 446 15 1050
Buckshot (1) 16 1583
buckshot (1) 12 1716
buckteeth (1) 15 388
bucolic (1) 14 928
bud (3) 5 570 14 808 16 1184
Budapest (2) 17 535 1908
Buddh (1) 9 284
Buddha (2) 5 328 12 197
buddhi (1) 9 69
budding (2) 14 1054 16 1869
budge (2) 6 950 11 1194
budgers (1) 18 162
Budget (1) 7 734
budget (2) 17 1455 18 579
budging (1) 16 28
Budgy (1) 14 1330
buds (1) 14 479
Buena (1) 13 1204
Buenas (2) 13 1208 15 216
buff (1) 6 180
buff (2) 15 536 3760
Buffalo (1) 16 404
buffalo (1) 14 1138
buffalos (1) 14 145
buffer (1) 8 1049
buffeted (2) 9 405 10 1117
bug (1) 14 1516
Bugabu (1) 6 441

bushel (1) 14 675
Bushmills (1) 18 696
bushranger (1) 9 1182
bushranger's (1) 15 1873
bushy (1) 7 331
busily (3) 14 279 16 269 681
business (41) 4 112 401 5 384 504 6 66
  217 316 7 144 208 8 131 601 10 371
  11 487 944 1013 12 452 967 1477 13 241
  14 662 1459 1587 15 325 2541 3765
  16 117 386 530 638 780 955 1285 1484 1826
  17 491 1914 18 49 297 1129 1344 1538
businessman (1) 1 669
businessmen (1) 6 625
businum (1) 15 2242
busk (2) 8 197 15 2976
buskined (1) 15 2810
buskins (1) 12 172
Buss (1) 3 378
bust (6) 6 191 11 361 387 15 3087 3258
  18 885
buster (1) 14 1440
bustle (1) 15 284
bustpads (1) 15 3250
Busy (1) 8 1185
busy (4) 12 971 16 1652 1786 18 1140
BUT (1) 7 272
But (251) 1 41 92 97 333 353 544 2 51 141
  238 262 278 395 406 3 4 167 318 449 4 80
  265 428 5 453 467 499 6 65 106 203 206 285
  335 432 536 550 630 643 783 878 988 7 55 71
  126 152 279 499 558 588 722 745 973 977 978 1010
  1012 1051 8 64 86 147 686 733 868 967 972 985
  1049 1142 9 160 181 208 237 240 254 362 467
  476 648 653 658 666 685 788 812 827 874 884 919
  963 978 1006 1077 1178 10 48 71 140 150 191
  489 545 552 569 682 825 949 1147 11 13 41 128
  133 220 329 347 363 545 627 697 776 835 875 888
  908 970 1003 1005 1071 1109 1121 1228 12 25
  134 290 391 651 702 789 1329 1360 1369 1372 1376
  1384 1419 1481 1665 1783 1850 13 33 40 45 78
  115 140 207 245 253 259 267 278 296 533 652 659
  687 706 748 775 783 864 877 890 950 1004 1088
  1189 1196 1225 1272 14 136 175 195 225 229
  264 301 341 377 418 420 429 432 483 547 593 622
  748 770 774 797 853 902 905 1010 1060 1131 1134
  1139 1149 1160 1328 1383 15 333 523 669 1369
  1397 2318 2375 2397 2409 2418 2642 2674 2736
  2740 3162 3171 4297 4382 4436 4471 4473 4535
  4576 16 11 24 179 241 248 284 506 530 766 815
  997 1098 1127 1164 1460 1492 1786 1790 1791
  1843
But (7) 1 384 591 2 305 7 862 9 138
  10 1251 11 694
but (420) 1 122 237 407 420 569 2 34 243 263
  368 394 3 98 140 4 59 506 511 5 170 333
  391 399 6 177 178 224 270 447 672 818 956 958
  7 214 338 463 489 572 730 806 809 819 8 463
  755 863 972 1086 1149 9 7 88 106 109 127 356
  360 369 384 388 408 473 498 529 556 692 804 868
  898 1046 1050 1073 10 12 81 501 544 692 750
  978 1058 1171 1208 1245 11 136 361 378 416
  433 658 717 815 1235 12 2 45 66 264 291 339
  346 349 617 631 645 726 735 772 841 970 978 1039
  1048 1139 1144 1171 1237 1339 1501 1602 1755
  1842 1899 13 5 10 17 22 57 84 99 114 124 126
  148 159 160 166 204 210 240 247 308 328 349 354
  357 358 361 362 367 376 382 394 401 414 419 427
  461 476 493 494 547 557 575 582 587 592 614 618
  649 678 680 760 769 866 1016 1095 1168 1179 1180
  1207 1230 14 18 47 56 63 115 116 121 142 213
  214 217 245 250 278 283 291 292 295 302 308 337
  356 358 365 401 417 426 437 448 458 459 480 492
  495 496 502 508 515 518 526 531 541 557 567 574
  589 610 624 634 736 744 748 757 772 790 805 864
  870 891 917 936 939 997 1054 1055 1071 1149 1151
  1210 1219 1242 1259 1336 1346 1347 1354 1364
  1372 1375 1400 1437 1438 1497 1508 1558
  15 106 199 593 873 1290 1323 2323 2402 2518
  2531 2982 3136 3450 3513 3606 3617 4070 4401
  4435 4741 16 4 12 29 31 32 70 80 96 108 117
  167 181 182 184 216 222 252 371 432 444 502 505
  551 615 708 737 757 770 803 812 894 897 937 972
  1015 1079 1081 1096 1099 1173 1185 1194 1238
  1247 1263 1288 1309 1445 1471 1557 1569 1615
  1639 1737 1761 1787 1883 1885 17 76 291 293
  371 383 465 565 642 655 1124 1276 1287 1504 1621
  1672 1916 1945 2160 2161 2196 18 12 17 19 32
  41 64 66 108 157 167 194 215 216 258 268 299 331
  338 355 361 410 422 439 447 514 527 528 529 619
  652 694 696 746 764 780 800 803 810 868 870 936
  951 954 983 996 1021 1046 1066 1161 1299 1316
  1366 1390 1407 1449 1534
but (11) 2 238 239 7 295 313 849 10 446
  12 515 14 649 17 419 1398
but (8) 15 148 292 668 901 906 2033 3942 4459
butcher (7) 7 211 212 8 880 9 1050
  10 826 18 842 1374
butchered (1) 14 546
butcher's (5) 2 312 9 131 14 1417
  15 3908 4628
Butchers (1) 6 608
butchers (2) 18 317 944
Butchers' (1) 8 725
Butler's (1) 8 27
Butt (7) 7 642 707 12 1102 16 9
  17 145 326 2057
Butt (1) 15 4684
butt (6) 4 22 8 376 12 1469 13 941
  16 582 17 1783
butt (1) 15 2556
buttend (2) 12 1336 15 2516
Butter (2) 8 438 13 65
butter (24) 1 334 4 11 45 51 238 274 278 298
  8 1 40 151 234 9 64 10 88 1055 1087
  12 115 1753 13 1294 15 2276 16 991
  17 250 18 249 273
butter (2) 15 1572 4179
buttercooler (1) 1 337
buttercups (1) 1 211
Buttered (1) 11 940
buttered (6) 1 447 4 389 12 988
  16 282 18 931 1244
buttered (1) 15 4168
butterflies (1) 14 790
butterfly (1) 13 157
buteries (1) 8 35
buttering (1) 8 152
Butterly (1) 1 527
Butterly (1) 15 1611
buttermilk (3) 5 497 12 356 15 1235
buttery (1) 17 1547
butting (3) 10 588 12 1322 15 2429
butting (1) 15 2631
buttocks (1) 9 88
buttocks (1) 15 4706
buttocksmothered (1) 15 2939
Button (1) 15 3440

button (8) 4 22 8 100 9 364 10 941
  13 115 872 15 2341 18 1029
buttoned (7) 3 477 4 538 7 228 9 821
  13 244 15 2542 18 672
buttoned (1) 15 284
buttonhole (1) 10 1156
buttonhole (2) 15 451 4037
buttonholes (1) 15 414
buttonhooking (1) 15 2815
Buttoning (1) 10 1141
buttoning (1) 5 457
buttonless (1) 6 101
Buttons (1) 18 816
buttons (12) 2 297 3 189 5 452 8 165
  613 13 1199 16 36 37 17 867 1431 1444
  1778
buttons (3) 15 4040 4936 4966
butts (1) 12 114
butty (1) 10 1169
buttytailed (1) 15 3368
buxom (1) 11 502
Buxton (1) 10 19
Buy (4) 9 948 11 230 13 1124 15 3131
buy (29) 2 230 3 499 4 146 523 6 394
  7 702 939 8 488 625 876 955 1061 1119
  9 95 514 10 869 11 1265 13 1124
  14 654 15 550 2934 3763 16 191 737
  18 252 404 405 469 1523
buybull (1) 15 2242
buying (3) 10 523 12 1651 18 407
buys (2) 2 359 16 738
Buzz (4) 5 450 9 207 15 2427
Buzz (2) 15 1837 1926
buzz (3) 11 796 13 1037 15 2418
buzzard (1) 15 3946
buzzed (2) 8 896 918
buzzing (1) 11 316
By (81) 1 359 2 70 329 3 5 45 59 490
  4 385 518 5 1 5 149 200 385 6 448 563 773
  866 7 533 751 853 895 8 802 968 9 257
  10 352 572 573 1240 11 49 151 156 185 219
  491 524 606 660 884 952 1078 1130 1134 1146 1207
  12 1424 1811 1812 13 1173 14 441 604 613
  1141 1410 1547 15 762 967 1226 1768 2538
  2679 3024 3032 3065 4371 16 1777 17 91 694
  727 729 733 768 1215 1229 1232 1954 1955 2210
  2274 2284 2294
By (1) 15 931
by (1117) 1 70 107 110 136 156 169 188 242 244
  245 269 367 386 389 401 428 434 461 476 490 555
  576 627 688 2 7 48 70 151 208 227 296 311 316
  336 341 343 344 354 370 375 427 3 17 68 92 149
  167 178 181 186 206 215 250 260 279 283 345 356
  391 411 422 463 4 50 89 141 146 151 164 183
  224 256 301 333 475 485 502 5 155 214 322 339
  341 344 353 445 458 487 521 568 6 37 41 64 79
  176 228 283 316 322 364 371 386 429 437 440 443
  445 449 450 467 488 500 504 515 593 631 653 672
  732 831 833 840 874 917 919 928 978 987 1014
  7 23 45 53 90 162 343 345 356 395 485 508 568
  597 701 716 720 776 793 821 949 960 969 8 59
  61 142 145 149 155 334 385 386 396 426 500 519
  540 561 572 586 588 654 741 806 807 861 901 946
  963 964 1065 1111 1140 9 4 12 39 134 155 159
  169 174 175 208 255 329 330 384 390 471 477 478
  479 494 521 524 635 685 744 850 870 929 930 933
  944 989 994 1009 1036 1040 1051 1125 1190 1214
  10 7 13 16 86 93 147 149 150 153 178 185 210
  265 305 314 372 388 507 532 569 592 593 601 643

C

Caesar's (1) 2 86
Café (1) 4 423
cafés (1) 16 1710
Caffrey (25) 13 12 14 16 24 26 29 30 31 35 243 249 251 253 306 352 354 382 481 492 678 682 711 715 754 767
Caffrey (8) 15 131 132 237 3995 4374 4415 4654
CAFFREY (12) 15 43 54 68 4001 4380 4389 4404 4592 4631 4650 4740 4777
Caffrey's (2) 15 41 4647
caftan (1) 15 249
cage (1) 14 415
caged (1) 16 1794
cagework (1) 3 304
Cahill (1) 1 361
Cahill (1) 1 361
Cahill's (1) 10 1202
Cain (1) 8 241
Cairns (2) 10 628 15 584
Cairns (1) 16 914
Cake (1) 17 1472
cake (7) 5 512 7 339 8 60 9 738 1138 18 199 453
cake (1) 15 335
Cakes (1) 15 1594
cakes (9) 4 423 6 500 501 8 75 10 1056 1058 17 1463 18 1554
cakes (1) 15 684
cakeshops (1) 8 416
cakewalk (1) 15 425
cakey (1) 3 153
calamitous (1) 17 2181
Calandrino (1) 9 836
Calcata (1) 17 1207
calced (1) 12 1684
Calculate (1) 17 589
calculated (5) 12 471 910 14 1184 16 1632 17 2261
calculating (1) 17 681
calculation (1) 17 1928
calculations (2) 17 462 1070
caldron (2) 3 219 15 1759
Caledonian (2) 12 1835 14 989
calefaction (1) 17 2038
calendar (3) 12 43 17 464 2275
Calf (1) 14 1455
calf (5) 4 525 12 1446 13 929 14 1299 17 1819
calf (1) 15 3360
calf's (2) 1 170 3 348
calfs (1) 18 945
Caliban (1) 1 143 9 756 15 1760
calibre (2) 14 1250 16 1220
Caliph (1) 15 3113
caliph's (1) 15 4324
calisthenics (1) 15 4042
Call (12) 3 90 278 386 7 1055 1056 11 640 871 13 910 1048 1213 15 859
CALL (1) 15 10
call (94) 1 24 542 607 3 223 413 4 26 98 363 5 31 108 509 7 176 339 974 1051 1057 8 119 538 752 1120 1130 1147 1159 1192 9 553 1049 10 28 158 462 1058 1067 11 12 313 314 316 634 855 869 1233 1245 12 337 685 777 1654 1667 1769 13 54 219 688 959 972 1020 1157 1227 14 1104 1113 1114 1119 1341 1344 1348 15 267 779 974 1681 1772 2206 3861 4295 4759 4926 16 4 293 298 503 854 891 1138 1170

1616 1871 1892 18 145 241 384 452 792 875 1256 1270 1370 1566
call (3) 6 355 10 573 17 824
call (3) 15 9 598 3950
Callan (9) 6 158 11 857 896 13 960 14 800 830 1395 15 1007 17 1847
Callan (1) 15 2611
callbox (1) 15 3031
callboy (1) 9 748
Callboy's (1) 6 861
Calle (2) 18 763 1465
calle (1) 15 216
called (87) 1 6 227 515 520 741 742 2 118 181 187 3 231 287 4 221 267 375 377 5 244 338 360 6 943 7 15 964 8 112 281 327 405 717 9 130 626 768 966 1088 10 70 11 324 449 715 1008 1132 12 35 37 571 1000 1339 1441 1887 13 51 203 306 352 474 646 678 686 746 869 872 945 1176 1263 14 444 604 619 973 1286 1331 15 540 1753 1301 16 9 130 146 360 648 852 961 1082 1161 1258 1416 18 43 162 336 616 817 840 992 1154 1584
called (1) 7 859
calligraphed (1) 17 1402
calligraphy (1) 17 683
Callinan (5) 7 691 10 555 568 572 17 2137
Callinan (1) 15 4341
CALLINAN (1) 15 1655
Calling (1) 15 666
calling (17) 1 282 629 2 183 3 376 4 146 7 106 157 8 120 655 9 169 12 804 1799 1914 13 1202 16 113 18 1025 1034
Callipyge (1) 15 1705
Callous (1) 11 834
callous (1) 9 97
callow (1) 15 3249
Callowhill (1) 17 168
Calls (1) 15 670
calls (25) 1 77 211 685 2 154 3 385 395 4 95 6 57 768 9 20 28 251 788 789 790 12 703 1332 1339 14 890 1344 1550 18 536 963 1255
calls (16) 15 67 928 1176 2943 3156 3169 3472 3538 3757 4524 4709 4714 4890 4891 4928 4962
calm (11) 1 27 224 4 512 6 460 13 1163 14 431 1357 16 708 17 190 1167 18 961
Calmer (3) 11 793 14 436 470
Calmer's (1) 14 429
calming (1) 14 425
calmly (5) 1 647 4 304 7 380 10 195 11 1105
calmly (1) 10 617
calmly (3) 15 2292 2586 2729
calms (1) 15 2737
Calomel (1) 13 1194
caloric (2) 14 1469 17 249
calorification (1) 17 265
Calpensis (1) 12 1710
Calpe's (1) 12 1003
Calpornus (1) 17 33
CALUMET (1) 7 464
Calvary (1) 15 4240
Calvary (1) 1 587
calve (1) 3 113
calves (4) 8 724 12 104 834 15 1052
Calypso (1) 18 837

Camaldolesi (1) 12 1680
Cambrensis (1) 12 1251
Cambrian (1) 12 1835
Camden (5) 9 1192 10 545 16 199 418 17 1975
Came (4) 7 456 13 1002 14 409 15 3418
came (190) 1 1 9 67 195 281 344 389 489 2 52 121 123 186 320 375 3 29 336 346 4 240 539 5 24 110 213 417 6 288 321 517 589 590 616 632 635 679 722 902 7 232 387 397 415 469 505 670 697 786 912 8 562 702 806 809 933 989 1167 1176 9 5 90 326 485 515 546 636 987 10 2 17 88 147 158 196 199 210 433 534 548 596 633 654 902 904 968 1033 1241 11 89 228 233 287 313 440 845 978 994 1031 1234 1252 12 2 127 209 244 393 967 971 975 1114 1121 1178 1248 1373 1393 1598 1689 1712 1727 1910 1914 13 48 54 139 177 281 350 457 462 505 531 550 641 886 1203 1299 14 108 110 125 128 320 490 529 548 589 15 523 574 584 1971 2194 3308 4858 16 128 131 192 721 862 950 1235 1237 1342 1365 1366 1373 1445 1471 1521 1557 1641 17 67 735 1275 18 34 47 77 171 373 423 493 499 566 608 667 697 780 824 872 924 956 975 1051 1054 1110 1319 1428 1446
came (3) 9 637 16 1252 17 813
camel (3) 14 1138 15 1526 16 1792
camel (2) 15 314 320
cameo (3) 16 1225 17 1794 1795
cameo (1) 15 285
camera (2) 10 420 16 1459
Cameron (2) 10 538 18 545
Cameron (2) 15 1403 4341
Camerons (2) 17 1987 18 556
camiknickers (1) 15 2404
camisole (1) 17 2095
cammin (1) 9 831
camp (2) 9 134 18 1414
camp (1) 15 4695
campaign (1) 17 1839
Campbell (7) 3 112 6 941 15 2190 16 661 908 1019 1355
camphire (1) 15 3232
camphorated (1) 17 1539
Camping (1) 6 448
camping (1) 14 1024
Camus (1) 12 1383
CAN (2) 7 614 1071
Can (23) 1 370 2 137 161 253 254 4 155 198 7 151 8 116 813 921 9 1102 10 314 429 11 257 1123 15 1007 1640 2292 2928 3132 16 618 1385
Can (1) 7 582
can (176) 1 43 74 340 552 565 647 2 51 94 234 289 322 339 361 410 417 3 8 26 282 4 29 48 5 112 220 262 471 514 531 537 6 218 656 7 35 154 155 156 160 617 623 627 798 824 952 976 981 988 991 8 93 563 662 760 852 884 955 1115 9 59 67 103 186 277 298 397 582 738 865 1085 10 51 390 421 479 679 826 950 1074 1082 11 783 969 976 1238 1245 12 464 921 1096 1237 1442 1547 13 173 443 590 756 968 1155 1193 1275 14 21 28 52 547 568 767 777 831 868 1063 1119 1229 1281 1287 1296 15 325 477 1082 1192 1350 1804 1966 1972 2198 2333 2350 2511 2805 3140 3205 3788 4235 4428 4782 16 246 730 758 786 815 891 1120 1139 18 52 96 170 237 277 282 297 369 386 420 492 520 566

567 583 855 873 894 960 988 1020 1025 1026 1165 1199 1276 1359 1361 1363 1388 1394 1399 1456 1476 1492 1522 1544 1548 1552

can (3) 1 261 456 9 733

Canaan's (1) 14 1436

Canada (5) 7 383 12 1084 1088 17 680 18 719

Canadian (2) 17 1644 1864

Canal (2) 10 1273 17 983

canal (8) 6 120 438 445 15 2141 17 567 18 108 391 555

canals (2) 17 177 222

canary (3) 3 254 9 644 10 58

canary (1) 15 4037

canarybird (2) 13 462 1299

cancan (1) 15 3886

cancelling (1) 17 1705

Cancer (1) 15 4187

cancrenous (1) 14 1289

Candahar (1) 14 1332

candescence (1) 17 107

candescent (1) 2 76

Candia (1) 15 2485

candid (2) 15 3043 16 781

Candidate (3) 14 964 998 1001

candidate (1) 16 72

candidly (2) 16 866 1110

Candle (2) 9 221 17 1023

candle (19) 1 333 12 1785 13 720 737 1166 16 846 17 107 111 112 114 117 120 124 589 590 1271 2070 18 139 1001

candle (1) 15 40

candleflame (1) 17 1326

candlelight (1) 9 417

candles (6) 5 432 6 582 12 1719 13 447 554 15 3889

candles (2) 15 1939 4689

candlestick (5) 17 1033 1312 1323 1328 1333

candlestick (1) 15 286

candlesticks (1) 11 1263

candour (4) 14 915 16 716 17 1427 18 744

cane (9) 8 1075 1082 1099 1105 1112 10 1116 11 1234 12 1344 17 1296

cane (2) 15 4038 4966

Canebrake (1) 12 1270

canebrake (1) 15 3421

canes (1) 12 99

Canice (2) 3 259 12 1706

Caniculus (1) 12 1696

canine (2) 12 201 734

caning (1) 12 1339

Canis (1) 17 1046

canister (1) 17 309

cannibal (1) 16 1211

Cannibals (1) 8 745

cannibals (1) 5 352

Canning (1) 12 235

Cannon (2) 8 831 16 1279

cannon (1) 12 1509

cannonballs (2) 10 13 12 575

cannonmouth (1) 12 672

cannonshot (1) 15 1565

cannot (10) 1 740 9 467 738 12 867 14 829 891 1226 1228 1229 1396

cannot (2) 1 586 598

cannot (1) 15 924

Canon (8) 13 448 491 496 552 572 621 674 1292

Canon (1) 15 1128

canon (2) 12 937 14 250

canons (1) 14 242

canopy (1) 12 1727

Can't (18) 3 325 5 186 6 844 989 8 140 421 562 563 610 10 701 11 714 860 13 1076 1247 15 644 2955 4724 16 784

can't (41) 1 54 74 120 121 122 192 348 4 40 130 448 5 559 6 206 400 8 139 893 1123 1149 10 730 11 688 901 973 12 21 680 764 1237 1628 1665 13 793 813 837 1004 1139 14 512 15 1998 2109 3783 16 480 816 1171 1646

can't (3) 7 582 12 428 17 817

cant (20) 18 85 102 104 239 355 466 487 507 595 628 937 1016 1019 1050 1084 1269 1392 1398 1529 1530

Cantalice (1) 12 1691

cantankerous (1) 18 1474

canteen (3) 2 309 14 1458 15 620

Cantekissem (1) 14 816

canter (3) 11 374 14 1139 16 1564

canters (1) 12 1506

canting (1) 14 1420

Cantrell (3) 5 193 389 11 214

Cantwell's (1) 11 185

Canv (2) 14 1231 1300

canvas (3) 6 869 8 310 9 923

Canvasclimbers (1) 9 156

CANVASSER (1) 7 120

Canvasser (3) 14 952 1004 15 1944

canvasser (1) 15 3496

Canvasser's (1) 15 1581

canvassers (1) 15 1428

Canvassing (1) 6 124

canvassing (3) 4 111 6 706 8 940

canyon (1) 14 1553

Caoc (1) 16 426

Caolte (1) 12 1129

Caoutchouc (1) 15 3905

Cap (1) 8 577

CAP (4) 15 2096 2102 2108 2113

cap (19) 5 67 7 42 984 8 838 10 9 201 239 255 1140 1220 1264 1267 11 1083 1249 13 142 590 14 758 17 1582 18 836

cap (15) 15 31 1026 1168 1259 1356 2049 2085 2095 3550 3739 3981 4167 4329 4410 4613

capable (4) 16 758 17 1087 1195 18 1230

capacious (2) 14 1195 17 1571

capaciousness (1) 12 160

capacity (3) 17 164 196 1616

capall (1) 15 1772

caparisoned (1) 15 1445

capbell (1) 15 4178

Cape (2) 12 1455 14 781

cape (3) 1 181 7 30 16 902

cape (2) 15 4019 4048

capecoat (1) 7 29

Capel (7) 4 360 10 368 12 314 1720 13 794 16 1422 17 1376

caper (2) 15 1887 1888

capered (1) 1 600

capering (2) 6 354 7 444

capers (1) 10 810

capers (1) 15 2157

capful (1) 14 1119

capiat (1) 14 1534

Capillary (1) 15 3354

capital (15) 5 71 10 381 1280 12 450 630 15 338 16 1853 17 679 1654 1661 1750 1792 1793 1794

capitalist (1) 9 711

capitalistic (1) 15 1394

capitals (1) 12 1733

capitis (1) 12 478

capo (1) 11 1245

capon's (1) 9 636

capon's (1) 15 3828

capotes (1) 14 776

Capped (1) 5 179

capped (2) 9 726 17 2098

Cappoquin (1) 18 779

capriciously (1) 12 1287

Capricorn (1) 17 195

capricorned (1) 14 1093

caps (11) 2 156 311 6 37 709 910 9 1169 10 77 13 14 571 15 2579 18 839

caps (1) 15 61

capsicum (1) 14 696

capsize (1) 16 650

capsized (1) 6 416

Capt (1) 16 1243

Captain (8) 5 560 12 182 192 15 1063 16 462 678 968

captain (9) 11 1082 16 966 1356 18 623 644 690 823 857 1583

captain (1) 16 1391

captain's (2) 4 215 16 1236

captions (2) 16 1236 17 1393

captivity (2) 4 225 226

capture (2) 8 555 10 1073

captured (2) 15 2664 16 1243

captures (1) 15 2011

capuchins (1) 12 1685

Car (2) 11 354 912

car (36) 5 460 6 409 7 640 667 8 347 10 120 128 135 229 504 556 558 775 972 992 1189 11 302 341 878 12 1588 1770 1799 1856 1906 15 1065 3319 4801 4832 4858 4864 16 309 1066 1879 1892 18 366

car (2) 16 1886 1894

car (9) 15 3738 3757 4317 4319 4860 4902 4905 4909 4916

carabineros (1) 18 756

Caramba (1) 14 1470

caramel (1) 8 149

carapace (1) 15 1257

Caraway (1) 14 1493

Carbine (1) 15 4752

carbon (2) 17 132 1549

carboned (1) 15 2746

carbonised (1) 17 1685

carbonised (1) 15 1956

carbuncly (1) 13 310

carcasefed (1) 15 1205

carcases (1) 14 1248

carcass (4) 3 286 348 6 773 18 1426

Card (3) 11 876 1128 15 3965

card (35) 1 684 4 243 251 253 259 261 5 25 54 60 65 319 419 6 57 8 257 261 264 9 586 589 606 10 250 436 542 12 439 660 1567 13 573 15 2525 3965 16 488 568 602 17 1780 18 717 842 1317

card (2) 15 726 729

Cardinal (1) 15 2653

CARDINAL (1) 15 2663

cardinal (2) 10 14 17 740

cardinal (3) 15 1421 2654 2656
cardinal's (2) 6 534 15 2651
cardrive (1) 17 2052
cardrivers (1) 14 1248
cards (8) 5 155 12 1024 14 658 16 1659 1853 17 504 18 1314 1429
cardsharping (1) 10 784
Care (1) 13 1105
Care (1) 15 1578
care (40) 1 46 99 231 5 216 6 3 801 804 993 1022 8 922 9 363 814 855 10 116 201 440 684 11 449 13 171 222 770 853 14 46 410 15 3016 3288 3601 4891 16 1790 17 700 728 1911 18 53 243 251 411 1096 1412 1434
care (2) 1 383 11 552
care (1) 15 164
cared (6) 13 267 433 14 464 15 566 16 1024 1839
career (4) 13 255 15 3043 16 1862 17 1609
careering (1) 18 785
careers (4) 16 1055 17 16 548 787
careful (8) 4 494 5 231 480 6 484 13 851 15 2361 17 389 18 120
Carefully (1) 16 1421
carefully (10) 2 210 3 501 4 251 541 6 586 12 718 1440 13 237 15 468 17 121
carefully (1) 15 904
Careless (3) 5 50 102 7 987
careless (1) 18 601
carelessly (2) 10 119 16 1506
carelessly (1) 15 1010
carelessness (1) 18 1015
cares (2) 10 140 16 662
Caress (1) 15 3680
caress (2) 2 46 14 678
caressed (3) 6 260 8 905 18 796
caresses (1) 13 725
Caressing (1) 13 902
caressing (2) 15 1343 2620
caretaker (7) 6 713 720 728 797 799 842 873
caretaker (1) 15 1236
caretaker's (1) 6 739
careworn (2) 10 236 13 374
Carey (5) 5 379 380 381 8 442 16 1054
carfuls (1) 10 340
cargo (1) 13 1164
caricature (2) 7 450 13 509
caring (2) 14 871 16 1212
carking (1) 16 662
Carl (1) 16 202
Carlisle (5) 1 698 8 337 10 747 16 418 17 1976
Carlo (2) 12 186 17 1696
Carlow (2) 8 802 15 1264
carman (1) 15 4424
Carmel (3) 8 148 12 1682 15 3435
Carmelite (1) 12 1247
Carmen (3) 9 1023 12 1250 15 2745
carmine (1) 17 1536
Carnal (1) 14 454
carnal (4) 6 246 17 1205 2278 2283
carnally (1) 15 948
carnation (1) 10 328
carneficem (1) 15 1488
carnem (1) 16 1093
carnival (1) 15 1690

carnivores (1) 15 710
carnose (1) 17 1998
caro (3) 3 396 10 359 14 294
carob (1) 10 434
Caroline (2) 17 1338 1347
Carpathians (1) 15 2416
carpenter (2) 17 1406 18 176
carpentry (1) 17 1601
carper's (1) 9 242
carpet (8) 3 369 4 89 150 10 1043 15 3183 3931 17 1526 18 21
carpet (1) 15 480
carpets (1) 18 1155
carping (1) 9 215
carping (1) 15 2258
Carr (3) 12 230 15 620
Carr (5) 15 48 60 3995 4462 4741
CARR (20) 15 66 615 619 626 4001 4373 4393 4409 4446 4466 4492 4565 4572 4596 4625 4643 4719 4745 4785 4795
carra (3) 11 38 50 1118
carracarracarra (1) 11 987
Carrantuohill (1) 12 1446
Carré (1) 15 4060
Carriage (1) 6 1015
carriage (33) 6 2 25 38 45 91 115 140 227 258 292 332 366 383 399 407 427 458 483 496 500 10 65 1178 1235 11 72 13 258 292 15 1029 3771 17 1502 1508 18 362 364 371
carriagepane (1) 15 650
carriages (7) 6 498 10 1185 1205 1238 1262 17 55 494
carriagesack (1) 17 1564
carriagewhip (1) 4 347
carriagewhip (1) 15 705
carriagewindow (1) 6 11
Carrick-on-Shannon (1) 16 1642
Carrickmines (1) 12 111
Carried (1) 15 1388
carried (19) 1 311 331 2 176 4 298 300 5 222 6 633 910 7 891 9 246 11 478 12 1280 14 992 15 3185 16 1387 17 161 708 1068 2308
carried (1) 16 1254
carries (2) 13 922 14 1160
carries (3) 15 816 2480 3575
Carrigaloe (1) 16 415
Carrion (1) 15 4591
carrion (1) 6 444
Carroll's (1) 11 88
carrot (1) 18 870
carrot (1) 15 4706
carrots (2) 8 927 18 1500
carrots (1) 15 3991
carrotty (1) 9 758
Carr's (2) 15 4472 4651
carry (17) 2 229 3 179 4 131 5 297 7 644 13 839 14 704 1493 15 1898 2688 2689 2691 3088 16 200 875 18 306 988
carrying (10) 8 364 10 471 535 1207 12 365 13 449 921 1045 14 54 15 3803
carrying (1) 15 1439
carryings (1) 15 869
cars (1) 7 1047
cars (1) 1 241
cart (9) 4 216 6 512 633 10 316 521 863 12 1222 13 865 15 3131
carted (1) 8 479
Carthusians (1) 12 1679

carting (1) 12 1395
cartload (1) 6 515
Cartoons (1) 18 1592
carts (1) 18 1592
Caruso-Garibaldi (1) 12 919
carve (1) 16 1394
carver (1) 8 471
carvings (1) 9 802
cascade (1) 15 3297
Cascades (1) 8 621
cascara (1) 4 510
case (81) 1 615 618 4 291 429 5 171 438 6 269 470 540 998 7 366 383 467 475 748 749 777 9 1071 10 627 630 965 12 1084 1094 1110 1429 13 310 14 53 61 65 204 207 253 308 958 969 972 987 1052 1177 1258 1262 15 742 761 2403 2444 4847 16 78 226 435 645 836 913 1069 1118 1185 1202 1308 1343 1379 1380 1385 1407 1469 1532 1672 1892 17 244 1826 2039 2078 2296 18 83 156 201 437 530 539 1444 1499 1549
case (1) 12 419
casemates (1) 18 791
Casement (1) 12 1545
caseroom (1) 7 196
cases (12) 7 163 8 1157 14 975 990 15 950 2440 3373 16 1308 1552 1608 1837 1891
Casey (1) 16 428
Cash (1) 17 1458
cash (7) 6 887 15 642 1985 3601 16 185 17 1692 1860
Cashed (1) 8 733
cashed (1) 5 304
Cashel (9) 8 302 9 1115 10 445 919 1102 1106 1261 11 1124 12 1460
Cashel (1) 15 2308
cashier (1) 7 113
cashregister (1) 11 382
casinos (1) 17 1717
casket (2) 12 1823 14 1135
caskhoop (1) 5 7
casque (1) 9 296
Casqued (1) 15 4611
Cassandra (1) 2 329
Cassidy's (1) 4 224
Cassidy's (1) 15 3045
Cassiopeia (4) 3 410 9 930 17 1123 2020
cassock (2) 11 1082 12 611
cassock (1) 15 4696
cast (15) 7 591 8 526 9 400 12 1040 13 297 444 449 595 1251 14 241 916 1511 15 978 16 397 17 868
cast (1) 7 246
cast (3) 15 1902 3227 3469
castagnettes (1) 11 1153
castanet (1) 15 2609
castanets (1) 18 1596
caste (2) 5 104 16 525
Casteele (1) 15 1731
castigation (1) 14 984
Castile (10) 11 8 14 54 329 331 1109 1271 12 185 14 1510 15 740
Castile (1) 7 591
casting (4) 7 892 12 1723 15 1391 16 1410
casting (1) 15 1747
castingbox (1) 7 184
Castle (4) 8 362 14 1336 15 750 16 1192

cent (6) 4 _135_ 6 _62_ 8 _337 384_ 17 _648_	chafed (1) 10 _295_	chances (2) 15 _869_ 18 _733_
Centaur (1) 15 _1064_	chaffering (1) 14 _1412_	chancre (1) 15 _1304_
Centigrade (1) 17 _1247_	chafing (2) 3 _455_ 14 _949_	chandelier (1) 17 _1534_
CENTRAL (1) 7 _1042_	chagrin (1) 16 _185_	*chandelier* (5) 15 _2041 2063 2281 3988 4244_
Central (1) 17 _1732_	chain (10) 2 _444_ 8 _279_ 10 _507 801 1277_	chandeliers (1) 13 _1090_

cent (6) 4 135 6 62 8 337 384 17 648
Centaur (1) 15 1064
Centigrade (1) 17 1247
CENTRAL (1) 7 1042
Central (1) 17 1732
central (3) 12 629 17 1423 1534
centralised (1) 17 1295
centre (6) 3 241 15 4433 16 482 17 1046 1428 1531
centre (2) 15 2479 4688
centred (1) 16 1549
centres (3) 12 473 14 1388 17 1914
centrifugal (2) 17 1214 1225
centripetal (2) 17 1214 1225
cents (1) 14 912
centuries (2) 9 214 18 666
centurion (1) 15 2600
centurionum (1) 14 709
Century (1) 17 1524
century (2) 14 743 15 3247
Ceppi's (1) 11 185
cerebral (2) 1 210 17 1768
cerebration (1) 17 382
cerecloth (1) 9 169
ceremonial (1) 14 943
ceremony (4) 12 1278 1819 14 946 17 1021
Ceres' (1) 15 2092
cert (2) 7 388 14 1514
Certain (1) 17 563
certain (44) 8 462 547 1171 9 1002 10 890 12 347 1500 13 42 340 769 14 16 156 423 439 449 680 963 1182 15 873 16 93 132 292 410 1035 1058 1194 1448 1579 1773 1869 17 37 389 492 646 694 695 743 912 1001 1776 1894 1969 2075 18 1008
certain (1) 8 68
Certainly (8) 8 1004 9 359 588 10 317 420 14 40 15 2218 2220
certainly (26) 4 513 5 425 492 9 588 596 10 28 11 824 13 390 14 10 1184 1276 15 2219 16 228 536 880 1057 1096 1254 1329 1476 1569 1717 1766 18 13 422
certificate (3) 17 1855 1864 1931
certified (2) 17 92 651
certify (1) 17 2077
certifying (1) 17 1403
certo (1) 3 132
cervical (1) 12 470
Cesar (1) 16 493
cespite (1) 10 346
cess (2) 10 269 17 1938
cessation (1) 17 463
cessile (1) 14 1409
cesspool (1) 15 3211
cesspools (1) 15 138
C'est (4) 3 162 169 9 579 15 2159
c'est (1) 3 183
C'était (1) 15 2585
c'était (1) 14 307
cette (3) 3 161 14 307 15 2583
Ceylon (2) 5 29 17 1980
Ceylon (1) 2 302
Ceylon (1) 15 3978
cf (4) 17 897 900 902 906
Cha (1) 12 1495
Chace (1) 12 422
chachachachacha (1) 5 428
Chacun (1) 15 661

chafed (1) 10 295
chaffering (1) 14 1412
chafing (2) 3 455 14 949
chagrin (1) 16 185
chain (10) 2 444 8 279 10 507 801 1277 14 858 1171 15 630 17 119 18 1166
chain (6) 15 15 1366 1379 1382 2051 4284
Chaîne (1) 15 4090
chained (2) 8 237 18 1391
chainies (1) 6 953
chaining (1) 18 1391
chainless (1) 17 1576
chain's (1) 10 313
chains (3) 15 2666 16 1777 1881
chains (1) 15 193
chair (19) 1 347 2 292 3 93 95 4 265 301 9 670 773 12 902 14 492 1209 15 1049 16 436 17 1296 1488 2109 18 663 1011 1372
chair (4) 15 1510 2083 2810 4095
chairman (3) 12 903 913 1874
chairman (1) 7 828
chairmen (1) 15 1831
chairs (9) 2 200 3 274 11 726 13 234 1088 16 1709 17 125 1288 1299
Chaldee (1) 14 156
chalice (4) 5 386 11 419 427
chalice (3) 15 1440 4692 4703
chalk (2) 14 636 16 1796
chalk (1) 15 649
chalked (1) 10 644
chalked (1) 15 3707
chalks (2) 8 334 13 407
chalkscrawled (1) 3 155
challenged (3) 9 656 14 412 15 277
challenges (3) 14 917 17 834 835
Chamber (1) 11 979
chamber (14) 6 986 10 408 1008 11 1022 12 1115 1347 13 190 14 796 15 3285 16 588 18 499 924 1136 1462
Chamberlain (3) 8 423 436 15 791
chamberlain (1) 15 1438
chamberpot (2) 4 330 16 1474
chambers (4) 9 279 11 966 14 36 18 1196
chambers (1) 9 354
Chameleon (1) 15 2342
chameleon (1) 14 1039
CHAMP (1) 7 1034
champagne (2) 15 3075 18 496
champagne (1) 15 452
champing (4) 3 56 5 214 8 843 12 109
champion (5) 9 766 12 881 918 14 628 16 1638
champion (1) 15 4146
champions (3) 12 964 1375 13 351
Chanah (1) 17 759
Chance (1) 13 1271
chance (19) 6 77 125 7 482 8 556 11 354 1256 12 1579 13 808 14 1348 15 1978 3625 16 85 584 714 17 2056 18 243 884 1192 1498
chanceable (1) 14 538
chanced (2) 14 497 16 224
chancel (1) 6 582
chancellor (2) 9 625 12 771
chancellor's (1) 10 627
chancery (1) 10 626

chances (2) 15 869 18 733
chancre (1) 15 1304
chandelier (1) 17 1534
chandelier (5) 15 2041 2063 2281 3988 4244
chandeliers (1) 13 1090
chandler's (1) 11 1013
Chang (1) 12 564
Change (4) 6 494 8 275 10 372 14 1572
change (46) 1 652 4 169 5 101 118 306 6 155 187 830 858 8 1072 9 148 205 10 1189 11 384 427 865 12 1606 13 641 879 921 1068 1099 14 510 1039 15 328 740 2397 16 545 625 1171 1172 1246 1247 1315 17 881 1867 1955 18 83 444 648 900 971 1341 1381
change (1) 15 4050
changeable (1) 14 1040
Changed (2) 5 268 15 3173
changed (21) 1 504 4 376 5 141 470 7 3 126 8 150 609 10 1194 11 693 12 1640 13 881 1115 1119 15 3153 16 366 1305 18 516 528 826 1483
changeling (1) 3 308
changeling (1) 15 4957
changes (6) 5 475 11 175 982 13 805 15 3406 17 500
Changez (1) 15 4103
Changing (3) 6 781 7 250 8 486
changing (3) 6 132 8 1048 16 1143
changing (1) 15 4026
Channel (1) 16 521
channel (4) 2 328 14 1288 16 1032 1154
channels (2) 17 1318 1698
chanson (1) 14 401
chant (6) 1 462 583 655 17 761 765 795
chant (1) 15 3227
chanted (2) 1 595 17 801
chanter (2) 11 1132 17 767
chanter's (1) 10 921
chanting (3) 5 406 9 1162 12 1721
chants (4) 15 73 1241 3640 3649
chanty (2) 14 648 16 972
Chap (6) 4 214 490 11 1035 1059 1266 13 876
chap (49) 1 28 154 3 399 4 212 292 5 37 544 6 159 690 825 889 7 292 341 987 8 101 176 471 674 691 712 808 1043 9 510 1080 10 438 1136 11 488 561 569 577 1228 1250 12 311 439 1323 1491 13 29 386 834 978 14 1566 15 3231 16 75 208 511 576 1385 18 964 976
chapbook (2) 2 42 14 627
chapbooks (1) 9 806
CHAPEL (1) 15 1531
chapel (8) 6 574 580 827 8 497 12 812 16 1768 18 139 709
Chapelizod (1) 7 732
chapels (1) 15 1425
chaperoned (1) 12 552
chapfallen (1) 6 1027
chaplain (1) 12 1520
chaplain (1) 15 1238
Chapped (1) 4 147
chapped (1) 10 846
chap's (4) 8 240 1114 13 875 16 1511
Chaps (1) 13 974
chaps (6) 5 434 6 980 13 1182 15 267 275 2680

chief (1) 15 1423
chiefly (6) 14 47 51 16 1206 1601 1731 17 1764
chiefly (1) 15 1401
chief's (1) 6 919
chieftain (2) 12 90 1262
chieftains (1) 12 91
Child (3) 7 852 10 589 12 1711
child (49) 5 233 6 53 325 820 7 969 8 383 480 9 211 406 421 422 837 876 1136 11 645 12 1232 1567 13 639 956 958 1109 1203 1219 14 169 171 554 831 892 1063 1065 1274 1542 15 1809 2579 3687 16 437 17 866 18 109 161 163 167 489 498 802 1168 1449
child (1) 10 139
child (4) 15 33 38 41 904
childbed (2) 3 396 14 113
childbirth (1) 6 624
childe (2) 14 160 161
Childermas (1) 14 103
childhood (6) 2 169 9 927 12 647 13 297 382 14 1275
childing (1) 14 177
Childish (1) 15 1349
childless (1) 14 122
childman (1) 17 2317
Children (2) 8 714 13 1250
CHILDREN (2) 15 17 21
children (44) 4 95 5 381 6 122 538 540 624 762 8 31 380 707 1072 1146 9 219 1135 10 727 12 547 551 1105 1508 1656 1682 1683 1687 13 19 30 895 977 1192 1233 14 849 1276 1328 15 1687 3273 16 480 17 580 720 2183 18 162 327 1130 1159 1241 1280
children (1) 7 858
children (3) 15 7 1822 3856
Children's (1) 13 956
children's (1) 1 269
children's (1) 15 15
Child's (1) 8 375
Child's (1) 17 1368
child's (5) 6 138 506 7 802 8 41 1097
Childs (6) 6 469 7 748 14 958 1017 1033 15 761
childs (2) 18 1258 1287
Chile (1) 16 489
chile (2) 14 1504 15 962
chill (2) 8 821 15 998
chillies (1) 14 696
chilling (1) 4 232
Chilly (1) 6 604
chilly (2) 13 10 15 2981
Chiltern (1) 8 515
chime (3) 13 625 17 1226 1529
chimed (2) 11 147 13 1286
chimera (1) 15 1392
CHIMES (1) 15 1363
chimes (1) 9 748
chimes (1) 15 1362
chimiques (1) 3 176
chimney (3) 14 1011 15 4313 17 151
chimneyflue (1) 17 258
chimneyflue (1) 15 2305
chimneypots (1) 15 1406
chimney's (1) 15 4285
chimneysweep (1) 12 7
chimneysweeps (1) 15 1429
chimpanzee (1) 15 1189

Chin (1) 9 1129
chin (10) 1 56 5 528 7 996 10 1068 1141 13 25 259 14 810 15 3485 18 897
chin (1) 15 2262
China (4) 8 621 16 459 903 18 1541
China (2) 6 983 17 1379
china (2) 1 108 11 90
Chinaman (1) 9 1129
Chinamen (1) 14 963
China's (1) 5 326
chinashop (1) 14 581
chinaware (1) 17 2104
chinchin (1) 12 600
chinchopper (3) 13 259
Chinee (1) 5 327
Chinese (7) 6 769 983 8 490 869 13 272 16 570 668
chink (2) 4 498 14 1501
chinked (1) 11 1269
chinks (1) 16 573
chinless (2) 9 1129 14 963
chinless (1) 9 1150
chinmole (1) 15 357
chintz (1) 13 233
Chip (1) 7 899
chip (3) 9 1005 10 312 16 867
chipped (3) 4 279 8 239 17 302
chippendale (1) 3 95
chipping (1) 12 681
Chips (4) 11 3 192 193 223
chips (5) 11 3 192 12 97 18 795
chirp (1) 10 565
chirp (1) 15 1268
chirping (1) 10 249
chirruped (1) 11 323
chirruping (1) 11 13
chiseller (1) 6 279
chits (2) 13 975 18 375
chitterling (1) 14 328
chivalrous (1) 12 287
chivalry (4) 7 566 12 289 659 13 336
chivvying (1) 15 3840
chivying (1) 9 161
Chloe (1) 14 1156
chlorate (1) 13 333
Chloroform (1) 5 481
chloroform (3) 5 481 17 626 18 1172
chlorotic (1) 14 1291
Chocolate (1) 17 1472
chocolate (1) 13 339
chocolate (4) 15 143 2700 2729 2736
chocs (1) 16 1565
chode (1) 14 326
choice (13) 5 18 28 11 1222 12 38 15 476 2351 2418 16 90 355 546 1019 1836 17 308
CHOIR (1) 15 4163
choir (9) 3 116 5 332 394 408 8 166 13 497 675 18 25 274
choir (2) 15 1953 4162
Choirboy (1) 11 612
choirstairs (1) 18 900
choke (2) 12 444 14 816
choked (6) 1 318 323 6 292 8 664 1031 10 500
choked (1) 15 1617
chokeechokee (1) 14 1518
chokers (1) 15 413

Choking (1) 12 784
choking (3) 11 167 14 563
choking (2) 15 2183 4186
chokingly (1) 13 734
chokit (1) 15 3828
choler (1) 14 862
Chon (1) 9 1129
chookchooks (1) 4 31
choose (2) 18 894 1389
chop (3) 8 660 12 445 18 910
chopine (1) 9 330
choppy (1) 16 651
chops (3) 13 1294 18 944
Chopsticks (1) 5 330
chord (5) 11 407 478 663 15 2500 17 9
Chords (1) 11 1005
chords (16) 1 246 250 11 20 407 452 529 663 737 767 791 831 840 999 1017 1030 1121
chords (1) 15 3502
Chortle (1) 15 1581
chortling (1) 15 425
Chorus (1) 17 1231
chorus (2) 8 623 11 1144
chorus (1) 1 277
chorus (1) 15 1954
Chorusgirl's (1) 11 1078
chose (6) 1 136 9 253 256 10 1046 11 391 16 1547
chosen (3) 2 45 9 256 14 1239
chosen (1) 7 865
choses (1) 14 792
Chow (3) 10 457 463 12 1495
Choza (1) 16 474
choza (1) 16 603
Chree (1) 15 2614
Chris (5) 7 691 10 555 568 572 15 1658
Chris (1) 15 4341
CHRIS (1) 15 1655
Chrished (1) 10 623
chrism (1) 14 131
Christ (26) 3 69 5 398 6 274 7 241 9 68 12 327 336 383 386 388 412 1808 14 281 1584 15 2195 2196 2205 2999 3006 4720 16 1084
Christ (1) 17 1394
Christ (1) 15 1493
Christ' (1) 12 1792
Christass (1) 15 4141
Christbaum (2) 15 1863 1864
christened (2) 11 206 14 1334
Christfox (1) 9 337
Christian (2) 10 78 17 1847
christian (14) 6 346 596 772 881 8 2 9 785 12 610 640 1688 14 322 15 1564 1754 16 162 17 96
Christianity (2) 8 666 17 1638
christianity (1) 17 32
christians (3) 8 49 9 783 10 1006
Christicle (1) 14 1579
christies (1) 15 410
Christina (1) 17 539
christine (1) 1 21
Christmas (6) 5 546 8 753 15 443 16 1836 17 422 18 62
christmas (1) 13 334
Christopher (2) 12 183 17 2137
Christ's (2) 1 659 14 83
Christum (1) 12 1750
Christus (1) 16 1092

clacked (4) 8 287 11 16 381 383
clacking (3) 1 148 2 95 10 830
clacks (1) 15 3893
clad (2) 6 39 12 1183
clad (2) 15 3234 3460
Claddagh (1) 18 866
Claffey (1) 8 153
claim (3) 10 946 12 1117 16 877
claimant (1) 16 1343
claimed (3) 13 351 614 17 1824
claims (1) 15 3276
Claire (2) 8 586 10 984
Clamart (1) 9 578
clambering (1) 3 115
clammy (3) 1 310 3 371 13 852
Clamn (1) 7 695
clamour (2) 2 122 4 136
clamour (1) 15 3963
clamoured (1) 13 355
clamped (1) 17 154
clamps (1) 6 440
Clan (1) 14 371
clan (1) 12 1008
Clanbrassil (4) 14 1047 16 78 17 142
  1869
clandestine (3) 15 3028 17 668 2251
clang (2) 15 4125 4663
clanged (2) 1 650 11 383
clanging (2) 7 10 8 477
Clank (2) 7 136
clank (1) 7 103
clanked (2) 5 313 7 101
clanking (3) 7 74 139 217
clans (1) 16 1595
Clap (2) 15 1593 2070
CLAP (4) 15 4438 4442 4514 4635
clap (5) 8 96 11 757 12 1100 14 435
  15 1593
Clapclap (2) 11 28 756
Clapclipclap (1) 11 757
Clapclopclap (1) 11 757
Clapham (2) 12 228 18 784
clapped (6) 6 1022 7 171 11 754 758
  16 831 18 1054
clapper (2) 10 691 11 973
clapping (6) 7 899 11 1160 12 1301
  13 383 14 775 887
clapping (2) 15 3900 3911
Clappyclap (1) 11 28
Clappyclapclap (1) 11 756
claps (3) 12 137 529 14 818
claps (3) 15 2630 3876 4005
Clara (1) 12 1685
Clare (4) 6 217 530 10 1114 17 622
Clarence (2) 7 629 11 189
Clarendon (1) 18 375
claret (7) 8 990 10 466 1219 11 119 422
  12 965 18 454
claret (1) 15 4035
claretwine (1) 14 1508
clarions (1) 15 1441
Clarke (1) 15 3355
clash (1) 15 4665
clashed (1) 16 776
clashing (1) 16 1862
clasp (2) 11 564 14 393
clasp (1) 15 4125
clasped (7) 3 47 6 209 226 9 878
  10 465 884 12 652

clasping (2) 1 166 6 556
clasping (2) 15 131 3550
claspknife (1) 16 578
clasps (4) 15 133 3215 3783 3815
class (8) 13 285 15 637 865 16 1731 1739
  17 54 18 362 367
classes (3) 16 82 1133 17 1618
classes (1) 16 1252
classic (3) 15 1468 3174 3267
classical (8) 2 329 11 280 14 1253
  16 1139 1716 1754 17 389 1611
classics (2) 7 605 14 705
classified (1) 14 976
classmates (2) 2 28 15 3309
classy (1) 18 1189
Clatter (1) 10 1031
clatter (1) 6 69
clattered (1) 17 283
clattering (4) 8 425 687 12 1857
  18 1544
clauber (1) 9 822
clause (1) 17 1667
clave (1) 12 1782
Claver (3) 5 323 380 10 144
claw (2) 10 1051 17 1527
claw (2) 15 2461 4764
clawed (1) 16 610
claws (4) 3 363 7 484 8 856 18 936
claws (2) 15 2436 4220
Clay (3) 6 906 10 1002 15 2932
Clay (2) 15 1174 1570
clay (10) 6 819 864 872 14 474 831 1321
  15 3967 16 1330 1508
clay (1) 15 1960 2481
Clean (5) 4 21 11 569 570 15 3100 3492
clean (35) 1 515 715 4 47 481 5 565
  6 106 237 911 981 7 32 8 818 1045 9 75
  639 12 983 13 450 638 797 847 1189
  14 342 478 1000 15 4461 17 1828 2123
  18 19 348 615 1124 1354 1356 1512 1553
clean (1) 15 335
Cleanchested (1) 3 77
cleaned (2) 4 455 10 32
cleaner (1) 17 281
cleaners (1) 18 471
cleaners (1) 15 1432
cleanest (1) 14 62
cleaning (3) 8 752 810 14 623
cleanlooking (1) 16 454
cleans (1) 4 481
cleanshaven (1) 18 873
cleansing (2) 16 936 17 215
Clear (4) 8 1100 12 1456 15 754 4025
clear (17) 3 239 275 4 265 7 375
  8 1099 9 714 11 397 781 855 13 907
  1207 16 1647 1703 1813 17 1344 18 688
  861
clear (1) 15 2047
cleared (4) 6 566 10 421 12 1432
  16 40
cleared (1) 15 4317
clearer (2) 8 702 16 1175
cleargrained (1) 17 1537
clearing (2) 1 83 13 546
clearing (1) 15 3328
Clearly (1) 5 112
clearly (1) 16 1647
clears (1) 15 1803
Cleary (1) 12 930

Cleave (1) 14 1414
cleaver (1) 15 4538
cleaves (1) 15 141
cleft (2) 1 135 7 860
cleft (2) 15 589 1327
clefts (1) 15 138
clemency (2) 15 1809 17 1617
clement (1) 2 45
clenched (1) 15 477
clenches (1) 15 3195
clenching (1) 7 627
Cleopatra (2) 9 883 12 188
Cleopatra (1) 9 252
clepen (1) 14 193
clergy (2) 12 925 927
clergyman (4) 10 418 426 17 1835
  18 353
clergyman's (2) 9 195 10 403
Clergymen's (1) 9 48
cleric (1) 17 540
clerics (1) 9 566
Clerk (1) 8 325
clerk (7) 9 184 10 1005 1015 12 1872
  14 895 15 3376 17 484
clerk (3) 15 896 1627 4356
Clerkenwell (1) 3 248
clerk's (1) 10 989
clerks (1) 14 347
Clery's (3) 5 194 13 159 234
CLEVER (1) 7 674
Clever (6) 5 330 484 7 675 13 922
  15 2535 2537
clever (7) 1 290 8 1117 9 308 312
  12 983 13 146 18 1175
Cleverest (1) 7 292
Cleverever (1) 15 2539
cleverly (1) 16 1286
Click (1) 3 420
click (1) 12 243
clicked (1) 10 375
clicking (1) 4 528
client (3) 15 942 968 976
client's (2) 15 946 951
cliff (4) 1 594 669 3 14 15 3375
cliff (1) 15 3378
Clifford (4) 11 897 17 1798 1842 2252
cliffs (3) 1 567 16 562 17 1974
Clifton (1) 17 1308
climate (3) 5 34 16 876 880
climates (1) 17 1518
climatic (1) 17 192
climax (1) 16 1365
climb (1) 18 977
climb (3) 7 295 314 9 1224
climb (1) 15 133
climbed (5) 3 283 6 332 15 3358
  17 84 1652
climbing (2) 18 1091 1233
climbing (1) 15 4668
climbs (3) 15 132 315 1842
clime (2) 12 1818 14 939
Clinch (1) 13 867
cling (1) 3 422
clinging (6) 1 680 3 423 10 202 441
  12 1775 13 338
Clings (1) 13 1022
clinker (1) 12 676
clinking (2) 11 782 1270
clip (4) 4 40 6 19 13 493 14 393

cochinchina (1) 18 1157
cochonneries (1) 9 641
Cochrane (3) 2 1 112 190
Cochrane's (3) 5 193 389 11 215
Cock (1) 3 453
Cock (1) 15 3980
cock (11) 9 257 11 38 50 987 1118 15 521 571 17 1265 18 1035 1352
cock (1) 2 102
cock (1) 15 2064
cockahoop (1) 12 1064
cockalorum (1) 13 1165
cockboat (1) 15 4142
Cockburn (2) 12 231 234
cockcanary (1) 9 644
Cockcarracarra (1) 11 1048
Cockcock (1) 11 988
cocked (7) 3 357 8 507 11 494 630 12 1334 16 1740 18 1171
cocked (4) 15 1252 1572 2630 2711
cockerel (1) 14 1392
cockhorse (2) 15 2944 3804
cockhorse (1) 15 2947
cocking (2) 11 141 14 560
cockle (1) 3 487
Cocklepickers (1) 3 342
cockles (5) 6 787 10 820 1276 13 313 1113
cockloft (1) 11 1198
Cockney (1) 1 299
cockney (1) 10 34
cock's (1) 7 663
cock's (1) 15 811
Cocks (1) 16 393
cocks (3) 11 964 13 830 15 3577
cockscomb (1) 15 3493
cockshout (1) 18 1544
cockspurred (1) 15 1058
cocktails (1) 15 2868
cocky (1) 15 3586
cockyolly (1) 15 3130
cocoa (8) 16 271 1621 1646 17 307 356 370 799 18 1330
Cocoanut (1) 13 957
cocoanut (1) 12 997
cocottes (1) 15 3885
cod (6) 5 552 12 1096 15 1871 3496 18 943
codding (2) 12 141 307
coddoubled (1) 15 4147
Code (1) 8 324
code (3) 7 756 15 969 17 772
codes (1) 17 2217
codfish (1) 8 21
codfish (1) 15 4334
codger (1) 4 111
codlings (1) 12 82
codology (1) 12 451
codpiece (1) 9 822
cod's (3) 12 214 410 841
cod's (1) 15 3845
cods' (1) 11 520
Coela (1) 15 2089
coelo (1) 13 574
coelum (2) 12 1741 14 1408
coexreligionist (1) 17 1899
Coffee (3) 13 961 16 792 17 1474
coffee (16) 3 219 7 654 8 510 11 486 16 331 355 360 602 785 807 1141 1170 1699 18 562 724 749

coffeehouses (1) 14 536
coffeeroom (1) 17 470
Coffey (2) 6 595 8 880
Coffey (1) 15 1238
COFFEY (1) 15 1240
coffey (1) 11 1036
Coffin (1) 6 509
coffin (26) 6 322 416 421 521 579 582 595 615 633 801 820 822 833 865 869 923 10 1163 1166 11 291 1035 12 1083 16 1304 1353 1728 17 1303
coffin (3) 15 3667 3674 4144
coffinband (1) 6 914
coffincart (1) 6 637
Coffined (1) 9 352
coffinlid (2) 10 208 210
coffins (1) 6 610
coffinships (1) 12 1372
cog (1) 15 202
cogent (1) 14 1278
Coghlan (2) 4 281 401
cogitated (1) 17 563
cogitation (1) 14 67
cogitations (1) 17 576
cognate (1) 17 858
cognisance (1) 14 330
cognisant (1) 16 1032
cohabitation (2) 14 1424 17 1959
cohabited (1) 16 1488
Cohen (5) 15 2967 3108 3208 17 2055 18 1213
Cohen (2) 15 2742 3479
Cohen's (3) 15 1287 4378 4882
Cohens (1) 18 1498
cohesion (1) 17 1062
coif (1) 15 3434
coifed (1) 14 1104
coiffeuse (1) 15 2320
coifs (1) 13 812
coign (1) 3 71
coigns (1) 9 1218
coil (1) 12 447
coil (1) 15 1346
coiled (3) 4 90 6 914 17 150
coiled (2) 15 1178 4557
coiling (1) 14 1107
coils (4) 8 1048 9 541 10 803 876
Coin (1) 16 371
coin (14) 1 457 459 2 85 4 168 10 223 238 253 11 371 382 13 576 15 3206 16 1619 17 987 1453
coin (2) 15 312 3540
Coincidence (5) 11 303 713 15 593 16 890 17 635
coincidence (7) 8 503 525 16 414 1222 1776 17 633 639
coincidences (2) 16 826 17 323
coined (2) 16 847 1379
coins (10) 2 201 449 4 182 10 700 708 11 384 14 286 17 301 1807 1928
coins (6) 15 1574 1813 3595 3604 3991 4010
coisde (1) 15 1771
coistrel (1) 9 455
coition (2) 15 2413 17 1809
coke (3) 16 102 212 942
col (1) 11 903
colander (1) 6 131
Cold (7) 4 231 5 390 6 1009 8 846 1006 1176 10 549

cold (52) 1 153 634 2 213 3 271 324 5 338 458 521 7 309 338 612 8 139 470 583 847 1124 10 459 805 907 11 34 13 578 852 876 1083 14 882 1106 1427 15 307 1030 1107 1805 2013 2197 2964 3492 4230 16 589 1014 1059 1316 17 233 238 245 1246 1539 18 264 304 555 906 916 950 1400
cold (4) 15 159 257 659 2263
coldcream (1) 11 939
coldly (2) 1 14 217
coldly (3) 15 1195 1677 3449
coldness (1) 10 1212
Coleman (4) 6 158 11 857 896 15 1007
Coleridge (1) 9 768
collapse (3) 8 36 17 17 37
collapses (1) 12 1479
collapses (2) 15 1555 4748
collapsible (1) 17 1435
collapsing (1) 6 257
Collar (1) 14 1489
collar (20) 1 479 513 3 302 4 489 5 101 528 529 6 511 576 7 395 821 8 191 10 1140 1145 1155 1268 15 2543 17 1431 1435 18 189
collar (3) 15 3844 4036 4696
Collard (1) 11 468
collars (1) 13 830
collateral (1) 17 1200
collation (3) 8 36 14 1291 17 354
colleagual (1) 17 2174
colleague (1) 9 90
colleagues (1) 12 588
collected (2) 17 647 2072
collected (1) 15 1815
collecting (2) 8 143 16 681
collection (4) 1 480 15 803 16 327 17 1840
collection (1) 15 1812
collective (2) 17 1646 1689
Collector (1) 12 24
collector (4) 1 394 9 609 12 1590 17 1938
Collector-general's (1) 15 4351
Colleen (1) 12 194
colleen (3) 12 690 14 1512
colleens (1) 15 919
College (11) 5 550 7 88 8 406 9 552 10 653 1105 1249 14 1324 17 145 1861 18 1257
college (15) 5 43 551 553 6 317 7 793 801 12 1459 13 134 135 14 494 590 15 4439 17 136 791 18 1332
Collide (1) 15 245
collide (1) 14 1365
colliding (1) 15 2042
collie (1) 8 48
Collins (3) 7 940 18 653 1153
Collis (9) 6 56 10 472 780 1191 11 390 521 1164 1227 12 268
Collis (1) 15 500
COLLISION (1) 7 414
collision (4) 15 639 16 916 17 1120 2182
collisions (1) 16 901
collops (1) 12 1614
Colman (1) 12 1700
colon (1) 12 622
colonel (3) 3 247 15 3082 16 996
colonel (1) 15 4356
colonial (1) 17 1643

corrected (1) 16 194
correction (2) 15 2883 17 715
correlative (1) 17 2220
correspond (1) 17 574
corresponded (1) 17 1493
correspondence (2) 9 319 17 2251
corresponding (1) 17 75
corridor (4) 2 118 181 205 9 592
Corrigan (3) 17 1240 2135 18 107
Corrigan (1) 16 1256
corroborated (1) 16 1021
corrosive (1) 17 684
corrugated (1) 17 322
corrupt (1) 9 149
corrupted (2) 7 843 844
corruptio (2) 16 759 760
corruption (3) 9 109 14 340 17 2185
corse (1) 14 295
corselet (1) 14 269
corsetlace (1) 15 2054
corsetlover (1) 15 3010
Corsets (1) 15 3257
corsets (2) 15 2976 18 446
CORTÈGE (1) 7 443
cortège (1) 10 1250
Co's (1) 17 306
cos (1) 14 1556
cose (1) 10 362
cosmetics (1) 15 2258
cosmic (1) 15 2196
cosmic (1) 15 1581
cosmos (1) 15 2197
cost (8) 8 98 10 937 13 1038 14 865
   15 3915 16 108 17 166 1740
costard (1) 9 243
costbag (2) 10 472 1191
costdrawer (2) 3 66 6 52
Costello (13) 14 192 193 229 313 324 401 416
   544 806 817 841 853 1208
Costello (2) 15 2151 2238
COSTELLO (1) 15 1795
coster (1) 15 3245
Costive (1) 4 510
costliest (1) 12 292
costliest (1) 10 609
costs (2) 3 80 6 890
costume (8) 11 1257 13 335 856
   15 2322 2870 16 714 17 1432 18 471
costume (4) 15 298 703 1058 2050
costumed (2) 15 3903 17 575
costumes (3) 12 1285 17 425 758
Cosy (2) 8 172 10 647
cosy (2) 13 11 239
Cot's (1) 14 1542
cotta (1) 12 621
Cottage (1) 17 1580
cottage (3) 3 70 10 1128 18 453
cottage (1) 13 313
cottagers' (1) 17 1598
cottages (1) 5 5
cotton (4) 5 352 8 1149 12 1514
   14 638
cottonball (2) 12 1349 16 1357
Cottonopolis (1) 12 1530
cottonwool (1) 13 153
Couch (1) 3 383
couch (4) 14 61 673 1151 15 3264
couchant (1) 2 429
couched (3) 4 306 12 200 14 927

Cough (2) 1 179 15 928
cough (6) 5 483 6 121 7 611 12 594
   13 616 18 353
cough (1) 15 2727
coughball (1) 2 443
coughed (1) 6 336
coughing (6) 2 444 10 634 11 167
   12 834 15 2190 3143
coughmixture (1) 14 1590
coughs (1) 10 632
coughs (7) 15 392 928 2057 2169 2313 2375
   2420
Could (19) 5 3 270 400 6 185 7 836
   8 111 196 610 768 1061 1111 11 696 979
   12 756 757 13 848 1122 15 490 17 1581
could (288) 1 91 157 407 411 551 2 160
   3 329 4 220 227 376 5 175 244 247 287 303
   401 6 83 188 401 445 623 807 808 809 816 962
   1029 7 152 172 230 844 999 1036 8 22 37 382
   420 573 831 836 1030 1037 1046 1119 9 227 470
   747 10 166 384 966 1030 1137 11 17 153 721
   1224 12 243 290 383 487 672 687 688 748 1230
   1305 1569 1768 13 30 81 90 107 191 219 220
   337 347 414 415 420 421 424 434 438 446 454 460
   478 483 495 513 515 524 537 540 545 556 558 575
   594 597 599 604 627 643 688 693 705 707 724 898
   951 1032 1046 1119 1249 14 49 149 230 268 430
   433 437 460 542 555 603 605 634 718 721 773 826
   870 892 965 1123 1124 1130 1142 1220 1292 1312
   15 797 951 952 978 1053 2351 2522 3037 3149
   3395 3586 3660 3680 3804 4951 16 14 68 105
   125 149 219 262 272 295 296 324 348 385 422 528
   529 658 743 755 823 877 907 932 995 1008 1037
   1143 1217 1220 1271 1447 1451 1454 1458 1460
   1493 1630 1679 1741 1788 1794 1821 1830 1833
   1834 1839 1852 1854 17 275 497 797 1050 1093
   1954 18 27 61 116 131 138 181 186 197 231 244
   267 269 293 300 319 394 404 412 419 430 433 443
   498 499 506 510 511 525 529 560 571 579 586 652
   659 699 735 739 743 754 788 795 799 807 829 859
   870 888 896 955 984 1002 1116 1127 1131 1141
   1163 1197 1346 1349 1415 1440 1460 1471 1478
   1482 1489 1525 1579 1580 1607
could (4) 6 814 11 402 17 419 824
Couldn't (10) 3 64 5 20 39 6 176
   8 162 666 673 9 1160 12 841 16 788
couldn't (41) 1 551 623 2 262 4 80
   5 127 6 765 967 8 180 458 546 978 9 94
   10 1171 1208 11 393 545 584 1235 1236
   12 66 436 856 13 77 230 321 477 731 861 944
   1271 15 2561 2579 3359 16 160 803 846 852
   1049 1110 1173 1892
couldnt (27) 18 73 76 110 116 164 179 194 212
   326 331 352 393 454 555 618 666 750 779 911 913
   929 970 995 1009 1030 1256 1379
council (5) 9 804 10 408 1008 14 948
   1199
Councillor (3) 10 970 971 17 601
Councillor (1) 15 4337
COUNCILLOR (2) 15 1387 3385
councillor (6) 7 105 122 145 149 975
   12 852
councillor (1) 15 1379
counsel (4) 12 1009 1187 14 207
   17 1427
counsel (1) 15 899
counselled (2) 14 908 16 1702
counsellors (1) 14 681
counsels (2) 17 241 248

Count (2) 12 561 16 1148
count (6) 13 1199 1249 14 1263 16 580
   18 506 779
count (1) 15 3548
Counted (1) 11 1225
counted (4) 3 447 12 984 14 339
   17 867
countenance (9) 9 310 12 246 1605 1619
   13 599 14 1206 16 397 17 339 438
countenance (1) 7 868
counter (20) 3 407 4 146 5 487 7 64
   8 336 822 993 9 1058 10 321 594 596
   11 90 109 328 12 1166 14 1225 1444
   16 357 457 1202
counteract (1) 17 1961
counteracting (1) 17 291
counterassaulted (1) 15 890
counterattraction (1) 16 930
counterbalance (1) 17 691
counterblast (1) 16 526
counterestimating (1) 17 345
counterflap (1) 7 69
counterjumper's (1) 6 70
counterledge (1) 11 178
counterproposals (1) 17 960
counterretort (1) 15 60
counters (2) 11 620 17 504
counters (1) 15 1577
Countess (1) 12 560
countess (2) 10 163 165
counties (1) 15 1546
counting (3) 4 445 6 824 12 214
counting (1) 15 26
countinghouse (2) 4 499 14 1417
countless (1) 14 1272
countries (2) 12 830 16 1039
countries (1) 15 1830
Country (2) 7 95 13 1072
country (47) 1 412 667 2 438 5 117
   6 134 940 943 7 87 9 710 927 1164
   10 723 949 11 1052 1061 1072 12 144 441
   500 540 1142 1582 1591 1628 1630 13 789
   14 142 360 15 795 1538 3387 4472 4473 4535
   16 736 988 1097 1171 1234 1397 1518
   17 1657 1989 18 710 931 1560
country (4) 7 830 831 10 735 11 1284
countrybound (1) 17 1575
Countrybred (1) 8 617
countryfolk (1) 9 708
countryfolk (1) 9 267
countryside (1) 14 617
countrystile (1) 14 980
counts (3) 15 2006 3606 3657
county (14) 4 127 6 216 8 802 12 16
   1090 1124 1855 16 1642 17 137 164 622 882
   1406 1606
coup (1) 16 1289
coup (1) 16 554
couped (1) 15 1051
couple (10) 14 1542 15 338 16 541
   17 81 1966 18 2 434 556 1526 1556
couple (2) 15 1601 2055
coupled (2) 16 1370 1486
coupled (1) 15 597
coupler's (1) 3 47
couples (3) 12 815 13 631 15 3037
couples (2) 15 2751 4151
coupon (1) 17 1384
coupons (1) 17 1808

crayfish (2) 15 2266 2273
crazy (5) 1 640 4 494 6 31 13 779
 18 1176
creak (2) 4 544 18 1208
creaked (5) 7 28 9 329 590 11 337 761
creaking (12) 6 1 25 26 131 508 7 177
 8 644 9 5 9 969 11 433 965
creaking (1) 15 2697
Creaky (1) 4 73
creaky (1) 4 49
Cream (2) 8 862 10 795
cream (21) 4 298 366 6 80 8 951 955 1180
 10 1087 1094 11 295 700 13 65 227 1025
 15 3805 16 179 17 311 364 799 1526
 18 292 1506
cream (1) 15 4035
creamery (1) 15 2276
creamfruit (2) 3 368 9 1208
creaminess (1) 13 225
creaming (1) 18 923
creamlaid (1) 17 1806
creams (2) 4 400 8 2
creamy (4) 8 778 10 1093 11 700
 15 3437
creased (2) 4 394 16 1465
creased (1) 15 816
creases (2) 3 447 17 1481
create (3) 9 43 14 865 18 1565
created (8) 9 1013 1029 10 149 150
 12 772 14 1002 16 567 17 1097
creating (1) 9 1130
Creation (2) 1 612 3 35
creation (6) 9 475 816 10 1075 12 1280
 16 1786 18 1198
creation's (1) 14 858
creations (1) 15 2980
Creator (5) 2 380 9 468 10 104
 14 403 15 1484
creator (2) 9 471 12 1354
creaturas (1) 12 1747
creature (15) 1 489 5 103 13 222
 14 302 732 764 854 981 1157 15 559
 16 729 731 17 370 1034
creatures (5) 10 140 14 228 766
 17 1134 2179
credence (1) 16 175
credentials (1) 16 1342
Credit (1) 17 1456
credit (5) 12 1825 13 1050 14 1475
 15 1538 16 246
credulously (1) 10 1195
cree (1) 7 50
creecries (1) 9 286
creed (2) 14 1451 17 403
creeds (1) 16 1133
creek (2) 1 678 715
creels (1) 12 82
creep (2) 9 143 14 1012
creep (1) 15 138
Creeper (1) 12 1272
creeper (1) 17 1507
creepers (1) 4 476
creeping (3) 3 273 9 145 15 2445
creeps (2) 6 1000 12 125
creeps (1) 15 2871
creepycrawl (1) 9 87
creepystools (1) 3 193
Cremation (1) 6 984
Crème (1) 8 878

crème (1) 8 878
Creole (1) 15 2189
crepitant (1) 15 2163
crept (3) 13 120 360 1177
crepuscular (1) 17 1134
crescendo (1) 16 998
crescent (2) 7 258 12 225
crescent (1) 15 1510
cresset (1) 15 137
Cressid (1) 9 884
Cressida (1) 9 401
crest (3) 9 925 12 1873 17 1610
crested (2) 3 297 7 345
crestfallen (1) 15 256
crests (1) 3 340
cretic (1) 7 369
cretonne (1) 17 2102
crevice (1) 17 121
crew (3) 12 1333 13 1164 15 3577
crew (1) 2 102
cri (1) 10 1216
criada (1) 18 1483
crib (2) 14 1383 18 497
Cribbed (1) 14 1486
cribbed (1) 15 824
crick (4) 3 19 7 1023 15 3209
Cricket (1) 5 558
cricket (2) 15 878 18 1089
cricket (2) 15 1434 4396
Crickey (2) 10 274 14 1540
cried (81) 1 28 44 66 296 346 452 708 733
 2 189 194 196 249 446 4 25 38 381 6 69 274
 282 390 7 256 329 336 353 359 442 507 619 649
 684 693 738 899 959 968 991 1019 8 998
 9 605 1053 10 269 273 444 451 690 11 11
 131 132 146 169 286 415 532 736 758 1074 1146
 1201 1215 12 510 1595 1600 1604 1611 1618
 1619 13 63 384 385 394 733 738 755 14 214
 309 418 775 812 816 1131 1134
CRIER (2) 15 860 1157
Cries (1) 4 90
Cries (1) 15 4664
cries (12) 1 602 2 116 428 10 187 646
 12 600 13 49 351 14 778 784 18 118
cries (9) 15 286 2461 2553 2602 3161 3936 3940
 3946 4652
crime (5) 8 1157 14 1022 1261 15 3043
 16 1055
crimes (3) 3 228 16 840 1000
Criminal (1) 14 1517
criminal (9) 9 850 14 1261 15 3681
 16 1056 1193 17 1600 2185 2189 18 992
criminality (1) 17 1002
criminals (1) 8 324
Crimmins (4) 10 721 725 731 749
crimps (1) 14 537
crimson (5) 5 343 357 17 1105 1365
 18 1598
crimson (4) 15 752 1442 1445 1520
crimsoned (1) 13 264
crimsoning (1) 13 454
cringing (1) 7 394
cringing (1) 15 1086
crinkled (2) 10 308 17 308
crinkly (1) 15 2970
crinoline (1) 15 283
cripples (1) 15 1614
crisp (5) 4 83 8 721 11 1024 12 1615
 15 2899

crispation (1) 15 3394
crispine (1) 15 285
crisscrossed (2) 11 795 15 2815
Crissie (2) 3 87 6 52
critical (1) 17 990
criticiser (1) 18 1088
Croagh (1) 12 1453
Croak (1) 11 1012
croak (1) 6 594
croak (1) 15 1241
croaker (1) 11 806
crock (1) 6 446
crockery (1) 17 312
Crocodile (1) 15 3218
crocodile (2) 11 1054 16 466
crocus (1) 11 1056
crocuses (1) 17 1556
Croesus (1) 15 3004
Crofter (2) 12 1589 1634
Crofton (6) 6 247 12 1589 1632 1670 1752
 1768
Crofton (1) 15 4350
CROFTON (1) 15 1678
crois (1) 3 169
Croisé (1) 15 4080
croit (1) 3 171
Croker (1) 12 196
cromlechs (1) 12 1448
Cromwell (3) 12 1507 1785 16 1122
crone (1) 1 404
crone (2) 15 29 32
crones (1) 14 527
cronies (2) 8 1152 9 694
Cronion (1) 14 1336
crook (1) 15 863
Crookback (1) 9 912
crookback (2) 9 985 14 855
crookbacked (1) 15 2151
Crooked (3) 10 586 11 891 13 952
crooked (10) 1 136 2 129 4 151 164
 6 597 10 331 11 244 13 485 15 3358
 18 836
crooked (2) 7 835 9 1224
crookeding (1) 18 957
crookedly (1) 15 386
crooking (1) 15 2281
crop (4) 4 197 8 215 16 1267 1789
crop (1) 15 1060
cropeared (1) 14 854
cropped (2) 16 505 1384
cropped (1) 15 62
Croppies (1) 2 276
cropping (2) 4 157 158
cropping (1) 15 986
Croppy (2) 6 145 11 991
CROPPY (2) 15 4531 4546
croppy (5) 11 1043 1074 1113 1140 1142
croppy (1) 15 4544
crops (1) 12 1370
Crosbie (1) 6 159
Cross (4) 7 6 11 853 17 1805 1813
Cross (1) 16 1738
cross (23) 4 129 5 330 6 746 7 134 1041
 8 567 1076 1077 1081 10 935 12 1029 1458
 13 260 1087 1206 14 584 15 174 700 2944
 16 920 17 1933 18 295 688
cross (4) 15 175 537 2660 4682
crossblind (6) 7 440 444 10 963 1197
 11 65 460

crossblind (1) 15 3730
crossbones (1) 12 664
crossbones (1) 15 501
Crossbuns (1) 8 36
crosscat (1) 13 677
crosscountry (1) 15 3951
crossed (22) 1 2 212 693 3 159 4 77 224 5 10 414 7 142 8 145 155 414 551 10 12 76 193 532 902 11 229 17 8 18 740 1075
crossed (4) 15 1520 1885 2678 3503
crosses (2) 1 12 6 929
crosses (1) 15 2031
crossexamination (1) 15 929
Crosseyed (1) 11 648
crossfire (1) 12 1293
Crossguns (1) 6 438
Crosshaven (2) 10 400 11 850
crossing (6) 7 132 8 368 582 10 1104 16 203 18 259
crossing (1) 15 2166
crosslacing (1) 15 2822
crosslaid (1) 17 127
Crosslegged (1) 9 280
crosslegged (1) 4 90
crosslegged (1) 15 2048
crosstempered (1) 16 1169
crosstree (1) 9 496
crosstrees (1) 3 504
crotchety (1) 11 471
Crotthers (5) 14 191 233 887 1204 1256
Crotthers (1) 15 2238
CROTTHERS (1) 15 1792
Crotty (1) 10 399
crouched (4) 3 355 10 859 14 421 17 855
crouched (1) 15 88
crouches (4) 15 29 584 2161 3729
Crouching (1) 1 400
crouching (2) 3 248 17 89
croup (1) 15 3120
croup (1) 15 3108
croups (1) 6 387
Crow (1) 15 4591
crow (1) 11 964
crowbar (2) 15 712 18 148
CROWD (2) 15 3964 4755
crowd (5) 6 63 7 783 16 552 1511 18 629
crowd (15) 15 63 137 141 173 1038 1191 1404 3960 4405 4423 4628 4722 4801 4817 4819
Crowded (1) 6 459
crowded (1) 18 182
crowded (1) 15 1555
Crowding (1) 2 96
crowds (4) 2 304 15 518 16 912
crowed (2) 7 367 13 383
CROWN (1) 7 14
Crown (7) 5 329 16 77 435 17 300 362 922 2019
crown (20) 4 69 283 6 233 472 7 86 8 688 1133 9 947 10 11 636 11 867 12 142 342 1224 1872 14 748 1540 16 243 17 1536 1622
crown (5) 15 896 1439 2252 3961 4034
crowned (3) 3 316 11 747 16 1201
crowned (1) 15 3823
crowning (2) 7 29 13 116
crowns (6) 2 220 221 4 83 12 1309 1714 15 2518

crowns (3) 15 1492 3546 3570
Crows (1) 15 3962
crows (1) 9 1156
crows (2) 15 2404 3827
CROZIER (1) 7 61
crozier (1) 3 53
Cruachan's (1) 12 85
crubeen (1) 7 951
crubeen (4) 15 158 256 668 672
crubeens (1) 15 311
Crucial (1) 15 933
crucial (1) 16 1535
crucifer (1) 12 1676
crucified (1) 3 156
Crucifix (1) 15 3465
crucifix (1) 8 19
crucify (2) 12 1327 1812
crude (1) 3 209
cruder (1) 14 1359
Cruel (4) 4 27 8 269 11 803 15 2939
cruel (7) 12 1061 13 659 15 559 562 1724 2904 2975
Cruelty (2) 4 349 12 1062
cruelty (2) 15 697 17 2183
Cruentus (1) 12 593
cruise (1) 13 1184
cruiskeen (1) 12 122
crumb (1) 8 78
crumbling (1) 6 994
Crumbs (2) 2 23 6 97
crumbs (3) 10 287 1128 17 2124
Crumlin (2) 13 1190 17 52
crumpled (6) 1 71 5 80 8 57 10 294 753 1096
crumpled (1) 15 738
crunching (1) 5 213
crunching (1) 15 674
crupper (1) 16 1877
crusader (1) 17 2021
cruse (1) 15 1487
cruses (1) 12 1715
Crush (1) 3 19
crush (5) 3 10 14 501 16 1515 18 1039 1040
crushed (7) 4 274 6 975 1018 7 901 8 396 12 39 18 778
crushed (1) 15 4285
crusher (1) 5 2
crushes (1) 15 3321
Crushing (1) 8 897
crushing (1) 13 440
Crusoe (2) 6 811 8 82
Crusoe (1) 6 813
Crusoe (1) 15 1848
crust (3) 1 446 14 749 18 990
crustcrumbs (2) 4 3 6 96
Crusted (1) 4 175
crusted (2) 3 374 8 1067
crusting (1) 4 232
Crusty (1) 8 1160
crutch (1) 15 130
crutch (1) 15 4141
crutched (1) 10 228
crutches (2) 10 8 12 1718
Crutchetts (1) 18 1469
crux (1) 16 1604
Cry (1) 12 1607
CRY (1) 15 4362
cry (34) 1 282 3 354 6 519 638 7 447

9 248 338 638 11 350 736 737 745 12 677 1103 1915 13 191 192 627 735 736 884 14 170 1025 1391 15 1392 4641 16 850 1174 18 176 673 1308 1535
cry (2) 2 355 9 1143
cry (5) 15 516 2272 2852 3469 4335
Crybabby (1) 15 3218
crying (9) 1 252 3 133 10 1165 11 168 12 840 13 1174 16 740 17 865 18 1449
crying (1) 15 3845
crypt (2) 6 971 973
cryptogram (1) 17 1800
crystal (7) 11 216 12 39 87 280 288 14 403 17 240
crystal (2) 15 1318 1548
crystalclear (1) 13 591
crystallised (1) 17 309
crytears (1) 14 1556
cubes (2) 2 156 17 1111
cubic (1) 17 164
Cubicle (1) 11 1015
cubicle (1) 17 932
cubicles (1) 11 1018
cubilibus (1) 14 1574
cubit (1) 10 561
cubs (1) 8 437
Cuchulin (1) 12 176
Cuck (2) 9 1025 15 3208
cuckold (4) 9 1021 1050 15 1117 1159
cuckolds (1) 15 1126
Cuckoo (5) 9 1025 15 1133 1134 1135
Cuckoo (9) 13 1289 1290 1291 1296 1297 1298 1304 1305 1306
cuckoos (1) 12 1572
Cuckoos' (1) 15 3175
cuckquean (1) 1 405
cuckstool (1) 4 500
cucumber (1) 8 759
cud (3) 8 675 1031 14 1041
cuddled (2) 10 587 13 29
cuddling (1) 4 178
cuddling (1) 15 1317
cudgel (1) 12 204
cudgels (1) 16 1397
cuff (1) 4 519
Cuffe (7) 6 392 12 837 13 914 14 571 15 1008 17 485 2139
Cuffe (1) 15 4338
cuffedge (1) 1 106
Cuffe's (2) 12 105 14 926
Cuffes (2) 18 510 1224
cuffs (3) 5 68 495 13 830
cuffs (1) 15 3846
Cui (1) 15 1369
cuin (1) 17 727
cuirasses (2) 15 1853 4665
cuisine (1) 8 335
cuius (1) 12 1746
cujuslibet (1) 14 708
cul (1) 9 34
Culdee (1) 12 195
culdees (1) 17 753
culinic (1) 15 1579
culled (1) 15 1032
Cullen (1) 17 632
Cullen's (1) 12 369
Culler (1) 5 560
culls (1) 12 105

culminating (2) 14 1260 16 513
Culo (1) 16 314
Culotte (1) 3 197
culpa (1) 11 1033
Culpepper (1) 14 1235
culprit (1) 13 61
Cult (1) 15 3012
cult (1) 15 2271
cultivate (1) 16 1219
cultivated (1) 17 1960
cultivation (1) 17 1701
cultivator (1) 17 1609
culture (2) 12 712 900
culture (1) 7 845
cultured (3) 10 581 13 548 16 1183
cum (3) 6 601 12 1743 1748
Cumberland (1) 5 229
cumbersome (2) 15 4112 4126
cumbrously (1) 15 4101
cummerbund (1) 15 300
Cummins (2) 12 1026 13 633
cuneiform (1) 17 772
Cunning (1) 8 338
cunning (6) 3 154 8 78 9 840 12 282
286 1776
Cunningham (67) 5 331 6 1 8 34 86 95
104 109 113 133 141 146 151 188 192 219 250 259
277 282 286 289 295 305 325 334 336 339 342 367
369 403 415 420 456 473 491 526 529 718 735 737
1006 1020 1024 7 165 10 956 959 964 967
975 978 983 987 993 999 1014 1023 1029 1032 1038
12 411 761 1587 16 504 17 1238
18 1266
Cunningham (1) 16 1257
Cunningham (3) 15 1140 3854 3857
CUNNINGHAM (2) 15 3859 3862
Cunningham's (4) 6 73 344 716 10 5
cunnythumb (1) 5 233
cunt (1) 4 227
CUNTY (4) 15 4440 4444 4633 4637
cuore (1) 15 351
Cup (4) 4 14 389 16 1242 17 324
Cup (1) 13 1175
cup (42) 1 436 450 4 333 359 5 369 532
6 379 419 7 388 8 814 1008 9 644 818
10 750 1093 11 163 12 244 281 288 794
1217 1898 13 1222 14 178 186 501 746 748
15 4814 16 331 355 360 750 1141 1338 1621
17 361 363 661 18 436 910 956
cupboard (2) 12 1231 13 971
cupful (1) 14 749
cupidity (1) 15 4275
Cupid's (1) 13 88
cupolas (1) 12 1734
Cuprani (1) 7 99
cups (8) 1 408 441 3 458 10 1083
14 277 419 17 299 18 934
cur (2) 12 1230 15 1082
curaçoa (1) 10 547
curate (4) 4 114 8 774 13 1127
14 1542
curates (1) 4 126
curb (2) 11 330 14 679
curb (1) 15 271
curbstone (12) 5 52 6 229 464 490 8 175
295 523 1075 1104 10 59 645 11 1190
curbstone (2) 15 196 506
curchycurchy (1) 15 4083
curd (1) 5 501

curdled (1) 15 1598
curdling (1) 4 366
curdog (1) 14 1420
curds (2) 13 958 17 314
Curé (1) 10 838
Cure (1) 6 307
cure (10) 5 365 477 479 6 61 7 96
13 902 14 657 15 3257 3274 16 955
cured (7) 2 339 340 341 13 113 291
15 199 16 1591
cures (3) 5 483 6 121 15 2389
curfew (1) 14 1338
Curiosity (2) 8 136 13 776
curiosity (6) 1 553 3 198 15 457
16 300 330 566
Curious (8) 4 28 415 5 223 504 6 130
11 622 13 1109 16 414
curious (8) 5 409 9 781 13 1040
14 344 1006 16 687 1176 18 539
Curiously (1) 15 1301
curiously (3) 4 21 10 357 16 1757
curiously (1) 15 2022
curl (1) 4 469
curled (6) 1 96 2 22 3 215 4 261
10 100 17 856
curled (1) 15 2083
Curley's (1) 12 1459
curling (3) 1 131 3 339 11 824
curling (3) 15 705 4167 4178
curlpapers (1) 15 2248
curls (3) 5 570 7 709 13 270
curls (1) 4 437
curls (2) 15 2587 4944
Curly (1) 8 883
curly (4) 15 3129 18 271 1312 1350
Curlycues (1) 11 1017
curlyheaded (1) 13 14
Curran (3) 2 256 7 740 12 501
currant (3) 15 2901 18 621 940
currants (1) 8 912
currants (1) 15 3368
current (5) 1 29 12 163 17 162 336 2176
currents (2) 14 1106 17 204
curricle (1) 17 1595
curriculum (2) 5 43
curried (1) 12 1357
cur's (1) 3 318
curs (1) 15 968
Curse (5) 5 132 10 690 13 1239
15 2934 2957
curse (13) 3 431 6 137 7 844 10 911
1119 11 285 12 684 1198 1785 13 1150
14 330 1037 15 2935
curse (1) 12 740
Cursed (2) 12 1667 15 3644
cursed (6) 1 209 8 1012 11 1041 1097
15 2937 18 953
curses (1) 12 740
cursing (4) 11 1200 12 1785 16 683
18 426
cursory (1) 16 336
Curtain (1) 13 857
curtain (6) 9 1041 10 598 604 11 1051
17 1175 18 1054
curtains (5) 8 626 10 633 646 647
15 3356
curtains (2) 15 605 4032
curtana (1) 15 1444
curtly (1) 10 1076

curtly (1) 15 2682
curtseyed (1) 1 461
curtseying (1) 10 181
curtseying (1) 15 4092
curvature (1) 10 662
curve (6) 1 742 3 356 4 253 10 653
13 935 17 208
curved (1) 6 253
curves (13) 8 823 920 921 1129 1180 10 564
13 796 15 3267 16 1448 1465 17 1296
2234
curves (1) 10 612
curves (4) 15 298 473 3723 4062
curvilinear (2) 17 150 2095
curving (3) 6 3 9 1124 11 83
cushion (1) 15 1520
cushions (3) 15 3411 18 367 664
cuspidors (1) 17 1532
cuss (1) 14 1548
cussedness (1) 16 297
custard (3) 8 355 12 95 1616
custody (2) 14 1381 15 1169
Custom (2) 11 1052 12 1839
custom (7) 3 236 6 36 714 10 750
11 1248 12 1342 14 360
customary (2) 16 144 1597
customer (1) 16 625
customers (2) 8 419 13 1050
Customhouse (3) 10 297 16 101 238
customhouse (1) 15 129
customs (3) 5 295 12 1254 14 26
Cut (4) 13 1084 14 1532 1570 15 274
cut (43) 1 206 4 154 389 392 5 235
6 432 7 26 33 8 777 9 940 10 327
11 519 12 461 980 13 117 154 579 592 704
774 911 14 497 797 1353 15 401 1153 1233
3713 4541 16 411 833 1429 1691 17 287 2093
18 31 285 422 514 602 986 998 1134
cut (1) 17 826
cutaway (1) 10 901
Cute (2) 4 111 12 1761
cute (1) 11 859
cutest (2) 14 1504 15 2203
cutlers (1) 12 620
cutlet (1) 8 761
Cuts (1) 16 480
cuts (3) 8 630 11 297 12 952
cutter (1) 11 881
cutting (11) 7 121 123 187 972 17 1514 1801
1814 1867 2102 18 159 472
cuttingly (1) 15 3183
cutty (1) 15 4679
cycle (3) 6 445 17 98 1576
cycles (1) 14 1080
cycleshop (1) 8 156
cycling (1) 17 1593
Cyclist (1) 15 233
cyclist (1) 5 551
cyclists (2) 13 436 1070
cyclists (1) 15 178
cyclone (1) 7 701
cyclonic (1) 12 1870
cygnets (1) 9 161
cygnets (1) 15 3840
cylinder (4) 15 1350 17 1326 1328 2159
cylindrical (2) 17 309 1045
Cymbeline (1) 9 1221
Cymbeline (1) 9 1021
cynanthropy (1) 12 714

danger (1) 15 3
dangerous (2) 9 103 10 776
dangerouslooking (1) 16 578
dangers (2) 13 1160 16 63
Dangle (1) 6 748
dangled (1) 8 298
dangled (1) 15 4127
dangles (1) 15 807
dangling (7) 1 514 2 287 5 118 8 316
 10 940 1103 1108
dangling (2) 15 2038 3845
Daniel (5) 6 750 10 93 15 1645
 17 444 1641
Daniel (1) 15 4683
dank (2) 5 302 15 1663
Danny (2) 16 657 664
Dannyman (1) 16 1052
Dans (1) 15 3536
dans (3) 3 161 14 307 15 2583
Dansez (1) 15 4103
Dante (3) 12 182 16 886 17 479
Daphne (1) 12 1270
dapper (1) 10 987
dapping (1) 14 520
darbies (1) 15 1043
Darby (1) 14 1419
d'Arcy (3) 8 181 10 539 17 2133
d'Arcy (1) 15 4342
DArcy (1) 18 1295
dArcy (1) 18 273
Dardanelles (1) 16 462
Dare (1) 7 930
dare (9) 1 536 3 451 9 659 853 12 870
 1108 14 1073 15 1115 2868
dare (2) 12 27 100
dared (3) 9 763 11 306 13 597
dared (1) 9 1149
daredevil (1) 15 1265
darem (3) 4 314 5 227 15 469
Daremo (1) 15 3002
Daren't (1) 6 793
daren't (2) 11 1194 12 1314
darent (1) 18 1078
Daresay (4) 4 68 5 12 7 266 13 828
daresay (4) 1 648 6 776 8 1098 16 243
Dargle (2) 7 1009 17 167
daring (1) 10 866
daringly (1) 15 3115
Dark (7) 4 89 5 156 6 486 8 1120
 9 1026 12 190 13 822
DARK (1) 15 749
dark (103) 1 6 60 250 268 630 2 86 158 171
 3 15 154 420 4 34 41 42 95 544 545 5 14 298
 570 6 435 533 752 7 70 816 945 8 1109
 1124 1142 9 442 573 603 923 1214 10 514
 790 805 11 42 149 151 706 974 1005 1006 1007
 12 298 446 1211 1557 1558 1566 13 108 116
 415 450 563 719 832 866 873 898 901 965 1015
 1070 1149 1260 14 268 374 379 597 1056 1124
 1132 15 1066 3176 3270 3321 16 192 590 879
 1088 1243 1434 1679 1782 17 267 331 612 616
 868 1037 1297 1365 2021 2182 2328 18 1040
 1315 1385 1411 1418 1429
dark (16) 15 134 213 301 361 667 748 1184
 2005 2257 2479 2482 3227 3386 3974 4078 4956
darkbacked (2) 10 315 520
darken (1) 18 216
darkened (5) 1 386 6 846 9 1006
 10 802 1226

darkened (1) 15 4669
darkening (1) 9 463
darker (5) 9 463 13 557 768 14 1368
 16 105
darker (1) 15 2831
darkerhued (1) 12 1282
darkest (1) 14 1345
darkest (1) 15 233
darkgreener (1) 9 30
darkhidden (1) 15 2272
darkies (1) 14 1557
Darkinbad (1) 17 2329
Darkly (1) 3 409
darkly (3) 6 476 12 349 18 1340
darkly (1) 15 1836
darkmans (1) 3 384
Darkness (1) 3 421
darkness (12) 2 73 160 362 3 45 274 409
 5 494 10 806 12 338 14 383 1069 1073
darkness (2) 15 2153 4245
darkrimmed (1) 7 560
Darkshawled (1) 15 3220
DARKVISAGED (1) 15 3110
Darling (3) 8 646 13 937 1069
darling (19) 2 315 5 255 264 6 888
 8 327 12 829 13 17 1106 1280 14 384
 1331 15 1064 2815 2882 3770 3914 18 817
 861 1311
darling (1) 4 287
darlint (1) 7 929
darned (3) 3 431 6 106 9 533
darning (1) 17 663
darted (2) 5 52 11 74
darting (1) 13 933
darts (4) 15 175 184 3502 3504
Darwin (2) 14 859 17 1644
das (1) 17 1885
Dash (1) 15 743
dash (2) 11 1026 17 1674
dashing (1) 10 788
dastard (1) 15 979
data (2) 2 163 17 1417
date (10) 2 12 12 574 16 178 1376 1422
 1654 17 32 901 1781 2276
dated (3) 15 392 17 1403 1792
datepalms (1) 15 297
dates (1) 17 60
dateshaped (1) 2 126
daub (2) 8 272 18 1128
daubily (1) 10 1221
dauby (3) 10 382 496 1221
dauby (1) 15 2985
Daughter (3) 7 201 340 11 507
daughter (44) 4 411 8 28 154 460 9 196
 314 424 647 678 1005 10 163 655 11 506 644
 12 227 399 1003 1113 13 325 918 14 87
 916 1073 15 572 778 973 3165 4585 16 133
 150 651 1414 1441 17 56 362 536 539 831 860
 942 943 944 18 882 893
daughter (1) 17 813
Daughter's (1) 10 884
daughter's (2) 8 559 9 422
DAUGHTERS (1) 15 1940
daughters (10) 2 7 8 467 9 693 830 852
 1192 12 1685 13 1107 14 374 15 1936
daughters (1) 15 1938
Daunt's (1) 16 906
Davenant (1) 9 643
David (12) 8 515 10 17 26 27 845
 12 234 15 1488 1834 2785 17 330 759 1107

David's (2) 15 2091 2092
Davis' (1) 12 916
Davitt (3) 16 1592 17 508 1649
Davitt (1) 15 4684
Davy (24) 7 28 8 697 732 809 815 824 833
 937 942 947 953 957 961 969 975 982 987 1013
 1026 11 867 13 1164 14 1578 16 423
 17 982
Davy (1) 9 909
Davy (2) 15 1122 4348
DAVY (3) 9 1185 15 1124 1696
Davy's (2) 7 669 672
Daw (2) 7 336 340
dawdled (2) 3 357 10 1145
dawdling (1) 10 1124
dawn (4) 4 84 14 1191 15 1542
 17 1248
dawned (1) 16 431
dawns (1) 6 1031
Dawson (5) 8 1028 1080 9 279 10 538
 743
Dawson (1) 15 4351
Dawson's (2) 6 151 7 276
DAY (2) 7 726 1063
Day (12) 2 287 3 463 4 432 536 8 991
 992 9 889 1213 13 1184 15 202 1126
day (230) 1 189 205 235 308 468 473 610
 2 93 200 262 286 287 363 3 33 241 246 315 411
 463 491 4 44 79 86 91 122 123 316 402 434 440
 463 5 33 102 182 208 285 307 397 466 476 505
 509 6 316 392 446 512 513 623 674 675 678 679
 765 830 855 924 933 7 260 261 285 287 382 526
 530 543 550 736 8 46 59 129 148 165 169 180
 215 423 473 477 494 537 595 949 9 154 187 377
 498 596 611 674 775 929 944 1044 1108 1204
 10 122 158 179 217 218 525 683 910 999
 11 199 263 807 905 913 1199 1253 1259 12 1
 49 285 662 1101 1111 1357 1377 1651 13 3 20
 181 217 219 255 463 844 889 1035 1214 14 267
 439 516 539 567 596 659 775 1050 1074 1339 1576
 15 645 1030 1453 1505 1525 1688 2129 2380 2409
 2412 2429 3065 3105 3683 3994 4562 16 73 157
 479 500 671 872 997 1237 1525 1556 1577
 17 16 76 95 178 281 655 923 1120 1198 1236
 1404 1724 1832 1846 1999 2071 2289 18 26 46
 62 211 280 328 335 349 354 371 474 481 506 669
 738 765 780 799 953 989 1013 1068 1095 1102 1133
 1179 1195 1270 1350 1408 1470 1541 1550 1572
 1573
day (5) 1 303 305 6 167 7 866 12 741
daybook (2) 10 97 207
daybreak (2) 1 401 17 1257
daydream (1) 13 195
DAYFATHER (1) 7 195
dayfather (2) 7 197 16 1258
dayfather's (1) 8 180
daylabourers (1) 7 859
daylight (7) 1 315 9 1112 12 67 1315
 15 593 17 1044 18 829
daylit (1) 9 592
day's (5) 3 250 4 85 12 25 549 16 968
DAYS (1) 7 737
Days (1) 15 3325
DAYS (1) 15 3330
days (73) 1 674 2 395 3 322 490 4 202
 6 66 869 7 266 795 8 266 282 289 304 316
 373 9 801 819 1044 1048 1097 10 14 159 410
 790 939 943 11 599 772 1019 12 43 646 1029
 13 22 297 321 334 344 655 667 1177 1268

65

12 252 394 512 762 816 1100 13 77 146 228 328 386 479 493 709 775 786 975 1190 15 488 556 1235 2877 2934 3023 3445 3472 4378 4474 4892 16 69 283 553 599 1028 1129 1146 1167 1339 1543 1579 1617 1627 1649 1761

didn't (1) 5 282

didnt (37) 18 12 122 202 211 216 243 310 354 356 432 439 441 623 651 667 671 673 681 708 727 757 777 835 1046 1047 1074 1092 1123 1288 1304 1320 1370 1386 1406 1477 1479 1582

didst (3) 14 373 1430

didst (1) 9 146

Die (2) 11 1019 15 3204

die (31) 1 167 205 4 395 5 204 6 380 8 216 9 796 10 91 11 1019 1102 12 500 1257 13 1237 14 204 211 215 250 393 439 440 1242 15 4471 4473 4474 16 444 1130 17 1990 18 231 455 794 883

die (3) 14 1432 15 1654 16 1816

die (1) 15 1557

diebus (1) 3 466

died (40) 3 142 234 6 36 378 549 809 867 887 968 7 751 873 8 157 159 219 9 172 216 217 676 725 726 10 404 682 11 162 767 1131 12 694 1131 1372 1651 13 315 14 101 102 267 517 16 1071 1317 17 623 18 117 697 726

died (1) 5 129

dienen (1) 9 491

dies (6) 4 352 392 424 8 487 9 1033 18 1247

dies (1) 15 1744

Diet (1) 14 1402

diet (3) 14 693 17 13 1707

Dietary (1) 17 249

dietary (2) 12 718 17 28

Dieu (3) 1 665 3 170 14 307

differ (1) 16 780

difference (8) 5 187 11 467 13 504 660 707 16 775 1526 17 525

differences (4) 16 312 17 893 908 1097

Different (3) 8 1131 13 875 16 1289

different (41) 7 1011 8 1096 1122 9 779 12 75 106 1428 1883 13 175 669 706 1037 1137 14 1187 1242 15 434 3073 16 512 572 814 1145 1314 1405 1523 1719 1724 1783 1848 17 41 503 892 972 1086 1143 1199 1221 1251 1483 18 246 1326 1390

different (3) 15 1751 1830 1849

differentiating (1) 14 1234

Differently (1) 17 891

differently (4) 17 887 889 1093 1916

difficult (5) 14 43 15 1996 4471 17 387 1754

difficulties (3) 2 343 17 343 441

difficultly (1) 14 849

difficulty (6) 10 131 14 1003 16 308 1447 17 700 1086

diffuses (1) 13 1039

diffusing (1) 17 1295

diffusing (1) 15 336

diffusion (4) 17 358 1257 1267 1319

Dig (1) 11 866

dig (4) 6 809 10 105 13 809 15 1116

digest (1) 14 1287

digested (1) 8 1033

digestion (3) 8 753 922 17 564

digests (1) 8 755

diggings (1) 16 1645

digidi (1) 14 1454

digit (1) 17 1080

digital (2) 17 682 1928

DIGITS (1) 7 1069

digits (1) 14 984

Dignam (58) 4 119 551 5 91 6 158 422 452 627 815 993 1008 7 80 8 219 479 10 4 534 771 1017 1028 1122 1133 1137 1140 1145 1150 1154 1172 1266 11 805 857 1244 12 315 317 321 329 330 389 392 395 404 762 772 781 13 115 315 317 318 956 962 14 474 15 1244 16 1245 1246 17 1240 1241 1255 1462 18 1261 1279

Dignam (4) 5 116 127 16 1249 1256

Dignam (3) 15 1205 1251 3837

DIGNAM (6) 15 1209 1217 1225 1229 1245 1253

Dignam's (11) 4 353 8 744 10 60 11 1205 12 761 13 861 939 1175 1225 15 1218 1258

Dignam's (1) 15 1257

Dignams (1) 18 48

dignified (1) 15 3826

dignity (6) 13 125 769 14 1006 1199 1323 16 1845

dignity (2) 15 1478 3243

dignum (1) 10 4

Digs (1) 14 1473

digs (1) 16 165

dil (1) 15 1651

dilapidated (1) 16 220

dilate (2) 11 707 12 474

dilated (1) 15 3815

dilating (1) 11 707

dilemma (2) 14 579 1002

Dillon (13) 6 1013 8 159 10 538 13 893 1107 15 1008 17 1336 2136 18 429 720 741 1502

Dillon (1) 15 4337

Dillon's (10) 6 697 1009 7 431 8 28 10 643 11 725 13 1091 15 3162 17 57 467

Dillon's (1) 15 3094

Dillons (2) 18 1313 1327

Dilly (19) 10 288 645 660 666 668 671 675 680 686 696 701 705 711 863 874 1227 15 4202 16 270 17 146

Dilly (1) 15 4147

dillydallying (1) 16 535

Dilly's (1) 10 855

dim (6) 1 225 245 247 11 465 14 1346 15 4943

dimber (1) 3 378

dime (1) 14 1586

dimension (2) 17 1048 1202

dimensions (5) 12 162 903 15 2358 3486 16 626

DIMINISHED (1) 7 1069

diminishing (3) 17 451 1067 1295

diminuendo (1) 9 907

diminutionem (1) 12 478

diminution's (1) 14 31

diminutive (2) 17 1322 1331

dimly (1) 16 190

dimple (1) 13 25

dimpled (1) 4 308

dimpled (1) 4 437

dims (1) 15 2041

Dimsey (2) 12 234

din (1) 10 713

Dina (2) 15 420 422

Dinbad (1) 17 2325

dine (1) 16 1572

Dineen (2) 9 967 968

diner (2) 8 689 11 288

diner's (2) 11 286 317

diners' (1) 11 479

dingdong (3) 8 582 11 564 12 1573

dinge (2) 6 1015 1021

dinged (1) 14 313

dinged (1) 15 936

Dingle (1) 12 1698

dingy (5) 3 250 10 114 598 604 632

dining (1) 18 82

Diningroom (1) 11 357

diningroom (2) 6 410 11 287

diningrooms (1) 7 940

dinky (1) 13 174

Dinna (1) 14 1522

Dinner (3) 8 870 11 359 17 1467

dinner (19) 5 546 6 964 7 503 8 160 237 411 10 537 13 891 14 623 16 1663 17 473 1525 1549 18 317 337 427 450 1055 1285

dinner (2) 15 450 1577

dinnerparty (1) 12 1387

Dinners (1) 11 523

dinnertime (1) 13 1054

dint (1) 14 856

dio (1) 9 1049

dioceses (1) 12 1886

Dion (1) 8 601

dip (1) 11 1259

diphthong (1) 3 127

Diplodocus (1) 15 2373

diploma (1) 9 59

diplomatically (1) 16 255

dipped (5) 1 38 5 459 11 860 12 1839 18 129

dire (1) 9 403

dire (1) 3 170

direct (8) 14 688 17 698 872 984 1179 1812 1820 2219

directed (4) 12 339 1881 16 935 17 368

direction (10) 13 227 16 35 237 698 1360 1661 1844 17 855 1262 1437

direction (1) 15 1888

directions (6) 7 956 12 76 17 356 1483 2302 18 681

directions (2) 15 1850 4038

Directly (2) 9 9 968

directly (4) 12 555 14 1225 16 1340 17 1296

directors (1) 15 1830

Directory (1) 17 1362

directory (2) 17 1526 1612

directress (1) 13 110

Dirt (1) 5 502

dirt (5) 5 524 6 465 519 18 72 1434

DIRTY (1) 7 921

Dirty (3) 4 481 12 998 15 385

dirty (20) 1 71 4 495 7 110 8 696 1159 10 102 12 433 13 52 797 868 1279 15 1890 3208 16 720 18 74 429 564 694 1094 1405

dis (1) 14 1448

dis (1) 15 1654

disabled (2) 15 796 17 1946

disagreeable (1) 15 1980

distinctly (4) 12 1443 16 22 1480 1609
distingué (1) 16 1477
distinguish (1) 14 1296
distinguishable (1) 12 604
distinguished (7) 12 106 468 1822 15 778 16 1350 17 1548 18 1344
distinguishedlooking (2) 5 331 13 543
distracted (1) 16 1798
distracting (1) 14 65
distraction (2) 17 436 1920
Distractions (1) 14 1022
distrained (1) 10 943
Distrait (1) 9 120
distrait (1) 15 3594
distress (1) 6 869
distressed (1) 16 1319
distressful (1) 16 1097
distressing (1) 14 972
distressingly (1) 9 128
distribute (1) 15 1568
distributing (1) 7 204
distributor (1) 17 1940
district (1) 12 86
district (1) 15 913
Districts (1) 13 703
distrusting (1) 17 240
disturb (4) 5 234 15 3249 17 288 2119
disturbance (1) 12 1861
disturbed (3) 6 743 8 146 16 942
disturbing (1) 4 74
disunion (1) 17 1224
disunited (1) 17 1965
disvested (1) 17 2072
dit (1) 14 306
ditches (1) 18 1563
ditchwater (1) 13 468
Ditto (1) 12 146
ditto (1) 17 1542
dittoed (1) 16 884
Dittoh (1) 14 1467
ditty (2) 11 443 16 144
diuretic (1) 17 1198
diurnal (1) 17 1262
Div (2) 14 1224 1286
divan (1) 17 668
divaricated (1) 15 3425
dive (1) 8 426
dived (1) 6 833
divergent (3) 14 955 15 2091 17 27
divers (5) 9 744 12 1723 14 38 140 16 1226
divers (1) 15 333
diversified (1) 16 329
diversion (1) 14 1518
diverting (1) 11 272
divestiture (1) 17 1479
divide (1) 12 348
divided (8) 6 385 11 831 12 634 16 1881 17 1655 1994 2176 18 437
dividend (1) 8 337
dividends (1) 17 1067
divides (1) 9 855
Divine (1) 15 4233
divine (8) 3 49 7 774 12 282 13 723 14 66 791 17 1205 1208
divine (3) 1 589 7 769 17 413
divined (1) 17 582
divinely (1) 15 1062
divinities (2) 17 1985 2078

divisible (2) 17 1065 1066
division (9) 10 473 628 13 152 16 51 78 132 17 884 1068
divisions (1) 17 1066
divisors (1) 17 1067
Divorce (1) 17 2202
divorce (1) 7 199
Divorced (1) 8 351
divorced (3) 9 1038 18 846 1127
divulge (1) 17 2000
divulged (4) 10 851 16 1194 17 510 1635
Dix (2) 14 1443 1472
Dixon (18) 8 429 14 125 189 229 259 334 355 469 505 582 589 614 623 665 703 726 801 1400
Dixon (1) 15 2238
Dixon (1) 15 1797
dizzily (1) 16 115
Dlugacz (1) 4 492
Dlugacz (1) 15 987
Dlugacz (1) 15 990
Dlugacz' (1) 11 884
Dlugacz's (2) 4 46 140
DO (1) 7 614
Do (84) 1 183 189 287 373 379 424 517 538 2 21 134 161 243 270 438 3 326 4 115 116 255 357 5 258 375 504 6 93 512 7 146 502 8 245 276 876 886 961 1077 1081 1087 9 197 214 251 303 429 542 651 653 725 1065 10 486 662 865 1158 11 39 409 487 578 832 868 908 993 12 1045 1046 1054 1088 1385 1654 1660 13 795 1162 14 1142 1167 15 442 539 747 1527 2539 2733 3023 3542 4295 4602 4784 4814 16 753 822 1425 1646
Do (1) 12 894
do (346) 1 28 89 158 353 468 506 642 2 55 56 134 137 283 289 331 374 415 420 439 3 16 132 192 222 320 421 4 68 98 126 214 258 425 5 107 174 176 244 245 247 251 252 253 363 372 377 445 556 557 6 79 103 192 194 617 657 700 762 792 809 860 891 1002 1003 7 35 151 154 156 160 256 330 496 510 617 627 651 693 711 783 815 886 1031 1051 8 35 202 203 328 332 402 535 538 558 574 596 599 824 889 933 934 972 985 1035 1092 1115 9 103 186 349 566 611 649 651 653 656 663 814 827 849 1118 1160 10 64 304 462 672 679 715 720 721 728 927 1317 1142 11 39 149 393 404 435 436 472 571 671 690 691 825 869 908 942 992 993 1049 12 381 708 777 842 859 1075 1135 1146 1254 1402 1419 1806 13 19 407 628 705 709 786 830 848 880 916 954 1020 1029 1048 1050 1151 1155 1196 1231 1255 1263 1271 1275 1280 14 130 137 156 237 362 417 442 443 591 814 1104 1144 1265 1276 1312 1430 1465 1474 1497 1509 15 398 399 437 642 745 779 871 977 983 1070 1111 1114 1485 1498 1634 1647 1873 2190 2191 2297 2350 2473 2541 2869 3132 3263 3445 3464 3693 3743 3903 4381 4590 4626 4720 4828 4870 16 149 165 168 181 345 412 616 736 749 765 800 1051 1395 1409 1445 1460 1700 1718 17 123 160 659 1032 18 34 38 46 71 76 77 84 85 89 101 111 131 138 155 170 193 233 236 238 244 251 278 315 354 367 418 455 469 628 696 795 821 827 895 906 928 936 963 983 987 1007 1060 1107 1108 1128 1161 1170 1197 1251 1281 1299 1313 1322 1366 1404 1413 1419 1436 1437 1459 1479 1482 1489 1506 1515 1525 1527 1529 1551 1561 1570
do (4) 1 361 5 282 6 814 9 798
do (1) 15 1495

Doady (3) 14 1320 1325 1337
doaty (1) 11 208
Doc (2) 12 1895 14 1243
doc (1) 14 1482
docile (1) 15 3057
docility (1) 17 221
Dock (2) 15 1367 16 49
dock (4) 10 297 12 1100 15 1169 16 225
docked (1) 15 3130
docket (3) 10 319 321 15 1249
dockets (2) 6 733 17 1865
dockleaves (1) 11 967
Dockrell's (1) 8 171
Dockrell's (1) 15 914
Docks (1) 17 1737
docks (2) 16 1077 17 223
Doctor (12) 5 478 13 310 14 94 96 576 810 1402 15 1210 2424 4402 17 650
doctor (14) 1 211 3 124 5 427 8 96 398 9 738 11 209 13 134 961 14 812 1312 18 576 1151 1169
doctor (1) 15 4359
doctors (5) 5 440 6 886 8 400 14 36 590
doctrine (2) 2 324 14 10
doctrines (2) 14 933 17 25
document (2) 16 455 17 1413
Documents (1) 17 1855
Dodd (1) 10 1193
Dodd (1) 15 1918
Dodder (2) 6 55 13 662
Dodge (1) 11 1181
dodge (3) 6 397 8 309 15 245
dodged (1) 10 512
dodger's (1) 12 998
dodging (3) 10 1149 12 4 16 211
doe (1) 14 712
d'œil (1) 16 554
Does (8) 6 860 931 8 38 769 9 419 10 1084 11 310 627
does (94) 1 138 231 2 238 3 420 497 4 149 151 337 429 5 105 240 258 286 360 500 522 6 194 341 671 700 706 816 889 990 7 205 215 230 261 306 8 329 448 528 852 940 980 981 1052 9 50 160 377 419 452 664 834 10 489 738 791 11 689 731 874 1256 1259 12 452 677 1590 1657 13 796 832 886 1155 1241 14 500 810 1102 1278 1374 15 639 714 744 2717 4588 4884 16 247 256 426 573 672 714 1453 17 607 18 54 225 269 521 592 709 844 949 1249 1272 1395 1430 1438 1490
does (1) 12 28
doeskin (1) 15 2051
Doesn't (9) 3 356 4 214 5 390 8 130 1056 11 911 912 1044 15 3615
doesn't (19) 1 207 607 5 189 6 194 368 400 804 7 128 8 325 732 804 955 10 872 11 104 697 833 12 844 15 4392 4486
doesn't (2) 1 383 12 362
doesnt (10) 18 142 386 592 1076 1200 1208 1251 1370 1518 1528
doffed (5) 5 319 9 489 10 30 1220 14 89
doffs (1) 15 3305
Dog (4) 3 310 8 366 15 1564 4708
dog (49) 3 187 286 294 298 332 343 349 4 451 7 211 212 8 861 9 475 11 1019 12 126 410 452 484 492 493 494 697 699 703 709

748 753 766 1162 1234 1766 1904 13 232 1240
14 808 1541 15 266 1890 2642 3644
16 1339 1607 1790 17 1890 18 14 615 635
813 1087
dog (3) 15 577 633 4945
dog-gone (1) 14 1582
Dogbiscuits (1) 6 501
dogcarts (1) 17 495
Dogdays (1) 15 662
dogged (1) 15 667
doggedly (1) 15 513
Doggerina (2) 18 613 622
doggone (1) 15 2194
doggy (2) 12 489
doggybowwowsywowsy (1) 8 849
doghaired (1) 14 987
dogma (2) 1 652 16 1129
dog's (4) 3 310 350 13 908 15 2786
Dogs (2) 10 765 13 1028
dogs (10) 3 376 6 78 127 444 12 453
13 974 15 4529 17 1952 18 418 1446
dogs (2) 15 482 1903
Dogs' (2) 6 125 8 847
dogs' (1) 12 625
dogsbody (4) 1 112 137 3 351 15 4178
dogsbody's (1) 3 352
Dogskull (1) 3 350
dogsniff (1) 3 350
dogvans (1) 17 1719
dogwhip (1) 15 4329
Doherty (1) 12 933
Doing (7) 4 132 5 269 6 238 7 176
8 767 11 1011 12 134
doing (49) 4 200 5 32 7 629 987 8 953
972 9 301 312 649 10 854 857 898 1011
11 354 487 887 12 12 300 395 488 506 784 813
818 997 1174 1192 1403 13 559 817 1003
15 195 385 585 682 3131 3803 16 680 711
1012 1230 1861 18 3 88 297 314 796 1012 1259
doings (1) 16 1187
Dolan (1) 15 3676
Dolan (1) 15 3668
DOLAN (1) 15 3670
dolce (2) 5 32 16 1705
doldrums (1) 14 1175
doldy (1) 15 149
doleful (1) 16 144
D'Olier (2) 15 3030 17 130
Doll (2) 11 56 1271
doll (5) 11 1170 17 868 18 306 917
doll (1) 15 289
dollarbills (1) 10 608
Dollard (45) 8 117 839 10 539 791 893 906
911 916 921 925 932 940 945 950 11 435 442
449 450 451 472 481 528 538 586 652 758 772 800
997 1074 1139 1151 1154 1157 1163 1168 1169
1173 1174 1175 1176 1214 1272 17 2138
18 1285
Dollard (2) 15 2604 4342
DOLLARD (4) 15 1664 1668 2608 2617
dollard (1) 11 1178
Dollard's (7) 6 145 10 901 908 1206
11 436 554 1011
dollop (1) 14 1438
doll's (1) 1 582
dolls (1) 17 575
dollwomen (1) 15 651
Dolly (3) 12 195 15 4419 18 1287
DOLLY (1) 15 4417

dolly (1) 13 150
Dollymount (3) 10 213 16 630 17 1715
dolman (1) 15 1015
Dolmetsch (1) 16 1765
Dolor (1) 11 1132
Dolores (2) 11 518 734
dolores (1) 11 1132
dolorous (1) 11 1133
dolours (1) 13 445
Dolphin (2) 10 504 11 189
dolphin (1) 12 1772
Dolphin's (9) 4 345 8 274 11 899
13 946 1105 1106 15 1770 17 1798 2083
Dolphins (1) 18 330
dolt (1) 14 327
domain (2) 16 1127 17 65
domain (1) 7 245
dome (3) 3 274 7 1011 9 1026
domed (2) 1 313 3 271
domestic (9) 11 1026 14 923 947
16 1474 1537 17 23 657 1632 1633
domestic (1) 15 903
domicile (2) 14 56 17 937
dominant (3) 11 736 15 2106 17 1166
dominating (1) 17 1119
domination (2) 7 557 15 2777
Domine (2) 6 601 7 557
domineering (1) 18 754
Dominenamine (1) 6 595
Domini (5) 7 422 11 1032 12 1721 1740
15 2089
Dominic (2) 12 1686 13 453
dominical (1) 17 98
Dominican (1) 13 451
Dominie (1) 3 19
dominions (2) 12 295 1517
domino (1) 15 2991
dominos (1) 17 661
Dominum (2) 12 1750 13 675
Dominus (1) 12 1742
domus (1) 17 1030
Don (11) 9 308 10 174 178 12 199 563
15 352 1064 1886 16 493 18 773 1428
Don (4) 8 1040 1053 11 965 16 1753
Don (1) 15 3673
DON (3) 15 1914 3675 4506
don (2) 12 961 15 2967
Dona (1) 15 3640
dona (1) 14 1474
Donal (1) 12 729
Donald (1) 15 3326
DONATE (1) 7 1021
donation (1) 17 1687
Done (6) 4 391 11 62 909 13 849 1268
15 3390
Done (1) 11 1294
done (70) 2 173 5 177 6 126 578 735 932
7 602 8 21 166 9 467 651 1012 10 767
11 599 635 12 448 627 1028 1154 1259 1567
13 85 224 243 337 458 14 61 63 372 431 438
472 524 745 918 1031 1071 1312 1343 1410
15 287 665 1466 2217 2221 4291 4474 4558
16 20 272 591 677 679 836 845 1300 1396 1679
17 287 1751 1964 2039 2214 2215 18 42 100
111 365 807
done (3) 2 14 6 731 9 551
done (1) 15 4915
Donegal (3) 7 505 12 1831 16 554
doner (1) 6 612

Doneraile (1) 8 974
dongiovannism (1) 9 458
donjon (1) 12 1137
donkey (2) 6 837 17 1577
donkeys (1) 18 1590
donna (1) 18 896
donna (2) 9 940 16 1437
Donnerwetter (1) 15 722
Donnez (1) 15 4103
Donnybrook (3) 5 561 7 1046 11 879
Donnybrook (2) 15 1883 3728
Donnycarney (1) 10 843
Donohoe's (1) 12 1917
Donor (1) 12 1526
donor (1) 16 1522
donor's (2) 17 1747
donought (1) 14 554
dons (2) 15 1168 2513
Don't (49) 1 171 235 2 229 6 124 408 854
7 49 541 544 790 8 23 535 547 663 695 728
9 936 10 856 11 138 639 814 12 242 320
877 1040 1762 1765 13 792 1188 14 1472
1492 15 370 398 518 554 1111 1561 2025 2880
2889 2904 2920 3049 3644 4251 4288 4756 4757
don't (133) 1 61 161 170 184 213 354 433 493
506 623 624 666 2 80 236 331 3 291 319
4 55 486 5 79 162 185 264 351 399 411 435 455
6 659 713 895 7 256 648 650 976 8 106 117
229 452 503 707 922 9 93 112 114 116 123 133
277 363 364 528 530 723 903 904 916 956 958 1069
1071 1072 1082 10 35 48 938 1023 1094
11 37 127 131 204 364 510 746 874 877 964 1201
1240 1265 12 314 453 465 522 692 761 954 1634
1793 13 753 783 853 863 870 878 925 1058 1085
1262 14 1477 1587 15 404 739 819 833 2220
2254 2911 3144 3200 3517 3528 3607 4299 4401
4493 4495 4513 4791 4797 4839 4874 16 202
251 443 464 893 1125 1412
don't (2) 1 362 12 515
dont (31) 18 55 166 168 208 262 279 324 337
439 460 620 657 887 964 976 978 1124 1144 1182
1236 1237 1250 1251 1431 1434 1440 1470 1513
1524 1565 1570
doom (2) 9 498 14 424
doom (1) 15 2013
Doomed (1) 8 68
doomed (1) 6 851
doomsday (1) 9 787
Dooooooooooog (1) 15 4711
Door (2) 9 889 11 845
door (127) 1 250 318 327 523 529 2 118 179
3 9 185 276 4 50 300 456 457 468 494 496 539
5 52 99 322 457 6 9 27 198 492 574 590 935
7 28 50 51 176 224 280 298 344 375 391 399 408
424 670 908 8 401 578 650 697 9 7 13 344
581 604 10 258 643 770 1211 1282 11 275
286 299 353 392 670 671 672 690 965 986 1028
1047 1281 12 249 252 408 1080 1784 1789 1796
13 676 1158 1175 14 123 167 318 488 494 835
1026 1398 15 1029 2696 2780 16 581 705 711
724 882 923 1361 1707 17 102 119 1032 1034
1218 1221 1271 1272 1282 1284 1287 1288 1542
18 216 257 334 335 343 364 530 533 990 1010
1011 1544
door (10) 15 150 2034 2629 2630 2699 2723
2742 2789 2926 4257
doorbell (1) 5 478
doorbrasses (1) 17 1508
doorcase (1) 10 212

drive (8) 6 347 10 515 12 1797 15 1528 3151 4932 17 1502 18 237
drivel (2) 9 1160 12 493
driven (1) 12 1365
driven (1) 15 3727
Driver (1) 8 1084
driver (5) 8 349 11 878 15 204 16 1878 1885
driver (1) 15 4348
drives (1) 14 1559
drives (1) 15 659
Driving (1) 3 471
driving (8) 6 301 8 514 9 462 846 12 1900 18 152 1302 1305
drizzle (1) 15 3149
drizzle (1) 15 3980
drizzling (1) 14 1064
Drogheda (1) 12 1508
Drol (1) 15 4708
droll (4) 8 54 10 34 11 165 14 732
drolls (1) 12 544
Droma (1) 12 1439
drone (3) 1 237 3 83 10 924
droned (2) 1 385 11 250
drones (1) 3 100
drool (1) 14 329
Droop (1) 15 3087
drooped (1) 14 1146
drooping (5) 5 210 8 1084 10 208 13 1167 14 1416
drooping (1) 15 2480
droops (3) 15 321 2076 4095
Drop (5) 8 444 510 1165 10 428 15 745
drop (16) 5 51 346 400 8 552 931 10 762 11 1140 1248 12 120 444 461 13 1109 15 4886 16 304 1498 18 802
dropblind (1) 11 462
dropped (9) 4 75 277 5 23 6 586 10 238 254 953 14 1299 17 1684
Dropping (1) 6 450
dropping (8) 3 344 6 440 855 8 912 10 665 12 711 16 921 18 251
dropping (3) 15 457 2466 3368
droppings (1) 4 479
Drops (1) 11 984
drops (1) 11 420
drops (1) 15 4016
dropsical (1) 15 1692
dropsy (1) 12 1785
drought (1) 14 475
drouth (7) 4 44 7 715 8 1085 12 710 13 1129 17 171 18 455
drouth (1) 9 1149
drouthy (1) 9 566
drove (22) 3 243 5 138 6 385 399 436 453 7 640 667 10 766 1072 1177 1247 1269 12 3 1371 1588 13 891 14 571 710 15 572 16 1066 18 947
drove (1) 17 805
Drover (1) 9 303
drover's (1) 6 390
Drown (1) 6 274
drown (4) 6 273 10 876 12 1327 18 1467
drowned (9) 1 675 3 322 471 7 199 8 1147 13 471 16 1683 18 855 960
drowned (1) 15 1919
Drowning (2) 6 988 15 4863
drowning (8) 1 62 3 317 328 5 170 6 428 10 875 16 292 17 1253

drowning (2) 15 1746 2211
drowns (1) 9 1002
drowsily (1) 16 583
drowsing (1) 8 1066
drowsy (3) 11 312 14 1386 16 375
drudge (2) 8 1099 12 1359
drudges (1) 12 1349
drug (1) 9 393
drugged (1) 15 2020
druggist (1) 15 340
Drugs (1) 5 474
drugs (5) 5 487 8 885 10 816 14 64 1034
druid (2) 9 1221 14 1165
druid (1) 15 2263
Druiddrum (1) 14 1455
druidism (1) 17 32
druids (1) 1 297
druids' (1) 8 13
druidy (1) 1 297
Drum (1) 11 1242
drum (5) 2 293 298 11 555 1228 17 303
drum (2) 15 1407 4017
Drumcondra (1) 11 518
drumhandle (1) 15 4015
drumhead (1) 12 483
Drumleck (1) 8 901
drummajor (1) 11 508
drummed (1) 15 750
Drummond (1) 9 386
Drumont (1) 3 231 493
drums (6) 5 112 7 74 12 93 527 18 685 1263
drums (1) 15 1059
drumthumped (1) 10 1249
Drunk (1) 6 354
Drunk (1) 15 2512
DRUNK (3) 15 2521 2536 2582
drunk (21) 1 297 6 726 8 48 978 9 552 726 10 1151 12 251 510 1394 13 964 966 15 266 360 769 2499 3868 16 89 209 18 1265 1437
drunkables (1) 14 1529
drunkard (1) 6 349
Drunkards (1) 13 1186
Drunkards (1) 15 4663
drunkards (1) 8 605
Drunken (1) 13 1216
drunken (14) 3 66 6 52 9 1159 14 178 188 194 230 262 329 1444 15 253 18 692 756 1264
drunken (1) 15 35
drunkenly (1) 15 3856
drunkenness (1) 11 1191
drunker (2) 18 929
Drunks (1) 15 636
drunks (3) 4 130 6 722 725
Dry (1) 11 258
dry (20) 3 500 4 14 473 5 488 8 986 9 536 10 1272 11 259 12 657 691 1435 13 1140 14 480 15 2448 2562 3770 16 672 17 193 234 18 1153
dry (1) 12 742
dry (1) 15 2399
drying (1) 13 918
dryingline (1) 3 156
Dth (3) 8 288 373
dth (2) 8 373
Du (5) 8 890 9 491 14 1432

du (1) 16 1239
Dub (3) 11 572 15 505 2789
dub (1) 2 430
dubbed (1) 16 1307
Dubedat (2) 8 889 890
Dubedat (1) 15 1586
Dubedatandshedidbedad (1) 15 4355
dubiosity (1) 16 574
dubious (1) 14 932
dubiously (1) 6 567
dubiously (1) 15 1993
DUBLIN (2) 7 79 921
Dublin (95) 1 75 2 283 288 3 471 4 129 5 68 279 389 6 65 202 451 960 7 6 702 915 923 931 1005 8 362 464 709 1110 9 150 310 518 10 409 669 774 11 357 900 12 34 36 257 385 509 534 542 1124 1305 1405 1557 1815 1875 13 465 782 14 1020 1335 1408 15 442 1009 1010 1127 1160 1167 1344 1364 1632 4607 16 42 119 215 258 441 550 843 1298 17 12 42 139 177 486 536 538 600 976 1253 1376 1678 1712 1721 1731 1732 1733 1734 1736 1737 1742 1869 1908 1982 2076 2082 2135 2137 18 92
Dublin (7) 2 285 7 964 9 415 12 417 418 17 419 1362
Dublin (12) 15 913 1078 1162 1378 1402 1415 1418 1520 1555 1930 1936 4670
Dubliner (2) 9 1036 12 970
Dubliners (1) 7 922
DUBLIN'S (1) 7 1021
Dublin's (8) 7 610 10 1133 11 268 12 962 15 4660 16 1435 1850
Dublins (3) 3 377 15 785 18 402
Dubosc (1) 15 761
ducats (1) 9 534
Duces (1) 3 82
duchess (2) 15 3006 17 432
duchesse (1) 8 883
Duck (1) 5 560
duck (12) 8 449 806 883 1006 12 757 14 712 15 46 47 58 59 72 3149
duck (1) 15 412
ducked (2) 12 970 15 852
duckling (1) 15 2346
duckloving (1) 15 2676
ducks (2) 12 838 16 951
ducks (1) 15 296
ducky (3) 13 609 15 556 2882
duct (1) 8 1048
ducts (1) 12 653
Dudley (8) 7 700 10 110 1176 1185 1214 1218 1222
Dudley's (1) 10 1185
duds (2) 8 318 14 1575
due (22) 8 984 9 271 12 549 1186 13 96 14 670 680 729 825 963 1176 1279 15 944 3106 16 50 924 1101 1490 1495 1696 17 982 1377
dueguard (1) 15 759
Duel (1) 17 2201
duellist (1) 17 723
duels (1) 15 4682
duennas (1) 14 1249
duet (1) 12 706
duet (1) 15 352
duets (3) 10 556 16 1655 17 664
Dufery (1) 17 1406
Duff (1) 8 442

E

elbow (12) 1 100 389 2 70 297 4 259 303 7 130 8 1090 10 987 12 1844 16 1233 1511
elbow (1) 15 2337
elbowdeep (1) 15 3089
elbowed (1) 3 178
elbowing (1) 15 4423
elbowlength (1) 15 1014
elbows (1) 8 689
elbows (1) 15 2574
elbowsleeve (1) 11 388
elder (7) 1 561 12 246 13 197 14 175 16 44 739 1568
elder (1) 15 249
Elderflower (1) 12 1274
elderflower (1) 8 172
elderly (8) 1 687 7 923 10 473 625 1194 14 888 16 553 1671
elderly (3) 15 78 356 1614
elder's (1) 9 19
elders (2) 9 722 12 1185
eldest (6) 2 25 6 567 8 364 16 131 17 537 2263
Eldorado (1) 5 215
eldritch (1) 14 1016
elect (1) 12 636
elect (1) 15 4454
elected (1) 15 2932
elected (1) 15 3461
ELECTOR (1) 15 1371
elector (1) 12 1392
Electors (1) 15 1366
Electric (2) 4 458 15 1689
electric (7) 6 868 8 572 13 150 151 15 3393 17 44 221
electrical (2) 12 1840 17 344
electricity (3) 8 927 16 769 17 1714
electrifying (1) 16 1374
electrocute (1) 12 1327
Electuary (1) 5 479
elegance (2) 14 713 1212
elegant (2) 14 995 17 1852
elegantly (1) 10 980
ELEISON (1) 7 559
eleison (1) 7 564
element (3) 12 545 14 1239 16 280
elemental (2) 9 71 73
Elements (1) 17 1398
elements (2) 16 647 17 132
Elephant (1) 6 253
Elephant (1) 15 4451
elephant (4) 11 606 12 1496 16 350
elephantgrey (1) 8 164
elephantiasis (1) 15 1778
elephantine (1) 15 2362
elephants (1) 18 166
Elephantuliasis (1) 15 2449
elevated (2) 17 1088 1189
elevates (2) 15 1128 4703
elevating (2) 3 120 17 1312
elevation (2) 17 2238 18 862
Eleven (3) 4 320 5 95 15 3606
eleven (32) 2 135 4 420 5 12 6 237 798 8 1058 9 36 1105 10 820 1276 12 1712 1859 13 22 389 500 726 14 1027 1562 15 551 1911 3210 3294 3560 3562 3579 3606 3609 3613 16 450 544 1326 17 91
eleven (1) 2 105
eleven (1) 15 4957

eleventh (2) 14 267 16 71
Elfin (1) 2 303
elicited (1) 15 1034
Elijah (11) 8 13 57 10 294 754 1096 11 867 12 1683 1916 14 1580 15 3375 17 332
Elijah (2) 12 1914 1915
Elijah (1) 15 2176
ELIJAH (2) 15 2188 2215
Elijah's (1) 10 1109
Elijah's (1) 15 2183
eliminating (1) 17 993
elimination (1) 17 1934
élite (3) 8 878 11 267 16 1704
Elixir (1) 6 430
elixir (1) 15 2321
Eliza (1) 9 630
Elizabeth (3) 9 678 757 17 482
Elizabethan (1) 9 149
eljen (1) 12 600
Elk (1) 14 1090
ell (2) 6 374 900
Ellen (2) 17 536 1795
Ellen (1) 15 4348
ELLEN (1) 15 282
ellipse (1) 15 2111
ellipses (1) 17 1555
elliptical (1) 17 1113
Ellis's (3) 5 237 17 1374 1495
Ellpodbomool (1) 17 406
ells (1) 12 155
elm (3) 12 1262 13 167 17 1977
Elmshade (1) 12 1269
elocutionary (1) 7 487
Elohenu (2) 7 209 15 3228
elongated (1) 15 1559
eloped (1) 18 373
eloquence (2) 7 736 14 764
eloquence (1) 15 1000
eloquent (2) 12 908 16 638
eloquently (1) 12 904
Elsa (1) 17 879
else (38) 1 207 505 3 75 135 430 6 663 676 738 836 845 7 214 9 747 13 364 430 603 673 885 1052 14 459 1292 15 3127 3477 16 1 151 775 1520 1651 1740 1768 18 39 44 640 745 865 1098 1172 1398 1588
else (1) 15 4914
elsewhere (3) 9 472 17 113 135
Elsinore (1) 1 567
Elsinore's (2) 3 281 9 479
Elster (2) 6 186 16 526
elucidate (1) 17 1177
Élus (1) 10 148
elvers (1) 15 2264
Elvery's (2) 6 253 11 606
Ely (1) 14 490
'em (2) 8 140 16 486
em (8) 3 400 13 792 1137 14 1447 17 737 1792 1794
emaciated (1) 14 1289
emaciated (1) 15 4157
emanated (1) 16 1323
emanating (2) 12 344 16 105
embalmed (3) 9 352 17 1338 1343
Embalming (1) 6 822
embankment (1) 16 123
embarazada (1) 18 802
embargo (1) 2 339

embarked (1) 16 745
embarra (1) 7 167
embarrassed (1) 2 212
embarrassment (1) 16 1467
embarrassment (1) 15 1993
embassy (1) 14 551
embattled (1) 1 663
Embedded (2) 11 42 1006
embedded (1) 12 1877
Embellish (1) 15 1667
embellished (1) 11 1031
ember (1) 16 278
embers (1) 13 293
embezzlement (1) 17 2184
embezzling (1) 5 546
embittered (1) 14 1358
Emblem (1) 15 208
emblems (1) 3 417
embodied (1) 15 1519
embon (2) 11 1106 13 1282
embonpoint (3) 10 616 622 16 1468
embonpoint (1) 15 2753
embossed (2) 12 292 17 1535
Embrace (1) 15 1819
embrace (7) 6 852 12 639 13 2 439 15 429 16 1842 18 332
embraced (2) 18 119 1408
embraces (4) 8 638 9 218 14 676 1322
embraces (2) 15 1516 1821
embracing (3) 16 518 18 203 1400
embracing (1) 15 3640
embraided (1) 14 324
embrasure (1) 15 2513
embrasures (1) 15 652
Embroider (1) 8 1118
embroidered (2) 12 1438 13 460
embroidery (1) 17 663
embroidery (1) 15 1927
embryo (1) 14 1295
embryologists (1) 14 1235
embryonic (1) 14 990
Emerald (1) 12 554
emerald (6) 9 102 12 1282 14 583 1105 15 877 17 1304
emerald (2) 15 1617 4524
emeraldgartered (1) 15 3117
emeralds (1) 12 668
emerged (3) 6 1006 17 1037 2269
emerged (1) 7 849
emergence (1) 17 1134
emergency (2) 16 1788 17 14
emerges (1) 15 156
emersion (1) 17 1133
Emery (1) 6 977
emigrant's (1) 15 1960
Emigrants (1) 6 389
Emigration (1) 16 1241
emigration (1) 17 1642
EMILE (2) 15 1914 4506
Emily (1) 17 947 1454
Eminence (1) 15 1420 2654
eminence (3) 17 710 713 1509
eminence (1) 15 4688
eminent (6) 8 332 526 12 731 14 902 15 1478 17 1748
eminently (1) 16 1291
emir's (1) 2 214
emitted (2) 17 1331 2061
emitting (1) 16 29

fang (2) 3 226 9 541
fangs (1) 13 1221
fanlight (1) 17 115
Fanned (1) 17 257
fanned (1) 7 595
fanned (1) 7 245
Fanning (8) 10 995 997 1001 1013 1017 1027 1030
Fanning (1) 15 1174
FANNING (1) 15 1175
fanning (1) 1 186
fanning (1) 15 4206
Fanning's (1) 10 1021
Fanny (3) 8 513 17 537 18 1267
fans (1) 15 4
fanshoals (1) 3 472
fansticks (1) 4 528
fantastical (1) 9 950
fantasy (1) 12 1450
Far (11) 4 218 444 6 837 11 1185 13 2 1176 1286 14 915
Far (1) 15 3382
far (84) 1 743 2 169 170 3 340 406 419 444 4 225 5 29 59 110 6 824 8 473 9 149 10 369 455 573 865 1106 11 31 1044 1046 12 501 525 786 1445 1789 13 61 80 178 363 427 484 627 696 718 728 759 1008 1054 1180 14 14 45 69 72 95 180 827 873 1165 1259 15 600 637 877 2090 3630 3687 16 14 21 603 850 989 1174 1234 1329 1477 1598 1610 1720 1893 17 5 7 490 1068 18 204 419 725 794 807 908 942 1165 1172
far (5) 5 32 7 327 830 16 1705 17 415
far (2) 15 1966 4330
Farabutto (1) 16 318
faraway (2) 11 273 15 982
Fare (2) 15 1968 2626
fare (9) 6 173 8 884 10 138 775 11 622 879 15 1287 16 42 508
fared (3) 9 496 14 73 112
Farewell (3) 11 591 15 1968 2626
Farewell (1) 11 590
farewell (7) 1 593 8 189 10 755 12 525 1816 16 1072 1415
farewell (1) 16 1390
farfamed (2) 12 1252 16 237
Farley (1) 5 333
FARLEY (1) 15 1711
farls (1) 3 210
farm (6) 4 154 8 950 12 16 14 685 15 1035 18 786
farmer (8) 12 510 13 999 14 582 589 619 16 133 17 1603 2135
farmer (1) 15 1611
farmer's (4) 8 559 12 115 14 525 592
farmers (1) 10 724
Farmhouse (1) 4 156
farmhouse (1) 15 571
farming (1) 17 1605
farmyard (1) 14 712
Farnaby (1) 16 1766
faroff (1) 14 1326
farraginous (1) 14 1412
farreaching (1) 16 769
Farrell (8) 7 403 8 302 9 1116 10 919 1102 1106 1261 11 1125
Farrell (1) 15 2309
Farrell's (1) 6 228
farrier's (1) 16 22

farriers (1) 15 1430
farrow (1) 15 4583
Farsaigh (1) 17 750
farseeing (1) 4 65
farst (1) 15 3853
fart (2) 12 1386 18 906
fart (1) 15 50
farther (16) 1 95 243 3 155 296 341 5 456 10 63 11 723 13 756 14 208 1379 15 1287 16 551 1163 1592 17 5
farther (4) 15 135 142 173 4912
farthest (1) 3 409
farthing (5) 7 733 11 621 16 145 17 1621 18 5
farthing (1) 4 289
farting (2) 12 841 18 1083
farts (1) 15 2958
fasciated (1) 14 394
fascinated (2) 13 541 15 3011
fascinated (1) 15 1336
Fascinating (1) 8 110
Fascination (1) 6 202
fascination (4) 8 462 512 15 3121 17 1850
Fashion (2) 13 149 804
fashion (26) 6 790 8 874 12 543 13 112 345 1201 14 686 690 739 777 893 15 968 2946 16 3 1083 1134 1378 1428 1594 1803 17 2260 18 456 515 969 1114 1304
fashion (1) 15 959
fashionable (5) 12 1266 13 197 15 3884 16 1825 17 1614
fashioned (1) 12 204
fashioned (1) 15 2482
fashions (1) 12 1777
Fast (1) 10 548
fast (17) 6 160 8 35 752 791 11 684 12 1260 14 169 198 638 16 87 277 343 943 1095 1190 18 1118 1389
fast (1) 15 2240
fasted (1) 9 210
fastened (1) 13 689
faster (2) 13 516 17 286
Fat (2) 7 48 11 1163
fat (42) 3 118 476 6 772 776 7 48 479 481 8 34 408 450 812 914 9 142 815 10 305 333 763 1230 1231 11 419 420 1143 1160 12 96 503 514 841 13 24 610 902 1201 14 369 15 2356 2555 2673 2896 18 114 411 1098
fat (5) 15 1608 1766 2857 2932 3128
fatal (2) 12 615 16 1064
fatchuck (1) 15 149
Fate (5) 11 726 732 1233 13 1239
fate (5) 9 464 13 99 15 2775 3687 16 502
fated (1) 16 1485
fates (1) 16 636
Father (127) 1 578 658 660 3 49 483 5 332 398 6 319 595 7 622 8 713 9 61 132 863 967 968 10 12 19 21 24 26 30 33 40 46 49 51 52 53 62 63 68 73 77 79 80 83 85 87 93 96 98 99 101 104 113 115 120 121 122 123 128 131 136 137 142 143 148 151 153 155 161 171 180 184 189 193 203 213 264 740 842 882 884 887 890 892 908 918 927 939 944 948 952 964 1173 11 437 466 479 483 532 540 587 602 604 774 799 990 1150 1215 12 178 1067 1727 13 377 448 490 496 554 555 573 621 677 1293 14 815 15 1671 1838 2272 3676 4840 17 145 2134 2140 18 107

Father (1) 16 1887
Father (5) 15 1129 1237 3668 4350 4693
FATHER (5) 15 1240 1711 3670 4698 4702
father (134) 1 557 561 700 3 68 112 199 470 4 61 5 204 205 571 6 53 284 529 577 7 690 950 8 29 420 9 179 380 388 390 481 553 814 820 828 844 860 864 865 867 868 869 875 10 18 39 53 289 291 666 696 1170 1172 1207 11 186 254 259 645 763 1017 1063 12 956 1082 1279 1640 1648 1805 1806 13 132 182 290 299 308 311 377 917 1039 1157 14 384 555 564 604 622 842 957 1034 1063 1119 1336 15 262 264 272 360 1291 1591 1963 2558 2572 16 254 436 666 1182 1569 1759 17 138 471 474 829 929 1636 1875 2082 18 31 107 112 113 117 130 316 377 403 508 622 644 678 690 722 766 890 982 983 1061 1088 1214 1306 1464 1583
father (4) 2 89 10 793 11 1074 17 1353
father (1) 15 906
Fatherhood (1) 9 837
fatherhood (1) 9 835
fatherless (1) 12 550
father's (18) 3 62 164 229 7 648 9 132 681 829 856 12 1640 13 276 15 3655 16 109 252 1659 1807 17 146
father's (3) 1 585 8 67 9 170
FATHERS (1) 7 841
fathers (9) 10 1004 12 442 1728 14 1467 15 262 2572 18 124 350 612
fathers' (1) 16 1747
fathership (1) 14 341
fathom (3) 3 470 16 296 566
fathoms (4) 1 673 3 470 9 1002 17 188
fatigue (5) 11 1007 17 1585 1758 2043 2152
fatiguing (1) 15 2380
fatlings (1) 12 89
fatness (1) 14 153
fatpapped (1) 15 2606
fatten (1) 18 538
fattened (1) 11 165
fattening (1) 14 1438
fattish (1) 18 664
fatto (1) 9 34
faubourg (1) 16 1161
faucet (1) 17 162
Faugh (1) 13 1149
fault (16) 5 469 6 573 7 419 11 1066 12 1156 16 966 968 1165 14 884 16 1073 1792 18 61 216 1078 1446 1516
fault (2) 15 633 4331
Faultfinding (1) 16 790
faultless (1) 12 592
faults (1) 13 312
fauna (2) 15 3353 17 225
faunal (1) 3 442
Faunman (1) 9 578
Fauntleroy (1) 18 1312
Faure (1) 3 234
Faut (2) 3 170 15 2094
favour (13) 1 407 2 289 7 890 9 668 10 334 12 402 789 14 562 683 17 675 1639 1862 18 1192
favourable (2) 12 553 17 1518
favourably (3) 13 1230 14 702 17 1845
favoured (2) 9 443 12 352
favoured (1) 12 428
favouring (1) 16 1752

Favourite (1) 17 644
favourite (14) 2 310 7 610 8 830 12 542 593 13 11 153 14 1237 15 448 16 427 560 1371 1483 1680
favourite (1) 15 3981
favourites (1) 16 1756
favours (3) 14 764 15 3080 3426
Fawcett (2) 6 158 11 858
fawn (1) 5 111
fawn (2) 15 537 1059
fawning (1) 3 345
Fay (1) 12 938
fay (1) 9 757
Fbhracht (1) 15 3490
fè (1) 7 722
fealty (1) 10 1197
Fear (2) 8 342 16 737
fear (36) 1 60 152 2 264 3 312 6 16 60 388 741 7 935 8 36 798 9 614 1025 1178 1210 12 216 263 918 1760 13 454 650 1187 1189 1267 14 425 429 1123 15 1346 2394 2445 2463 16 1179 17 1765 18 454 801 1391
feared (2) 12 1868 14 93
fearful (2) 1 8 18 570
fears (4) 1 152 11 1073 12 481 13 172
feasible (1) 16 1136
FEAST (1) 7 203
Feast (1) 8 148
feast (7) 8 322 14 1125 1351 15 4735 17 94 144 1116
feastday (2) 12 1112 14 758
feasted (1) 14 200
feat (1) 17 2264
feather (3) 8 351 14 904 18 972
feather (1) 15 2859
Featherbed (2) 10 555 13 892
featherbed (2) 3 478 18 428
Feathered (1) 7 340
feathered (1) 15 3420
featherfans (1) 1 255
feathering (1) 16 1875
feathers (1) 12 1287
feathers (1) 15 2048
featherskins (1) 15 2552
feathery (1) 7 345
featly (1) 9 1142
feature (1) 8 811
featureless (1) 15 1143
features (10) 1 380 7 89 9 509 11 614 14 756 15 3487 16 302 396 1328 17 1103
features (5) 15 2728 2958 3009 3456 4223
February (5) 3 181 14 482 15 1030 17 411 1654
Febuary (1) 12 420
fecal (1) 15 3033
fecit (2) 7 1056 12 1741
Fecking (1) 11 619
fecking (1) 14 562
Fécondateur (1) 14 778
fecund (1) 14 155
fecundation (1) 14 687
fecundity (1) 17 1156
Fed (1) 2 71
fed (7) 2 166 4 143 480 6 621 8 395 481 12 754
fee (7) 8 399 14 682 15 2779 3474 16 291 17 1465 1504

feeble (2) 15 259 2074
feebleminded (1) 15 1801
feebly (1) 10 692
feebly (1) 15 3335
feed (15) 5 217 6 604 781 992 8 34 382 408 652 865 930 9 160 13 1186 14 693 18 35
feeding (6) 2 71 6 379 7 136 8 243 719 10 859
feeding (1) 15 1324
feeds (1) 5 34
feefarm (1) 17 1519
Feefawfum (1) 3 293
Feel (14) 3 494 5 505 6 105 843 1003 8 495 640 1042 1110 10 622 13 824 15 498 2820 2860
feel (90) 1 648 666 2 253 262 3 238 4 9 79 83 5 250 359 361 362 401 410 6 203 602 843 1003 7 594 8 42 1110 1131 9 27 101 323 387 461 813 815 974 11 32 54 182 707 738 794 840 894 969 1101 1136 1217 1254 12 796 867 13 561 707 734 778 823 828 829 852 859 1089 1095 1101 1273 14 870 1012 15 1308 2981 3334 3769 16 814 1057 1403 1462 1719 17 1245 18 87 96 103 150 300 331 554 583 585 590 615 637 902 903 1050 1060 1364 1470 1514 1607
feelers (2) 2 72 4 42
Feeling (1) 8 1131
feeling (24) 1 309 707 4 516 5 293 6 77 8 1105 9 1197 10 1231 11 668 1127 12 751 1172 13 87 224 997 14 920 15 210 16 1049 1706 17 810 1312 18 114 808 1004
feeling (4) 15 797 1984 1993 3513
feelings (9) 12 790 798 13 191 14 903 1283 15 3136 16 173 1631 17 830
Feels (1) 5 132
feels (5) 3 145 8 575 9 10 11 644 13 1064
feels (5) 15 201 256 260 669 1296
fees (4) 2 29 15 836 16 1841 17 1743
feet (71) 1 244 2 186 447 3 16 30 147 205 268 270 272 278 327 339 371 374 5 44 6 105 672 850 7 451 877 8 10 58 616 618 1106 9 948 10 404 757 11 687 698 1152 12 172 200 694 1162 1779 13 103 210 287 14 529 856 1427 15 307 498 1201 1605 2197 2573 2781 2847 16 559 1326 1327 1330 1508 1864 17 84 86 87 120 154 170 1243 18 226 257 679 884 906 1206 1405
feet (1) 1 464
feet (10) 15 312 579 1886 2045 2485 2853 3983 4045 4694
feetmeat (1) 15 257
feetshuffling (1) 15 2169
feetstoops (1) 7 393
feety (1) 8 819
Fehrenbach's (2) 10 535 1123
feigning (3) 7 593 14 813 1157
Fein (6) 8 458 9 239 12 1574 1624 18 383 1227
Fein (1) 12 523
fein (1) 12 523
feintruled (1) 17 1806
Felicitously (1) 9 446
felicity (1) 14 748
feline (1) 16 870
Félix (1) 3 233

Felix (3) 12 1691 15 1504 17 722
felix (1) 14 1239
Fell (3) 13 310 890 15 3713
fell (49) 1 315 2 217 375 3 14 350 4 326 6 48 417 683 701 732 872 7 573 593 747 8 161 244 580 910 10 251 253 986 1052 11 1021 1064 12 617 13 47 499 599 1168 1179 1270 14 416 448 893 1128 1136 15 3273 3595 3720 16 125 506 625 863 887 1473 18 133 490
fellaheen (1) 7 911
fellmongers (1) 15 1433
Fellow (5) 6 1013 8 673 10 513 16 580 678
fellow (129) 1 127 156 3 182 223 4 356 492 5 92 119 212 366 378 469 479 6 177 178 244 311 672 679 737 740 807 829 891 968 980 7 292 307 312 398 997 8 182 220 403 420 458 463 553 682 701 861 967 984 1107 1112 1144 9 614 824 10 383 479 905 1143 1146 11 70 153 281 438 450 471 1200 12 10 65 233 270 272 687 688 693 823 885 892 957 1055 1215 1239 1332 1580 1589 1604 1629 1661 13 205 807 829 1001 1061 14 506 739 783 806 1366 15 205 600 663 1098 1613 1800 2616 2671 3138 4874 16 68 205 529 641 653 684 846 949 1553 18 243 390 551 561 683 703 741 782 921 1041 1143 1311 1337 1409 1417 1478
fellow (2) 1 584 5 129
Fellowchristians (1) 15 1753
Fellowcountrymen (1) 15 1771
fellowcountrymen (1) 9 516
fellowcraft (1) 15 759
fellowfaces (1) 17 1184
fellowplayer (1) 9 746
fellow's (5) 6 818 8 753 12 1065 13 973 15 2120
Fellows (2) 11 1077 13 1050
fellows (29) 1 522 7 600 707 8 37 99 439 923 1007 10 748 784 11 154 12 443 482 1347 13 17 14 190 505 678 15 95 4052 16 27 66 847 869 1183 1601 1859 18 1170 1591
fellowship (1) 14 187
Fellowthatsolike (1) 15 4340
fells (1) 17 1702
felly (1) 6 490
felonsetting (1) 16 1052
felony (1) 17 2186
Felt (3) 6 522 8 854 13 796
felt (57) 1 123 225 4 72 327 449 460 5 78 250 7 29 8 1108 1135 1136 1141 9 836 868 10 70 11 293 692 1178 12 338 13 136 149 341 365 429 560 643 649 652 828 941 969 1178 1197 14 51 59 119 15 1054 2782 3243 16 406 762 1216 1221 1723 18 132 149 301 393 500 513 646 1062 1140 1351 1452 1579
felt (1) 10 611
Female (1) 12 547
FEMALE (1) 15 1875
female (33) 10 473 625 1194 13 85 1253 14 340 687 923 943 15 2221 2777 3010 16 713 895 931 1449 17 280 671 865 1216 1812 1998 2038 2078 2090 2124 2160 2216 2232 2277 2279 2284 2288
female (1) 9 24
female (4) 15 1614 2167 2482 2620
female's (2) 15 4540 16 720
FEMALES (1) 7 1014

females (12) 6 999 10 80 12 695 14 67 674 972 1289 1455 17 999 1411 1949 2291
feminam (1) 15 2372
feminine (9) 13 12 14 865 15 4376 16 1552 17 290 2053 2219 2221 2294
feminine (1) 15 2432
Femininum (1) 15 319
femininum (2) 10 849 861
FEMINIST (1) 15 1465
femme (2) 8 597 9 1135
femmes (1) 14 1494
fence (2) 11 1104 15 235
fencibles (1) 14 655
fender (1) 15 3188
fenians (1) 2 272
Fenius (1) 17 750
fennel (1) 4 91
fennygreek (1) 15 2363
fens (1) 17 227
Ferdinand (1) 17 723
ferenti (1) 10 841
Fergus (2) 12 1127 15 4932
Fergus (1) 1 241
Fergus' (1) 1 249
Ferguson (2) 15 4950 16 1560
ferial (1) 7 813
Fermanagh (1) 5 438
Fermé (1) 3 187
ferment (1) 8 671
fermenting (1) 7 82
fernfoils (2) 11 45 1108
ferns (4) 1 535 8 900 912 13 1179
ferocious (1) 18 630
ferocious (1) 15 4720
ferociously (1) 16 469
ferociously (1) 15 2928
ferons (1) 9 641
ferox (1) 15 712
Ferrando's (1) 3 100
Ferreol (1) 12 1692
ferreteyed (1) 4 152
ferreteyed (1) 15 987
ferry (2) 6 448 10 1098
ferrywash (1) 10 754
Fertiliser (1) 14 660
fertilising (1) 14 685
fertility (1) 17 2274
ferule (1) 1 628
fervent (1) 12 611
fervour (1) 14 311
fervour (2) 15 917 3406
festal (1) 15 1398
festivities (1) 16 1835
festivity (2) 15 1679 1681
festooned (1) 17 1803
festooned (1) 15 4921
fetch (4) 5 188 8 184 14 526 15 3088
fetched (6) 1 337 4 182 209 11 1204 14 400 725
fetching (1) 15 558
fete (1) 18 292
fêted (1) 16 1859
fetid (1) 16 22
fetor (1) 15 1796
Fetter (3) 9 651 11 907 16 1763
fetterchain (1) 15 313
fettered (1) 2 50
fettered (1) 15 4692

fetters (1) 12 1715
feudalism (1) 9 626
Fever (1) 11 940
fever (7) 1 226 7 165 12 977 1107 18 389 397 868
feverpits (1) 6 986
Few (2) 8 438 11 824
few (72) 1 113 548 3 143 4 203 404 5 225 6 551 565 873 887 908 1028 7 759 8 355 758 9 222 535 708 746 10 71 939 943 12 445 494 691 1368 1550 13 106 953 1278 1288 14 211 801 15 999 1967 3743 3789 4901 16 18 185 198 219 322 325 508 902 1025 1191 1275 1329 1367 1438 1457 1631 18 148 321 423 455 504 556 603 698 740 743 772 776 1057 1063 1415 1481 1526 1531
few (1) 7 857
few (1) 15 156
fez (1) 18 1495
fez (1) 15 728
Fff (3) 11 58 1247 1288
Ffoo (1) 5 208
ffrenchmullan (1) 12 670
fiacre (1) 14 492
Fiacre (3) 3 193 12 1291 1702
fiancée (1) 12 667
fiat (1) 14 1070
fib (1) 15 404
fibre (2) 10 300 17 305
fibres (1) 1 645
Fibres (1) 8 1136
fichue (3) 3 161 14 307 15 2583
fickle (1) 13 584
fiction (3) 9 844 15 1023 17 323
fictitious (1) 16 497
fiddle (2) 11 1161 15 2679
fiddlefaddle (1) 18 1156
Fiddlefaddle (1) 11 1195
fiddles (1) 11 574
fiddlestrings (1) 13 826
fiddling (1) 16 1206
fidelity (1) 17 1545
fides (1) 16 498
fidgets (3) 4 458 8 683 18 1010
Fido (1) 15 663
fidus (2) 6 49 16 54
fie (1) 9 72
field (28) 1 401 2 154 185 193 310 3 336 415 418 6 763 764 9 862 10 180 186 12 402 1309 1447 13 754 14 761 1129 1154 1386 15 3949 3966 16 531 1797 17 63 1603 2188
field (1) 15 3975
Field (5) 2 415 12 828 850 855 15 1249
Field (1) 8 339
fieldaltar (1) 15 4689
fieldglasses (2) 8 552 17 492
fieldglasses (1) 15 538
fieldlark (1) 12 161
fieldmarshal (2) 7 543 12 1383
fieldmarshals (1) 8 708
fields (11) 6 764 877 8 642 9 37 933 10 264 12 91 14 476 598 16 1728 18 1560
Fields (1) 8 902
fieldwork (1) 17 1593
fiendish (1) 15 1754
fiends (1) 9 495
fierce (4) 10 1002 1114 1261 15 2555

fierce (1) 15 4623
Fierce (1) 4 346
fiercely (1) 15 2552
Fiercely (1) 15 316
fiery (2) 2 144 3 193
fife (1) 15 1407
fifenote (1) 11 5
fifenotes (1) 11 218
fifteen (9) 2 135 5 310 6 620 696 968 8 1059 9 16 13 842 16 608
Fifteen (8) 4 135 141 415 5 310 6 485 8 31 13 890 15 359
fifteenth (1) 4 415
fifth (6) 6 394 679 9 672 11 1271 12 1859 15 4371
Fifth (1) 12 1306
fifthly (1) 17 440
fifths (1) 15 2073
fifty (15) 5 396 6 610 7 923 8 60 869 895 9 831 10 1134 11 1197 12 961 13 1137 14 476 518 15 2416 16 389
Fifty (1) 16 393
fiftyfive (1) 1 547
fiftythree (1) 7 924
Figather (1) 11 150
Figatner (1) 15 4357
Figatner's (1) 11 149
figged (1) 15 2942
Figgis' (1) 3 427
fight (16) 2 395 430 12 976 999 13 245 356 1082 14 1313 1342 15 967 4461 4632 4760 16 1306 18 395 699
fight (1) 2 397
fight (1) 15 4682
fighting (7) 8 714 12 1329 1356 15 780 2641 4593 18 642
figlia (1) 14 303
figlio (1) 14 303
Figne (1) 16 1454
figrolls (1) 2 22
figs (2) 11 150 12 93
figtrees (1) 18 1599
figuratively (1) 16 607
figure (38) 1 319 6 199 252 255 730 876 7 43 8 533 9 44 269 603 10 315 521 908 12 151 612 630 13 83 155 543 969 14 1045 1049 1211 15 2977 3102 16 105 112 128 665 675 1326 1445 1506 1855 17 783 18 448 891
figure (10) 15 212 214 248 748 1191 1236 2085 2262 3479 4956
FIGURE (1) 15 217
figured (1) 16 509
figures (11) 2 129 3 297 4 141 9 990 10 97 393 11 832 16 1699 1886 17 862 1750
figures (2) 15 1706 3220
Figures (2) 15 39 3408
Filberts (1) 10 953
filches (1) 9 919
file (6) 4 475 7 302 383 444 8 407 16 1372
file (2) 15 1325 3951
filed (2) 10 310 16 1494
files (5) 7 409 597 634 653 9 586
filibeg (1) 9 1148
filibegs (1) 2 266
filibegs (1) 15 2178
filibustering (1) 9 1148
Filii (1) 1 351

firstnamed (1) **17** 251
firstrate (2) **16** 519 1222
firstshot (1) **12** 1527
firtree (1) **18** 790 824
firtrees (1) **17** 1584
fish (22) **3** 478 **4** 220 **8** 79 86 858 867 891 **12** 73 214 1055 1254 1753 **13** 1162 **14** 548 693 **16** 275 867 **17** 430 900 **18** 546 939 1421
Fish (1) **15** 154
fished (1) **6** 283
Fisher (1) **17** 1647
fisherman's (1) **14** 251
fishermens (1) **18** 975
fishes (7) **3** 472 **6** 88 **12** 81 1724 **14** 150 152 720
fishes (1) **15** 1569
fishes' (1) **8** 892
fishful (1) **12** 71
Fishgluey (1) **10** 622
fishgods (1) **1** 366
Fishguard-Rosslare (1) **16** 533
fishingcap (1) **15** 1741
fishingrods (1) **17** 1563
Fish's (1) **6** 520
fishslicers (1) **18** 433
fishwoman (1) **18** 1067
fishy (1) **8** 79
fissure (1) **17** 374
fist (6) **8** 892 **10** 126 127 **12** 1471 **14** 313 **16** 975
fist (3) **15** 477 2942 4747
fistic (1) **12** 976
fists (2) **3** 103 **10** 834
fists (1) **15** 3195
fit (14) **1** 114 **5** 167 **11** 359 523 581 608 **12** 30 98 **13** 323 954 **15** 854 3458 **18** 893 1113
Fit (2) **11** 1161 **15** 2789
fitly (2) **13** 444 **14** 1118
fitments (1) **17** 1530
fitness (1) **14** 905
fits (5) **1** 110 **15** 3257 **16** 601 1275 **18** 211
Fits (1) **10** 745
fitted (5) **4** 296 382 **6** 587 **14** 254 **17** 1522
Fitted (1) **8** 168
Fitter (1) **12** 398
fittest (3) **14** 794 1285 **16** 1602
Fitton (1) **9** 638
Fitz (1) **16** 1066
Fitzedward (1) **15** 4687
Fitzgerald (4) **3** 314 **7** 305 **10** 448 785
Fitzgerald (1) **15** 4686
Fitzgeralds (1) **10** 439
Fitzgibbon (4) **7** 794 798 **10** 47 **17** 139
Fitzgibbon (1) **15** 4343
Fitzgibbon's (2) **7** 823 **14** 494
Fitzharris (3) **7** 641 **16** 324 1044
Fitzmaurice (6) **8** 302 **9** 1116 **10** 919 1102 1106 1261
Fitzmaurice (1) **15** 2308
Fitzpatrick (1) **17** 544
Fitzsimon (1) **12** 90
Fitzsimons (2) **10** 1146 1148
five (74) **1** 673 **2** 258 **3** 8 197 470 **4** 131 284 **6** 939 **8** 126 384 385 481 790 1016 **9** 134 537 1020 **10** 117 389 396 648 680 974

976 **11** 189 881 1024 **12** 37 41 323 327 442 517 533 800 1122 1425 1556 1562 1565 1663 1761 1909 **13** 166 1172 1232 **14** 1126 1371 1450 **15** 647 1149 1643 1647 2416 3034 3476 3606 3906 **16** 509 838 1326 **17** 86 96 122 150 298 307 662 1690 1836 1882
five (2) **8** 778 **12** 428
five (1) **15** 1825
Five (15) **1** 365 **3** 12 470 **6** 539 540 **8** 1059 **9** 205 **10** 2 377 647 **11** 805 866 **14** 1467 1477 **15** 1183
fivebarred (1) **8** 348
fives (1) **17** 1552
fiveseater (1) **15** 547
fix (3) **7** 431 **14** 145 795
fixe (1) **10** 1068
fixed (10) **8** 247 432 **10** 1084 1218 **13** 563 **15** 733 1158 **17** 1053 2014 2264
fixes (3) **15** 1262 2005 4160
fixing (1) **5** 495
fixtures (1) **17** 418
fizz (2) **12** 1025 **15** 4861
Fizz (1) **8** 865
fizzing (1) **15** 3851
fjords (1) **17** 219
flabbergasted (2) **12** 337 **16** 1273
flabbily (1) **3** 30
flabby (1) **4** 106
flabbyarse (1) **12** 1568
flag (11) **8** 161 **9** 155 **12** 1307 1308 1541 **14** 480 1128 **15** 3948 **16** 899 1113
flag (1) **15** 1411
Flag (1) **6** 869
flagellate (2) **18** 495 963
flagged (1) **1** 315
FLAGGER (1) **15** 1458
flagon (4) **10** 1237 **11** 360 **12** 1616 **14** 742
flagons (1) **10** 1237
flags (2) **6** 130 **12** 1839
Flaherty's (1) **15** 2676
flahoolagh (1) **12** 691
flair (1) **14** 1359
flakes (1) **17** 2125
Flakes (1) **8** 271
flambeau (1) **14** 675
flambeaus (1) **14** 354
flame (8) **2** 10 **3** 240 248 **10** 404 **11** 668 **13** 667 **17** 106 124
flame (3) **15** 2289 3232 4244
flames (1) **14** 145
flames (2) **15** 1927 1936
flaming (3) **1** 620 **3** 391 **13** 366
flaming (1) **7** 522
flaming (1) **15** 514
flan (1) **3** 214
Flanagan (1) **12** 938
Flanders (1) **18** 658
flange (1) **17** 103
flank (2) **10** 1021 **14** 1210
flanks (2) **6** 390 **10** 1096
flannel (1) **18** 961
flannel (1) **15** 875
flannelette (1) **13** 1235
flannels (1) **15** 4396
flap (1) **5** 78
Flap (1) **8** 768
Flapdoodle (1) **8** 382
flapper (1) **15** 2340

flapping (6) **1** 707 **8** 51 61 83 **10** 811 821
flapping (1) **15** 2476
flaps (1) **15** 365
Flaps (1) **8** 63
flare (1) **10** 398
flaring (1) **15** 137
flash (12) **1** 130 **3** 477 **5** 130 **6** 988 **9** 662 **10** 759 **12** 1024 **13** 513 1070 **14** 1387 **15** 370 **18** 885
flashed (4) **6** 199 322 **10** 1111 **13** 590
flasher (1) **15** 167
flashes (1) **12** 529
flashes (5) **15** 1207 2071 2257 2308 4126
flashing (5) **2** 159 **4** 23 **5** 335 **13** 1138 **16** 1652
flashing (2) **15** 3988 4058
Flashing (1) **15** 415
flashlight (1) **15** 1588
flaskets (1) **12** 92
flasks (1) **16** 925
flat (21) **1** 721 **3** 418 419 **4** 274 **7** 448 **8** 393 631 **10** 1258 **11** 602 836 847 848 864 **12** 982 **15** 3566 3629 **16** 864 **17** 324 1675 **18** 451 1250
flat (2) **15** 1343 2575
Flat (2) **3** 418 **5** 279
flatcaps (1) **14** 537
flatcut (1) **8** 1106
flatfoot (2) **13** 1259 **15** 3176
Flathouse (1) **15** 3957
flatly (1) **11** 247
flatly (1) **15** 3442
flats (1) **18** 856
flattened (1) **5** 239
flattening (1) **11** 74
flatter (1) **9** 874
Flatter (1) **9** 874
flattered (1) **15** 1998
flatteries (1) **14** 451
flatteringly (1) **14** 452
Flatters (1) **13** 884
Flattery (1) **8** 575
flatties (1) **15** 1922
flatulence (1) **7** 96
flatulent (1) **12** 1392
flaunted (1) **9** 1100
flaunting (1) **15** 3847
Flavin (1) **12** 934
flavour (1) **8** 720
flaw (2) **4** 211 **9** 1219
Flaw (1) **11** 619
flawless (1) **13** 583
flaws (1) **3** 375
flax (1) **12** 1243
flaxenhaired (1) **15** 3355
Flaxseed (1) **6** 124
flay (1) **15** 1083
flayed (2) **12** 168 1357
Flayed (1) **8** 726
flayers' (1) **3** 305
flea (1) **15** 3184
Flea (1) **8** 799
fleas (1) **18** 935
flecked (1) **13** 211
flecks (1) **15** 1275
fled (1) **6** 169
fled (1) **6** 164
fleece (1) **14** 1419
Fleece (1) **15** 4451

188 231 233 245 286 294 307 320 323 328 342 350
376 377 380 393 396 409 411 423 429 458 474 501
513 519 545 552 553 557 559 564 569 578 605 608
680 695 703 705 706 723 760 773 781 793 797 832
854 857 860 886 908 931 934 938 943 946 976 981
984 992 1008 1019 **7** 4 18 51 88 95 96 124 153
159 194 223 248 263 265 293 306 311 313 319 375
388 403 417 432 455 466 475 477 553 583 612 616
625 630 635 645 654 667 686 711 725 729 736 738
741 745 795 815 935 949 951 973 982 983 997 998
1004 1008 1044 **8** 2 3 21 25 30 36 39 56 69 75 81
96 99 115 138 151 161 188 190 195 204 208 259
263 290 321 322 324 334 335 342 344 355 356 357
376 389 392 399 412 415 424 429 430 435 463 469
471 492 510 515 588 605 613 628 634 655 690 701
714 723 729 733 771 814 826 827 828 856 863 871
886 940 953 998 1003 1008 1027 1061 1073 1096
1119 1125 1129 1130 1145 1148 1155 1163 1164
1173 1182 1188 1191 **9** 27 39 53 70 130 132 141
173 186 215 216 265 282 310 322 369 375 438 442
451 454 518 520 527 537 539 559 562 566 569 577
587 639 644 658 663 664 693 694 746 747 752 757
759 783 785 795 804 810 814 870 879 895 904 925
972 981 1036 1037 1071 1081 1082 1131 1167 1195
1206 **10** 9 10 12 20 33 114 120 135 172 274 322
329 390 394 400 461 468 482 505 526 621 648 656
657 699 701 706 719 723 744 748 779 837 847 863
869 893 898 910 915 935 943 974 982 985 1001
1011 1019 1021 1085 1114 1124 1134 1144 1146
1148 1156 1168 1193 1200 1207 1269 **11** 34 51
88 105 110 111 125 127 187 211 234 247 260 264
277 288 289 317 347 350 359 365 422 444 486 523
555 581 608 671 688 692 698 711 765 834 844 846
857 870 877 935 960 1001 1002 1015 1035 1042
1060 1079 1083 1101 1102 1110 1113 1139 1144
1187 1188 1199 1222 1228 1231 1267 **12** 10 21
41 80 88 90 98 120 123 126 142 162 185 236 237
242 261 269 271 297 357 358 359 365 368 379 398
442 445 448 453 479 482 487 497 500 507 509 536
540 545 550 580 604 621 629 630 638 652 659 678
681 702 709 732 748 754 767 771 781 790 804 823
833 834 835 837 847 861 869 895 901 909 945 951
961 962 963 976 978 1032 1048 1061 1088 1093
1101 1108 1123 1124 1125 1140 1147 1169 1172
1223 1233 1254 1255 1264 1315 1321 1323 1336
1359 1377 1379 1384 1390 1424 1425 1462 1476
1481 1517 1574 1601 1608 1642 1644 1668 1673
1730 1731 1753 1756 1761 1779 1791 1792 1799
1811 1817 1849 1854 1899 1900 1908 1913
13 17 29 52 53 54 119 134 136 149 171 179 180
182 185 196 216 222 223 226 233 236 238 240 242
244 256 278 288 300 308 314 320 323 330 340 355
356 373 374 375 376 377 381 388 389 417 440 444
452 454 461 463 469 487 500 504 509 516 526 566
568 585 588 593 601 607 643 649 650 653 663 667
672 744 748 787 789 790 794 796 798 804 813 816
840 843 866 870 884 894 896 899 902 911 912 918
919 920 954 969 970 987 1005 1028 1073 1081 1122
1123 1132 1143 1152 1156 1161 1167 1177 1183
1184 1195 1203 1206 1212 1220 1221 1222 1228
1236 1237 1244 1254 1257 1271 1281 1288
14 15 28 47 49 51 75 78 83 97 108 109 117 119
120 129 130 132 133 136 139 143 160 162 163 165
168 174 177 179 181 196 198 199 200 204 210 217
220 240 249 250 252 257 261 268 269 270 272 273
274 275 279 280 284 287 301 309 320 324 330 342
344 350 353 356 359 361 373 378 379 382 404 411
422 430 434 439 445 460 464 470 472 481 488 501
507 510 513 521 523 525 526 531 533 536 547 561

570 571 575 584 589 594 602 604 611 624 629 636
655 657 663 682 686 689 691 695 699 710 719 736
751 758 762 777 788 792 798 802 805 825 836 839
853 854 859 868 871 873 890 903 911 929 936 947
954 990 1004 1016 1018 1031 1050 1051 1053 1054
1065 1076 1077 1120 1124 1127 1149 1158 1186
1221 1233 1250 1278 1295 1309 1311 1317 1339
1340 1353 1359 1398 1405 1433 1440 1461 1467
1470 1497 1498 1504 1509 1511 1522 1535 1542
1553 1561 1566 1573 1590 **15** 65 93 211 235 279
332 381 385 405 411 429 434 477 493 495 498 526
566 586 603 620 638 640 642 644 647 669 670 700
701 709 720 750 780 794 833 886 892 940 955 970
979 1040 1046 1088 1093 1100 1145 1231 1254
1272 1283 1289 1372 1393 1397 1516 1564 1594
1643 1673 1674 1685 1686 1687 1688 1691 1737
1760 1776 1809 1922 1936 1941 1942 1943 1944
1945 1946 1947 1948 1949 1950 1951 1952 1954
1963 1964 1985 1998 2070 2105 2231 2258 2259
2331 2360 2374 2394 2422 2447 2558 2566 2580
2702 2739 2789 2806 2824 2866 2885 2893 2934
2941 2944 2964 2966 2980 3022 3043 3086 3090
3127 3136 3138 3142 3178 3186 3249 3257 3321
3335 3538 3556 3580 3607 3693 3698 3866 3886
3888 3914 3926 4003 4024 4196 4197 4202 4238
4268 4275 4312 4403 4407 4434 4470 4472 4473
4487 4569 4606 4639 4713 4742 4797 4863 4869
4875 **16** 5 7 25 32 39 46 50 65 67 70 72 75 80
104 120 158 165 170 184 186 200 201 202 209 213
214 222 224 236 241 251 271 273 274 285 291 305
324 329 338 345 368 380 385 406 407 420 421 424
436 482 483 492 511 536 541 543 546 548 549 550
553 589 590 634 643 656 695 698 711 732 753 757
766 769 779 788 795 796 799 805 811 813 823 836
873 880 907 911 918 926 936 941 950 967 974 999
1007 1008 1019 1024 1031 1033 1042 1048 1058
1061 1066 1070 1075 1078 1085 1086 1089 1096
1123 1137 1141 1153 1154 1161 1179 1185 1194
1205 1219 1220 1222 1239 1274 1300 1308 1341
1352 1396 1404 1430 1436 1444 1445 1447 1457
1458 1461 1462 1465 1470 1492 1494 1519 1532
1546 1548 1551 1584 1603 1604 1611 1620 1621
1630 1635 1650 1667 1684 1693 1699 1707 1733
1736 1751 1752 1754 1755 1766 1788 1796 1824
1830 1836 1837 1842 1843 1850 1854 1855 1863
1865 **17** 89 92 125 126 136 172 175 215 233 236
314 354 356 357 358 365 372 386 394 418 437 452
485 487 492 507 508 514 549 550 565 569 636 648
652 663 688 737 767 787 798 844 853 896 924 973
983 984 1008 1092 1138 1218 1307 1400 1401 1410
1455 1465 1484 1518 1544 1548 1558 1561 1615
1616 1638 1650 1651 1657 1665 1678 1691 1710
1711 1714 1716 1718 1719 1720 1723 1724 1739
1740 1741 1744 1757 1814 1820 1824 1862 1879
1884 1913 1930 1937 1945 1965 1980 2004 2031
2075 2147 2157 2159 2203 2295 **18** 4 5 6 18 20
44 60 69 72 98 100 113 117 121 140 157 177 197
199 202 210 228 229 235 239 258 261 262 275 276
302 304 312 317 318 324 327 346 358 361 367 378
396 403 411 416 417 423 425 432 435 436 438 454
471 474 483 490 495 509 510 527 530 537 538 547
560 568 571 574 587 603 619 625 628 675 684 685
688 691 707 714 719 746 762 773 776 796 799 800
801 805 842 863 866 898 925 930 935 942 943 947
952 956 964 984 989 990 993 1001 1002 1004 1016
1023 1025 1033 1041 1043 1055 1056 1057 1065
1068 1071 1072 1090 1093 1096 1102 1112 1121
1126 1129 1143 1153 1156 1162 1168 1178 1183
1186 1209 1210 1211 1212 1232 1236 1243 1246

1249 1255 1280 1289 1293 1298 1308 1309 1310
1317 1319 1320 1323 1328 1339 1349 1350 1351
1368 1371 1377 1380 1381 1389 1392 1398 1412
1415 1422 1426 1429 1430 1435 1439 1455 1473
1480 1490 1492 1493 1502 1510 1519 1526 1537
1541 1543 1556 1563 1564 1567 1572 1578 1595
for (21) 2 14 106 **7** 321 **8** 68 **9** 551 726
807 1014 1152 **10** 139 612 621 1255 **12** 29
222 422 **14** 650 **16** 1250 **17** 398 803
for (22) **15** 32 74 147 311 323 1501 1570 1575
1579 1619 1702 1710 1812 1984 2668 3219 3317
3757 3953 3957 4149 4914
foraneous (1) 14 383
forbear (1) 14 718
forbearance (2) 10 1094 14 868
forbid (1) 14 873
forbidden (2) 13 1038 17 1989
forbidding (3) 12 858 14 979 1008
Force (2) 12 1481 15 3243
force (14) 5 46 **12** 9 556 1361 1364 1475
15 2197 2976 16 1132 1214 17 102 1857
forced (4) 16 687 1213 17 1162 1668
forcemeat (1) 4 143
forceps (2) 8 375 12 1718
forces (3) 17 402 2028 2188
forcible-feeble (1) 16 986
forcibly (3) 12 904 16 1045 1182
forcingcase (1) 15 1035
ford (1) 10 930
fordo (1) 14 83
fordone (1) 11 162
fore (9) 6 584 10 340 12 1308 15 2357
16 289 1283 17 1485 1810 2099
fore (1) 15 2682
forearm (5) 1 438 3 77 8 627 12 616
17 1818
forearm (2) 15 759 2076
foreboard (1) 8 127
forecast (2) 9 134 14 861
foreclosure (1) 17 1668
forefathers (2) 10 1012 12 907
forefinger (5) 1 588 2 345 5 77
10 1069 1188
forefinger (8) 15 134 2012 2058 2337 3124
3394 3751 3916
forefingers (1) 7 132
foregoing (1) 16 1013
foregone (1) 16 1601
forehead (11) 5 7 8 374 1108 9 436
10 958 1051 13 328 1137 14 775 1109
15 1468
forehead (6) 15 312 959 1164 2152 2894 3656
forehoofs (1) 3 338
Foreign (2) 12 138 17 1658
foreign (11) 12 554 599 13 658 1210 1302
14 1370 15 942 3924 16 958 1176
17 685
foreigner (1) 13 416
foreigners (1) 16 591
foreigns (1) 15 3887
foreland (1) 17 1716
foreleg (1) 10 1232
foreleg (1) 15 320
forelock (1) 14 601
forelock (1) 15 2721
foreman (7) 7 108 125 130 147 154 159 180
foreman (1) 15 1140
foreman's (2) 7 85 135
foremost (2) 16 1693 1785

foremother (1) 8 576
forensic (2) 7 735 14 978
forepassed (1) 14 273
forepaws (1) 3 360
forepaws (1) 15 2574
foresaid (1) 14 288
foresaw (1) 5 567
foresee (5) 2 401 8 215 9 178 16 1834
　17 1581
foresight (2) 14 63 772
foreskin (1) 13 979
Forest (1) 12 1295
forest (6) 8 881 9 580 879 14 712
　15 2448 3353
forest (1) 7 247
Forester's (1) 15 3305
Foresters (1) 12 1268
forests (2) 9 822 17 261
foretell (1) 9 435
foretold (1) 9 1051
Forfeits (1) 15 3511
forger (1) 15 1159
forgeries (1) 16 781
forgery (1) 17 2184
forges (1) 15 8
Forget (4) 3 184 5 294 15 1108 3867
forget (38) 1 197 2 11 272 3 58 5 289
　6 854 7 541 544 545 8 845 9 440 723
　10 39 11 146 613 623 779 940 12 644
　13 257 275 299 438 807 843 14 371 1068 1522
　1588 15 1360 3200 17 79 18 112 270 460
　1117 1144
forgetfully (1) 9 240
forgetmenot (1) 5 265
forgets (3) 6 710 14 912 18 1250
forgetting (8) 9 241 11 307 14 1263
　16 649 1267 1383 18 943 1534
Forgive (2) 15 1929 3151
forgive (8) 6 299 485 13 437 14 89
　15 477 1108 4742
forgiveness (1) 16 1538
forgiving (1) 13 765
Forgot (1) 9 1134
forgot (22) 3 407 5 468 6 831 7 166
　231 325 8 372 9 241 1134 1140 10 444
　1245 11 314 1210 13 333 15 2226 3151
　17 701 18 253 288 694 1527
Forgotten (3) 4 60 11 807 13 1115
forgotten (22) 1 307 308 3 263 4 365
　5 232 6 872 8 521 9 151 975 11 392
　12 1842 14 912 987 15 720 2126 2384 2764
　4433 16 19 17 78 1419 18 1472
Fork (1) 13 993
fork (11) 1 43 3 218 4 296 385 8 237
　657 673 689 11 848 12 136 13 992
fork (2) 15 2159 2601
forkfingers (1) 11 683
forkful (1) 4 390
forks (4) 8 718 12 1532 15 2708
　18 433
forlorn (4) 11 331 13 1232 14 1551
　16 1293
forlornlooking (1) 18 1255
forlornly (2) 15 1323 2451
form (56) 1 314 386 404 2 75 76 179
　3 280 414 4 21 6 249 8 295 465 1127
　9 208 248 10 997 1118 11 719 720 1253
　12 241 639 668 920 1287 13 503 969
　14 662 957 1209 1516 15 2098 3028 3424

16 895 948 984 1057 1100 1449 1521 1572 1733
　17 260 527 625 649 780 1193 1663 1844 1966
　2123 2124 18 324
form (2) 7 769 11 665
form (7) 15 26 248 1572 2179 2697 4927 4947
formalities (1) 13 397
formation (2) 17 199 872
formativus (1) 14 1238
formed (5) 2 68 5 163 16 330 17 1055
　1995
former (13) 12 1876 14 894 1262
　15 1506 16 322 1328 1662 17 250 578 957
　959 1296 1642
former (1) 15 1508
formerly (3) 12 715 17 512 1870
former's (1) 16 494
formidable (3) 12 165 16 585 17 1827
formidavit (1) 10 205
forming (1) 17 1222
Formless (1) 9 61
formless (1) 9 49
Forms (1) 6 487
forms (17) 2 75 76 196 3 280 6 487 488
　8 928 9 208 209 10 342 1225 11 434
　12 1776 17 218 1097 1143 2228
formulated (1) 17 1710
fornicating (1) 12 803
fornication (1) 14 369
foror (1) 11 552
Forrest (2) 12 229 1277
forsaken (1) 11 954
forsooth (1) 14 1423
Fort (4) 16 418 17 1975
forte (1) 18 1508
forte (1) 17 1309
Forth (1) 11 216
forth (44) 1 447 527 4 539 5 79 6 678
　7 434 572 8 531 1176 9 381 750 1200
　10 222 252 253 433 553 700 922 11 1157
　12 49 287 454 1136 1441 1598 13 6 626
　14 75 109 117 176 209 375 390 473 873 1120
　1348 15 2117 2435 16 868 1197 1306
forth (3) 7 328 9 96 1043
forth (3) 15 1236 2606 4017
forthbringing (1) 14 63
forthcoming (4) 12 863 16 268 1696 1856
forthflowing (1) 3 467
fortitude (1) 14 822
fortnight (7) 5 485 8 587 832 12 21
　13 333 508 16 1318
fortunate (2) 15 1048 16 1824
fortunately (2) 14 16 16 1512
Fortune (2) 11 373 12 820
fortune (4) 8 331 11 370 12 822
　17 1933
fortuned (1) 14 232
fortune's (1) 3 312
fortunes (3) 7 569 14 535 17 1750
Forty (1) 12 1529
forty (9) 9 681 13 464 902 15 2572 3107
　4198 16 214 1551 18 51
forty (1) 15 1549
fortyfive (1) 12 1917
fortyfoot (2) 1 600 12 1263
fortyfour (1) 8 326
fortyone (1) 12 1864
fortythreebutton (1) 15 3079
Forward (2) 14 1443 1562
forward (45) 1 9 135 326 389 564 594 2 81

123 375 3 123 137 358 5 263 421 7 174
　8 108 809 1091 9 5 90 291 485 585 10 233
　240 246 664 757 796 933 952 11 233 12 660
　1773 13 217 481 742 14 14 235 1365
　15 2847 16 1053 17 2308 18 875 1116
forward (28) 15 141 164 184 192 222 372 513
　578 613 632 704 1038 1246 1267 1585 2146 2479
　2571 2698 2885 3044 3195 3242 4045 4251 4447
　4551 4611
fossicle (1) 17 1440
fossilised (1) 17 261
Foster (1) 16 1583
foster (1) 14 863
Foster's (1) 17 1775
fostersister (1) 16 151
Fottrell (1) 12 1872
FOTTRELL (1) 15 895
fou (3) 14 1505 1565
fought (8) 12 977 1379 13 582 14 1313
　1342 15 794 4606 16 1042
fought (1) 7 428
foul (8) 3 476 4 316 6 701 9 632
　10 808 14 457 464 15 842
foul (1) 15 2942
Found (2) 3 471 6 348
found (54) 1 684 4 294 467 5 23 25 172
　433 6 479 725 7 199 8 865 1191 9 18
　483 583 609 1041 1089 10 1144 11 407 408
　876 12 722 728 1216 13 159 211 342 512 645
　14 38 433 527 550 627 1180 1214 15 1799
　2087 3245 16 18 185 975 1620 1683 1768
　17 388 18 58 68 236 381 501 1084 1393
Foundation (1) 6 320
foundation (1) 8 12
founded (8) 5 465 9 841 12 221 787
　14 252 15 2642
foundered (1) 7 566
Foundling (1) 12 547
foundry (1) 15 170
fountain (2) 6 191 8 711
fountain (1) 15 1328
Four (13) 1 293 296 297 4 487 6 231
　10 646 837 1190 11 385 445 1242 14 1137
　17 320
Four (1) 15 1440
four (77) 4 11 272 285 298 5 307 309 6 91
　582 7 32 220 385 410 654 882 939 941 8 733
　9 37 552 677 988 1011 10 116 240 395 483
　1237 11 188 305 308 309 352 392 683 962 1073
　12 1241 1443 1444 1829 13 16 173 725 847
　1068 14 142 461 462 598 816 912 1151 1181
　1371 15 868 887 1022 3119 3258 3264
　16 838 1091 1697 17 91 95 114 152 300 303
　355 375 402 1305 18 333 466 741
four (3) 15 921 2240 3750
Fourbottle (1) 10 768
fourcorners (1) 15 1602
fourflushers (1) 14 1583
fourfold (1) 11 684
fourhundredandeighth (1) 9 518
fourleaved (1) 12 668
Fourpence (1) 5 511
fourpence (6) 1 444 5 308 309 10 670
　16 1697 17 233
fourpenceworth (1) 7 939
fours (2) 3 344 16 1045
fours (1) 15 2852
Fourteen (1) 15 3103
fourteen (1) 17 1863

fourth (2) 17 715 1207
fourthly (1) 17 436
fourths (1) 16 628
fourwalker (1) 16 1784
fourwheeler (1) 16 26
fourworded (1) 3 456
Foutinus (1) 14 236
fowl (4) 6 1009 8 722 17 1687 18 1589
fowl (1) 12 422
fowlingpiece (1) 15 3160
fowlrun (1) 17 1568
fowls (1) 4 2
Fownes's (1) 10 1227
Fox (3) 9 340 15 1762 16 1323
fox (11) 2 115 148 8 342 11 248 13 199 15 1695 3464 3486 3577 3610
fox (2) 15 2039 3952
foxeyes (1) 4 186
Foxford (1) 12 1246
Foxrock (1) 15 547
Foxy (1) 3 112
foxy (2) 12 13 67
foxy (1) 15 1000
Fr (1) 12 930
fracas (1) 16 1497
fraction (5) 14 283 15 429 17 846 927 1277
fractions (1) 17 1882
fractious (1) 15 711
fracture (1) 12 469
fractured (1) 17 2102
Fragende (1) 15 3652
fragility (1) 13 84
fragment (4) 7 270 15 3038 17 1491 1926
Fragments (1) 6 461
fragments (6) 6 488 8 75 17 320 724 1494 1950
fragrance (1) 4 306
fragrant (4) 13 371 372 14 1363 1367
Fraidrine (1) 9 1084
Frail (1) 9 1218
frail (3) 7 835 9 1036 15 1067
Frailty (2) 12 1227 15 3277
frame (5) 3 82 4 372 12 174 13 581 17 1297
Framed (1) 2 300
framed (2) 14 664 15 3263
franc (1) 17 1682
français (1) 12 1389
France (4) 3 257 9 108 12 1381 17 1739
Frances (1) 14 1330
Francis (10) 10 108 12 1026 1684 14 350 1110 17 93 144 627 1641 2140
Francois (1) 18 488
francs (1) 9 629
Francy (1) 12 180
frangibility (1) 17 2212
Frank (6) 9 440 14 545 552 554 841 17 1175
frank (2) 1 180 12 656
frankeyed (1) 12 152
Franklin (2) 12 187 14 469
franklin (4) 14 172 177 190 217
Frankly (1) 15 565
frankly (6) 1 51 10 341 15 3032 16 295 1459 1714
Franks (2) 8 98 15 2633
Frantic (1) 7 928

FRANZ (2) 15 1914 4506
frate (1) 3 385
fraternity (2) 12 1086 16 835
fratres (1) 14 366
fratricidal (1) 14 958
fratricide (2) 7 748 15 761
Frau (1) 15 3652
fraud (1) 5 391
frauds (1) 12 1581
fraudulent (1) 17 1939
Frauenzimmer (1) 3 30
Frauenzimmer (1) 15 4145
fraught (1) 17 285
fray (1) 9 447
frayed (2) 6 160 7 487
fraying (1) 1 101
freak (1) 18 311
freckled (1) 5 184
freckled (1) 15 340
Fred (2) 2 256 9 1082
Freddy (2) 13 318 18 1293
Freddy (1) 15 3845
FREDDY (1) 15 3848
Frederick (9) 8 1088 1138 1151 12 1096 1121 1875 14 1329 17 94 334
Frederick (1) 15 1162
Free (6) 8 770 12 1543 15 1630 1693 1695 3936
free (44) 1 626 636 2 226 388 6 915 934 8 962 1037 9 36 117 1016 10 69 733 11 413 814 12 692 1373 1450 13 673 14 768 1151 1501 15 631 1693 1695 4738 16 340 796 866 17 105 132 867 897 1219 1596 1828 1865 2163 18 427 909
free (1) 1 590
free (6) 15 301 441 1570 2300 4447 4966
freed (4) 1 182 8 499 10 361 17 1725
freedom (1) 15 1519
freefly (1) 11 160
freehold (1) 14 682
freely (5) 12 577 980 1519 17 88 103
freely (1) 15 4049
freelyfreckled (1) 12 153
Freeman (3) 15 1944 18 504 1227
Freeman (13) 4 101 5 49 6 884 7 43 66 652 8 941 953 1188 9 586 11 856 859 1123
FREEMAN (1) 15 1531
Freeman's (7) 7 44 118 9 595 15 812 17 336 1459
Freemans (1) 18 600
freemason (2) 12 300 18 382
freemasons (1) 18 1227
freemasons' (1) 8 1151
freemen (1) 15 1376
Freer (1) 11 1182
frees (1) 9 721
frees (1) 15 4095
freewheel (2) 13 632 17 1576
Freeze (1) 8 512
freeze (2) 14 1010 16 1632
freezing (1) 17 1246
fren (1) 14 1556
French (34) 1 425 543 2 249 3 198 5 526 7 887 8 857 891 9 115 123 315 766 1065 1101 10 182 867 869 1228 12 1297 1378 1385 13 486 877 14 363 552 553 777 15 700 2710 16 1287 17 1398 18 1189 1235
Frenchy (2) 12 804 14 1503

frend (1) 14 1539
frenzied (1) 12 985
frenzy (1) 17 1148
frequency (1) 17 2149
frequent (5) 6 487 17 670 1574 1927 18 1169
frequentative (1) 17 382
frequented (1) 17 555
frequently (8) 1 393 16 504 1062 17 55 657 682 1283 1419
frere (1) 14 192
Fresh (3) 4 136 9 1090 15 359
FRESH (1) 9 1187
fresh (32) 1 601 4 44 483 5 501 505 6 623 990 999 7 612 8 729 818 948 1003 9 341 10 818 11 211 619 12 652 664 849 13 10 14 1217 15 3893 16 433 632 1727 17 233 317 1594 1831 18 938 1501
fresh (1) 15 4140
freshcheeked (1) 10 1216
freshened (1) 1 573
fresher (1) 17 282
freshest (1) 14 883
freshets (1) 17 206
freshfound (1) 15 4335
freshly (2) 4 120 14 1129
freshness (1) 13 127
freshprinted (1) 5 58
fret (1) 7 380
fretted (2) 1 102 11 331
Freytag (1) 17 1383
friar (3) 9 560 14 1525 16 169
friar's (1) 14 336
friars (4) 12 1679 1681 1684 1686
Friction (1) 13 1084
friction (1) 17 105
Friday (12) 5 128 6 811 812 12 508 13 187 16 273 1576 17 932 18 69 594 939 1107
Fridays (2) 15 869 18 1550
Fried (2) 4 45 8 151
fried (7) 1 317 3 97 4 3 11 520 12 627 13 1294
Friend (3) 4 440 12 824 15 1950
friend (58) 3 168 450 5 134 6 41 454 710 723 7 648 735 953 8 219 9 856 10 966 11 376 476 957 12 54 221 365 776 861 1223 14 97 362 594 653 665 717 779 1154 1368 1590 15 490 688 1283 1636 1772 2246 2396 2417 2437 3400 3998 4390 4786 4874 16 109 265 281 471 858 1070 1323 1526 1594 17 1401 18 612 727
friend (2) 5 115 7 830
friend (1) 15 4346
friendlier (1) 16 1136
friendliness (2) 5 150 16 301
Friendly (1) 17 1659
friendly (8) 1 35 283 6 327 9 290 10 358 14 549 16 1803 18 1533
friendly (2) 15 329 4469
friend's (4) 10 945 14 272 16 498 821
Friends (2) 12 130 554
friends (27) 2 290 4 404 6 523 8 225 9 647 723 11 566 961 12 131 523 716 1609 1814 13 9 50 665 809 14 639 15 1601 3688 16 145 1191 17 1832 2010 18 1086 1393 1456
friends (2) 12 362 16 1253
friends (1) 15 1426
friendship (5) 1 308 14 198 17 12 1641 18 1270

friers (1) 16 867
Friery (1) 18 1070
frieze (1) 17 1536
frieze (1) 15 386
frigging (1) 18 88
fright (5) 6 281 11 1259 12 1855
　13 913 18 338
fright (1) 15 4186
frighted (1) 9 342
Frightened (1) 13 1202
frightened (1) 18 1002
Frightening (1) 13 1191
frightens (1) 13 1128
frightful (3) 11 79 14 143 18 791
frightfully (1) 13 146
frigid (3) 14 882 16 1337 17 202
Frigidian (1) 12 1700
frigidity (1) 17 1149
Frillies (1) 15 1950
frillies (2) 11 1188 13 1281
frillies (1) 10 609
frilly (1) 15 2982
fringe (4) 7 248 11 637 12 1283
　17 1293
fringe (3) 15 2871 4366 4722
fringed (1) 15 2743
fringes (1) 15 2979
Frisco (1) 14 1585
frisk (1) 15 591
FRISKY (1) 7 1070
frisky (1) 3 255
frittered (1) 16 85
Fritz (1) 15 713
Fritz (1) 15 1578
frivol (1) 15 428
frivolity (1) 14 899
Fro (2) 11 47 1113
fro (13) 1 314 582 7 826 9 329 377 1190
　11 47 571 1113 13 21 719 752 14 1482
fro (5) 15 2020 2157 2670 4585 4910
frock (5) 7 802 14 1144 15 2966
　18 612 858
frock (1) 15 471
frockcoat (4) 6 842 8 310 10 57 738
frockcoat (2) 15 935 4035
Frockcoats (1) 10 795
frocks (1) 15 2978
frocktails (1) 10 762
Froedman (1) 17 93
froeken (1) 3 234
froggreen (1) 3 210
Froggy (1) 15 1578
Frogmore (1) 6 550
frogs (2) 8 164 18 1219
frogsplits (1) 15 4124
frogwise (1) 1 680
frolic (1) 8 402
frolicsome (1) 13 37
FROM (1) 7 841
From (52) 1 497 503 2 16 378 3 33 47 296
　4 105 5 52 6 77 198 382 8 27 297 708
　9 111 586 692 834 10 141 425 718 1034 1132
　1196 1202 1223 11 313 515 954 1079 12 155
　173 525 1869 13 660 1169 14 554
　15 2401 3289 16 1029 17 67 164 850 852
　854 1321 1355 1835 2196
From (2) 7 523 9 1225
From (15) 15 132 138 143 213 605 1164 2478
　3232 3957 4054 4166 4317 4690 4709 4714

from (887) 1 1 53 62 65 86 109 125 141 160 172
　203 213 242 266 269 281 316 319 324 338 344 346
　355 392 399 406 428 478 491 498 501 520 528 580
　612 619 645 663 684 727 741 2 70 86 121 142
　146 154 157 167 181 209 221 241 244 279 283 293
　296 313 376 377 421 428 443 3 29 35 43 71 110
　131 147 194 211 219 278 282 297 304 317 340 346
　357 376 407 413 453 473 480 500 4 12 17 60 64
　66 95 102 109 126 147 154 157 165 182 186 192
　203 224 240 251 271 279 308 310 322 333 341 385
　416 418 539 5 4 19 49 110 181 221 234 260 267
　319 370 417 418 6 11 24 38 72 96 154 205 229
　257 288 302 329 358 374 400 437 451 507 586 652
　685 717 724 819 911 991 1006 7 11 31 93 134
　150 184 232 239 256 304 355 367 371 401 411 426
　437 469 475 487 506 571 678 697 748 777 814 819
　931 940 941 950 972 975 982 1038 1044 8 29 45
　74 76 78 80 88 127 196 198 214 233 235 255 295
　311 403 406 444 460 518 523 534 569 572 576 602
　621 635 661 683 684 688 720 726 737 747 809 840
　881 933 937 957 1010 1098 9 82 136 149 150 203
　211 233 235 236 238 242 269 326 338 369 377 384
　388 473 475 482 546 552 581 621 636 647 681 740
　755 759 775 779 782 825 832 838 880 895 919 933
　934 937 966 983 988 994 1000 1001 1016 1037 1058
　1086 1219 1222 10 41 46 62 76 88 117 134 199
　202 221 222 238 251 252 285 312 313 328 342 349
　394 421 422 440 458 465 470 472 496 513 526 561
　565 654 683 698 786 809 815 817 818 821 863 867
　902 914 928 941 950 1013 1031 1041 1093 1098
　1116 1127 1146 1177 1184 1200 1211 1221 1227
　1230 1233 1273 1278 11 59 81 93 112 113 143
　216 254 304 321 338 365 407 424 437 454 460 472
　620 677 678 679 855 875 1008 1082 1111 1156 1269
　12 83 90 99 110 111 112 113 159 164 203 209 233
　285 298 342 344 352 374 441 459 492 501 532 538
　578 585 587 597 631 653 671 710 720 752 893 911
　915 980 1067 1090 1135 1136 1180 1200 1243 1247
　1252 1357 1391 1446 1526 1527 1532 1579 1593
　1635 1666 1682 1814 1834 1837 1882 1888 1908
　13 62 71 94 177 194 205 216 226 260 316 322 420
　457 515 519 578 620 626 635 641 658 667 689 706
　723 728 736 756 874 875 917 924 1002 1053 1116
　1119 1124 1166 1175 1204 1210 1250 14 45 95
　109 153 191 261 279 291 318 376 382 390 394 399
　426 450 466 495 498 514 543 560 575 597 661 671
　682 698 702 705 725 749 754 770 777 778 811 827
　836 851 875 913 915 923 927 940 998 1028 1036
　1046 1059 1075 1125 1156 1166 1170 1172 1205
　1214 1217 1219 1271 1296 1299 1337 1338 1354
　1370 1376 1495 1585 15 306 462 585 670 953
　998 999 1019 1035 1064 1068 1169 1211 1356 1367
　1516 1658 1754 1776 1780 1896 1900 1901 1981
　2092 2545 2578 2784 2900 2995 3005 3187 3188
　3251 3375 3395 3418 3493 3500 3636 3873 4233
　4541 4593 4641 4886 4953 16 23 105 136 153
　287 292 327 349 372 375 376 419 445 446 451 453
　472 542 552 557 563 566 597 660 661 708 729 733
　741 744 750 758 773 791 809 840 843 855 876 946
　1054 1083 1112 1117 1155 1181 1192 1214 1221
　1234 1235 1241 1254 1323 1346 1372 1416 1503
　1511 1517 1524 1534 1597 1599 1640 1641 1657
　1672 1692 1758 1765 1798 1812 1848 1859 1877
　17 2 28 29 32 41 68 88 129 148 152 171 223 224
　241 259 262 265 269 271 273 278 346 379 384 390
　417 431 436 442 480 495 555 573 616 671 713 724
　770 882 935 977 995 1000 1006 1007 1013 1019
　1022 1037 1046 1053 1091 1113 1125 1128 1129
　1130 1132 1140 1204 1211 1217 1236 1281 1286

　1288 1297 1324 1429 1436 1439 1448 1510 1512
　1515 1516 1557 1574 1596 1634 1637 1660 1684
　1725 1739 1782 1784 1786 1801 1805 1813 1820
　1841 1844 1887 1924 1925 1933 1989 1993 2001
　2016 2018 2035 2057 2075 2087 2110 2112 2188
　2209 2220 18 131 241 293 298 301 314 344 382
　393 399 417 451 589 593 599 612 650 658 683 698
　717 718 719 756 780 831 858 871 899 918 933 941
　944 970 976 995 1019 1030 1143 1153 1177 1210
　1214 1336 1346 1357 1370 1443 1485 1571 1588
from (12) 1 597 2 355 4 288 348 7 831
　849 8 183 11 344 673 16 1249 17 1372
from (116) 15 39 41 42 50 78 125 135 156 197
　309 320 352 372 424 577 598 683 689 726 738 910
　911 926 928 1028 1079 1163 1260 1269 1362 1404
　1446 1494 1510 1546 1554 1598 1605 1748 1750
　1764 1842 1844 1880 1954 2022 2051 2147 2148
　2149 2150 2162 2167 2174 2176 2252 2263 2291
　2661 2684 2686 2698 2700 2725 3168 3235 3341
　3363 3378 3383 3469 3470 3525 3538 3568 3619
　3641 3674 3710 3740 3757 3795 3952 4019 4031
　4064 4076 4121 4127 4145 4146 4179 4189 4256
　4261 4315 4319 4320 4330 4418 4502 4666 4670
　4676 4681 4689 4703 4780 4905 4912 4937 4959
FROM (1) 15 846
fromage (1) 3 220
fronds (1) 3 463
fronds (1) 15 3951
frons (1) 15 1880
front (32) 3 131 4 85 5 73 6 24 567 583
　995 8 189 476 1100 10 1210 11 558
　13 131 147 926 15 2322 2357 16 102 212
　830 17 54 515 735 1272 1288 1508 1778
　18 47 788 877 1515 1585
front (6) 15 2049 2085 2479 4318 4694 4697
frontal (1) 17 872
frontdoor (1) 13 44
fronted (1) 10 992
frontlet (1) 6 321
frontlets (1) 10 1243
fronts (1) 9 1202
frostbound (1) 15 1046
frosted (1) 15 650
frosty (1) 15 701
frostyface (1) 18 336
froth (2) 5 317 12 686
frown (1) 9 122
frowned (9) 1 64 191 2 440 6 101
　8 1078 10 921 1109 1110 18 708
frowning (10) 4 341 5 10 8 990 9 79
　671 10 561 1111 11 103 16 476
　18 1173
frowningly (1) 16 676
frowns (1) 14 1374
frowns (7) 15 2034 2105 2722 3528 3631 3664
　4930
frows (1) 16 1811
frowsy (1) 11 1252
frozen (6) 2 317 3 307 420 8 583
　15 1032 18 555
frozen (1) 7 768
Frseeeeeeeeeeeeeeeeeeeeefrong (1)
　18 874
frseeeeeeeefronnnng (1) 18 596
fructified (1) 14 1413
frugal (1) 13 1125
fruit (15) 4 207 5 296 6 500 773 958
　8 273 336 535 862 10 177 303 14 1148 1321
　1371 17 1039

gentlemen (2) 7 828 862
gentlemen (1) 15 1436
gentlemen's (1) 12 589
gentlest (1) 7 245
Gentlewoman (1) 18 447
gentlewoman (2) 13 99 14 874
Gently (1) 13 832
gently (31) 1 3 167 4 75 5 213 6 110
    141 540 587 7 438 478 8 293 1090 1136 1141
    9 793 10 126 619 714 834 11 863 948 1115
    12 845 13 439 1256 14 175 795 15 2886
    16 921 1779 17 1489
gently (6) 15 467 743 1339 1595 2770 3509
gentry (3) 3 105 14 1494 17 1607
gent's (1) 15 270
gents (4) 1 22 14 1534 1544 15 4538
genuflected (1) 13 675
genuflecting (1) 15 1496
genuflection (1) 17 1495
genuine (7) 1 21 13 88 16 721 781 822
    1209 1653
genuinely (2) 12 551 14 1252
genus (1) 16 328
genus (1) 16 1852
Geo (2) 8 332 527
geographical (2) 17 1913 1970
geological (1) 17 1058
geometrical (2) 17 574 1693
Geometry (1) 17 1398
George (28) 4 151 8 426 9 301 439 994
    11 562 567 758 815 819 881 924 947 1038 1158
    1212 1282 12 228 1391 1872 15 1488 4371
    4638 16 559 17 424 600 1227 2171
George (2) 15 1908 4349
George (1) 15 895
George's (6) 4 78 544 10 297 13 500
    17 8 578
George's (2) 15 1184 1493
Georges (1) 18 1231
Georgina (5) 9 195 15 122 443 3620
    18 172
Ger (2) 10 43 15 2462
Geraghty (4) 12 20 36 67 100
Geraghty (1) 15 4358
Gerald (10) 7 798 10 1179 1223 1235
    12 928 15 2462 3009 3011 3012
Gerald (2) 15 4355 4686
Geraldines (2) 10 449 930
geraniums (2) 15 3799 18 1601
Gerard (2) 9 651 16 1763
Gerard's (1) 11 907
German (4) 1 667 6 84 12 1392
    16 1812
german (2) 14 592 18 95
Germans (2) 8 555 16 1001
Germany (3) 6 370 9 766 15 4455
germs (2) 14 1280 17 1061
gert (1) 14 1482
Gertrude (4) 13 198 566 17 1847 2255
Gerty (55) 2 36 10 1206 12 1494
    13 72 78 79 93 97 101 139 148 166 172 193 194
    207 223 264 300 304 325 328 331 332 356 360 366
    404 446 495 509 522 525 527 540 545 568 575 578
    589 599 616 634 686 687 756 757 770 935 944 1300
    1301 17 1847 2255
Gerty (1) 15 372
Gerty (2) 15 374 383
Gerty's (6) 13 107 115 171 289 355 581

gesabo (1) 18 1493
gestation (1) 14 728
gested (1) 14 193
gesticulating (1) 12 1907
gesture (7) 2 277 6 225 7 664 776
    12 291 14 743 15 105
gesture (1) 15 3562
gestures (5) 2 367 368 6 489 15 116
    16 392
gestures (3) 15 2661 3905 4370
Get (27) 3 116 282 4 358 5 82 6 679
    1032 7 342 8 120 135 677 697 1172 9 1211
    10 706 11 586 605 1122 1181 12 1176
    14 1457 1562 15 928 3985 4202 4726 4768
    4809
get (227) 1 43 194 292 388 497 506 2 178 307
    417 3 187 256 291 456 4 60 73 126 197 360
    495 5 19 95 114 174 189 198 217 462 502 530
    6 178 246 537 539 564 608 779 808 830 870 998
    1004 7 83 105 155 187 188 192 304 309 351 439
    918 988 1051 8 46 47 84 193 218 444 459 554
    573 661 967 1057 1059 1079 1124 1157 9 277
    452 748 10 279 372 384 420 514 589 662 668
    669 683 684 893 1159 1166 11 686 803 807 929
    12 21 66 484 487 506 688 1034 1046 1384 1565
    1799 13 86 132 405 477 524 568 605 785 813
    853 875 913 916 1026 1032 1034 1038 1083 1101
    1162 14 597 1477 1526 1558 15 369 647 657
    745 1099 2260 2561 2711 2887 3059 3073 3207
    3472 3581 3628 4511 4724 4896 16 11 15 149
    180 184 200 203 250 451 625 671 788 1290 1715
    18 1 14 15 23 28 32 51 57 157 186 196 223 239
    298 346 408 412 454 460 466 467 505 508 518 537
    576 583 602 603 607 651 718 754 804 806 854 870
    877 892 901 926 939 943 954 956 977 988 1012
    1044 1048 1102 1104 1135 1147 1170 1243 1275
    1359 1371 1380 1431 1457 1471 1494 1498 1548
    1549 1556 1579
get (2) 1 590 12 428
getatable (1) 16 556
Getonouthat (1) 7 350
Gets (1) 11 1182
gets (20) 5 503 6 606 675 947 8 470 487
    829 979 9 1159 11 116 1090 12 444 1199
    13 1098 16 240 18 364 374 537 661 1397
gets (1) 15 3550
Getting (4) 4 92 5 124 8 209 784
getting (58) 3 15 4 400 5 153 295 332
    6 16 57 204 212 397 454 741 746 8 38 179 317
    719 773 9 761 794 10 20 12 30 754 1022
    1784 13 260 346 538 557 1195 1212 15 369
    2204 16 311 924 1551 1603 18 51 58 301 451
    474 559 601 914 929 943 1007 1027 1079 1099 1150
    1155 1223 1273 1274 1323 1541
getup (2) 16 662 1446
gev (1) 14 1523
geysers (1) 17 207
Ghaghahest (1) 15 24
Ghahute (1) 15 20
ghastly (2) 12 530 15 1768
ghastly (1) 15 4322
Ghemara (1) 17 754
ghesabo (1) 13 990
Ghetto (1) 10 591
ghetto (1) 17 757
Ghimel (1) 15 1623
ghimel (1) 17 738
Ghost (3) 7 622 9 493 14 226
ghost (22) 1 556 2 152 6 754 755 1000

    1001 7 237 8 20 508 9 147 150 165 174 175
    215 380 470 478 1018 12 326 14 1033
    15 2068
ghost (1) 15 4548
ghostbright (1) 10 1052
ghostcandle (1) 1 274
ghostcandled (1) 3 396
Ghostly (1) 1 274
ghostly (1) 14 1015
ghost's (1) 9 667
ghosts (5) 8 730 9 1045 12 1201
    14 1088 1114
ghoststory (3) 2 55 9 141 15 3053
ghostwoman (1) 3 46
Ghoul (1) 1 278
ghoul (1) 15 4200
ghouleaten (1) 15 1208
Già (3) 3 493 494 9 941
giant (4) 6 752 769 12 1262 18 609
giantantlered (1) 14 1094
Giantkiller (1) 12 197
Giant's (1) 17 1975
giant's (1) 12 1877
Giants (1) 16 849
giants (3) 9 1045 12 656 18 597
giants (1) 7 247
giants (1) 15 1511
Gib (1) 18 617
gibbed (1) 12 72
gibbering (2) 15 2602 3044
gibbosity (1) 14 855
giblet (1) 4 2
Gibraltar (23) 4 60 211 11 515 12 1249
    13 1204 15 1731 3289 16 611 879 17 52
    1386 1983 2083 18 136 326 440 501 607 864 914
    1164 1463 1602
giddily (1) 15 4151
Giddy (2) 15 3375 4210
giddy (6) 1 171 7 1012 14 790 15 2553
    2719 4094
giddy (1) 15 1275
Gift (1) 11 1094
gift (13) 4 284 12 1823 14 758 15 106
    16 1807 17 375 1336 1338 1339 1344 1347
    1746 18 1296
gifted (1) 16 260
gifts (4) 1 335 16 1389 17 909 2010
gig (1) 15 572
gigant (1) 3 292
giggle (1) 15 3722
gigglegiggled (1) 11 164
gigglegold (1) 11 159
giggles (1) 18 212
giggling (3) 11 158 12 1165 18 1052
giggling (1) 15 2685
giglot (1) 9 666
Gilbert (2) 9 894
Gilbert's (1) 9 898
Gilbey (1) 17 306
gild (1) 13 655
gilded (4) 1 170 5 213 11 421 15 3083
gilded (1) 15 4127
gildedlettered (1) 11 119
gilds (1) 15 3012
Gilead (1) 14 931
Gillen's (1) 15 144
Gillespie (1) 18 723
Gillett (2) 12 227 228
gillie's (1) 15 2177

goodwill (1) 16 1098
Goodwin (7) 4 291 8 188 193 11 466 17 2134 18 336 1333
Goodwin (2) 15 4018 4047
Goodwin's (4) 4 294 8 166 185 11 1055
Goodwins (1) 18 263
goodygood (1) 14 1488
Goooooooooood (1) 15 4716
Goose (1) 8 404
goose (5) 3 164 478 8 468 15 3178 16 1399
goose (1) 15 1908
gooseberried (1) 9 628
gooseberries (1) 12 98
gooseberry (1) 17 1924
goosefat (1) 15 2074
goosegog (1) 14 1517
goosegrease (1) 8 469
Goosepond (1) 12 565
Goosestep (1) 8 407
goosestepping (1) 15 2240
gopherwood (1) 15 2321
gorbellied (1) 9 778
Gordon (6) 6 370 419 12 225 15 3003 16 1241 18 691
gores (1) 18 447
gores (1) 15 514
gorescarred (1) 2 12
Gorey (1) 11 1063
gorge (1) 8 672
Gorgeous (2) 11 198 18 674
gorgeous (5) 10 554 11 921 14 1536 15 824
gorges (1) 3 225
gorget (1) 15 4035
Gorgias (2) 7 1035 9 621
gorging (1) 15 706
Gorgonzola (1) 8 764
Gorman (2) 12 931 937
gormandising (1) 16 812
gorse (1) 12 158
gorsespine (1) 15 3372
Gort (1) 12 1561
gosa (1) 13 499
goshawks (1) 15 4667
gospel (5) 5 416 12 1849 14 929 16 829 1395
gospel (1) 15 4689
gospeller (1) 14 1579
gospellers (1) 9 803
Gospeltrue (1) 14 1517
Gospodi (1) 16 463
gossamer (2) 13 1020 14 1104
gossip (2) 9 187 14 540
gossoon (1) 3 245
Got (29) 3 242 4 62 233 6 82 123 510 887 937 993 1010 1015 7 668 8 99 158 334 395 10 605 720 11 432 861 1001 1076 13 1216 14 1472 1478 15 602 780 2206
got (152) 1 684 3 241 363 4 135 260 399 490 5 148 184 242 469 6 122 279 282 470 727 885 7 81 82 102 482 652 655 688 950 8 194 256 282 353 377 424 427 429 460 506 831 9 206 226 895 10 330 501 671 680 696 698 784 1145 1161 11 253 12 881 967 971 1034 1573 1768 1789 1843 1850 1897 13 31 186 260 437 486 553 555 635 786 840 1129 1144 1194 14 327 498 511 614 632 635 817 1471 1500 1547 1590 15 70 643 701 1534 1971 2201 2205 2219

2517 2578 3011 3663 4882 16 75 89 161 168 173 176 205 658 787 828 900 1018 1076 1190 1238 1283 1340 1347 1546 1662 1821 18 17 45 111 187 197 210 217 254 283 380 458 480 511 572 575 643 664 676 732 777 803 815 864 884 1015 1084 1090 1155 1178 1192 1193 1256 1303 1573
got (1) 12 810
Gothic (1) 17 1383
Gott (1) 17 1886
gotten (1) 14 541
gouger (1) 13 788
gougers (2) 12 693 18 711
Gough (1) 15 795
Gould (1) 11 720
Goulding (30) 6 51 56 8 320 10 471 472 1191 11 354 390 521 523 570 609 643 768 784 786 797 828 1028 1070 1164 1227 13 846 15 4174 17 141 539 952 18 1299
Goulding (1) 15 499
GOULDING (1) 15 2788
Goulding's (1) 11 343
Gounods (1) 18 274
gourme (1) 15 2094
goût (1) 15 662
gout (2) 13 321 17 1946
gouts (1) 15 4548
Goutte-d'Or (1) 3 252
gouty (4) 11 52 452 1152 15 3209
governed (2) 14 212 18 1435
Government (1) 15 1551
government (13) 4 193 8 465 12 862 999 1576 13 1056 15 2760 3375 16 967 1097 17 1697 1838 1865
Governor (1) 18 1466
governor (4) 7 511 10 1040 1213 15 4410
Governor's (1) 17 1386
governor's (1) 4 62
governors (1) 18 1585
gown (4) 1 31 508 6 80 18 1496
gown (7) 15 1366 1819 2074 2743 2809 2877 3857
gowned (2) 1 314 13 102
gowns (1) 10 609
gowns (1) 15 2239
goy (1) 15 253
Grab (1) 13 1086
grab (1) 12 426
grab (1) 15 6 4764
grabbed (1) 12 1249
grabbing (2) 12 1315 14 1393
grabs (1) 15 2884
Grace (8) 8 675 12 1274 13 1055 1069 1280 14 434 16 558 1241
Grace (1) 15 1422
grace (18) 5 22 6 874 7 62 476 593 776 8 471 9 75 1077 11 214 215 661 12 294 1441 14 422 1084 15 3204 17 1427
grace (3) 15 2661 4022 4030
graced (2) 7 772 12 1278
graceful (5) 9 1162 12 725 13 83 155 698
graceful (1) 11 724
graceless (1) 2 179
gracelessness (1) 2 168
graces (2) 14 1252 16 1832
gracias (1) 18 1472
gracing (1) 15 4031
gracious (4) 8 339 12 291 14 748 906
graciously (4) 9 117 10 1201 12 1524 1883

graciously (1) 15 4464
gradation (2) 17 201 1316
gradations (1) 17 2301
grade (7) 4 69 5 24 11 876 1128 12 1859 14 687 17 649
grade (2) 15 720 1787
grades (1) 17 552
gradient (2) 14 1559 17 169
gradual (5) 12 1722 17 927 1319 2238 2245
Gradually (1) 5 475
gradually (8) 12 340 14 25 16 361 17 86 116 268 654 2122
graduate (1) 12 659
graduated (1) 17 92
graduates (1) 13 1088
graf (1) 7 541
Graft (1) 10 736
Grafton (5) 8 614 702 10 1150 13 931 18 524
Graham (3) 8 6 11 606 17 331
grahamise (1) 14 1516
Grain (1) 2 327
grain (3) 5 187 13 1028 14 346
grained (1) 1 16
grains (2) 13 1017 17 1890
grainy (1) 3 147
graize (1) 15 2675
grameful (1) 14 95
gramercy (1) 14 225
grammar (2) 14 633 18 1473
grammatical (2) 17 743 2217
grammes (1) 6 682
GRAMOPHONE (2) 15 2170 2210
gramophone (2) 6 963
gramophone (3) 15 605 2115 2168
grampus (1) 11 576
granados (1) 14 910
Grand (6) 1 435 12 1369 15 1505 17 176 435 983
grand (23) 1 434 6 120 1033 8 208 876 9 311 10 385 11 468 12 1022 1267 15 1917 4509 16 525 555 1696 1736 1855 17 422 18 402 1070 1093 1262 1358
grand (2) 15 900 4454
grandacious (1) 14 1530
grandam (1) 14 299
granddaddy's (1) 9 678
granddam (1) 15 1757
granddaughter (1) 9 693
grandees (1) 15 1417
Grandest (1) 11 828
grandest (2) 3 100 14 1587
GRANDEUR (1) 7 483
Grandfather (1) 10 813
grandfather (8) 1 556 2 152 9 425 869 16 133 1669 17 1909 18 1005
grandfather (1) 15 1256
grandfather's (1) 17 1353
Grandjoker (1) 12 559
grandly (1) 7 349
grandmother (5) 2 115 3 361 12 838 14 633 15 3610
grandmother (1) 15 3953
grandmothers (1) 9 853
grandoldgrossfather (1) 15 3866
grandp (1) 9 426
grandpapa (2) 13 232 343
grandpa's (1) 9 1039
grandson (3) 1 555 9 869 15 261

grew (10) 1 225 2 111 3 294 8 361 10 578 12 1004 14 343 1124 15 3302 16 1615

grew (1) 8 783

Grey (4) 4 218 230 6 744 7 686

grey (49) 1 86 118 120 122 491 689 739 3 114 4 221 223 227 322 534 535 5 370 6 130 423 635 745 746 830 973 974 7 83 305 505 8 312 10 633 1050 1161 11 67 12 1281 1684 13 199 211 741 1177 1235 1286 14 701 1080 1366 16 666 752 17 153 18 142 710 1274 1573

grey (15) 15 284 538 939 1163 1204 1257 2035 2924 3316 3960 4078 4158 4223 4330 4705

greybearded (1) 15 2923

greyedauburn (2) 9 652 11 907

greyeyed (1) 9 258

greyhound (1) 15 708

greying (1) 9 830

Greyish (1) 6 242

greyish (2) 10 261 16 338

greylunged (1) 14 1244

greyly (1) 7 572

Greystones (1) 6 82

grianauns (1) 12 1448

grid (1) 15 1031

griddlecakes (1) 13 224

Gridiron (1) 15 3701

grief (15) 3 429 5 204 6 161 181 428 461 9 10 11 736 1031 12 652 13 48 181 1119 15 4239 4863

Grier (1) 17 539

grievances (1) 16 986

grieve (1) 15 1998

grieved (3) 14 222 275 672

grievous (1) 14 471

Griffin (1) 15 766

Griffith (5) 3 227 4 101 8 462 12 1538 1574

Griffith (1) 15 4685

Griffith's (1) 5 71

Griffiths (1) 18 386

grig (1) 6 761

grigged (1) 18 214

grike (1) 3 285

grill (3) 5 54 60 8 661

grilled (2) 4 4 6 760

grilse (1) 12 72

grim (4) 1 625 12 612 13 1161 16 1527

grimace (3) 4 166 7 418 10 1018

grimaced (3) 10 141 11 126 16 612

grimacing (2) 15 2678 3900

Grimes (2) 6 186 16 526

grimly (1) 7 1072

grimly (1) 15 1180

Grimm (1) 9 958

grimy (1) 15 3

Grin (1) 16 439

grin (2) 14 1015 16 724

grin (2) 15 148 2762

grind (2) 16 545 986

Grinding (1) 16 306

grinding (1) 10 1114

grinding (1) 15 27

grinds (1) 15 2860

grindstone (1) 17 1563

grinned (2) 7 473 11 377

grinning (5) 6 79 10 705 1152 14 335 18 1287

grinning (1) 15 4220

grins (1) 15 2123

grip (3) 5 139 7 343 419

grip (1) 15 4946

Gripe (1) 15 930

gripe (1) 10 807

griped (1) 11 998

gripes (1) 15 4532

gripeth (1) 14 108

gripped (3) 8 297 651 16 1005

gripping (1) 10 341

gripping (2) 15 613 3982

grips (1) 15 35

Griselda (1) 9 620

Grissel (2) 14 987 15 3867

grist (2) 9 748 16 706

gristle (3) 8 660 11 570 13 876

Grizzled (1) 10 756

grizzled (1) 16 1016

groan (1) 7 329

groaned (1) 9 773

Groangrousegurgling (1) 15 4112

groaning (3) 1 110 8 373 480

groans (2) 15 27 161

groatsworth (2) 3 177 9 245

groceries (1) 15 3178

grocer's (2) 13 333 15 1805

grocers (2) 12 1730 17 983

grog (4) 8 766 986 11 271 18 692

Grogan (3) 1 357 375 14 732

Grogan (1) 15 1763

GROGAN (2) 9 1186 15 1716

Grogan's (2) 1 370 10 89

groggy (1) 12 967

groin (1) 8 787

groom (1) 14 346

groove (4) 9 615 10 373 468 16 1230

grope (1) 9 759

groped (1) 3 499

gropes (1) 15 3456

groping (3) 8 376 9 810 10 400

gros (1) 3 166

gross (5) 7 826 9 758 10 811 15 3038 17 1786

Grossbooted (1) 7 21

grossbooted (1) 7 23

Grosvenor (2) 5 99 8 347

grot (2) 14 453 461

grotesque (1) 9 435

grotesque (2) 15 1607 3904

grotto (1) 15 3235

ground (28) 3 351 448 5 45 6 476 554 636 637 766 877 7 820 8 857 9 106 272 10 745 11 913 12 166 13 248 14 90 158 613 750 1037 15 1061 16 940 1772 17 1512 1527

ground (8) 15 247 1247 1258 1552 2083 2854 3955 4256

groundlings (1) 9 157

grounds (2) 13 630 17 1551

groundsman (1) 17 1609

groundswells (1) 17 206

group (4) 13 318 16 310 475 725

group (2) 15 3551 4771

grouped (1) 14 1328

grouping (1) 16 1783

groups (1) 8 409

grouse (1) 12 124

grouse (1) 15 3414

grousing (1) 12 709

Grove (2) 18 623 644

grove (2) 6 928 14 1363

grove (1) 7 322

Groves (2) 18 690 1583

Grow (1) 4 482

grow (10) 4 85 5 8 6 75 11 364 12 1412 13 477 14 610 1346 15 1606 16 995

grow (2) 15 2831 4920

growing (7) 1 60 4 475 6 769 13 1202 15 3319 16 996 18 1150

Growl (1) 11 1200

growl (2) 12 263 1766

growled (10) 1 380 10 8 230 234 242 911 1063 11 586 1163 16 972

growlers (1) 16 461

Growling (1) 12 709

growling (3) 12 407 706 707

growling (4) 15 28 101 582 673

growls (3) 9 156 11 1143 12 202

growls (2) 15 693 4618

grown (5) 1 554 14 605 15 3171 17 2003 18 30

grownups (1) 13 896

Grows (1) 6 20

grows (4) 13 1267 14 613 1098 18 1551

grows (2) 15 993 1206

growth (9) 1 652 7 816 9 855 12 157 14 390 1387 17 44 1005

groynes (1) 12 1732

Grub (1) 8 701

grub (2) 1 335 8 56

grudge (2) 6 297 12 546

gruel (1) 18 1355

gruelling (1) 12 963

gruesome (3) 6 470 12 531 16 49

gruff (1) 2 286

gruffly (1) 7 407

gruffly (1) 15 4618

grumbled (1) 10 239

grumbling (3) 3 225 6 465 10 724

Grundy (1) 16 1204

grunt (1) 4 56

grunt (1) 15 2931

grunted (1) 11 134

grunting (3) 7 401 944 12 109

grunting (3) 15 322 2852 4544

gruntlings (1) 14 872

grunts (1) 15 3177

Guarantee (1) 10 630

guarantee (2) 16 246 17 1746

guaranteed (3) 12 834 17 590 1528

guarantor (1) 4 361

guard (6) 8 240 12 480 803 13 1095 14 321 18 368

guard (1) 15 4955

guarded (1) 16 300

guardedly (1) 1 603

guardhouse (1) 18 833

Guardian (1) 9 599

Guardians (1) 17 177

guardians (3) 12 1678 15 787 16 81

guarding (1) 13 4

guards (1) 15 4618

Guelph-Wettin (1) 12 1401

guess (3) 9 884 14 527 18 825

guessed (1) 13 75

Guesswork (1) 16 1293

guest (22) 10 *432* 12 *1825* 14 *182 897*
15 *3198* 17 *252 360 363 364 366 375 402 636
726 774 795 937 940 945 956 1036*
guest's (2) 17 *375 709*
guests (4) 8 *39* 10 *1225* 15 *4370*
17 *1548*
guffaw (1) 8 *605*
guffaw (1) 15 *589*
guffaws (2) 15 *2999 3006*
Guggenheim (3) 15 *1856 1857* 17 *1749*
guid (1) 9 *817*
guidance (1) 17 *1991*
guidance (1) 15 *1547*
Guide (1) 17 *712*
Guide (2) 10 *839* 17 *1368*
guide (5) 6 *317* 8 *1091* 13 *672* 16 *281*
17 *1724*
guidewheel (1) 15 *192*
Guido (1) 3 *318*
guiiiide (1) 18 *678*
guilds (1) 15 *1426*
guileless (1) 13 *745*
guiltless (2) 9 *243* 15 *1769*
guilty (6) 6 *474* 9 *180 364* 15 *763 946*
2234
guilty (1) 15 *898*
Guinea (1) 14 *1517*
guinea (12) 1 *155 291* 2 *256 257 258*
4 *503* 9 *1085* 11 *616 902* 13 *1061*
16 *1231* 18 *1169*
guineas (12) 2 *256 258* 8 *554 1060*
10 *647 745* 11 *189* 15 *1183* 16 *508 1766
1774 1782*
Guinness (2) 11 *769* 12 *1454*
Guinness's (7) 5 *388* 7 *45 497* 10 *774*
13 *1268* 15 *2896 2933*
Guinness's (1) 15 *1749*
guise (1) 14 *345*
guitar (4) 17 *664* 18 *1335 1337*
guitar (1) 15 *2489*
gules (2) 15 *3949 4638*
gulf (1) 17 *1156*
Gulfer (1) 9 *285*
gulfs (1) 17 *218*
gulfstream (2) 1 *476* 17 *204*
gull (3) 3 *335* 15 *2331 3437*
gull (2) 8 *62 549*
gullet (3) 8 *234 659* 12 *1432*
gullets (2) 3 *218* 18 *1278*
gullies (1) 17 *214*
Gulls (1) 15 *1188*
GULLS (1) 15 *685*
gulls (4) 8 *52 76 79* 11 *867*
gulls (2) 15 *683 4669*
Gulp (2) 8 *701*
gulped (1) 11 *431*
gulping (1) 13 *1161*
gulpings (1) 14 *1097*
gulps (1) 15 *310*
Gum (1) 14 *1509*
Gum (1) 15 *4145*
gum (1) 10 *808*
gum (1) 15 *3232*
gumbenjamin (1) 15 *2363*
gumboots (1) 14 *1442*
gumchewed (1) 13 *876*
gumheavy (1) 3 *443*
gumjelly (1) 8 *909*
Gumley (8) 7 *645 648 649* 12 *1101*
16 *109 944 1726*

gummed (1) 17 *1386*
Gummy (1) 15 *4578*
GUMMY (2) 15 *4584 4736*
gummy (1) 11 *570*
gumption (1) 6 *747*
gums (1) 8 *660*
gun (7) 12 *1337 1355 1477* 13 *1116*
14 *1449* 15 *2348* 16 *394*
gunboat (1) 16 *727*
guncarriage (1) 6 *550*
guncase (1) 1 *58*
gunfire (2) 13 *1206* 18 *688*
Gunn (5) 11 *1050* 16 *860* 17 *420 426*
18 *1111*
gunners (1) 15 *1530*
gunpowder (2) 3 *216* 10 *442*
gunpowder (1) 15 *1928*
gunrest (4) 1 *9 30 37 67*
guns (4) 13 *1193* 15 *1526* 16 *1497*
18 *679*
guns (1) 15 *4662*
gunwale (2) 3 *287 480*
gurgles (2) 15 *20 3057*
gurgling (4) 1 *12 14* 8 *659* 16 *929*
gurls (1) 6 *785*
gurnard (1) 12 *71*
Gurrhr (1) 4 *38*
Gus (1) 15 *3259*
gush (2) 4 *106* 11 *708*
gushed (3) 10 *277* 13 *738* 14 *1028*
gushes (1) 11 *708*
gushingly (2) 15 *460 2614*
gusset (1) 8 *272*
gussets (1) 17 *1583*
gussetted (1) 15 *2402*
gust (1) 8 *192*
Gustav (1) 17 *1383*
Gustave (1) 9 *50*
gusto (2) 8 *760* 16 *1634*
gut (2) 11 *834* 12 *171*
Gutenberg (1) 12 *191*
guts (11) 1 *412* 2 *318* 5 *185* 8 *437 892*
12 *214 1795* 13 *995 1073* 15 *3143*
17 *218*
guts (1) 12 *746*
guttapercha (1) 5 *218*
gutted (1) 15 *4611*
gutter (3) 8 *124* 10 *513 703*
gutterpress (1) 16 *1482*
gutters (1) 8 *129*
gutters (1) 15 *1406*
guttersheet (1) 7 *734*
guttersnipe (1) 7 *447*
guttural (1) 17 *747*
guttural (1) 15 *3227*
guvnor (1) 14 *1499*
guy (1) 14 *1546*
guzzling (1) 14 *1436*
Gwendolen (1) 15 *1586*
Gwynn (2) 9 *723* 13 *857*
gym (1) 15 *2869*
gymnastic (2) 17 *2262 2266*
gyration (1) 17 *521*
gyrations (1) 17 *1108*
gyved (1) 11 *684*

H

H (6) 6 *462* 9 *283* 10 *1237 1258* 11 *893*
16 *1239*
H (1) 12 *430*
H (1) 15 *1177*
h-Eireann (2) 12 *859 899*
H₂O (1) 14 *1511*
H E L Y 'S (2) 10 *310 379*
H E L Y S (1) 8 *126*
H F (1) 17 *1841*
H G (1) 10 *1222*
H H (1) 18 *121*
H J (2) 10 *96* 12 *364*
H J (1) 16 *1255*
H M S (1) 18 *837*
H M S (1) 13 *15*
H P B's (1) 9 *71*
H R H (2) 12 *1892* 18 *500*
H T (1) 10 *652*
Ha (9) 7 *758* 8 *693 894* 11 *702 1110*
12 *1050* 14 *1398* 15 *3755 3818*
ha (9) 4 *70* 5 *24* 8 *594* 11 *876*
12 *1050* 15 *3755 3818*
Habaa (1) 13 *398*
Habeas (1) 12 *1893*
Habeas (1) 6 *741*
Habemus (1) 15 *1488*
Haben (1) 17 *1383*
habiliments (1) 15 *2399*
habit (14) 6 *422* 13 *291 452* 14 *25 322
866 930 1357* 15 *3243* 16 *1188 1597 1715*
17 *1960* 18 *1234*
habit (5) 15 *1207 1255 1927 3434 3456*
habitable (1) 17 *2230*
habitation (2) 17 *836 892*
habits (5) 15 *1361* 16 *66* 17 *911 2193*
18 *1198*
habitual (3) 16 *65 1487* 17 *154*
habitually (3) 16 *631* 17 *1757 1769*
Habsburg (1) 7 *540*
Habsburgs (1) 8 *872*
hachures (1) 17 *1972*
hack (1) 14 *1139*
hacked (1) 1 *349*
Hackett (1) 12 *935*
hacking (1) 3 *305*
hackle (1) 5 *67*
hackleplume (1) 15 *4613*
Hackney (1) 7 *1047*
hackney (3) 11 *878* 15 *1065* 17 *494*
hackney (2) 15 *4147 4317*
hackneycar (1) 15 *3726*
hackneyed (1) 16 *1850*
Had (24) 2 *48* 4 *350* 6 *82 232 363 529 873*
8 *633 698* 10 *602* 11 *1256* 13 *99 290 916*
14 *1513* 17 *46 388 487 519 540 858 987 1259
1916*
Had (1) 8 *778*
had (777) 1 *103 105 108 109 149 216 217 266
270 320 327 399 440 543 573 581 603 634 660*
2 *15 35 45 69 123 140 142 146 147 166 178 187*
3 *41 106 147 265 327 367 448* 4 *36 54 64 152
206 261 420 489 515 517 522 529* 5 *318 324 371
396 406 438 480 498 552* 6 *29 75 80 106 295 311
442 446 472 544 586 705 727 747 799 828* 7 *134
258 433 533 600 602 794 814 816 823 947 986*
8 *31 82 117 149 155 163 169 251 265 331 379 380*

425 495 559 567 600 758 800 802 903 908 937
9 $_{176\ 245\ 252\ 349\ 454\ 455\ 619\ 629\ 630\ 634\ 665}$
$_{680\ 708\ 805\ 894\ 1108\ 1192}$ **10** $_{13\ 32\ 65\ 105\ 119}$
$_{123\ 132\ 137\ 138\ 140\ 146\ 150\ 167\ 169\ 191\ 379\ 545}$
$_{552\ 558\ 572\ 593\ 635\ 673\ 719\ 746\ 874\ 1057\ 1124}$
$_{1204\ 1209\ 1210}$ **11** $_{101\ 197\ 262\ 264\ 314\ 378\ 473}$
$_{474\ 488\ 491\ 643\ 921\ 1020\ 1040\ 1041\ 1042\ 1043}$
$_{1121\ 1173\ 1209\ 1225\ 1254}$ **12** $_{16\ 30\ 238\ 339\ 349}$
$_{350\ 352\ 357\ 365\ 367\ 370\ 373\ 513\ 530\ 540\ 557\ 571}$
$_{587\ 617\ 628\ 647\ 671\ 774\ 776\ 821\ 891\ 892\ 964\ 965}$
$_{1137\ 1185\ 1186\ 1187\ 1215\ 1224\ 1296\ 1390\ 1393}$
$_{1426\ 1478\ 1550\ 1600\ 1611\ 1725\ 1728\ 1736\ 1806}$
13 $_{1\ 33\ 43\ 45\ 84\ 85\ 94\ 100\ 111\ 112\ 115\ 117\ 127}$
$_{130\ 166\ 173\ 177\ 194\ 206\ 211\ 225\ 226\ 235\ 270\ 293}$
$_{297\ 299\ 313\ 318\ 322\ 327\ 330\ 342\ 367\ 370\ 375\ 377}$
$_{416\ 420\ 428\ 431\ 432\ 436\ 461\ 473\ 475\ 476\ 481\ 484}$
$_{503\ 504\ 518\ 540\ 541\ 548\ 569\ 580\ 584\ 585\ 601\ 634}$
$_{644\ 648\ 657\ 658\ 687\ 692\ 703\ 711\ 721\ 728\ 746\ 747}$
$_{749\ 757\ 760\ 892\ 907\ 915\ 1001\ 1013\ 1035\ 1054\ 1091}$
$_{1158\ 1214\ 1240\ 1274}$ **14** $_{23\ 39\ 52\ 58\ 60\ 72\ 88}$
$_{89\ 91\ 99\ 115\ 118\ 126\ 127\ 135\ 177\ 192\ 197\ 204\ 207}$
$_{210\ 221\ 223\ 229\ 255\ 258\ 265\ 266\ 267\ 271\ 278\ 287}$
$_{330\ 336\ 338\ 339\ 358\ 412\ 430\ 437\ 438\ 447\ 453\ 465}$
$_{495\ 508\ 531\ 535\ 541\ 543\ 550\ 552\ 554\ 563\ 569\ 575}$
$_{586\ 590\ 624\ 633\ 653\ 654\ 657\ 658\ 659\ 667\ 681\ 698}$
$_{699\ 716\ 718\ 726\ 736\ 743\ 755\ 756\ 760\ 772\ 773\ 811}$
$_{819\ 820\ 822\ 838\ 843\ 845\ 846\ 860\ 861\ 876\ 884\ 895}$
$_{909\ 923\ 924\ 945\ 997\ 1013\ 1110\ 1126\ 1149\ 1153}$
$_{1159\ 1160\ 1161\ 1181\ 1201\ 1202\ 1223\ 1310\ 1311}$
$_{1313\ 1329\ 1347\ 1496\ 1525\ 1549}$ **15** $_{392\ 409\ 434}$
$_{548\ 566\ 645\ 869\ 892\ 979\ 1019\ 1033\ 2415\ 2572\ 2579}$
$_{2719\ 2951\ 3104\ 3139\ 3176\ 3601\ 4196\ 4759\ 4875}$
16 $_{20\ 36\ 66\ 98\ 107\ 120\ 132\ 134\ 135\ 139\ 144\ 145}$
$_{146\ 187\ 217\ 218\ 226\ 230\ 257\ 273\ 303\ 321\ 367\ 368}$
$_{444\ 501\ 502\ 544\ 561\ 570\ 615\ 630\ 634\ 639\ 647\ 649}$
$_{651\ 675\ 709\ 712\ 716\ 734\ 736\ 754\ 797\ 798\ 830\ 837}$
$_{901\ 902\ 905\ 908\ 917\ 925\ 929\ 931\ 955\ 1042\ 1056}$
$_{1058\ 1063\ 1070\ 1075\ 1078\ 1145\ 1178\ 1181\ 1190}$
$_{1191\ 1213\ 1303\ 1331\ 1342\ 1361\ 1373\ 1396\ 1404}$
$_{1450\ 1478\ 1508\ 1526\ 1558\ 1582\ 1584\ 1608\ 1625}$
$_{1659\ 1660\ 1662\ 1663\ 1666\ 1672\ 1732\ 1753\ 1757}$
$_{1773\ 1805\ 1807\ 1847\ 1853\ 1863\ 1878}$ **17** $_{75\ 78}$
$_{136\ 172\ 174\ 176\ 179\ 261\ 325\ 327\ 331\ 335\ 337\ 338}$
$_{349\ 385\ 390\ 404\ 410\ 417\ 452\ 479\ 481\ 483\ 488\ 491}$
$_{498\ 503\ 520\ 521\ 555\ 557\ 558\ 563\ 660\ 676\ 678\ 682}$
$_{693\ 698\ 703\ 718\ 787\ 852\ 853\ 855\ 857\ 861\ 862\ 864}$
$_{868\ 875\ 885\ 903\ 904\ 905\ 906\ 909\ 923\ 947\ 977\ 978}$
$_{980\ 1019\ 1072\ 1092\ 1124\ 1127\ 1144\ 1145\ 1195}$
$_{1198\ 1236\ 1261\ 1281\ 1283\ 1284\ 1286\ 1288\ 1293}$
$_{1355\ 1486\ 1497\ 1634\ 1635\ 1637\ 1642\ 1646\ 1652}$
$_{1760\ 1803\ 1845\ 1894\ 1903\ 1905\ 1912\ 1963\ 1987}$
$_{1988\ 2126\ 2149\ 2198\ 2274\ 2283\ 2286\ 2292}$ **18** $_{5}$
$_{7\ 41\ 56\ 58\ 64\ 114\ 130\ 132\ 149\ 153\ 174\ 183\ 196\ 218}$
$_{261\ 264\ 286\ 293\ 301\ 307\ 309\ 317\ 321\ 324\ 338}$
$_{378\ 406\ 421\ 433\ 487\ 524\ 536\ 569\ 570\ 576\ 582\ 587}$
$_{615\ 620\ 637\ 642\ 650\ 671\ 674\ 711\ 719\ 724\ 765\ 787}$
$_{799\ 811\ 816\ 819\ 820\ 848\ 857\ 905\ 916\ 919\ 927\ 972}$
$_{985\ 1034\ 1055\ 1072\ 1106\ 1119\ 1121\ 1152\ 1160}$
$_{1168\ 1169\ 1179\ 1208\ 1294\ 1296\ 1414\ 1442\ 1464}$
$_{1467\ 1473}$

had (9) **7** $_{830\ 862\ 863}$ **9** $_{138\ 1147\ 1150}$
10 $_{15}$ **11** $_{781}$ **17** $_{1352}$
had (3) **15** $_{900\ 904\ 909}$
haddies (1) **15** $_{503}$
Haddington (1) **10** $_{1274}$
haddock (2) **12** $_{72}$ **15** $_{3681}$
haddy (1) **18** $_{930}$
Hades (1) **15** $_{967}$
hadn't (17) **1** $_{440}$ **5** $_{211}$ **6** $_{93}$ **8** $_{1112}$

11 $_{182\ 1182}$ **12** $_{251}$ **13** $_{357\ 437\ 872}$
15 $_{640}$ **16** $_{170\ 180\ 1086\ 1178\ 1292\ 1787}$
hadnt (9) **18** $_{282\ 348\ 360\ 442\ 835\ 872\ 1180}$
$_{1239\ 1441}$
haec (1) **7** $_{1056}$
haft (1) **6** $_{912}$
HAG (1) **15** $_{4758}$
hag (5) **3** $_{232\ 493}$ **4** $_{224}$ **13** $_{1046}$
18 $_{1399}$
hag (1) **15** $_{3045}$
Hagadah (1) **15** $_{1623}$
hagadah (1) **7** $_{206}$
Hagar (1) **14** $_{925}$
haggadah (1) **17** $_{1878}$
haggard (1) **16** $_{704}$
haggard (1) **15** $_{3161}$
haggles (1) **15** $_{606}$
haggling (1) **16** $_{350}$
hagiographical (1) **17** $_{752}$
Hah (1) **15** $_{4871}$
hah (2) **15** $_{4871}$
Haha (1) **15** $_{220}$
Hai (1) **15** $_{3950}$
Haihoop (1) **15** $_{3949}$
haihooping (1) **15** $_{2091}$
Hail (4) **5** $_{431}$ **7** $_{312}$ **15** $_{4387}$ **18** $_{136}$
hail (6) **9** $_{38\ 610}$ **10** $_{987}$ **15** $_{4952}$ **16** $_{29}$
17 $_{217}$
hailed (3) **1** $_{106}$ **10** $_{970}$ **11** $_{339}$
Hailer (1) **17** $_{2324}$
hailing (1) **10** $_{1189}$
hails (2) **16** $_{419}$
Hainau (1) **17** $_{869}$
Haines (61) **1** $_{49\ 162\ 284\ 318\ 328\ 334\ 344\ 352}$
$_{359\ 365\ 393\ 425\ 426\ 430\ 439\ 449\ 469\ 474\ 478\ 487}$
$_{488\ 491\ 520\ 537\ 541\ 545\ 553\ 558\ 562\ 566\ 572\ 603}$
$_{609\ 611\ 615\ 618\ 633\ 639\ 642\ 645\ 693\ 715\ 718\ 730}$
9 $_{91\ 306\ 513\ 559\ 1114\ 1130}$ **10** $_{1044\ 1048\ 1054}$
$_{1060\ 1068\ 1076\ 1082\ 1091\ 1224}$ **14** $_{1012\ 1032}$
Haines (1) **15** $_{4695}$
HAINES (2) **15** $_{4700\ 4704}$
Haines's (2) **1** $_{666}$ **2** $_{42}$
Hair (5) **1** $_{136}$ **5** $_{81}$ **11** $_{301\ 941}$ **13** $_{840}$
hair (96) **1** $_{15\ 76\ 117\ 186\ 689}$ **2** $_{124\ 139}$
3 $_{114\ 374}$ **4** $_{242\ 371\ 436\ 445\ 489}$ **5** $_{22\ 28}$
$_{109\ 529\ 571}$ **6** $_{19\ 238\ 395\ 575}$ **7** $_{332\ 345\ 821}$
8 $_{266\ 333\ 903\ 916\ 1084\ 1129\ 1135\ 1137}$
9 $_{1139}$ **10** $_{382\ 797\ 876}$ **11** $_{7\ 81\ 82\ 83\ 166}$
$_{222\ 348\ 547\ 942\ 1235\ 1239}$ **12** $_{157\ 997\ 1176}$
13 $_{116\ 211\ 454\ 475\ 509\ 513\ 563\ 571\ 739\ 834\ 838}$
$_{1281}$ **14** $_{753\ 1116\ 1484}$ **15** $_{2321\ 3141\ 3163}$
$_{3392\ 3484}$ **16** $_{271\ 338\ 597}$ **17** $_{730\ 785\ 896}$
$_{902\ 1208\ 1889}$ **18** $_{59\ 163\ 213\ 271\ 478\ 563\ 593}$
$_{638\ 752\ 1064\ 1134\ 1312\ 1321\ 1603}$
hair (21) **15** $_{41\ 285\ 302\ 876\ 1016\ 1346\ 2005}$
$_{2049\ 2060\ 2587\ 2628\ 2702\ 2857\ 2884\ 2985\ 3234}$
$_{3267\ 3740\ 4083\ 4159\ 4764}$
hairbrush (1) **15** $_{3077}$
haircombs (1) **15** $_{4057}$
hairdresser (1) **10** $_{743}$
hairdresser's (2) **15** $_{144\ 2247}$
haired (1) **10** $_{636}$
hairgrowth (1) **15** $_{1326}$
hairoil (1) **5** $_{21}$
hairoil (1) **15** $_{1487}$
hairpin (3) **4** $_{335}$ **16** $_{1795}$ **18** $_{750}$
hairpins (2) **8** $_{200}$ **18** $_{212}$
hairs (6) **6** $_{239\ 745}$ **15** $_{1785\ 3000}$ **17** $_{1438}$
$_{1777}$

hairsbreadth (1) **16** $_{409}$
hairshirt (1) **15** $_{1805}$
Hairy (1) **12** $_{829}$
hairy (6) **6** $_{361}$ **8** $_{807}$ **15** $_{53}$ **18** $_{416}$
$_{1385\ 1387}$
hairy (1) **15** $_{4705}$
hairylegged (1) **12** $_{154}$
hairynostrilled (1) **15** $_{2604}$
Haja (1) **13** $_{392}$
haja (1) **13** $_{392}$
Hajajaja (1) **15** $_{1598}$
Hak (1) **15** $_{2603}$
hake (1) **9** $_{1159}$
halberdiers (1) **15** $_{4611}$
Halcyon (1) **15** $_{3324}$
Halcyon (1) **15** $_{3325}$
HALCYON (1) **15** $_{3330}$
halcyon (2) **13** $_{334\ 344}$
hale (2) **12** $_{165}$ **14** $_{75}$
haled (1) **1** $_{329}$
Half (14) **1** $_{733}$ **2** $_{93}$ **5** $_{73\ 532}$ **6** $_{284}$
$_{798}$ **8** $_{875}$ **11** $_{540}$ **12** $_{1017\ 1055\ 1319}$
13 $_{1277}$ **15** $_{1527}$ **16** $_{243}$
Half (1) **15** $_{1208}$
half (102) **1** $_{130}$ **2** $_{258}$ **3** $_{58}$ **4** $_{148\ 504}$
$_{537}$ **7** $_{575\ 999}$ **8** $_{119\ 337\ 438\ 452\ 881\ 952}$
$_{1133}$ **9** $_{629}$ **10** $_{169\ 499\ 535\ 744\ 1123\ 1137}$
11 $_{211\ 700\ 814\ 831\ 867\ 1045\ 1061\ 1192}$
12 $_{142\ 487\ 821\ 1025\ 1052\ 1053\ 1054\ 1055\ 1224}$
$_{1670}$ **13** $_{203\ 395\ 522\ 532\ 732\ 764\ 847\ 877\ 1006}$
$_{1136\ 1192\ 1268\ 1280}$ **14** $_{616\ 780\ 816\ 1585\ 1590}$
15 $_{616\ 722\ 1021\ 2144\ 2417\ 3049\ 4392}$ **16** $_{161}$
$_{236\ 300\ 395\ 431\ 698\ 877\ 1160\ 1266\ 1409}$ **17** $_{87}$
$_{306\ 522\ 880}$ **18** $_{252\ 425\ 440\ 533\ 580\ 600\ 708}$
$_{755\ 827\ 1068\ 1185\ 1243\ 1246\ 1291\ 1364\ 1373\ 1425}$
$_{1486\ 1586\ 1590\ 1596}$
half (5) **15** $_{2699\ 2759\ 3439\ 3565\ 3583}$
halfbaked (1) **16** $_{1290}$
halfcastes (1) **15** $_{3947}$
halfclosed (1) **4** $_{247}$
halfcrazy (1) **16** $_{1186}$
halfcrown (1) **15** $_{253}$
halfcrowns (2) **2** $_{220}$ **16** $_{194}$
halfempty (1) **17** $_{305}$
Halffed (1) **8** $_{470}$
halffilled (1) **17** $_{229}$
halfmasticated (1) **8** $_{660}$
halfmile (1) **10** $_{651}$
halfmoon (1) **15** $_{465}$
halfnaked (1) **8** $_{888}$
halfpenny (2) **7** $_{708}$ **17** $_{316}$
halfseasover (1) **5** $_{72}$
halfshut (1) **18** $_{153}$
halfsilk (1) **17** $_{2092}$
halfstood (1) **11** $_{118}$
halfturned (1) **18** $_{302}$
halfway (2) **1** $_{37}$ **4** $_{256}$
halfwon (1) **14** $_{1053}$
halfyear (1) **17** $_{1862}$
halibut (1) **12** $_{72}$
Hall (3) **5** $_{152}$ **7** $_{456}$ **17** $_{435}$
hall (32) **4** $_{49\ 52}$ **7** $_{391\ 395\ 816}$ **8** $_{922\ 1037}$
$_{1151}$ **9** $_{977\ 1130\ 1168\ 1192}$ **10** $_{970\ 1110}$
11 $_{690\ 1021\ 1273}$ **12** $_{897\ 1181}$ **14** $_{86\ 183}$
$_{421\ 797\ 1201\ 1301\ 1579}$ **17** $_{627\ 1502\ 1522}$
18 $_{123\ 375\ 605}$
hall (1) **17** $_{822}$
hall (5) **15** $_{2033\ 3824\ 4271\ 4314\ 4320}$
halldoor (6) **4** $_{75}$ **9** $_{570}$ **17** $_{115\ 116\ 1507}$
18 $_{1406}$

hankered (1) 14 536
hankering (1) 16 1805
hanks (1) 4 140
Hanlon (1) 8 891
Hanlon's (1) 4 36
Hanna (1) 15 1104
Hannibal (1) 12 1893
Hannigan (1) 3 204
Hanoverians (1) 12 1390
Hans (1) 12 567
Hanukah (1) 15 1624
hap (1) 14 269
hapless (1) 12 661
happed (1) 14 126
happen (9) 4 448 449 6 432 13 878 896
　　15 883 4951 16 443 18 282
happened (20) 1 193 4 429 12 674
　　14 1183 15 2566 4866 16 40 42 43 107 108
　　444 890 918 1405 1450 1534 1535 1838 18 1058
happening (3) 5 133 10 91 16 152
happens (5) 12 853 15 4732 16 1385
　　18 357 1223
happied (1) 9 1054
Happier (1) 8 170
happier (2) 2 389 8 608
happily (3) 1 580 12 916 14 1239
happiness (7) 13 655 14 273 677 726 751
　　825 18 744
happiness (1) 15 913
Happy (4) 8 170 200 13 1088
happy (27) 1 583 4 81 5 219 246 359
　　6 227 8 409 612 9 1177 10 1061
　　11 297 810 811 12 646 1292 1519 1754
　　13 20 1105 14 305 734 763 1311 1314 1315
　　1402 15 2351
Harakiri (1) 12 564
harassed (1) 7 168
harassed (1) 15 1994
harbinger (1) 14 1100
harbour (9) 1 671 2 326 11 851
　　12 1303 14 519 16 417 965 17 1710
　　18 872
harbourmasters (1) 16 646
harbourmouth (1) 1 83
harbours (2) 12 1301 16 960
Harcourt (2) 8 192 18 550
Hard (8) 4 63 6 794 7 956 8 318
　　11 839 14 477 15 1232 3566
hard (47) 2 100 436 3 418 6 22 518
　　8 146 378 9 10 10 454 898 11 670 672
　　697 915 1219 12 63 427 13 132 347 464 869
　　1242 14 114 116 204 365 416 475 572 925 1049
　　1064 1124 1181 15 1304 2880 2987 16 948
　　1095 1736 18 529 577 1057 1199 1208 1382
hard (1) 16 979
hard (7) 15 1058 1309 2451 2752 2835 2943
　　4275
hardearned (1) 12 546
harden (1) 13 870
hardened (1) 18 992
hardening (1) 15 3456
hardest (1) 16 186
hardheaded (1) 14 1228
hardhumped (1) 15 2383
hardihood (1) 14 27
hardly (7) 9 851 11 1258 16 9 174 1832
　　18 647 1462
hardly (1) 9 1143
hardon (1) 15 3090

Hardwicke (4) 12 399 17 7 602
　　18 1420
hardworking (3) 12 1104 1109 16 869
Hardy (1) 8 362
hare (3) 3 334 8 869
harebell (1) 9 652
harelip (1) 14 984
hares (1) 8 713
harimon (1) 17 729
Hark (3) 14 1088 1569 15 3998
hark (1) 14 1397
harkee (1) 14 356
harking (2) 11 798 15 442
harlequinade (1) 17 426
harlot (1) 15 3039
harlot's (1) 15 4641
harlot's (1) 2 355
harlots (3) 3 366 9 1207 15 3930
harm (17) 1 202 606 5 149 6 623 889
　　8 267 770 12 326 13 885 1278 15 3695
　　16 1624 1660 18 41 108 1463 1517
harman (1) 14 1519
harmless (2) 8 870 16 870
harmonial (1) 15 2205
harmonically (1) 17 1570
Harmony (1) 11 879
Harmony (1) 15 3727
harmony (3) 9 444 11 737 12 591
harm's (2) 6 270 13 955
Harmsworth (1) 7 733
harness (5) 8 514 10 450 1035 15 700
　　16 941
harness (1) 15 4919
harnessed (1) 17 224
harnesses (2) 8 615 634
Harold's (2) 7 6 15 699
Harolds (1) 18 295
Haroun (2) 3 366 15 3113
Haroun (1) 15 4325
HARP (1) 7 370
Harp (1) 8 600
harp (5) 8 606 11 580 581 14 1350
　　17 1244
harp (1) 15 2629
harped (1) 11 1030
harping (3) 3 266 11 644 663
harpoon (1) 16 1795
Harpooning (1) 8 715
harps (3) 11 583 12 1308 1713
harpsichording (1) 11 324
harpstrings (1) 1 245
harpy (1) 6 518
Harriers (1) 15 272
Harrington (1) 15 1378
HARRINGTON (1) 15 1381
Harris (3) 9 440 17 1399 1582
Harris (1) 15 3222
Harrison's (2) 8 233 310
Harris's (1) 8 552
harrowed (1) 9 496
harrowing (1) 16 586
Harry (18) 3 92 9 647 14 592 613 619
　　623 630 15 1182 4392 4399 4484 4602 4770
　　4793 16 1341 18 818 861 1026
Harry (4) 1 597 17 802 804 806
Harry's (1) 14 618
Harsh (1) 9 576
harsh (1) 7 346
harsh (2) 15 2184 4111

harshed (1) 6 490
harsher (1) 12 728
harshly (1) 1 327
harshly (1) 15 2545
Hart (1) 17 1254
Harty (1) 17 173
harumscarum (1) 18 1470
harvest (1) 14 522
harvestmoon (1) 8 602
Harvey (4) 8 441 10 630 13 417
　　18 1055
Has (21) 3 25 4 457 5 285 6 234 373
　　543 706 900 7 985 8 1155 9 390 519
　　11 392 12 873 13 1068 14 912 929
　　15 307 1295 3202 16 777
Has (1) 12 744
has (254) 1 41 323 547 552 2 49 373 437
　　3 36 77 94 95 276 4 358 428 492 504 529
　　5 148 183 272 306 395 6 36 226 617 630 762
　　763 828 899 7 135 155 261 463 641 742 785 800
　　909 949 8 64 118 206 212 230 304 340 441 463
　　616 868 951 984 1008 1098 9 41 48 54 58 112
　　147 151 159 161 166 172 186 215 290 303 304 309
　　322 379 397 424 456 460 466 475 477 478 504 583
　　611 668 672 682 685 809 864 865 921 923 1009
　　1011 1013 1029 1031 1056 1138 1155 1164
　　10 559 751 846 865 935 944 946 1068 11 84
　　496 561 695 959 1003 1026 1161 1209 1260
　　12 65 66 360 476 545 606 707 720 721 725 731
　　736 862 1046 1068 1106 1265 1494 1556 1557 1602
　　1883 1889 13 195 296 443 613 736 911 951 1056
　　1099 1153 1195 1223 1244 1253 14 18 228 245
　　442 520 524 553 564 664 783 791 807 811 905 906
　　913 918 976 983 995 1009 1018 1221 1227 1277
　　1280 1304 1323 1336 1340 1403 15 70 824 837
　　969 972 1002 1121 1464 1468 1770 1776 1781 1782
　　1801 2271 2284 2331 2357 2380 2498 2590 2796
　　2964 3141 3296 3425 3540 3631 3687 4006 4074
　　4474 4557 16 751 772 879 1097 1123 1158 1727
　　17 1763 2320 18 22 50 81 111 144 168 349 411
　　564 726 827 935 1075 1105 1198 1210 1235 1277
　　1368 1383 1385 1401
has (3) 7 770 9 799 16 1810
has (10) 15 414 862 1205 1826 2483 2746 2748
　　4317 4965
hasarded (1) 16 262
hash (2) 9 576 16 1606
hashbaz (1) 15 4619
Hasn't (3) 8 228 10 943 15 4762
hasn't (4) 1 42 10 518 12 455 16 787
hasnt (2) 18 154 1321
hasp (1) 6 256
Hast (2) 9 483 12 1612
hast (9) 14 370 372 377 378 379 380 1410 1413
hast (1) 8 1053
haste (6) 2 224 9 163 888 10 358 1236
　　11 889
hastened (3) 11 1081 13 204 16 1152
hastening (2) 8 141 10 1233
hastens (1) 15 4326
hastily (2) 1 65 4 384
hastily (2) 15 729 1508
Hastings' (1) 2 301
hasty (6) 2 205 8 1183 9 603 10 988
　　11 433 14 843
hasty (1) 15 2023
Hat (2) 3 182 17 1026
hat (128) 1 491 519 582 601 3 174 241 390
　　417 438 487 4 66 69 293 294 485 5 21 25 28

139 319 347 355   6 40 129 199 234 303 452 587
709 824 873 875 1015 1018 1021 1022   7 29 172
331 351 457 469 638 957   8 166 297 416 507 606
1168   9 298 299 946 1123   10 30 56 81 102 215
360 901 1201 1244   11 302 882 1122 1252
12 384 397 1046 1092   13 156 276 335 368 478
506 509 515 677 795 838 1032 1234   14 86 104
698 1049   15 92 195 549 3770 4590 4894
16 2 220 494 705 790 1336 1513 1517 1740
17 85 117 629 707 708 1033 1923 2103   18 84
227 296 472 521 705 713 798 837 971 1089 1402
1573

hat (37)   15 27 270 465 539 543 720 726 807 936
1058 1480 1787 1928 2033 2060 2072 2245 2250
2252 2586 2588 2657 2684 2698 2859 3306 3764
3857 3876 4033 4123 4499 4579 4749 4805 4921
4945

hātākāldā (1)   12 354
hatbrim (1)   10 211
Hatch (2)   14 1064   15 364
hatched (1)   3 417
hatchet (2)   15 762   17 1563
hatching (1)   11 1024
hatching (1)   15 3707
Hate (4)   5 82   6 1012   8 716   11 1069
hate (28)   8 494 696   11 1068   12 524
13 1232   15 376 518 1977 4534   16 657 672
898 1102   18 31 44 106 323 333 387 491 518 725
876 936 942 952 1038 1458

hated (3)   12 1467   13 47 294
hater (1)   3 109
Hates (1)   8 1119
hath (12)   9 257   11 904 1055   12 448
14 177 297 361 381 400 402 1038   15 4701
hath (1)   13 315
Hathaway (2)   9 180 240
hating (1)   17 237
hatless (1)   16 1517
hatless (1)   15 3372
Hatpin (1)   8 239
hatrack (1)   18 544
hatrack (1)   15 3823
hatred (4)   12 1418 1481 1482 1485
Hats (1)   15 1459
hats (20)   2 367   5 356 415   6 37 59 174 656
719   8 126 654   10 832   11 494 688 852
12 1325 1334   14 1394   18 129 631 1420
hats (5)   15 499 590 758 1573 3962
Hatten (1)   14 377
hatter (1)   11 883
hauberk (2)   15 1915 4507
Hauck (1)   15 2745
haud (1)   16 175
Hauding (1)   14 1495
haught (1)   14 413
haughtiness (1)   7 805
haughtiness (1)   7 839
HAUGHTY (1)   7 1032
haughty (4)   5 103   10 470   11 97 1261
haulage (1)   6 443
Hauled (1)   3 480
hauled (1)   10 502
hauling (1)   12 705
hauls (2)   15 288 3524
haunch (1)   10 451
haunch (1)   15 316
haunches (4)   5 218   8 727   10 810
14 1084
haunches (1)   15 3129

haunt (2)   6 1001   16 560
haunted (1)   14 1037
Haunting (1)   8 502
haunting (3)   13 111 422   16 1332
haunts (2)   12 374   15 395
Hauptmann (1)   17 869
hausi (1)   16 1764
hauteur (1)   13 97
Have (47)   1 322 440   2 91   3 139   5 507
6 188 220 755 963   7 154 651 652 654   8 135
467 469 713 756 1097   9 18 552   11 34 261 526
527 1240   12 869 1668   13 964 974 995 1118
14 808 1123 1470 1508   15 259 493 1347 1985
2197 2524 2711 2764 4238   16 611 807
Have (1)   12 810
have (627)   1 54 89 91 117 128 151 161 180 209
296 412 469 516 524 533 548 554 609 648   2 51
141 219 225 237 238 259 278 290 291 321 349 389
410 420   3 98 130 158 183 263 288 290 296 298
376 475   4 73 203 326 328 365 418 483 485 489
5 3 172 179 248 249 250 255 277 294 320 355 356
373 391 429 470 473 499 501 524   6 70 77 83 92
98 163 216 221 259 338 346 353 405 406 407 415
578 610 620 755 797 808 832 867 919 932 944 958
7 171 172 198 499 706 740 744 763 787 884 915
917 923 945 976 1002   8 53 79 125 133 136 150
162 213 214 239 318 331 355 382 421 422 427 462
480 488 498 508 521 553 764 771 782 831 846 926
930 980 1029 1038 1049 1108 1111 1116 1126 1145
1160 1161 1192   9 2 43 82 86 141 176 184 188
256 277 289 318 334 348 349 371 445 565 596 709
739 754 812 815 847 876 971 1012 1015 1064 1094
1113 1167   10 45 139 191 288 430 698 711 749
862 1058 1062 1070 1084 1280   11 208 272 276
658 696 714 869 939 969 1123 1127 1200 1206 1226
1249   12 3 47 161 275 383 434 453 595 749 758
789 845 876 892 919 1147 1200 1233 1245 1312
1317 1364 1399 1406 1463 1567 1590 1650 1850
1854 1862 1868 1875 1887 1899   13 11 43 101
102 104 107 114 180 191 231 235 240 271 316 318
319 422 484 487 512 583 628 658 733 778 782 816
819 833 853 855 861 885 942 958 995 1019 1031
1046 1048 1082 1126 1142 1146 1148 1163 1182
14 14 25 27 35 37 104 119 137 176 196 230 320
354 366 410 432 433 526 741 777 779 781 833 837
838 882 889 902 903 908 918 939 1080 1112 1125
1142 1147 1180 1280 1314 1320 1342 1454 1509
1531   15 111 287 399 524 638 641 643 646 665
669 720 721 743 745 843 950 952 967 998 1009
1066 1100 1171 1505 1506 1677 1683 1778 1783
1793 1799 1810 1836 1968 2126 2198 2205 2270
2376 2384 2389 2397 2408 2453 2525 2526 2538
2641 2717 2738 2757 2775 2782 2794 2898 2993
3083 3129 3198 3204 3206 3215 3254 3285 3388
3392 3397 3398 3405 3449 3475 3486 3520 3522
3607 3625 3644 3734 3764 4233 4433 4436 4460
4470 4563 4847 4858 4870 4894   16 71 72 163
176 187 306 357 443 456 477 517 737 752 836 871
886 895 974 1001 1025 1044 1051 1061 1071 1151
1157 1233 1300 1302 1346 1351 1447 1456 1473
1665 1801 1839 1849 1860   17 275 352 455 457
460 461 549 551 906 935 1076 1614 1839 1871 2003
2126   18 8 19 20 21 55 65 111 142 143 148 150
165 167 181 219 242 283 319 320 339 343 365 372
376 387 394 397 422 430 434 436 443 447 450 457
462 475 498 502 510 511 571 597 599 604 615 627
651 652 668 710 725 777 829 847 853 857 869 896
903 931 948 961 977 979 1006 1031 1061 1063 1080
1081 1082 1087 1095 1100 1101 1104 1122 1143

1149 1170 1209 1210 1226 1254 1288 1303 1341
1344 1377 1382 1429 1438 1444 1448 1449 1456
1459 1460 1462 1478 1484 1493 1494 1509 1519
1525 1535 1539 1542 1552 1558
have (17)   1 300 304 591   4 289   7 846 849
864 866 867   10 15   11 1292   12 28 427
13 927   17 412
have (2)   15 905 2017
haven (3)   11 853   12 1358   13 444
Haven't (3)   6 556   8 204   15 4278
haven't (7)   6 695 845   7 482   12 1390
15 3663 4570   16 421
havent (5)   18 660 827 886 1403 1472
Having (6)   4 273   5 110 266   12 355
14 834   17 229
having (109)   1 160 446 620   2 83 147 203
4 334 455   5 271 407   7 873   8 365 799 1033
9 679 835   10 626 723 778 842 1006 1117
11 129   12 119 498 584 694 913 1061 1912
13 255   14 42 427 508 570 680 741 765 801 868
1001 1304   15 400 1963 2118 2625 3080 4394
16 19 107 214 322 340 423 494 496 645 878 918
952 1063 1134 1218 1315 1375 1377 1443 1519
1527 1606 1610 1684 1692 1698 1874   17 238
378 456 460 628 630 748 799 856 903 925 1074
1137 1402 1486 1909 1910 1911 1923 2068 2098
2277 2279   18 44 166 223 416 603 728 913 1079
1117
having (1)   15 3952
havoc (1)   14 482
Haw (3)   11 527 1240   15 3733
haw (2)   11 527   15 3733
Hawhorn (1)   11 23
hawked (2)   11 186   13 1221
hawker (2)   6 500   17 1937
hawker's (2)   10 316 521
hawkers (1)   7 698
hawking (1)   18 1094
Hawkins (1)   17 436
hawklike (1)   9 952
hawks (2)   12 1719   14 1566
hawthorn (2)   11 633   18 1292
hawthorn (1)   15 1448
Hawthornden (1)   9 386
Hawthorne (1)   12 1276
hay (9)   4 173   10 98 210 216   12 688
14 603   15 3493   17 1586 1604
Haye (1)   10 372
Hayes (2)   12 189   15 550
Hayes (1)   15 4357
hayfever (1)   14 1425
hayforks (1)   15 3958
hayjuice (1)   10 221
hayloft (1)   3 66
hayseed (1)   17 1584
haytedder (1)   17 1565
hazard (3)   5 211   6 171   17 571
haze (1)   15 987
Hazeleyes (1)   12 1270
hazelnuts (1)   12 1293
He (873)   1 4 9 20 24 30 35 44 51 54 56 57 64 67
75 86 95 99 121 122 123 130 152 185 203 216 223
230 290 298 309 324 349 363 368 385 397 410 454
465 472 494 508 511 530 534 549 555 558 579 581
588 593 600 616 618 627 630 632 688 704 707 710
727 735   2 22 62 82 116 128 151 176 184 188 208
221 241 242 250 282 292 296 303 320 345 352 353
375 376 427 440 444   3 48 77 80 94 95 100 152
158 159 166 173 206 260 265 268 276 278 283 299

317 335 348 355 358 361 397 437 447 451 489 498 500 503   **4** 2 12 23 34 39 43 48 52 58 70 74 77 100 103 105 135 140 145 154 157 162 174 186 191 201 243 250 253 261 271 277 278 283 286 296 298 304 327 328 338 344 345 374 382 387 389 394 420 424 426 432 449 460 465 467 472 475 485 494 495 512 515 529 537 538   **5** 3 10 47 54 61 65 76 124 143 166 213 221 223 226 229 237 260 276 290 318 338 345 353 354 369 371 413 438 452 456 458 461 467 478 487 517 522 528 542 549 550 567 568 **6** 9 10 50 69 72 74 93 95 114 127 129 169 194 209 260 303 306 311 349 358 375 433 451 492 496 503 505 533 544 569 587 621 636 646 685 699 706 710 728 763 785 804 826 853 883 884 887 893 897 905 934 971 1022   **7** 73 88 109 118 124 126 128 155 161 183 196 204 222 226 235 258 261 325 331 339 371 377 390 405 408 415 421 424 432 450 458 465 470 475 487 493 571 576 592 625 634 641 653 688 694 720 742 744 751 755 768 777 788 797 800 802 809 817 825 827 860 870 893 901 904 908 954 960 991 1028 1037 1060 1067   **8** 57 74 106 118 125 155 175 186 219 230 256 270 299 304 309 312 323 368 371 414 419 426 457 551 564 586 589 590 620 627 641 678 697 702 732 735 782 790 795 800 834 839 840 844 866 940 955 958 1008 1039 1078 1090 1143 1169 1186   **9** 5 30 35 60 74 114 115 122 141 168 245 246 256 265 329 365 390 434 448 454 456 474 478 493 501 506 520 549 563 569 586 589 606 608 614 653 683 697 710 726 732 741 745 766 781 824 829 835 855 878 894 898 921 923 965 995 1016 1018 1020 1021 1030 1041 1047 1057 1061 1075 1092 1128 1133 1162 1166 1177 1179 1190 1210 **10** 8 12 16 19 32 37 70 88 128 174 175 186 187 191 195 208 233 242 246 312 327 339 395 415 432 436 446 450 453 461 468 478 482 491 544 561 564 570 579 580 591 597 603 606 607 634 635 655 664 678 686 700 708 836 867 895 899 902 913 926 944 952 960 1001 1072 1074 1080 1082 1086 1088 1089 1093 1114 1131 1139 1157 1158 1170 1270 **11** 46 153 193 195 197 205 217 222 232 235 239 250 251 253 262 264 266 273 275 283 292 302 346 371 395 401 427 433 437 450 451 471 474 478 483 493 514 535 538 583 610 644 687 778 786 790 796 810 822 823 833 849 859 895 916 917 928 930 934 994 1001 1033 1068 1120 1140 1172 1175 1281 1283   **12** 168 267 335 370 374 409 460 594 775 848 947 988 990 1210 1550 1640 1675 1806 1911 1915   **13** 22 199 200 203 235 421 423 449 453 459 517 613 743 747 801 1098 1179 1239 1246 1270 **14** 104 247 348 421 432 533 540 563 586 684 921 1010 1012 1027 1034 1043 1063 1068 1111 1116 1123 1125 1128 1155 1162 1185 1322 1341 1346 1374 1421 1515   **15** 339 616 662 750 766 873 885 886 953 980 981 1016 1018 1021 1022 1045 1051 1054 1069 1070 1111 1117 1153 1456 1468 1712 1741 1769 1770 1776 1780 1800 1801 1803 1805 1807 1810 2245 2385 2466 2526 2561 2572 2573 2601 2651 2665 2673 2676 2784 3011 3028 3138 3140 3445 3769 4187 4273 4378 4392 4443 4486 4513 4568 4600 4726 4727 4741 4762 4786 4873 **16** 106 131 148 170 181 186 188 215 233 261 281 287 395 411 448 468 472 568 604 692 822 830 835 902 922 953 1071 1081 1082 1086 1088 1117 1142 1298 1300 1305 1306 1333 1448 1495 1542 1740 1743 1774 1789 1803   **17** 63 124 161 349 355 488 530 616 617 637 777 780 839 844 993 1012 1264 1435 1436 1443 1447 1449 1451 2109 2241 2320 **18** 178 1519 1520

He (8) **5** 129 **7** 524 866 **10** 15 **12** 31 **17** 805 807

He (116) **15** 25 31 99 147 151 155 159 164 168 175 184 196 222 226 229 297 310 315 335 356 366 501 604 632 649 667 689 807 816 900 923 933 965 995 999 1163 1179 1205 1206 1213 1255 1265 1268 1317 1318 1444 1491 1521 1558 1886 1928 2014 2023 2031 2032 2161 2164 2186 2247 2248 2263 2264 2272 2274 2306 2479 2480 2482 2483 2485 2571 2657 2668 2677 2710 2711 2713 2728 2829 2901 3063 3575 3594 3629 4020 4034 4038 4039 4110 4121 4153 4243 4285 4314 4320 4332 4333 4449 4454 4543 4548 4615 4674 4728 4747 4748 4925 4928 4934 4944 4946 4959 4965

he (2805) **1** 6 9 11 19 28 34 37 45 46 51 53 63 66 72 77 82 88 97 106 112 116 122 134 136 141 143 148 150 162 168 183 185 202 204 222 225 235 243 258 331 333 339 353 365 374 378 380 381 406 411 424 431 458 474 476 478 491 503 504 512 513 515 519 525 527 534 547 549 556 565 574 577 580 607 622 645 647 673 684 685 704 708 720 724 739 742 **2** 14 36 69 131 134 174 178 187 189 193 200 207 209 211 222 251 262 294 298 346 354 358 360 388 389 400 406 409 424 429 437 446   **3** 4 6 52 64 80 125 126 127 165 166 167 231 234 246 249 251 263 270 295 320 333 337 345 356 360 365 367 406 408 441 461 470 473 474 480 486   **4** 3 6 24 30 35 49 54 64 72 81 112 120 135 142 143 149 152 156 167 188 211 230 247 251 258 264 265 267 273 275 280 291 292 297 300 309 310 320 321 336 340 341 352 354 358 362 375 381 386 390 392 394 408 420 427 440 462 467 470 497 500 506 507 508 515 516 529 538 541   **5** 7 8 15 17 21 28 48 52 55 56 68 89 111 115 116 118 126 128 151 165 167 186 191 196 197 200 214 221 231 263 267 275 300 319 324 334 371 379 386 387 395 396 416 418 471 472 493 513 541 **6** 33 36 41 44 56 57 93 97 108 120 132 138 142 191 194 196 232 245 251 269 272 274 281 282 283 289 297 298 300 308 311 314 344 353 362 368 432 433 442 469 510 530 535 538 544 570 572 576 578 579 581 596 598 615 616 617 623 626 629 630 643 647 649 679 684 693 700 703 715 717 722 724 731 732 733 747 751 762 767 786 806 808 809 826 829 860 865 866 867 877 878 885 888 894 895 899 923 924 926 958 972 974 978 1012 1026   **7** 34 68 69 71 74 87 102 113 122 129 134 135 139 145 153 160 171 188 197 205 212 215 228 248 258 266 267 279 284 292 306 318 336 339 365 376 382 388 401 415 435 460 481 492 493 494 506 521 538 545 548 562 586 588 594 599 612 616 629 630 635 645 648 664 671 698 728 751 756 789 813 814 817 818 822 873 919 961 973 974 977 978 981 986 987 992 993 996 1036 1038 1061 1062 1072   **8** 27 31 44 51 54 78 93 102 118 121 128 137 159 174 177 180 216 246 251 259 263 289 301 306 313 317 363 380 424 432 441 463 475 487 502 505 506 525 529 606 639 650 662 665 784 797 802 842 867 893 934 939 942 944 945 946 950 953 955 960 976 980 981 1003 1006 1012 1098 1107 1110 1111 1112 1117 1128 1135 1138 1140 1145 1173   **9** 9 12 13 20 39 91 92 112 127 131 142 160 171 176 177 192 219 226 227 236 246 253 254 280 284 292 302 303 304 305 311 318 332 339 348 349 351 359 360 393 419 424 427 442 446 452 455 457 470 473 475 476 477 478 487 489 508 510 513 515 523 529 531 537 543 546 548 556 560 569 575 578 580 591 592 602 613 614 624 631 652 656 657 660 663 665 671 672 676 680 682 691 692 695 712 713 725 731 742 763 764 774 788 789 790 804 817 818 830 845 854 867 868 891 895 896 919 925 932 936 962 969 971 983 984 1004 1009 1012 1018 1021 1022 1031 1033 1054 1056 1071

1077 1084 1101 1104 1134 1138 1158 1167 1191 1197 1208   **10** 2 11 27 28 30 32 33 36 37 39 48 59 66 79 97 114 118 170 175 196 210 211 224 230 302 322 325 329 336 364 371 386 423 433 438 439 444 445 446 450 455 457 465 467 476 489 492 501 503 506 510 512 522 525 530 545 552 566 573 577 581 593 595 635 638 641 662 673 679 687 695 703 719 747 756 769 869 900 904 908 923 934 941 943 950 953 980 997 1004 1007 1019 1021 1026 1034 1048 1057 1061 1066 1068 1072 1084 1089 1092 1094 1109 1112 1115 1119 1123 1138 1141 1144 1151 1155 1167 1169 1171 1173 1188 1234 1245 **11** 24 43 90 91 100 101 104 135 141 206 210 219 243 247 255 257 260 272 280 281 291 314 318 329 333 337 342 354 373 374 389 391 392 432 453 463 485 501 520 522 549 554 556 561 573 588 589 605 615 623 633 635 644 648 667 671 695 697 719 738 747 780 781 782 783 786 787 799 800 854 889 901 907 911 913 917 918 924 928 930 949 959 986 994 1003 1009 1013 1025 1026 1032 1040 1041 1042 1060 1064 1090 1092 1132 1161 1165 1170 1172 1173 1191 1204 1211 1212 1222 1235 1248 1253 1265 1266 1267   **12** 3 16 27 28 29 65 66 67 100 120 122 126 129 131 132 136 137 144 147 148 149 150 155 170 202 209 216 220 224 240 257 259 261 265 267 277 290 305 337 345 348 349 352 357 366 367 377 379 382 383 396 398 403 405 410 414 432 433 434 435 436 441 443 444 466 480 484 485 486 487 492 494 495 496 503 509 510 511 614 615 632 645 671 673 681 682 699 702 703 704 705 748 749 751 759 762 770 774 775 776 781 782 786 795 801 805 806 808 816 819 821 835 880 895 948 957 959 962 974 990 1020 1025 1028 1033 1043 1046 1054 1060 1068 1069 1078 1080 1093 1100 1103 1122 1130 1140 1143 1144 1210 1212 1217 1219 1222 1227 1229 1230 1232 1306 1311 1314 1333 1343 1344 1345 1357 1359 1362 1393 1406 1410 1414 1417 1426 1433 1434 1469 1470 1471 1478 1479 1481 1485 1487 1488 1505 1506 1512 1522 1529 1531 1534 1550 1555 1556 1564 1569 1570 1582 1591 1595 1597 1599 1600 1607 1613 1619 1622 1631 1632 1635 1638 1647 1655 1657 1659 1665 1666 1736 1737 1744 1755 1756 1763 1768 1777 1778 1785 1788 1789 1798 1803 1808 1811 1843 1844 1847 1853 1854 1897 1898 1901 1903 1904 1908 1909   **13** 47 55 77 133 134 136 137 138 140 141 143 145 146 149 183 186 201 202 204 206 241 243 246 247 248 249 250 259 309 312 314 319 321 339 347 383 388 390 395 397 411 416 420 421 423 424 428 429 431 432 433 434 436 439 452 454 456 457 483 491 494 495 502 504 537 539 540 544 546 547 548 554 557 558 559 574 584 585 594 597 656 667 671 676 693 704 724 726 728 730 731 733 743 744 745 747 749 800 841 848 849 881 886 915 976 983 985 993 1047 1056 1059 1082 1111 1119 1120 1130 1146 1154 1156 1178 1219 1220 1221 1225 **14** 60 74 84 87 89 94 99 102 108 109 110 112 119 120 129 130 131 132 133 137 148 163 164 165 170 171 172 175 178 180 181 194 196 197 198 202 210 221 227 229 230 234 236 239 240 250 252 254 258 260 261 262 264 266 270 273 275 280 281 285 287 289 310 315 327 335 336 338 339 341 342 361 381 401 412 415 417 419 420 426 430 431 432 433 434 435 437 438 439 440 441 443 448 471 500 501 502 507 508 520 530 531 532 533 535 539 541 542 543 545 547 549 550 551 553 557 559 560 565 568 573 575 579 580 585 589 591 593 594 599 603 605 607 610 614 621 624 625 627 632 634 635 636 638 653 658 661 667 672 678 679 681 689 692 696 698 704

710 716 717 720 723 725 727 745 746 752 755 756
763 765 771 774 782 820 823 835 838 839 840 841
846 854 860 861 866 870 876 880 890 902 911 912
913 914 917 929 931 945 965 989 999 1006 1007
1015 1019 1023 1025 1030 1041 1045 1062 1140
1160 1181 1184 1192 1193 1228 1241 1245 1249
1251 1262 1303 1307 1329 1352 1401 1405 1473
1474 1509 1521 1547 1549 1561 1576   15 585
648 766 824 857 887 893 951 954 1018 1020 1029
1032 1033 1047 1053 1054 1061 1067 1071 1115
1145 1169 1171 1359 1384 1462 1561 1782 1804
1808 1894 1898 2126 2223 2234 2367 2462 2463
2706 2786 3030 3031 3032 3034 3036 3037 3141
3163 3610 3647 3718 3720 3800 3940 4279 4286
4290 4293 4303 4374 4378 4394 4493 4495 4515
4517 4757 4759 4775 4778 4873 4884 4886   16 3
11 13 14 25 38 71 73 74 75 76 82 86 90 92 93 95
105 108 109 110 117 119 129 144 146 149 153 155
161 170 173 176 180 182 183 185 187 189 190 191
192 205 206 209 216 217 218 220 221 226 230 231
235 239 242 243 246 248 256 257 258 262 270 272
282 287 294 295 296 298 299 301 303 304 306 307
321 324 340 348 351 356 358 359 366 368 378 385
386 391 392 396 398 401 402 430 453 484 485 490
495 499 501 502 504 509 515 517 527 571 573 578
582 585 586 599 603 608 610 614 615 622 624 628
630 634 651 655 658 660 670 673 679 683 684 685
699 700 709 710 711 712 716 720 723 730 743 744
745 748 755 762 787 797 800 802 803 807 828 831
836 837 841 848 853 859 865 866 872 873 887 904
905 916 920 924 925 952 954 955 964 966 969 974
975 976 984 985 987 995 997 1001 1004 1005 1024
1031 1033 1037 1049 1054 1057 1058 1060 1063
1067 1070 1075 1078 1079 1089 1109 1116 1119
1131 1133 1146 1147 1148 1149 1166 1173 1178
1180 1181 1183 1188 1190 1196 1201 1210 1216
1217 1221 1227 1228 1229 1230 1233 1238 1246
1258 1268 1270 1271 1295 1299 1301 1303 1304
1311 1313 1315 1317 1325 1335 1336 1344 1346
1357 1359 1371 1372 1387 1388 1394 1396 1404
1405 1408 1411 1422 1424 1425 1426 1440 1441
1447 1450 1456 1458 1462 1464 1470 1472 1476
1478 1479 1491 1505 1516 1518 1522 1556 1558
1559 1561 1567 1569 1572 1575 1582 1583 1584
1588 1591 1592 1593 1595 1598 1607 1608 1609
1611 1614 1615 1617 1619 1620 1623 1635 1637
1641 1648 1650 1658 1660 1662 1672 1673 1682
1687 1693 1697 1698 1702 1708 1714 1721 1723
1731 1738 1746 1753 1755 1756 1757 1758 1761
1764 1768 1773 1787 1790 1792 1796 1800 1806
1807 1810 1812 1817 1818 1819 1821 1828 1832
1834 1838 1839 1841 1842 1852 1853 1854 1860
1863 1866 1869 1877 1878 1889   17 67 68 69 72
75 77 78 84 90 100 101 106 109 119 229 237 248
285 293 325 337 349 362 366 368 371 384 385 388
390 402 404 410 459 476 487 497 498 521 530 531
555 563 606 633 636 639 693 698 706 707 710 810
830 834 850 852 853 864 875 885 906 909 947 979
980 990 1007 1019 1070 1072 1083 1092 1146 1151
1177 1259 1261 1269 1270 1271 1283 1321 1355
1356 1421 1424 1480 1483 1603 1616 1634 1635
1642 1645 1657 1754 1760 1761 1763 1765 1894
1905 1923 1924 1925 2013 2017 2019 2060 2125
2126 2128 2130 2149 2210 2251 2256   18 1 2 4
14 17 22 25 29 30 31 34 36 37 39 41 45 46 48 51 54
60 64 65 73 76 77 81 93 94 97 98 107 108 110 112
113 115 116 122 124 125 130 140 141 142 143 144
148 149 150 154 167 170 171 173 175 176 178 179
183 184 185 187 188 194 196 197 198 203 208 210

222 225 226 227 234 246 247 251 255 257 258 260
265 268 270 273 274 276 277 278 281 282 283 284
286 293 294 297 301 302 303 306 307 309 310 315
317 318 319 321 322 328 329 330 331 333 338 342
343 345 349 350 356 359 360 361 362 363 364 367
380 382 383 385 386 387 389 390 391 392 393 397
404 411 413 419 421 423 424 425 426 439 440 447
452 453 454 457 458 461 485 486 487 488 493 496
500 501 502 503 504 506 510 512 519 520 522 527
528 529 533 535 536 547 560 561 564 566 567 569
571 575 577 578 581 584 586 592 618 624 625 634
643 648 649 655 658 671 682 684 694 697 708 713
722 724 728 732 735 737 743 762 764 769 771 774
777 778 780 781 787 796 799 800 801 814 817 818
819 820 824 828 835 836 853 857 866 872 889 891
892 894 899 927 929 932 949 951 955 960 963 964
966 968 980 981 983 985 987 988 989 992 993 1000
1001 1002 1008 1013 1017 1019 1020 1022 1027
1046 1054 1062 1076 1087 1091 1092 1094 1097
1101 1106 1108 1112 1119 1121 1123 1124 1135
1139 1140 1144 1154 1155 1158 1160 1163 1164
1172 1175 1178 1179 1181 1185 1186 1191 1192
1197 1198 1199 1200 1201 1203 1205 1210 1213
1217 1223 1225 1228 1229 1230 1235 1238 1246
1249 1250 1251 1254 1258 1272 1277 1278 1281
1284 1285 1288 1290 1292 1294 1295 1296 1299
1301 1302 1304 1309 1311 1313 1314 1321 1324
1325 1326 1327 1329 1330 1331 1333 1334 1349
1354 1361 1362 1363 1364 1366 1368 1379 1386
1394 1395 1397 1401 1406 1421 1422 1424 1427
1428 1430 1445 1451 1452 1457 1460 1461 1476
1477 1482 1486 1488 1489 1490 1491 1492 1493
1510 1520 1521 1524 1526 1527 1528 1530 1537
1546 1549 1572 1576 1577 1578 1580 1582 1604
1605 1607

he (22) 2 66 4 514 7 580 863 864 9 22
23 24 25 550 1043 10 614 12 28 31 427
16 405 703 1252 1886 17 819 828 1352
he (208) 15 132 136 151 156 158 160 171 173
193 201 209 220 241 260 296 333 468 513 577 666
672 705 714 720 741 742 744 759 769 843 901 904
906 909 959 961 1085 1109 1168 1191 1234 1246
1262 1521 1601 1602 1603 1605 1606 1607 1608
1609 1610 1611 1613 1936 1966 1968 2027 2049
2073 2094 2105 2148 2160 2185 2207 2209 2222
2307 2312 2374 2392 2404 2420 2427 2433 2435
2436 2441 2442 2455 2465 2467 2476 2499 2549
2553 2555 2556 2574 2600 2602 2621 2623 2629
2660 2669 2682 2699 2714 2723 2739 2787 2847
2897 2911 2936 2942 2945 2946 2958 2959
2962 3006 3067 3081 3087 3088 3090 3108 3127
3144 3202 3211 3212 3215 3276 3335 3373 3465
3477 3534 3545 3584 3606 3610 3622 3631 3720
3751 3763 3783 3792 3820 3827 3876 3893 3904
3916 3935 3940 3945 3949 4013 4033 4044 4152
4170 4298 4312 4325 4387 4414 4426 4427 4429
4436 4456 4460 4462 4472 4481 4538 4554 4555
4570 4796 4808 4814 4821 4826 4839 4869 4883
4890 4891 4896 4919 4922 4926 4930 4936 4937
4939 4951 4952 4955 4965 4966

Head (10) 1 181 8 396 9 405 11 1193
12 1831 14 1417 15 3948 16 168 1651
17 1400
Head (1) 15 3378
HEAD (1) 15 2637
head (153) 1 13 233 237 289 418 582 742
2 198 405 3 83 114 241 4 20 248 495 528
5 110 124 279 295 313 314 347 6 1 59 119 479
509 580 655 765 784 925 1023 1025 7 104 290

433 821 825 8 145 297 375 520 687 873 901 1079
1124 1126 9 100 253 446 546 1111 1190
10 102 132 240 246 305 455 633 658 664 962
1198 1262 11 64 141 421 687 688 804 941 955
12 55 342 459 611 774 836 1046 1323 1615 1850
1878 13 118 142 264 268 385 504 510 513 589
745 898 942 999 14 192 216 630 643 743 1026
1057 1213 1327 15 209 274 1050 2126 2376
2968 3374 4214 16 30 122 180 385 617 763 1201
1400 1781 17 85 243 1033 1712 1777 1889 2110
2111 2112 2312 18 364 478 522 546 770 886
1061 1095 1253 1267 1350 1487 1532 1573
head (3) 4 438 7 863 17 826
head (54) 15 125 322 499 513 936 1000 1173
1487 1510 2036 2040 2082 2178 2264 2288 2309
2334 2441 2460 2482 2587 2620 2631 2636 2658
2682 2711 2712 2830 2884 3215 3254 3291 3360
3436 3551 3658 3664 3668 3673 3764 3876 3900
4255 4284 4556 4674 4696 4697 4821 4827 4910
4912
headache (4) 5 255 285 12 1660 13 778
headaches (1) 13 327
headband (4) 4 70 5 24 26 320
headband (1) 15 726
headborough (2) 14 555 565
headed (2) 12 1676 15 233
headed (1) 15 1412
headgear (3) 12 1871 14 1393 16 1524
headhanger (1) 16 1785
heading (1) 10 982
headland (4) 1 224 11 590 592
headless (2) 9 295 11 1219
headlight (1) 15 186
headline (1) 2 129
headlong (1) 15 1528
headpiece (1) 4 101
headrent (1) 17 1666
Heads (2) 8 755 827
heads (19) 2 301 366 5 343 356 357 6 658
825 839 8 520 11 159 177 12 532 605
14 151 16 276 1202 18 669 1241 1242
heads (9) 15 1147 1151 1424 1460 1749 2020
4387 4578 4678
Headshake (1) 6 916
headsman (1) 12 596
headstall (1) 15 1445
headstrong (1) 13 45
heady (1) 8 1172
heah (2) 18 701
healed (1) 14 128
Healer (1) 14 296
healer (1) 14 937
healing (4) 12 1724 13 435 17 213 891
heals (1) 17 1826
heals (1) 15 1844
Health (2) 12 241 14 1545
health (15) 6 301 430 10 915 12 820 1076
1077 1502 13 216 389 14 38 181 932
16 86 510 731
health (1) 3 201
health (1) 15 1798
healthier (1) 8 536
Healthy (2) 5 406 13 1062
healthy (4) 6 329 14 1274 18 165
Healy (3) 7 800 12 194 14 494
Healy (1) 15 4343
heap (5) 1 725 2 370 12 503 14 1448
16 104
heaped (3) 1 722 2 213 370

heaping (1) 16 1399
heaps (1) 16 1860
heaps (1) 15 4476
Hear (7) 1 665 6 75 11 458 930
  12 1317 15 1532
hear (115) 1 251 487 665 2 9 42 110 244 376
  3 10 23 4 405 5 153 186 203 262 400 409
  6 144 213 268 717 789 899 1003 7 128 130 257
  310 393 834 8 33 162 283 289 336 9 80 95
  306 517 618 971 10 21 942 1171 11 98 136
  260 294 315 335 389 671 672 677 711 722 794 839
  842 911 924 932 945 975 1005 1049 1061 1085 1091
  1139 1213 1245 12 243 749 988 1036 1317
  13 409 699 874 1004 1122 14 96 136 437 515
  521 524 664 966 1066 1535 15 1216 1658 2217
  2334 3804 3831 4439 16 758 862 1143 1748
  1893 17 797 1204 1242 2017 18 164 182 617
  721 933 1131
hear (3) 9 1143 17 819 824
hear (3) 15 899 924 3757
Heard (4) 11 853 14 435 436 15 3395
heard (108) 1 257 282 534 609 2 47 91 181
  3 125 126 465 4 54 58 470 5 95 127 181 213
  6 24 530 532 7 299 793 877 8 46 771 943
  9 13 353 480 569 805 10 186 472 626 645
  11 1 65 112 113 240 278 338 345 395 443 457 545
  549 611 633 650 678 679 780 782 787 823 849 930
  934 935 1143 1173 12 108 280 352 459 707 920
  942 1143 1193 13 267 304 14 104 170 202
  338 339 426 952 15 574 640 721 2911 3230 3270
  4441 16 287 379 973 1011 1078 1147 1419 1757
  17 777 810 830 1228 2061 18 140 634 1000
  1309 1383 1462
heard (4) 1 584 6 147 7 838 839
heard (11) 15 367 1136 1258 1408 2686 2697
  2727 2734 3220 3297 3340
hearer (1) 16 660
hearers (1) 14 667
hearing (14) 2 428 3 281 7 162 1029
  9 155 11 670 916 936 948 1105 14 80 260
  545 926
hearing (2) 15 2406 2705
hearkened (1) 14 118
hears (2) 9 145
hearse (4) 6 407 416 436 504
hearsedrivers (1) 15 4883
hearses (2) 6 449 15 1687
HEART (1) 7 1
Heart (12) 6 305 320 954 1010 8 7 220
  12 1097 13 670 15 290 4232 4233
Heart (2) 1 463 15 1125
Heart (2) 15 1583 4450
heart (103) 1 102 217 2 84 140 4 2 244
  5 261 6 127 347 352 551 643 670 672 674 787
  793 868 874 955 7 58 303 854 999 8 7 650
  789 1169 1179 1190 9 105 110 402 480 750 1000
  10 823 877 11 659 669 720 1083 12 147
  165 231 405 545 795 892 1777 13 8 137 173 215
  326 411 430 445 671 700 763 1201 14 268 410
  414 422 635 679 750 844 862 1055 1071 1219 1341
  1345 1480 15 474 559 1188 1232 1358 1516
  1606 1998 2620 2688 2689 2691 2883 3884
  16 502 507 18 234 275 330 634 733 1362 1561
  1608
heart (3) 1 463 7 428 472
heart (2) 15 758 4221
heartbalm (1) 13 435
Heartbeats (1) 11 1107
heartbroken (1) 13 577

heartburn (1) 7 241
heartening (1) 15 3946
heartfelt (1) 12 1516
hearth (6) 1 314 8 196 14 1210 1372
  16 270 17 1527
hearth (1) 15 3538
hearthdreaming (1) 17 906
hearthrug (1) 18 266
hearthrug (1) 15 2048
hearths (2) 12 1255 13 296
hearthstone (1) 17 125
heartily (9) 7 99 8 16 10 407 12 583
  649 14 722 1121 15 2208 4461
heartless (1) 15 767
heartpocket (1) 15 738
heartrending (2) 10 726 12 654
heart's (2) 8 152 14 604
hearts (14) 2 84 171 6 551 644 676 930
  7 928 9 1036 10 835 11 676 13 279
  375 14 791 1130
heartscalded (1) 8 230
heartstrings (1) 11 714
hearty (4) 12 914 1826 13 242 14 702
heass (2) 18 700 702
Heat (2) 13 1012 17 263
heat (22) 4 80 201 8 789 898 11 446 525
  764 14 680 715 992 15 401 2784 3323
  16 876 17 262 313 380 18 416 607 662 910
  920
heated (3) 14 1000 16 310 1083
heated (1) 15 2753
heath (1) 2 148
heathen (4) 5 327 9 720 13 402
  18 429
heather (2) 8 903 13 1139
heather (1) 15 3397
heatless (1) 17 856
heatseated (1) 11 764
Heatwave (1) 5 563
Heave (1) 14 1463
heave (2) 13 1281 17 2054
heaved (1) 14 643
heaven (34) 2 147 3 193 4 217 5 342
  6 449 562 651 788 9 66 329 496 1051
  10 291 12 245 406 530 1911 1914 13 214
  279 14 96 748 1029 1410 15 1769 1933 2201
  3578 3581 3889 4738 16 1129 18 1558
heaven (2) 2 104 107
heavenbeast (1) 17 1139
heavenborn (1) 17 1243
heavengrot (1) 17 1139
Heavenly (1) 5 558
heavenly (3) 5 445 9 62 11 1122
heavenman (1) 17 1140
heaven's (1) 14 1098
Heavens (1) 17 1373
heavens (6) 9 929 10 568 12 532
  14 422 1098 18 135
heaventree (2) 17 1039 1139
heavenward (1) 15 961
heavenworld (1) 12 345
heaves (1) 15 31
heavied (1) 14 97
Heavier (1) 15 1301
heavier (2) 6 522 16 1281
heavily (8) 1 332 5 313 6 536 16 375
  620 922 923 984
heavily (3) 15 36 185 3553
Heaviness (1) 4 463

heaving (3) 11 1106 16 1468
heaving (2) 10 616 622
heaving (1) 15 909
Heavy (2) 3 290 7 223
Heavy (1) 15 4661
heavy (37) 1 327 535 3 288 4 58 66 208
  460 5 131 464 6 864 7 425 8 233 287
  311 421 475 1066 9 545 10 277 356 932 942
  12 405 14 514 605 1066 1258 1384
  15 2673 16 583 808 1736 18 416 422 660
  870 1138
heavy (5) 15 2076 2747 2830 2839 4856
heavybraked (1) 14 520
heavyfooted (1) 11 1152
heavyhooved (1) 12 110
heavylooking (1) 10 1167
heavystringed (1) 8 296
heavyweights (1) 10 833
hebdomadary (1) 17 1898
Heber (1) 17 751
Heblon's (1) 17 650
Hebrew (5) 12 1091 17 678 724 738
  18 834
Hebrews (1) 16 1268
hecat (1) 11 343
hectic (1) 7 293
hectic (1) 15 994
He'd (3) 7 989 8 509 16 665
He'd (1) 17 820
he'd (23) 6 16 114 808 7 978 8 36 846
  1154 10 1159 11 913 12 437 491 684 816
  845 895 1088 1146 1363 1477 1854 1898 14 616
  1510
hed (40) 14 1540 18 32 35 116 140 167 232
  241 267 283 297 309 354 454 503 505 508 590 696
  764 820 821 857 905 956 999 1007 1096 1121 1162
  1253 1299 1307 1310 1356 1377 1402 1429 1462
  1506
hedge (4) 10 199 14 563 1155 17 1514
Hedges (1) 7 265
hedges (1) 13 1172
Hee (10) 11 40 916 917 918 1004 1283
  15 510 3807 3818
hee (23) 11 40 916 917 919 1004 1283
  15 510 3807 3818
heed (1) 5 79
Heehaw (1) 11 1255
Heel (1) 15 202
heel (9) 1 221 12 1783 13 32 932
  14 503 15 711 2869 4236 16 1003
heel (6) 15 417 2044 2860
heelclacking (1) 15 2734
heeled (1) 6 91
heelless (1) 15 875
heelmarks (1) 15 3183
heels (19) 1 169 628 4 403 6 605 7 912
  986 8 618 9 603 12 369 444 836
  13 170 486 1121 14 1393 15 2862 3083
  3119 3374
heels (4) 15 2038 2178 2312 4332
heeltapping (1) 15 4024
Heenan (2) 10 832 12 955
hefty (1) 12 960
Hegarty (1) 17 537
Hegarty's (1) 15 3174
hegemony (1) 17 194
hegoat's (1) 15 2992
heifer (3) 4 153 159 14 502
heifers (1) 12 106

Heigho (6) 11 858 15 1186 4086
Heigho (8) 4 546 547 548 17 1233 1234
heigho (2) 17 1233 1234
Height (1) 4 29
height (10) 6 3 9 643 13 114 762 975 16 112 17 148 1322 2002 18 390
heights (3) 8 77 15 1033 1529
heir (11) 6 43 7 542 12 1010 14 272 562 945 16 151 1199 1344 17 534 538
Heirloom (1) 15 1313
heirs (2) 12 49 51
Hek (2) 15 2268 2603
held (59) 1 4 107 135 309 588 620 660 2 128 387 3 367 4 157 162 333 5 57 6 497 840 7 382 834 1065 8 564 9 446 519 862 1208 10 9 11 239 252 313 461 561 661 813 832 1015 1204 11 195 567 745 854 859 931 934 947 12 46 1071 13 31 101 734 14 8 104 894 1150 15 886 3625 16 579 1015 17 1519 18 625
held (2) 15 1059 1589
HELEN (1) 7 1032
Helen (6) 2 391 7 536 1039 9 622 12 236 1271
Heligoland (1) 12 1258
heliotherapy (1) 17 295
Heliotrope (1) 13 1009
heliotrope (1) 14 1106
He'll (7) 7 439 973 9 513 12 1020 14 578 15 641 4780
He'll (1) 1 590
he'll (13) 5 529 6 61 539 663 7 973 8 985 10 395 11 1023 12 701 1029 1098 13 1048 15 4896
he'll (1) 17 827
Hell (5) 7 128 10 1006 11 861 12 1330 14 1446
hell (42) 1 506 3 425 5 446 6 477 858 1002 7 482 672 9 401 496 846 10 460 1072 1082 1143 12 262 434 1190 1197 1354 1357 1631 1755 1856 14 621 1021 1543 15 1754 2522 2546 2908 3205 3889 4212 4233 16 641 18 332 731 1364 1477 1536 1568
Hellenic (2) 1 42 17 2078
Hellenise (1) 1 158
HELLO (1) 7 1042
Hello (32) 3 39 4 346 5 84 85 194 452 520 6 831 7 381 665 692 8 140 737 738 1162 10 389 394 401 740 741 882 883 11 356 12 434 1011 1012 1013 1014 15 811 3757
hellohello (1) 6 966
Hellohellohello (1) 6 965
hellprate (1) 14 411
Hell's (1) 10 559
hell's (2) 14 382 1575
hellsgates (1) 15 578
helm (1) 14 644
helm (2) 15 1915 4507
helmet (1) 18 1586
helmet (1) 15 4958
helmets (1) 8 407
helmsman (1) 12 1773
helotic (1) 17 1936
Help (1) 7 594
help (35) 2 164 430 6 65 8 984 1119 9 68 163 1078 10 136 12 1039 1133 1300 14 622 640 1192 1193 1539 15 648 2126 2222 2438 2928 4720 16 1049 1619 18 9 104 886 1084 1211 1219 1276 1398

helped (11) 1 618 4 418 6 83 1020 9 386 10 1080 14 1313 15 780 16 1847 17 119 18 1529
helping (5) 7 468 8 690 13 448 14 1405 18 1020
helpless (1) 11 1053
helpmate (2) 3 41 375
helps (2) 4 137 9 1079
helterskelter (2) 8 439 13 684
helterskelterpelterwelter (1) 15 4363
Hely (2) 15 1008 17 2139
Hely (1) 15 4337
Hely's (8) 6 703 969 8 126 142 158 11 296 13 642 17 1785
Hely's (1) 15 479
Helys (2) 18 561 1224
hem (2) 15 1585 2743
hemisphere (1) 17 2242
hemispheres (2) 17 2229 2232
hemlock (1) 9 239
hemorrhage (2) 17 1091 2287
hen (3) 12 845 846 14 184
Hence (3) 5 367 15 2408 17 906
Henceforth (1) 15 2965
henceforth (2) 15 1386 17 1871
henchmen (3) 12 1835 16 1330 1499
hencods' (1) 4 3
henev (1) 11 29
Hengler's (3) 4 349 16 412 17 975
henna (2) 15 2060 2586
HENNESSY (2) 15 1914 4506
Hennessy's (1) 15 2233
Henny (2) 13 1112 18 322
Henpecked (1) 15 3706
henpecked (1) 15 111
Henri (1) 15 3003
henroost (1) 15 1695
Henry (62) 2 334 5 62 241 249 253 303 6 169 568 571 690 695 704 707 715 1007 1019 1021 1025 7 731 8 951 10 779 937 982 993 1002 1006 1018 1215 1216 1229 11 296 861 888 889 896 1080 1187 1261 1262 12 180 267 1308 1461 1720 14 1442 15 730 733 753 1769 16 661 851 908 1354 17 579 1240 1797 1841 2104 2134 2252 18 654
Henry (2) 6 164 16 1257
Henry (11) 15 1141 1174 1570 1626 1847 2478 2492 2627 4336 4349 4683
HENRY (4) 15 1628 2488 2619 2634
hens (2) 4 479 11 964
hentrusion (1) 14 1448
Her (71) 1 210 250 255 266 268 273 275 276 3 377 4 28 315 325 378 415 430 435 528 5 14 134 346 347 6 87 190 379 479 552 645 8 247 355 542 1065 9 215 880 10 1209 11 76 575 808 938 943 1056 1183 12 294 1498 13 83 89 164 168 189 224 316 517 591 654 1011 1188 1199 1201 1230 14 89 94 518 1152 15 1189 2355 4555 16 437 916 1433 17 1159
Her (2) 10 611 13 947
Her (10) 15 313 1309 2082 2746 2747 2752 2753 2830 4030 4159
her (1456) 1 90 93 94 103 104 108 109 138 140 167 208 212 252 256 257 265 268 270 271 274 339 391 397 401 402 404 405 407 410 411 418 419 420 422 424 426 438 439 440 457 501 655 664 685 2 73 140 141 143 166 312 347 393 3 32 35 46 131 209 210 212 246 253 330 331 373 374 375 376

378 379 393 394 395 396 398 399 400 401 422 424 425 428 429 469 504 4 7 12 22 23 29 33 34 35 43 61 74 95 147 148 151 165 168 171 172 176 178 238 248 253 254 256 257 259 265 276 277 285 286 298 304 305 306 318 321 333 334 338 344 359 366 367 371 378 379 422 423 433 436 445 451 455 457 458 470 487 521 524 525 527 531 532 533 5 6 7 13 48 61 100 102 106 109 120 134 138 139 154 155 195 222 234 235 276 285 295 298 346 348 373 376 377 400 423 428 432 460 492 494 495 6 13 53 67 70 83 155 168 221 238 239 240 247 350 379 380 480 484 518 519 545 547 551 555 646 695 696 705 748 753 754 852 939 7 711 928 949 8 29 38 70 112 144 145 146 153 167 168 169 172 181 182 184 186 188 191 192 195 196 197 198 199 200 204 208 218 228 235 239 250 255 264 266 268 269 270 272 282 287 290 293 309 312 313 332 340 343 344 347 348 350 352 356 357 363 374 375 395 396 398 417 447 450 480 542 560 590 617 628 837 838 848 903 904 905 906 908 909 910 913 914 915 936 972 973 1061 1127 1128 1129 1130 1132 9 37 73 161 241 249 251 254 341 427 448 461 539 540 541 611 615 619 630 633 644 652 667 672 673 675 676 677 679 681 682 686 691 696 697 712 713 724 789 803 805 806 809 825 827 871 934 937 986 1011 1160 10 20 31 126 127 128 129 134 135 136 167 168 170 200 202 238 239 262 268 269 275 286 300 321 327 334 369 383 386 388 440 510 558 559 560 562 605 606 660 678 686 706 766 809 810 811 859 867 870 875 876 1080 1081 1194 1207 1210 1220 1221 1227 1232 1281 11 45 66 74 95 103 115 118 123 136 140 141 142 144 155 163 164 165 166 167 181 195 201 202 203 216 222 238 244 247 250 286 293 312 331 333 347 360 361 363 365 367 378 387 398 406 410 413 414 421 463 502 536 546 547 563 591 592 596 639 645 660 662 680 691 706 707 714 725 726 730 738 755 807 813 815 817 844 866 870 931 941 949 954 1046 1057 1058 1060 1088 1091 1106 1107 1110 1114 1123 1159 1167 1175 1237 1238 1255 1260 1264 12 161 248 294 298 401 503 506 507 508 637 639 640 642 644 661 677 781 782 783 785 812 813 840 841 842 847 849 1002 1005 1052 1064 1113 1157 1166 1167 1172 1279 1394 1395 1396 1534 1660 1801 13 7 27 36 37 54 60 62 72 79 82 85 87 88 95 96 98 99 100 101 102 103 104 111 116 118 119 121 122 124 125 131 137 138 147 153 155 162 168 169 170 173 180 181 184 188 189 190 191 195 202 203 204 209 210 212 213 215 220 229 242 253 264 265 268 270 273 276 288 289 290 292 297 299 304 320 327 328 329 330 331 336 341 352 356 357 358 360 361 366 368 369 370 372 380 385 405 411 412 413 424 425 426 429 430 434 438 439 440 443 445 453 454 475 478 479 480 483 484 485 486 495 496 498 502 503 506 508 509 514 515 516 517 519 522 524 531 537 544 550 557 560 561 562 563 564 568 575 577 578 580 582 585 587 588 592 599 601 614 617 618 631 634 636 637 638 639 640 641 644 648 649 653 658 660 671 672 689 691 692 695 696 697 698 701 702 707 712 723 724 729 734 735 736 758 761 762 763 764 769 772 774 777 787 796 800 803 809 836 838 839 841 849 855 862 868 871 872 883 884 889 890 892 893 900 911 917 918 920 921 922 923 928 929 945 950 962 972 998 1003 1007 1010 1011 1013 1022 1024 1091 1092 1094 1137 1195 1196 1197 1202 1203 1204 1221 1231 1241 1254 1257 1260 1284 1285 14 47 50 53 55 57 65 69 70 81 84 85 86 88 89 90 91 93 104 112 118 120 122 137 176 178 206 207 210 221 222 240 242 245 246 253 295 302 319 321 323 345 451

453 458 459 502 511 512 513 515 516 643 644 688
725 733 755 757 758 764 790 795 796 805 818 827
830 875 883 885 890 893 894 917 919 924 980 981
982 983 1036 1039 1040 1054 1066 1081 1082 1083
1105 1130 1133 1134 1135 1142 1144 1149 1150
1153 1157 1158 1159 1267 1277 1307 1308 1316
1318 1319 1320 1321 1326 1328 1353 1369 1378
1412 1414 1424 1437 1438 1475 1478 1495 1524
1552 15 57 94 95 360 540 566 573 797 949 979
980 1145 1233 1288 1289 1290 1723 2314 2322
2342 2344 2345 2359 2448 2549 2550 2552 2600
2602 2645 2768 2818 2827 2880 2986 2994 3005
3143 3162 3163 3185 3293 3355 3358 3387 3424
3538 3580 3611 3634 3767 3789 3800 3803 3815
3931 4178 4376 4582 16 138 271 437 546 706
721 722 723 726 732 734 799 872 907 912 917 999
1000 1003 1009 1042 1061 1063 1065 1211 1355
1356 1371 1373 1382 1387 1428 1431 1438 1443
1445 1459 1467 1538 1541 1547 1549 1606 1644
1746 1749 1750 17 140 487 488 489 503 504 505
506 507 508 688 691 695 696 864 867 875 876 878
881 896 897 898 902 910 924 926 1118 1160 1161
1162 1163 1164 1166 1167 1168 1169 1884 2082
2180 2241 2275 18 6 7 8 9 10 11 12 13 14 28 29
36 56 63 66 67 68 69 70 159 160 162 172 174 183
187 188 191 193 194 195 214 215 216 218 219 235
236 243 269 376 418 441 476 477 478 480 481 486
489 490 496 498 499 526 527 541 565 575 614 624
641 642 652 667 668 675 719 721 727 742 749 751
752 753 755 758 759 828 878 917 935 993 998 1006
1009 1013 1014 1017 1018 1020 1021 1025 1026
1027 1029 1030 1031 1033 1035 1036 1037 1039
1043 1047 1048 1049 1053 1056 1062 1064 1065
1066 1069 1070 1074 1076 1081 1082 1083 1098
1099 1101 1111 1156 1157 1210 1252 1253 1255
1268 1282 1283 1393 1397 1408 1447 1458 1467
1480 1503 1595

her (19) 1 384 4 290 5 281 7 328 858
9 22 23 10 608 612 614 615 617 622
11 1285 13 948 17 825

her (227) 15 30 32 34 69 81 86 88 89 285 286
288 297 298 300 301 311 312 313 316 328 329 357
361 365 369 373 387 388 437 441 466 468 472 473
492 579 752 753 765 863 1016 1026 1028 1060 1081
1103 1114 1117 1280 1296 1319 1332 1343 1346
1510 1715 1717 1763 1821 1970 1984 1994 2006
2011 2015 2016 2017 2025 2032 2051 2052 2054
2057 2058 2060 2075 2077 2079 2082 2083 2084
2167 2281 2288 2290 2291 2292 2300 2301 2302
2303 2561 2586 2588 2713 2745 2751 2752 2764
2768 2800 2809 2811 2812 2829 2830 2847 2851
2860 2873 2875 2877 2884 2885 2901 2912 2925
3009 3068 3167 3168 3169 3233 3235 3254 3267
3279 3285 3291 3383 3394 3436 3456 3459 3459
3463 3465 3469 3472 3483 3489 3506 3524 3525
3531 3546 3565 3575 3589 3649 3695 3708 3710
3776 3796 3799 3803 3812 3837 3838 3839 3840
3841 3843 3846 3863 3911 4000 4005 4010 4030
4088 4096 4118 4159 4160 4161 4168 4182 4189
4217 4218 4232 4238 4275 4315 4320 4361 4418
4580 4693

herald (1) 9 1059
heraldic (1) 15 1433
herb (2) 5 479 17 891
herbalist (2) 9 652 16 1763
Herbert (1) 9 443
herbivorous (1) 15 388
herbs (1) 5 476
Hercules (4) 10 569 12 1249 1893
17 1052

Herd (1) 14 296
herd (1) 15 3321
herds (3) 3 339 12 89 102
herdsmen (1) 7 846
Here (64) 1 347 677 2 83 3 61 267 351
399 405 4 277 337 5 541 7 231 8 403
640 9 348 1206 10 610 677 706 872 900 983
11 141 605 739 994 1002 12 274 303 433 818
1436 13 427 1286 14 738 1489 1552
15 130 1043 1085 2286 2733 2911 2942 2957 3091
3413 3524 3528 3695 3763 3783 4010 4251 4268
4281 4286 4566 4770 4793 4817 16 471
here (213) 1 25 60 63 162 567 630 712 740
2 42 192 200 220 234 290 341 349 393 401 404
3 2 39 97 244 282 289 300 390 414 434 435
4 131 232 233 327 331 407 476 484 5 53 222
263 356 376 384 395 480 559 6 8 98 346 374 429
510 512 584 640 644 676 722 749 758 804 900 960
978 997 7 76 142 348 411 608 635 650 665 692
996 1016 8 80 432 594 623 673 680 695 699 976
1133 9 89 310 384 515 585 819 922 10 284
307 386 412 413 421 422 467 476 489 519 733 772
785 840 846 854 973 995 11 356 569 570 723
739 821 866 1111 1211 1255 1260 12 100 130
304 490 917 1141 1158 1165 1241 1361 1431 1673
1812 13 51 259 1171 1176 1211 1233 1254 1260
1267 14 285 301 318 408 725 794 1223 1336
1465 1477 1504 1572 15 81 174 395 401 523 603
642 812 843 1118 1197 1278 1471 2193 2284 2525
2541 2873 2875 3082 3105 3129 3529 3543 3743
3871 3930 3967 4024 4302 4303 4415 4436 4461
4471 4628 4773 4894 16 471 683 853 893 894
1223 1644 17 1098 18 13 503 584 610 989
1079 1146 1215
here (4) 7 490 494 12 28 16 1810
hereabouts (2) 15 2314 16 426
herebefore (1) 14 288
hereby (4) 7 890 12 49 15 1504
17 1870
Hereditary (1) 8 174
hereditary (5) 10 157 12 1347 15 1505
1525 1777
heredity (1) 15 945
herein (1) 12 49
hereinafter (2) 12 35 37
Heremon (1) 17 751
hereof (1) 14 339
Here's (8) 8 403 468 11 370 13 1053
14 1491 15 2105 4732 4770
here's (6) 1 482 8 813 12 836 13 258
here's (2) 1 587 3 201
heresiarch (3) 1 659 3 52 9 862
heresiarchs (1) 1 656
Heresiarchus (1) 15 2643
heresies (1) 1 656
heresy (1) 5 327
Hereupon (2) 14 313 16 1682
hereupon (1) 16 666
herit (1) 14 867
Herman-Joseph (1) 12 1703
Hermes (1) 15 2269
hermetic (1) 7 783
hermetists (1) 9 282
Hermit (2) 8 879 12 190
hermosa (1) 13 1209
Hero (1) 17 644
hero (16) 1 62 6 289 10 492 503
11 340 342 1274 12 155 609 639 644 1008
14 1331 15 1744 16 1005 1643

Herodotus (1) 12 196
Herod's (1) 14 1422
heroes (4) 9 623 12 83 176 1213
heroes (1) 15 4680
heroes' (1) 10 834
heroic (1) 15 781
heroically (1) 16 38
heroine (1) 15 4418
heroines (1) 12 176
heron (1) 12 1287
Herpyllis (1) 9 724
Herr (4) 9 1073 12 468 566 17 869
herring (3) 3 97 12 1057 16 1661
herringbone (1) 8 1106
herringpies (1) 9 627
Herring's (1) 8 810
herrings (5) 12 81 512 13 1033 1187
16 273
herrings (1) 15 502
hers (14) 1 398 8 377 13 161 341 525 1103
14 90 884 1329 15 3884 16 719 17 2124
18 218 639
Herschel (1) 17 1110
hersel (1) 14 1523
herself (36) 4 261 303 428 5 189 269 495
8 971 9 260 11 215 556 935 12 637 1172
13 102 161 165 176 219 293 440 458 572 644 762
1016 14 402 1130 15 1288 2552 16 722
17 924 18 5 761 1071 1076 1361
herself (7) 15 1744 2053 2166 2744 4024 4095
4206
Hertwig (1) 14 1236
Herz (1) 17 1886
Herzog (2) 12 17 33
Herzog (2) 15 3222 4358
He's (87) 1 128 155 431 605 4 312 5 333
6 63 111 149 190 301 374 381 643 926 7 299
461 8 229 245 262 797 829 940 960 962 982 983
9 93 95 203 514 570 10 438 439 492 525 581
685 758 893 897 935 936 948 11 73 77 457 458
1001 12 257 331 379 390 392 995 1492 1545
1556 1558 1635 13 942 14 1512 1586 1587
1590 15 369 627 1283 1540 1762 3141 3873
4208 4363 4439 4488 4602 4757 4796 4891
16 382 690 1022
He's (2) 5 126 129
he's (51) 3 63 4 340 5 67 107 187 194
6 831 850 992 7 431 688 692 8 262 430 1159
9 820 10 523 917 1173 11 621 631 838 859
966 12 30 55 320 385 403 437 752 854 988 1045
1548 1551 1554 1584 1630 1648 13 759 846
15 640 3230 3803 4297 4486 4744 4756 4874
he's (1) 15 4145
hes (53) 14 1473 18 17 81 83 105 120 206
228 268 289 356 363 411 415 421 482 578 601 823
825 826 925 926 1044 1199 1204 1208 1224 1253
1256 1274 1300 1301 1310 1316 1326 1328 1332
1339 1344 1345 1375 1394 1400 1432 1442 1491
1522 1530
Heseltine (2) 10 1177 1222
hesitate (2) 9 133 12 877
hesitates (2) 15 2014 2031
hesitating (1) 9 3
hesitating (1) 15 4927
hesitation (1) 16 1712
hesitation (1) 16 4017
Hesouls (1) 9 285
Hesperus (1) 16 845
hest (1) 15 4547

1191 1193 1206 1216 1225 1349 1352 1354 1356
1397 1514 1516 1518 1544 1550 1554 1560 1561
15 174 204 206 264 287 639 661 750 762 779 871
893 980 1016 1020 1037 1068 1071 1072 1083 1093
1103 1104 1105 1115 1116 1168 1172 1262 1564
1618 1727 1736 1737 1760 1762 1783 1785 1800
1884 1894 1896 1900 1929 2231 2254 2542 2566
2579 2618 2769 2916 2918 2922 2944 2951 2953
3039 3085 3142 3230 3498 3634 3778 3780 3873
4230 4233 4259 4269 4279 4304 4378 4390 4392
4394 4399 4426 4484 4487 4602 4626 4720 4724
4726 4737 4739 4742 4746 4756 4757 4763 4782
4784 4788 4797 4813 4874 4882 4883 4892 4901
4951 **16** 2 12 15 108 130 146 149 157 163 168
173 183 194 196 198 213 234 358 361 375 379 389
407 412 431 498 499 516 531 566 581 632 633 658
716 719 804 824 830 831 837 847 859 862 872 904
905 919 927 932 935 946 967 973 1023 1041 1045
1066 1084 1085 1179 1182 1234 1269 1274 1299
1300 1302 1303 1330 1333 1335 1351 1352 1375
1422 1456 1473 1478 1508 1516 1520 1522 1526
1529 1555 1560 1565 1594 1597 1605 1613 1615
1616 1618 1619 1651 1687 1699 1721 1724 1775
1818 1834 1857 1865 1868 1871 **17** 136 288 328
351 362 392 402 417 509 558 576 626 639 645 674
686 835 836 837 839 840 877 884 886 896 921 924
926 989 1153 1157 1250 1256 1426 1430 1639
1752 1902 1934 2091 2264 **18** 16 18 20 21 26 39
41 42 46 48 50 52 57 58 72 73 81 82 85 86 87 90 93
96 103 119 125 154 155 156 157 167 168 170 179
182 183 186 189 190 191 192 193 196 197 200 202
203 208 220 221 223 233 241 249 259 262 263 270
272 277 279 280 282 284 287 288 291 294 295 300
302 303 305 314 341 352 355 357 360 366 371 374
379 381 387 404 407 412 417 426 429 445 452 459
461 492 494 506 507 511 515 525 529 530 532 537
538 543 565 576 579 587 588 591 594 602 604 616
655 661 678 693 708 716 718 735 740 763 772 774
776 777 778 779 783 788 797 800 809 811 812 814
815 822 825 839 840 843 846 853 861 864 866 868
896 902 903 913 926 931 933 946 947 948 953 954
962 963 969 984 998 1004 1021 1044 1046 1080
1089 1092 1094 1111 1112 1114 1138 1152 1156
1158 1162 1168 1171 1172 1176 1180 1186 1195
1204 1209 1215 1226 1229 1231 1232 1234 1243
1245 1249 1251 1252 1255 1256 1257 1260 1276
1280 1290 1293 1302 1304 1305 1312 1316 1328
1330 1331 1339 1342 1350 1351 1353 1363 1364
1366 1368 1370 1400 1402 1422 1427 1448 1476
1479 1486 1493 1498 1504 1505 1509 1510 1511
1513 1514 1515 1516 1523 1525 1527 1530 1538
1539 1550 1552 1565 1573 1574 1578 1580 1604
1605 1607

him (17) **4** 348 **5** 121 126 **6** 167 **10** 609
617 621 **12** 27 28 100 **17** 821 822 823 824
him (78) **15** 16 25 75 101 124 144 145 146 178
179 186 214 271 298 317 461 482 487 514 591 632
653 958 1129 1234 1237 1256 1270 1281 1317 1340
1377 1519 1520 1587 1611 1612 1702 1703 1887
1903 1929 1990 1998 2012 2014 2015 2022 2025
2032 2300 2612 2629 2686 2710 2729 2830 2962
3227 3317 3469 3479 3604 3625 3763 3875 3904
3990 4182 4327 4335 4431 4457 4544 4747 4922
Himself (8) **1** 660 **9** 493 494 526 863 875
himself (192) **1** 36 42 61 97 216 508 556 558
618 693 704 714 **2** 299 **4** 100 506 537 538
5 354 461 478 480 **6** 2 6 112 276 298 529 532
562 647 681 860 935 **7** 264 348 465 468 1037
8 38 99 137 664 813 **9** 241 435 454 456 464 475

559 742 837 868 875 965 997 1052 1119 **10** 7 22
208 228 229 233 240 246 409 482 644 667 713 742
1021 **11** 104 467 1191 1199 **12** 29 119 655
675 775 804 919 1223 1306 1332 1406 1435 1558
1581 1640 **13** 299 307 350 433 504 540
14 542 578 591 611 624 626 663 693 713 714 727
731 834 890 897 907 945 1020 1033 1045 1062 1154
1186 1192 1193 1297 1347 **15** 953 1047 1806
3031 3769 3778 4443 **16** 129 225 303 305 340
386 496 634 653 679 821 837 846 885 938 956 1086
1188 1219 1293 1300 1348 1459 1557 1577 1613
1635 1839 1854 1863 **17** 79 88 126 253 276 364
372 385 637 1616 1756 2127 2129 2211 2286
18 4 121 131 284 694 906 982 1062 1213 1229
1251 1377 1455
himself (1) **9** 115
himself (21) **15** 673 758 930 1222 1885 2033
2495 2535 2678 2958 2959 3549 3783 3815 3900
4388 4426 4447 4469 4930 4934
Hinbad (1) **17** 2324
hind (3) **6** 500 **14** 607 **16** 1785
hindbar (1) **8** 809
hindering (1) **12** 1488
hinderparts (1) **3** 54
hindhead (1) **10** 580
hindleg (2) **3** 357 358
hindpaws (1) **3** 359
hindquarter (1) **4** 161
hindquarters (1) **8** 716
hindquarters (1) **15** 316
Hindu (1) **6** 548
Hindustanish (1) **14** 525
hinges (1) **17** 116
hint (4) **7** 119 **13** 531 569 **16** 1192
hinting (1) **15** 3125
hints (2) **15** 3251 **16** 323
hip (7) **4** 72 **6** 22 494 **7** 228 **8** 1191
12 1283 **15** 2330
hipbones (1) **18** 415
hiphip (1) **12** 600
hippodrome (1) **14** 1217
Hippogriff (1) **15** 2325
Hips (1) **6** 207
hips (5) **4** 148 **8** 168 **10** 811 **16** 892
18 447
hips (1) **15** 2602
hipshaker (1) **16** 1784
hipshot (1) **15** 2151
Hiram (1) **12** 561
Hire (2) **6** 446 **15** 2374
hire (1) **16** 25
Hired (1) **3** 187
hired (2) **1** 213 **17** 494
Hirsch (3) **15** 1858 **17** 1749
hirsute (1) **17** 1112
HIS (1) **7** 326
His (223) **1** 131 156 159 233 237 289 514 660
729 **2** 82 124 143 246 357 375 **3** 61 102 147
205 225 229 328 338 347 359 370 401 402 408 446
451 499 **4** 66 81 148 181 215 244 421 **5** 8 24
25 27 77 79 89 203 **6** 49 57 64 65 242 260 529
765 768 803 815 831 848 914 **7** 16 62 81 660 709
772 816 819 820 825 834 977 **8** 3 10 17 40 70 88
138 189 287 302 322 396 424 475 511 533 562 576
580 606 637 650 672 694 747 792 855 919 986 1034
1078 1129 1162 1169 1180 1183 1191 **9** 117 228
242 366 432 440 478 494 497 521 531 546 579 615
625 687 744 753 863 881 932 947 1023 1109
10 44 123 149 185 356 564 620 762 797 1111

1155 1161 1195 1201 1245 1247 1267 1278
11 52 420 445 452 631 698 1040 1228 **12** 171
922 1135 1403 1498 1515 1516 1608 1609 1639
1737 1817 **13** 54 56 412 548 563 694 801 911
1116 **14** 99 176 288 660 701 934 1024 1032 1165
1341 **15** 954 1170 1562 1629 1799 3106 3680
3681 4214 **16** 4 133 145 482 583 597 624 710
759 1006 1241 1513 1614 **17** 348 368 433 608
1137 1320 1759
His (3) **6** 146 **8** 778 **9** 1171
His (23) **15** 806 993 1162 1206 1207 1296 1319
1420 1422 1500 2265 2484 2654 2658 2682 2686
2712 2830 3063 3439 3982 4284
his (2646) **1** 12 13 25 30 31 33 35 38 50 56 57
64 65 75 86 95 96 100 101 102 111 115 121 122 123
125 132 143 147 148 152 156 168 173 182 185 186
187 188 203 217 221 223 225 226 232 237 266 292
298 309 329 346 363 364 368 378 379 380 385 446
447 448 451 468 479 491 502 508 510 511 513 514
515 518 528 530 534 540 550 556 559 564 570 580
582 594 601 602 606 616 618 619 620 621 627 628
631 632 643 645 652 657 679 681 687 689 690 693
695 704 707 710 722 742 **2** 16 17 23 24 28 43 44
62 70 84 90 114 115 125 126 128 130 142 148 151
153 164 165 167 170 176 177 181 188 193 197 205
208 211 212 218 224 236 241 248 250 251 261 268
282 283 292 293 294 296 305 307 320 345 352 382
386 387 388 399 405 422 424 426 430 436 443 444
446 448 **3** 5 10 14 16 17 51 52 53 58 63 66 68 76
77 80 82 83 105 109 110 111 114 122 124 125
126 140 147 150 168 211 217 220 223 226 228 230
241 247 250 251 265 268 270 277 278 284 295 327
328 329 335 339 347 348 354 358 360 361 362 372
373 375 387 397 406 410 417 438 439 446 477 481
489 499 500 503 **4** 6 23 54 66 67 69 72 103 112
113 115 141 143 148 163 175 177 182 186 230 231
232 247 256 279 280 283 293 299 300 382 391 393
394 395 407 427 439 447 460 461 468 489 495 497
498 500 501 507 508 513 516 530 538 541 **5** 5 13
20 21 22 23 24 25 26 27 28 38 42 49 50 57 58 60 65
77 80 100 107 110 111 150 164 180 192 202 204
205 208 221 235 261 267 268 275 279 306 313 314
319 328 329 345 355 371 372 379 417 421 429 436
439 469 476 512 517 518 519 521 525 528 529 535
536 567 568 570 **6** 1 3 51 59 60 66 67 72 74 75
76 86 95 96 101 105 110 119 129 136 141 143 161
169 178 192 196 200 209 225 227 229 232 236
253 254 257 260 262 275 277 287 299 301 306 333
335 336 343 347 350 358 363 390 430 439 443 451
465 471 491 492 494 495 496 500 503 510 511 569
575 576 580 586 587 590 591 593 595 605 631 636
643 648 652 673 680 685 691 694 709 716 719
720 746 763 766 772 786 787 795 799 807 808 809
815 822 824 831 840 848 849 852 857 865 873 875
876 878 880 895 908 909 912 915 925 927 928 933
935 954 978 1007 1008 1010 1015 1021 1022 1025
1029 **7** 29 30 34 42 47 49 57 74 87 112 114 121
125 131 132 139 144 147 165 166 171 173 182 183
187 198 199 204 206 207 215 226 227 229 248 250
251 259 262 263 274 277 290 300 318 331 332 340
351 361 367 371 372 379 419 421 433 439 448 451
458 459 460 467 469 473 480 492 493 494 532 539
540 542 560 587 593 595 597 624 627 630 638 653
663 664 728 732 733 738 742 751 760 762 767 777
778 798 806 809 810 815 821 824 825 835 860
882 896 901 957 959 972 982 986 988 991 996 1055
1065 1068 **8** 4 39 78 108 127 128 161 182 189
230 270 297 298 311 312 313 314 358 360 364 411
423 424 427 442 458 487 504 506 509 510 512 513

534 553 562 564 566 574 580 594 595 600 601 603 614 627 637 651 657 659 674 679 682 684 685 688 689 690 691 694 701 709 713 735 737 742 766 768 777 786 787 790 795 796 804 810 818 819 820 839 840 843 845 854 873 881 893 894 897 899 933 934 937 951 952 954 957 975 979 984 985 986 990 1001 1005 1008 1020 1028 1035 1046 1050 1075 1079 1084 1085 1096 1097 1099 1104 1105 1111 1127 1128 1136 1137 1140 1141 1142 1143 1152 1154 1155 1173 1175 1176 1191 9 13 17 29 46 59 74 77 82 90 100 101 132 136 152 167 171 172 173 175 176 218 219 220 225 235 236 246 248 252 253 254 263 284 295 296 304 312 326 363 365 378 390 406 420 422 427 434 438 457 463 471 476 480 489 501 504 509 522 527 545 546 570 582 603 607 629 638 645 658 670 693 694 697 712 721 722 723 724 732 741 745 746 748 750 752 759 780 788 789 790 791 792 805 813 814 816 822 823 826 829 833 836 855 856 867 868 869 875 878 879 885 887 894 896 911 913 921 922 923 924 926 929 931 946 955 984 988 1001 1002 1003 1005 1006 1007 1010 1016 1032 1033 1041 1062 1076 1077 1086 1088 1100 1109 1116 1135 1138 1157 1170 1199 1202 1210 10 1 2 7 10 30 32 37 43 46 69 79 81 86 98 117 118 144 154 161 184 188 189 193 201 203 207 210 211 215 216 217 221 230 240 245 246 264 281 313 324 330 335 348 360 386 401 423 432 436 443 461 465 513 544 551 561 564 565 579 596 598 607 619 633 634 635 638 643 649 655 660 664 665 667 671 672 686 688 691 708 755 756 757 761 762 778 779 784 789 812 813 831 832 834 842 885 896 899 903 913 915 933 940 941 942 952 953 954 958 964 974 1001 1002 1013 1014 1015 1018 1036 1044 1048 1049 1050 1051 1052 1060 1065 1066 1068 1072 1074 1077 1091 1093 1105 1108 1114 1115 1117 1137 1140 1141 1143 1145 1155 1162 1168 1169 1171 1182 1187 1188 1199 1201 1219 1220 1231 1234 1245 1246 1247 1264 1267 1268 1269 1273 1277 11 67 86 90 105 146 156 170 192 216 241 259 265 267 271 274 284 346 365 366 373 377 419 427 470 483 490 535 557 564 588 589 600 611 619 621 627 630 643 644 647 648 676 682 684 687 696 721 722 768 769 780 784 788 795 802 834 854 856 859 916 927 930 1011 1021 1027 1033 1042 1051 1052 1060 1063 1065 1070 1071 1082 1114 1131 1152 1161 1201 1230 1241 12 3 7 10 21 30 47 49 50 55 56 122 132 136 137 139 156 164 165 169 173 174 200 203 214 247 253 254 305 326 344 345 348 367 370 371 375 381 384 390 397 410 443 466 486 488 496 501 502 514 517 519 545 557 585 586 588 593 594 607 610 611 613 614 615 616 617 635 641 643 644 645 646 659 660 667 672 673 674 682 685 686 693 710 711 716 721 724 774 806 808 811 821 830 833 836 848 892 920 923 950 957 972 974 978 980 981 988 1009 1023 1026 1027 1046 1051 1063 1065 1066 1080 1081 1090 1092 1115 1162 1173 1210 1211 1212 1230 1231 1288 1301 1312 1313 1314 1323 1326 1335 1336 1358 1362 1369 1389 1403 1404 1415 1432 1434 1444 1469 1471 1491 1505 1507 1509 1512 1517 1520 1523 1528 1530 1544 1548 1553 1564 1565 1574 1580 1582 1583 1591 1595 1597 1598 1612 1628 1649 1650 1663 1673 1687 1739 1744 1753 1772 1777 1798 1800 1805 1808 1817 1844 1853 1854 1898 1900 1907
13 23 24 25 31 34 46 47 51 56 59 77 129 132 134 138 142 144 173 182 211 212 213 215 220 236 241 244 247 248 258 260 301 309 310 311 312 317 320 322 336 349 378 388 389 393 396 399 402 412 415 422 440 449 450 451 495 504 514 516 536 538 543 545 546 550 556 559 560 572 573 585 594 596 607 609 610 611 612 613 622 623 629 632 652 654 655 657 677 690 692 694 700 707 708 734 788 800 802 834 846 851 875 881 892 910 962 973 982 1035 1042 1062 1082 1107 1109 1121 1134 1138 1144 1158 1162 1169 1171 1179 1205 1216 1224 1247 1256 1266 1270 1287 14 22 73 83 91 93 100 104 109 129 134 136 137 147 162 164 181 190 197 198 199 213 232 234 236 255 256 264 266 267 269 271 272 273 276 313 329 330 337 341 343 358 361 384 397 400 410 411 413 414 415 416 419 420 423 425 430 433 472 473 499 509 519 525 539 540 542 546 551 554 555 557 558 564 566 571 583 587 588 593 596 597 599 600 601 603 606 607 611 617 620 621 623 630 631 633 636 637 653 654 657 667 679 686 689 692 695 698 702 706 707 710 713 714 717 718 722 727 730 741 752 753 765 775 814 819 838 845 851 857 861 863 880 881 889 893 894 905 909 910 912 914 918 920 921 925 931 933 937 944 976 993 994 996 1012 1023 1026 1028 1033 1036 1047 1049 1052 1055 1062 1063 1116 1123 1124 1125 1139 1148 1162 1163 1189 1204 1205 1208 1214 1295 1308 1321 1329 1350 1376 1419 1469 1474 1494 1513 1540 1547 1549 1554 1566 1578 1590
15 92 171 235 262 369 572 648 662 665 700 739 780 848 869 926 955 973 979 981 1047 1048 1054 1063 1067 1071 1091 1104 1118 1254 1283 1291 1453 1526 1594 1755 1759 1779 1782 1929 2092 2093 2426 2433 2457 2523 2525 2541 2542 2545 2600 2666 2675 2718 2784 2786 3012 3035 3131 3140 3174 3209 3309 3444 3610 3671 3720 3828 3836 3868 4273 4428 4569 4570 4762 4789 4799 4863 4894 4949 16 5 19 30 36 44 53 54 60 62 66 68 96 97 103 109 117 130 165 177 181 184 185 186 214 220 222 223 230 233 241 247 265 269 270 282 289 291 292 334 339 342 348 357 359 367 371 387 389 391 392 394 395 396 422 430 431 432 445 448 454 465 468 472 495 504 525 575 576 579 582 585 588 594 597 617 651 655 657 666 667 673 674 682 684 690 700 714 716 730 731 734 762 768 777 788 797 811 812 822 825 829 833 836 838 840 853 858 861 901 916 919 920 924 926 928 932 934 939 942 947 950 952 956 969 970 975 976 984 986 988 1005 1006 1010 1015 1023 1024 1025 1056 1059 1064 1065 1069 1071 1076 1084 1092 1111 1141 1150 1169 1175 1176 1187 1210 1216 1233 1236 1237 1265 1268 1272 1275 1276 1290 1293 1301 1303 1305 1312 1313 1315 1316 1317 1320 1321 1322 1325 1326 1330 1336 1337 1344 1353 1359 1368 1393 1394 1395 1396 1399 1400 1421 1422 1440 1448 1471 1497 1517 1520 1527 1539 1554 1555 1567 1568 1581 1587 1591 1597 1609 1619 1627 1637 1638 1652 1657 1659 1673 1677 1692 1693 1715 1716 1717 1721 1739 1743 1745 1785 1786 1793 1795 1797 1804 1807 1808 1827 1830 1831 1841 1845 1853 1860 1861 1862 1864 1867 1868 1874 1875 1878 1879 1893 17 56 59 72 73 84 85 86 88 91 111 114 117 118 138 139 141 142 146 148 231 238 252 289 291 319 322 331 339 340 342 359 361 362 363 364 365 368 374 375 380 382 383 392 402 404 410 469 492 497 519 520 521 522 523 557 561 564 576 578 616 636 658 660 674 709 774 775 795 834 852 855 859 860 867 888 921 924 925 927 933 945 951 979 1011 1012 1018 1033 1040 1173 1177 1194 1262 1274 1275 1286 1312 1313 1323 1324 1348 1355 1356 1401 1408 1426 1430 1435 1436 1450 1451 1452 1480 1484 1486 1487 1488 1490 1606 1609 1623 1634 1635 1636 1640 1646 1652 1755 1769 1844 1875 1906 1909 1923 1925 2001 2005 2006 2009 2013 2109 2111 2115 2116 2122 2124 2133 2143 2145 2154 2180 2211 2269
18 1 3 24 25 30 31 32 35 43 51 59 61 79 95 97 105 115 116 117 119 122 124 145 153 182 195 206 222 226 227 228 230 234 240 249 257 272 276 278 288 296 300 304 306 310 312 317 319 338 343 350 364 365 384 403 415 416 419 422 428 452 454 502 521 532 542 543 547 568 569 575 583 587 625 634 648 661 679 689 692 693 695 700 701 713 715 717 735 762 771 799 800 813 816 818 824 835 836 837 873 890 906 930 932 959 961 970 982 990 991 994 1000 1002 1005 1019 1056 1061 1078 1086 1088 1089 1090 1093 1094 1114 1115 1136 1138 1162 1171 1173 1176 1187 1193 1200 1201 1202 1203 1206 1209 1218 1223 1225 1234 1235 1240 1250 1258 1259 1260 1265 1273 1276 1277 1279 1280 1287 1290 1292 1301 1306 1311 1322 1325 1350 1352 1354 1369 1372 1375 1387 1407 1422 1424 1431 1432 1443 1454 1479 1485 1489 1505 1509 1510 1512 1516 1521 1522 1526 1538 1543 1573 1577 1586 1597 1608

his (25) 1 567 4 348 6 165 166 7 839 863 868 9 909 1042 1043 1044 1149 10 611 16 1249 1251 1886 17 802 826 827 1353

his (412) 15 14 31 65 73 74 75 99 124 125 135 137 161 187 197 201 209 222 256 291 292 315 316 321 323 357 385 414 441 451 452 457 465 477 480 499 506 514 516 532 538 562 577 584 616 633 659 663 664 693 694 704 720 738 758 769 772 793 806 807 809 811 832 843 876 900 908 936 937 958 959 974 992 995 1085 1107 1147 1164 1173 1178 1179 1180 1203 1204 1213 1244 1251 1252 1255 1260 1262 1275 1297 1309 1316 1339 1415 1484 1499 1566 1587 1598 1600 1605 1613 1617 1702 1775 1787 1826 1841 1843 1844 1850 1880 1886 1909 1913 1915 1919 1928 1961 1962 1964 1984 1993 2006 2011 2012 2023 2036 2037 2038 2039 2049 2058 2072 2084 2145 2146 2148 2149 2157 2159 2162 2211 2216 2223 2248 2263 2264 2272 2273 2290 2302 2307 2309 2310 2334 2337 2339 2355 2366 2371 2383 2392 2415 2420 2432 2435 2441 2451 2460 2467 2486 2487 2489 2491 2524 2545 2555 2556 2570 2574 2575 2598 2601 2602 2606 2609 2618 2620 2621 2623 2624 2625 2627 2628 2629 2630 2631 2636 2641 2657 2658 2659 2660 2668 2669 2677 2678 2683 2684 2700 2702 2705 2711 2724 2725 2728 2830 2831 2839 2847 2853 2857 2859 2860 2894 2936 2945 2957 2958 2973 3063 3089 3090 3094 3102 3108 3124 3128 3161 3195 3196 3202 3215 3219 3305 3363 3386 3420 3461 3530 3550 3551 3595 3604 3628 3649 3655 3656 3658 3687 3692 3695 3713 3722 3738 3739 3763 3773 3788 3809 3815 3844 3878 3893 3930 3940 3952 3975 3987 3988 3990 4012 4013 4020 4022 4027 4034 4037 4039 4040 4048 4121 4168 4171 4178 4179 4223 4243 4255 4320 4324 4328 4332 4410 4414 4428 4436 4456 4460 4464 4472 4477 4502 4507 4532 4549 4556 4560 4568 4570 4597 4614 4644 4694 4696 4705 4742 4748 4749 4770 4780 4793 4799 4805 4821 4827 4860 4890 4908 4910 4912 4915 4918 4921 4927 4934 4944 4946 4955 4959 4965 4966 4967

hising (1) 3 462

hising (1) 1 384

hismy (1) 3 487

hisn (1) 14 1501

hisses (1) 12 913

hissing (1) 18 1119

hissing (1) 15 186

Hissss (2) 11 36 984
hissss (1) 11 964
hist (2) 14 318 410
historians (1) 14 33
historic (6) 10 407 409 12 960 16 558
1361 1497
historic (1) 15 1580
historical (5) 7 793 15 2446 16 1891
17 752 1600
historical (1) 15 1845
historically (1) 17 575
historicity (1) 9 48
histories (1) 9 753
History (6) 2 377 7 684 9 811 13 1093
15 4371 16 1120
History (3) 17 1367 1385 1416
history (19) 1 649 2 46 247 325 381
7 677 9 992 10 439 12 666 1235 1417
1481 14 1016 15 4607 16 816 1000 1070
1514 1525
history (1) 7 850
hit (11) 7 280 12 243 13 1217 1219
15 3247 4290 4756 4788 16 7 10 1745
hitch (1) 16 505
hitches (1) 15 959
hitching (1) 15 4142
hither (2) 13 626 14 451
Hitherto (1) 14 1005
hitherto (2) 15 1385 17 580
hitting (2) 12 695 15 2914
hives (1) 17 1060
hives (1) 7 847
H'lo (1) 15 4501
Hlo (1) 3 440
Hm (9) 13 1007 1009 1029 1042 15 3622
3631
Hmmm (1) 15 2702
Hnhn (1) 15 492
Ho (12) 12 1595 14 451 15 2946 2993
3743 3786 3818 3912 3946 4156 4925 17 620
Ho (2) 15 3893 16 314
ho (13) 14 1570 15 67 618 2345 2993 3786
3818 3912 4547
ho (1) 10 344
hoard (4) 2 215 370 10 814
hoarded (1) 9 743
hoarding (1) 10 1273
Hoardings (1) 6 184
hoardings (2) 5 193 10 141
hoards (1) 9 785
Hoarse (1) 2 274
Hoarse (1) 15 4663
hoarse (6) 1 275 7 6 334 11 1097
12 202 13 700
hoarse (3) 15 51 1241 3962
hoarsed (1) 11 589
Hoarsely (1) 11 589
hoarsely (1) 10 614
hoarsely (6) 15 478 991 1922 2340 3809 3812
hoarsened (1) 1 381
hoary (3) 11 1008 12 611 14 1424
Hoax (1) 15 2340
hob (5) 1 268 4 12 17 158 159 161
hobbies (1) 12 1253
hobbledehoy (1) 6 271
hobbledehoy (1) 15 3333
hobbles (1) 1 168
hobbles (1) 15 32
hobbling (1) 3 303

hobby (1) 6 447
hobbyhorse (1) 15 3720
hobbyhorse (1) 15 4127
hobbyhorses (2) 15 2719 4109
HOBGOBLIN (1) 15 2156
hobgoblin (1) 15 2150
hobgoblins (2) 15 1393 2068
hobnailed (1) 4 160
hobnobbing (1) 12 1024
hoc (1) 9 770
hoch (1) 12 600
Hock (1) 8 876
hock (2) 11 119 422
Hockey (2) 2 92 119
hockeystick (2) 15 3982 3988
Hockeysticks (1) 2 153
hocuspocus (1) 16 1109
hodden (1) 14 701
Hodges (1) 3 426
hoe (1) 17 1565
hog (3) 13 882 15 1890 3043
hoggets (1) 14 569
hogjowled (1) 14 1582
hogo (1) 13 1032
Hog's (1) 15 1983
hog's (1) 12 1615
hogs (1) 12 1717
hogs (1) 15 4143
hogshead (1) 3 383
hogwash (1) 18 453
Hoh (1) 11 919
Hoho (2) 11 442 12 996
Hohohohohohoh (1) 15 4879
Hohohohohome (1) 15 4899
Hohohohome (1) 15 4879
hoi (1) 14 1481
hoi (1) 16 335
hoik (1) 12 1570
hoisted (3) 5 99 6 632 13 1172
hoisted (2) 15 1409 1620
Hok (1) 15 2603
Hokopoko (1) 12 564
hoky (1) 15 2679
Hokypoky (1) 5 362
Holà (1) 15 3941
Hold (18) 3 418 9 89 10 454 898 905 906
11 372 866 12 427 1852 15 117 797 2616
2618 2916 3059 3680 4251
hold (35) 1 70 166 4 207 7 729 9 789
830 833 11 450 451 639 1120 12 26 1661
1800 1843 13 122 954 992 1162 14 768 866
890 1071 1193 15 2526 3783 16 846 917 1588
1662 17 196 18 197 907 1314
hold (2) 15 1078 2929
holden (1) 12 1123
holder (2) 14 683 1042
holdeth (1) 14 250
holdfast (1) 1 491
holdfasts (1) 17 151
Holding (2) 8 531 13 923
holding (26) 1 109 250 4 168 5 7 344 417
6 460 519 588 7 424 510 8 270 610
10 363 383 1230 11 930 12 978 1315 1789
13 653 685 14 78 86 16 30 17 112
holding (10) 15 704 898 988 1237 1239 2031
3750 4920 4945 4958
holdings (1) 16 1732
holds (6) 9 35 764 788 11 1034 17 617
835

holds (22) 15 124 158 404 668 808 992 1499
1787 1984 2265 2307 2501 2636 2957 3751 3792
3842 3916 4000 4456 4697 4966
Hole (1) 12 1072
hole (24) 1 600 5 296 6 610 800 855 860
906 8 929 12 756 1459 13 998 14 1037
1195 16 79 522 17 210 1215 18 151 766
902 1089 1092 1165 1522
hole (1) 15 1573
Holeopen (1) 12 1878
Holes (1) 9 948
holes (5) 4 48 11 1089 13 817 1027 1248
holiday (4) 4 452 12 992 17 1204
18 952
holidays (2) 11 195 13 317
holies (1) 17 2045
Holiness (1) 14 434
Holland (1) 17 1740
holland (1) 17 235
Hollandais (1) 3 220
hollandais (1) 3 221
Hollands (1) 16 377
holler (1) 14 1512
hollering (1) 14 1440
Holles (21) 8 282 430 10 1101 11 488
13 841 14 1 491 1302 1399 15 2519 2987
16 717 17 860 969 18 561 704 1217 1245
1286
Hollow (2) 13 1115 15 3154
Hollow (1) 15 3156
HOLLOW (1) 15 3157
hollow (7) 1 115 2 154 215 226 12 528
14 1560 17 1275
hollow (3) 15 1210 2044 4160
Holly (1) 12 1270
hollyberries (1) 12 1294
HOLLYBUSH (1) 15 1877
hollybush (1) 2 115
Holmes (1) 15 1849
Holocaust (1) 8 1147
holocaust (1) 17 2051
Holohan (3) 5 96 7 642 643
Holohan (1) 15 4346
HOLOHAN (1) 15 1726
Holy (16) 5 431 6 621 764 7 622 9 61
493 12 765 1067 1112 1886 14 226 872
15 2115 2866 3142 16 773
holy (43) 1 644 2 114 3 129 5 439 460
6 563 819 9 664 764 11 198 1017 12 68
510 609 1093 1145 1300 1402 1631 1704 1811
13 289 395 459 490 14 100 220 248 251 597
1525 15 437 1713 3466 3901 16 1791
17 1206 1982 2045 2048 18 361 1137
holyeyed (1) 9 30
holyeyed (1) 15 2262
Holyhead (2) 13 1243 16 503
Holyoake (1) 12 1278
homage (4) 2 300 6 709 9 611 15 3405
homage (1) 15 1495
hombre (1) 13 1209
Home (3) 1 740 8 30 17 1790
home (110) 3 163 199 4 95 340 416 5 3 9
246 381 6 125 943 7 150 230 700 8 34 181
194 284 472 612 635 743 946 951 9 755 1000
10 554 707 11 297 845 1004 1015 1016 1051
1229 1258 1259 12 353 398 510 517 625 1029
1365 1370 13 177 298 317 324 404 530 601 641
854 891 921 967 970 1054 1111 1154 1212 1217
14 68 501 710 929 1056 1086 1131 1259 1417

15 266 401 453 495 547 1593 3185 3985 4419
4511 4866 4876 4883 4897 16 548 645 949 1145
1383 1605 1607 1627 1644 17 597 18 347 553
1087 1187 1226 1233 1272 1283 1424 1443 1456
1550
home (5) 5 144 6 165 10 235 248
16 420
homecoming (1) 16 423
homegrown (1) 15 1034
homeless (1) 16 1566
homelife (1) 16 1177
homeliness (1) 14 1360
homely (4) 5 496 10 183 13 239
16 1571
homely (1) 15 907
homemade (1) 18 881
Homer (1) 9 1165
homer (1) 14 1418
Homer's (1) 9 110
Homerule (2) 8 473 13 1079
homerule (2) 4 102 103
homes (2) 13 297 15 788
homespun (2) 8 533 9 269
Homestead (1) 2 412
Homestead (1) 9 271
homestead (1) 15 2275
homeward (1) 4 231
homicide (2) 12 1662 17 1766
homijah (1) 17 764
homiletic (1) 17 752
homily (1) 14 696
hominess (1) 13 224
homing (1) 3 505
Homo (1) 5 329
homo (3) 5 402 11 975 16 328
homogeneous (1) 17 1620
homonymity (1) 17 633
Homonymous (1) 12 1697
homophonous (1) 17 443
homothetic (2) 17 199 1333
Hon (1) 14 493
Honest (2) 12 308 15 1970
honest (8) 9 593 14 534 841 1524 15 944
16 1484 17 1656 18 1020
honestly (2) 15 558 16 1700
honey (8) 1 334 337 476 2 197 9 558
15 2377 2417 17 2233
honey (1) 15 3981
honeycombed (1) 6 766
honeying (1) 9 1087
honeymilk (1) 14 1436
Honeymoon (1) 9 1173
honeymoon (3) 12 1295 13 238 18 984
honeysauces (1) 9 627
Honeysuckle (1) 12 1274
honing (1) 12 615
honking (1) 5 131
honorary (1) 15 1425
honorificabilitudinitatibus (1) 9 926
honoris (1) 17 1613
Honour (2) 13 96 17 2010
Honour (2) 15 729 1162
honour (21) 2 287 437 7 304 8 746
9 453 10 749 11 1149 12 753 1188 1284
13 96 663 694 14 321 842 15 885 1033
1456 1523 3994 16 1113
Honourable (3) 10 1213 12 865
15 1608
Honourable (2) 15 1414 4550

HONOURABLE (5) 15 1057 1080 1087 1097
1113
honourable (17) 5 105 106 7 265
10 1178 1179 1223 1235 12 240 580 861 862
867 873 1893 13 373 14 26 15 1161
honourable (1) 15 4453
honourablest (1) 14 200
Honoured (1) 15 4607
Honoured (1) 12 419
honoured (5) 10 175 12 1342 14 35
15 3769 18 500
honoured (1) 12 428
honours (3) 12 818 16 359 1583
Hoo (1) 6 950
hood (1) 13 384
hood (1) 15 4324
hooded (1) 15 314
HOOF (2) 15 2819 2823
hoof (4) 1 496 732 14 561 16 940
hoof (3) 15 321 2810 2811
hoofirons (1) 11 1
hoofs (10) 2 311 6 25 26 386 8 424
10 1233 11 59 65 113 17 615
hoofs (2) 15 4662 4919
hoofthuds (2) 8 615 641
Hook (2) 3 474 15 2827
hook (7) 7 705 8 726 858 12 970
14 1552 15 2891 18 494
hook (1) 15 2148
Hooked (1) 7 341
hooked (2) 4 299 16 1673
hooking (1) 4 521
Hooks (1) 9 807
Hoondert (1) 15 3111
Hoop (1) 15 3947
hoop (2) 7 997 17 876
Hooper (6) 6 950 7 456 687 17 1339 1344
2140
Hoopla (1) 15 3574
hoops (2) 3 154 9 786
Hoopsa (4) 14 5 15 2025
hoopsa (3) 14 5 6
Hooray (2) 2 384 15 1375
hoose (3) 12 834 14 573 1539
hoot (1) 15 4664
Hoots (1) 14 1532
Hop (2) 7 644 15 3076
hop (2) 5 389 12 283
hop-of-my-thumb (1) 12 17
HOPE (1) 7 905
Hope (13) 4 465 509 6 663 744 8 498 617
804 10 386 11 859 1103 1255 12 1021
13 1213
hope (47) 1 501 2 433 5 90 188 6 222
369 547 553 7 907 8 217 9 58 305 323 437
438 903 916 10 895 1173 11 742 12 588
788 1756 13 180 377 14 1024 1120
15 2316 2558 16 615 675 1293 17 835
18 11 258 332 731 912 925 1048 1140 1142 1207
1210 1321 1328 1332
hope (3) 11 685 710 17 398
hoped (2) 11 197 17 885
hopeful (1) 14 1334
Hopeless (2) 13 1233 1266
hopeless (1) 7 329
hopelessness (1) 9 828
hopes (5) 3 166 227 6 929 13 172
16 1659
hopes (1) 15 311

Hoping (1) 6 857
Hoping (1) 6 167
hoping (2) 13 179 14 949
hoping (1) 12 428
hopk (1) 11 712
hopped (1) 1 64
hopping (2) 13 1128 18 922
hopping (1) 15 3844
Hoppy (2) 5 96 110
Hoppy (1) 15 4346
HOPPY (1) 15 1726
hops (1) 1 168
hops (1) 15 2032
hopscotch (1) 5 231
hor (1) 15 4547
Horace (1) 12 181
HORATIO (1) 7 1063
Horatio (1) 11 762
horde (3) 1 656 3 304 15 1394
hordes (1) 12 1372
Horeb (1) 14 376
Horhorn (3) 14 2 3 4
Horhot (1) 15 4547
horizon (2) 9 932 17 1268
horizontal (2) 15 3154 17 298
horizontally (1) 17 582
Horn (6) 1 732 11 23 526 527 1254
14 781
horn (6) 11 432 527 1240 13 952 14 234
15 3734
horn (1) 15 2744
hornbeam (1) 17 1514
Hornblower (4) 5 555 557 10 1264
18 1257
Hornblower (1) 15 4329
HORNBLOWER (1) 15 1897
hornblower (1) 15 4126
Horne (5) 8 282 14 74 78 834 1302
Horned (1) 15 250
horned (2) 14 1059 1093
horned (1) 7 768
Horne's (10) 14 85 86 205 332 421 501 504
724 1201 1403
hornhandled (1) 16 818
hornies (2) 8 422 14 1553
horning (1) 15 2461
hornmad (1) 9 1023
hornpipe (1) 15 4142
hornrimmed (1) 17 1878
Horns (1) 14 376
horns (11) 2 336 3 117 6 395 9 635
12 1312 1718 14 145 578 579 586 617
horns (2) 15 1619 4690
horquilla (1) 18 751
horrible (5) 1 625 12 615 13 870
14 129 1097
Horrid (1) 11 4
horrid (4) 6 424 11 183 184 14 839
horrifying (1) 16 858
horror (8) 1 275 3 329 4 230 14 1010
1014 16 913 1791 18 1137
horror (1) 15 4186
horrors (1) 16 588
horrorstruck (1) 15 4176
Horryvar (1) 14 1522
Horse (4) 6 510 8 1084 16 198
17 2135
HORSE (2) 15 4878 4898
horse (37) 1 732 5 526 6 441 8 343 507

Hurry (6) 1 466 4 173 263 422 8 1190 12 279
hurry (9) 2 184 4 413 501 6 322 7 419 12 1755 13 806 16 1627 18 1118
Hurrying (1) 9 825
hurrying (3) 1 244 4 231 7 436
Hurt (1) 15 3720
hurt (16) 3 189 7 419 13 579 1071 1197 1220 14 466 1464 15 2901 3136 4938 16 680 1296 1609 18 570 575
hurted (1) 15 4757
hurting (1) 6 613
hurtling (1) 12 1880
hurtness (1) 13 60
hurts (1) 15 4414
Husband (4) 5 429 8 242 13 964 14 1319
husband (38) 5 100 6 545 8 226 358 9 677 678 1037 10 1233 1281 11 927 13 236 966 1230 14 221 769 15 1017 3706 16 440 1062 1356 1380 1533 1540 18 160 218 235 355 418 485 828 893 1099 1112 1256 1267 1275 1393 1397
husband (1) 10 608
husbandly (1) 14 184
husbandman (1) 14 615
husband's (4) 9 668 10 169 170 14 885
husband's (1) 15 3841
Husbands (1) 11 874
husbands (3) 15 3210 18 221 1392
husbandwords (1) 9 448
Hush (2) 7 393 14 1575
hush (4) 1 333 7 783 11 674 13 720
Hushaby (1) 11 1019
hushed (1) 3 36
Hushmoney (1) 17 2205
husht (1) 12 265
huskily (1) 15 81
husks (1) 15 2496
husky (3) 11 5 218 13 203
hussars (2) 16 1391 18 401
hussy (1) 15 382
hussy's (1) 14 924
hustled (1) 7 408
hutched (1) 14 1373
Hutchinson (1) 10 1010
Hutchinson (1) 15 1414
Huuh (2) 14 1088 1089
huuh (1) 14 1128
Huuuh (2) 6 390 391
Huzzah (1) 14 1131
Hy (2) 8 97 15 2633
Hyacinth (2) 13 1009 1027
Hyde's (2) 9 94 514
hydrants (1) 17 217
hydraulic (3) 17 221 1572 1711
hydrocephalic (1) 15 2151
hydrochlor (1) 15 1651
hydroelectric (1) 17 1712
hydrogen (2) 17 132 212
hydrokinetic (1) 17 190
hydrophobe (1) 17 237
hydrophobia (1) 12 710
hydros (2) 16 520 1654
hydrostatic (1) 17 190
Hyena (1) 15 4200
hyena (1) 15 714
hyenas (2) 12 1371 15 969
Hyg (1) 14 1243

Hygiene (1) 8 751
Hygiene (1) 15 1709
hygiene (1) 17 241
hygienic (1) 17 1543
hygrographic (1) 17 1529
hygrometric (1) 17 209
hymen (3) 8 11 14 349 17 2212
hymn (1) 15 2088
hymn (1) 17 414
hymns (1) 16 1742
Hynes (29) 6 111 504 719 735 736 878 880 884 891 895 898 919 925 7 76 105 111 115 117 8 1058 12 5 908 1152 13 1046 1243 15 1191 16 1248 1254 17 1239 18 38
Hynes (1) 16 1260
Hynes (2) 15 1612 4342
HYNES (2) 15 1194 1659
hyperborean (1) 1 92
hyperduly (1) 17 1207
hyperphrygian (1) 15 2090
hypertrophied (1) 15 1232
hypnotic (2) 17 848 852
Hypnotised (1) 11 1059
hypnotised (1) 5 73
hypocrite (1) 15 1757
hypocrites (1) 18 1375
hypostasis (2) 3 124 17 783
hypotenuse (1) 17 1994
hypothesis (3) 14 988 17 1092 2084
hypothetical (2) 14 986 17 660
Hypsospadia (1) 15 1789

I

I (2619) 1 0 43 60 61 63 79 112 117 120 127 138 152 157 166 167 170 184 189 192 197 202 205 213 214 218 249 251 290 291 292 307 310 311 339 342 347 353 357 358 372 374 416 428 430 433 469 480 488 490 493 498 499 501 505 506 516 517 524 533 542 547 566 577 605 611 623 624 631 636 638 647 648 666 677 684 709 739 740 2 9 11 20 80 91 135 168 191 222 233 234 235 237 238 251 259 262 264 268 269 278 290 291 314 321 324 331 338 341 343 349 377 389 395 401 402 413 415 417 420 424 425 430 433 437 3 2 11 14 15 18 23 25 26 45 58 60 61 65 70 126 136 140 158 174 179 190 223 229 236 237 238 245 246 256 257 258 267 276 280 282 293 296 298 307 308 311 323 324 327 329 331 366 367 390 407 412 418 419 425 434 435 439 442 448 450 452 455 479 485 494 495 496 498 499 4 28 31 63 73 76 79 80 94 98 156 203 232 233 285 294 320 331 371 399 400 405 408 409 432 486 488 490 519 529 5 37 79 90 95 97 107 112 115 121 127 141 170 175 179 188 199 203 207 211 236 239 242 243 244 245 247 248 249 250 251 252 253 254 255 258 265 289 297 311 320 331 336 359 373 380 385 395 400 422 425 427 433 468 469 470 495 503 504 522 526 534 537 550 6 19 21 36 51 60 70 83 105 106 114 131 152 154 168 173 185 197 203 205 213 216 222 243 268 274 300 367 369 400 405 408 433 445 449 454 456 527 532 536 547 559 570 578 592 595 619 621 640 650 656 662 666 690 693 695 696 701 712 713 718 736 742 743 751 755 776 820 821 828 831 845 862 880 884 889 894 895 898 916 938 939 940 969 982 996 998 1000 1002 1003 1007 1011 7 119 129 152 155 171 172 189 218 225 227 230 231 256 260 284 294 351 376 393 413 481 489 508 532 555 563 594 612 616 617 633 639 679 683 722 729 743 747 763 792 805 815 824 884 885 891 902 907 915 917 952 961 972 975 976 978 986 988 989 997 999 1019 1057 1059 1061 1066 1072 8 22 46 52 60 84 106 110 112 116 117 131 133 137 141 142 145 146 149 150 165 172 184 186 213 214 215 217 220 231 242 250 278 279 281 306 308 321 327 328 352 354 371 402 425 426 427 429 452 481 495 508 542 544 552 567 571 573 584 608 613 662 685 692 696 735 758 782 786 815 824 827 831 836 844 852 854 875 882 885 888 890 906 908 913 915 923 942 943 944 945 947 949 952 963 964 967 976 987 1003 1044 1057 1059 1083 1084 1096 1098 1119 1126 1142 1153 1154 1167 1171 1182 1184 1188 1189 1191 1192 9 27 39 45 47 63 64 93 94 101 127 136 177 179 184 193 202 205 208 210 212 224 271 277 302 303 305 320 323 353 362 363 369 375 379 382 383 384 385 387 390 438 443 445 457 461 465 487 508 515 517 520 526 527 535 580 609 610 614 662 668 685 696 725 727 731 761 778 813 814 815 825 847 858 860 875 876 891 903 916 935 950 962 963 974 981 1015 1056 1071 1078 1082 1088 1094 1109 1113 1118 1130 1131 1140 1154 1167 1178 1200 1206 1207 1210 10 225 323 336 384 390 426 442 444 459 462 476 493 506 517 525 540 545 550 552 556 558 562 563 569 593 669 675 676 680 684 695 698 699 703 721 730 733 734 744 823 824 826 840 859 863 872 894 897 911 934 936 937 946 953 964 974 1019 1023 1067 1068 1069 1076 1077 1091 1094 1120 1137 1171 1172 11 17 32 54 73 98 114 124 128 132 149 150 152 176 181 182 187 189 198 204 206 210 219 229 236 260 263 272 276 278 295 307 345 356 358 372 375 393 428 448 463

473 480 481 485 508 510 533 558 570 583 584 633
638 642 648 649 650 655 658 689 691 715 721 722
725 730 731 732 790 805 807 843 844 845 857 858
861 863 865 874 887 891 892 894 910 969 980 1066
1069 1080 1089 1096 1110 1120 1123 1126 1136
1145 1182 1204 1210 1212 1217 1224 1233 1239
1243 1244 1247 1254   **12** 1 3 4 6 9 13 20 21 24
30 53 55 57 58 59 60 61 62 66 122 136 141 146 207
210 213 233 240 241 242 243 251 252 255 260 262
274 307 311 312 314 315 378 381 383 387 392 421
424 448 453 459 513 522 677 686 697 698 702 751
757 760 762 769 787 789 791 792 795 798 811 820
826 827 852 855 856 861 867 876 884 893 942 945
988 994 996 1000 1027 1029 1051 1055 1058 1060
1110 1167 1176 1203 1215 1224 1260 1360 1362
1393 1410 1412 1430 1431 1465 1467 1485 1502
1534 1535 1548 1549 1554 1555 1559 1561 1562
1563 1564 1570 1573 1603 1609 1623 1627 1647
1651 1655 1667 1754 1756 1783 1812 1847 1849
1903 1909   **13** 26 52 71 72 262 527 590 775 776
778 779 781 784 785 786 787 799 826 828 831 832
833 837 840 842 843 844 845 859 860 861 862 867
868 871 878 882 883 898 908 914 918 920 921 922
929 937 943 949 951 961 966 985 986 1001 1005
1007 1009 1016 1036 1044 1046 1049 1076 1085
1091 1092 1098 1099 1101 1104 1109 1113 1121
1125 1142 1190 1194 1197 1199 1200 1207 1216
1227 1232 1241 1255 1258 1263 1274 1276 1279
14 171 259 302 452 515 521 524 567 568 572 581
665 748 749 757 762 770 773 776 777 779 795 811
817 818 823 826 828 832 842 844 886 890 891 903
1015 1017 1019 1022 1113 1115 1121 1134 1142
1144 1149 1150 1155 1161 1322 1368 1411 1420
1422 1474 1481 1495 1507 1514 1518 1525 1526
1535 1557 1586   **15** 44 56 81 91 93 94 163 204
208 225 228 232 253 264 277 325 332 338 339 355
375 378 385 395 399 402 404 405 421 433 434 435
452 457 467 476 496 510 518 519 523 524 546 557
562 566 573 603 627 639 640 641 645 658 669 682
699 700 709 714 715 720 739 762 775 776 777 786
794 797 802 803 804 819 830 833 835 867 868 869
873 876 877 880 887 892 947 949 967 970 974 980
983 998 1003 1009 1010 1012 1019 1020 1028 1033
1062 1066 1081 1082 1086 1095 1167 1188 1190
1191 1201 1211 1218 1230 1231 1234 1262 1293
1301 1308 1323 1336 1360 1367 1471 1485 1498
1542 1634 1640 1645 1647 1681 1685 1723 1736
1739 1769 1772 1783 1785 1789 1793 1804 1807
1809 1817 1966 1968 1972 1977 1980 1984 1996
2091 2101 2190 2200 2204 2217 2218 2219 2220
2221 2226 2227 2229 2231 2234 2246 2253 2254
2258 2270 2316 2322 2323 2325 2369 2375
2376 2381 2388 2389 2392 2408 2430 2437 2455
2463 2472 2473 2496 2508 2519 2522 2525 2526
2533 2542 2546 2547 2558 2621 2625 2703 2717
2725 2736 2740 2755 2757 2777 2778 2782 2794
2805 2806 2807 2817 2826 2864 2868 2882 2885
2894 2897 2898 2911 2916 2918 2920 2928 2932
2951 2970 2986 2987 2988 2993 3010 3020 3022
3023 3024 3049 3050 3052 3054 3057 3068 3084
3104 3125 3136 3140 3146 3147 3151 3162 3181
3191 3205 3208 3215 3243 3248 3257 3263 3267
3270 3272 3273 3275 3285 3288 3318 3334 3353
3355 3358 3365 3388 3397 3405 3473 3475 3496
3498 3520 3533 3586 3606 3644 3655 3663 3680
3693 3698 3706 3714 3716 3718 3719 3743 3764
3783 3789 3791 3831 3914 3922 3935 3938 4068
4173 4174 4186 4187 4202 4203 4297 4299 4304
4306 4313 4378 4381 4401 4405 4410 4414 4426

4428 4433 4436 4441 4469 4470 4473 4474 4479
4487 4493 4497 4513 4534 4535 4570 4575 4576
4582 4590 4604 4651 4741 4742 4782 4791 4797
4801 4813 4824 4843 4863 4866 4868 4873 4875
4882 4883 4886 4894 4950 4951   **16** 155 160 161
163 198 202 203 242 243 246 251 254 256 258 279
281 284 345 389 412 419 420 421 439 451 459 460
461 463 465 466 467 470 570 576 656 665 670 671
728 731 750 757 758 764 766 767 768 780 784 815
816 851 880 890 891 898 969 1082 1083 1084 1086
1099 1120 1125 1130 1132 1133 1138 1152 1155
1160 1161 1163 1164 1167 1355 1411 1412 1419
1470 1643 1678 1679 1708 1709 1800   **17** 34
1793 1869 1871 1883   **18** 10 11 14 16 19 26 31
33 38 39 43 44 46 47 53 55 58 59 64 66 67 68 70 72
73 79 84 85 87 90 91 104 106 107 108 112 113 114
115 116 121 122 123 124 125 129 132 133 134 135
139 143 144 146 148 149 153 154 156 158 163 166
167 168 171 177 179 180 181 183 184 186 187 189
193 196 198 199 200 201 204 208 209 211 212 213
214 217 219 220 233 235 240 241 247 248 249 250
251 253 254 256 258 259 261 262 263 267 268 269
270 271 272 273 274 277 279 286 287 288 291 294
300 302 303 305 308 310 312 313 314 317 320 321
323 324 325 326 328 330 332 333 336 338 340 341
343 344 346 347 348 352 365 366 367 368 373 374
378 379 381 386 387 391 393 397 398 404 405 406
411 412 413 422 429 430 432 433 434 438 439 443
447 450 455 457 459 461 462 463 467 468 469 474
475 476 477 479 480 482 491 493 498 501 503 508
511 513 514 515 516 517 518 520 521 524 527 529
532 533 535 536 546 550 554 555 557 558 560 561
562 565 569 570 571 574 576 578 579 582 583 584
585 587 588 592 595 600 605 606 614 618 619 621
629 633 636 637 639 641 644 645 646 647 650 651
652 653 654 655 656 657 660 662 663 664 665 668
671 673 676 694 697 698 699 704 705 708 718 719
721 725 727 730 731 732 733 734 735 736 737 739
742 748 749 750 757 762 763 764 765 768 771 772
774 776 777 779 783 787 788 789 790 797 799 800
803 809 810 811 812 814 815 818 819 821 822 823
825 827 830 834 836 840 841 843 845 846 851 856
858 859 861 863 865 867 873 876 877 882 883 886
887 889 896 902 903 905 910 911 912 913 914 915
916 919 920 922 924 925 931 933 935 936 938 939
940 942 952 964 967 969 970 971 976 977 978 979
983 986 987 995 998 999 1000 1009 1010 1011 1015
1017 1019 1021 1029 1030 1031 1034 1036 1038
1044 1045 1048 1049 1050 1051 1055 1057 1062
1063 1066 1067 1070 1073 1074 1077 1080 1084
1085 1092 1095 1098 1102 1103 1104 1107 1113
1115 1116 1117 1119 1121 1124 1125 1131 1132
1133 1134 1137 1138 1139 1140 1141 1142 1144
1146 1149 1151 1152 1154 1157 1160 1161 1162
1163 1165 1167 1169 1171 1172 1179 1180 1181
1182 1184 1187 1190 1194 1195 1197 1205 1207
1208 1210 1213 1214 1215 1231 1235 1236 1244
1245 1248 1250 1251 1252 1257 1259 1270 1276
1277 1293 1300 1303 1304 1305 1306 1309 1310
1312 1313 1314 1315 1320 1321 1323 1324 1325
1326 1327 1328 1332 1334 1338 1346 1349 1351
1352 1354 1356 1358 1360 1361 1362 1363 1366
1369 1378 1381 1383 1392 1398 1399 1401 1405
1410 1412 1415 1422 1423 1425 1430 1432 1434
1442 1444 1445 1446 1448 1449 1451 1452 1455
1458 1459 1461 1463 1467 1469 1470 1471 1472
1474 1475 1476 1478 1479 1482 1483 1496 1499
1504 1506 1512 1514 1516 1518 1523 1524 1525
1528 1530 1534 1540 1544 1547 1548 1550 1551

1552 1553 1554 1557 1564 1565 1569 1570 1573
1574 1575 1576 1578 1579 1580 1581 1582 1584
1602 1603 1604 1605 1606 1608
I (47) **1** 260 361 456 586 589 592 596 597
2 251 253 **6** 147 670 852 **7** 582 830 831 832
838 839 **8** 67 1070 **9** 98 170 247 1143 1144
10 15 445 446 **11** 344 402 552 665 1292
12 27 29 100 **16** 1743 **17** 817
i (8) **12** 265 419 420 423 427 428 **16** 314
i e (2) **16** 537 879
I H S (1) **5** 372
I H S (1) **15** 1935
I N R I (1) **5** 372
I O U's (1) **15** 1814
Iacchia (1) **15** 2573
Iago (4) **2** 240 **9** 911 1023 1027
Iagogo (1) **15** 3828
Iagogogo (1) **15** 3829
iambing (1) **9** 1125
iambs (1) **3** 23
Iar (2) **12** 1125 1134
Ibsen (1) **16** 52
Icarus (1) **9** 953
Ice (1) **8** 862
ice (1) **16** 332
ice (1) **15** 5
icebergs (3) **16** 461 901 **17** 220
icecaps (1) **17** 192
icecream (2) **10** 229 **16** 309
icecreamers (1) **16** 867
icefloes (1) **17** 220
ich (1) **15** 257
Ichabudonosor (2) **15** 1862
Ichthyosauros (1) **15** 2373
icicles (1) **18** 792
icily (1) **13** 592
Icky (1) **15** 1272
ickylickysticky (1) **15** 4321
icy (1) **18** 918
I'd (18) **5** 170 175 179 **6** 301 806 **7** 96 200
8 35 982 **12** 698 1036 **13** 262 269 1207
15 1737 4847 **16** 200
I'd (1) **4** 289
Id (38) **18** 19 54 85 86 115 118 127 187 188 193
231 345 371 446 484 709 782 822 954 961 998 1039
1081 1136 1344 1398 1402 1404 1433 1449 1467
1484 1493 1494 1501 1503 1556 1557
ide (1) **11** 484
Idea (2) **8** 871 **11** 901
idea (55) **1** 545 578 623 **4** 200 535 **5** 249
330 350 352 360 **6** 213 217 678 771 823 886
7 146 149 193 947 1019 1062 **8** 20 33 93 378
457 539 784 1110 **10** 479 1083 1084 **11** 482
12 550 **13** 264 757 864 1123 **15** 1095 2446
16 182 218 642 800 1034 1054 1074 1137 1562
1616 **18** 81 151 282 1004
Ideal (1) **6** 944
ideal (5) **4** 155 **9** 1022 **13** 209 211
16 553
ideal (1) **13** 646
idealistic (1) **15** 1781
ideas (9) **1** 192 **8** 138 1156 **9** 49 51 53
12 1574 **16** 1585 **18** 1407
ideated (1) **17** 608
idée (1) **10** 1068
idee (1) **10** 344
identical (6) **16** 839 1079 1331 1608 1775
17 363
identically (1) **16** 642

362 386 399 422 430 442 446 **3** 4 7 15 16 26 31
33 36 38 45 63 66 73 95 98 101 106 107 110 118
122 126 127 130 131 137 151 153 163 166 167 175
178 179 186 189 193 205 212 223 235 248 251 254
266 268 270 280 281 284 287 300 303 304 305 306
315 318 319 324 326 333 342 355 356 361 363 377
378 388 393 399 410 411 415 420 421 427 429 440
442 448 450 459 462 468 469 476 490 499 **4** 6 7
18 39 41 42 51 52 53 65 68 69 72 79 80 81 84 90 95
99 102 104 113 120 127 134 141 143 147 159 160
162 172 174 176 178 179 198 201 202 204 205 206
207 212 213 216 220 223 240 266 272 273 286 293
294 299 300 328 331 343 355 362 370 371 385 392
393 395 399 401 403 406 413 417 422 424 429 433
436 439 458 462 468 469 474 479 482 490 495 498
524 531 533 534 541 543 544 **5** 13 15 32 35 36
37 38 40 42 49 51 78 80 85 103 108 109 111 124
128 133 139 151 154 172 184 185 195 197 198 199
204 216 230 246 261 267 275 279 280 290 291 296
301 302 303 305 314 328 334 335 342 345 346 354
357 358 362 363 365 367 369 374 396 397 401 404
408 417 418 426 434 435 436 437 438 443 459 460
461 463 465 467 471 475 495 497 503 504 509 518
544 552 556 560 561 563 567 **6** 2 6 9 14 15 16 19
21 22 24 31 39 58 63 71 75 76 78 83 97 108 122
126 159 168 172 180 181 184 190 193 201 202 222
225 232 237 248 257 269 281 292 301 314 327 338
347 348 354 360 370 395 401 406 414 422 432 435
461 478 479 483 516 521 527 530 546 550 551 555
558 563 567 571 581 583 585 589 598 602 604 609
610 616 619 624 629 632 643 644 648 650 661 665
672 681 697 700 703 705 709 711 713 719 720 725
744 747 752 754 757 759 763 766 771 778 790 792
799 805 815 819 820 821 822 824 825 826 828 829
830 839 841 851 852 854 858 861 865 868 870 878
885 891 892 906 915 923 939 940 952 963 964 969
975 982 988 989 995 1004 1008 1015 1025 **7** 16
29 32 36 47 51 52 64 70 73 83 89 90 91 101 112
119 124 131 133 136 145 155 169 177 181 193 198
200 201 204 207 224 233 259 280 281 286 293 299
306 309 311 315 338 339 341 345 350 367 377 391
396 405 415 419 426 431 436 444 450 451 459 461
462 466 470 479 481 482 490 492 494 497 505 510
534 542 558 574 587 592 600 606 612 616 617 618
619 620 621 627 629 632 647 669 680 688 705 708
709 720 721 731 735 738 742 747 748 751 757 764
786 802 805 816 826 835 854 889 890 901 902 906
924 932 934 940 955 963 968 969 974 976 983 986
987 1003 1015 1023 1038 1044 1047 **8** 6 11 14 19
23 31 41 47 60 94 95 97 100 131 136 145 151 152
157 158 177 185 188 193 196 200 206 212 213 229
236 240 248 250 251 281 282 287 310 311 315 317
318 321 327 336 344 350 352 353 358 359 362 364
366 369 379 395 398 399 403 404 406 409 410 411
421 423 428 430 431 432 442 444 459 460 463 472
474 478 483 488 489 497 500 504 516 517 531 532
533 540 547 556 557 568 577 596 597 602 611 612
613 616 618 624 626 642 643 650 664 685 697 705
709 710 720 733 747 768 786 788 797 801 802 809
822 824 828 837 838 848 858 866 867 873 874 875
877 882 887 890 892 897 902 903 907 914 921 925
929 939 942 944 948 951 958 960 969 971 973 976
988 989 1020 1037 1039 1043 1045 1066 1072 1076
1080 1081 1084 1100 1108 1111 1112 1124 1126
1127 1142 1147 1148 1152 1156 1160 1165 1168
1171 1175 1176 1177 1191 **9** 4 11 37 63 66 74 85
94 101 102 104 105 109 113 115 117 128 131 133
134 142 154 156 158 159 164 167 172 174 195 214
225 230 246 248 249 250 252 253 260 269 278 279

292 297 302 310 318 323 337 338 340 352 356 357
366 383 390 393 403 406 412 427 434 441 444 451
452 455 456 457 462 464 465 466 467 469 477 480
486 498 509 518 538 556 559 561 570 577 578 582
592 593 609 611 619 622 624 634 649 654 657 660
666 669 670 672 680 694 695 711 713 721 722 724
743 747 752 760 766 779 780 782 784 800 801 804
809 818 821 823 829 837 843 859 867 876 879 880
881 882 883 887 894 896 897 899 901 912 914 921
922 923 924 926 927 929 930 948 957 965 983 986
990 998 1002 1003 1007 1009 1012 1013 1014 1019
1021 1024 1033 1035 1041 1049 1050 1051 1054
1071 1073 1075 1088 1089 1090 1108 1117 1119
1164 1192 1193 1200 1211 1218 1219 **10** 2 10 14
22 31 36 56 74 86 90 97 100 105 106 115 116 128
131 140 147 149 154 156 158 159 165 174 175 176
186 187 193 196 200 208 222 230 237 246 258 260
271 275 276 277 291 292 299 300 302 307 317 324
334 348 358 365 369 371 394 395 398 401 403 406
407 409 412 416 428 436 439 443 476 479 482 484
499 512 514 517 526 527 530 540 544 564 568 570
580 587 606 626 627 629 630 644 669 671 672 675
703 708 721 722 755 759 762 766 769 770 771 778
783 790 794 795 805 806 808 820 825 833 896 902
912 915 933 937 949 980 987 992 1008 1009 1010
1022 1025 1027 1035 1045 1048 1082 1087 1090
1111 1125 1131 1138 1142 1146 1150 1158 1160
1165 1169 1173 1179 1196 1197 1200 1210 1229
1231 1234 1241 1245 1248 1260 1262 1263 1269
1271 1275 1281 **11** 10 11 42 46 49 70 72 75 83
86 87 89 106 108 118 119 125 134 139 145 147 155
167 175 197 206 220 227 232 236 242 250 264 277
291 294 296 297 313 316 351 353 354 357 363 366
368 374 383 384 397 413 418 438 453 471 476 485
488 492 516 523 524 525 546 548 558 569 572 573
576 586 588 602 618 619 620 632 633 634 639 643
647 660 661 675 679 684 691 705 706 721 722 723
725 733 736 748 764 772 775 780 784 785 788 789
793 798 811 821 828 842 850 851 876 880 893 905
913 931 943 946 956 958 966 971 974 975 993 1014
1017 1019 1023 1024 1032 1035 1051 1054 1057
1058 1059 1071 1080 1085 1090 1091 1095 1097
1113 1115 1120 1130 1135 1136 1139 1142 1153
1157 1164 1182 1193 1197 1198 1201 1207 1225
1230 1238 1250 1252 1254 1257 1259 1260 1274
1281 **12** 9 10 16 25 34 36 42 48 55 60 69 70 75
79 88 116 119 121 122 127 132 139 157 161 164
169 171 172 186 202 215 222 245 249 250 253 263
264 267 272 282 289 291 292 312 314 345 348 349
351 352 355 359 368 370 381 385 394 399 401 409
410 439 459 461 463 472 474 476 504 507 516 517
518 525 535 543 545 556 570 572 586 588 592 598
599 605 606 608 610 613 616 625 630 631 632 634
639 645 648 650 657 662 663 666 668 674 675 681
682 686 689 705 706 710 712 721 726 728 730 738
756 758 775 776 794 802 805 822 832 835 839 858
865 868 870 872 897 898 900 902 907 914 917 920
921 950 952 958 963 965 966 976 981 984 989 996
1009 1023 1024 1025 1026 1027 1041 1049 1072
1075 1082 1087 1089 1092 1098 1100 1112 1113
1115 1116 1117 1123 1130 1132 1134 1137 1151
1156 1157 1160 1161 1166 1171 1173 1178 1181
1183 1186 1187 1192 1203 1204 1205 1210 1222
1226 1236 1237 1238 1242 1243 1247 1250 1254
1280 1285 1286 1287 1289 1295 1298 1302 1303
1312 1314 1325 1326 1327 1331 1334 1342 1348
1354 1355 1365 1368 1369 1371 1372 1382 1394
1403 1422 1425 1428 1433 1436 1443 1446 1450
1472 1487 1497 1509 1515 1517 1519 1528 1530

1531 1536 1542 1551 1552 1553 1557 1564 1565
1566 1574 1609 1621 1635 1636 1647 1651 1658
1659 1662 1666 1714 1716 1755 1769 1772 1781
1786 1795 1815 1824 1837 1839 1845 1849 1854
1858 1859 1861 1865 1866 1867 1876 1878 1881
1886 1897 1912 1917 **13** 1 2 7 13 14 18 21 25 34
36 37 52 55 57 62 79 80 87 91 98 99 101 112 117
118 121 127 129 131 132 133 135 137 138 147 151
152 165 170 173 182 189 190 194 197 200 201 203
212 216 220 222 226 227 234 235 239 251 255 259
276 286 291 292 293 298 301 303 304 324 325 326
334 338 339 342 345 349 369 378 379 383 402 410
412 421 438 446 449 452 453 456 469 471 491 494
498 500 504 511 514 516 518 533 542 548 549 557
564 565 576 586 587 592 600 602 604 606 610 614
618 622 624 632 636 637 642 648 652 660 666 667
671 672 684 691 696 701 705 712 720 728 730 738
741 748 751 754 758 762 774 780 781 782 786 789
794 806 808 811 815 817 825 827 832 833 835 836
840 841 865 866 867 873 876 877 878 892 896 899
909 918 921 926 931 933 950 957 961 963 964 965
971 973 975 976 978 986 991 995 997 998 999 1000
1002 1016 1024 1053 1055 1062 1064 1066 1074
1079 1090 1091 1099 1105 1106 1111 1112 1115
1121 1124 1125 1126 1129 1130 1136 1140 1141
1147 1149 1150 1153 1159 1164 1166 1182 1184
1185 1187 1190 1191 1201 1215 1218 1221 1224
1234 1241 1244 1250 1251 1259 1267 1268 1270
1278 1284 1286 1292 **14** 10 23 24 34 40 43 46
54 56 57 61 65 68 70 76 77 82 85 86 88 96 97 102
104 105 111 113 114 115 119 127 129 132 137 140
141 144 145 148 150 152 154 156 162 164 165 174
182 185 200 205 208 209 211 224 225 234 237 246
248 253 258 262 265 273 275 288 292 304 308 314
315 322 328 334 336 337 343 345 346 350 359 360
368 369 379 385 386 388 398 403 408 409 419 421
430 433 435 438 448 453 455 461 467 471 474 475
484 487 497 500 509 510 511 517 520 523 526 527
530 535 542 548 550 552 553 572 577 581 583 588
596 597 598 599 602 603 606 609 610 612 614 615
619 620 621 625 627 630 643 645 651 655 659 663
669 675 676 682 683 692 697 721 724 728 730 736
739 745 749 750 759 762 765 768 769 771 778 780
781 783 787 788 789 791 793 797 801 809 812 817
820 828 834 852 857 884 885 890 895 896 900 903
921 926 927 931 938 944 946 948 964 967 969 971
975 976 981 990 994 995 998 1002 1007 1011 1013
1021 1026 1036 1043 1044 1046 1048 1049 1058
1064 1069 1070 1075 1078 1084 1098 1103 1107
1111 1131 1132 1135 1138 1144 1145 1148 1150
1153 1156 1157 1158 1159 1168 1175 1180 1195
1196 1197 1198 1199 1200 1204 1209 1211 1215
1227 1242 1243 1245 1250 1255 1256 1257 1258
1259 1260 1261 1263 1266 1267 1270 1275 1276
1278 1279 1284 1285 1291 1292 1296 1298 1301
1302 1309 1316 1317 1321 1323 1328 1335 1340
1341 1345 1349 1354 1358 1359 1364 1367 1369
1371 1372 1378 1382 1383 1385 1387 1395 1403
1404 1405 1411 1417 1433 1435 1436 1442 1448
1456 1463 1473 1475 1485 1502 1518 1521 1546
1548 1549 1553 1554 1556 1559 1566 1575 1580
1588 1590 **15** 57 92 93 109 117 163 202 207 209
330 333 360 364 369 370 395 409 420 421 422 441
442 445 505 519 547 548 557 558 572 573 585 637
662 669 680 709 739 742 743 745 747 777 786 788
795 796 825 830 834 835 848 852 854 868 878 885
887 896 928 941 946 950 951 955 968 975 977 982
985 1009 1017 1019 1031 1033 1045 1046 1047
1052 1053 1054 1065 1071 1100 1116 1126 1156

1169 1188 1224 1230 1289 1295 1301 1369 1384
1391 1396 1454 1481 1544 1594 1632 1643 1660
1663 1674 1693 1695 1715 1731 1736 1758 1770
1781 1790 1801 1802 1807 1809 1873 1878 1895
1899 1958 1963 2118 2120 2135 2140 2189 2199
2202 2208 2218 2227 2233 2236 2313 2321 2322
2324 2346 2356 2357 2358 2366 2372 2398 2413
2414 2415 2416 2432 2440 2442 2449 2456 2470
2497 2539 2578 2579 2580 2643 2665 2696 2782
2783 2784 2789 2814 2818 2827 2862 2866 2867
2869 2893 2899 2908 2946 2965 2978 2981 2987
2991 2992 3000 3010 3022 3029 3030 3031 3033
3037 3042 3057 3073 3083 3085 3088 3107 3137
3143 3154 3175 3185 3188 3199 3207 3209 3211
3245 3246 3248 3259 3263 3264 3279 3285 3311
3318 3335 3354 3483 3489 3535 3578 3663 3671
3764 3767 3770 3804 3891 3907 3909 3949 3998
4183 4197 4202 4204 4306 4376 4378 4381 4402
4411 4436 4455 4460 4479 4484 4540 4586 4602
4606 4626 4720 4738 4752 4791 4793 4847 4861
4868 4870 4882 4884 4886 4897 4901 4953   **16** 3
6 10 15 16 19 20 34 50 53 61 62 64 71 73 77 78 80
81 90 92 102 109 117 119 122 125 129 131 137 140
150 152 154 157 160 162 165 166 168 173 180 181
183 184 187 188 191 192 195 198 199 200 204 207
211 212 217 219 223 224 225 235 236 237 248 250
252 255 256 258 260 267 269 272 276 279 281 282
285 289 290 291 302 308 310 311 325 326 329 332
341 342 343 346 354 364 368 371 382 412 428 432
434 436 448 459 461 464 470 473 476 491 493 499
510 513 528 532 534 540 542 545 548 550 552 554
560 564 568 571 573 576 578 579 587 589 593 594
595 598 601 604 606 607 609 612 615 622 638 639
640 649 653 658 662 668 670 678 681 682 686 698
713 717 730 731 748 750 761 765 770 773 775 779
781 794 802 812 828 830 833 838 840 850 851 861
862 865 867 868 875 878 881 887 889 890 894 895
900 903 912 914 917 924 930 942 944 945 947 948
950 954 957 965 972 973 975 976 986 987 989 993
995 996 999 1000 1007 1013 1016 1028 1035 1039
1041 1042 1051 1056 1068 1076 1077 1082 1083
1085 1090 1091 1100 1103 1111 1118 1119 1120
1123 1125 1127 1128 1129 1134 1135 1138 1139
1142 1144 1152 1158 1173 1176 1184 1188 1189
1194 1198 1200 1203 1211 1212 1218 1219 1225
1229 1240 1248 1266 1269 1275 1277 1287 1288
1290 1299 1308 1309 1311 1312 1326 1333 1334
1335 1338 1342 1343 1344 1345 1350 1353 1356
1360 1373 1374 1376 1377 1381 1383 1385 1391
1393 1397 1398 1400 1401 1404 1421 1428 1429
1433 1444 1445 1446 1448 1449 1451 1455 1458
1459 1469 1473 1478 1486 1490 1493 1494 1495
1496 1498 1510 1511 1515 1518 1520 1521 1523
1525 1527 1532 1535 1536 1541 1544 1546 1548
1557 1559 1561 1562 1579 1580 1581 1583 1584
1586 1588 1589 1592 1594 1595 1598 1602 1612
1619 1623 1624 1626 1627 1636 1642 1645 1654
1655 1661 1663 1665 1669 1674 1677 1678 1679
1697 1699 1700 1710 1713 1716 1718 1721 1727
1729 1732 1735 1736 1738 1739 1742 1743 1744
1745 1747 1750 1753 1756 1759 1760 1762 1763
1768 1780 1782 1790 1791 1792 1793 1801 1803
1808 1809 1825 1826 1827 1832 1833 1835 1836
1838 1841 1843 1845 1846 1853 1854 1861 1871
1878 1891 1892 1893   **17** 3 9 20 24 30 31 34 35
39 46 51 52 54 57 58 59 66 75 88 89 91 93 111 127
131 135 136 137 138 139 140 141 143 145 146 153
154 162 164 177 183 185 186 187 188 190 191 194
196 201 202 205 209 210 213 214 217 218 220 221

222 227 228 233 234 238 244 250 251 253 255 260
261 266 267 268 269 272 279 280 289 294 303 308
325 329 330 331 333 339 340 355 358 364 369 374
376 384 387 391 393 404 436 440 442 447 448 450
452 454 455 457 459 461 467 468 469 470 471 476
479 481 484 486 489 498 513 514 515 519 521 523
542 545 547 563 576 581 600 603 609 610 612 623
624 628 630 639 645 649 667 668 671 674 679 683
687 688 694 695 696 709 728 732 735 737 738 748
749 757 758 759 761 772 775 777 780 787 795 831
846 855 856 858 860 861 862 872 879 894 897 901
906 907 913 914 916 918 931 932 961 966 972 976
977 980 982 1001 1004 1009 1011 1023 1042 1046
1047 1049 1051 1053 1054 1058 1059 1060 1063
1065 1066 1071 1077 1084 1088 1097 1103 1118
1121 1122 1124 1127 1129 1130 1143 1144 1147
1148 1154 1159 1183 1187 1193 1194 1197 1206
1212 1215 1220 1226 1236 1237 1238 1239 1240
1241 1244 1251 1252 1260 1262 1277 1279 1281
1284 1288 1293 1306 1311 1322 1326 1328 1329
1348 1359 1398 1406 1410 1412 1415 1417 1421
1422 1424 1426 1428 1430 1432 1437 1438 1442
1444 1447 1458 1480 1482 1495 1500 1504 1511
1518 1530 1553 1554 1594 1595 1599 1608 1611
1613 1616 1618 1619 1623 1626 1628 1635 1636
1638 1639 1640 1641 1645 1651 1656 1663 1664
1667 1668 1678 1683 1684 1685 1686 1692 1693
1699 1703 1720 1721 1728 1731 1750 1761 1763
1767 1770 1777 1788 1799 1802 1803 1824 1826
1827 1844 1850 1851 1856 1862 1870 1873 1876
1878 1879 1888 1889 1891 1894 1907 1914 1917
1918 1919 1936 1939 1969 1970 1977 1993 1996
2019 2025 2026 2039 2049 2051 2056 2059 2071
2077 2099 2130 2131 2138 2147 2149 2160 2163
2170 2172 2179 2181 2188 2191 2213 2222 2229
2230 2242 2252 2261 2265 2289 2290 2296 2313
2316 2317 2329   **18** 2 7 16 30 44 45 48 50 56 62
68 75 78 83 91 94 98 105 115 116 119 123 125 136
139 149 151 153 154 155 156 168 177 181 187 192
194 197 198 200 201 208 211 213 226 228 235 238
240 242 247 255 258 260 264 266 267 269 271 278
286 292 294 295 306 307 310 317 319 323 326 336
338 351 352 362 366 367 370 377 380 390 394 398
401 404 406 407 409 413 420 435 437 440 446 460
462 466 467 468 475 479 482 495 497 500 502 510
514 524 530 539 540 557 561 562 564 565 573 579
582 597 599 602 608 611 616 617 629 631 632 634
635 641 642 647 648 650 652 655 658 662 663 681
684 685 687 694 699 703 704 709 710 711 731 733
736 737 740 741 747 748 749 751 754 757 763 764
766 771 774 775 782 788 790 804 806 807 813 816
828 829 830 831 841 844 849 850 864 870 874 877
880 890 895 903 905 911 914 915 920 922 926 927
932 954 958 959 961 963 974 975 978 979 980 982
991 992 996 998 1000 1009 1010 1013 1018 1025
1026 1032 1037 1038 1040 1041 1042 1053 1058
1059 1061 1069 1074 1079 1086 1089 1091 1093
1094 1103 1106 1111 1112 1113 1116 1118 1120
1122 1133 1139 1144 1150 1158 1165 1167 1180
1182 1189 1192 1198 1201 1202 1206 1211 1213
1216 1222 1223 1228 1235 1238 1239 1242 1245
1252 1256 1261 1262 1264 1265 1267 1280 1281
1286 1289 1290 1297 1303 1304 1306 1307 1309
1311 1319 1321 1325 1329 1334 1335 1343 1346
1347 1353 1354 1359 1360 1365 1369 1371 1373
1375 1376 1379 1388 1396 1403 1406 1409 1413
1418 1419 1429 1430 1431 1435 1439 1446 1447
1448 1453 1458 1460 1461 1462 1463 1465 1466
1467 1475 1476 1479 1481 1482 1486 1489 1490

1491 1492 1497 1498 1499 1501 1502 1503 1504
1505 1515 1516 1517 1521 1530 1541 1542 1546
1549 1551 1554 1555 1557 1558 1569 1573 1577
1585 1586 1587 1591 1593 1594 1599 1603

in **(69)** **1** 362 598 **2** 104 239 253 **3** 203
4 515 **6** 147 165 601 618 983 **7** 320 321 323
750 768 770 828 831 839 868 869   **8** 416
9 288 304 366 500 733 1173 1174   **10** 16 161
194 197 368 608 611   **12** 362 419 420 422 427
478 1118 1291 1324 1721 1740 1801   **13** 948
14 406 962 1574   **15** 1654   **16** 780 1231 1250
1251 1800 1868   **17** 397 412 650 814 1379 1388
1503

in **(359)** **15** 15 30 34 36 40 48 61 73 86 126 132
134 139 148 248 249 269 270 283 285 286 292 298
300 310 317 321 329 340 386 387 388 412 413 416
450 451 452 471 480 481 482 501 536 538 543 582
584 651 652 653 684 703 704 728 752 753 772 808
814 863 875 900 902 907 912 918 933 935 939 957
958 986 988 1007 1014 1016 1026 1058 1081 1117
1128 1139 1151 1162 1163 1177 1179 1191 1210
1216 1238 1259 1265 1279 1304 1318 1328 1355
1366 1378 1380 1382 1408 1412 1419 1442 1469
1477 1480 1493 1508 1509 1519 1548 1553 1558
1565 1571 1572 1573 1583 1595 1603 1609 1614
1617 1741 1750 1775 1819 1825 1826 1829 1849
1853 1873 1883 1885 1888 1898 1904 1915 1927
1935 1938 1939 1960 1961 1962 1964 1970 1977
2005 2016 2019 2035 2044 2045 2050 2051 2053
2071 2074 2075 2133 2150 2152 2177 2178 2184
2216 2239 2240 2245 2247 2248 2273 2288 2299
2303 2337 2412 2432 2451 2452 2489 2513 2574
2602 2609 2618 2630 2636 2655 2656 2658 2660
2705 2712 2722 2728 2743 2745 2812 2830 2835
2851 2854 2858 2859 2860 2923 2925 2943 2947
2957 3028 3089 3090 3111 3124 3144 3160 3168
3211 3221 3225 3227 3234 3279 3297 3305 3316
3325 3328 3340 3377 3382 3386 3394 3408 3411
3416 3418 3420 3434 3456 3459 3460 3530 3549
3594 3642 3649 3707 3723 3739 3760 3773 3809
3821 3822 3823 3826 3838 3857 3942 3962 3979
3988 3996 4013 4016 4017 4018 4019 4026 4034
4038 4039 4048 4055 4057 4058 4061 4077 4078
4100 4124 4141 4144 4148 4157 4166 4168 4221
4238 4244 4264 4310 4318 4327 4329 4335 4396
4449 4465 4476 4477 4498 4507 4532 4578 4611
4612 4657 4673 4679 4681 4693 4695 4742 4747
4771 4805 4838 4858 4910 4911 4912 4920 4945
4955 4957 4959

IN **(1)** **15** 1560
inaccessible **(1)** **12** 112
inactive **(1)** **17** 1185
inadequate **(3)** **12** 796 **16** 1186 **17** 214
inadvertence **(2)** **17** 5 833
Inadvertently **(1)** **15** 2314
inadvertently **(2)** **16** 1513 **17** 81
inadvisable **(1)** **16** 1312
inaffirmative **(1)** **17** 1163
Inagh **(1)** **12** 1452
inalienably **(1)** **17** 1099
inall **(2)** **11** 29 **15** 512
inalterably **(1)** **17** 1098
inanition **(1)** **17** 37
inanity **(1)** **17** 2225
Inasmuch **(1)** **17** 896
inasmuch **(4)** **16** 12 116 **17** 2274 2285
inaudibly **(3)** **15** 937 4959 4962
inaugurate **(4)** **10** 1268 **17** 962 963 964
inaugurated **(2)** **14** 1531 **15** 1002

131

infallibly (1) 16 1829

infamy (4) 9 672 14 1584 15 1757 3351

infancy (4) 16 564 1520 17 1006 1355

Infant (1) 15 916

INFANT (1) 15 1875

infant (8) 12 1120 13 396 14 1240 15 942 17 865 18 497 582 781

infanticide (2) 6 346 14 1261

infanticides (1) 14 962

infantile (4) 15 1756 17 864 1791 1952

infantilic (1) 15 1579

infantry (1) 12 1892

Infant's (1) 15 1580

infant's (1) 8 658

infants (5) 10 587 14 987 1260 16 477 17 1899

infare (1) 14 84

Infatuated (1) 11 1110

infatuated (1) 15 2837

infatuation (1) 16 1552

inferior (2) 17 733 1811

inferiorly (1) 15 2413

Infernal (1) 15 1199

infernal (3) 6 607 15 2935 17 1135

inferno (1) 14 1018

inferred (1) 17 2215

infidel (2) 17 836 843

infinite (8) 2 50 9 1012 13 748 14 521 1079 17 580 1043 1112

infinite (1) 15 2176

infinitely (6) 12 735 13 193 16 784 1740 17 993 1054

infinitesimal (3) 17 1056 1276 1762

infinity (4) 17 1141 2086 2087 2131

infirm (2) 17 488 1890

infirmarian (1) 14 943

infirmary (1) 17 136

inflamed (1) 15 1020

inflammable (2) 16 1392 17 105

inflammably (1) 17 2150

inflated (2) 7 315 17 494

inflexible (1) 13 694

inflicted (3) 15 2869 16 1064 17 1448

infliction (1) 6 957

Influence (3) 5 33 15 665 2739

influence (20) 2 342 344 7 261 12 385 13 985 1088 14 244 15 4760 16 67 411 1828 17 13 17 26 44 292 847 1118 2204 2205

influenced (1) 12 1408

influences (2) 15 2737 17 1152

Influential (1) 15 3688

influential (1) 14 1334

influenza (1) 6 124

influx (1) 16 556

Inform (1) 15 3146

informant (1) 17 483

information (5) 12 1138 15 1034 16 1029 17 633 2005

informed (5) 14 255 820 16 163 205 1068

infracostal (1) 17 1448

infrequent (1) 17 669

infused (1) 14 248

infusion (1) 17 357

ingemiscit (1) 3 466

ingenious (2) 14 858 1267

Ingersoll (1) 15 2199

ingle (2) 14 1058 16 270

ingleside (2) 17 1282 1289

inglorious (1) 14 870

ingoing (1) 8 476

ingots (2) 12 81 14 1417

Ingram (1) 10 790

ingredients (1) 17 358

ingress (4) 17 1034 1219 1274 1286

inhabit (1) 12 1737

inhabitability (1) 17 1083

inhabitants (2) 17 226 892

inhabitants (1) 15 1553

inhabitation (1) 17 1022

inhaled (4) 16 55 17 1490 1493

inhaling (4) 4 379 5 21 487 14 1245

inherent (3) 15 823 16 116 828

inherit (1) 17 1499

inherited (1) 17 23

inhibition (2) 14 669 17 2175

inhibitions (1) 17 2271

Inhibitory (1) 17 1431

inhibitory (1) 14 669

inhuman (1) 17 2038

inhuman (1) 15 3044

inimitable (1) 12 544

Inisfail (1) 12 68

Inishark (1) 4 138

Inishboffin (1) 4 138

Inishturk (1) 4 138

initial (8) 9 931 12 1540 16 1614 17 166 679 1264 1693 1828

initial (1) 15 3108

initialled (4) 4 66 12 1539 16 718 17 2099

initially (1) 17 450

Initials (1) 8 528

initials (2) 7 17 12 1873

initiated (2) 14 1169 17 2170

initiation (1) 17 378

iniurias (1) 3 466

injected (1) 1 209

injected (1) 15 213

injection (1) 15 2316

injects (1) 8 342

injun (2) 12 308 14 1524

injunction (1) 14 981

injured (1) 15 977

injuries (3) 15 4847 16 1064 17 2204

injury (1) 16 1511

injustice (1) 12 1474

ink (16) 2 126 139 3 217 11 822 847 13 273 642 16 668 718 1345 17 1379 1402 18 1053 1128 1193

inkbottle (1) 8 137

Inked (1) 6 160

inkeraser (1) 8 141

inkhorns (1) 12 1715

inkle (1) 14 985

inkling (1) 15 2389

inkshining (1) 10 31

inlaid (2) 17 1284 1290

inlaid (1) 15 2480

inland (2) 7 341 16 645

inlets (1) 14 677

inmate (4) 14 724 16 1056 17 1944 1945

inmost (2) 6 670 12 654

Inn (1) 15 4452

inn (1) 11 249

innate (3) 13 97 17 1002 1623

innately (1) 15 976

inner (18) 1 321 530 4 1 382 6 495 7 297 344 375 387 411 469 670 697 904 908 8 161 11 520 17 1542

innings (1) 6 1004

Inniskillings (1) 15 1063

Innocence (3) 11 298 639 15 1188

innocence (3) 13 910 14 792 15 3458

innocent (8) 2 36 6 474 9 365 1195 12 648 14 1190 1291 18 1311

innocent (2) 15 915 4055

innocents (2) 8 754 14 1423

Inn's (1) 12 1863

Inns (1) 15 1366

Innuendo (1) 7 150

innuendo (2) 16 1209 1594

innumerable (2) 12 102 17 1076

innumerable (1) 15 315

inoculated (1) 15 2590

inodorous (1) 17 2092

inoffensive (1) 15 3276

inoperative (1) 14 941

inquest (1) 6 359

inquired (3) 16 484 611 1774

inquirer (1) 14 1240

inquirers (1) 14 44

inquiring (1) 16 1288

inquisition (2) 14 1215 16 1121

inquisitional (1) 9 1159

inquisitive (1) 16 242

inquisitively (1) 15 438

inquit (1) 9 811

in's (1) 9 541

insane (2) 1 129 17 1165

insanity (3) 6 339 14 1550 15 1964

insatiable (1) 16 1805

inscribed (1) 17 1864

inscriptions (1) 17 772

inscrutability (1) 17 1166

inscrutable (1) 16 598

Insect (1) 17 592

Insects (2) 13 1143 15 2412

insects (2) 12 82 15 2421

insecure (1) 17 1672

insecurity (1) 17 1413

insemination (1) 14 970

insensible (1) 17 1450

insentient (1) 17 2062

Insert (1) 17 1833

inserted (6) 13 1042 17 72 601 1451 1878 2111

inserting (1) 17 1215

insertions (1) 12 1283

inserts (1) 15 4032

Inshore (1) 1 243

inside (35) 4 70 5 24 314 6 82 154 576 1011 7 384 8 132 375 752 871 10 1165 11 566 1129 1179 13 184 185 796 887 15 82 1283 2220 16 27 106 453 472 1029 18 142 180 181 585 765 811 1221

inside (2) 10 446 612

inside (2) 15 726 1028

insides (5) 6 424 8 1050 14 513 18 633 1149

Insidious (1) 8 730

insignia (1) 15 4451

insignificant (2) 9 77 13 503

insincere (1) 15 1977

insinuated (1) 16 1163

insinuating (1) 17 1940

insist (1) 15 3052

insisted (1) 18 1310

insistence (1) 15 2752

545 555 556 562 606 631 641 649 700 708 **2** 31
41 74 75 86 101 108 113 152 170 174 183 189 195
201 219 237 243 244 247 251 259 339 340 346 350
359 360 362 377 383 406 416 420 **3** 8 13 38 50
65 86 104 107 120 126 127 140 145 207 212 253
282 295 299 306 377 421 435 439 444 474 491 495
496 502 **4** 30 40 46 80 112 131 149 205 215 216
235 236 264 319 375 405 406 419 451 478 485 492
542 **5** 12 31 40 41 43 46 68 71 91 92 95 104 105
118 172 191 199 200 206 222 245 290 334 341 361
364 373 393 408 463 467 501 527 564 566 **6** 33
42 44 63 67 74 97 126 132 152 159 196 203 207 212
217 219 221 237 240 244 246 248 268 271 285 314
335 341 342 345 392 405 454 456 469 470 481 506
510 524 537 561 564 566 568 571 580 613 629 644
645 649 650 651 657 665 690 693 700 751 768 804
805 806 822 825 843 848 849 866 867 880 894 895
923 941 954 981 987 988 990 1001 1018 **7** 25 49
68 90 96 106 113 149 166 167 214 224 233 234 260
262 269 330 347 435 456 463 501 511 530 545 546
553 556 557 583 588 644 645 648 659 661 667 669
671 672 736 788 800 802 879 887 889 890 892 909
925 967 977 984 1036 **8** 13 14 41 58 64 65 81 86
87 95 109 110 156 178 204 235 237 244 257 259
260 281 301 302 306 328 349 384 409 447 462 465
493 494 502 520 525 547 572 585 588 590 594 606
662 686 742 775 787 807 831 851 898 939 948 953
976 1000 1009 1013 1080 1137 1145 1163 1168
1172 **9** 27 47 50 53 63 66 69 84 88 91 100 106
109 134 141 147 150 151 154 155 165 166 177 179
185 188 232 250 274 290 297 298 301 305 307 309
312 334 357 359 362 364 371 378 382 390 391 407
420 422 432 443 452 460 461 471 472 476 478 480
520 522 525 542 543 553 569 584 609 614 626 639
653 657 671 673 679 714 752 756 782 793 796 802
810 813 816 826 828 832 833 837 838 840 844 855
856 881 882 884 885 898 903 916 923 924 927 928
931 942 950 975 977 989 990 998 1004 1005 1009
1010 1012 1018 1020 1021 1023 1027 1028 1033
1037 1044 1049 1072 1074 1075 1078 1097 1158
1178 1199 **10** 274 294 382 401 409 410 431 438
454 476 480 511 522 581 602 669 685 687 730 733
754 771 790 844 875 889 891 894 900 918 945 947
980 995 1061 1074 1089 1094 1138 1139 1170
11 6 14 22 43 94 96 104 152 230 260 269 298 303
354 369 385 446 512 554 573 628 634 635 641 646
670 681 713 824 825 829 830 831 832 836 837 862
867 883 889 907 911 915 916 917 938 945 968 969
980 982 1036 1107 1149 1173 1242 1244 1254 1255
1264 1265 1275 **12** 70 78 87 108 122 138 216
271 272 374 377 386 397 432 503 522 549 657 684
692 710 713 717 728 735 737 765 772 787 823 846
847 852 856 863 868 872 880 945 988 990 993 1006
1043 1048 1059 1062 1071 1078 1135 1165 1175
1207 1226 1227 1259 1307 1313 1330 1352 1386
1398 1417 1421 1422 1430 1465 1467 1483 1486
1491 1498 1544 1550 1565 1578 1622 1630 1631
1632 1633 1647 1659 1665 1666 1673 1778 1802
1847 1860 1867 1868 **13** 7 46 66 72 96 189 209
444 566 744 774 777 795 816 855 878 879 894 940
960 979 984 987 993 997 1008 1014 1017 1019 1025
1043 1059 1065 1066 1071 1110 1117 1126 1127
1131 1188 1200 1201 1237 1239 1262 **14** 7 9 13
17 18 20 33 43 64 67 69 74 107 108 153 189 223
226 227 259 268 281 282 292 294 295 298 301 350
386 387 391 392 398 444 445 449 453 494 496 509
513 518 544 582 613 629 780 786 793 796 809 825
830 833 847 848 872 902 908 911 913 914 926 930
934 935 937 940 1016 1017 1018 1021 1022 1024

1030 1035 1037 1038 1040 1041 1043 1045 1048
1058 1060 1062 1065 1073 1076 1078 1079 1085
1086 1087 1100 1101 1137 1138 1139 1140 1152
1153 1165 1229 1233 1234 1240 1241 1262 1263
1264 1267 1272 1284 1302 1303 1317 1322 1352
1373 1398 1407 1419 1420 1421 1424 1437 1474
1500 1558 1573 1576 1580 **15** 94 129 167 204
231 371 445 458 463 493 496 639 730 738 750 765
769 804 826 835 880 940 942 943 953 954 967 975
981 1028 1117 1153 1158 1171 1197 1210 1220
1222 1224 1233 1356 1359 1391 1397 1456 1527
1542 1543 1544 1561 1562 1629 1656 1679 1712
1731 1753 1757 1759 1768 1770 1775 1777 1780
1789 1793 1796 1798 1799 1800 1803 1810 1871
1899 1922 1965 1974 1996 2028 2087 2088 2089
2091 2093 2095 2097 2098 2105 2129 2191 2203
2245 2312 2313 2314 2321 2327 2344 2355 2374
2375 2395 2402 2409 2424 2426 2444 2462 2489
2496 2516 2531 2635 2651 2696 2740 2759 2762
2775 2789 2932 3022 3086 3116 3138 3153 3163
3199 3274 3277 3302 3340 3355 3464 3493 3505
3513 3516 3520 3522 3546 3592 3594 3606 3613
3620 3676 3713 3767 3775 3851 3888 4176 4197
4286 4293 4303 4403 4415 4416 4424 4433 4434
4436 4470 4471 4487 4493 4495 4515 4568 4656
4840 **16** 59 128 232 233 249 258 264 282 283
298 346 416 437 546 660 679 683 684 719 732 733
738 756 758 764 766 780 850 876 877 895 897 1046
1092 1095 1096 1140 1154 1159 1270 1390 1392
1689 1719 1802 **17** 597 603 730 833 834 1099
1883 1884 2128 2130 **18** 19 51 60 94 95 124 142
145 155 163 176 208 261 276 287 325 347 356 385
386 437 442 450 455 464 559 605 609 617 660 736
775 826 898 902 912 939 946 953 964 968 994 1027
1033 1094 1121 1124 1133 1145 1149 1169 1177
1230 1240 1250 1261 1273 1291 1301 1302 1326
1327 1335 1405 1440 1473 1486 1510 1519 1533
1539 1563 1579

is (32) **1** 198 **2** 65 **3** 382 387 **5** 144
6 147 164 **7** 490 494 857 858 **8** 416 **9** 550
726 733 1043 **10** 524 571 572 734 **11** 322 629
710 **12** 428 810 1508 **16** 593 1252 1348 1681
17 416 644

is (50) **15** 965 987 1005 1258 1265 1318 1407
1444 1447 1508 1519 1521 1548 1588 1619 1626
1984 2035 2042 2047 2146 2185 2186 2264 2306
2309 2686 2697 2734 2743 2747 3220 3297 4037
4159 4319 4333 4450 4454 4456 4669 4674 4706
4796 4914 4915 4919 4925 4928

Isaac (2) **7** 707 **12** 1736
Isaac (1) **15** 4684
Isaacs (2) **14** 1447 **17** 792
Isabella (1) **12** 236
isabelle (1) **15** 3980
Iscariot (1) **15** 1176
Iscariot (1) **15** 1918
Iscariot's (1) **11** 439
Ise (1) **14** 1504
Isidore (1) **12** 1690
Isis (2) **7** 856 **9** 279
Island (9) **10** 114 781 **12** 998 1642
14 102 **15** 2195 **17** 141 1722 1977
Island (1) **14** 660
island (12) **1** 158 **7** 1067 **12** 1861 1876
14 345 582 587 612 640 682 **16** 548 1036
islanders (1) **1** 393
islands (9) **11** 946 **13** 1018 **16** 521 1211
17 198 199 1976 2230 2231
Isle (4) **3** 128 **6** 270 279 **12** 554

isle (2) **3** 153 **7** 150
isles (1) **17** 2231
Isn't (12) **1** 77 **6** 267 290 **8** 208 787 939
12 990 1490 1623 1638 **15** 1462 4607
Isn't (1) **10** 735
isn't (15) **1** 51 568 623 **5** 8 93 **7** 169 909
8 119 **9** 308 362 **10** 910 **12** 993 1360
15 3528 4281
isnt (5) **18** 465 1003 1109 1198 1410
isolated (2) **17** 1166 1266
isolation (1) **17** 756
Isolde (1) **12** 192
Isolde's (1) **12** 1455
isosceles (1) **16** 886
isosyllabic (1) **12** 735
Israel (4) **12** 1791 **13** 1220 **15** 1400
17 750
Israel (4) **7** 209 857 **15** 3228 **17** 1030
israelite (1) **12** 778
Israelitic (1) **17** 1637
Israel's (1) **14** 72
issue (13) **2** 330 **12** 1132 **14** 68 515 877
16 1038 1136 **17** 336 901 2277 2281 2288 2291
issued (4) **12** 163 862 869 **17** 1861
issuing (1) **3** 402
issuing (1) **15** 4532
ista (1) **15** 84
istas (1) **12** 1747
Istria (1) **15** 1907
istsbeg (1) **18** 876
IT (7) **7** 77 203 614
It (208) **1** 137 138 146 207 249 281 408 552 631
649 742 **2** 67 85 174 208 339 **3** 90 459
4 13 223 226 326 398 511 533 **5** 285 360 492
6 104 342 434 476 553 671 748 755 906 **7** 45
155 166 398 403 478 503 748 804 807 842 887 909
1023 1036 **8** 122 154 824 948 1168 **9** 154 165
663 714 810 838 929 1002 1004 1009 1012 1076
10 74 103 122 151 155 179 253 468 494 858 1124
11 116 302 315 382 543 654 657 717 745 796 811
824 829 849 862 872 980 1244 **12** 360 363 604
960 976 982 1043 1071 **13** 109 116 214 282 331
399 406 428 484 557 566 579 638 767 940 944 1002
1139 1277 **14** 33 321 582 672 859 928 997 1022
1037 1072 1101 1104 1165 1223 1241 1311 1398
1432 **15** 129 277 708 739 1067 1108 1210 1224
1769 1793 2088 2089 2097 2203 2228 2233 2271
2374 2380 2775 2783 2901 2988 3009 3011 3276
3293 3294 3354 3424 3427 3513 3634 3930 4847
16 346 488 539 582 728 757 816 876 918 1034
1095 1100 1270 1282 1329 1553 1718 1833
17 75 642 834 836 1153 1755 1826
It (9) **6** 164 **7** 490 494 830 **8** 783 **9** 799
1013 **17** 514 1397
It (5) **15** 1326 1548 3630 4317 4680
it (2072) **1** 34 41 42 74 77 82 91 116 138 150 158
162 179 184 214 231 235 250 295 307 309 320 323
340 349 359 371 372 374 400 409 425 428 435 451
454 488 489 490 496 520 530 533 542 547 551 552
553 562 568 577 606 607 609 614 616 618 619 623
630 632 637 710 722 724 **2** 7 8 61 113 189 195
200 209 221 224 225 229 230 246 262 282 322 339
340 349 418 443 **3** 8 11 16 95 121 168 182 223
275 282 290 298 323 324 349 357 365 367 413 458
465 471 474 484 489 491 497 498 **4** 13 28 37 40
54 61 62 64 73 79 80 81 85 99 130 133 146 151 156
157 173 181 182 200 207 216 221 227 257 273 278
293 296 297 298 300 331 349 354 355 357 359 363
365 372 375 386 387 388 390 393 394 395 429 456

457 467 468 485 492 501 511 517 530 532 537
5 12 15 26 29 31 41 49 50 51 78 92 93 95 127 128
132 134 153 181 185 200 208 211 221 235 242 261
267 269 274 275 276 300 319 320 326 328 336 346
348 351 352 357 359 361 365 370 373 387 390 399
406 408 409 412 424 441 453 456 469 470 471 484
498 499 503 504 509 527 531 534 537 541 544 552
559 567 **6** 10 16 17 22 36 61 66 77 79 81 121 122
127 131 133 152 159 168 213 245 247 248 267 268
271 278 290 308 309 331 336 340 341 347 360 412
424 432 453 470 479 510 521 532 572 587 589 611
614 615 616 617 619 621 623 633 675 687 753 762
767 768 784 785 792 802 812 816 817 820 843 844
850 861 874 934 936 940 941 942 954 955 956 963
975 981 984 993 1030 1031 **7** 25 26 88 92 103
105 124 125 126 128 136 137 153 155 161 167 169
176 188 193 205 213 218 223 227 228 234 240 241
269 277 319 338 347 364 372 424 431 463 467 475
481 493 521 545 549 601 603 616 617 618 621 627
639 644 648 658 664 676 679 686 702 712 742 764
768 775 784 800 817 836 860 890 891 907 909 930
936 947 967 975 976 1012 1025 1039 1051 1055
1056 1057 **8** 21 22 23 24 37 38 42 46 60 65 85 86
97 106 112 128 136 137 143 153 161 165 168 187
217 235 237 240 256 257 260 267 281 321 342 348
349 355 381 387 402 421 432 470 489 497 531 537
544 559 562 563 571 576 581 592 610 613 630 660
661 666 676 683 684 689 716 717 721 730 744 749
760 769 773 782 784 788 796 804 806 823 839 851
861 871 872 884 885 898 908 920 927 930 948 951
967 968 983 996 1009 1015 1019 1023 1029 1032
1036 1046 1091 1108 1109 1110 1129 1130 1134
1163 1171 1172 **9** 20 50 80 95 116 127 141 156
174 177 185 188 193 195 197 204 227 247 256 290
298 302 308 310 313 318 331 362 367 379 418 420
452 470 525 529 542 551 559 584 623 626 668 739
780 782 783 804 812 818 834 858 916 923 930 932
936 942 950 1002 1006 1010 1011 1012 1028 1038
1047 1068 1072 **10** 23 38 70 84 105 133 209 239
254 279 284 313 317 322 371 372 410 421 447 454
468 482 488 489 499 527 528 538 548 553 554 578
589 593 602 603 605 635 637 641 649 666 676 687
716 737 738 744 746 751 758 783 797 813 863 864
872 889 891 910 937 1038 1051 1058 1069 1094
1138 1141 1155 1157 1159 1160 1161 1162 1164
1165 1166 1172 1208 1231 **11** 94 96 121 122 277
298 304 305 315 363 366 407 408 421 422 446 487
545 573 580 586 602 613 616 618 642 644 652 653
679 683 687 688 701 713 723 745 746 796 803 821
830 835 837 844 871 872 888 930 931 940 941 945
948 969 970 1011 1025 1052 1080 1082 1087 1090
1113 1145 1149 1173 1181 1191 1196 1210 1229
1230 1249 1254 1265 1267 **12** 59 63 66 70 138
143 216 243 253 258 318 358 366 372 383 390 440
448 455 461 496 511 585 616 657 676 677 684 700
710 720 722 737 749 753 770 771 777 787 842 851
853 886 895 921 942 956 962 976 994 1016 1038
1049 1061 1062 1086 1089 1113 1168 1188 1247
1330 1339 1352 1353 1360 1384 1386 1417 1421
1427 1445 1475 1552 1555 1557 1571 1573 1574
1578 1587 1588 1601 1630 1635 1640 1646 1655
1662 1764 1795 1838 1850 1854 1868 1869 1897
1907 1909 **13** 31 43 44 91 95 104 113 117 118
127 129 150 159 161 163 173 186 193 204 208 233
247 254 255 269 285 300 309 310 327 332 337 352
353 354 356 363 364 372 379 388 397 411 423 431
443 458 464 467 473 476 477 478 479 521 528 532
542 545 547 548 555 559 565 567 568 569 579 583
600 604 606 617 618 628 637 642 646 651 652 659

666 680 684 692 713 714 717 721 722 727 738 739
744 746 759 760 775 782 786 790 792 795 796 816
824 832 845 848 853 859 860 866 869 874 883 923
924 942 944 950 952 959 973 983 1003 1008 1012
1013 1014 1016 1017 1019 1020 1021 1025 1026
1030 1037 1038 1043 1066 1069 1102 1109 1122
1126 1142 1154 1157 1192 1198 1219 1225 1228
1229 1240 1247 1250 1259 1261 1265 1267 1272
1299 **14** 15 21 40 43 69 112 114 115 117 126
138 142 152 154 156 170 171 172 175 204 212 213
232 255 257 262 270 279 291 309 319 324 341 342
351 360 365 392 419 422 425 447 455 459 460 461
512 530 531 535 545 548 561 566 631 634 636 654
656 664 665 698 703 706 718 734 746 750 773 785
791 809 811 847 848 873 876 885 893 902 905 913
915 917 918 924 940 997 1016 1037 1048 1054 1099
1100 1104 1105 1108 1115 1124 1139 1145 1156
1163 1167 1186 1191 1195 1197 1204 1210 1226
1229 1234 1264 1286 1297 1307 1309 1317 1322
1325 1339 1357 1360 1381 1399 1409 1428 1429
1454 1472 1513 1528 1548 1558 1586 1588 1590
1591 **15** 44 56 70 71 360 400 476 477 488 541
550 552 556 557 558 585 593 603 639 657 665 669
670 701 714 743 744 747 813 819 893 928 947 970
1028 1031 1034 1054 1066 1088 1091 1233 1308
1323 1353 1523 1542 1607 1615 1681 1736 1819
1836 1966 1974 1975 1996 2066 2087 2088 2097
2120 2135 2191 2206 2231 2366 2375 2516 2523
2525 2526 2527 2535 2538 2539 2706 2711 2736
2740 2784 2868 2877 2893 2935 2941 2957 2970
3006 3023 3043 3075 3091 3130 3139 3144 3199
3200 3207 3243 3359 3446 3447 3464 3472 3473
3515 3520 3540 3558 3606 3625 3663 3671 3713
3775 3799 3804 4170 4178 4183 4187 4306 4410
4416 4436 4467 4473 4474 4513 4554 4570 4602
4636 4821 4847 4870 4881 4896 **16** 6 9 15 20 29
31 32 33 39 40 42 59 60 75 78 93 108 120 135 150
158 164 167 171 172 176 180 188 193 202 213 222
224 240 243 263 269 270 272 277 283 284 294 296
298 323 332 353 356 392 407 411 439 444 458 468
473 474 499 506 507 531 533 539 544 545 553 556
557 561 562 566 567 568 579 580 607 627 628 632
633 637 639 640 645 649 665 680 710 721 740 751
756 766 767 785 793 798 803 807 808 809 816 819
820 826 827 834 836 865 891 897 909 917 927 928
934 938 940 954 974 976 991 1025 1026 1038 1041
1046 1049 1057 1065 1090 1097 1102 1120 1165
1168 1170 1205 1206 1207 1216 1218 1219 1233
1238 1248 1254 1262 1265 1269 1274 1293 1299
1308 1309 1315 1317 1324 1334 1336 1346 1364
1369 1372 1379 1386 1402 1405 1406 1419 1423
1444 1445 1449 1453 1454 1460 1461 1473 1478
1479 1491 1493 1500 1515 1516 1519 1530 1532
1533 1534 1569 1575 1586 1596 1601 1603 1604
1610 1613 1615 1617 1618 1628 1657 1659 1660
1687 1727 1729 1750 1755 1761 1774 1775 1783
1784 1791 1807 1844 1845 1849 1859 1863 1871
1892 **17** 9 74 130 162 163 291 589 599 617 896
905 955 981 1008 1139 1140 1322 1325 1326 1404
1405 1780 1832 1839 1883 **18** 19 24 32 34 36 37
48 50 53 54 60 64 65 66 72 74 76 77 85 92 95 97 98
99 100 101 102 109 110 111 112 113 114 125 132
138 140 142 145 147 152 155 156 158 163 169 173
175 187 196 197 206 211 214 222 236 240 241 250
251 255 264 266 278 279 281 286 287 288 298 301
312 314 316 318 319 320 324 325 327 331 338 340
344 346 350 360 362 367 375 378 379 386 395 397
399 406 408 409 412 417 418 420 431 451 456 460
463 465 467 478 480 485 498 504 511 514 515 517

520 527 530 531 541 544 547 549 551 554 555 557
558 565 577 580 586 590 592 600 605 606 608 613
616 635 639 651 652 655 659 666 667 673 675 676
677 693 707 710 737 739 749 751 762 765 766 770
780 781 783 790 798 803 809 816 818 821 830 831
836 841 860 869 870 889 895 897 903 911 915 920
923 927 939 947 956 979 991 1008 1023 1029 1031
1032 1051 1056 1058 1073 1074 1081 1084 1095
1108 1109 1110 1117 1121 1125 1133 1141 1143
1144 1150 1152 1154 1161 1163 1164 1166 1167
1177 1181 1193 1195 1197 1208 1210 1213 1214
1223 1249 1251 1252 1270 1274 1276 1295 1297
1298 1300 1303 1304 1305 1316 1319 1321 1325
1331 1353 1355 1357 1383 1385 1386 1393 1394
1398 1412 1413 1422 1424 1433 1435 1438 1440
1446 1449 1450 1452 1472 1475 1479 1483 1485
1490 1492 1502 1513 1515 1517 1518 1521 1524
1526 1527 1533 1537 1547 1551 1563 1570 1575
1584

it (21) **1** 463 591 **4** 438 **5** 127 147 283 284
288 292 **6** 731 **7** 243 317 838 **9** 1043
10 445 572 734 **12** 363 **17** 414 805 820
it (38) **15** 101 321 502 729 912 974 1005 1310
1327 1346 1717 2044 2174 2257 2289 2586 2588
2631 2636 2657 2700 2712 2714 2860 3089 3502
3531 3621 3641 3642 4033 4039 4210 4551 4749
4902
Ita (1) **12** 1710
ITALIA (1) **7** 754
Italian (19) **1** 638 639 642 **4** 347 **8** 721 758
9 767 840 **11** 825 851 **16** 576 881 1655
17 939 962 2137 **18** 1015 1302 1476
Italian (1) **15** 1430
italianos (1) **16** 866
Italians (1) **16** 310
italics (2) **12** 722 **14** 660
Italy (2) **9** 922 **16** 868
itancy (1) **18** 744
itch (3) **5** 529 **9** 356 **11** 1083
itching (3) **2** 114 **13** 493 **18** 902
It'd (1) **12** 1661
it'd (1) **12** 1795
itd (2) **18** 1434 1488
Item (2) **9** 1116 **14** 1542
item (2) **11** 615 **15** 2343
items (1) **4** 147
Iterum (1) **9** 848
ITHACANS (1) **7** 1034
i'the (2) **9** 283 580
itinerant (1) **14** 896
itinerary (1) **17** 11
It'll (1) **1** 673
itll (3) **18** 1341 1358 1536
It's (83) **1** 150 206 285 326 498 555 572 674
2 321 **3** 72 **4** 341 **5** 41 45 162 **6** 138
213 331 498 617 737 771 831 843 1024 **7** 89 181
977 **8** 42 54 94 258 284 571 949 **9** 123 529
558 775 **10** 220 322 656 695 872 1077 **11** 84
793 827 836 **12** 140 464 1152 1190 1539 1765
13 252 682 686 869 907 968 1019 **15** 399 743
823 842 2201 2202 3130 3162 3171 3543 4488 4851
16 671 786 889 1098 1101 1129 1720
it's (72) **1** 209 210 212 290 434 442 **4** 509
5 148 239 358 360 469 **6** 108 189 329 744 943
7 214 975 989 **8** 111 179 301 536 563 784 891
966 1086 1142 **9** 528 529 558 **10** 467 945
11 703 946 1244 1291 **12** 512 1481 1482 1541
1586 **13** 590 825 879 990 1015 1017 1040 1077
1087 1088 1153 **15** 478 2196 2908 2999 3020

137

3143 3560 16 770 782 811 848 898 1136 1137 1576 1644

it's (1) 1 198

Its (3) 1 628 4 297 17 185

its (280) 1 15 70 103 125 270 309 315 528 689 2 200 3 153 230 417 441 451 459 4 13 386 500 5 78 131 184 232 260 317 354 6 27 140 582 583 588 801 876 913 7 174 176 177 501 621 8 75 89 266 376 621 835 1082 9 269 474 631 632 659 802 810 851 10 209 313 349 404 858 924 941 1052 1066 1088 1116 1196 1210 11 316 745 947 1239 12 530 922 1259 1265 1367 1858 13 1 87 168 297 326 511 517 531 648 951 1016 1299 14 14 34 669 673 682 938 939 1113 1185 1198 1299 1365 1388 1404 15 975 2324 16 28 50 138 428 473 550 557 561 564 638 646 758 792 928 948 1433 1489 1586 1587 1736 1753 1823 1824 1827 1862 17 86 102 103 116 124 125 132 185 186 188 189 190 191 192 193 195 196 198 200 201 202 205 208 211 212 213 214 216 217 220 222 223 224 226 227 279 306 344 490 607 735 856 874 899 1065 1077 1081 1145 1154 1216 1217 1221 1286 1294 1297 1298 1303 1306 1322 1328 1410 1511 1513 1771 2099 2163 2192 2220 18 18 35 44 100 101 140 225 241 334 354 356 374 438 465 492 539 548 581 636 728 731 745 797 821 823 843 854 869 915 951 959 996 1003 1021 1027 1057 1078 1101 1122 1137 1151 1199 1237 1256 1303 1318 1355 1378 1379 1386 1397 1399 1444 1455 1457 1459 1463 1516 1518

its (2) 7 243 246

its (14) 15 27 186 1255 1550 2006 2085 2150 2266 2273 2481 3531 4220 4689

itself (48) 2 68 3 488 490 6 175 177 975 7 345 764 8 47 499 755 9 1002 1003 1004 10 403 12 1075 1760 1866 13 278 1039 1093 14 54 1359 15 1802 2117 2118 2119 2120 2908 16 598 1291 1293 1458 1459 1525 1584 17 645 858 1849 2213 18 436 469 517 905 1121 1544

Iubilantium (1) 15 4165

Iubilantium (2) 1 738 17 1231

iubilantium (1) 1 277

iudicia (1) 10 197

iusti (1) 15 3865

iustitiae (1) 10 197

iustum (1) 10 4

iuventutem (1) 15 123

IV (1) 16 559

Ivan (1) 16 1851

I've (11) 7 997 12 141 269 13 1214 15 4002 4832 4897 16 379 432 458 655

I've (1) 10 1254

Ive (4) 18 470 890 1136 1515

Iveagh (2) 5 304 11 1014

Ivers (1) 12 929

Ives (1) 12 1702

ivied (1) 13 626

ivory (4) 3 315 9 473 10 190 12 1246

ivory (3) 15 1014 2743 4966

ivorylike (1) 13 88

Ivy (1) 6 855

ivy (2) 10 118 17 1507

ivytod (1) 12 1293

J

J (23) 5 325 6 264 278 286 8 1158 10 56 600 1193 1239 12 934 938 1100 13 646 14 1256 1584 15 1262 1752 1921 16 1287 17 587 791 982 1786

J (1) 16 1260

J (3) 15 1918 2145 3223

J A (1) 10 652

J B (2) 10 1259 15 835

J C (2) 4 314 6 222

J F X (1) 17 1648

J H (1) 15 1230

J J (71) 7 282 290 297 301 365 382 409 424 437 451 462 466 478 499 502 545 600 625 700 727 741 746 755 760 767 775 777 782 800 813 819 872 906 958 1000 1062 1064 10 236 433 442 453 458 12 1016 1018 1020 1022 1032 1043 1048 1071 1077 1085 1091 1159 1192 1202 1235 1399 1407 1542 1546 1630 1633 1646 1653 1669 1848 15 938 966 997 1644

J J (2) 15 973 992

J L (1) 17 1308

J P (3) 12 1894 15 793 1008

Ja (1) 15 257

ja (2) 13 392

jab (1) 12 968

jabber (1) 3 387

Jack (37) 5 546 6 645 7 285 381 456 996 998 8 419 645 800 10 43 401 413 454 699 984 12 196 814 815 1013 1076 1588 1638 1656 1670 1751 1768 1799 14 305 15 1088 1153 16 1456 17 1238 1282 18 755 818 1272

Jack (1) 14 405

Jack (3) 15 1140 3327 4396

jack-in-the-box (1) 15 3668

jackanapes (1) 14 1392

jackass (1) 9 791

jackboots (1) 15 1058

jackdaw (1) 15 837

jacket (10) 7 131 458 8 838 10 1245 16 445 17 375 18 471 1030 1448 1497

jacket (5) 15 299 450 1741 2054 3981

jackets (1) 2 311

Jackjohn's (1) 14 407

jackknife (1) 16 656

Jacko (1) 10 951

jackpriests (1) 3 117

Jackson (2) 10 652 17 424

Jacky (18) 12 1355 13 13 16 41 43 45 52 61 63 245 346 467 472 678 685 715 767 934

Jacky (3) 15 132 237 241

Jacob (5) 12 1119 1737 1825 15 262

Jacob (1) 17 1030

Jacob's (2) 7 210 14 1057

Jacob's (1) 15 2481

Jacobs (1) 15 1241

Jacobs' (1) 12 495

Jacquard (1) 12 1246

Jacques (1) 15 1847

jade (1) 15 2043

jaded (1) 10 1236

jadegreen (1) 12 1287

jady (1) 14 1515

Jaffa (3) 4 194 212 8 635

jagged (1) 1 100

jail (4) 11 772 12 1457 16 833 18 993

jail (1) 12 420

jailbirds (1) 9 853

jailbreaking (1) 17 2187

Jailer (1) 17 2322

Jake (1) 15 2189

jakers (1) 12 1175

Jakes (1) 7 622

jakes (3) 4 494 539 15 3207

jalap (1) 1 156

jalaps (1) 14 373

jam (3) 2 37 15 2202 18 940

James (28) 2 215 4 491 6 447 8 337 442 457 9 47 312 10 601 929 991 1216 11 879 12 881 932 1086 1690 1698 14 1548 15 1018 1534 16 55 17 543 544 577 632 1557 1647

James (1) 15 3727

Jameson (2) 12 1753 18 1333

Jamesons (1) 8 1025

James's (4) 10 674 718 720 1215

Jamesy (1) 18 1128

jamjam (1) 11 705

jamjars (1) 17 317

Jammed (1) 5 341

jammed (1) 15 4264

Jammet's (2) 13 900 15 4862

jampuffs (1) 8 232

Jane (1) 7 201

Janeiro (1) 12 1371

Janey (1) 1 323

jangled (1) 12 174

Jannock (1) 14 1523

Jans (1) 16 1811

January (4) 17 422 471 1204 2281

Januarys (1) 18 604

Japanese (3) 4 117 17 1531 1570

japanesily (1) 15 3858

Japers (1) 11 473

Japhet (1) 1 561

Jappies (1) 14 1560

Japs (1) 16 1001

jar (6) 5 295 8 951 10 301 11 365 13 1130 17 311

jar (1) 15 3792

Jarlath (1) 12 1706

jars (1) 4 202

jars (1) 15 2184

jarvey (14) 4 439 10 568 775 960 12 1771 1797 1850 1900 15 4881 16 42 444 464 709 908

jarvey (3) 15 4323 4908 4911

jarvies (4) 6 173 16 335 442 843

jaspberry (1) 13 272

Jasperstone (2) 15 1866 1867

jaundice (1) 7 135

jaundiced (1) 14 1290

jaunes (2) 3 233 15 4501

jaunt (1) 15 4147

jaunted (6) 11 15 304 330 456 498 763

jauntily (1) 10 1241

jaunting (3) 11 302 12 1770 18 366

jaunty (4) 11 245 579 640

jauntyhatted (1) 15 4034

jaw (9) 6 849 8 313 663 1034 12 969 1800 14 254 15 4411 16 1268

jawbo (1) 13 28

jawbreakers (2) 12 466 18 566

jawing (1) 10 1128

jaws (3) 3 347 11 1055 12 711

jaws (3) 15 2157 2467 2624

Jay (1) 14 1444
jay (2) 1 336 14 1420
Jays (1) 15 596
jays (2) 15 589 596
Jaysus (1) 9 1160
Je (1) 3 169
je (1) 3 169
jealous (6) 1 640 10 167 14 320
   15 1995 18 184 485
Jealousy (1) 17 2162
jealousy (7) 13 364 601 16 297 1115
   17 2155 2195 18 1392
Jean (1) 12 1267
Jean (1) 15 1847
Jeep (1) 16 1812
jeer (4) 7 338 9 752 14 416 864
jeering (1) 12 701
jeering (2) 15 485 3985
jeers (1) 15 2990
Jeffs (1) 10 1259
Jehovah (1) 9 609
Jehovah (1) 7 491
Jehu (1) 16 25
jehudi (1) 17 764
jejune (1) 1 45
jellibees (1) 18 687
jellily (1) 15 3242
jelloids (1) 13 84
jelly (2) 1 681 18 315
Jem (2) 10 1148 16 1022
Jemina (1) 13 947
Jenatzy (1) 14 1560
jennets (1) 7 93
Jenny (3) 11 699 12 1175 15 3969
jennyass (1) 9 792
jeopard (1) 14 253
Jeremiah (1) 12 199
jeremies (1) 14 1428
Jericho (1) 15 4419
jerked (5) 2 382 6 1025 10 8 229
   11 362
jerkily (2) 7 458 994
jerkily (1) 15 806
jerkin (2) 15 1177 1775
jerkined (1) 3 304
jerking (1) 5 528
jerks (5) 2 62 5 78 10 7 246 15 3472
jerks (6) 15 15 25 65 2602 3882 4543
jerky (1) 4 539
Jerome (3) 6 513 665 768
Jerome (1) 15 4671
Jerry (1) 15 4484
jerrybuilt (1) 8 491
jerrymandering (1) 12 1575
Jersey (2) 17 305 18 849
jersey (2) 18 481 1148
jersey (1) 15 4450
jerseys (1) 15 3326
Jeru (1) 15 2209
Jerusalem (6) 7 207 12 1473 1571
   13 1089 15 2171 17 1982
Jervis (2) 10 505 17 1252
Jeshurum (1) 14 370
Jesified (1) 14 1486
jessamine (3) 13 1011 17 2094 18 1601
jesse (1) 3 429
Jessie (1) 17 426
Jessie (1) 12 422
Jest (1) 9 1153

jest (5) 1 35 12 1658 15 207 16 1530
   18 775
jester (2) 2 44 9 1110
jester's (1) 15 4166
Jesu (1) 14 168
jesuit (9) 1 8 45 209 500 10 147 162
   14 1487 16 1747 17 16
jesuits (2) 9 754 18 381
Jesurum (2) 15 1858
Jésus (1) 3 167
Jesus (33) 1 608 3 14 68 6 163 7 533
   557 9 48 10 657 698 12 30 66 150 424 513
   816 1393 1569 1711 1793 1811 1812 1901 1909
   14 1588 15 2199 2680 4232 4288 16 363
   17 137 1203 18 497 1104
Jesus (2) 15 1579 4476
Jesus' (1) 1 287
Jesusjack (1) 18 163
Jesusmario (1) 7 57
jet (6) 3 219 4 385 10 31 221 13 802
   16 616
jet (2) 15 86 136
Jetez (1) 15 2094
jets (1) 1 690
jetsam (1) 17 1686
jeunesse (1) 15 2094
jeux (2) 15 2161 2162
jew (24) 2 350 359 8 1159 9 763 1209
   10 980 12 1628 1631 1635 1647 1761 1804
   1805 1808 15 1686 16 1082 1084 1638 1641
   17 530 810
jew (4) 1 585 12 1801
jew (1) 15 2145
jewbaiting (1) 9 749
jewel (3) 14 677 15 3107 3861
jewel (1) 6 355
jewelled (1) 15 3407
jewelled (1) 15 312
jewellery (1) 17 1937
Jewels (1) 13 1070
jewels (1) 13 102
jewels (1) 15 1813
jewess (1) 18 1184
Jewgreek (1) 15 2097
jewies (1) 12 452
jewish (2) 17 96 759
jewjesuit (1) 9 1159
jewman (2) 10 916 12 1811
Jewman's (1) 15 534
jew's (4) 9 750 17 830 942 1244
jew's (3) 17 805 807 813
Jews (2) 9 783 16 1119
jews (18) 1 667 2 347 438 6 771 7 490
   8 1073 9 785 10 698 12 1798 15 847
   16 1122 17 1639 18 91 687 834 1204 1247
   1588
jews (1) 7 845
jews' (1) 10 412
jewy (1) 12 30
Jeyes' (1) 15 1574
jib (2) 13 774 16 833
jibes (2) 1 500 14 235
jibs (1) 8 428
jig (2) 11 977 14 1498
Jigajiga (1) 15 1138
Jiggedy (1) 11 579
jiggedy (2) 11 578
jiggered (1) 14 1509
Jigjag (2) 15 1138

jigs (1) 7 366
jigtime (1) 12 976
Jilted (1) 13 774
jilted (1) 18 742
Jim (2) 12 179 15 797
Jimmy (7) 6 464 10 982 993 1006 1018
   12 1039 15 2578
Jimmy (2) 15 1626 4349
JIMMY (1) 15 1628
Jinbad (1) 17 2322
Jing (1) 11 689
jing (1) 11 457
jingbang (1) 10 569
Jingle (14) 11 15 19 212 245 330 456 458 498
   568 640 687 762 812 869
jingle (5) 8 615 11 15 245 579 883
jingle (2) 15 415 1136
jingled (5) 4 59 7 459 11 524 884
   16 941
jinglejaunty (1) 11 290
jingles (2) 15 4903 4916
Jingling (4) 8 634 641 11 304 458
jingling (4) 4 303 7 459 11 15
   18 1131
jingling (3) 15 1081 4317 4919
jingly (2) 11 606 18 1212
Jingo (1) 15 2959
jingo (1) 6 866
jink (2) 13 28
jinkleman (1) 15 3024
jinks (1) 15 487
Jippert (1) 15 2549
jiujitsu (1) 16 67
jivic (1) 12 341
Jno (1) 16 1256
jo (1) 9 1126
Joachim (1) 3 108
Joachim's (1) 10 852
Joan (2) 9 677 14 1419
Job (1) 6 15
job (45) 3 256 456 4 133 5 12 179 456
   6 20 121 178 571 622 630 679 885 7 215 546
   8 143 158 422 506 1067 9 1159 10 288
   11 910 12 1328 13 860 955 1154
   15 1288 2430 3132 16 148 157 203 234 523
   654 656 945 1319 18 196 364 561 1084
jobber (1) 12 237
jobs (3) 1 641 15 2990 16 975
Jock (1) 14 1489
jock (2) 15 2434
jockeycap (1) 15 74
jockeyed (1) 2 326
jockeys (2) 12 1404 16 1197
jocosely (2) 16 1779 17 368
jocoserious (1) 17 369
Jocular (1) 15 2441
jocundly (1) 14 238
Joe (131) 7 639 703 8 344 423 436 11 611
   12 5 6 8 12 19 23 52 54 56 58 59 60 61 62 65 130
   134 139 141 143 145 147 198 206 210 211 233 238
   241 266 272 302 309 316 318 320 322 326 332 335
   412 421 427 433 438 456 458 460 463 481 521 681
   683 698 749 755 758 765 768 818 820 823 825 827
   831 837 850 854 857 880 886 941 943 951 990 993
   1014 1019 1038 1041 1050 1057 1078 1084 1094
   1143 1145 1149 1154 1175 1176 1233 1299 1351
   1390 1402 1409 1411 1412 1413 1429 1434 1436
   1466 1502 1503 1511 1540 1558 1559 1564 1627
   1655 1675 1786 1798 1813 1852 1900 15 565
   791 1008 17 1239 18 818 1068

Joe (2) 7 582 12 420
Joe (3) 15 4338 4342 4349
JOE (1) 15 1659
joey (1) 14 1516
Jog (1) 11 977
jog (1) 2 287
jogged (3) 7 174 11 607 977
joggerfry (1) 4 139
jogging (1) 6 29
jogging (2) 15 2137 3733
joggled (2) 11 766 883
jogjaunty (1) 11 524
jogs (1) 15 3983
Johann (1) 9 492
Johannes (3) 9 1061 16 1812 17 784
John (169) 2 279 286 5 1 322 6 222 307
568 571 690 695 704 707 710 715 740 1007 1019
1021 1025 7 106 740 793 823 1067 8 13 500
706 839 950 1066 1084 9 18 43 58 79 100 122
126 141 152 214 225 232 273 359 392 408 412 516
618 655 660 675 708 737 763 795 834 886 924 949
970 993 1027 1054 1064 1070 1098 10 1 10 107
174 178 213 658 746 752 778 893 936 968 973 979
986 989 995 997 1001 1013 1015 1017 1021 1025
1026 1027 1030 1033 1040 1049 1050 1212 1226
1229 11 762 882 959 1243 12 55 178 187 267
272 620 929 932 1178 1206 1258 1317 1319 1338
1341 1379 1414 1419 1421 1475 1486 1490 1538
1573 1586 1623 1628 1692 1702 1704 1753
13 283 1035 1293 14 349 1213 1523
15 730 1516 3994 16 130 142 428 968 1192
1769 1774 17 790 1240 1339 1344 1399 1647
1648 1656 2045 2134 2140 18 1333 1383
John (4) 9 882 1126 16 1257
John (14) 15 995 1130 1141 1174 1236 1412
1516 2248 3673 4336 4343 4352 4685
JOHN (8) 15 1175 1243 1248 1512 1533 2256
3304 3675
johnnies (1) 18 128
Johnny (4) 7 264 8 860 13 1154
16 1076
Johnny (2) 16 981 982
johnny (2) 14 1575 15 837
John's (1) 12 276
Johnson (3) 12 1039 15 122 3620
Johnson's (1) 9 195
Johnston (2) 17 418 542
johnyellows (1) 15 4509
Join (1) 15 2192
join (6) 7 357 11 358 14 1447 15 2208
4868 18 1016
joined (5) 1 726 2 209 12 1132
14 1009 16 459
Joiner (1) 1 607
joiner (1) 14 305
joiner (1) 1 586
joining (2) 12 650 17 1750
joining (2) 15 1887 1888
joins (2) 15 1107 4911
joint (2) 8 717 13 130
joints (2) 10 549 13 1065
jointures (1) 14 674
joke (11) 5 430 6 790 793 795 9 307
15 740 1768 3831 16 179 1796 18 1376
Jokes (1) 11 647
Jokes (1) 17 442
jokes (4) 6 57 787 16 759 1530
Joking (1) 15 2204
Joking (1) 15 4476

joking (2) 1 118 608
jollification (1) 10 553
jollily (1) 11 442
Jolly (5) 4 417 6 1009 8 363 10 889
11 1231
Jolly (1) 9 26
jolly (9) 8 394 12 1616 13 362 14 315
644 15 45 4863 18 168 615
jollypoldy (1) 15 149
jolt (2) 6 25 10 558
jolting (1) 15 3319
Joly (1) 8 574
Joly (1) 15 4344
Jonah (1) 10 782
Jones (3) 8 140 16 424 1535
Jones' (1) 13 1164
Jones-Smith (2) 15 1865 1866
jordan (1) 9 807
jorum (1) 12 1395
José (1) 9 1022
Joseph (13) 1 607 5 423 12 804 908 1694
13 140 14 305 570 15 1834 17 485 601
905 2139
Joseph (3) 1 586 3 162 16 1260
Joseph (4) 15 1414 1612 1955 3222
Josephine (1) 17 1846
Joseph's (3) 4 136 10 80 16 1453
Josie (8) 8 273 13 814 15 441 17 1846
18 169 203 843 1253
Josssticks (1) 5 329
jot (1) 16 600
jot (1) 15 4367
jotter (1) 10 381
jotting (2) 4 519 6 878
joult (1) 18 427
Journal (7) 7 44 118 964 9 595 17 336
1459
journal (3) 14 504 16 602 1682
journalic (1) 15 1582
journalism (3) 7 631 690 16 1653
journalist (2) 3 231 494
journalist (1) 15 1612
journey (4) 6 466 9 1032 10 120
18 1318
joust (2) 2 315 15 4636
Jousts (2) 2 316 317
Jove (5) 1 359 5 521 6 371 9 539
11 219
jovially (1) 15 2609
Jovian (1) 17 1095
Jowl (1) 14 463
jowl (1) 1 32
jowl (1) 15 2491
Joy (2) 8 908 12 180
Joy (1) 17 1783
joy (16) 5 268 8 908 10 1074 11 172
707 969 970 12 244 13 161 428 14 176
309 1321 15 2551 18 1178
joy (1) 15 73
Joybells (1) 15 1492
joybells (1) 10 156
joyed (1) 14 355
joyful (3) 10 933 11 969 14 950
Joyfully (1) 9 556
joyfully (1) 9 549
joygush (1) 11 709
joylessly (1) 6 54
joyous (2) 10 159 13 126
joyously (1) 2 262

joyride (1) 15 2201
joys (4) 11 970 14 771 15 2815 3019
J's (2) 8 53 11 1180
Juan (1) 15 1064
Jubainville's (1) 9 93
Jubilee (1) 14 1547
jubilee (1) 17 429
Juda (2) 14 1383 17 58
Judaic (1) 17 1900
judaicus (1) 15 1796
Judas (5) 9 1200 11 438 15 1176 2573
16 98
Judas (3) 9 1043 1044 15 4730
judashand (1) 15 2277
Jude (1) 15 1917
Jude's (1) 12 229
Judge (4) 9 65 520 1017 16 430
judge (8) 3 106 6 342 8 598 9 152
12 1037 14 1577 15 4490 16 303
judged (1) 12 787
judgers (1) 14 864
judges (4) 8 1160 9 688 12 1114
14 213
judging (1) 18 1230
judgment (3) 10 630 17 689 692
judgments (2) 9 11 15 1481
judicial (1) 15 1162
judicium (1) 6 601
Judith (1) 9 677
jug (7) 1 388 397 4 36 15 116 117 129
17 312
Jugged (1) 8 869
jugginses (1) 5 215
juggle (1) 16 1130
juggler's (1) 15 1604
juggling (2) 8 958 11 832
juggling (1) 15 2161
jugs (1) 13 272
jugular (1) 15 1183
juice (5) 8 795 1048 10 761 17 1924
18 1128
juices (3) 8 342 12 284 14 154
juicy (4) 6 394 790 10 308 18 1503
jujube (2) 15 4454 4477
jujubes (1) 8 4
jujuby (1) 15 4123
Julia (2) 8 417 17 140
Julian (2) 12 1690 17 99
Juliet (1) 12 1492
Juliet (1) 9 455
Julius (6) 2 48 12 188 17 58 536 2134
18 1375
July (1) 7 124
jumble (1) 13 234
Jumbo (1) 12 1496
Jumbo (1) 15 2604
jump (5) 4 29 13 909 15 637 16 1616
18 629
jumped (7) 9 606 1054 13 474 14 656
15 4195 16 1037 18 762
jumpers (1) 16 1017
jumping (6) 1 346 6 88 11 8 181
15 2910 18 851
jumps (3) 15 1260 3757 4109
jun (1) 14 505
junction (4) 8 560 15 2193 17 156 1730
juncture (1) 14 1178
JUNE (1) 7 1063
June (16) 6 803 8 868 9 154 10 376

kipkeeper (1) 15 3498
kipper (2) 8 802 12 957
kippered (1) 15 502
Kippur (3) 8 36 752 15 1624
kips (2) 9 552 14 1573
Kirschner (1) 15 2190
kirtles (1) 14 489
Kisászony (1) 12 561
Kish (5) 3 267 4 434 13 1180 1268 16 650
Kish (1) 15 3382
kish (1) 8 894
Kismet (2) 15 641 1108
kismet (2) 11 1233 13 1062
Kiss (4) 8 647 13 817 832 15 2942
kiss (38) 3 398 399 400 4 405 5 413 6 756 7 711 981 991 9 541 12 1134 13 204 214 533 817 859 886 14 380 15 488 2892 2942 3586 3906 18 102 105 106 190 275 875 1047 1351 1402 1405 1406 1520 1575 1595
kiss (2) 3 384 10 611
kiss (2) 15 492 2683
Kissed (1) 8 916
kissed (24) 4 450 8 642 906 913 915 916 12 641 13 60 871 889 1091 1102 1225 14 380 15 3264 17 2241 18 286 330 391 672 769 1604
Kisses (1) 15 1267
KISSES (1) 15 1271
kisses (2) 4 444 15 3801
kisses (7) 15 1269 1587 1607 3267 3340 3589 4321
kissing (10) 4 450 8 846 11 691 13 532 810 15 3121 18 53 274 770 1141
kissing (2) 15 4959 4964
kissy (1) 12 1495
kit (1) 14 1211
kit (1) 15 1873
kitchen (30) 1 266 4 6 8 267 432 6 952 8 23 704 882 10 259 17 104 110 112 122 142 143 258 297 811 933 1521 1559 18 59 198 335 1000 1094 1330 1431 1481
kitchenwench (1) 14 690
kite (1) 7 445
kite (1) 15 2137
Kithogue (1) 15 18
kittenishly (1) 15 2709
Kitty (6) 12 1276 14 787 811 15 2196 4726 18 479
Kitty (17) 15 2050 2082 2302 2586 2709 3506 3542 3549 3568 3589 3640 3666 4111 4121 4260 4323 4728
KITTY (15) 15 2056 2065 2078 2130 2577 2716 2879 2921 3410 3555 3569 3794 3806 3817 4108
KITTY-KATE (1) 15 2225
Kittylynch (1) 15 4123
Kitty's (2) 15 3550 4387
Klook (12) 12 846 847 849 15 3710
knack (1) 16 685
knacker's (1) 12 835
knackers (1) 15 4484
Knaplock (1) 17 1400
knave (2) 3 312 12 1596
Knee (1) 7 420
knee (21) 4 300 6 492 587 7 421 9 296 11 410 12 137 13 696 729 15 3116 3118 3140 16 437 855 1521 17 127 135 18 772 1138
knee (1) 15 3402

kneebreeches (3) 15 1883 2245 3760
kneecap (1) 6 613
Kneel (1) 1 640
kneel (7) 1 93 207 5 369 6 584 7 853 14 750 18 309
kneel (2) 15 322 1939
kneelength (1) 15 2816
kneeling (5) 3 125 127 6 765 13 287 17 135
kneels (1) 18 1197
knees (20) 1 276 3 77 103 4 23 254 501 542 5 416 6 29 209 228 7 63 251 11 728 12 156 169 15 2983 3120 16 1538
knees (3) 15 2263 2943 4780
knelt (14) 1 91 5 342 343 419 6 460 584 586 587 11 1032 12 610 13 497 553 15 2807 17 126
Knew (2) 8 29 11 1256
knew (104) 1 403 2 35 242 262 368 369 371 372 3 223 450 4 61 418 419 5 395 6 595 7 102 532 8 50 149 457 10 11 32 170 1024 1208 11 338 485 1092 1172 12 297 668 782 801 1005 1564 13 82 127 139 163 164 192 223 300 431 561 580 584 602 604 634 650 693 700 880 898 1044 14 117 302 303 482 999 1112 15 574 1995 2518 2533 2769 16 67 119 173 206 713 1755 17 530 531 1761 18 46 54 75 178 214 323 328 332 343 387 515 886 955 1013 1085 1092 1181 1208 1362 1385 1422 1428 1449 1475 1579
knew (1) 2 238
knickerbockers (1) 13 244
knickers (13) 13 724 15 2403
Knife (4) 8 237 15 4539 16 576 577
knife (21) 1 364 7 934 8 346 459 657 673 685 686 689 11 30 848 12 619 16 816 818 1059 1065 18 365 485 487 1458 1480
knifeblade (1) 1 55
knifed (1) 2 49
knifeful (1) 8 682
Knight (1) 10 748
knight (5) 3 314 9 310 816 14 184 15 4636
knight (1) 15 3461
knighterrant (1) 14 1061
knights (3) 12 446 14 174 15 3080
knights (2) 15 4615 4681
knitted (1) 18 1448
knitting (2) 17 663 18 91
knives (6) 3 305 12 1532 14 144 16 592 821 18 1075
knob (2) 6 614 11 1114
knobbed (1) 15 1180
Knobby (1) 15 3698
knobby (1) 10 339
knobs (3) 6 946 14 965 15 3139
Knock (5) 5 365 11 689 804 1047 15 3436
knock (22) 2 154 3 92 4 62 417 10 1147 11 986 1238 13 968 1170 14 892 1337 15 3087 16 765 893 17 82 283 18 450 1200 1234 1300
knocked (9) 6 911 10 517 1148 12 382 1597 1600 14 423 16 1336 1514
knocker (2) 6 27 11 987
Knocking (1) 6 678
knocking (10) 3 5 4 465 5 167 6 433 8 397 9 636 12 975 16 1740 18 353 1011

knockingshop (1) 16 580
knockkneed (1) 2 315
Knockmaroon (1) 7 661
knockmedown (1) 12 502
knockout (1) 12 983
knocks (2) 14 514 18 504
knot (4) 15 2081 2805 2807 18 640
knot (1) 15 4366
knots (1) 15 2829
knotted (2) 10 776 15 710
knotting (1) 1 478
knotty (2) 15 2422 16 774
knotty (1) 15 3958
knout (1) 15 2892
Know (15) 3 258 7 233 8 879 9 1153 10 562 602 11 826 865 892 13 1024 14 289 1474 15 4299 16 416 484
know (311) 1 53 61 493 698 2 20 21 237 238 243 244 270 413 438 439 3 176 222 229 231 234 4 115 116 214 5 91 96 97 185 216 252 258 371 6 18 406 484 512 691 736 790 804 806 884 887 891 895 916 1007 7 145 149 150 153 157 189 310 502 532 563 630 643 711 732 798 814 902 8 117 134 207 246 325 429 441 444 547 578 581 717 828 859 884 885 942 967 977 987 1107 1142 1166 9 94 103 112 115 116 123 158 177 237 247 277 360 363 364 400 429 467 470 508 528 530 632 827 847 883 903 904 956 958 962 1069 1082 10 166 445 493 537 540 550 582 663 672 675 731 897 1008 11 280 376 510 544 639 642 689 738 826 851 889 955 971 1045 1047 1082 1197 1243 12 233 252 314 320 453 888 949 1027 1045 1046 1058 1162 1240 1385 1419 1506 1548 1603 1636 1660 13 71 72 142 274 397 423 437 464 533 567 656 751 775 829 836 839 863 908 925 972 1085 1089 1160 1188 1226 1249 1262 14 459 566 725 776 1145 1368 15 404 421 434 739 740 819 980 1062 1192 1321 1338 1996 2204 2254 2542 2562 2866 3084 3125 3273 3288 3445 3481 3496 3517 3693 4192 4297 4306 4381 4401 4486 4487 4582 4784 4813 4874 16 378 420 783 1022 1126 1155 1617 1838 18 87 113 115 142 158 166 168 171 187 188 189 202 206 233 299 311 345 422 439 461 473 481 491 533 710 719 727 801 835 880 887 964 990 1081 1126 1162 1167 1182 1207 1222 1236 1250 1277 1370 1398 1411 1431 1440 1470 1506 1510 1529 1530 1534 1536 1569 1570 1582
know (1) 5 282
Knowall (1) 12 838
Knowing (1) 9 338
knowing (13) 11 1258 13 1021 15 948 3052 16 707 946 1115 1521 1532 18 282 1065 1401 1485
knowing (1) 15 4367
knowledge (9) 6 793 9 469 471 687 14 798 15 2095 16 1754 17 696 741
Known (1) 2 332
known (33) 3 435 483 7 631 1075 8 983 9 350 429 11 269 12 371 475 554 715 844 888 13 194 436 14 958 1186 1302 15 785 1385 2453 4192 16 305 17 91 947 1013 1020 1117 1140 1141 1872 2008
known (1) 7 849
Knows (6) 4 203 6 951 8 55 769 1102 11 561
knows (66) 1 117 150 161 434 2 406 4 112 428 5 331 411 6 53 244 358 549 879 974 8 504 749 844 9 614 824 10 570 11 177 461 644 645 1114 12 988 1208 1482

1648 13 171 927 1143 14 396 817 847 1063 1341 1443 15 635 2126 3525 16 155 282 1683 18 83 179 234 461 519 590 827 847 909 1003 1108 1149 1172 1341 1430 1439 1453 1501 1518 1588

knuckle (2) 8 1067 18 409
knuckle (1) 15 693
knuckledusters (1) 12 576
knuckledusters (1) 15 1180
knuckles (1) 15 3698
knuckly (1) 8 1031
Kobberkeddelsen (1) 12 564
Koch's (1) 2 332
Kock (4) 11 500 987 15 1023 18 969
Kock (1) 15 3045
Kock's (1) 4 358
Koehler (1) 2 258
Koh-i-Noor (1) 15 1499
kohol (1) 15 1319
Kok (1) 15 2603
Kol (1) 15 1408
Kolod (1) 17 763
Kop (1) 15 796
Kosher (4) 4 277 8 751 15 495 1623
Kossuth (1) 15 1847
Kostka (1) 12 1704
Kraa (1) 11 60
Kraaaaaa (1) 11 1291
Kraahraark (1) 6 965
Kraandl (1) 11 60
kraark (1) 6 965
kraɲ (3) 11 1290
Krandlkrankran (1) 11 1290
Kratchinabritchisitch (1) 12 566
kreutzer (1) 14 1422
Kriegfried (1) 12 569
Kristos (1) 9 62
Kristyann (1) 14 1539
kronia (1) 12 600
krowawr (1) 15 4609
krpthsth (1) 6 966
Krugers (1) 18 395
kudos (2) 16 1153 1519
Kuh (1) 14 1432
Kuk (1) 15 2603
kwawr (1) 15 4609
kybosh (1) 12 1578
KYRIE (1) 7 559
Kyrie (2) 7 563 564
kyries (1) 14 347
Kyrios (1) 9 622
Kyrios (1) 7 562

L

L (9) 6 882 12 187 912 14 1230 1300 16 1262 1265 17 1822 18 1264
L (2) 16 1260 17 401
L-n-h-n (1) 12 542
L B (2) 15 2424 17 1841
L B (1) 15 1554
L J (1) 12 930
L L D (2) 12 928 17 1612
L M (1) 4 518
Là (3) 4 314 5 227 15 469
là (2) 15 3894
La (7) 11 892 894 15 3247 17 1986 18 398 626
La (7) 3 167 5 228 11 17 415 15 1020 2385 4090
la (13) 8 586 9 16 641 10 984 11 892 894 12 563 18 774 1189 1428
la (24) 3 233 252 5 227 228 7 717 8 596 878 883 890 10 346 11 404 682 764 1240 13 1209 14 1536 1545 15 122 469 2094 16 319
la-amp (1) 8 590
label (4) 14 1164 17 357 603 1386
labelled (1) 16 355
labelled (1) 15 817
labels (1) 17 2099
Lablache (1) 11 1150
Labour (1) 9 753
labour (10) 8 378 11 265 14 265 967 1414 15 1394 1688 3476 16 1153 17 1533
labours (3) 14 1058 1214 1258
Laboursaving (1) 15 1392
laburnum (1) 17 1569
Lacaus (2) 8 623 13 862
lace (9) 5 370 11 726 12 1244 15 1053 2815 2826 2982 17 2096 18 900
lace (2) 15 2829 4693
laced (2) 12 173 15 2975
laceflare (1) 5 139
lacefringe (1) 3 337
laceknots (1) 17 1483
lacerated (6) 17 320 1489 1490 1491 1494 1926
laces (3) 5 118 10 244 17 1484
laces (1) 15 2812
lachrymal (1) 12 653
Laci (1) 15 3002
lack (5) 2 29 12 962 14 218 15 643 3464
Lackaday (1) 12 1602
lacking (2) 10 1083 14 1199
lacklustre (1) 15 4870
laconic (2) 17 682 2273
LACQUEY (1) 15 3095
lacquey (6) 10 281 643 649 688 691 712
lacquey (1) 15 3094
lacquey's (1) 15 4140
Lacus (1) 14 1092
lacustrine (1) 17 227
Lad (1) 15 207
lad (6) 10 566 12 1335 1344 1392 14 1371 15 3142
ladder (4) 1 529 531 16 1377 17 1564
ladder (2) 15 314 1554
laddered (1) 18 443
ladders (2) 12 11 18 793
laddies (1) 10 1249

laden (1) 7 848
Ladies (7) 11 655 15 452 708 2030 4538 16 1207 17 1829
ladies (21) 8 888 9 283 339 1090 10 1246 11 960 12 552 598 1780 14 537 1255 15 448 1891 2817 3066 3883 16 523 1837 18 255 742 1045
ladies (2) 7 828 862
ladies (5) 15 917 1078 1401 1446 4677
Ladies' (1) 13 1235
ladies' (10) 4 481 6 791 12 589 15 3320 3400 16 1557 17 153 1304 2092 2093
ladies' (1) 15 499
lads (2) 15 788 16 671
Lady (14) 7 700 8 148 340 877 10 628 12 197 1269 13 288 458 14 516 1369 15 742 1677 16 1808
Lady (1) 16 913
lady (53) 3 430 5 156 7 949 8 327 9 442 638 647 10 59 164 191 238 1176 1208 1218 1276 11 336 1256 12 247 661 662 814 1223 1498 13 101 14 134 185 266 505 690 723 778 817 821 916 15 1011 1066 2289 2718 2947 3924 4407 4775 4786 16 526 713 1428 1440 1545 17 1832 1836 1853 18 500 1361
lady (2) 15 1586 4348
ladychapel (1) 3 122
Ladylike (1) 11 106
ladylike (4) 11 336 711 13 618 15 3082
ladylove (1) 13 336
Lady's (2) 5 113 6 377
Lady's (1) 13 151
lady's (8) 6 447 9 73 11 563 661 16 1433 17 375 1569 2103
Ladys (1) 18 897
ladyships (1) 14 608
Ladysmith (2) 15 1526 18 388
Laemlein (1) 15 1907
l'aer (1) 7 721
Laetabuntur (1) 14 1574
laetificat (1) 15 123
Lafayette (2) 14 1221 16 1435
lag (1) 14 420
lagan (1) 17 1686
Lager (2) 11 288
lager (1) 15 510
laggard (1) 2 184
lagged (4) 8 421 12 801 1899 16 209
lagging (3) 8 127 10 968 16 103
lagging (1) 15 4076
lagoons (3) 3 454 17 201 218
Lahore (1) 18 1148
laid (50) 1 44 319 457 502 722 2 209 3 113 500 4 182 253 261 5 155 6 226 977 7 121 615 9 215 219 589 654 722 800 1011 10 210 591 965 1009 1207 11 177 259 600 948 1112 1132 12 1366 1744 13 319 636 735 14 183 474 15 880 3081 4874 16 709 1426 17 1728 18 3 1022 1314
laid (1) 1 464
laid (1) 15 4333
lain (3) 14 245 16 1300 17 857
lair (3) 3 251 15 2456 17 2118
lair (1) 15 32
Laird (1) 17 1735
laissez (1) 2 324
lait (1) 3 165
laity (1) 12 938

lake (5) 3 453 4 219 17 897 1155 18 985
lake (1) 15 986
lakecontained (1) 17 203
lakes (3) 12 1451 17 1978 18 1562
lakes (1) 15 1324
lakeshore (1) 4 155
lakin (1) 9 638
Lal (2) 2 288
Lal (1) 2 284
lala (1) 5 228
Lalage (1) 14 1143
Lalor (1) 17 1647
Lalouette's (1) 1 214
Lamb (3) 8 9 14 1580 15 3638
lamb (8) 7 210 8 11 483 10 1133 12 115 962 981 15 3483
Lambay (1) 14 682
Lambay (1) 14 660
Lambe (1) 15 3636
Lambert (46) 3 315 6 111 503 539 556 560 562 564 568 572 692 702 706 715 828 7 234 242 251 260 268 278 313 316 333 355 357 361 364 10 236 399 401 407 417 420 426 428 430 431 443 459 782 11 783 12 1010 1752 15 3868 17 1239
Lambert (1) 16 1260
Lambert (1) 15 1141
Lambert's (5) 7 239 10 758 11 780 785 788
Lambes (1) 18 1548
lambkin (1) 15 4967
lamb's (2) 14 269 15 747
lambs (1) 12 103
lame (6) 13 771 1094 15 3149 3466 16 1607 18 346
lame (1) 15 4141
lamentation (1) 11 793
Lamentations (1) 15 1931
lamented (2) 3 34 12 1119
lamenting (1) 16 957
Lamh (1) 12 1211
Lammermoor (1) 12 190
lamp (22) 9 225 347 10 1103 13 144 294 631 1171 1172 15 1234 4268 4271 16 1470 17 506 1174 1178 1525 1541 2300 18 143 912 1547 1597
lamp (6) 15 33 99 133 136 2491 4284
lampglow (1) 15 61
lamplight (1) 9 292
Lamplighter (1) 13 633
lamplighter (1) 13 629
lamppost (1) 12 702
lampposts (1) 8 299
lampposts (1) 15 1405
lamp's (1) 15 4269
lamps (3) 4 441 12 1717 13 1090
lamps (1) 15 4
lampset (1) 15 165
Lancashire (1) 17 1733
lance (1) 2 425
lancecorporal (1) 15 96
lancers (2) 18 402
lances (1) 1 664
lancet (1) 1 152
lancets (1) 17 1520
lancinating (1) 14 1089
Lancs (1) 18 389
Land (2) 13 1079 14 1518

land (76) 1 10 2 47 3 154 327 4 86 195 219 223 5 316 6 316 460 819 7 208 273 276 873 1061 8 35 464 577 10 733 12 68 70 85 89 207 215 446 501 601 1259 1348 1370 1373 1536 1671 13 102 122 658 1080 1158 14 87 153 375 377 439 444 447 482 610 989 1086 1200 1437 15 631 947 1517 1901 16 606 1007 1351 1416 17 193 1501 1623 1988 1996 2016 2230 2231 18 1188 1318
land (2) 7 271 833
land (2) 15 914 3384
landaus (1) 17 495
landbreeze (1) 15 4078
landed (9) 6 283 9 711 12 765 981 1378 15 4863 16 1191 17 1607 18 683
Landing (1) 17 1737
landing (5) 1 194 4 464 7 218 10 1168 18 1221
landing (1) 15 2035
landings (1) 12 400
landlady (2) 6 832 16 1566
landlady's (1) 6 59
landless (1) 3 253
Landlord (2) 8 486 14 1531
landlord (5) 10 943 946 11 533 959 14 1531
landlord's (1) 12 1606
landlubber (1) 16 503
lands (6) 3 392 488 14 140 495 925 17 2230
landscape (2) 8 893 17 1598
landshadows (1) 15 4076
landslip (1) 6 766
landward (1) 3 473
Lane (5) 11 899 14 1137 16 1279 17 1981 2076
lane (34) 3 379 4 178 5 2 222 6 39 639 708 7 74 924 8 1031 9 651 10 310 1130 11 907 1251 1254 12 14 213 230 13 901 987 14 1446 1572 15 207 16 21 515 713 1763 17 1244 18 635 1120 1229 1384 1420
lane (5) 15 42 50 3047 4819 4917
lanes (2) 15 598 919
laneway (1) 4 102
Lang (1) 14 1490
Langtry (1) 18 481
Language (3) 3 387 5 261 11 709
language (40) 1 434 3 288 4 96 6 667 7 555 564 776 8 65 466 9 454 10 1007 1011 1012 11 298 849 12 679 681 1182 1204 13 38 944 14 552 609 634 853 1023 1203 1400 15 106 1691 4726 16 311 341 345 346 17 240 340 1535 18 767
language (2) 7 845 869
languages (6) 16 352 17 725 731 741 745 748
languages (1) 15 1825
languid (2) 5 571 13 97
languideyed (1) 15 4076
languidly (1) 3 461
languor (3) 11 736 14 199 507
languorous (2) 15 3303 3306
Lank (1) 10 876
lank (1) 10 858
lank (1) 15 4160
lankylooking (1) 6 805
Lanner (2) 15 4044 18 269
Lansdowne (1) 10 1277
lantern (1) 6 998

lantern (1) 15 2257
Lanternjaws (1) 3 112
lanterns (2) 11 1014 18 986
lanterns (1) 15 178
Lanty (1) 12 1585
Lap (2) 3 166 5 336
lap (10) 4 38 43 47 6 459 8 195 849 12 1171 15 573 3075 3985
lap (1) 15 3254
lapboard (1) 3 80
lapel (2) 15 536 992
lapels (1) 15 4035
lapidaries (1) 15 1431
lapidary's (1) 10 800
lapin (1) 3 166
Lapland (1) 14 1482
lapped (4) 3 163 165 4 46 8 1032
lapping (2) 8 161 12 749
laps (1) 3 173
lapse (2) 17 114 697
Lapses (1) 15 3835
lapses (1) 17 505
lapses (1) 15 905
Lapwing (5) 9 953 954 976 980
laqueo (1) 15 4730
Laracy (1) 15 4350
larboard (2) 12 1774 1775
Larby (1) 18 1590
larceny (1) 17 1630
Larch (1) 12 1284
Larches (1) 12 1259
Larchet's (1) 15 2519
lard (2) 8 151 18 1404
lard (1) 15 1429
larder (3) 12 1603 1620 17 1547
larders (1) 8 35
lardy (1) 12 502
lardyface (1) 12 1477
Laredo (1) 18 848
large (42) 1 331 4 304 5 370 545 6 344 422 481 707 7 29 8 228 9 13 75 10 380 828 901 995 1001 1002 12 91 151 541 716 902 924 1814 1822 1837 13 1235 15 2978 16 537 644 862 955 989 1428 1434 1634 1826 17 1313 1777 1778 18 1521
large (16) 15 301 320 413 817 929 1382 1854 1938 2661 2748 2752 2985 3363 3457 3842 3843
largefooted (1) 10 215
largelidded (1) 5 150
largely (5) 16 1114 1207 1492 1493 1586
largenosed (1) 12 153
larger (3) 9 11 17 158 310
largesize (1) 14 1530
largesized (1) 16 1633
largest (2) 12 1303 17 1415
lark (4) 5 14 8 321 12 269 15 3334
larks (1) 7 449
larn (1) 14 1503
larrup (1) 15 2231
Larry (7) 4 105 113 10 230 11 952 18 452
Larry (1) 12 543
Larry (2) 15 3046 4338
LARRY (1) 15 1672
L'art (1) 9 425
larum (1) 14 736
las (2) 14 1441 18 1465
lascar's (1) 15 957
lascivas (1) 14 708

145

Lascivious (1) 3 238
lascivious (2) 3 238 468
lascivious (1) 15 3394
Lash (1) 15 710
lash (1) 18 467
lashed (1) 15 1100
lashers (1) 8 728
lashes (3) 3 441 11 1104 13 108
Lashings (1) 10 547
lass (3) 13 36 15 4074 4130
lass (1) 10 1251
Lassalle (1) 17 723
lasses (1) 15 4676
lassie (1) 15 1739
lassitude (1) 16 349
lassoes (1) 3 453
lassos (1) 15 3959
lassy (1) 11 502
Last (17) 6 224 459 679 852 996 7 986
    8 558 9 599 1207 11 54 689 1047 1064 1066
    12 184 14 1456 15 3985
Last (3) 11 590 1176 16 1738
Last (1) 15 3979
last (159) 1 93 127 212 285 541 700 2 415
    3 52 365 4 145 507 531 5 59 95 128 181 195
    242 243 403 422 463 469 563 6 126 142 236 300
    469 577 578 635 657 663 677 815 853 7 277 445
    456 569 702 998 8 17 189 246 279 418 419 663
    9 391 518 587 836 913 972 1010 1035 10 146
    225 460 476 570 1167 11 220 420 650 726 1025
    1099 1178 1220 1271 1275 1284 12 379 525 609
    652 958 1311 1363 1571 1618 1726 1849 1906
    13 2 5 159 346 474 562 624 692 762 966 1143
    1161 1166 1240 14 107 109 395 458 482 516 914
    1332 15 392 701 868 977 2129 2643 2994 3426
    3449 3484 3761 16 209 270 934 1072 1498 1555
    1698 17 94 238 1309 2004 2128 2129 2130 2142
    2143 2279 18 77 131 156 163 176 219 374 451
    459 477 604 718 799 1032 1042 1077 1117 1151
    1158 1222
last (4) 15 30 907 4081 4148
lasted (1) 5 406
lasting (1) 16 746
lastlap (1) 10 651
Lastly (1) 14 1213
lastmentioned (1) 17 675
lastnamed (2) 16 555 17 250
lasts (2) 13 952 17 1832
latch (1) 17 102
latchkey (3) 4 72 5 468 17 73
Late (1) 10 860
LATE (1) 15 1381
late (37) 3 34 5 53 6 85 319 348 7 80
    975 10 479 534 1123 1280 11 640 1067
    12 227 234 1119 1174 1179 1816 13 84 528
    531 1212 14 654 718 858 15 2741 2779 3198
    16 47 1245 1611 17 325 947 2082 2143
    18 343
late (2) 10 614 16 1248
late (2) 15 1378 3841
lately (10) 3 63 5 545 6 98 774 11 261
    16 132 1227 18 384 1009 1018
lateness (1) 17 2029
latent (4) 14 680 15 1780 17 209 695
Later (2) 1 718 6 156
later (15) 5 128 509 7 998 9 394 459 1048
    10 490 14 1026 15 646 16 326 358 1450
    1866 17 1277 1637
later (1) 15 156

lateral (1) 17 1571
laterally (1) 17 2314
latere (1) 15 77
latest (1) 12 1180
lath (3) 10 402 423 432
lather (4) 1 2 64 310 17 279
lathered (2) 1 39 95
lathering (1) 17 284
Latin (12) 1 519 3 117 174 5 349 350 419
    6 602 7 555 11 1034 14 629 995
    16 176
latitude (2) 17 1621 2304
latitudes (1) 14 66
latration (1) 17 1951
latria (1) 17 1208
latrines (1) 15 3066
Latten (1) 15 1088
latter (14) 7 575 9 498 12 1877 14 694
    16 322 697 1168 17 251 578 858 957 958 1327
    1957
latterly (1) 16 1847
latter's (1) 16 494
lattice (4) 12 1597 13 336 18 1339 1595
lattiginous (1) 17 1043
l'attosca (1) 9 374
Laud (1) 9 1223
laud (1) 7 883
laudable (2) 14 822 16 644
laudanum (2) 5 482 14 1023
Laudate (1) 13 675
lauded (1) 15 1051
laugh (33) 1 605 2 28 6 275 292 297 543
    791 7 1028 9 31 458 1157 10 544
    11 556 12 30 514 1393 1426 13 36 127 270
    1200 1218 14 238 904 1016 15 2993 3007
    3826 16 161 1160 17 442 18 536 1535
laugh (4) 15 3211 3755 3828 4873
laughed (39) 1 131 258 491 2 27 34 261
    4 295 7 1060 8 604 912 9 30 60 126 567
    575 1016 1061 1190 10 49 529 11 78 176 182
    474 479 533 558 774 12 649 1781 13 38 256
    263 358 14 237 18 123 1195 1323
Laughing (3) 1 141 9 1104 15 2001
Laughing (2) 15 4057 4678
laughing (47) 1 36 44 603 2 444 6 149
    1013 7 99 251 8 191 9 391 573 1086
    10 863 1057 1089 11 72 728 903 1157
    12 250 269 277 278 310 765 808 809 1036 1045
    1424 1848 1856 13 589 609 1188 15 570 829
    969 3901 16 685 1530 18 211 248 819 1090
    1586
laughing (1) 4 514
laughing (6) 15 3666 3786 3807 3918 3920
    4490
laughingly (1) 16 232
laughingstock (1) 17 1942
laughs (1) 13 653
laughs (21) 15 618 1098 1610 2095 2432 2590
    2866 3165 3610 3820 3900 4433 4522 4814 4821
    4824 4860 4868 4869 4883 4897
Laughter (1) 1 132 11 1080
Laughter (2) 15 50 1732
laughter (21) 1 166 560 2 27 116 443 446
    6 257 7 232 334 10 576 1065 11 143 147
    160 167 174 176 538 14 730 16 1359
laughter (2) 9 905 917
laughter (8) 15 367 483 894 923 2123 2133
    2618 3911
launch (2) 9 551 16 960

launched (2) 12 638 16 1761
laundered (1) 15 2248
laundry (3) 15 2988 18 1414 1416
Laur (1) 5 477
laurel (2) 11 117 13 1171
laurels (1) 16 1746
Laurence (2) 7 1012 12 1698
Laurence (1) 17 1388
l'avait (1) 14 306
lavatory (2) 15 3320 18 256
laved (1) 5 568
lavender (2) 10 57 17 1815
lavender (2) 15 816 4036
Lavery (1) 12 932
lavished (1) 14 716
Law (4) 5 44 7 605 10 1103 14 443
law (41) 3 92 5 41 6 181 474 867 1028
    7 500 755 8 230 9 687 11 982 12 247
    1010 1049 1114 1122 1136 1235 13 55
    14 213 242 1169 1272 1279 15 969 1480 1642
    2781 4434 16 81 874 1193 1204 17 180 720
    842 996 1627 1789 1790
law (1) 7 869
law (1) 15 1428
lawbooks (1) 8 230
lawdeedaw (1) 3 96
lawful (2) 14 875 1322
Lawksamercy (1) 14 812
Lawn (2) 3 492 9 648
lawn (8) 1 174 10 1111 12 122 890 952
    14 490 1362 17 876
lawn (1) 15 2184
lawnmower (1) 17 1571
lawnmower (1) 15 2524
lawnmowers (2) 15 2513 2537
lawnsprinkler (1) 17 1572
Lawrence (1) 17 1116
laws (6) 9 478 785 13 456 16 769
    17 758 1695
Lawson (2) 15 1862
lawyer (1) 14 494
Lawyers (1) 10 470
Lay (6) 6 819 7 898 8 576 11 1025
    12 688 14 1559
lay (61) 1 2 181 249 711 2 22 126 169 417
    3 258 286 348 408 437 4 183 226 243 6 508
    582 8 906 910 913 935 9 149 220 249 817 914
    1193 10 938 11 929 1220 12 23
    13 209 1179 14 112 128 150 223 237 361 452
    1135 1151 1321 1413 1540 15 106 551 1693
    3000 3106 3865 4204 16 819 1095 1232
    17 296 1617 18 6 789
lay (1) 15 4920
layer (2) 8 379 15 2356
Laying (1) 6 17
laying (6) 6 583 1028 7 379 14 254 1122
    1163
layman (2) 14 256 17 541
lays (3) 3 80 12 846 847
lays (1) 15 678 3583
Lazarillo (1) 16 493
Lazarus (2) 6 678 9 419
Lazenby's (1) 13 314
lazily (2) 4 174 8 89
Lazy (2) 7 618 15 3671
lazy (4) 5 30 316 10 7 16 617
lb (2) 17 308 18 1555
lbs (1) 18 1556
Le (4) 14 778 15 1858 17 1110

Le (3) 3 196 9 120 10 147
le (1) 9 858
le (8) 3 162 170 14 307 15 2585 3896 4045 4046 4103
Lead (2) 1 139 18 381
lead (9) 8 518 9 408 12 447 14 420 1487 1549 16 1283 1617 18 382
lead (1) 15 907
leaded (1) 7 146
leadenfooted (1) 7 723
leader (6) 1 535 4 101 7 378 12 1595 16 1325 1392
leader (1) 15 4336
leader's (2) 16 1497 1498
leaders (5) 3 243 10 1036 1037 13 112 15 4530
leaders' (1) 10 1243
Leading (2) 6 351 15 853
leading (10) 9 598 12 968 14 1083 1129 16 526 1537 1565 17 2005 18 926 1580
leading (2) 15 748 1961
leadpaper (1) 17 308
leadpapered (1) 5 18
leads (4) 9 735 14 389 17 836 18 514
leads (2) 15 2014 2248
leaf (1) 3 441
leaf (2) 15 906 4503
leafage (2) 7 247 253
league (7) 9 323 12 683 857 15 220 1527 18 1188
leagues (2) 13 1018 17 194
Leah (6) 5 194 6 185 13 1212 15 496 17 2079 2257
Leahy's (2) 3 29 13 1173
leaked (1) 5 315
leaks (1) 17 214
leaks (1) 15 2167
Lean (3) 8 1036 9 817 16 1720
lean (9) 2 139 4 475 6 778 7 816 9 471 13 721 14 1476 15 2327 16 1887
lean (1) 9 99
leaned (14) 1 13 100 2 17 82 4 338 10 89 212 575 13 695 715 717 941 1114 1287
Leaning (1) 1 82
leaning (10) 4 87 113 7 433 9 152 407 13 744 16 457 17 896 18 797 1116
leaningplace (1) 1 528
Leanjawed (1) 6 517
leans (4) 15 212 2574 3549 3738
Leap (2) 12 1459 17 1978
leap (3) 13 208 590 14 1071
leap (3) 15 414 1265 4543
leaped (3) 2 443 7 660 11 746
leapers (1) 15 4675
leapfrog (1) 15 323
leaping (6) 1 601 2 120 10 795 1037 14 81
leaping (7) 15 1324 1750 2947 3979 4128 4332
leaps (8) 15 139 165 226 1373 1586 3876 4244 4674
leapyear (2) 8 733 18 1575
Lear (5) 9 185 188 401 912 990
Lear (1) 15 4685
Learn (4) 6 84 757 7 96 15 3119
learn (21) 2 404 406 5 429 7 915 8 574 858 1115 9 233 10 869 11 1264 13 138 924 1058 14 555 634 16 284 1121 18 772 1005 1006 1362

Learned (1) 15 2805
learned (13) 2 35 6 991 9 1113 12 608 926 1009 1114 14 453 15 2124 16 1138 17 1072 1760 18 933
learned (1) 7 830
learner (1) 2 403
learning (4) 11 842 12 1448 14 824 18 1565
learningknight (5) 14 125 128 135 136 160
learnt (1) 9 236
Leary (1) 17 34
lease (3) 6 796 16 547 17 1519
Leask's (1) 5 2
least (44) 3 1 5 148 484 6 224 794 8 575 9 215 216 11 549 569 679 12 654 13 5 660 14 218 418 885 1348 1566 15 309 3029 4575 16 119 245 284 731 812 820 1047 1084 1130 1137 1596 1623 1762 17 833 1761 1957 18 208 438 537 619 854 907
leat (1) 12 819
leath (1) 15 220
Leather (1) 5 179
leather (15) 2 200 208 3 447 4 70 524 5 23 320 6 101 8 239 9 337 14 1489 17 1372 1391 1532 18 988
leather (1) 15 726
leathern (1) 10 821
Leave (7) 6 890 11 807 12 1107 14 283 15 380 4782 4821
leave (35) 1 307 3 452 4 380 5 529 6 538 8 21 325 557 9 692 712 1199 10 30 697 1205 11 17 121 1113 1123 13 611 1008 14 168 201 1123 15 869 1723 2360 3206 16 252 1457 17 1220 18 241 408 670 801 1075
leave (2) 9 1042 11 402
leaves (13) 2 448 3 141 444 465 4 315 5 30 9 341 10 17 11 674 963 14 1117 18 73 852
leaves (5) 15 3238 3342 3453 3954 4110
leavetakers (1) 9 326
leavetaking (2) 11 325 17 2052
Leaving (1) 4 496
leaving (16) 6 912 11 95 12 753 1291 13 408 14 587 16 126 241 1487 17 112 694 18 601 693 913 989 1221
leaving (1) 15 301
Lebanonian (1) 12 76
Lecher (1) 14 356
Lecherous (1) 15 122
lechers (3) 15 4320 4322 4326
leching (1) 9 560
lecking (1) 18 936
lecture (3) 15 3076 17 1600 1882
lecturer (1) 9 1101
lectures (1) 16 796
Led (1) 8 861
led (23) 2 307 3 367 7 485 508 893 1029 9 602 10 779 932 952 11 358 363 390 12 509 1136 1683 1688 14 73 201 668 16 93 1721 17 943
led (2) 17 822 823
led (1) 15 4328
Leda (1) 12 283
ledge (1) 3 500
ledge (1) 15 1843
Ledwidge (1) 16 859
Lee (2) 9 419 15 4196
lee (1) 5 230

leech (2) 8 1165 9 750
leeches (1) 14 207
Leedom's (1) 15 3189
Leolee (1) 15 1274
leer (1) 1 500
leered (1) 5 535
Leering (1) 15 372
leering (1) 5 539
leering (2) 15 2986 3044
leers (1) 15 4869
Lees (1) 18 517
lees (1) 8 934
Leeson (3) 3 429 7 669 17 170
leet (1) 9 788
Left (2) 6 456 13 1200
left (128) 1 117 217 524 2 10 4 73 203 5 203 204 205 518 6 95 200 375 458 587 637 7 10 916 8 354 490 609 627 1082 1103 9 15 159 254 691 697 1007 1094 1135 1155 10 69 468 625 686 698 1018 1137 1231 1234 11 54 496 1178 12 207 720 968 970 982 1068 1229 1854 13 134 692 773 819 926 1287 14 121 379 409 622 748 1154 1216 1496 15 261 262 264 474 669 1190 1528 2271 2498 2547 2573 2782 2848 3309 4053 4381 4420 4881 16 23 187 562 565 633 924 1291 1526 1666 1703 1721 17 4 121 158 161 1217 1288 1436 1442 1448 1452 1571 1614 2312 2313 2314 2315 18 5 317 370 481 622 708 781 798 865 890 958 1015 1057
left (4) 8 1070 1074 9 247 16 703
left (31) 15 20 73 127 223 481 482 1297 1309 1841 1881 2265 2273 2305 2307 2339 2478 2479 2668 2712 2723 2725 2745 2764 4317 4456 4694 4934 4959 4966
Leftabed (1) 9 706
lefthand (1) 16 390
lefthanded (1) 14 628
Leftherhis (2) 9 701 703
lefts (1) 12 966
Leg (3) 14 1491 1538 15 1607
leg (25) 4 15 18 321 5 561 7 686 787 8 963 1007 12 702 1023 13 557 15 46 47 58 59 72 601 2270 16 562 17 2102 2312 2313 18 5 109 945
leg (1) 9 1147
leg (6) 15 2052 2281 2932 2943 4032 4141
legal (14) 6 56 8 1152 9 687 844 11 343 12 585 1867 15 1630 16 525 1069 1441 1524 17 665 2204
legal (1) 15 500
legem (1) 12 1747
legend (7) 4 69 9 991 14 659 17 796 801 812 1781
legend (1) 15 649
legendary (1) 12 1442
legends (1) 5 18
legends (1) 15 1399
Leger (1) 15 1840
Legers (1) 8 973
Legget (1) 15 4043
legging (1) 14 1399
legibility (1) 17 583
legible (1) 15 1826
Legion (1) 15 729
legion (1) 12 713
legitimate (4) 14 919 16 262 793 1533
legplates (1) 15 1854
Legs (1) 15 2179
legs (26) 1 31 447 681 3 17 4 384 430

5 411　6 236　7 57 63 730　8 118 1099
10 13　11 578　13 698 995 1087　15 2672
16 852　17 1527 2315　18 587 810 1035 1241
legs (3) 15 212 3784 4543
Lei (3) 10 345 346　15 2504
Leinster (3) 10 1263　12 85　17 339
leisure (1) 16 1275
Leith (1) 14 1565
Leitrim (1) 4 127
Leixlip (1) 6 450
leman (2) 2 393　14 231
lemon (9) 1 340　3 208 209　8 1 745 889
15 493 2298 2901
lemon (1) 15 335
lemonade (3) 12 691　17 905　18 554
lemonflavoured (1) 17 232
lemonjuice (1) 13 90
Lemon's (3) 8 6　11 606　17 331
Lemons (1) 13 1043
lemony (1) 5 512
lemonyellow (1) 5 569
Lemur (1) 15 4176
Lend (3) 1 69 293　15 2922
lend (7) 2 17　10 670 782　11 658
13 819　16 183 523
lender (1) 17 1667
lenders (1) 17 1667
lendeth (2) 1 727　14 261
Lenehan (92) 7 300 387 393 401 416 417 420
442 447 465 468 475 496 504 507 513 574 587 590
595 606 611 675 682 690 695 759 778 875 891 1028
8 829 844　10 395 484 490 494 498 511 517 522
524 529 536 541 551 575 579 1204　11 228 233
240 256 263 289 338 362 372 377 387 395 404 415
428 431　12 1178 1208 1215 1218 1226 1265
1318 1389 1536 1548 1554 1622 1649　14 173
191 217 338 417 506 529 1122 1127 1137 1161
16 146　17 2137
Lenehan (5) 15 1142 2238 3728 3739 4342
LENEHAN (5) 15 1700 1733 3742 3747 3752
LENEHAN'S (1) 7 577
Lenehan's (4) 7 437 984　11 328　16 1285
Lenehans (1) 18 426
length (10) 1 15　8 565　10 313　13 1091
14 949　15 4953　16 378 1286　17 86 374
lengthened (1) 7 560
lengthens (1) 15 993
lengthwise (2) 5 49　17 2040
lengthy (3) 16 601 988 1843
lenses (2) 7 826　8 554
Lent (1) 3 168
lent (15) 4 348　5 180　7 119　9 192 255
747 1084　12 530　13 104　14 857
16 195 1291　17 1376　18 655 1474
Lentulus (1) 17 784
Léo (1) 3 167
Léo (1) 14 306
Leo (9) 12 848　14 1524　15 1272 1274 1383
1594 1673　17 1213
Leo (1) 15 712
Leonard (10) 6 142　8 989 994 996 998 1005
1018 1024 1027　12 801
Leonard (1) 15 1142
LEONARD (3) 15 1633 1637 1728
Leonardo (1) 16 887
Leonard's (3) 15 203　17 49 50
Leop (2) 14 504 507
leopard (1) 2 214
leopards (1) 15 3990

Leopardstown (2) 15 544 546
Leopold (67) 4 1　5 206 498　6 126 364 882
8 871　10 592　11 519 628 642 768 1262
12 559 1006 1695　13 744 1060　14 126 128
133 138 160 162 170 182 195 197 238 252 264 271
330 566 1041 1044 1074 1076 1077 1236　15 260
261 721 753 1158 1364 1473 1475 1488 1561 3153
3444　17 405 1126 1612 1614 1788 1816 1855
1875 1883 1885 1906 1911 2002
Leopold (1) 17 1881
Leopold (3) 15 1848 3224 3329
leopold (1) 11 637
Leopoldi (1) 15 1855
Leopoldleben (1) 15 275
Leopoldo (1) 10 524
Leopold's (1) 17 1580
Leopopold (1) 15 1274
leper (1) 15 4157
leperyards (1) 14 36
leprechaun (1) 12 1787
leprous (2) 3 481　10 804
Les (5) 14 1494　15 2162 4090 4098
les (3) 3 235　12 1209 1389
lesbic (2) 9 852　15 3906
Less (2) 12 1690　17 885
less (32) 3 68　11 191　12 813 1405 1412
13 1082　14 63 275 690 804 1240 1308
15 2297　16 306 866 1206 1651　17 9 288
1009 1057 1193 1223 1514 1903 1953 2119 2182
2195 2248　18 711
lessee (2) 16 1048　17 420
lessen (1) 17 866
lesser (2) 17 1124 1619
Lessing (1) 15 3609
lessons (2) 17 911　18 1302
lest (5) 10 39　14 23 270 980　17 2060
Lesurques (1) 15 761
LET (1) 7 905
Let (59) 1 177 279 506　3 73　4 457　5 364
6 646 919 920 1003　7 133 160 649 792 900 930
8 250 294 410 511 735 740　9 719 877 971
10 606 769　11 445 446 541 803 1264
12 786 1074 1788　13 268 1039 1041 1265 1276
14 311　15 1108 1168 1962 1975 2807 2951
3115 3191 3778 3873 4434 4473 4756 4760
16 785 920 1171
Let (3) 7 491 494　11 1291
Let (1) 17 414
let (135) 1 88 279 476 480　2 413 442 446
3 237 386 464 501　4 142 273 277 387　5 8
189 294　6 611 817 951 990　7 654 1056
8 199 421 740 844 931　9 230 496 724 759
10 51 404 594 664 856　11 138 160 955
12 3 124 684 707 789 947 1062 1075 1156 1315
1766 1853 1901　13 95 320 356 361 397 726 836
860 924 993 995　14 160 187 210 222 645 664
905 933 1139 1304 1307 1337 1344 1346 1415
15 670 775 2231 2402 3388 3947 4886　16 7
303 304 692 750 1082 1219 1231 1269 1540 1636
17 162 1841　18 8 39 86 117 118 156 191 201
202 252 287 410 585 740 800 811 822 877 892 906
909 946 1081 1086 1104 1129 1191 1245 1249 1258
1509 1510 1527 1531 1544
let (3) 7 835　9 1224　11 1074
Lethal (1) 6 986
lethargy (1) 5 34 474
lethargy (1) 17 2225
Lethe (1) 14 1114
Let's (4) 11 389　15 528 530 3334

Let's (1) 15 1581
lets (1) 12 1143
lets (1) 15 672
lett (1) 11 861
Letter (4) 5 156　11 1123　13 1247
16 1241
letter (73) 2 290 417 421　3 58 405　4 251
252 253 257 280 310 394 427　5 61 65 70 79 80
221 237 242 243 251 263 268 275　6 66 168 364
744　7 181 530　9 317　10 5 39 46 51 53
11 1187　12 426 708　13 779 787 844 877
1136　14 530 1156　15 233 392 1017 1071 1249
1802 1967 2508 2779　16 1534　17 882 1194
1627 1841 1844　18 47 318 328 698 717 718 731
1235 1318
letterbox (3) 4 286　7 932　10 53
lettercards (1) 7 18
lettered (1) 7 42
lettering (1) 17 2099
letternumber (1) 17 1378
letterpress (1) 17 1392
Letters (2) 5 372　11 1078
Letters (1) 17 1375
letters (35) 2 156 433　3 139 430　4 243 249
487　5 55　7 18　8 126 132　9 1101
10 1207　11 648　12 304 305 309 316 412
13 322 1261 1266　14 363 555　15 380
16 1363 1486　17 98 748 1359 1797 1799
18 741 949 1176
letters (4) 15 1078 1554 1826 2436
letterwriter (1) 18 742
Letting (1) 4 256
letting (17) 6 484　7 382　12 706 884 1103
1160 1563 1567 1755 1765 1769　13 759
16 616 1875　18 200 1165
Lettuce (1) 4 482
lettuce (1) 13 314
leucodermic (1) 17 785
Leugarde (1) 12 1692
Levant (1) 4 212
Levanted (1) 6 887
levanter (1) 18 607
levee (1) 15 1012
level (11) 1 233　5 316　7 176　11 1011
13 388　14 1132　17 186 224 355 1593
level (1) 15 147
levelheaded (1) 16 219
levels (2) 9 281　12 347
Levenston's (2) 8 1139　15 4043
Lever (3) 16 968 1076
Lever (2) 16 981 982
lever (3) 5 180　10 488　17 522
Leverage (1) 10 477
leverage (1) 17 103
levin (1) 14 81
levitates (1) 15 4476
levites (1) 18 687
levity (2) 14 901　15 940
levying (1) 16 991
Lewd (1) 15 1189
lewd (2) 14 311 935
lewd (1) 15 4322
lewdly (1) 9 1025
lewdly (1) 15 1350
Lewers (1) 18 443
Lewis (1) 10 1107
Lewy (2) 15 1861 1862
Lex (1) 14 1029
lex (2) 3 48　7 756

412 486 506 597 679 696 712 715 717 722 730 815 829 905 960 993 995 1030 1133 14 107 120 322 427 811 1264 1316 1378 1444 15 437 853 1361 3268 3286 3778 3938 16 69 104 357 687 707 816 908 1094 1506 18 11 153 194 209 218 228 307 308 337 372 386 464 473 476 479 589 593 876 888 1013 1036 1134 1145 1198 1234 1288 1304 1320 1349 1408 1441 1482

look (1) 11 724

look (1) 15 933

Looked (4) 4 76 9 1123 11 1073 13 936

looked (105) 1 14 30 83 185 580 2 27 125 246 387 4 201 250 304 456 5 333 394 6 11 255 313 349 353 358 476 544 685 699 893 971 7 183 254 255 432 818 870 8 173 270 843 931 1180 9 225 295 590 872 946 965 1210 10 123 327 334 342 601 703 895 1052 1169 1226 1231 11 206 275 366 405 549 722 727 728 1056 1076 12 1280 13 121 141 339 340 449 609 680 690 1085 1229 14 91 272 1275 15 448 558 16 710 1146 1172 1405 1427 1434 1440 1466 1470 1781 1803 18 30 258 346 413 528 645 647 842 893 1054 1581

looked (1) 16 1894

lookeron (1) 16 1046

lookin (1) 16 1001

Looking (13) 2 388 3 333 5 494 6 238 344 8 51 56 429 569 12 1032 13 1204 1206 16 1400

looking (101) 1 181 324 329 3 427 5 119 167 401 415 6 35 86 204 510 **519** 575 661 897 7 254 296 297 716 763 997 8 **169** 741 1185 1188 1191 9 291 569 10 27 212 394 666 671 738 1131 11 73 77 234 858 859 1045 1158 12 368 967 1081 1162 1315 1321 1754 1756 1764 13 365 412 423 495 497 502 539 546 558 599 697 733 766 818 986 1164 1303 15 400 750 880 1283 2295 16 673 676 690 891 1689 1695 18 41 87 249 257 296 399 428 529 573 649 703 787 843 851 1001 1044 1184 1353 1502

looking (1) 15 926

lookingglass (3) 1 146 154 483

lookingglass (1) 4 288

lookout (4) 6 411 15 3086 16 188 1778

Looks (9) 6 424 607 7 173 223 11 1259 13 1054 1078 1232 14 1403

looks (20) 5 102 6 437 596 597 785 786 8 41 618 923 9 381 1154 14 844 15 1456 17 1340 18 542 1037 1279 1304 1354 1483

looks (13) 15 105 184 297 408 958 1234 2668 2762 2800 3542 3621 4413 4947

looloo (1) 15 4920

loom (1) 3 467

loom (1) 15 37

looms (3) 2 87 12 1243 14 1099

looms (1) 15 4888

loonies (1) 8 478

loooooves (1) 18 897

Loop (3) 5 138 16 101 933

Loop (1) 15 911

loop (1) 12 1174

looped (2) 4 322 11 704

loophole (1) 16 1488

looping (1) 6 802

Loopline (1) 10 295

loops (2) 2 130 6 720

Loose (2) 3 239 373

loose (28) 1 31 103 271 479 560 3 471

4 59 77 435 6 279 426 7 598 663 817 8 313 542 9 509 10 901 11 81 12 169 13 1188 14 39 540 1105 15 3289 17 1582 2117 18 593

loose (4) 15 387 2184 3844 4746

loosebox (1) 15 2019

Loosen (1) 15 926

loosen (2) 8 100 12 841

loosened (2) 16 1355 17 1484

loosening (2) 4 460 16 1686

loosening (1) 15 4644

loosens (1) 15 4946

looser (1) 15 4075

loosing (1) 9 806

loped (1) 3 347

lopes (1) 15 3989

Lopez (1) 9 750

loquat (1) 12 1004

Lorcan (1) 10 1011

Lorcan (1) 15 1379

LORCAN (1) 15 1387

Lord (70) 1 335 727 3 295 464 5 304 434 6 299 353 640 901 7 557 558 680 8 41 163 749 1006 1161 9 1056 1078 10 156 961 11 549 1206 12 449 685 1225 1516 13 851 892 929 938 940 14 168 227 261 613 15 635 1171 1364 1954 2647 4238 4713 16 130 142 1682 17 2136 18 110 175 209 378 584 588 595 656 666 821 831 847 915 1003 1142 1147 1214 1341 1410 1430 1487

Lord (5) 15 1378 1845 4686

LORD (2) 15 1381 4395

lord (70) 2 301 3 374 5 306 7 106 601 794 8 160 227 709 830 1162 9 454 625 658 661 1048 10 157 163 167 537 627 657 765 785 1010 1040 1184 1208 1210 1212 1276 11 544 547 548 12 771 1132 1260 13 258 1200 14 74 320 371 592 617 619 623 630 683 905 907 1116 1332 1391 1527 15 822 835 844 893 953 1008 16 1279 1283 1346 1538 1785 17 444 18 185 428 1311 1324

lord (3) 15 1414 1415 1438

lordling (1) 9 453

lordly (2) 12 112 1865

Lords (1) 18 1204

lords (7) 7 565 9 1008 10 1203 12 286 14 1170 16 136 1198

Lordship (1) 9 521

lordship (2) 15 826 18 1432

lordship (1) 15 1415

lordships (1) 12 1603

lordships' (1) 12 1408

lore (2) 9 238 10 816

Loré's (1) 11 150

Loreto (1) 13 288

lorries (1) 5 1

lorry (1) 15 1704

Los (1) 3 18

Lose (2) 7 227 13 1050

lose (14) 2 230 420 5 529 6 178 218 572 8 225 241 827 845 11 1193 14 675 868 15 641

losel (1) 14 328

loses (2) 10 1066 13 802

Losing (1) 7 303

losing (1) 18 1438

loss (7) 6 547 9 476 14 1125 15 1118 16 295 17 345 352

loss (1) 6 166

losses (1) 17 346

losses (1) 15 1432

LOST (1) 7 551

Lost (3) 5 132 6 545 11 22

Lost (2) 9 19 753

lost (79) 3 149 243 330 333 4 67 179 5 371 6 394 457 679 7 553 569 8 228 556 686 9 422 752 10 151 570 1062 11 22 407 408 478 632 634 635 636 641 642 646 678 802 840 870 927 1113 1242 12 1216 1241 13 79 444 627 657 803 1189 14 868 939 1101 1126 1133 1552 15 208 232 643 753 1527 1782 2635 3444 3607 4862 16 187 900 915 1244 17 2001 18 117 255 424 425 514 561 804 967 1062 1084 1576

loft (1) 17 1405

lost (4) 5 281 7 59 11 629 740

Lot (4) 4 418 5 488 8 84 11 913

lot (43) 5 79 6 308 607 783 7 96 197 8 409 568 720 10 460 569 11 1161 12 689 1325 13 480 14 1183 1195 1533 15 640 2223 2807 2867 2934 3088 3783 16 76 88 993 1340 1445 1480 1646 1837 18 179 411 518 519 548 878 879 1039 1275 1459

lot (1) 15 4366

Loth (1) 14 86

loth (1) 14 201

lotion (8) 5 462 8 628 1192 11 940 1128 13 1044 15 332 18 459

Lot's (1) 16 980

Lots (3) 6 675 10 588 13 1147

lots (3) 4 68 13 1004 15 3885

lots (1) 3 166

Lottery (1) 17 1808

lottery (5) 8 185 12 777 1898 16 642 18 1225

lottery (1) 15 1577

Lotty (1) 15 3355

Lotus (1) 9 283

Lou (1) 14 1448

Loud (2) 11 1089 14 408

loud (20) 1 110 275 422 654 2 365 4 545 7 162 183 611 1028 10 940 11 94 693 987 12 165 13 265 15 398 3826 3892 17 2061

loud (2) 15 1184 3211

loudlatinlaughing (1) 3 194

loudly (16) 1 227 411 419 2 29 4 32 7 17 991 10 456 712 884 11 936 1175 12 1597 14 402 16 957 1883

loudly (13) 15 1158 2866 3042 3132 3610 3667 3757 3797 3893 3900 4281 4752 4768

Lough (1) 12 1454

lough (4) 4 281 403 10 164 17 1974

Loughlinstown (1) 12 1457

loughs (1) 17 218

Louis (7) 3 287 6 221 885 9 283 12 1708 13 646 15 3119

Louisa (1) 14 1330

lounge (3) 17 57 1522 1530

lounged (2) 8 1066 10 94

loup (1) 15 3915

Lourdes (3) 5 365 7 949 15 3436

lourdily (1) 3 32

lousy (2) 1 500 9 1134

lout (2) 12 509 516

Louth (1) 16 133

Lout's (1) 3 291

Louy (1) 13 1107

lovable (2) 13 37 15 1799
Love (25) 6 758 7 883 8 649 9 429 659
 10 437 928 947 948 1202 11 533 681 1069
 1226 12 1485 1490 1491 1493 13 653 1237
 15 742 2009 2424
Love (2) 11 459 553
Love (3) 15 932 4146 4695
LOVE (2) 15 4700 4704
love (124) 1 48 102 3 88 246 451 4 355
 404 410 5 271 6 479 997 8 145 589 590 645
 963 1006 9 423 448 449 460 631 632 781 845 985
 1039 10 371 657 847 11 20 597 709 737 742
 12 523 1489 1493 1499 1628 13 104 138 156
 200 210 390 438 440 669 671 672 735 816 973 1094
 1196 1280 14 201 361 1476 1552 1567 15 11
 112 385 627 760 825 826 1086 1693 1891 1974 2610
 2621 2773 3321 3504 3888 3914 3924 4239 4535
 16 439 719 887 1061 1385 1734 17 1623
 18 35 80 103 192 193 235 242 328 348 366 397
 482 623 736 922 933 967 1056 1059 1063 1291
 1335 1409 1426 1455 1493 1503 1554 1557
love (4) 11 530 782 12 1508 13 313
Lovebirch (3) 10 602 12 1269 15 1018
Loved (1) 13 1199
loved (28) 2 140 142 9 424 660 10 37
 11 1177 12 297 13 312 434 584 628 634
 1236 14 255 1325 15 1323 4203 16 719
 1383 17 1634 18 480 812 851 920 1409
loveful (1) 15 912
lovekin (1) 14 1475
Loveless (1) 3 253
loveletter (1) 18 735
Loveletters (1) 15 1582
loveliest (1) 1 97
loveliness (3) 13 541 648 14 1221
lovelock (1) 13 834
lovelorn (1) 11 301
lovelorn (1) 15 146
Lovely (12) 4 124 5 29 431 8 928
 9 731 733 10 723 11 580 638 713 939
 12 78
lovely (63) 1 97 117 390 4 398 400 5 296
 6 610 8 464 928 1065 10 646 11 581 591
 921 1078 1080 1175 1176 12 79 80 602 1451
 13 121 162 192 232 338 399 519 635 740 800 801
 906 1272 14 1159 15 1067 2717 2980 3799
 3883 18 132 366 390 391 399 405 420 477 606
 612 619 620 847 938 984 1147 1349 1352 1455 1501
lovely (2) 4 443 7 271
Lovemaking (2) 16 1240 1289
Lovephiltres (1) 5 482
lovephiltres (1) 15 2599
Lover (2) 3 246 9 1022
lover (9) 3 245 422 9 260 657 14 769 1134
 18 355 1365 1595
lover (1) 15 3168
lover's (1) 3 211
Lovers (1) 13 1100
lovers (4) 3 468 8 935 12 545 14 351
lovers (1) 15 4361
lovers' (3) 13 129 185 16 1565
Love's (3) 11 682 15 455 2506
Love's (5) 4 314 5 157 9 753 15 4190
 17 1307
love's (6) 1 253 11 325 326 681 13 757
 15 2814
love's (1) 1 240
Loves (1) 18 598
loves (18) 9 852 12 1493 1494 1495 1496
 1497 1498 1499 1500 1501 15 2552 18 877
 1340
loveshivery (1) 11 531
lovesoft (1) 11 680
lovesome (1) 14 87
Lovesongs (2) 9 94 514
lovesongs (3) 9 103 12 724 15 3459
lovesongs (1) 11 928
lovewords (1) 15 3796
Lovey (1) 14 1475
lovey (2) 12 1495 13 1284
loving (6) 12 639 14 844 1319 15 3036
 3265 16 1536
lovingcup (1) 12 1527
lovingly (1) 13 3
lovingly (1) 15 2814
Low (4) 10 683 11 42 1005 1081
low (34) 2 394 3 301 455 4 496 5 89 460
 6 713 7 461 9 31 330 10 1201 11 93
 328 363 630 674 1168 12 1183 1267 13 302
 1011 14 536 801 806 836 1340 1536 15 852
 3191 16 1300 1430 17 1268 18 277 1034
low (6) 15 74 564 992 1130 2489 4017
lowbacked (2) 16 1886 1894
lowcorsaged (1) 15 1014
lowcut (1) 11 1056
lowcut (1) 15 4036
lowdown (1) 6 63
lowed (1) 1 402
Lower (6) 10 1270 1271 16 1192 17 3 967
 2258
lower (27) 2 334 6 848 7 147 8 56 562
 9 554 10 1180 11 909 1222 12 347 713
 15 2359 16 796 1630 1882 1894 17 85 296
 298 330 1045 1452 1727 2055 18 68 449 1547
lower (1) 15 1764
lowerclass (1) 14 1298
lowered (3) 6 12 11 462 17 86
lowered (2) 15 1151 3664
lowering (1) 12 1783
lowers (1) 3 90
lowest (8) 12 384 533 13 302 14 923
 15 2665 16 629 1214 18 426
lowing (5) 4 159 6 385 11 963 12 109
 13 1149
lowly (1) 1 404
lowlying (1) 9 932
lowneck (1) 18 1269
lownecks (1) 18 10
lowpower (1) 17 1808
lowringing (1) 8 615
Lowry (1) 6 158
Lowry's (1) 10 495
Lowry's (1) 12 747
Low's (2) 14 572 17 491
lows (1) 3 326
lowsized (1) 10 1028
lowskimming (1) 3 335
lowspirited (1) 16 304
Loyal (2) 7 569 17 1622
loyal (5) 7 553 554 10 159 1264 15 1631
loyal (1) 15 1555
loyally (1) 14 1342
loyalty (1) 14 908
Loyola (2) 1 231 9 163
Lozenge (1) 8 3
lozenges (3) 10 803 15 2710 17 574
Ltd (2) 8 142 17 1785
Lub (1) 15 2268

lub (1) 9 1109
Lubber (1) 9 1106
lubber (2) 9 1107 1110
lubric (1) 16 1378
Lubricate (1) 8 759
Lucan (1) 18 271
Lucas (1) 7 739
Lucia (1) 6 852
Lucifer (1) 15 3599
Lucifer (1) 3 486
lucifer (2) 17 105 131
luck (29) 6 330 8 403 800 839 10 916
 12 8 1230 1850 13 179 185 1157 14 1161
 15 55 208 981 2827 2935 3969 4462 16 176
 233 240 1228 1233 1658 18 140 867 869 1480
luckily (1) 13 349
luckless (2) 14 783 1140
luckpenny (1) 14 1066
luck's (1) 15 1290
Lucky (4) 8 187 377 425 15 594
lucky (5) 12 1100 13 180 226 16 1063
 1339
lucky (1) 15 2025
lucrative (1) 16 793
lucre (1) 16 1842
Lucrece's (1) 9 473
Lucy (2) 9 1134 12 1709
Ludamassy (1) 14 1555
ludendo (1) 16 1764
Ludwig (2) 12 194 16 859
luff (1) 14 643
lug (1) 9 390
lugged (2) 3 35 16 1672
lugs (2) 11 353 12 1907
lugs (1) 15 4333
lugubriously (1) 15 1214
lugubru (1) 15 146
Lugugugubrious (1) 11 1005
Lui (1) 3 182
lui (3) 9 941 14 780 16 316
lui-même (1) 9 114
Luigi (1) 18 975
Luitpold (1) 12 468
Luke (5) 8 274 13 1106 17 1261 1338
 1347
Lukewarm (2) 7 224 15 3793
lukewarm (1) 4 143
lukewarm (1) 15 158
lull (1) 7 761
Lullaby (1) 11 1019
Lulls (1) 5 367
lum (1) 14 1490
lumbago (1) 7 949
lumbering (2) 15 4133 4148
lumberroom (2) 2 121 154
lumbershed (1) 17 1561
luminary (2) 16 1069 17 1160
luminiferous (1) 17 263
luminosity (1) 12 340
luminosity (1) 15 2570
luminous (5) 8 19 17 1120 1171 1189 1267
Lump (1) 3 88
lump (14) 2 227 259 4 274 5 362 6 52
 909 933 8 366 468 9 1039 16 1354 1787
 17 309 18 281
Lumpmusic (1) 11 1006
lumps (5) 1 353 10 1086 12 576
 15 3139 18 1404
lumps (1) 15 6

MacDonogh (1) 12 1440
MacDowell (15) 10 1126 1206 12 1494
    13 79 83 101 166 194 207 264 366 566 770 1300
    1301
MacDowell (1) 15 372
Macduff (1) 7 898
mace (2) 10 1009 14 696
mace (1) 15 1382
macebearer (1) 10 1009
MacFadden (2) 12 578 582
MacFlimsy (1) 13 35
M'Gillicuddy (1) 12 1833
M'Gillicuddy's (1) 12 112
M'Glade's (1) 8 130
M'Guckin (1) 11 611
M'Guinness (2) 10 61 62
M'Guinness (1) 15 4348
M'Guinness's (1) 10 267
MacHale's (1) 12 1585
machine (6) 6 990 7 174 201 15 1199
    3908 17 92
machine (1) 15 1260
machineries (1) 7 82
Machines (2) 7 80 15 1391
machines (3) 2 230 7 101 183
Machree (1) 14 1497
machree (1) 11 1160
machree (1) 9 775
Macht (1) 15 3653
MacHugh (19) 7 237 256 270 299 325 348 378
    394 407 461 470 484 501 547 637 697 791 937
    11 268
MacHugh (1) 7 578
MacHugh (1) 15 927
MacHugh's (1) 7 334
macin (1) 11 1250
M'Intosh (5) 6 895 15 1561 1564
    16 1265 17 2066
M'Intosh (1) 16 1261
Macintosh (1) 6 894
Macintosh (1) 15 1560
macintosh (5) 6 805 825 10 1271
    12 1498 13 1062
macintosh (3) 15 1558 1565 2307
Mack (1) 1 323
MacKay (2) 15 1858 1859
MacKenna (1) 9 113
M'Keown (1) 12 412
Mackerel (2) 8 405 15 3331
MacKernan (1) 2 258
Mackey (1) 17 1557
Mackintosh (1) 14 1552
mackintosh (1) 14 1546
Mack's (1) 15 1285
MacLir (1) 9 191
MacLir (1) 15 2262
MacLir (1) 15 2267
MacMahon (2) 3 164 12 183
M'Manus (1) 12 935
MacMurragh (1) 12 178
MacMurrough's (1) 2 393
macro (1) 9 841
macrocosm (1) 17 1014
macruiskeen (1) 14 1497
M'Swiney's (1) 6 71
MacTrigger (1) 8 749 777
Mad (2) 8 513 14 1152
mad (20) 1 581 9 1117 13 713 781
    15 662 2908 3151 16 1187 18 192 225 238
    289 677 806 845 1087 1176 1395 1532 1608

Madagascar (1) 14 345
Madagascar (1) 17 1374
Madam (14) 7 609 683 14 1405 15 392
    3534 3767 3867 4042 16 798 1437 1745
    17 1308 1823 18 716
madam (2) 15 3464 4638
Madame (4) 6 693 10 1130 13 109
    14 987
Madame (1) 6 243
madame (1) 3 254
madame (2) 6 224 237
Madcap (1) 13 270
Madden (14) 7 389 9 582 10 511
    14 190 203 210 219 423 506 1001 1126 1129 1209
    1519
Madden (1) 15 2238
MADDEN (1) 15 1788
maddening (2) 13 511 14 1519
Madden's (1) 14 1519
madding (1) 16 552
Made (5) 4 8 8 337 13 787 1199 1272
made (177) 1 12 156 200 421 547 692 2 242
    392 3 17 45 333 439 4 166 504 5 29 306
    462 469 552 7 74 109 134 259 375 421 533 569
    630 686 793 1041 8 198 329 337 761 958 9 7
    164 226 392 454 519 766 784 10 105 118 915
    916 1001 1018 1021 1202 1236 11 208 243 696
    767 880 1007 1061 1239 1258 12 371 426 815
    880 908 942 958 962 1183 1613 1626 1810 1853
    1901 13 128 229 279 494 541 542 702 868 899
    942 949 976 1027 1217 1279 14 84 144 221 292
    338 370 530 641 679 705 720 996 1195 1204
    15 476 776 873 1021 1784 2088 2398 2708 3198
    3533 3866 4455 4701 16 23 38 100 498 722 922
    1193 1306 1362 1443 1491 1570 1625 1684 1734
    1745 1760 1769 1837 17 315 404 515 558 715
    732 924 2317 18 37 154 157 176 185 251 263
    307 328 394 403 418 441 444 459 460 483 486 495
    535 536 539 586 637 670 675 814 1138 1153 1514
    1519 1570
Madeleine (1) 3 213
Madeline (1) 3 22
Mademoiselle (1) 15 716
madhouse (2) 13 659 18 996
madly (1) 18 242
madman (1) 18 1406
madness (4) 3 110 8 358 14 1436
    15 1768
madness (1) 15 4173
madonna (1) 9 839
madonna (1) 16 314
madre (1) 14 303
Madrid (3) 11 733 18 617 736
Madrid (1) 16 1432
madrileno (1) 18 720
Mady (2) 11 861 1188
maelstroms (1) 17 207
maestro (2) 3 6 10 360
Maeterlinck (2) 9 1042 1131
Mafeking (1) 9 754
Maffei (1) 4 348
Maffei (1) 15 703
MAFFEI (1) 15 707
Magdalen (2) 1 169 15 402
Magee (7) 9 412 451 780 819 820 870 951
Magee (1) 9 1150
MAGEEGLINJOHN (1) 9 900
Magennis (3) 7 782 787 788
magenta (1) 15 249

Maggot (2) 15 570 17 2136
maggot (1) 18 223
maggots (1) 6 783
maggoty (2) 6 1004 11 1263
Maggy (9) 10 261 272 278 280 285 289 292 872
    16 274
Magherafelt (1) 13 646
magic (5) 13 652 14 147 155 15 3622
    16 410
magician (1) 9 62
Maginni (4) 8 98 10 56 600 1239
Maginni (1) 15 4032
MAGINNI (6) 15 4041 4059 4079 4089 4097
    4102
MAGISTRA (1) 7 754
magistrate (2) 15 1372 17 1610
magistrates (1) 8 438
Magmagnificence (1) 15 2845
magnanimity (1) 17 2173
magnates (2) 12 1514 16 1826
magnates (1) 15 1376
magnesium (1) 15 1588
Magnetic (1) 13 990
magnetic (2) 13 984 17 1844
magnetising (1) 17 583
magnetism (3) 13 987 17 26
magnificent (3) 12 903 16 1388 18 478
magnified (1) 14 1098
magnifying (1) 17 1809
magnitude (4) 14 1099 17 1073 1119 1123
magnitudes (1) 17 1105 1143
magnopere (1) 14 710
magnum (1) 8 1153
magnum (1) 15 1487
Magnus (2) 15 1863
Magories (1) 8 860
Magrane (1) 17 1641
Maguires (1) 12 1314
Mah (1) 15 1400
Mahak (1) 15 4462
mahamahatma (1) 9 281
mahamanvantara (1) 3 144
Mahar (1) 15 4618
maharajahs (1) 15 1417
Maher (1) 12 932
Maher (1) 16 1888
Mahogany (1) 12 1273
mahogany (2) 12 618 18 724
mahone (1) 9 775
Mahony (1) 16 74
Mahound (1) 14 147
maid (11) 4 474 9 453 10 158 11 1192
    13 522 14 231 595 834 15 3086 16 739
    17 1847
maid (1) 9 423
Maiden (1) 13 858
maiden (3) 14 1551 16 135 18 1292
maiden (2) 9 617 13 947
maidenhair (4) 11 45 222 1108 1135
Maidenhead (1) 15 81
maidenhead (1) 15 359
Maiden's (1) 3 322
Maidens (1) 15 2547
maidens (1) 12 79
Maid's (1) 14 350
Maids (1) 8 602
maids (3) 12 1284 18 28 250
maids' (1) 14 562
maidservant (1) 9 791

Mail (1) 10 973
mail (4) 2 43 9 165 15 760 2806
Mailboat (1) 13 1242
mailboat (3) 1 83 575 12 854
mailcars (1) 7 16
mailed (1) 12 673
mailed (1) 15 4508
Mailer (1) 17 2324
mailvans (1) 7 1048
maimed (1) 17 1941
maimed (1) 15 582
Maimonides (4) 2 158 14 247 17 711
714
Maimonides (1) 15 1846
Maimun (2) 15 1864
Maimy (1) 13 1107
Main (1) 17 632
main (9) 5 457 8 1000 12 1915 13 331
14 560 646 16 45 1015 17 1713
Maindorée (1) 15 1827
Mainly (1) 7 97
mainly (1) 14 401
mainprise (1) 12 1139
mains (1) 17 166
mains (1) 15 4080
maintain (1) 14 11
maintained (2) 12 535 16 86
maintaining (1) 14 203
maintenance (1) 17 1624
Maior (3) 17 1047 1993 1996
Mairy (2) 11 870 13 803
Mairy (1) 5 281
Mais (2) 14 746 15 2093
maison (2) 8 586 10 984
Maister (2) 9 895 896
Majestad (1) 18 762
majestic (1) 14 402
majestic (1) 7 855
Majesty (13) 8 3 10 1195 12 294 1498
1499 1515 1516 1608 1609 1817 15 1182 1629
17 433
majesty (1) 13 396
Majesty's (3) 7 16 12 1403 15 1170
majesty's (1) 12 1009
majolicatopped (3) 17 1284 1290 1321
Major (3) 6 768 16 1441 17 2082
Major (2) 15 4612 4622
MAJOR (2) 15 4617 4751
major (8) 10 786 11 997 13 1108
14 916 17 55 801 1102 1420
Majorgeneral (1) 15 779
majority (3) 14 1259 15 780 18 1058
makar (1) 15 4462
Make (15) 1 713 4 80 173 476 5 509
6 83 8 472 9 158 10 772 11 1091 1265
13 1003 15 1103 1353 4628
Make (1) 9 808
make (154) 1 54 354 480 490 2 264 3 490
4 64 404 433 5 287 395 492 499 6 65 218
400 445 754 868 876 980 7 128 153 265 542
8 163 234 342 713 955 978 9 142 163 491 949
1068 10 106 384 597 11 445 814 940 979 981
12 312 713 756 1041 1108 1109 1131 1257 1305
1327 1387 1737 13 90 257 273 438 486 571 598
629 653 660 883 1057 14 130 132 155 359 441
458 594 621 665 1446 15 274 488 897 1088 2805
2892 2893 2990 3006 3073 3187 3780 4202 4479
4609 16 105 385 433 518 754 951 1039 1209
1224 1362 1543 1853 17 61 70 877 929 1003

2201 18 4 42 86 96 101 138 150 187 195 216
231 273 342 441 554 618 640 730 835 854 881 897
901 920 980 995 1120 1123 1195 1196 1251 1304
1364 1386 1408 1445 1492 1505 1509 1515 1539
make (3) 1 362 592 17 820
makebelieve (1) 16 1481
makee (1) 15 961
Maker (1) 14 224
maker (1) 14 293
makers (1) 12 1825
Makes (4) 4 83 5 387 6 602 13 861
Makes (1) 17 398
makes (32) 1 162 357 358 475 5 359 513
7 215 1012 9 80 228 985 996 10 1078
11 841 12 676 13 775 778 826 977 1211
15 205 235 1606 2738 3143 18 99 331 452 637
1460
makes (8) 15 32 531 1812 2297 2723 3402 3950
4298
Making (3) 3 250 6 978 8 1173
making (40) 1 194 671 6 17 98 178 7 417
8 412 555 892 10 921 985 11 618
12 252 656 1793 14 488 15 259 3504 4875
16 308 975 1188 1696 1801 17 882 1829
18 93 151 320 360 427 531 605 729 765 1002
1063 1147 1276 1491
making (1) 1 590
making (1) 15 3562
Mal (2) 14 495 499
Malachi (23) 1 41 139 518 682 712 3 302
9 305 369 492 553 1056 1099 12 177 1728
14 196 651 1163 1164 1213 1488 15 1772 4171
17 1316
Malachi (1) 14 660
Malachi (1) 15 4693
MALACHI (2) 15 4698 4702
Malachias (1) 14 1031
Malachias' (1) 14 1010
Malachi's (2) 14 233 524
maladies (1) 17 1001
maladroit (1) 2 366
malady (1) 14 39
Malaga (1) 8 24
Malahide (10) 3 243 10 155 156 157
14 683 1496 15 638 16 137 293
Malahide (1) 15 1493
Malaria (1) 12 564
Male (2) 5 196 12 547
MALE (1) 15 2018
male (23) 3 235 9 855 10 1278 12 476
1646 14 729 15 2398 2966 3177 16 936
17 534 537 777 780 890 1215 1811 1899 2072
2124 2157 2216 2281
male (8) 15 1614 1821 2017 2687 2697 2705
2727 2985
Maledicity (1) 14 771
maledictive (1) 12 1448
malefactor (1) 12 1140
malefactors (1) 17 2021
maleficent (1) 17 17
males (8) 9 255 434 11 202 14 993 1233
15 3035 17 1432 1950
malice (4) 9 1087 12 1072 14 235 833
malicious (1) 2 27
Malign (1) 14 829
malignant (1) 17 1764
malignant (1) 15 4220
maligned (1) 9 244
malingering (1) 17 2185

Mall (2) 10 101 17 983
Mallarmé (2) 9 109 112
mallet (1) 3 18
Mallon (1) 16 1192
Mallow (1) 18 357
Malone (2) 17 545 547
Maloney's (1) 16 166
Malora (1) 12 563
malorum (1) 16 175
Malt (1) 3 86
malt (2) 9 746 15 2418
malt (1) 14 406
Malta (1) 18 795
Malthusiasts (1) 14 1415
maltjobber (1) 9 742
Mamma (5) 6 862 13 1190 15 281 3851
mamma (2) 6 863 15 3513
mammal (1) 15 2356
mammamufflered (1) 15 3333
mammary (1) 17 1443
mamma's (1) 15 202
Mammoth (1) 15 1329
mammoth (2) 3 207 14 1091
mammy (1) 14 1521
Mamy (2) 14 1330 18 1502
MAN (2) 7 781 1054
Man (11) 6 270 279 7 151 9 1030
12 185 186 14 1551 15 1974 2552 2554
Man (2) 13 1060 17 1645
Man (1) 15 2179
MAN (3) 15 1560 3110 4779
man (384) 1 61 468 675 680 687 695 714
2 252 266 3 46 188 242 254 322 328 331 367
478 483 4 89 127 5 100 106 153 156 175 207
250 6 39 74 180 202 229 303 329 335 341 344
439 561 599 708 752 772 809 934 983 7 81 117
196 200 293 706 788 818 852 853 8 5 121 294
335 343 420 446 504 574 656 658 659 662 663 677
806 825 922 934 976 982 1023 1067 1102 1156
9 62 165 181 228 237 310 402 423 432 449 524
768 788 815 830 836 838 897 952 1020 1032 1039
1040 1052 1073 1203 10 25 36 44 48 129 132
199 200 604 685 741 883 890 915 987 1046 1147
1264 11 85 169 301 448 536 584 695 756 1062
1131 1192 12 55 127 271 396 596 755 880 881
972 976 980 981 995 1104 1110 1125 1497 1543
1546 1556 1586 1604 1654 1663 13 8 207 210
223 249 301 306 407 433 439 629 657 672 694 859
873 874 914 992 994 1034 1130 1138 1223 1232
14 71 72 73 80 85 96 100 101 108 111 118 121
134 181 183 237 245 260 267 361 364 396 451 479
692 714 814 861 888 895 1000 1008 1038 1179 1227
1345 1374 1433 1448 1524 1539 15 306 385 688
739 775 777 797 842 928 976 977 980 1093 1100
1153 1395 1464 1498 1530 1534 1540 1561 1715
1737 1753 1799 1800 2027 2259 2522 2545 2550
2554 2564 2962 3084 3118 3137 3138 3174 3198
3716 3892 4382 4402 4808 16 44 70 141 160 194
201 202 224 260 288 292 462 537 540 576 601 647
686 730 732 739 768 814 832 836 1058 1137 1179
1208 1302 1328 1342 1381 1440 1476 1505 1514
1544 1568 1719 1724 1794 1891 17 30 110 111
113 117 331 613 1350 1829 1836 1889 1941
18 11 30 102 104 118 210 224 231 235 271 323
370 385 386 412 474 482 509 542 590 684 715 722
769 888 911 976 988 1056 1062 1142 1147 1158
1198 1228 1245 1265 1274 1310 1345 1396 1401
1404 1429 1501
man (4) 6 730 12 1801 14 650 16 648

man (6) 15 38 1558 1565 2035 4360 4782
man-o'-war (1) 13 56
manacles (1) 15 2666
manage (3) 1 551 4 518 11 973
managed (3) 16 528 1148 18 379
management (1) 16 861
manager (3) 10 746 12 364 18 512
managers (1) 15 1830
managing (1) 16 1273
managing (2) 15 1830 4356
Mananaan (1) 3 57
Mananaan (2) 9 190 191
Mananaun (1) 14 1029
Mananaun (1) 15 2262
MANANAUN (1) 15 2267
Manchester (1) 12 1514
manchild (3) 14 267 272 17 2317
mandarin's (1) 15 2249
mandement (1) 14 137
mandoline (1) 17 664
mandolines (1) 18 986
mane (2) 3 110 12 1772
mane (1) 15 3975
maneater (1) 15 712
maneaters (1) 16 470
Manfield's (1) 15 2814
manflower (1) 5 264
manfully (1) 14 1313
Mangan's (2) 10 534 1123
manger (2) 8 366 14 602
mangiD (1) 7 206
mangle (1) 16 275
mangled (1) 13 1054
mangling (1) 17 2039
mango (1) 12 1537
mango (1) 15 320
mangongwheeltracktrolleyglarejugger-
  naut (1) 15 643–644
Mangy (1) 12 485
mangy (4) 12 120 1231 18 436 452
manhandle (1) 15 4757
manhole (1) 10 494
manhole (1) 15 1263
manholes (1) 10 498
manhood (2) 13 1101 16 1388
manifest (1) 14 45
manifestation (1) 2 381
manifesting (1) 16 1670
manifestly (1) 16 1687
maninthestreet (1) 15 4347
manipulated (1) 17 735
Mankind (1) 15 1356
mankind (3) 12 1249 14 83 364
manless (1) 11 1012
manly (5) 8 935 12 911 13 210 14 1046 16 690
Manna (1) 8 79
manned (1) 14 642
Manner (1) 9 1212
manner (23) 1 54 2 75 7 895 9 468 12 48 287 685 14 163 201 237 262 809 972 1256 15 1071 16 739 841 1679 17 21 358 1329 1553 18 195
manner (1) 7 848
manners (10) 9 149 11 92 14 1213 15 2028 4586 17 920 1251 18 320 927 1368
Manningham's (1) 9 633
Manning's (1) 8 426
mano (2) 5 227 15 469

manoeuvre (1) 16 930
manoeuvring (1) 16 1799
Manola (1) 18 441
Manorhamilton (1) 15 3006
Man's (2) 6 479 17 1944
man's (29) 1 421 2 193 241 3 152 335 4 352 6 573 670 7 261 806 8 509 9 87 812 10 172 11 778 13 565 566 14 1123 1342 1414 15 853 1278 2550 3132 16 676 718 1355 1890 17 120
man's (2) 14 650 17 1353
man's (2) 15 386 2033
mans (3) 15 3904 18 28 484
Manse (1) 14 455
manservant (1) 9 791
manshape (1) 3 413
Mansion (1) 8 186
mansion (2) 10 416 16 137
mansion (1) 14 405
mansions (1) 14 290
manslaughter (1) 17 2189
Mansmell (1) 13 1036
Mantailored (1) 8 164
Mantamer (1) 15 3062
mantel (1) 17 1528
mantelpiece (6) 2 265 7 359 13 462 1292 17 1323 1334
mantelpiece (1) 15 2053
mantelshelf (1) 7 433
mantilla (1) 10 31
mantillas (1) 18 633
mantle (2) 5 235 16 1498
mantle (6) 15 1026 1442 1477 1490 2282 2479
mantles (1) 7 327
mantrap (1) 15 93
manu (1) 15 3546
manual (4) 15 1688 4197 16 813 17 1188
Manufacture (1) 15 1708
manufacture (1) 15 1806
Manufactured (1) 17 600
manufactured (1) 15 1393
manufacturer (3) 8 3 17 1176 2105
manufacturers (1) 15 1431
manufacturing (1) 8 1157
Manuo (1) 12 804
manure (2) 4 477 15 3212
manures (1) 17 1559
Manus (1) 12 1439
manuscript (1) 2 296
Manx (2) 7 150 15 3129
Many (6) 2 394 6 298 573 13 10 15 1799 3026
Many (2) 15 1745 1902
many (65) 2 196 389 390 394 3 340 5 10 6 227 516 538 644 797 960 8 212 380 825 885 9 539 1044 1097 10 140 599 11 558 12 176 297 552 595 924 1104 1207 1658 1774 1826 13 296 375 512 781 819 1017 14 116 124 139 446 563 564 673 1057 1265 1429 15 3054 3176 16 1355 1417 1550 17 24 67 466 991 1074 1624 18 719 775 1216 1334 1582
many (4) 9 32 415 14 406 16 1253
many (3) 15 1566 1845 4672
map (3) 16 627 17 1913 18 378
Mapas (1) 12 1455
Maple (1) 12 1273
M'appari (3) 11 587 594 16 1757
mapped (1) 5 440

maps (1) 17 1970
maraschino (1) 11 517
Marathon (2) 7 254 255
marauders (1) 16 124
Marble (1) 16 1451
marble (3) 5 458 12 1252 17 1335
marble (1) 7 770
marble (1) 15 1129
marbles (2) 5 233 236
marcato (1) 9 1179
Marcella (1) 16 850
Marcello (1) 15 2087
Marcellus (1) 1 653
March (6) 6 374 803 7 652 12 573 14 1458 17 1336
March (1) 12 1828
march (8) 4 85 11 1246 12 1190 15 3500 18 401 1219
march (3) 15 49 1426 1436
marchand (1) 14 776
Marche (2) 18 613 858
marched (2) 3 205 8 123
marches (1) 14 139
marches (1) 15 513
marching (8) 3 24 6 509 8 363 406 411 478 13 1154 18 689
marching (1) 15 2240
marchpane (1) 9 627
Marcus (2) 10 508 15 571
Mare (1) 14 1516
mare (9) 9 622 10 567 11 764 766 885 12 1221 14 1083 1129 1162
mare (2) 3 22 24
mare (1) 15 3727
mare's (2) 11 525 15 775
mares (1) 12 104
marfeast (1) 17 1942
Margaret (1) 9 646
margarine (1) 6 397
Margate (4) 8 1065 16 519 520 18 1346
marge (2) 8 42
margerain (1) 14 331
margin (1) 17 1488
marginal (2) 17 1381 1392
Marha (1) 12 560
Maria (7) 12 1383 15 203 17 1909 18 275 306 757 1465
Maria (1) 10 585
Maria (1) 15 1509
Marie (6) 10 380 495 1141 1220 18 872
mariée (1) 14 1453
maries (1) 3 297
Marina (2) 9 406 421
mariner (5) 9 1211 11 1026 13 64 16 844 1669
mariner's (2) 16 423 675
mariners (2) 3 157 12 88
Mario (3) 7 53 54 55
Mario (1) 15 2485
Marion (27) 4 244 245 311 444 5 154 6 693 10 371 11 496 500 502 12 227 1006 1710 13 843 14 266 15 306 325 345 16 798 1437 1745 17 56 365 411 1178 1984 18 256
MARION (7) 15 305 318 327 346 350 3768 3777
Marionette (1) 15 540
marionette (1) 15 3882
MARION'S (1) 15 3811
marital (2) 14 934 1259

Maritana (2) 18 1293 1297
Maritana (1) 16 493
Marius (1) 17 1110
Mark (7) 2 346 5 73 12 1476 14 292 1379 15 209 3922
mark (15) 4 331 5 178 7 631 804 10 574 12 1530 1565 14 413 985 15 2316 16 1345 17 604 18 569 1097 1512
marked (15) 8 1155 13 912 14 1014 15 550 1153 1779 1789 4443 16 330 775 1010 17 981 1776 1879 18 531
marked (3) 15 1553 1935 4455
Market (1) 17 1726
market (9) 9 394 14 603 16 993 1105 17 430 486 1985 18 545 1589
marketnet (2) 8 364 10 136
markets (3) 12 136 1651 18 1499
marking (1) 16 718
Mark's (1) 6 183
Marks (1) 17 577
marks (4) 4 195 17 359 366 371
marks (1) 15 4328
marksmanship (1) 16 407
Marks's (2) 11 1261 1274
Marlborough (2) 7 940 16 166
marmalade (1) 1 170
maroon (2) 17 507 1372
marquee (2) 15 3843 3855
MARQUESS (1) 7 552
marquess (1) 17 1656
Marriage (1) 6 945
marriage (15) 7 98 11 874 13 195 14 1276 15 433 1055 1699 3028 3264 3277 17 2120 2274 18 678 758
marriageable (2) 9 830 13 963
marriages (3) 9 1052 12 223 14 306
Married (6) 11 173 180 13 1152 15 2755 3622 3632
married (49) 3 65 6 323 831 8 150 158 9 674 1005 1059 11 169 523 12 398 503 1064 13 197 657 709 873 14 1551 15 94 385 776 1093 2228 3209 3252 3620 3634 3833 16 132 134 1386 1550 18 40 120 167 217 410 624 720 774 821 826 843 896 1152 1254 1299 1326 1389
married (1) 16 1887
marries (2) 9 959 12 1052
marrow (1) 16 1633
Marrowbone (1) 18 1384
marrowbones (1) 16 1303
marrows (1) 12 95
Marry (2) 9 193 13 978
marry (7) 6 548 704 13 1208 15 3701 18 232 238 1158
marry (1) 9 1151
marrying (3) 13 837 18 103 412
Mars (3) 12 359 15 3657 17 1114
mars (1) 9 854
marsala (1) 18 538
Marsh (1) 15 3084
MARSH (1) 15 3099
marsh (2) 11 1012 12 1257
Marshal (1) 12 183
marshal (2) 10 1007 1049
marshal (2) 15 1412 1438
Marshall's (1) 16 1243
marshal's (1) 8 505
marshes (1) 17 227

marshlands (1) 15 4666
Marsh's (1) 3 107
Martello (2) 1 542 13 44
Martha (19) 5 257 289 6 743 7 53 11 27 229 715 742 835 897 12 1709 13 782 806 1214 14 1101 15 2981 17 1798 1842 2252
Martha (6) 7 58 11 713 735 16 1753 1756
MARTHA (2) 15 751 764
martha (1) 11 738
Martha's (1) 5 266
Martian (1) 17 1095
Martin (101) 5 331 6 1 8 34 73 86 95 103 104 109 113 133 141 144 146 151 187 192 219 250 259 277 282 286 289 295 305 325 334 336 339 342 343 367 369 403 415 420 456 473 490 526 529 537 564 716 718 735 737 1006 1020 1024 1028 1029 7 165 10 956 959 964 967 973 975 978 983 986 992 999 1014 1023 1028 1032 1038 12 237 411 761 762 1486 1587 1588 1621 1625 1635 1639 1644 1665 1668 1669 1673 1694 1758 1764 1767 1771 1797 1806 1890 13 417 16 504 17 1238 18 1055 1266
Martin (2) 6 147 16 1257
Martin (2) 15 1140 3854
MARTIN (1) 15 3862
martinet (1) 15 3025
Martin's (1) 6 354
Martyn (1) 9 307
Martyn's (1) 9 307
martyr (3) 8 12 12 609 17 1116
martyrs (2) 11 1101 12 1689
marvel (2) 14 154 171
marvellous (5) 12 714 14 138 177 260 1306
marvellously (1) 14 146
Marx (1) 12 1804
Mary (41) 1 375 5 289 431 6 219 7 52 8 451 454 9 646 675 10 65 163 165 280 372 12 1494 1504 1709 1720 13 8 289 378 639 805 14 76 189 334 1329 1573 15 290 861 2578 2981 4718 17 142 538 952 18 56 136 952 1385
Mary (2) 1 382 13 312
Mary (1) 15 862
MARY (5) 15 866 872 879 884 891
marybeads (1) 3 387
Maryborough (1) 18 358
Mary's (5) 10 408 433 929 14 703 17 757
Marys (1) 18 1387
masculine (5) 17 289 668 2218 2222 2294
masculinely (1) 15 1466
Masetto (1) 18 1507
mashed (4) 8 699 11 553 608
mashtub (1) 12 678
mashtub (1) 15 4149
mask (2) 9 326 887
masked (3) 1 173 2 274 15 1690
masked (2) 15 2514 4082
masks (2) 5 353 13 1191
masks (1) 15 424
Masoch (1) 10 592
Mason (2) 6 662 15 1945
mason (2) 5 75 8 973
mason (1) 15 4455
masonic (2) 15 450 4298
masonry (2) 2 9 3 249
masonry (1) 15 4245
masquerading (1) 15 822

Mass (1) 13 1122
Mass (1) 16 1738
mass (24) 1 108 653 5 342 404 422 6 499 603 7 353 9 896 10 261 1225 11 299 12 283 805 1290 1867 15 2344 17 1204 1433 18 141 213 753 757 862
mass (2) 15 2149 4695
Massa (2) 12 1521 14 1557
Massachusetts (1) 15 4453
Massage (1) 5 502
massage (1) 5 505
Massboy (1) 11 612
massboy (2) 5 418 448
masse (1) 12 1266
Massed (1) 15 4630
massed (1) 2 369
Masses (1) 5 436
masses (3) 14 1385 17 260 18 5
masseurs (1) 15 1428
Massey (1) 11 98
massgoing (1) 18 1503
masshouse (1) 17 757
massive (1) 17 1528
massive (1) 15 2742
Massor (1) 17 754
masspriest (1) 14 99
massproduct (1) 17 369
masstime (1) 11 1041
mast (1) 3 148
Master (36) 8 882 10 46 52 534 1122 1137 1140 1145 1150 1154 1265 13 40 41 43 45 49 54 61 346 607 14 334 337 349 350 355 410 417 423 424 15 3062 17 1494 1635 18 488 580
Master (2) 9 583 12 431
Master (6) 15 3326 3327 3328
master (27) 1 637 2 44 3 81 157 295 354 5 289 7 735 8 98 227 448 973 9 66 12 203 1115 1116 1343 1605 13 672 14 1303 15 760 2759 4569 16 916 1538 1860
master (1) 17 819
master (5) 15 1177 1437 2724 2855 4956
Mastering (1) 10 638
Masterly (1) 10 792
mastermystic (1) 7 784
Masterpiece (1) 18 1238
Masterpiece (1) 10 586
masterpiece (2) 4 370 14 976
masterpieces (1) 17 1601
master's (2) 2 45 15 1247
Masters (1) 10 1133
masters (9) 1 638 7 911 9 412 12 1385 1444 1599 1602 1614 15 3174
Masterstroke (1) 4 502
masterstroke (1) 8 279
masterstroke (1) 4 514
Masterstrokes (1) 15 817
mastery (2) 12 162 14 193
Mastiansky (5) 4 205 6 770 17 58 2134 18 417
Mastiansky (3) 15 1904 3223 4357
MASTIANSKY (1) 15 1906
masticate (1) 14 1287
mastiff (1) 15 673
Mastino (1) 16 888
mastodon (1) 14 1091
mastodontic (1) 12 1836
masts (2) 12 1304 14 642
masts (1) 15 1398

masturbated (1) 9 1152
Mat (8) 6 697 1008 1009 11 725 13 1091 1106 15 3162 18 1313
mat (1) 18 226
matador (1) 18 626
match (18) 5 103 7 466 764 8 768 10 1135 12 645 940 1322 13 15 158 716 15 602 1061 3626 17 105 131 18 1089 1422
match (3) 15 3622 3628 3630
Matcham (2) 8 278 11 903
Matcham (1) 4 513
Matcham's (1) 15 817
Matcham's (1) 4 502
matchbox (2) 6 952 7 762
matched (1) 13 976
matches (5) 7 223 463 11 620 13 1140 17 1305
matches (1) 15 3597
matchless (1) 12 538
mate (2) 16 683 920
Mater (6) 1 205 8 430 14 809 1474 17 1254 18 380
Mater (4) 5 397 6 375 16 1139 1744
Material (1) 7 557
material (3) 9 433 17 2062 2206
maternal (3) 14 1284 16 1570 17 1355
Maternity (2) 14 1301 17 968
maternity (2) 14 45 1445
mates (1) 6 912
matey (1) 14 1502
mathering (1) 18 520
Mathew (2) 6 320 11 763
matin (1) 3 210
matinée (1) 13 417
matinée (1) 7 575
matresfamiliarum (1) 14 708
matriculated (1) 14 556
matriculation (1) 17 553
matrimonial (9) 16 1399 1482 17 910 1336 1338 1339 1344 1347 2197
matrimonially (1) 17 2197
matrimony (2) 17 1640 2196
matris (2) 2 165 9 843
matrix (1) 14 969
matron (2) 14 322 886
matronly (1) 13 1234
matrons (1) 15 2449
matted (1) 15 2049
Matter (1) 15 4873
matter (63) 1 207 2 195 321 323 4 190 6 981 7 305 745 8 100 12 372 760 832 1118 1144 1644 13 615 1059 14 205 301 574 681 1174 15 411 711 2087 2345 3033 3615 16 32 178 222 224 411 474 492 527 541 644 732 746 752 779 896 1037 1207 1366 1494 1514 1518 1540 1650 1834 1863 17 1137 2226 18 18 142 710 1020 1032 1149 1174 1408
mattered (2) 13 428 673
matters (8) 5 77 9 128 13 12 14 8 621 16 305 1362 1365
Matterson's (1) 15 2896
Matthew (7) 1 173 9 821 17 57 467 1253 1336 2136
Matthew (1) 15 2514
mattress (5) 14 1498 15 2580 17 2041 2116
maturation (1) 14 43
mature (5) 9 1020 16 1643 17 1432 2037 2236

maturer (2) 14 770 15 844
maturing (1) 15 1813
maturity (4) 17 1006 1355 1356 1964
matutinal (4) 17 40 282 1265 2038
Maud (5) 3 233 5 70 12 1273 13 857 17 1779
maudlin (1) 9 357
maugre (1) 14 264
Maul (1) 8 447
maul (1) 8 728
mauling (2) 12 705 16 1633
mauls (1) 15 673
maun (1) 14 1538
Maunder (1) 11 1199
Maundy (1) 15 1569
Maureen (1) 12 688
Maurice (1) 11 1124
Maurice (1) 15 1611
mausoleum (1) 6 534
mauve (6) 6 326 7 721 13 176 14 1105 15 2740 17 1680
mauve (6) 15 2040 2278 2406 2476 4285 4965
mavourneen's (1) 12 59
mavrone (1) 9 564
maw (1) 15 30
Mawkish (1) 8 907
mawkish (1) 8 851
maxillary (1) 14 965
maxim (3) 6 473 7 556 13 46
maxime (1) 9 770
Maximilian (1) 7 541
Maximum (1) 5 532
Maximum (1) 15 3976
maximum (5) 17 456 457 582 583 1659
Maximum II (1) 16 1289
Maxwell (2) 10 59 191
May (32) 2 324 3 441 7 632 8 190 218 589 888 9 1056 10 336 1138 12 1276 1412 13 127 978 14 816 1362 1563 15 1617 3791 4068 4173 4525 17 95 1376 1404 1449 18 80 140 229 781 1299
May (1) 17 1782
may (60) 3 48 5 171 444 7 92 885 936 8 163 190 771 1160 9 173 370 383 384 450 782 843 844 884 10 749 11 255 257 12 787 861 918 1430 1646 14 19 747 936 1058 1121 1162 1166 1229 1277 1322 1325 1339 1346 1490 15 830 1171 1191 1484 1894 2088 2419 2438 2798 3607 4066 16 158 353 897 1160 17 2003 18 667 1427
Māyā (1) 12 358
Maybe (5) 7 129 9 665 11 985 12 332 13 967
maybe (5) 1 399 5 93 6 607 18 21 1161
Maybrick (1) 18 234
Mayers (1) 18 1294
Mayhap (1) 13 104
mayhap (2) 13 439 14 902
mayhem (1) 17 2185
Maynooth (4) 9 1008 12 1403 1459 15 2533
Mayonnaise (1) 8 354
mayonnaise (1) 15 3753
Mayor (2) 17 2136 18 428
Mayor (1) 15 1378
Mayor (1) 15 1381
mayor (11) 7 106 8 160 709 10 537 1010 1276 13 258 892 15 1008 1364 17 444
mayor (2) 15 1414 1415

mayoral (2) 15 1378 1382
mayoralty (1) 12 823
mayoress (1) 10 1277
mayors (1) 15 1416
maypoles (1) 15 1398
May's (1) 4 526
maze (2) 3 154 6 876
mazer (1) 14 282
mazurka (1) 7 450
Mazzoth (1) 15 1624
mazzoth (1) 5 358
m'baad (1) 17 729
McCann (1) 2 256
MCMIV (1) 17 99
MCoys (1) 18 1267
MDCCXI (1) 17 1400
Me (19) 3 410 6 76 8 8 917 9 572 820 951 11 645 12 1040 14 1466 1496 15 1075 1077 2953 3363 3502 4278
Me (1) 13 927
me (893) 1 47 89 136 137 161 162 171 180 183 210 213 220 274 276 279 419 469 480 481 503 548 567 614 625 629 637 640 641 2 20 30 71 98 99 131 169 200 234 247 268 278 289 294 307 340 376 430 433 3 31 35 39 48 71 74 90 115 133 163 167 182 219 228 250 256 260 279 282 295 306 309 325 328 356 365 367 413 414 424 434 435 436 452 490 4 29 95 210 241 251 398 401 523 5 55 82 96 119 178 185 191 242 245 247 248 251 258 269 373 426 455 494 6 68 77 94 104 246 299 349 353 358 375 381 382 448 483 545 609 613 646 743 770 819 879 883 888 904 1004 1012 1016 7 122 207 282 398 404 431 531 616 642 645 782 789 790 792 842 883 998 1035 1056 1072 8 174 217 230 250 251 285 306 325 328 329 350 353 374 405 430 432 497 538 613 633 647 683 698 733 735 740 760 787 800 803 839 879 880 899 904 905 907 909 910 915 916 917 961 1023 1042 1058 1098 1126 1174 1175 1178 9 55 82 113 163 221 256 322 332 352 357 372 483 539 576 601 614 671 673 719 740 820 827 877 919 1078 1079 1084 1113 1154 1202 1208 1217 10 51 329 386 416 418 439 559 670 680 683 745 747 769 782 825 846 847 865 876 934 937 938 950 967 1138 1170 11 127 138 152 207 234 252 257 342 351 384 445 446 487 541 658 732 734 742 754 755 868 869 871 888 891 974 995 1256 1259 1266 1267 12 15 141 211 400 460 504 677 678 698 762 774 778 786 792 795 798 839 1002 1109 1149 1225 1437 1555 1566 1610 1618 1659 1788 1809 13 458 780 788 797 814 823 829 833 836 845 859 872 875 890 900 925 939 949 963 971 1006 1008 1025 1039 1041 1046 1048 1057 1102 1145 1199 1202 1207 1209 1219 1229 1239 1253 1272 1279 1282 1284 14 292 368 370 371 372 373 377 379 547 622 751 759 772 774 783 787 789 806 814 816 1018 1021 1024 1027 1055 1162 1168 1170 1443 1466 1468 1470 1478 1481 1496 1515 1521 1524 1525 1555 1572 15 55 93 205 211 277 306 385 398 399 429 461 478 493 554 573 638 660 729 739 766 775 880 885 886 998 1016 1021 1022 1028 1045 1054 1060 1061 1064 1065 1068 1069 1071 1082 1099 1108 1115 1190 1192 1235 1263 1321 1485 1673 1677 1771 1819 1896 1936 1962 2009 2201 2206 2207 2220 2222 2231 2323 2343 2427 2429 2498 2523 2526 2681 2739 2764 2768 2769 2807 2868 2893 2911 2914 2922 2934 2935 2951 3009 3049 3052 3053 3075 3151 3191 3243 3245 3263 3264 3357 3359 3395 3424 3427 3476 3477 3481 3509 3534 3538 3557 3559 3572 3584 3601 3680

melting (5) 1 333 5 432 568 14 759 15 4206

mem (1) 17 739

Member (3) 7 87 8 443 17 1401

member (7) 9 885 12 211 437 861 17 858 2143 18 1186

member's (1) 12 868

members (8) 10 448 12 634 865 924 14 947 16 1199 17 1235 2150

members (2) 15 1567

membrane (1) 11 540

memento (1) 18 866

mementos (1) 15 876

memetipso (1) 14 366

MEMORABLE (1) 7 358

Memorable (1) 16 1104

memorable (1) 14 959

memorial (2) 6 191 550

Memoriam (1) 17 1462

Memories (1) 1 265

memories (5) 14 1345 16 1308 17 503 864 875

Memory (1) 15 3215

memory (35) 1 215 265 650 2 7 8 273 4 137 6 457 8 178 899 9 208 245 246 249 427 10 416 11 87 627 12 519 644 13 438 14 706 988 1074 1346 1360 15 1358 1662 1783 2737 3520 4187 4372 16 754 17 1916

memory (1) 15 902

memory's (1) 13 1142

Men (4) 6 758 8 653 9 1207 10 727

men (130) 1 62 669 2 158 364 3 215 228 234 317 435 468 5 384 6 546 624 625 789 833 7 308 715 722 8 130 445 511 653 670 935 1120 9 254 356 359 430 453 675 1045 1191 10 94 105 144 768 888 894 1166 11 56 79 311 416 992 1008 1140 1276 12 69 481 655 971 1130 1189 1264 1475 1482 1779 1891 13 207 236 663 668 701 748 794 837 923 1206 14 151 193 289 442 488 537 640 901 15 762 780 788 1754 3257 3791 4183 4193 4402 4461 4595 4853 16 560 751 796 1325 1544 1551 1813 17 514 1838 1946 18 51 237 369 396 420 472 583 598 632 688 817 853 886 1057 1108 1219 1236 1284 1346 1348 1356 1380 1388 1520

men (1) 11 617

men (3) 15 5 50 1447

menace (4) 1 662 3 116 14 31 326

menaced (1) 1 655

menagerer (1) 15 325

mend (3) 5 77 18 714 1015

mendacious (1) 17 687

mendancers (1) 15 3474

mended (1) 18 901

Mendelssohn (5) 12 1804 16 1755 17 712 713 722

Mendelssohn (1) 15 1847

Mendes (1) 15 1755

Mendicancy (1) 17 1938

mendicancy (1) 15 1689

mending (1) 14 699

Mendoza (1) 17 723

Menelaus (2) 2 391 7 537

Menelaus' (1) 9 622

menfriends (1) 15 3175

menial (1) 17 1632

menopause (2) 14 971 17 1000

Men's (1) 10 341

men's (12) 2 318 6 127 8 671 9 1168 11 974 13 273 282 14 100 15 596 16 309 561 17 1817

men's (1) 15 2924

mens (3) 18 550 557 1265

mensa (1) 9 716

menstruate (1) 13 783

menstruation (1) 17 999

ment (1) 7 167

mental (13) 5 474 7 623 16 788 813 17 39 384 515 674 850 2157 2160 2285

mentality (2) 7 556 17 1004

mentally (2) 15 3030 16 1845

menthol (1) 13 328

mention (15) 7 734 9 439 673 679 11 540 12 826 13 1047 14 1472 15 2246 16 159 240 867 17 2251 2256 18 387

MENTIONED (1) 7 552

mentioned (16) 9 744 14 382 15 796 854 1758 2827 16 76 107 1338 1756 17 687 716 718 721 1613 1915

mentions (2) 9 718 720

mentis (1) 12 1044

Menton (18) 6 568 690 695 704 715 1007 1010 1019 1021 1025 10 937 1229 15 731 1230 1943 17 1240 2134 18 38

Menton (1) 16 1257

Menton (2) 15 1141 4336

Menton's (6) 6 707 8 262 321 10 779 1028 12 267

Mentor (1) 15 1943

Mentre (1) 7 719

menu (1) 8 447

mer (1) 15 2519

mer (1) 11 264

Mercadante (3) 5 403 11 975 12 1804

Mercadante's (1) 16 1737

Mercalli's (1) 12 1860

mercantile (1) 17 1899

Mercator's (1) 17 186

mercenary (1) 17 1852

mercerised (1) 12 1281

Mercer's (3) 8 1163 10 1269 13 1167

mercers (1) 8 620

mercers (1) 15 1431

merchandise (1) 7 848

merchant (8) 2 359 7 143 12 34 14 373 15 572 16 738 17 1628 2171

merchants (3) 2 350 12 1248 17 1558

Merchants' (4) 10 315 520 17 600 2049

Merci (2) 14 1491 15 220

merci (1) 15 122

Merciable's (1) 14 189

mercies (1) 13 790

Merciful (2) 14 820 15 1951

merciful (4) 11 680 12 335 13 304 18 134

merciful (1) 15 2687

merciless (1) 2 149

mercilessly (1) 13 587

Mercurial (3) 1 518 15 4171 17 1095

mercurialised (1) 15 748

MERCURY (1) 15 749

mercury (1) 15 213

Mercury's (1) 1 601

Mercy (2) 12 1853 14 1139

mercy (17) 6 163 346 8 1161 11 679 1206 12 125 1607 13 316 748 14 879 15 1171 1481 4233 4238 16 94 17 487 18 960

mercy' (1) 11 127

Mercy's (1) 14 506

merde (1) 15 3940

mère (2) 12 1653 14 1453

Mere (1) 11 970

mere (5) 12 787 13 223 14 526 899 18 1405

Meredith (2) 9 994 14 1486

Meredith (1) 15 3327

merely (11) 9 868 14 56 16 222 564 640 734 1066 1153 1360 1471 1885

Meretricious (1) 15 2332

merge (1) 17 769

merging (1) 1 246

meridian (1) 17 2304

meridional (1) 17 1996

merit (2) 16 911 17 648

merited (1) 16 545

merlins (1) 15 4668

mermaid (4) 11 300 1235 1236

mermaid's (1) 11 222

mermaids (1) 11 300

mermaids' (1) 16 1631

merrily (2) 13 263 381

merriment (1) 12 650

merriment (2) 15 2669 4911

Merrion (6) 10 1104 1108 1265 11 493 14 491 1579

Merry (2) 9 758 806

merry (13) 8 754 9 873 986 10 324 12 1620 13 17 14 132 341 1040 15 2739 4563 4638 16 1626

merry (2) 1 300 304

merry (2) 15 3773 3857

merryandrew (1) 14 534

merrying (1) 1 306

Mersey (1) 15 1183

Mervyn (1) 6 609

Mervyn (1) 15 4551

MERVYN (5) 15 1057 1080 1087 1097 1113

mes (2) 7 507 14 1449

Mesdames (1) 15 4355

Meseems (1) 14 172

meshes (1) 7 1068

Meshuggah (2) 8 314 15 1625

mesial (1) 9 615

Mesias (4) 6 831 11 881 15 1302 17 2171

Mesias (1) 15 1908

MESIAS (1) 15 1910

mesmerised (1) 14 1175

mess (3) 5 925 9 576 892 14 541 16 275

mess (1) 15 934

message (6) 8 933 9 556 12 357 13 1257 16 490 17 1677

message (1) 15 1502

Messages (1) 12 1881

messages (2) 15 3030 3034

Messenger (2) 5 545 7 762

Messenger (1) 15 1125

messenger (3) 1 400 406 12 244

messengerboy (1) 18 340

messengers (2) 12 1605 1608

Messer (1) 9 374

Messiah (5) 12 1642 1647 15 1834 1907 2601

Messiah (1) 8 1163

Messiah (1) 15 1954

milks (1) 15 2457
Milksop (1) 14 663
milkwhite (2) 4 34 12 1772
milkwhite (1) 15 1444
milkwoman (1) 1 498
milky (3) 10 570 13 854 17 1044
mill (2) 9 748 16 706
mille (1) 14 746
milled (1) 17 981
millennium (1) 14 234
Miller (2) 8 1045 12 234
Miller (1) 7 582
Millevoye (1) 3 233
Millicent (6) 14 1101 17 362 829 860 1775 1857
milligramme (1) 14 1397
milliner (1) 10 1131
millingtary (1) 14 1462
million (11) 5 305 307 311 9 629 15 1302 2401 16 990 1035 17 165 171 1690
millionaire (1) 3 6
MILLIONAIRESS (1) 15 1461
millions (15) 5 310 326 10 145 149 12 1240 1256 13 1017 15 722 16 990 17 197 1062 1079 18 1115
millstones (1) 12 1719
millwheels (1) 17 221
millwrights (1) 15 1427
Milly (37) 4 250 251 293 409 412 444 6 87 121 445 8 163 200 206 760 874 11 843 1066 13 785 798 918 1187 14 371 15 540 17 362 861 903 929 1775 1794 1857 18 159 291 571 717 1004 1025 1257 1326
Milly (1) 4 287
Milly (1) 15 3167
MILLY (1) 15 3170
Milly's (3) 4 284 8 171 1097
Millys (3) 18 850 1167 1489
mimber (1) 12 825
mimic (1) 14 732
mimicking (1) 15 571
mimicry (1) 14 736
Mimosa (1) 12 1274
Mina (17) 8 277 479 11 517 661 759 760 774 816 818 954 1167 1176 1177 14 1337 17 2054 18 159
Mina (3) 15 3730 4345 4691
MINA (1) 15 3798
Minagold (1) 11 48
minagold (1) 11 1213
minarets (1) 5 550
Minbad (1) 17 2324
mince (2) 2 331 10 549
minced (1) 8 750
mincepies (1) 14 1478
minches (1) 17 219
Mincing (2) 17 1981 2076
mincing (3) 10 714 15 3119 18 469
mincingly (1) 15 3914
Mincius (1) 9 1124
Mind (10) 3 291 8 294 10 402 872 1020 11 73 12 1559 15 177 3502 16 848
Mind (1) 12 362
mind (74) 2 15 43 4 6 142 428 6 162 571 753 872 1031 7 564 649 824 8 394 425 887 9 28 382 667 1016 10 48 175 866 936 1077 11 243 770 771 914 12 370 1120 1565 13 77 544 776 846 882 900 1044 14 253 319 611 641 866 880 15 364 644 2398 3075 3558

3826 16 4 53 1183 1211 1222 1272 1325 1471 1586 1739 1797 1808 17 658 1408 18 94 114 193 516 1146 1251 1352 1515
minded (1) 14 266
mindful (1) 10 1203
minding (3) 7 645 12 1101 16 117
mind's (5) 2 72 8 1127 9 1016 14 10 16 269
minds (8) 8 948 9 52 10 1061 12 9 13 1154 14 864 16 1532 1580
Mine (7) 2 170 232 4 139 6 862 12 1598 1613 13 1201
mine (39) 1 631 2 85 3 105 263 328 394 414 6 830 1012 7 530 8 219 554 9 483 580 10 431 11 376 12 1466 13 670 14 1065 15 968 2621 2775 2792 2965 3505 3696 4874 16 471 897 1694 18 116 329 638 728 800 893 1415
mine (3) 7 750 17 416
mineral (4) 7 1048 16 11 17 260 567
mine's (1) 14 1487
mines (1) 17 1001
Minette (1) 9 642
mingere (1) 9 762
mingled (3) 12 643 14 770 16 1890
mingling (4) 4 306 14 357 15 433 3319
mingling (1) 15 3302
Mingo (1) 9 762
miniature (2) 16 1225 17 573
minim (1) 14 349
minimes (1) 12 1685
minimising (1) 17 1382
minims (3) 15 1651 1652 1653
minimum (1) 17 1533
minion (2) 9 1139 14 185
minions (1) 12 1136
minishing (1) 14 391
minister (2) 10 948 14 1445
ministering (1) 13 326
ministers (2) 14 1247 16 1395
Minnie (2) 15 2745 3223
minnows (1) 3 476
Minor (2) 15 982 2500
minor (5) 11 893 16 1510 17 812 1102
minorates (1) 14 383
minors (2) 14 340 17 2185
Minotaur (1) 14 994
minstrel (2) 11 268 1025
minstrel's (1) 10 255
Minuet (1) 11 965
minuets (1) 15 4045
minus (2) 11 836 17 1444
minute (15) 4 53 5 125 520 6 514 7 28 233 628 8 360 1177 10 589 16 1288 17 1059 18 1104 1354 1423
minute's (1) 14 1399
minutes (19) 6 86 8 481 791 9 16 10 318 12 323 380 14 1181 15 646 2941 16 483 1457 17 114 918 1516 18 423 587 1043 1183
minutes (1) 3 187
minutes' (1) 16 1104
minutiae (1) 14 1294
minutiae (1) 16 637
M'invitasti (1) 8 1041
minx (1) 13 922
minxi (1) 9 762
mio (1) 11 595
miracle (2) 1 453 15 1838

Miracles (1) 10 838
miracles (2) 1 612 18 759
miraculous (1) 16 45
mirada (1) 18 512
Mirage (1) 13 1079
mirage (1) 15 297
Miranda (1) 9 421
Mirandola (1) 3 144
mire (3) 14 1218 16 1772 1882
mired (2) 3 376 16 1878
Miriam (5) 8 350 9 449 15 2994 2997 3000
Miriam (1) 15 4360
Mirror (1) 11 1046
mirror (37) 1 2 17 38 121 130 135 141 143 148 243 3 137 4 293 531 9 221 10 644 742 1027 11 214 690 13 162 192 919 920 1260 14 1044 1060 1160 15 2991 3820 3907 17 516 1342 1344 1348 1357 18 414
mirror (5) 15 145 148 2053 2303 3821
mirrored (1) 11 423
mirrors (4) 2 159 11 421 17 1183 18 1155
mirrors (1) 15 4058
mirth (5) 1 263 11 162 14 218 343 734
mirth (1) 15 4910
mirthful (1) 15 4913
mirthfully (1) 9 1191
Mirthless (1) 2 27
mirthless (1) 2 34
mirthprovoking (1) 12 543
Mirus (3) 8 1162 10 1268 13 1166
Mirus (1) 15 4109
Mirus (1) 15 1494
mis (2) 3 161 15 2583
misadventure (3) 6 364 13 56 16 1338
misapprehension (2) 16 1167 17 1018
misappropriation (1) 17 2184
misbegotten (1) 9 985
misbehave (1) 15 1070
misbelieving (1) 14 151
misbirth (1) 3 36
miscarriages (1) 14 961
miscellaneous (2) 16 327 17 2090
mischance (1) 16 39
mischief (3) 12 359 13 530 18 513
mischievously (1) 14 1150
Mischna (1) 17 754
misconception (1) 14 1176
Misconduct (1) 12 1170
misconduct (3) 9 963 15 1021 16 1483
misconducting (1) 12 1172
miscreant (1) 9 373
misdeeds (1) 15 3076
misdemeanant (1) 15 1807
misdemeanants (1) 16 1492
misdemeanour (1) 15 944
mise (1) 14 306
miser (1) 18 6
miserable (1) 15 766
misericord (1) 14 127
Misericordiae (1) 17 1255
Misericordiae (1) 6 376
miseris (1) 16 175
Misery (3) 10 880 11 967
misery (5) 2 228 5 204 14 1466 16 1600 17 1946
misery (1) 15 932
misfortune (2) 16 253 18 525

misfortunes (1) 12 1164
misgiving (1) 17 701
misguidedly (1) 16 1607
misha (1) 14 1526
mishinnah (1) 14 1526
mislaid (2) 12 1725 15 2757
misleading (1) 3 83
misled (1) 7 568
misnomer (1) 16 1275
misprints (1) 16 1267
Miss (82) 7 940 9 306 10 368 375 962
  1178 1198 11 67 81 92 115 118 126 134 136 143
  147 163 164 203 236 237 240 250 360 380 382 405
  460 542 562 770 813 818 897 1159 1167
  12 1268 1270 1271 1272 1273 1274 1275 1276
  1284 13 275 532 598 633 14 800 829
  15 2219 2221 3030 3077 4541 16 1557 1559
  17 56 140 411 425 1847 18 26 723 878 879
Miss (1) 15 4354
miss (52) 4 167 169 493 5 453 6 125
  8 889 890 11 64 66 68 69 72 95 103 107 116
  122 123 128 129 141 143 146 181 183 194 208 213
  225 232 277 280 284 318 346 377 403 760 818 819
  820 954 955 1038 1170 15 174 3077 16 887
missa (1) 12 1884
missed (6) 6 161 9 513 10 797 1058
  13 358 18 1596
missed (1) 16 405
Misses (1) 12 1275
misses (1) 16 1563
misshapen (1) 14 855
missies (1) 18 376
missile (2) 1 518 15 4606
missiles (1) 17 1952
missing (6) 12 714 1240 14 858 16 185
  17 1395 2001
Mission (1) 5 323
Mission (1) 15 1888
mission (3) 10 6 144 15 1054
Missionary (1) 3 192
missionary (2) 8 745 15 1802
missioner (1) 13 283
missive (1) 16 498
missus (9) 5 148 183 8 452 9 72
  10 540 550 15 885 1675 2759
missy (1) 10 336
mist (4) 14 1062 1327 17 217 18 637
mist (1) 15 2727
Mistake (3) 6 329 844 13 1217
mistake (11) 7 534 9 226 487 10 567
  12 437 13 494 1125 16 1306 1412 1591
  18 730
Mistaken (1) 15 760
mistaken (1) 6 103
mistakes (2) 9 228 15 2100
misted (1) 13 648
Mister (1) 12 838
mister (7) 9 558 12 1802 14 1446
  15 177 2439 3985
Misters (1) 15 3888
mistletoe (2) 12 1294 15 463
Mistress (2) 14 510 15 3062
mistress (8) 8 576 9 638 723 13 57
  15 2970 3071 17 667 18 1365
mistress (1) 15 3069
mistress (1) 15 321
mistrust (1) 8 1092
mists (1) 18 876
misty (3) 2 125 3 124 13 54

misunderstanding (1) 15 4600
misunderstood (2) 15 776 16 1596
mit (1) 15 2464
Mitchel (1) 17 1648
Mitchell's (1) 9 307
Mitchelstown (1) 12 874
mite (3) 13 1230 14 1321 15 559
mitigants (1) 17 1620
mitigating (1) 17 848
mitre (1) 3 53
mitre (1) 15 1854
mitred (2) 11 915 12 1678
mitres (2) 1 656 11 571
mittens (1) 15 284
Mity (1) 8 755
Mitzvah (1) 15 1624
mix (3) 8 871 9 761 12 284
mix (1) 15 1652
Mixed (1) 15 1699
mixed (17) 8 787 9 794 12 73 912 1658
  13 1011 1128 15 433 854 1699 1701
  16 519 17 830 1706 1718 18 941 950
mixedup (1) 18 179
mixolydian (1) 15 2090
mixture (4) 9 761 14 1236 17 799
  18 1535
mixup (2) 12 965 15 636
Mizpah (1) 17 1781
Mizrach (1) 17 1263
Mizraim (1) 15 1901
Mkgnao (1) 4 16
Mm (1) 7 116
Mn (1) 4 57
Mnemo (3) 15 2390 2737 3311
mnemotechnic (4) 15 2385 17 766 1422
  1424
Mo (1) 15 1041
mo (3) 5 532 9 539 14 278
mo (1) 9 366
moan (1) 14 1092
moaned (1) 9 1155
moaning (3) 1 61 14 1095 18 814
moaning (1) 15 4232
Moat (1) 12 231
moated (1) 18 898
Mob (1) 4 350
Mob (1) 15 1761
mob (4) 8 437 463 9 840 10 35
mob (1) 15 2612
mobbed (1) 12 986
mobcap (1) 15 283
mobile (2) 1 126 9 547
mobility (1) 17 1143
mobled (1) 9 800
mobsmen (1) 16 64
mocassins (1) 15 3160
mock (3) 9 979 13 1059 14 416
mock (2) 15 2288 2299
mocked (2) 3 318 14 1152
Mocker (1) 9 690
mocker (1) 9 543
mocker's (1) 9 544
mockers (2) 1 657 9 492
mockery (8) 1 34 116 210 661 7 601
  15 3891 4178
mockery (1) 15 329
Mocking (1) 15 2789
mocking (3) 2 159 4 344 7 445
mocking (2) 15 2123 4058

mockingly (1) 4 30
mockingly (2) 15 2055 3165
mocks (1) 14 846
mocks (1) 15 3733
mockturtle (2) 8 232 271
modality (4) 3 1 13 425 15 3630
Modder (1) 17 1252
mode (1) 17 264
Model (1) 17 311
model (7) 4 154 9 59 76 15 1035 2817
  17 647 18 1416
model (1) 15 916
modelled (1) 5 356
models (1) 10 1216
moderate (1) 14 1309
moderately (2) 17 1594 1852
moderation (1) 12 1195
moderator (1) 15 1424
Modern (1) 17 1802
modern (10) 12 353 730 1339 14 1280
  16 514 1590 17 581 772 793 1773
modern (1) 15 1825
moderns (1) 15 3903
modes (1) 15 2090
modest (3) 12 884 14 1042 16 799
modestly (1) 15 3120
modesty (3) 14 804 15 977 3892
modicum (1) 14 1414
modifications (2) 17 2250 2267
modified (2) 17 737 960
modulated (1) 17 795
modulations (1) 17 725
modus (1) 17 1030
Mogg (1) 15 4539
mohammadan (1) 17 97
Mohammed (1) 5 235
Moher (1) 17 1974
Mohicans (2) 12 185 16 1698
Moi (2) 3 169 235
moi (2) 3 183 15 2159
moiety (2) 3 78 17 927
Moira (3) 6 248 10 786 15 2519
moirette (1) 17 2096
Moisel (3) 4 209 8 392 17 1254
Moisel (1) 15 3223
Moist (1) 3 209
moist (3) 4 181 11 563 18 114
moist (4) 15 466 1310 2007 3457
moistened (2) 8 899 17 1485
moistens (1) 15 2486
Moisture (1) 5 112
moisture (3) 9 68 14 1385 1407
MOLARS (1) 7 1033
molars (1) 15 694
mole (5) 3 279 356 9 378 391 474
molecular (1) 17 1062
Molecules (1) 9 205
molecules (2) 9 377 17 1062
molefur (1) 15 549
mole's (1) 15 958
molestful (1) 14 51
molestors (1) 17 1632
Molesworth (3) 8 1080 1087 10 163
Moll (5) 14 509 1498 15 3151 3184
Molldopeloob (1) 17 407
mollificative (1) 14 353
mollify (1) 14 953
Molloy (2) 12 928 17 1308
Molly (63) 4 203 206 292 5 272 332 372 397

937 7 100 8 604 1125 10 606 12 1502
13 998 14 573 1528 15 53 55 1988 2063
3695 3816 4183 17 1265
More (2) 1 464 17 712
more (274) 1 151 161 195 200 334 436 2 29
145 404 433 3 1 131 133 422 423 4 75 79 135
227 359 5 27 211 251 293 298 299 387 561
6 17 92 141 201 284 332 365 412 487 546 554 602
665 843 907 947 1002 7 257 380 825 883
8 83 108 387 458 655 661 792 845 888 1118 1190
9 27 38 444 609 618 625 635 868 1051 1073 1134
10 77 164 334 625 680 696 912 1052 1169 1188
11 4 71 82 98 176 184 770 790 791 802 810 914
935 1175 12 209 331 352 497 515 599 728 729
733 735 1151 1188 1342 1400 1462 1536 13 83
169 271 432 476 557 591 722 842 994 1200
14 13 28 143 164 195 284 343 364 442 493 514
558 564 656 711 783 837 838 859 868 878 903 939
1055 1087 1118 1128 1152 1162 1320 15 235
670 873 892 1193 1600 1692 1783 1968 1988 2126
2194 2417 2778 2964 3436 3459 3602 4487
16 21 49 62 260 306 352 480 483 534 542 544 629
674 697 706 721 726 736 777 804 814 954 993 1042
1181 1206 1209 1349 1430 1499 1519 1529 1539
1651 1658 1757 1807 1812 1828 1883 17 122
311 377 386 511 517 657 676 703 853 874 885 970
989 1008 1070 1093 1142 1146 1197 1287 1516
1675 1884 1903 1927 2190 2194 2195 2273
18 30 102 168 202 339 474 502 **687** 728 840 865
886 908 915 927 1189 1240 1244 **1272** 1328 1451
1498 1536
more (10) 1 239 264 455 463 2 57 64
3 445 11 928 17 827
more (4) 15 564 2073 2342 4210
Moreau (1) 9 50
Morecambe (1) 17 1736
Moreover (1) 17 897
moreover (1) 12 1071
more's (2) 9 945 15 1990
Morgan (1) 17 1749
morganatic (1) 15 1508
morgue (2) 6 885 16 48
moribund (2) 17 1050 1947
Morituri (1) 15 1557
Morkan (2) 17 140
Morkan's (1) 8 417
Morley (1) 17 1656
mormon (1) 15 1156
morn (4) 11 14 325 326 1109
morn (1) 11 322
Morning (2) 4 233 525
Morning (1) 15 4081
morning (108) 1 4 232 242 292 390 399 406
459 562 2 422 426 3 124 4 51 84 173 188
189 416 474 490 526 5 4 22 379 524 6 58 78
114 153 352 604 681 788 1033 7 62 80 166 786
8 125 147 220 256 347 867 10 462 553 829
1077 11 1205 12 332 374 401 593 910
13 117 127 184 239 786 788 902 965 1018 1046
1134 1196 1224 1259 14 567 1046 15 205 333
886 2498 2895 4897 16 228 450 1144 1297 1472
1561 1713 17 144 626 1720 18 327 444 479
572 642 685 717 748 760 856 927 933 1144 1314
1360 1429 1491 1496 1498 1502 1587
morning (3) 4 288 10 557 16 1248
morning (3) 15 815 4054 4061
mornings (4) 1 442 443 4 159 12 1046
Morny (1) 8 831
Morocco (2) 12 1472 18 859

morocco (1) 17 1365
Morose (1) 3 385
morose (1) 16 301
Morpheus (1) 16 948
Morphy (1) 10 1259
morrice (2) 2 155 9 1169
Morris (1) 13 1225
morris (1) 15 2045
Morrow (1) 3 79
morrow (1) 15 2410
morrow (1) 11 552
morsel (3) 8 77 673 18 431
Mort (1) 14 551
mort (2) 3 373 14 1494
Mortacci (1) 16 318
Mortal (3) 8 924 15 3240 3245
mortal (8) 6 527 623 926 12 374 1189
15 941 16 995 1063
mortality (2) 14 1241 1268
mortally (1) 9 466
mortals (5) 13 94 14 8 30 53 16 1596
Mortar (1) 5 477
mortar (1) 2 213
mortarboard (1) 15 4696
mortarboards (1) 8 429
mortgage (1) 15 1640
mortgaged (1) 6 536
mortgagee (1) 12 764
mortgagee's (1) 12 774
mortgaging (1) 15 981
mortgagor (2) 12 770 774
mortified (1) 6 1014
mortify (1) 17 1164
Mortimer (1) 14 1334
Mortis (1) 14 1092
mortis (1) 12 478
mortuary (4) 6 574 8 497 11 1035
15 3889
mortuary (1) 15 1207
mortuis (1) 6 794
Mosaic (2) 7 756 15 969
Mosaic (1) 15 1165
mosaic (2) 15 2043 4100
Mosenthal (2) 5 200 15 264
MOSES (1) 7 1054
Moses (24) 2 158 4 156 7 757 1061
9 607 10 463 845 12 17 33 1093 1901
14 247 15 571 572 847 1855 17 711 712
713 714 2070
Moses (2) 7 833 862
Moses (6) 15 987 1846 3222 4357
Moses' (2) 10 508 813
mosey (2) 1 284 8 318
moslem (1) 15 1686
mosque (3) 5 549 550 17 1982
mosques (1) 4 93
mosquito (1) 18 665
Moss (1) 12 1068
mossoo (1) 14 1506
mossy (1) 7 245
MOST (1) 7 78
Most (20) 3 236 4 3 6 599 7 274
9 492 10 727 728 11 104 610 1148
12 294 13 284 14 1456 1464 1499
15 1151 1629 1951 3863 16 95
Most (2) 9 808
most (122) 3 178 236 237 5 34 6 108
7 463 747 889 8 400 9 12 195 328 359 503
522 543 593 784 1029 1049 1118 1164 1195

10 59 409 850 1182 11 256 268 634 655 981
1026 12 25 80 553 610 623 624 658 666 797 897
904 1104 1185 1722 1820 13 285 303 304 345
367 378 396 490 903 14 8 9 22 194 296 331 332
353 387 456 536 732 735 779 805 831 842 901 916
978 1201 1235 1256 1305 1349 1412 1530 1585
15 524 778 820 823 1072 1099 1160 1472 1796
1805 1809 2463 2508 3042 3426 16 58 96 427
519 782 896 948 949 1039 1049 1398 1640
17 197 245 518 874 1772 1827 18 1357
most (2) 6 147 16 1251
most (3) 15 1422 1745 2855
mostly (3) 16 1616 1641 17 301
mostly (1) 7 580
mote (1) 12 1237
motes (1) 1 174
Moth (1) 15 2468
moth (2) 15 2462
moth (3) 15 2042 2406 2461
mothball (1) 18 406
Mother (8) 1 375 10 463 12 184 1231
13 1065 14 215 732 15 1287
Mother (2) 15 1582 1763
Mother (11) 9 1186 15 1716 4172 4181
4188 4194 4201 4211 4216 4231 4237
mother (96) 1 78 80 85 88 91 93 107 122 195
205 208 215 218 279 357 370 3 32 86 200 492
4 94 5 439 6 65 66 329 820 7 583 8 30
9 107 179 235 376 424 643 665 833 10 682
12 399 814 956 1300 1648 13 320 325 327 918
1203 1234 14 58 241 248 249 257 296 834 842
958 1082 1123 1299 1376 1402 15 279 381 1817
1963 1990 2192 2702 2990 3467 4170 4180 4186
4192 4949 16 138 150 152 658 1804 17 142
468 943 1836 1884 18 283 846 994 1185 1306
1440 1441 1454
mother (2) 1 198 13 948
mother (1) 15 4157
mother-of-pearl (1) 15 451
motherhood (2) 14 120 1318
mothering (1) 14 446
motherless (1) 12 551
motherlight (1) 14 1316
Mother's (2) 9 221 14 1433
mother's (17) 1 189 204 2 143 315 3 185
8 706 9 879 11 1042 13 316 329 897
14 109 544 1048 15 2228 4137 16 1520
mother's (1) 1 585
Mothers (1) 14 456
mothers (6) 9 852 14 51 69 75 15 4372
18 890
Mothers' (1) 8 392
motherwit (2) 13 75 14 1404
motif (1) 12 1286
motion (13) 7 885 9 1033 10 628
14 1528 15 4042 16 1464 1694 17 39
264 1168 2306 2307 2309
motionless (3) 7 1043 17 1345 1346
motions (1) 14 862
motive (2) 9 956 16 566
motives (3) 11 633 12 791 16 116
motley (2) 2 309 9 486
motor (2) 7 341 15 1687
motor (1) 15 1775
motorcar (2) 9 802 10 759
motorgoggles (1) 15 1775
Motorman (1) 15 194
motorman (2) 15 187 192
mots (2) 10 1142 15 4868

2054 2055 2079 2256   18 4 234 256 417 476 481
513 531 612 654 657 718 748 785 845 846 947 1068
1082 1111 1466 1474
Mrs (1) 1 361
Mrs (19) 15 386 531 2923 3837 3856 4338 4339
4344 4348 4349 4352 4358 4360 4550 4691
MRS (38) 15 389 394 403 430 436 446 454 459
470 486 491 520 525 529 542 553 561 567 575 1013
1025 1036 1044 1057 1074 1076 1080 1087 1090
1092 1097 1102 1110 1113 1714 1818 2927 3859
M's (1) 14 499
Much (2) 6 425   11 1001
Much (1) 9 1013
much (162) 1 92 293 395   3 97   4 134 276
398 425 463   5 242 250 510   6 172 177 181 291
307 522 889   7 299 915   8 54 769 775 811 962
998   9 316 318 360 395 535 974   10 288 371
605 887 980   11 182 548 618 810 995 1090 1245
12 13 723 730 1075 1312 1664 1871   13 85 86
192 595 611 907 940 1048 1095   14 131 348 357
382 432 522 540 615 683 697 978 1034 1127 1364
1476   15 210 566 658 1088 1151 1564 2313 2463
2496 2500 3037 3098 3783 3885 3887 3901 3915
4838   16 89 145 175 188 241 279 284 382 429
439 565 680 736 828 967 1033 1123 1157 1182 1226
1292 1400 1456 1469 1562 1859   17 657 1657
18 7 18 22 69 155 179 193 201 211 217 263 441
456 457 464 470 476 526 568 581 735 788 880 897
999 1002 1003 1030 1122 1169 1229 1434 1507
1517 1518 1536 1546
muchacha (1) 13 1209
muchee (1) 15 961
Muchibus (1) 7 780
muchinjured (1) 16 1081
muchly (1) 11 299
muchneeded (1) 16 1846
muchtreasured (1) 12 1438
muchwhat (1) 14 419
muck (2) 7 986   12 1427
mucking (2) 12 770 1578
mucks (1) 8 617
mucksweat (1) 15 2750
mucosities (1) 15 3473
Mud (2) 10 114   15 274
mud (2) 15 330   18 793
mud (1) 15 272
mudcabins (1) 12 1366
mudchoked (1) 6 444
muddled (1) 16 1415
Muddy (1) 10 807
muddy (3) 15 277   18 223 267
mudflake (1) 15 197
mudflats (1) 5 316
mudslinging (2) 16 1331 1504
mudsplashed (1) 2 308
Mürzsteg (1) 2 334
muff (2) 15 3139   18 434
muff (2) 15 1028 1103
Muffled (1) 11 1249
muffled (3) 11 294   12 527   18 1263
muffled (2) 15 27 1258
muffler (2) 3 371   18 295
muffler (2) 15 1617 4524
mug (4) 3 95   12 1415   16 808 1169
muggyish (1) 16 915
Muglins (1) 1 576
mugs (2) 9 627   16 842
Muhammad (1) 12 189
mulberrycoloured (1) 9 1193

mulberrytree (1) 9 1033
Mulcahy (3) 6 717 723 726
Mulcahy (1) 6 731
Mulch (1) 4 481
mulcted (1) 15 2331
mule (2) 14 1421   15 95
mules (1) 7 93
mulieris (1) 10 168
Mull (1) 14 1205
mull (2) 17 2093   18 265
Mullaghmast (1) 7 880
mulled (1) 8 196
Mullee (1) 14 1453
Mullett's (1) 16 33
Mulligan (144) 1 1 17 41 47 50 59 64 71 85 92
111 115 121 127 138 147 179 184 191 197 219 221
228 229 287 293 296 318 323 330 338 342 346 353
355 360 373 388 391 393 408 416 427 431 435 440
446 451 471 485 494 499 502 510 523 531 534 539
543 546 554 559 564 569 579 657 660 678 687 692
697 703 717 720 721 722 726 733   2 255 430
3 112   6 49 63   7 583   9 41 305 369 485 504
507 515 554 568 573 605 645 655 716 726 731 773
792 794 951 978 1025 1053 1086 1099 1100 1119
1125 1142 1155 1170 1204 1209   10 746 1043
1049 1055 1071 1087 1224   11 154   14 495 651
655 666 697 704 719 727 730 964 998 1213 1242
1452   15 1772 4170   16 264 281 287
Mulligan (2) 9 1176   14 660
Mulligan (2) 15 2239 4166
MULLIGAN (3) 15 1774 4169 4177
Mulligan's (11) 1 40 201 281 313 377 461
9 545   10 1065 1080   14 700   17 1316
Mulligan's (1) 3 201
mulligatawny (1) 8 271
Mullingar (12) 4 250   5 321   6 89 444
8 206   13 927   14 499 1495   15 3165
16 509   17 882 891
Mullins (1) 16 1022
mullioned (1) 12 1732
multicoloured (5) 5 193   9 1194   17 499
2063 2098
multifarious (1) 14 1289
Multifarnham (1) 12 860
multiform (1) 17 2064
multiple (2) 15 3473   17 761
multiplication (2) 17 1933 1965
multiplicit (1) 14 389
multiplied (4) 4 141   11 830   17 1707
1963
multiply (3) 8 33 385   14 677
multiplying (3) 4 226   12 1724   17 1586
multisecular (1) 17 195
multiseminal (1) 14 974
multitude (3) 12 533 1313   14 1095
multitude (1) 15 2677
multitudinous (2) 9 1194   17 2064
multitudinous (1) 15 2623
multos (1) 9 771
Mulvey (7) 13 889 1282   17 870 2133
18 818 845 1582
Mulveys (2) 18 655 748
mumbled (2) 8 908   16 1091
mumbles (3) 15 923 2833 4839
mumbling (1) 10 852
mumbling (1) 15 291
Mummed (1) 9 412
mummer (4) 1 97 98   9 554 1155
Mummer's (1) 14 1486

mummers (1) 9 1167
mummery (1) 2 155
mummies (1) 6 822
mummy (2) 4 404   18 1432
mummy (1) 15 3378
mummycases (1) 9 352
mummy's (1) 4 399
mumps (2) 14 1425   18 1049
Mumpsypum (1) 11 1079
mum's (1) 8 40
Munchday (1) 8 693
munched (4) 1 385   8 128 692   16 620
munching (1) 15 690
municipal (6) 6 406   14 1294   15 1685
16 1726   17 175 430
Munro (1) 10 652
Munster (2) 12 84   15 1018
mur (2) 11 860 888
mural (2) 17 1535 1560
Muratti's (1) 17 2094
Murder (4) 6 478 482   9 575   14 958
murder (17) 3 180   5 382   7 632 661 749
9 129 569 570   12 1345 1794 1847   13 1192
15 1393   17 844 2190   18 224 998
murder (1) 12 422
Murdered (1) 6 471
murdered (6) 6 469 478   9 179 1035
14 276   15 2676
Murderer (1) 6 481
murderer (3) 14 1017   15 235   18 1419
murderer (1) 12 425
Murderer's (2) 6 476   14 1037
murderer's (1) 6 478
Murderers (1) 13 1255
murderers (3) 14 1095   16 1331 1813
murderous (1) 9 137
murders (2) 16 591   18 993
muriatic (1) 15 2395
murk (1) 14 1072
murk (2) 15 8 2178
Murmur (1) 14 223
murmur (7) 9 425 559 1119   11 675 947
12 675   14 836
murmur (3) 15 675 1329 3796
Murmured (1) 11 896
murmured (10) 1 97   2 240   7 237 499
9 265   11 631 1168 1169 1172 1176
Murmuring (1) 12 1819
murmuring (11) 5 263 344 349   7 409 462
10 713 843 919   12 71 639   14 1029
murmuring (3) 15 1330 1332 3308
murmurs (13) 15 375 741 769 829 1328 1456
2620 2814 3680 4931 4941 4951 4953
Murphies (1) 16 364
Murphy (9) 12 178 237 932   16 415 440 452
959 1727   17 1738
Murphy's (3) 16 415 726   17 2258
murrain (1) 14 326
Murray (11) 7 25 34 40 49 55 62   12 313
327   16 1475   17 1648   18 1024
Murray (1) 15 4342
Murray's (1) 7 31
Murren (1) 8 397
Murren's (1) 6 942
Murtagh (1) 12 191
Murthering (1) 9 579
Mus (1) 12 1895
muscle (2) 11 512   15 2783
musclebound (1) 15 2604

muscles (5) 15 3104 16 853 17 243 516 524

Muscovy (1) 14 577

Muscular (1) 6 596

muscular (3) 12 638 15 1069 17 1950

muscularity (1) 17 2216

muse (4) 7 609 11 265 711 12 539

mused (6) 9 359 1119 11 206 210 219 13 293

Musemathematics (1) 11 834

muses (1) 15 1707

Museum (2) 8 1169 16 1451

museum (11) 5 328 8 921 1173 9 515 610 13 1215 15 1791 16 890 17 2048 18 541 1202

museum (1) 15 1704

mush (1) 6 994

mushroom (2) 8 492 14 786

mushrooms (3) 8 722 12 95 13 880

Mushy (1) 13 887

mushy (1) 16 1487

Music (8) 5 399 8 769 11 703 904 1182 15 1948 17 12

Music (1) 15 1707

music (60) 1 22 251 4 531 5 342 394 403 405 8 186 9 1035 10 363 365 539 1239 1248 11 706 730 825 830 853 926 964 970 979 980 1049 1052 1055 1060 1081 1128 1244 12 1199 13 409 499 856 14 1252 1428 15 105 1278 1368 1965 16 518 972 1733 1735 1737 1739 1741 1751 1802 1823 1848 17 417 441 1266 1306 2049 18 381 1552

music (2) 7 768 17 413

music (4) 15 1318 1332 2014 2501

Musical (3) 11 555 560 726

musical (10) 12 687 13 591 15 3247 3528 16 1835 1850 17 20 664 2176 18 980

Musichall (1) 4 426

musichall (3) 9 108 10 495 497

musicrest (1) 17 1306

musicroom (1) 15 1991

musicroom (1) 15 2040

Musing (1) 11 223

musings (1) 9 76

musk (1) 1 256

musketeer (1) 15 1059

muskin (1) 14 676

muskperfumed (1) 1 263

Muskrat (1) 13 1028

Muslin (1) 8 614

muslin (2) 14 1144 18 292

mussels (1) 13 1233

Must (70) 3 187 400 4 60 73 210 234 328 347 360 465 5 19 297 409 6 77 227 484 512 607 830 843 7 205 715 8 28 369 403 427 504 547 554 566 572 584 592 623 628 640 1108 1127 1132 10 748 781 11 187 219 560 699 1000 1127 1268 1287 13 855 885 959 1036 1063 1212 1227 1231 1243 1254 1274 14 1231 1479 1520 15 199 2497 2740 2970 3100 3628 3721

must (151) 1 42 79 112 467 647 2 67 262 263 406 3 60 167 174 4 326 409 418 5 29 69 95 434 470 6 154 340 353 545 554 621 666 742 750 767 783 791 844 7 197 351 787 814 998 1072 8 21 53 71 245 306 318 462 613 1044 1111 1121 1128 1167 9 70 311 334 444 611 727 832 1099 1102 1201 11 208 229 272 738 872 875 913 970 1000 1061 1126 1210 1247 1248 12 285 876

1147 1485 1543 1567 1669 13 207 547 562 652 870 884 895 921 1095 1147 1182 14 439 441 767 877 882 886 931 1072 1276 1306 1375 15 523 1234 1690 2396 2803 3199 3286 3799 3889 4183 4437 4569 16 456 477 671 974 1094 1101 1151 1164 1208 1258 1473 18 77 118 143 148 150 219 242 343 387 405 455 584 790 869 927 1040 1056 1061 1209 1288 1553

mustachioed (1) 10 350

Mustard (2) 8 780 10 382

mustard (5) 8 789 819 850 14 616 15 2433

mustard (1) 15 2985

muster (1) 12 1835

musterred (1) 8 742

mustn't (4) 3 58 6 640 7 485 11 940

musty (1) 9 410

mutable (2) 17 1350 1354

Mute (1) 11 223

Mute (1) 15 3044

mute (8) 1 105 213 272 3 345 6 137 9 136 17 863 2235

mute (4) 15 1956 2575 4911 4912

mutely (4) 4 69 6 488 8 639 10 195

mutely (1) 15 32

mutes (2) 6 521 579

mutilated (1) 14 1247

mutilated (1) 15 1213

mutiny (1) 17 2186

Mutoscope (1) 13 794

mutter (1) 15 39

muttered (5) 5 532 10 908 1112 14 1019 16 1687

muttering (2) 2 297 14 1088

muttering (3) 15 292 481 4819

mutters (1) 15 220

Mutton (1) 15 3483

mutton (7) 4 4 45 8 195 926 13 1294 14 1547 18 945

mutton (1) 15 3991

muttonchop (1) 8 361

muttoning (1) 10 184

muttonleg (1) 15 284

mutual (14) 11 574 12 788 14 1003 15 1393 3049 16 821 1099 1331 1526 1600 17 769 1668 1959

mutually (2) 14 1190 17 973

muy (1) 18 1472

muzzle (1) 6 596

muzzle (1) 15 659

muzzling (1) 12 709

My (113) 1 41 628 708 2 168 340 3 16 61 164 174 279 399 454 487 494 498 5 148 151 183 6 76 82 131 203 376 613 713 1001 7 367 419 728 892 8 152 178 331 424 648 710 1179 1190 9 39 145 296 486 947 977 981 1202 10 540 865 1170 11 61 512 687 825 868 871 969 972 975 1072 1095 12 994 13 869 894 1080 1102 1142 14 787 1021 1491 1512 15 287 657 730 765 777 793 834 942 976 1008 1062 1247 1263 1504 1542 1600 1612 1744 2228 2312 2750 2988 3081 3171 3215 3258 3553 3935 4027 4044 4074 4115 4433 4478 4557 4706 16 419 780 876 1645 1800 18 897

My (9) 1 585 2 89 9 423 10 1242 1256 13 313 16 1231 17 644 1881

my (673) 1 48 54 69 152 189 204 218 251 273 287 553 667 718 721 2 29 72 191 227 247 346 395 417 421 3 2 16 46 237 246 272 275 292 296

305 307 310 312 324 327 368 378 390 414 420 4 19 112 167 169 361 399 404 409 485 492 519 5 15 16 82 169 172 179 187 190 204 243 253 254 341 375 436 452 495 566 6 22 66 70 71 105 126 170 364 375 819 888 1000 7 87 106 192 448 457 477 504 588 648 729 747 887 981 991 8 165 187 320 352 367 370 394 416 431 769 903 904 907 916 1016 1098 1133 1139 1166 1171 9 35 41 80 202 261 357 370 378 379 390 820 876 903 904 916 919 947 948 981 1008 1078 1164 10 415 736 738 840 866 873 877 912 1019 1160 1172 11 121 125 249 252 375 477 599 633 714 722 833 865 876 914 1066 1095 1113 1114 1122 1149 12 3 4 7 207 211 236 243 434 522 678 688 699 702 790 796 798 836 860 893 895 1002 1040 1072 1089 1106 1222 1232 1376 1429 1491 1563 1570 1599 1602 1609 1673 1759 13 252 385 535 590 613 712 824 835 846 871 877 941 945 971 983 1006 1044 1165 1199 1216 1260 1276 14 282 283 357 368 369 370 375 378 379 380 505 591 622 664 748 749 750 759 762 763 772 779 780 789 794 795 796 811 841 890 1020 1022 1024 1114 1143 1153 1343 1391 1457 1463 1471 1480 1492 1521 1525 1541 1558 1567 1584 1590 15 11 117 163 203 232 260 261 306 345 375 384 398 627 643 647 669 701 708 709 714 754 766 777 822 824 835 844 868 888 946 951 953 1011 1017 1019 1029 1031 1033 1046 1048 1049 1051 1053 1098 1100 1116 1210 1302 1368 1513 1634 1636 1640 1662 1673 1725 1737 1769 1770 1772 1773 1881 2100 2101 2135 2229 2270 2293 2334 2423 2442 2446 2495 2496 2522 2594 2610 2614 2625 2688 2689 2691 2772 2782 2794 2795 2806 2814 2820 2860 2889 2895 2897 2899 2908 2935 2970 2979 3050 3073 3083 3104 3107 3137 3142 3178 3208 3210 3265 3279 3286 3318 3387 3388 3402 3457 3504 3505 3546 3566 3663 3720 3770 3828 3866 3940 4012 4066 4202 4203 4204 4235 4238 4239 4303 4370 4407 4448 4460 4473 4513 4535 4566 4568 4569 4586 4598 4645 4701 4775 4786 4791 4827 4875 16 155 159 415 421 438 452 543 657 664 719 1109 1137 1437 1636 1680 1796 17 662 1885 18 15 40 53 55 62 63 74 77 78 79 86 109 129 146 149 153 173 189 190 200 212 216 246 248 253 257 261 262 263 265 267 273 275 276 282 285 286 287 301 303 306 313 317 321 330 348 377 392 430 431 432 434 450 459 462 465 516 522 523 529 533 551 563 575 587 592 593 606 607 613 634 646 662 663 665 672 673 700 701 704 745 762 765 770 771 772 778 793 797 798 809 810 811 825 837 841 846 850 862 863 875 880 885 888 889 890 892 900 901 902 905 907 910 912 914 922 925 957 971 988 1033 1063 1064 1095 1103 1133 1135 1139 1140 1149 1162 1176 1184 1193 1200 1215 1253 1268 1275 1298 1302 1316 1339 1353 1359 1369 1379 1383 1384 1387 1399 1402 1427 1446 1467 1471 1487 1506 1508 1511 1514 1520 1521 1522 1528 1531 1532 1533 1564 1574 1575 1576 1603 1605 1606 1607

my (41) 1 463 585 2 251 253 4 287 288 6 148 7 525 828 829 9 96 98 1126 1145 10 15 16 139 793 11 530 551 729 1284 1291 12 31 419 428 640 740 745 746 13 646 16 703 1348 1390 17 397 818 819

my (1) 15 4336

Myers (1) 15 1930

Myler (9) 8 801 10 1133 1135 12 947 955 960 967 971 972

Myles (37) 7 307 357 361 380 382 453 457 474 480 532 539 549 585 605 627 644 649 676 684 705

728 773 777 797 802 907 956 967 981 991 1004
1008 1015 1031 1051 1074   16 1273
Myles (2) 15 806 1142
MYLES (1) 15 810
Mynheer (1) 12 565
myopic (1) 17 1928
Myra (1) 12 1273
myriad (2) 14 1108 17 1059
myriadislanded (1) 3 394
myriadminded (2) 9 768 769
Myriorama (1) 18 40
Myrtle (1) 12 1273
Myrto (1) 9 236
myself (71) 1 434 517 606 4 520 5 171 250
461 6 522 7 681 997 8 52 404 428 875 885
9 384 559 10 825 12 996 1224 1564
13 824 848 943 1083 15 873 1021 2226 3084
4470 4554 4869 16 163 751 851 18 68 71 85
99 133 135 177 181 252 348 445 584 585 638 647
648 699 776 904 920 923 1012 1056 1078 1165 1179
1195 1379 1381 1433 1451 1467 1484 1508 1526
mysteries (1) 14 1169
Mysterious (2) 5 290 13 1015
mysterious (2) 13 1 14 1107
mysterious (2) 7 324 855
mysteriously (1) 15 3631
mysterium (1) 14 348
Mystery (1) 13 1060
mystery (9) 1 253 8 871 9 839 1072
10 371 14 608 1032 15 461 17 1177
mystery (2) 1 240 15 4190
mystery (1) 15 4360
mystic (2) 3 38 9 27
mystical (4) 9 835 838 13 374 16 762
Myth (1) 15 1579
myth (1) 10 1082
myths (1) 9 957

N

N (1) 17 2304
n-og (1) 9 413
N B (1) 17 1651
N g (1) 15 154
n g (1) 4 108
N. IGS./WI. UU. OX/W. OKS. MH/
   Y. IM (1) 17 1801
N W (1) 17 2303
Na (1) 12 884
na (1) 12 193
na (4) 9 413 12 859 898
nab (1) 14 1514
Nacheinander (1) 3 13
nachez (1) 14 1526
nachez (1) 15 279
nack (1) 12 427
Nadir (1) 17 1946
nadir (1) 15 2176
nae (3) 14 1505 1565
nag (1) 12 1855
nag (4) 15 3980 3982 3990 4140
naggin (4) 4 224 9 239 14 1441
17 312
Nagle (2) 12 198
Nagle's (2) 10 385 16 207
Nagles (1) 12 1832
nag's (1) 12 1850
nags (1) 5 210
nags (1) 15 4143
Nagyságos (1) 12 1816
nail (7) 6 432 8 701 13 1243 15 3474
16 445 1353 17 1486
nailed (2) 9 495 10 785
Nailer (1) 17 2323
nailfile (1) 17 594
nailless (1) 15 3492
Nails (1) 8 20
nails (14) 4 63 5 374 6 19 200 201 203 777
10 802 13 119 273 14 516 15 2971
17 1602 18 700
nailscraped (1) 15 3987
nailstudded (1) 15 1179
nainsook (1) 13 724
Naked (2) 4 372 9 541
Naked (2) 3 134
naked (15) 3 41 390 468 4 347 5 567
8 922 14 108 109 564 15 2344 18 440
560 1246 1347 1447
naked (3) 15 1705 1706 4692
nakedness (2) 3 235 15 2313
nakkering (2) 11 52 1152
nakkering (1) 15 2609
Namby (1) 14 1537
Name (5) 9 65 14 1074 15 718 4804
17 403
name (207) 1 34 41 54 140 193 435 2 12 130
181 430 3 176 451 4 149 197 358 5 14 169
172 200 248 379 383 6 64 97 569 595 603 704
726 881 882 896 918 7 142 182 977 8 148 176
180 302 513 890 893 1099 1114 9 169 176 350
420 508 607 659 691 696 853 866 879 901 903 916
919 921 924 927 928 949 986 10 3 43 44 156
947 974 1109 1160 11 149 150 501 502 640 714
715 826 844 1032 1055 1065 1080 1172 1173
12 17 143 294 640 661 713 731 1023 1028 1086
1135 1200 1227 1544 1639 1640 1811 13 15 65

658 856 945 1138 1228   14 295 449 546 580 632
653 867 1033 1068 1127 1145 1423 1497 1584
15 398 573 739 741 754 765 1360 1562 1809 2312
2524 3277 3406 4401 4799 4826 4926   16 135
159 205 208 237 364 365 370 415 495 679 839 907
966 1092 1305 1344 1381 1636 1765 1853
17 404 410 603 679 716 719 904 1389 1419 1424
1579 1782 1798 1847 1848 1867 1872 2002
18 95 483 614 617 657 818 841 847 946 1240
1416 1466 1467 1473 1526
name (4) 7 859 13 947 16 1348
17 401
name (1) 15 1826
named (16) 4 407 6 1002 12 20 1589
14 356 430 453 467 685 15 547 3084
16 233 686 1239 17 3 18 773
Nameless (2) 15 1143 4339
NAMELESS (2) 15 1144 1148
nameless (1) 12 571
namely (3) 16 713 837 1372
Names (2) 9 901 13 1099
names (24) 1 403 4 222 6 878 880
7 948 9 412 912 983 11 1069 12 666 826
13 372 15 2246 3210 16 363 1194 1370
1486 1563 1775 17 444 18 844 1463 1464
namesake (2) 6 233 9 173
namesakes (1) 12 1639
Namine (1) 15 1241
Naminedamine (1) 11 43
Nancy (2) 18 726 728
Nankeen (1) 15 2249
Nannan (2) 7 128 12 825
Nannannanny (1) 15 3370
Nannan's (1) 12 857
Nannetti (7) 7 123 188 975 8 1057
10 970 12 850 17 601
Nannetti (1) 15 4337
NANNETTI (1) 15 3385
Nannetti's (4) 7 75 121 11 186 13 1242
NANNYGOAT (1) 15 3369
nannygoat (1) 8 911
nannygoat (1) 15 3367
nans (1) 3 316
nantee (1) 14 1466
Nao (3) 13 68 70 74
nap (4) 3 439 6 1022 8 265 17 661
nape (4) 7 47 8 904 14 597 17 246
nape (1) 15 4890
napecomb (1) 11 166
Napier (1) 18 1214
napkin (3) 8 657 658 810
napkin (1) 15 507
Napkinring (1) 11 647
napkins (4) 11 571 912 915 18 1207
Naples (1) 17 1990
Napoleon (3) 12 187 15 3835 16 363
Napoleon (1) 17 1381
Napoleon (1) 15 465
Napoleonic (1) 15 2721
Napper (1) 3 260
napping (1) 5 178
nappy (1) 14 1489
Narcissus (2) 17 1428 2034
Narcotic (1) 5 272
narcotic (2) 16 285 17 1918
nard (1) 14 346
narrated (4) 15 952 16 491 17 639 1906
narration (4) 17 638 2267 2269 2273
narrations (1) 17 1912

narrative (3) 14 740 17 653 1756
Narrator (2) 17 2303 2314
narrator (12) 14 745 16 570 17 640
  1917 1918 1921 2250 2265 2272 2284 2288 2302
narrator's (1) 17 2298
narrow (4) 1 612 2 327 9 342 17 1722
narrowing (1) 4 35
narrowly (1) 1 174
narrowshouldered (1) 15 269
nasal (3) 16 663 17 872 1091
nasally (1) 15 2415
nascent (1) 17 1050
Nasodoro (1) 15 1827
Nassau (3) 8 551 10 1154 1247
nasturtiums (1) 12 1040
Nasty (2) 8 419 13 63
nasty (5) 10 514 15 3039 16 68 1511 1872
Nat (2) 12 860 869
natality (1) 14 1268
natation (1) 17 1594
nates (1) 15 1880
Nathan (1) 5 203
Nathan's (1) 5 203
natheless (1) 14 152
Nation (1) 12 917
nation (15) 12 891 1195 1370 1419 1422 1424
  1430 1570 1796 14 13 23 56 17 16 32
National (7) 4 136 6 171 12 1268
  14 1301 16 1451 17 968
National (3) 7 44 17 336
National (1) 15 3305
national (18) 1 469 668 7 976 8 369 1043
  9 309 1108 12 236 1418 14 684 15 1790
  16 782 840 17 24 758 1646 1675 2048
national (1) 9 1174
national (1) 15 4674
Nationalgymnasiummuseumsanatorium-
  andsuspensoriumsordinaryprivat-
  docentgeneralhistoryspecialprofessor-
  doctor (1) 12 567–568
Nationalised (1) 17 1658
nationalist (1) 7 620
nationality (1) 16 878
nation's (2) 2 348
Nations (1) 11 1289
nations (3) 12 1418 15 3387 4648
NATIVE (1) 7 326
native (6) 6 819 11 991 13 1080
  14 938 15 631 946
natives (2) 12 1547 16 603
nativity (1) 14 976
Natürlich (1) 3 321
natural (43) 3 178 6 108 848 10 871
  11 1249 12 464 672 13 117 478 791
  14 428 688 986 1360 15 1211 2364 2796 2894
  3355 16 639 769 896 987 1215 1670 17 294
  925 995 1307 1745 1828 2068 2178 2179 2217 2279
  2284 2290 18 268 325 1181 1196
naturale (1) 10 168
Naturally (2) 15 4849 16 1324
naturally (3) 16 1071 18 1191 1394
Nature (7) 7 94 8 498 11 1061 13 955
  14 790 1277 16 546
nature (52) 1 265 3 166 4 28 5 484
  6 329 8 684 9 435 859 870 1156 11 1094
  12 335 355 13 213 455 457 539 661 1055 1203
  14 34 228 392 580 760 922 930 1267 15 1068
  1101 1687 1742 1799 3820 16 65 826 1203 1364
  1556 1656 17 185 911 1827 2163 2178 2179
  18 244 1093 1369 1386 1559 1563

nature (1) 15 903
natured (2) 17 2179 2180
naturelles (1) 3 177
nature's (7) 7 499 13 456 14 17 21 1237
  1270 1306
natures (2) 17 2180 18 1059
naught (1) 11 869
naughties (1) 15 2994
naughtn't (2) 9 72 73
Naughty (3) 5 273 13 1106 15 562
naughty (17) 5 245 247 252 255 266 8 327
  612 11 201 715 869 1187 13 252 1263 1280
  15 559 1610
Naumann (1) 6 158
Nausea (1) 13 1187
nauseated (1) 14 854
nauseous (1) 15 3038
nautical (1) 16 726
naval (1) 17 1835
Navan (1) 16 996
navel (4) 3 42 5 503 570 12 957
navelcord (3) 3 36 6 914 14 980
navelcords (1) 14 300
navels (1) 18 291
navigable (1) 17 223
navigation (1) 17 1723
navigator (1) 16 1011
navvies (1) 4 213
NAVVY (5) 15 608 612 621 628 4608
navvy (9) 15 35 133 134 140 173 513 518 607
  620
Navy (1) 15 730
navy (7) 2 25 12 1329 1346 1356 13 154
  15 743 17 870
navy (1) 15 2050
Nay (8) 9 913 12 669 13 297 14 923
  1071 15 1645 3240 4638
nay (7) 14 136 215 794 1098 15 2389
  16 793 1844
ne (4) 12 1139 14 137 149
ne (3) 3 114 169 6 618
Neagh (1) 17 1974
Neagh's (1) 12 1454
neap (1) 17 191
Near (12) 5 232 6 453 862 935 10 83
  11 305 1269 12 497 13 777 1242
  15 2785 3630
Near (1) 15 1324
near (95) 1 680 688 2 292 3 321 419
  4 238 253 338 5 366 465 6 372 585 1003
  7 391 576 963 8 199 217 404 689 806 9 156
  546 722 782 961 1004 10 244 451 655 904 1046
  11 391 392 845 912 940 1167 1180 1258 1269
  12 3 17 150 328 397 512 526 618 774 801 1102
  1469 1854 1878 13 61 79 319 355 631 1032 1247
  1260 1274 14 532 1122 1149 1474 1501
  15 4554 16 9 172 212 629 631 868 1431 1763
  1783 1825 1893 17 1282 18 58 550 673 722
  753 762 769 783 975 1044 1414 1575
near (1) 13 313
near (6) 15 315 1702 1903 3628 4217 4927
Nearer (1) 13 1201
nearer (14) 1 281 3 265 336 4 158
  5 213 6 25 996 7 1003 9 329 14 929
  15 3626 16 110 361 1117
nearer (3) 15 4182 4217 4331
nearest (4) 14 718 1457 15 474 17 1512
Nearing (1) 7 199
nearing (3) 3 3 4 78 16 1314

Nearly (2) 6 906 8 629
nearly (12) 6 261 8 193 627 10 137
  12 207 973 13 184 867 18 550 573 823
  1511
Neary (1) 10 744
Neat (3) 4 513 13 922 16 694
neat (8) 4 512 5 543 6 767 8 346
  12 966 13 150 638 17 1508
'neath (1) 7 246
Neatly (1) 11 369
neatly (8) 1 71 123 549 5 346 7 204
  10 100 305 12 618
neatsleather (1) 9 5
Neaulan (2) 12 1267 1295
Neave's (1) 12 1652
Nebeneinander (1) 3 15
nebeneinander (2) 3 17 447
Nebo (1) 14 376
Nebrakada (2) 15 319 3463
Nebrakada (1) 10 861
nebrakada (1) 10 849
Nebukim (1) 17 712
nebula (2) 17 1049 1080
nebulae (1) 17 1108
Nebulous (1) 15 2167
nec (1) 12 635
necessaries (1) 17 1543
necessarily (2) 16 1842 17 941
necessarium (1) 9 770
necessary (12) 9 828 12 617 15 1980
  4576 16 353 742 805 870 918 17 126 1745
  2159
necessities (1) 17 924
Necessity (1) 9 297
necessity (6) 16 1371 1656 17 996 1410
  1960 2031
Neck (2) 7 63 15 1183
neck (37) 1 39 559 2 124 139 3 372
  4 225 350 5 377 6 511 576 7 47 48 663
  8 914 10 896 11 115 123 12 149
  13 573 1026 14 1085 1193 1426 1480
  15 1170 2397 3210 4597 4644 17 244 1436
  18 173 301 385 1511
neck (10) 15 322 752 1928 2084 2492 2571
  2659 2860 3550 4532
neckarching (1) 17 897
neckcloth (1) 7 817
neckfillet (1) 15 1970
necklace (2) 4 285 18 859
necklaces (1) 15 1815
necks (4) 5 343 7 1023 10 653 13 810
necktie (2) 13 845 17 1435
Nectar (1) 8 927
nectar (1) 8 925
nectarbowl (1) 11 263
nectarous (1) 12 288
Ned (66) 6 111 503 539 556 559 562 564 568
  572 692 702 706 715 828 7 233 239 242 251 260
  268 278 313 316 330 333 351 354 355 357 361 364
  10 399 401 407 414 417 420 428 431 443 459 757
  782 11 780 785 788 12 1011 1016 1017 1020
  1021 1033 1076 1097 1095 1097 1329 1377 1424
  1534 1632 1650 1668 1753 1848 17 1239
Ned (1) 15 1141
Need (1) 8 863
need (20) 4 196 9 27 11 546 12 917
  1441 1601 13 650 14 64 721 826 1588
  15 833 1234 2246 3365 4313 16 1463 1464
  1842 1859

62 65 98 102 112 120 137 142 149 297 324 356 448
458 470 473 475 486 498 514 516 527 544 573 715
729 733 737 864 872 888 949 953 960 967 1022
1032 1066 1128 1174 1241 1253 1260 1296 1316
1329 1355 1368 1390 1391 1408 1458 1535 1550
1564
no (15) 1 239 264 590 2 57 64 3 445
7 846 847 10 1252 11 928 12 31 744
16 1249 17 827
no (6) 15 1764 3227 4148 4925 4928
NO (1) 8 101
No-one (13) 2 42 3 138 159 5 53 230
6 315 8 493 504 911 1138 11 570 1289
13 319
no-one (21) 3 139 308 5 262 7 102
8 876 9 519 10 669 11 395 404
12 1026 1239 13 128 430 524 634 697 729
15 360 820 16 786 1301
Noah (4) 15 1855 3868 17 750
nob (1) 18 1258
nobble (1) 15 2200
nobbling (1) 12 1389
nobis (4) 7 1056 9 773 13 442 15 3640
NOBLE (1) 7 552
Noble (2) 7 836 15 4413
noble (18) 7 1037 9 194 973 10 176 177
12 86 246 281 902 1010 1775 1866 14 746 827
905 1395 15 699
noble (2) 15 1916 4507
Nobleman (1) 8 575
nobleman (6) 10 84 788 13 658 1053
16 217 18 773
nobler (2) 7 478 12 1445
noblest (4) 9 65 12 403 14 663 902
NOBLEWOMAN (1) 15 1463
nobly (2) 11 956 12 632
nobly (1) 15 1464
Nobodaddy (2) 9 787 14 419
Nobody (5) 4 499 6 333 365 13 925
16 485
Nobody (1) 15 934
nobody (16) 12 545 1069 15 666 1727 3202
16 907 1184 1320 18 10 159 309 339 1076
1353 1407 1542
nobodyd (1) 18 1411
noch (1) 9 491
noches (2) 13 1209 15 216
noctambules (1) 16 326
noctambulist (1) 17 930
noctibus (1) 3 466
nocturnal (10) 14 1036 15 3032 17 46
1134 1160 1496 1643 1940 2037 2057
nod (5) 5 556 7 36 10 908 11 253
12 1230
nod (2) 15 1380 4915
nodded (17) 1 672 704 5 164 6 35 661
7 123 278 637 8 291 1014 10 54 702 870
11 496 799 800 16 402
Nodding (1) 6 172
nodding (11) 3 439 6 419 7 952
10 200 897 924 927 1076 11 1193 16 383
1818
nodding (2) 15 4021 4912
noddy (1) 10 766
noded (1) 11 704
nodes (2) 15 2089 17 1440
nods (7) 15 1280 1988 2592 2710 3636 4490
4849
nohow (2) 14 1504 17 2012

Noir (1) 17 426
Noise (1) 8 179
noise (20) 1 162 7 425 574 882 9 85 330
11 965 981 13 1129 14 124 408 426 1126
15 2120 3998 16 929 939 1772 17 288
18 1002
noiseless (3) 9 7 8 15 3276
noiseless (1) 15 4672
noiselessly (2) 2 299 6 228
noises (3) 5 4 7 217 17 282
noisily (1) 6 47
noisily (2) 15 2476 4722
Noisy (1) 6 74
noisy (4) 5 132 13 16 18 712 1142
noisy (1) 15 2240 4366
Nolan (12) 10 968 973 979 986 990 995 1015
1025 1033 1041 1212 12 1178
Nolan (2) 15 4352 4353
NOLAN (2) 15 1533 3304
Nolan's (1) 8 950
Nolasco (1) 12 1682
Nom (1) 1 665
nom (2) 15 2093
nomad (1) 7 846
Noman (1) 17 2008 2011
Nombre (1) 10 148
nomen (2) 9 236 15 1869
nomenclature (1) 17 1154
nominally (1) 12 764
nominate (1) 15 1504
nomine (3) 1 351 11 1032 12 1740
nominedomine (1) 11 1244
nominis (1) 12 1749
Non (3) 3 220 6 601 15 4228
non (1) 18 1508
non (11) 4 327 5 224 6 238 9 941
11 541 826 15 473 4227 16 813 1558
non-compo (1) 17 590
non-intellectual (2) 17 437 439
non-political (2) 17 437 439
non-topical (2) 17 437 439
nonce (3) 16 11 1275 1621
noncommittal (1) 16 1091
Nonconformist (1) 17 789
noncorrosive (1) 15 4214
nondescript (2) 13 972 16 328
nondescript (1) 15 3316
None (5) 3 96 11 224 13 34 14 1475
15 3871
none (34) 3 308 7 1036 12 1252 1308
13 71 278 292 751 14 116 179 738 790 999
1076 1308 1411 1543 15 3206 4281 16 302
866 944 988 1170 1465 1743 1750 17 69 714 797
2008 18 439 1445 1457
none (3) 9 137 17 824 1352
nonentity (1) 17 2007
Nones (1) 10 191
nones (1) 10 195
nonesuch (1) 10 858
nonexistence (1) 17 69
nonexquisite (1) 11 465
nonluminous (1) 17 1121
nono (1) 13 400
nonpareil (1) 17 1392
nonperishable (2) 12 33 44
nonplussed (1) 16 12
nonsense (4) 7 202 708 18 384 1052
nonsensical (2) 16 1267 18 1178
nonstop (1) 15 2193

noodles (1) 14 1058
noodly (1) 16 1789
nook (2) 8 737 13 11
Nookshotten (1) 9 315
Noon (1) 3 216
noon (4) 3 303 443 4 527 14 385
noon (4) 15 932 4057 4061 4081
noonday (1) 15 2358
noonreek (1) 8 233
noose (1) 12 427
noose (1) 15 4554
nooses (1) 2 234
Nor (4) 3 107 9 440 11 1282 12 1057
nor (51) 2 35 6 804 7 843 9 238 457
1030 10 1119 11 1282 1283 12 1055
13 503 14 137 179 213 319 323 364 382 397
398 431 441 446 689 837 851 867 1199 1202 1396
1561 15 941 942 3867 16 218 17 1502
2130 18 679 1022 1308 1315 1316 1368
nor (4) 7 847 865 867 16 405
Nore (1) 3 259
Norma (1) 12 1278
normal (6) 16 692 1489 17 2 269 932 1704
normally (2) 14 1274 17 1087
Norman (5) 1 128 9 317 12 1170 1173
1499
normative (1) 14 1264
Norse (1) 9 994
North (23) 4 109 236 7 16 359 360 10 73
85 752 12 1444 1890 15 1017 1367 16 27
459 629 1406 17 143 486 490 1715 1726 1730
1736
North (1) 16 1255
North (1) 15 3980
north (14) 1 672 2 275 4 194 7 940
8 709 10 111 12 989 16 1406 17 7 94
146 204 1237 1517
northeast (2) 3 159 9 203
Northern (4) 16 46 17 2018 2085 2088
Northern (1) 9 598
northern (1) 10 1182
Northumberland (2) 10 1277 17 1653
northwest (3) 4 102 104 8 474
northwest (1) 15 1469
Norton (1) 15 1983
Norwegian (2) 4 215 16 907
Nos (1) 14 1533
nos (1) 6 618
Nose (1) 6 13
nose (50) 1 162 2 387 3 130 182 4 175
5 184 6 101 308 801 849 7 226 8 679 846
1154 10 1187 11 164 173 1051 1156
12 967 1064 1314 13 31 114 130 141 204 269
310 311 420 524 900 965 1042 14 584 889 1333
16 992 1673 1865 17 2316 18 24 55 145
693 912 1029 1173 1201
nose (14) 15 135 247 250 937 1026 1208 2152
2383 2420 2436 2831 2986 3840 3954
Nosebag (1) 5 211
nosebags (1) 5 216
nosed (1) 4 456
nosehole (1) 3 481
nosejam (1) 8 727
noseless (1) 15 4159
nosepaint (1) 16 663
noserag (2) 1 69 73
noserags (1) 1 113
nosering (1) 15 2891
noses (3) 5 216 8 461 847

nosewings (1) 11 142
Nosey (28) 8 737 766 786 799 813 817 828 836
843 940 943 945 949 954 958 962 966 971 978 983
988 995 1000 1009 1021 10 479 488 1217
Nosey (1) 15 1142
Nosey (3) 15 1639 1646 1719
nosing (1) 3 349
nosing (1) 15 4722
nostra (1) 9 831
nostrae (1) 14 708
nostre (1) 15 3536
nostria (1) 14 1534
nostril (1) 3 500
nostril (1) 15 135
nostrils (11) 4 208 379 5 58 512 6 275
10 620 11 144 12 159 14 587
15 1759 17 1490
nostrils (1) 9 1224
nostrils (4) 15 89 2561 2748 3361
nostrum (2) 12 1740 1750
nostrums (1) 14 932
Not (109) 1 333 718 2 45 367 424 3 189
236 4 72 328 371 425 435 5 154 232 239 329
363 394 6 71 181 245 282 788 899 950 8 58
59 84 119 389 531 577 588 627 695 791 820 926
943 1063 1137 1172 1174 9 130 360 10 166
729 826 925 11 17 187 190 281 352 375 392 445
540 618 1052 1090 1193 12 53 60 1232 1639
1664 13 473 930 1071 1074 1136 **1165** 1220
1253 1275 14 35 870 1352 1466 **1543** 1589
15 309 398 524 819 854 955 1293 13**06** 2373 2446
2500 2826 2962 3311 4473 4576 4600 4869 4938
16 145 522 1120 1841 17 1017 1499 1604 1903
Not (1) 6 730
Not (1) 15 934
not (766) 1 52 62 102 118 140 143 150 156 210
218 374 398 407 421 546 570 605 611 635 717 740
2 7 48 49 160 249 354 360 373 380 395 401 402
3 8 45 48 61 63 107 130 159 237 244 263 267
276 295 322 324 329 367 386 391 394 408 421 451
452 498 4 44 99 187 219 428 494 509 511
5 32 148 172 235 243 245 246 251 253 271 273
333 375 384 469 6 36 133 152 224 329 342 369
549 552 553 571 662 718 744 831 848 858 881 923
1002 1004 1028 7 89 144 153 463 530 548 563
567 731 734 805 815 818 872 887 894 895 975
8 83 86 116 130 328 344 389 473 578 612 851 905
933 949 983 1078 1086 1092 1125 1127 1145
9 2 70 103 106 160 167 178 232 237 243 247 331
348 350 397 424 427 445 459 470 473 487 521 525
589 659 666 671 692 712 805 815 827 834 839 853
865 867 993 999 1011 1012 1015 1030 10 12 38
61 74 146 150 166 167 169 172 291 378 382 391
581 676 750 887 917 945 967 994 1030 1036 1157
1231 11 38 61 153 239 240 246 296 358 378 546
548 621 674 770 771 810 815 818 819 820 859 876
905 955 956 994 1043 1067 1087 1105 1110 1144
1249 1281 1282 1283 12 9 44 285 323 507 654
657 672 713 720 723 732 752 888 957 1043 1203
1259 1481 1539 1603 1608 1609 1611 1630 1757
1842 1914 13 5 10 58 91 109 122 191 199
200 211 245 251 252 267 279 308 348 379 405 420
433 436 454 502 593 603 637 664 697 705 729 841
842 852 879 907 912 928 957 979 1045 1095 1103
1105 1142 1197 1211 1220 1239 1263 14 20 24
33 34 44 47 48 52 56 65 89 136 143 165 171 211
218 221 239 278 282 284 293 303 319 336 372 381
420 430 433 434 437 438 440 464 492 713 718 743
804 810 838 847 850 873 877 881 883 910 914 918

921 924 929 987 1012 1051 1072 1073 1074 1114
1121 1123 1126 1130 1140 1145 1154 1156 1167
1171 1176 1179 1196 1276 1290 1293 1347 1348
1353 1368 1389 1394 1403 1417 1421 1429 1476
1571 15 93 105 106 129 253 260 261 519 526
837 867 941 948 949 967 971 972 1171 1224 1290
1613 1801 1936 1965 2009 2117 2246 2295 2314
2321 2464 2516 2525 2680 2706 2794 2873 2875
2953 2957 3036 3037 3149 3175 3240 3279 3285
3388 3392 3458 3465 3477 3487 3489 3522 3660
3693 3761 3867 4187 4227 4290 4397 4407 4426
4428 16 4 25 48 60 64 119 120 129 136 182 188
204 217 219 230 242 245 278 290 295 302 324 325
345 358 444 454 483 491 496 501 507 555 556 596
624 631 635 649 652 715 724 734 737 739 742 778
812 827 828 848 849 867 1008 1031 1067 1078 1085
1086 1127 1153 1178 1193 1194 1205 1212 1217
1262 1266 1288 1308 1350 1367 1369 1380 1392
1404 1418 1445 1446 1447 1460 1466 1480 1513
1532 1539 1559 1587 1608 1615 1684 1692 1695
1720 1729 1765 1773 1781 1804 1806 1859 1870
1883 17 79 82 225 349 391 531 558 588 607 628
630 657 699 839 840 850 852 878 881 883 924 941
1070 1093 1139 1359 1421 1514 1515 1625 1772
1838 1850 1884 1903 1958 1962 1964 2060 2064
2115 2124 2160 2161 2180 2190 2198 2201 2202
2203 2205 2286 18 17 22 34 35 39 44 53 60 62
81 82 83 123 126 145 165 166 174 175 215 225 244
268 280 299 322 352 379 411 444 456 462 492 517
558 568 589 591 698 705 707 740 743 810 889 897
903 912 925 927 928 940 949 951 987 999 1006
1017 1021 1022 1035 1059 1069 1075 1101 1158
1168 1195 1242 1275 1278 1295 1303 1305 1325
1328 1332 1342 1345 1371 1391 1399 1401 1412
1443 1445 1450 1460 1477 1484 1488 1492 1507
1511 1518 1537 1557
not (12) 2 65 6 731 7 845 8 416 9 98
10 15 11 402 552 782 1289 14 317
not (4) 15 898 933 2329 4366
notably (3) 14 1283 15 4435 16 91
notch (1) 16 524
notches (1) 17 981
note (21) 3 438 7 97 8 594 9 999
10 922 1073 11 397 561 624 630 781 1024
12 728 1584 14 683 1380 16 1821
17 1793 1822 1830
note (1) 7 243
note (2) 15 1317 1318
notebook (3) 6 878 9 75 523
notebook (1) 15 4799
notebooks (1) 15 926
NOTED (1) 7 178
noted (2) 12 659 14 729
Notepaper (1) 17 1466
notepaper (4) 6 603 10 369 11 826
17 1806
Notes (1) 11 13
notes (14) 1 366 2 209 7 94 10 8
11 161 632 1195 12 602 920 13 1011
14 286 15 2517 18 277
notes (1) 15 2147
noteworthy (1) 12 915
nothandle (1) 4 333
Nother (1) 3 199
Nothing (16) 4 48 200 6 21 180 562 781
8 988 10 738 11 571 887 13 672 1104
1267 14 1381 15 2546 4568
Nothing (1) 9 1013
nothing (81) 1 177 207 612 3 35 94 98

4 355 428 6 328 890 948 8 135 390 858 1016
1081 9 131 360 392 635 10 274 1009
11 224 808 12 708 729 1038 1143 1160 1247
1432 1795 13 364 788 811 843 943 1073
14 34 50 747 15 1183 2224 2360 3513 3645
4303 4600 16 32 94 98 120 179 251 547 740 818
838 864 1024 1142 1265 1380 1705 1794
17 1953 18 17 105 138 282 331 495 518 745
999 1057 1244 1369 1558
nothing (2) 1 455 2 254
nothings (1) 16 1364
Nothung (1) 15 4242
Notice (1) 5 461
notice (21) 5 322 6 205 796 8 487
10 1158 11 107 246 247 12 763 876
13 160 14 612 15 328 1642 16 125 283
490 1445 17 1868 1870 18 70
noticed (19) 4 529 8 944 12 924
13 461 569 962 1239 1300 1302 16 734 925
1869 18 247 272 429 437 592 668 1017
notices (3) 7 198 8 744 17 602
noticing (1) 13 521
notion (7) 13 473 14 460 881 15 2525
16 517 18 705 1486
notions (1) 9 445
notorieties (1) 16 1201
Notoriety (1) 7 509
notorious (4) 12 25 101 14 926 15 1562
notoriously (1) 16 1497
Notre (1) 9 1098
Notts (1) 16 1684
notwithstanding (2) 16 1337 17 178
nought (15) 3 39 11 224 13 977
14 443 459 480 560 610 871 1149 1292 17 285
1068 2196
nought (1) 15 1266
noun (1) 18 1473
nourish (1) 16 498
nourished (1) 8 952
nourishing (2) 16 91 17 215
Nous (1) 9 641
nous (3) 3 220 14 306 16 595
Nova (2) 15 1544 17 1051
novel (3) 9 108 994 18 1474
Novelette (1) 13 110
novelty (2) 16 1850 17 1771
November (2) 13 222 17 2280
novena (1) 13 452
novetur (1) 14 347
novices (1) 15 3450
Now (60) 1 631 2 319 342 420 3 424
4 65 167 226 492 5 287 359 552 6 805 806
7 102 218 688 8 119 173 226 502 525 571 1159
9 199 315 10 314 467 483 731 1069 11 648
709 794 984 1014 1247 12 954 1022 13 26
319 814 1271 14 180 187 281 1062 15 404
1231 2208 2473 2792 2828 2966 3012 3676
16 240 331
now (373) 1 131 180 224 254 311 373 417 422
496 668 2 30 134 161 189 195 201 212 234 354
395 3 25 27 48 126 227 317 323 389 419 435 451
475 4 204 223 226 232 233 389 401 410 420 430
444 445 450 512 5 72 252 255 289 382 547 565
6 8 60 131 171 219 344 384 397 423 432 453 494
509 543 627 857 894 961 979 1024 7 71 173 199
338 543 693 706 739 740 886 930 972 8 97 230
262 282 325 334 339 430 606 608 733 735 752 786
829 917 1023 1044 1103 9 60 89 192 205 341 384
479 619 802 978 993 1114 1199 10 42 66 84 476

oats (5) 5 213 9 308 410 15 4841
  18 1560
obdurately (1) 15 1642
obedience (2) 14 336 1007
obedient (4) 7 136 11 601 603 12 1185
O'Beirne's (1) 15 212
obeisance (2) 10 1203 12 1183
obeisance (1) 15 960
obelisk (3) 3 275 12 1455 14 685
O'Bergan's (1) 12 290
obese (1) 6 973
obese (2) 15 1256 2127
obesity (1) 15 1622
obey (3) 6 126 17 118 2017
obey (1) 15 1121
obeyed (1) 17 667
obituaries (1) 8 139
obituary (4) 6 795 7 198 8 744 17 602
object (19) 6 818 12 1584 1880 14 689
  999 1166 15 978 16 286 330 445 706 750 793
  17 911 1679 1840 1930 2220 2296
object (1) 15 3595
objected (1) 16 777
objection (3) 8 1120 15 2710 17 878
objectionable (1) 15 1029
objective (2) 2 165 9 843
objects (11) 12 80 589 16 671 17 1311
  1333 1340 1840 1873 1888 2097 2101
objects (1) 15 1764
objurgations (1) 14 920
oblate (1) 15 4427
Obligated (1) 14 1471
obligation (2) 6 890 17 1204
Oblige (1) 10 5
oblige (2) 16 815 18 842
obliged (6) 6 889 10 426 11 655
  17 460 461 1965
obligingness (1) 14 741
oblique (3) 11 292 365 17 1174
obliterate (2) 14 1022 1034
obliterated (3) 16 488 17 1374 1916
oblivion (2) 5 365 16 1309
oblivious (3) 12 648 14 29 922
obliviously (1) 16 632
oblong (3) 6 767 12 116 17 1541
O'Bloom (1) 12 216
O'Brien (5) 4 491 6 226 15 1645
  17 1370 1648
O'Brien (2) 15 1953 4683
O'Brienite (1) 16 1503
obscene (1) 15 1065
obscenely (1) 15 664
obscenity (1) 15 3042
obscure (3) 2 159 17 1346 2242
obscure (1) 7 855
obscurely (1) 8 639
obscurity (5) 12 160 17 1037 1135 2029
  2068
obscurity (1) 15 2167
obsequies (1) 16 1253
obsequious (3) 10 709 1181 12 1599
observance (1) 12 1342
observants (1) 12 1685
observation (4) 16 220 1149 17 41 557
observations (1) 14 1188
observatory (1) 12 1859
Observe (2) 15 2332 2344
observed (15) 9 708 10 100 599 12 1879
  14 700 904 15 1064 2329 2801 16 239 748
  1150 17 1210 1481 2149

observer (2) 17 1044 2147
observer's (1) 14 1359
observes (1) 15 4515
observing (2) 16 819 17 498
obsession (2) 7 493 17 939
obsolescent (1) 17 1218
obsolete (3) 17 571 1524 1630
obstacle (1) 11 841
obstacles (1) 7 244
obstetrician (1) 14 951
Obstetrics (1) 15 1710
obstetrics (1) 14 977
obstreperous (1) 13 396
obstropolos (1) 14 1569
obstructing (1) 12 10
Obtain (2) 17 514 1397
obtain (4) 17 73 2074 2078
obtainable (2) 6 462 17 1557
obtained (4) 17 1075 1712 1784 1786
obtaining (2) 17 1216 2183
obtunding (1) 17 25
obtuse (1) 17 2161
obverse (1) 17 1057
obviate (1) 16 1858
obviating (4) 17 2031 2032 2033 18 449
Obvious (1) 15 2446
obvious (2) 15 823 16 81
Obviously (1) 15 2356
obviously (5) 16 593 1045 1389 1427 1554
O'Callaghan (2) 6 236 16 1185
Occam (3) 3 123
occasion (19) 12 135 632 663 671 1318 1817
  14 331 647 16 254 284 494 629 1217 1334
  1430 1694 17 393 951 1453
OCCASIONAL (1) 7 178
occasional (1) 16 391
Occasionally (3) 17 1923 1924 1925
occasionally (4) 10 81 14 988 16 849
  17 53
occasioned (1) 16 1358
occasions (5) 6 654 14 875 17 58 372
  1871
occasum (1) 3 487
occident (1) 14 244
occiput (1) 15 1993
occluded (1) 17 1998
Occult (1) 15 2269
occult (1) 8 530
occultation (1) 17 2000
occulted (1) 14 395
occultly (1) 9 104
occupant (2) 16 1199 17 2144
occupants (3) 10 120 12 1868 16 387
occupation (3) 15 802 16 1504 17 2264
occupations (1) 17 515
occupied (10) 16 859 1686 1797 17 1071
  1289 1302 1408 2032 2035
occupier (1) 17 1670
occupies (1) 15 2168
Occupy (1) 4 451
occur (4) 15 948 3890 16 1038 1195
occurred (4) 12 658 16 15 250 1496
occurrence (5) 14 950 15 946 16 605
  1515 17 344
Occurrences (1) 7 734
occurrences (1) 16 152
occurs (1) 16 332
Ocean (2) 3 483 10 630
ocean (7) 11 516 12 376 13 1147
  14 561 16 844 17 186 1156

ocean (1) 15 2274
oceanflowing (1) 17 203
oceangoing (1) 13 1148
oceangreen (1) 11 49
oceans (1) 11 696
oceansong (1) 11 378
Ochone (2) 15 4587
O'Ciarnain's (1) 12 898
O'clock (1) 11 386
o'clock (9) 4 117 8 852 10 553 12 604
  801 1122 13 1170 16 450 1572
oclock (1) 18 1232
o'clock's (1) 11 1242
O'Connell (14) 2 271 5 70 6 641 710 711
  740 750 7 1041 8 44 10 599 703 779
  12 90 17 330
O'Connell (2) 15 1236 4683
O'CONNELL (2) 15 1243 1248
O'Connell's (1) 2 269
O'Connor (9) 8 302 9 1116 10 435 919
  1102 1106 1261 13 1232 17 544
O'Connor (1) 15 2308
o'cook (1) 15 2438
octave (2) 11 684 15 2112
octaves (1) 15 2523
October (4) 17 239 948 1454 2276
octopus (2) 8 520 530
octopus (1) 15 2177
octuplets (1) 15 1823
ocular (2) 15 2442 17 2203
Ocularly (1) 15 2444
odalisk (1) 15 1332
Odd (1) 15 650
odd (17) 1 641 2 62 5 225 6 790
  7 266 8 856 12 1236 13 809 14 518
  16 215 902 1275 1310 1730 18 698 1416 1543
odd (1) 15 1766
Oddly (1) 9 441
odds (4) 12 948 16 636 1244 17 1676
oder (1) 14 308
odes (1) 14 1119
Odessa (1) 16 678
O'Dignam (1) 12 374
odious (2) 14 28 15 1167
O'Donnell (5) 7 541 12 179 1382
  15 1863
O'Donoghue (2) 15 4687 4688
O'Donohoe's (1) 10 1122
O'Donovan (1) 12 199
odoriferous (1) 14 353
odour (14) 1 104 105 271 272 2 145
  12 453 13 1028 1121 14 1146 15 105
  16 56 17 1490 1493 18 1160
odour (2) 15 652 2015
odours (4) 10 87 15 3320 17 1493 2015
O'Dowd (3) 12 513 840 17 482
O'Dowd (1) 15 4338
Odyssus (1) 17 33
odz (1) 3 293
O'er (1) 11 1126
o'er (5) 3 14 6 448 11 708 15 1965 3437
o'er (5) 1 567 7 246 8 63 550 17 805
oer (1) 18 876
OF (12) 7 1 14 20 38 78 141 203 236 464 737
  781 962
Of (54) 1 219 220 666 2 83 3 175 226 243
  491 4 108 429 6 251 780 867 7 34
  8 179 520 873 1118 9 527 988 1113 10 781
  11 157 500 1275 12 1043 13 396 903

1117 1118 1119 1120 1121 1122 1124 1125 1126
1127 1128 1129 1134 1135 1136 1137 1138 1139
1150 1155 1163 1168 1169 1170 1171 1174 1176
1180 1184 1185 1186 1189 1194 1198 1199 1200
1204 1208 1211 1212 1213 1240 1241 1243 1244
1249 1250 1253 1255 1256 1257 1260 1262 1263
1264 1267 1268 1278 1279 1281 1282 1283 1284
1285 1286 1287 1288 1289 1290 1291 1293 1300
1302 1303 1304 1305 1308 1309 1310 1311 1315
1320 1322 1325 1327 1334 1336 1344 1348 1349
1352 1354 1355 1356 1365 1370 1372 1373 1374
1375 1382 1383 1385 1388 1391 1394 1395 1397
1402 1403 1404 1405 1408 1417 1426 1427 1432
1433 1439 1440 1442 1443 1445 1448 1451 1453
1454 1456 1460 1461 1463 1469 1477 1479 1483
1485 1492 1504 1508 1509 1512 1514 1515 1516
1517 1518 1519 1523 1524 1526 1527 1528 1529
1531 1547 1561 1564 1568 1571 1575 1576 1579
1583 1584 1585 1589 1595 1601 1604 1614 1615
1616 1619 1638 1642 1647 1650 1652 1655 1658
1661 1663 1676 1678 1679 1681 1682 1683 1684
1685 1686 1687 1688 1690 1692 1694 1698 1702
1703 1706 1707 1708 1709 1711 1714 1718 1727
1729 1731 1736 1737 1738 1751 1755 1765 1769
1775 1777 1779 1780 1781 1783 1785 1786 1790
1792 1793 1796 1801 1814 1816 1817 1818 1820
1821 1822 1823 1824 1826 1827 1828 1829 1830
1831 1833 1835 1837 1838 1839 1840 1843 1853
1859 1860 1861 1862 1863 1864 1865 1866 1867
1869 1870 1871 1872 1873 1874 1875 1876 1877
1878 1879 1880 1881 1882 1885 1886 1887 1888
1891 1892 1897 1898 1901 1909 1912 1913 1914
1916 1917   **13**   2 4 7 8 26 29 32 34 36 38 42 49
57 58 74 81 84 85 86 87 89 90 94 99 100 107 110
112 116 117 118 121 122 127 128 130 131 139 142
144 145 147 148 150 153 156 157 164 169 172 180
187 190 193 195 198 201 204 206 213 215 224 225
228 232 249 250 264 265 268 279 281 282 284 285
286 287 288 289 290 295 298 299 300 301 302 309
310 320 321 329 330 332 333 334 336 364 365 367
368 371 372 373 374 378 381 384 389 390 402 405
406 410 416 419 422 424 427 430 438 442 444 445
447 452 454 455 457 462 464 465 466 469 476 480
483 489 490 496 500 503 508 510 513 514 519 524
527 530 538 543 549 551 552 554 560 561 563 572
579 580 584 586 591 594 597 603 609 610 625 627
628 633 634 635 637 639 642 645 648 658 661 666
670 671 687 694 700 701 703 704 708 711 713 716
722 726 727 731 735 738 739 742 743 747 748 749
757 758 761 763 768 769 774 779 785 786 791 793
801 802 803 804 805 816 820 823 839 853 856 860
865 868 874 877 885 886 897 903 907 910 913 914
926 927 929 935 941 943 944 949 955 963 964 965
969 972 975 978 983 987 991 1003 1004 1005 1008
1009 1012 1013 1017 1021 1022 1025 1026 1027
1038 1040 1042 1048 1061 1066 1069 1071 1072
1079 1084 1092 1094 1102 1105 1107 1109 1121
1130 1131 1135 1148 1150 1152 1155 1158 1159
1160 1162 1167 1169 1173 1175 1177 1178 1179
1185 1187 1188 1214 1219 1222 1223 1226 1243
1246 1248 1250 1252 1262 1267 1283 1299   **14**   9
10 11 13 14 15 16 17 19 21 22 26 30 31 35 40 43 44
46 55 56 57 64 65 67 68 73 90 91 101 108 116 119
123 124 127 130 134 139 141 142 145 147 150 153
154 155 156 158 163 165 168 171 173 176 179 181
184 187 188 189 190 192 193 194 195 205 206 207
209 211 220 221 225 227 230 232 233 237 239 241
242 243 244 245 246 247 252 253 255 256 261 265
266 267 268 269 270 271 274 280 281 282 283 286

288 292 293 295 298 300 302 305 315 321 322 324
326 328 329 330 331 334 338 339 340 344 345 346
351 352 354 355 357 359 360 363 367 371 373 374
375 376 379 380 381 384 385 386 388 394 395 396
397 399 403 408 414 415 422 424 426 427 435 436
439 443 444 447 449 456 460 465 467 471 474 482
486 487 491 498 501 502 504 505 508 509 513 519
522 524 525 526 529 533 534 538 539 541 544 547
548 549 551 556 562 565 566 569 577 579 583 586
587 590 595 596 597 598 602 603 604 608 612 614
615 616 622 624 628 629 631 633 634 637 638 640
641 642 646 647 656 657 658 661 662 664 665 666
668 670 673 676 677 680 681 682 683 686 687 688
690 693 694 695 696 697 700 703 706 710 711 712
714 715 721 724 727 730 732 734 735 736 739 742
743 744 746 749 750 752 753 756 759 761 763 764
766 767 769 773 774 776 777 780 782 786 788 792
793 796 798 799 803 805 806 807 814 815 816 821
826 827 830 831 832 833 834 835 836 840 841 846
847 848 849 851 852 853 854 855 856 857 858 859
860 861 862 863 865 866 867 869 871 872 873 878
879 881 883 884 888 889 892 893 896 897 899 900
901 904 905 906 907 911 912 913 915 916 920 921
922 923 925 929 931 932 933 934 935 937 943 946
947 948 949 951 952 954 955 956 959 960 963 964
966 967 968 969 970 971 972 974 975 977 979 981
983 984 986 987 988 989 990 993 994 995 996 998
1000 1002 1006 1012 1013 1017 1020 1021 1028
1029 1033 1038 1042 1043 1045 1048 1052 1053
1057 1058 1060 1063 1065 1066 1073 1074 1075
1076 1079 1080 1082 1084 1086 1087 1088 1089
1090 1095 1099 1100 1103 1104 1106 1108 1109
1110 1112 1113 1114 1116 1119 1124 1125 1126
1127 1128 1135 1142 1144 1145 1147 1158 1162
1167 1169 1170 1171 1174 1175 1176 1178 1182
1183 1185 1189 1190 1193 1195 1196 1197 1198
1199 1201 1202 1204 1205 1207 1209 1210 1211
1213 1214 1215 1216 1218 1220 1221 1227 1231
1232 1233 1236 1237 1238 1239 1247 1248 1250
1252 1253 1254 1257 1258 1260 1261 1262 1263
1266 1269 1271 1272 1273 1274 1276 1279 1282
1283 1284 1285 1290 1291 1293 1294 1298 1299
1301 1302 1305 1306 1307 1308 1310 1318 1321
1323 1324 1325 1326 1328 1331 1332 1335 1345
1351 1354 1356 1359 1360 1362 1363 1364 1369
1370 1371 1374 1375 1377 1380 1381 1382 1383
1384 1387 1388 1390 1392 1394 1397 1399 1403
1404 1414 1418 1423 1425 1428 1434 1436 1441
1445 1447 1455 1456 1465 1467 1469 1474 1475
1478 1479 1486 1492 1493 1495 1503 1510 1511
1514 1529 1537 1540 1542 1543 1549 1552 1562
1580 1584   **15**   46 47 58 59 72 94 106 112 117
129 170 203 206 208 209 210 233 235 245 261 262
264 290 384 395 398 401 402 429 434 435 447 467
497 510 548 549 551 554 557 559 564 565 586 611
640 644 646 655 658 665 670 688 697 701 713 714
716 721 740 744 746 747 750 760 765 772 775 776
778 779 781 785 787 788 789 803 821 822 824 826
836 837 840 842 844 845 847 855 865 873 878 883
885 940 942 945 947 949 950 952 953 954 968 969
971 981 982 1002 1004 1009 1017 1019 1020 1023
1030 1031 1032 1034 1035 1047 1048 1050 1061
1062 1063 1070 1099 1104 1118 1126 1151 1158
1160 1167 1220 1230 1231 1232 1233 1250 1254
1336 1350 1353 1357 1358 1364 1366 1368 1370
1383 1394 1396 1452 1456 1468 1472 1498 1507
1517 1529 1543 1545 1564 1629 1630 1632 1642
1643 1656 1662 1674 1677 1683 1685 1686 1687
1692 1720 1731 1737 1742 1754 1755 1756 1758

1759 1777 1778 1779 1782 1784 1789 1790 1798
1802 1805 1809 1898 1901 1907 1917 1936 1941
1942 1943 1947 1949 1950 1962 1963 1965 1967
1971 1974 2081 2087 2089 2090 2093 2094 2098
2117 2140 2141 2166 2197 2218 2231 2233 2254
2269 2271 2275 2293 2312 2315 2320 2321 2324
2329 2330 2332 2340 2341 2344 2346 2356 2357
2359 2361 2362 2363 2364 2365 2372 2380 2389
2394 2400 2412 2413 2416 2417 2418 2423 2424
2439 2440 2448 2449 2464 2473 2496 2498 2516
2523 2533 2535 2538 2541 2545 2547 2548 2550
2551 2575 2643 2647 2653 2667 2679 2681 2690
2703 2718 2750 2779 2780 2781 2782 2784 2795
2815 2817 2818 2826 2827 2835 2839 2861 2868
2869 2892 2893 2896 2899 2910 2932 2976 2979
2980 2982 2992 3003 3006 3012 3025 3028 3029
3038 3042 3043 3049 3053 3075 3078 3080 3085
3086 3107 3116 3118 3121 3131 3137 3141 3154
3174 3178 3186 3187 3191 3204 3230 3231 3243
3247 3248 3249 3268 3272 3273 3275 3295 3306
3311 3320 3321 3322 3323 3353 3358 3375 3387
3398 3399 3411 3424 3436 3444 3458 3467 3476
3486 3493 3500 3513 3533 3534 3566 3581 3601
3625 3630 3638 3650 3687 3692 3799 3800 3805
3861 3867 3868 3871 3882 3890 3892 3901 3902
3904 3906 3922 3930 3948 3965 4002 4042 4106
4137 4139 4170 4178 4212 4232 4235 4281 4291
4297 4299 4354 4371 4372 4413 4419 4420 4428
4433 4434 4435 4439 4443 4462 4469 4470 4490
4509 4515 4539 4541 4570 4585 4587 4590 4597
4628 4644 4735 4791 4817 4847 4862 4873 4874
4949 4953   **16**   2 6 8 10 16 19 22 23 24 25 28 30
35 36 37 38 39 41 44 45 46 47 48 52 55 57 58 62 63
65 66 67 68 69 76 77 80 81 83 87 88 89 90 94 95 96
97 99 101 102 103 104 105 106 109 110 112 115
116 118 123 130 131 132 133 134 136 137 139 142
147 148 150 151 161 165 167 169 172 173 175 177
178 179 180 182 186 195 196 205 206 208 211 212
219 222 223 224 225 227 231 236 237 238 240 249
256 260 262 263 265 275 276 277 280 285 292 296
300 301 302 310 311 323 325 327 328 330 331 332
333 335 338 340 342 343 350 352 354 355 356 360
362 371 375 376 379 385 387 397 411 415 425 427
428 430 434 435 442 445 453 456 466 468 471 473
475 477 478 482 497 498 499 500 502 510 511 513
514 515 518 522 526 527 529 532 533 535 537 539
541 542 544 545 547 549 552 554 556 560 561 563
566 568 574 580 583 585 588 590 591 593 595 597
598 600 606 611 616 617 622 625 626 628 632 635
638 639 640 641 649 662 663 674 675 679 686 688
692 693 694 698 704 705 706 709 710 712 713 714
722 723 724 725 726 739 740 741 744 745 748 752
754 757 759 761 762 763 769 770 772 774 777 778
780 781 782 784 785 786 794 801 802 804 805 806
807 809 810 813 816 821 826 827 830 832 833 834
838 839 840 854 856 859 860 861 863 870 877 886
890 892 893 896 897 901 903 907 908 909 910 913
914 922 923 924 925 926 928 931 933 934 937 939
940 942 946 947 948 950 952 955 956 958 968 969
970 971 972 977 978 987 988 990 991 997 999 1000
1002 1004 1007 1008 1010 1012 1022 1025 1027
1029 1032 1035 1038 1039 1040 1043 1047 1052
1055 1056 1058 1059 1061 1064 1067 1068 1073
1074 1076 1077 1088 1089 1090 1094 1098 1102
1107 1109 1112 1113 1114 1119 1120 1135 1136
1138 1141 1142 1143 1144 1145 1152 1153 1155
1158 1160 1170 1174 1175 1179 1180 1182 1183
1184 1185 1186 1189 1192 1193 1194 1195 1198
1199 1200 1201 1202 1207 1209 1210 1214 1219

1222 1223 1224 1225 1230 1232 1238 1242 1243
1245 1247 1248 1262 1265 1267 1276 1285 1289
1291 1305 1308 1310 1313 1317 1319 1321 1324
1325 1330 1332 1335 1340 1344 1351 1354 1355
1358 1359 1360 1363 1366 1375 1376 1377 1379
1380 1382 1384 1386 1387 1388 1389 1391 1393
1395 1397 1399 1401 1403 1405 1407 1410 1414
1422 1429 1430 1431 1432 1435 1440 1441 1445
1448 1451 1461 1462 1463 1466 1468 1469 1471
1476 1477 1480 1481 1482 1484 1494 1495 1498
1499 1500 1502 1503 1506 1508 1511 1512 1513
1514 1519 1521 1523 1524 1525 1526 1527 1530
1538 1543 1546 1547 1550 1552 1553 1556 1563
1564 1565 1572 1578 1581 1584 1588 1590 1591
1595 1596 1599 1600 1602 1606 1612 1613 1621
1622 1624 1625 1629 1633 1634 1635 1640 1648
1650 1652 1656 1658 1661 1662 1666 1668 1672
1677 1679 1683 1685 1687 1696 1698 1704 1705
1708 1715 1723 1724 1727 1728 1729 1730 1733
1737 1739 1741 1744 1750 1751 1752 1755 1758
1759 1761 1762 1772 1775 1780 1781 1783 1786
1787 1789 1791 1793 1794 1795 1797 1798 1801
1802 1803 1804 1811 1812 1813 1820 1826 1827
1834 1835 1836 1837 1840 1842 1843 1850 1852
1856 1857 1859 1860 1861 1864 1865 1872 1874
1877 1881 1882 1883 1889 1890 1891 1893   **17** 5
6 13 14 16 17 18 21 22 23 26 28 30 31 32 33 34 35
36 38 39 40 41 44 52 55 59 60 63 65 71 72 75 86 87
89 91 93 94 95 102 103 108 110 111 114 116 121
122 124 127 128 129 130 133 136 137 138 139 140
141 142 143 144 145 146 148 150 153 156 164 165
166 167 168 169 171 172 174 175 176 178 179 180
182 183 186 187 188 189 190 193 195 197 198 199
201 211 212 213 218 220 226 227 231 238 239 240
241 243 244 245 246 247 249 250 251 252 253 255
256 257 259 260 261 262 264 265 267 268 270 272
273 281 285 286 288 289 296 300 301 303 304 305
306 307 311 312 317 318 319 320 323 324 327 332
333 336 338 339 340 343 345 346 355 359 361 363
365 366 371 374 375 378 379 380 385 386 389 392
393 394 410 418 420 421 422 426 428 429 430 431
432 433 435 438 439 441 444 447 448 450 456 458
463 464 467 468 469 470 471 476 477 479 480 482
483 485 487 489 490 491 498 499 500 502 503 505
506 516 518 522 523 532 534 535 536 538 539 543
545 546 547 552 553 556 557 563 564 565 569 571
573 581 582 583 587 590 599 602 604 608 609 623
624 625 626 627 628 629 630 631 646 648 650 651
652 653 668 671 672 674 675 676 679 680 681 682
683 684 685 688 689 690 691 693 696 699 709 711
712 713 716 718 720 724 725 730 731 732 733 735
738 741 743 745 747 749 750 751 753 754 755 756
758 759 760 761 765 766 768 771 778 780 782 783
786 790 794 799 801 809 812 829 833 835 839 842
845 846 847 848 850 854 855 859 861 862 864 868
872 875 879 881 888 890 891 894 897 898 899 900
902 903 905 907 911 912 913 914 915 916 918 921
922 927 929 933 936 937 938 939 942 945 951 952
953 954 956 957 962 963 964 965 968 969 970 971
973 975 977 980 982 983 990 991 996 997 998 999
1000 1003 1004 1005 1009 1015 1020 1021 1022
1029 1032 1034 1037 1038 1039 1041 1042 1043
1045 1046 1048 1049 1050 1051 1052 1055 1057
1058 1059 1060 1061 1062 1063 1064 1065 1066
1071 1072 1073 1074 1075 1076 1077 1078 1079
1080 1081 1083 1084 1085 1086 1087 1089 1094
1096 1099 1101 1103 1104 1105 1107 1108 1109
1111 1112 1114 1115 1116 1118 1119 1121 1122
1123 1124 1125 1126 1128 1129 1130 1131 1132

1133 1134 1135 1142 1143 1146 1147 1148 1149
1151 1153 1155 1156 1162 1166 1167 1168 1173
1174 1177 1183 1184 1187 1192 1193 1195 1196
1197 1200 1201 1203 1204 1206 1207 1208 1212
1213 1215 1216 1220 1221 1222 1223 1224 1226
1227 1228 1235 1236 1243 1244 1246 1247 1248
1256 1257 1258 1259 1260 1261 1262 1266 1267
1272 1275 1277 1279 1286 1288 1294 1296 1298
1300 1301 1304 1306 1307 1316 1318 1319 1323
1324 1327 1328 1331 1332 1335 1336 1337 1338
1339 1340 1342 1343 1344 1347 1350 1358 1359
1375 1382 1387 1389 1401 1402 1403 1404 1408
1410 1411 1412 1413 1414 1417 1419 1423 1424
1427 1428 1431 1432 1433 1436 1438 1439 1440
1443 1444 1450 1451 1452 1454 1479 1480 1482
1484 1485 1486 1488 1489 1490 1493 1494 1495
1499 1500 1501 1505 1511 1514 1515 1520 1533
1536 1537 1542 1545 1555 1556 1573 1579 1581
1585 1588 1589 1590 1594 1596 1598 1599 1600
1603 1604 1608 1609 1610 1616 1618 1619 1620
1621 1623 1624 1625 1627 1629 1630 1631 1632
1633 1636 1639 1640 1642 1643 1644 1648 1649
1650 1651 1652 1653 1654 1655 1656 1658 1659
1660 1661 1662 1663 1665 1666 1667 1668 1670
1671 1675 1676 1679 1685 1687 1689 1691 1692
1693 1694 1695 1696 1699 1700 1701 1702 1703
1704 1705 1706 1707 1708 1709 1711 1712 1713
1714 1715 1716 1719 1720 1721 1725 1730 1731
1732 1738 1740 1741 1746 1748 1752 1753 1754
1755 1756 1760 1762 1764 1766 1767 1772 1773
1775 1776 1779 1781 1782 1783 1784 1786 1789
1790 1791 1793 1795 1796 1799 1806 1808 1812
1814 1815 1817 1819 1826 1828 1829 1831 1836
1840 1845 1850 1851 1852 1855 1856 1858 1859
1860 1861 1864 1865 1867 1868 1870 1872 1875
1876 1877 1878 1879 1880 1882 1885 1887 1889
1890 1891 1893 1897 1898 1899 1900 1901 1905
1907 1909 1910 1911 1913 1914 1916 1918 1919
1921 1924 1925 1926 1927 1928 1931 1932 1933
1934 1936 1937 1938 1940 1943 1944 1945 1946
1949 1950 1951 1952 1955 1957 1959 1960 1961
1966 1969 1970 1971 1974 1976 1978 1982 1983
1984 1987 1988 1989 1990 1992 1993 1994 1996
1997 1998 1999 2000 2002 2010 2011 2013 2015
2018 2020 2021 2023 2028 2029 2030 2031 2032
2034 2037 2038 2039 2042 2044 2045 2046 2047
2051 2052 2053 2054 2055 2061 2062 2068 2072
2074 2075 2077 2078 2079 2081 2082 2083 2084
2085 2088 2090 2092 2093 2094 2095 2096 2097
2104 2106 2109 2110 2112 2116 2118 2119 2120
2123 2124 2125 2128 2129 2133 2136 2140 2143
2144 2150 2152 2158 2159 2164 2165 2167 2168
2170 2171 2173 2178 2180 2181 2184 2185 2186
2187 2191 2197 2198 2204 2206 2207 2210 2212
2214 2215 2216 2218 2223 2224 2225 2226 2230
2231 2232 2233 2234 2235 2237 2241 2244 2253
2255 2256 2257 2259 2260 2261 2263 2264 2265
2266 2269 2271 2273 2274 2275 2278 2279 2281
2282 2284 2287 2288 2289 2291 2296 2300 2301
2303 2304 2306 2309 2313 2315 2316 2329   **18** 2
5 8 9 10 14 17 27 29 33 35 36 37 43 52 55 57 61 66
67 79 94 96 97 100 112 116 118 119 124 126 127
129 139 140 144 147 150 152 153 154 156 158 160
161 163 164 172 174 176 179 185 186 189 191 195
196 198 200 201 203 211 213 215 218 231 232 234
237 243 246 250 251 254 264 268 273 286 287 288
289 294 307 308 316 321 324 325 326 335 342 356
358 360 361 366 368 372 375 376 378 383 387 389
395 399 401 405 411 412 413 426 431 435 436 439

442 445 446 451 453 455 458 459 463 468 469 475
478 480 482 483 486 487 488 489 491 494 496 498
499 500 504 506 509 514 516 518 527 530 539 541
542 543 546 552 554 556 557 559 562 568 569 570
571 580 582 583 588 591 597 598 600 602 603 605
608 611 617 618 620 625 629 631 633 634 635 636
637 641 648 650 651 652 653 654 657 659 663 665
666 670 674 677 686 693 695 696 697 699 700 702
703 713 714 726 742 747 750 752 753 755 759 762
767 773 777 781 786 798 799 805 806 812 816 817
819 828 829 835 845 849 854 860 861 863 877 878
879 884 889 890 891 902 904 910 919 925 931 932
933 937 939 941 943 944 945 951 952 959 960 965
968 973 974 978 979 985 986 992 997 1002 1005
1006 1008 1017 1019 1020 1024 1026 1027 1029
1030 1036 1038 1039 1040 1050 1058 1059 1060
1065 1068 1072 1078 1079 1080 1083 1095 1099
1105 1107 1114 1115 1117 1123 1128 1129 1132
1137 1143 1144 1157 1164 1175 1177 1178 1184
1186 1188 1199 1205 1209 1210 1213 1219 1226
1227 1230 1232 1239 1241 1243 1249 1258 1260
1261 1267 1273 1275 1276 1286 1292 1296 1300
1302 1303 1304 1305 1309 1317 1319 1325 1330
1331 1333 1335 1339 1346 1355 1356 1357 1374
1375 1380 1384 1393 1396 1401 1403 1404 1405
1407 1413 1420 1421 1422 1424 1425 1426 1441
1443 1447 1453 1456 1459 1462 1464 1468 1471
1473 1479 1482 1493 1495 1498 1500 1509 1512
1515 1517 1525 1526 1534 1535 1544 1545 1553
1554 1556 1558 1560 1562 1563 1564 1568 1574
1576 1582 1585 1589 1592 1594 1602

of (126) **1** 455 463   **2** 78 294 305   **3** 257
4 346 369 513   **5** 147 281   **6** 146 148 186 355
7 243 244 247 320 322 323 327 427 579 591 617
750 768 769 770 771 829 832 838 839 846 847 848
856 863 865 867 868 869 1057   **8** 748 778 1071
1074   **9** 19 94 115 137 266 514 523 583 612 726
758 798 1001 1063   **10** 557 585 591 606 641 735
793 838 1254   **11** 226 685 710 1176 1289
12 362 417 420 422 427 740 744   **13** 1174 1213
14 407   **15** 1024 1125   **16** 1248 1252 1253
1298 1421   **17** 401 442 640 644 734 825 1367
1369 1373 1380 1381 1385 1391 1394 1395 1398
1416 1645 2260

of (414) **15** 1 3 6 8 15 29 30 36 38 41 50 61 75
78 86 135 136 138 140 147 149 173 174 191 243
249 250 260 271 288 297 310 314 335 340 357 361
367 450 482 500 502 509 516 536 579 581 590 605
653 683 693 726 729 752 753 759 770 793 807 808
815 863 875 896 902 905 907 908 909 910 912 913
920 936 939 960 986 992 994 996 1000 1015 1026
1038 1081 1122 1128 1136 1139 1140 1143 1162
1163 1184 1204 1208 1236 1237 1239 1266 1268
1318 1325 1326 1327 1329 1330 1333 1340 1341
1373 1376 1378 1402 1407 1411 1413 1415 1416
1418 1419 1420 1421 1423 1424 1425 1426 1432
1436 1437 1439 1441 1448 1477 1487 1490 1491
1502 1508 1511 1519 1520 1546 1547 1549 1550
1554 1555 1566 1567 1572 1573 1576 1577 1578
1580 1582 1585 1601 1608 1609 1619 1703 1705
1708 1748 1751 1764 1766 1798 1814 1829 1830
1831 1832 1846 1887 1919 1927 1928 1930 1937
1938 1953 1993 1994 2005 2012 2015 2016 2017
2019 2032 2039 2040 2041 2043 2045 2047 2048
2052 2053 2073 2074 2079 2123 2148 2149 2150
2159 2175 2177 2179 2186 2216 2249 2252 2261
2262 2268 2270 2272 2274 2290 2291 2300 2307
2308 2334 2461 2485 2487 2489 2501 2537 2570
2587 2607 2625 2654 2659 2677 2684 2724 2810

394 395 452 464 469 472 485 492 514 598 600 604
617 630 637 683 685 687 692 700 736 746 751 768
784 786 802 831 833 837 897 957 975 976 990 993
998 1037 1062 1063 1082 1083 1084 1094 1095
1097 1130 1137 1153 1162 1170 1207 1212 1213
1225 1240 1269 1291 1328 1330 1374 1377 1399
1416 1499 1536 1537 1583 1592 1594

old (9) **1** 382 **2** 356 **5** 161 **8** 748 **9** 26
10 16 **12** 810 **16** 702 **17** 419
old (5) **15** 1601 2186 4223 4330 4359
older (10) **4** 86 **8** 268 **9** 991 **14** 173
13 1322 **17** 472 504 **18** 476 624 1470
oldest (3) **4** 223 225 **12** 1308
Oldfashioned (1) **4** 292
Oldfellow (1) **15** 3828
oldish (1) **4** 149
oldly (1) **2** 345
oldmaidish (1) **16** 742
oldtime (1) **13** 336
Ole (1) **12** 984
ole (1) **14** 1441 1443
oleaginous (1) **14** 1056 **17** 303
O'Leary (1) **16** 427
O'Leary (1) **15** 4685
O'Lees (1) **14** 37
oleograph (1) **17** 1542
Olhausen's (1) **15** 155
Oliphant (1) **15** 96
Olive (1) **12** 1272
olive (4) **8** 760 **12** 1713 **17** 1507 2003
olive (1) **15** 2747
olivepress (1) **14** 154
Olives (2) **4** 196 202
olives (6) **4** 195 **5** 296 **8** 758 **12** 1005
17 303 **18** 1481
Olivetans (1) **12** 1680
olivetrees (1) **4** 202
Olivet's (1) **1** 599
ollav (1) **9** 30
ollave (1) **15** 2261
Ollebo (1) **17** 409
O'Loughlin's (1) **3** 377
O'Madden (19) **7** 505 508 572 589 592 598
609 623 641 695 696 725 774 888 896 1029
10 410 **11** 270
O'MADDEN (1) **15** 1694
Omaha (1) **12** 1324
O'Malley (1) **16** 558
Omar (2) **15** 117 **17** 1982
O'Mara (1) **16** 208
omega (2) **17** 1994 1995
Omelette (1) **15** 3918
omelette (2) **15** 3912
omens (1) **17** 1167
OMINOUS (1) **7** 871
Ominous (1) **14** 1092
ominous (1) **12** 527
omission (1) **18** 1538
omissions (2) **18** 1170
omitted (1) **17** 2251
omitting (1) **14** 65
omlet (1) **15** 3909
omne (1) **16** 1852
Omnes (1) **12** 1722
omnes (3) **13** 675 **14** 1533 **15** 84
omnia (2) **10** 197 **12** 1746
omnipollent (1) **14** 16
omnipotens (1) **14** 1445
Omnipotent (2) **15** 1955 4713

omnipotent (1) **1** 297
omnipotentiam (1) **14** 297
omnipresent (1) **17** 263
Omnis (2) **3** 396 **14** 294
omnis (1) **14** 347
OMNIUM (1) **7** 604
omnivorous (3) **14** 1287 **15** 2439 2448
O'Molloy (40) **7** 282 290 297 301 365 382 409
424 437 451 462 467 478 499 502 545 600 625 700
727 741 746 755 760 767 775 777 782 800 813 872
906 958 1000 1062 1064 **10** 433 442 453 458
O'Molloy (1) **15** 992
O'MOLLOY (4) **15** 938 966 997 1644
O'Molloy's (3) **7** 819 **10** 236 **12** 1008
O'Molloy's (1) **15** 974
omophorion (1) **3** 54
Omphalos (1) **14** 685
omphalos (3) **1** 176 544 **3** 38
ON (2) **7** 938 1033
On (76) **1** 273 **2** 126 201 278 364 448
3 133 181 336 **4** 49 72 132 216 234 271 434
6 162 440 442 464 627 **7** 22 930 **8** 370 595
1060 **9** 839 982 **10** 107 467 483 599 970 1199
1204 1277 **11** 103 188 189 865 1105 1112
12 618 1291 1351 **13** 263 **14** 86 1496
15 172 200 1525 2474 2848 3254 4562 4660
16 629 774 796 841 865 1529 1610 1752 1770
17 158 298 302 317 614 733 792 876 878 881
1996
On (5) **1** 302 305 **7** 522 **9** 1146 **12** 743
On (12) **15** 28 141 312 2032 2273 2309 2745
4143 4315 4688 4691 4965
on (1836) **1** 2 3 14 37 38 40 63 64 70 82 83 100
131 136 174 181 208 221 232 246 268 274 275 276
307 319 330 334 346 349 360 364 401 411 427 438
447 487 502 511 513 520 534 543 575 579 603 622
627 628 630 679 689 700 716 718 725 743 **2** 58
60 82 84 85 87 128 148 183 190 196 200 210 217
246 247 248 283 286 287 293 308 322 324 331 339
362 365 371 392 424 429 440 447 **3** 15 39 46 94
103 114 141 148 154 155 163 193 207 209 259 263
284 286 291 301 302 307 312 326 333 336 344 348
350 387 415 417 418 427 438 443 446 449 455 500
504 **4** 7 13 15 23 37 85 87 92 94 100 145 148 150
155 161 182 212 237 242 243 253 259 266 274 297
301 303 304 306 334 347 362 364 380 386 387 400
403 406 408 469 480 485 486 500 501 509 512 519
522 524 527 532 **5** 6 28 30 36 38 57 66 71 80 89
99 107 139 152 194 202 229 276 295 322 323 328
340 356 371 372 377 378 404 405 416 525 528 540
545 555 556 **6** 4 22 47 54 58 59 60 75 80 83 129
145 149 156 160 180 212 217 218 236 240 252 253
272 278 284 346 351 359 363 368 375 386 390 399
416 420 430 433 439 443 453 454 459 489 508 511
549 559 582 587 598 603 623 656 685 715 739
742 756 780 781 782 802 807 815 833 850 865 873
875 884 909 911 912 918 930 946 949 953 954 964
1011 1022 1027 1031 **7** 9 17 22 48 57 64 97 103
108 118 121 140 143 158 169 171 196 217 241 242
251 255 263 266 275 305 307 316 351 354 379 383
390 410 426 433 445 450 457 461 469 490 492 493
540 547 593 615 629 653 676 687 729 744 755 763
800 803 809 885 898 899 935 936 949 957 977 984
985 986 994 1000 1001 1005 1010 1017 1029 1067
8 4 18 20 34 36 44 48 58 70 77 79 82 85 89 100
109 115 126 133 156 167 185 189 190 198 209 211
240 242 247 272 281 292 315 317 330 338 347 354
371 373 382 387 399 402 427 432 436 439 440 443
447 452 458 477 479 485 490 505 506 508 509 512

537 555 556 561 562 576 586 613 617 631 637 654
659 675 683 689 712 719 727 741 753 789 791 812
813 815 827 858 861 865 866 884 893 896 897 900
903 911 913 952 955 973 990 1016 1020 1031 1050
1096 1104 1107 1121 1127 1129 1149 1155 1158
1161 1165 1166 1172 **9** 3 5 6 45 105 155 164 203
219 220 257 281 295 365 367 378 411 440 476 495
497 506 549 553 570 608 629 654 667 676 717 753
761 807 812 819 825 839 925 932 946 979 991 995
1010 1022 1038 1057 1083 1101 1153 1159 1162
1190 1217 **10** 20 33 69 70 79 98 104 108 111
114 127 129 144 172 209 213 217 249 253 263 268
303 315 364 375 381 393 402 424 425 426 478 480
496 521 525 542 554 555 556 575 579 594 634 635
641 647 660 686 690 708 747 754 757 783 789 803
811 814 822 872 899 913 938 945 953 960 1009
1023 1038 1047 1059 1077 1095 1110 1114 1119
1137 1140 1145 1151 1168 1174 1182 1186 1189
1195 1209 1210 1218 1224 1268 **11** 6 8 90 98
109 198 231 240 285 299 302 304 309 310 312 337
342 347 358 372 375 387 395 409 417 430 442 449
451 458 485 486 498 525 555 557 574 586 598 615
625 644 714 761 767 772 778 802 803 804 836 864
866 879 895 913 939 944 950 979 986 1001 1008
1056 1076 1086 1088 1146 1152 1182 1189 1199
1206 1207 1220 **12** 9 21 23 26 57 136 137 141
151 175 219 225 258 346 347 359 361 375 379 384
401 409 410 448 454 455 465 499 502 503 537 553
555 592 645 647 662 667 670 688 695 704 706 763
764 771 772 788 803 813 845 851 874 884 899 947
966 967 972 975 997 998 1040 1046 1051 1061 1063
1066 1092 1098 1103 1111 1131 1143 1149 1160
1166 1179 1190 1198 1213 1222 1224 1230 1264
1265 1281 1296 1298 1309 1331 1336 1339 1347
1358 1378 1391 1394 1415 1441 1447 1478 1504
1516 1547 1550 1556 1567 1578 1583 1584 1588
1590 1719 1731 1755 1764 1769 1770 1785 1792
1798 1799 1817 1822 1825 1829 1835 1844 1852
1876 1898 1907 **13** 3 4 5 9 15 33 37 58 74 95
102 117 124 133 142 162 163 178 181 184 185 188
237 247 248 269 273 295 309 310 316 317 321 328
332 364 405 407 409 419 422 426 429 431 462 471
480 485 486 493 500 501 506 508 510 514 524 562
563 566 596 598 607 612 621 637 677 686 713 714
716 726 729 733 735 756 764 765 768 773 775 784
799 805 808 822 841 844 846 866 888 893 910 911
919 920 928 991 997 1004 1008 1024 1032 1035
1038 1044 1051 1062 1065 1081 1083 1085 1095
1097 1114 1132 1134 1137 1139 1144 1156 1158
1160 1180 1203 1212 1225 1229 1230 1241 1246
1251 1259 1261 1271 1292 1302 **14** 19 30 55 72
84 108 120 143 148 158 170 173 195 201 251 267
269 346 382 408 418 423 447 462 480 503 509 511
520 531 548 561 579 585 597 600 607 612 613 626
642 657 661 726 736 818 835 844 887 968 979 1014
1018 1037 1046 1047 1050 1060 1081 1087 1106
1122 1127 1131 1138 1139 1147 1151 1178 1185
1187 1191 1200 1210 1238 1297 1314 1336 1356
1373 1398 1401 1408 1414 1449 1452 1453 1457
1460 1484 1499 1501 1502 1516 1558 1569 1572
1579 1580 1581 1583 1586 1591 **15** 53 172 333
423 462 519 528 546 549 552 557 586 602 613 650
699 713 767 777 869 880 945 980 981 1018 1022
1033 1037 1061 1063 1066 1091 1111 1171 1263
1288 1301 1353 1526 1543 1614 1640 1737 1772
1773 1800 1804 1966 2070 2081 2192 2197 2226
2233 2316 2320 2333 2345 2358 2376 2429 2433
2474 2498 2526 2719 2795 2880 2886 2895 2916
2918 2951 2986 3016 3024 3050 3052 3076 3084

3086 3109 3119 3121 3130 3268 3286 3294 3303
3306 3320 3346 3405 3472 3474 3566 3681 3780
3875 3888 3909 3912 3967 3969 4109 4117 4233
4238 4240 4251 4297 4310 4364 4415 4562 4660
4741 4814 4817 4858 4862 4863 4864   16 5 13 27
31 32 54 60 68 69 79 82 95 96 112 118 121 144 149
155 156 172 174 177 200 214 220 223 233 254 255
276 277 282 302 355 358 367 393 422 425 437 445
457 459 474 493 497 509 510 513 517 520 523 534
539 562 574 575 591 600 626 631 639 641 642 649
655 667 674 690 705 707 711 712 720 742 745 746
756 763 792 794 806 808 823 831 853 863 872 885
900 906 909 911 912 914 915 930 939 945 948 983
984 988 992 999 1006 1014 1034 1036 1037 1045
1055 1064 1069 1072 1078 1081 1088 1101 1102
1126 1131 1156 1174 1182 1190 1204 1213 1217
1274 1276 1280 1281 1284 1293 1302 1306 1324
1328 1330 1333 1347 1373 1375 1381 1397 1399
1406 1426 1427 1428 1432 1448 1449 1458 1481
1496 1502 1504 1530 1545 1546 1548 1549 1551
1557 1570 1577 1601 1603 1606 1615 1623 1632
1659 1689 1698 1708 1710 1715 1717 1720 1721
1729 1733 1758 1771 1786 1799 1809 1810 1818
1822 1838 1845 1851 1861 1866 1867 1872 1875
  17 13 27 28 29 43 44 48 54 56 58 70 75 84 85 94
106 116 121 126 135 144 148 157 158 173 180 214
229 286 296 299 319 356 372 384 393 404 411 418
431 435 470 477 486 488 493 522 603 623 626 629
643 655 748 796 897 915 921 932 951 981 983 1026
1033 1114 1118 1174 1216 1221 1243 1262 1268
1294 1312 1313 1321 1322 1323 1333 1336 1359
1386 1389 1402 1436 1443 1453 1488 1502 1540
1542 1546 1554 1566 1593 1596 1653 1661 1662
1663 1686 1692 1695 1716 1754 1780 1831 1943
2021 2039 2093 2097 2099 2103 2105 2106 2107
2109 2142 2145 2186 2241 2276 2277 2280 2303
2313 2316   18 9 20 29 41 45 51 59 62 64 68 70
77 88 92 108 109 117 155 163 171 173 178 183 184
190 198 200 205 206 207 215 220 223 226 236 239
254 257 266 274 275 289 290 293 295 298 300 309
326 331 332 348 351 353 365 366 374 376 380 382
396 400 410 415 421 425 432 438 447 458 465 466
473 477 478 492 506 518 521 523 608 612 613 640
644 652 657 660 663 664 667 670 672 675 692 695
701 704 707 724 752 758 760 768 778 780 782 785
788 817 826 834 836 842 858 860 861 865 884 885
892 900 906 907 913 934 951 956 965 966 972 980
1005 1007 1012 1022 1023 1028 1030 1031 1035
1037 1040 1046 1048 1053 1064 1077 1089 1096
1097 1099 1103 1105 1110 1124 1125 1126 1132
1136 1138 1143 1147 1154 1171 1184 1186 1193
1196 1197 1201 1202 1218 1221 1223 1227 1231
1244 1246 1258 1270 1277 1289 1292 1293 1312
1314 1318 1336 1369 1372 1382 1397 1412 1421
1428 1438 1443 1460 1462 1479 1508 1512 1526
1527 1568 1572 1580 1584 1591

on (20) 5 129   6 167 187   7 243 246 316 867
  9 1043 1151   10 524 608 611   12 363 420 515
1397   13 1060   16 703 1738 1886

on (160)   15 8 25 33 61 74 100 124 139 152 186
192 212 229 241 251 312 366 468 472 499 500 506
531 538 577 649 663 678 759 793 832 863 917 936
987 992 1005 1257 1266 1324 1339 1405 1440 1444
1484 1490 1491 1492 1499 1510 1520 1586 1587
1704 1775 1822 1826 1841 1871 1915 1918 1955
2006 2034 2039 2048 2052 2072 2084 2145 2184
2262 2286 2305 2467 2574 2588 2601 2620 2631
2658 2659 2661 2705 2734 2751 2829 2847 2852
2860 2931 2937 3068 3108 3367 3374 3386 3457

3502 3575 3583 3621 3640 3687 3723 3729 3764
3784 3844 3846 3863 3876 3878 3880 3911 3946
3980 3982 4020 4021 4027 4033 4039 4045 4091
4095 4141 4146 4153 4160 4180 4312 4320 4326
4349 4360 4366 4450 4456 4472 4507 4549 4579
4580 4665 4679 4691 4693 4709 4714 4722 4910
4934 4946 4947 4955 4964

Onan (1) 17 2054
ONCE (1) 7 221
Once (12)   6 677   9 356 657 669   11 1042
  14 88   15 274 639 1230   17 57 833 1260
Once (1) 12 917
once (110)   1 475 579   2 169 411   3 146 223
  4 51 244 420   5 13 27 106 236 304 347   6 484
830 884 960 961   7 773 819 820 825   8 29 134
607 733 734 977   9 57 71 341   10 77 322 540
605 1052   11 582 647 1013 1041   12 581 891
1188 1659   13 51 92 353 415 701 815 825 880
915 962 986 1093 1102 1302   14 234 878 904 951
1304 1550   15 272 1109 2200 2533 2807 3043
3833 4173   16 64 323 398 534 651 765 850 889
954 1005 1333 1521 1700 1839   17 58 386 546
565 676 852 853 854 975 980   18 57 100 129 161
247 263 512 804 874 1190 1392
once (1) 12 427
once (2) 15 2073 2158
oncoming (1) 14 72
ONE (1) 7 1007
One (86)   1 22   3 25 35   4 510   5 137 309
411 497   6 12 291 545 554 611 675 725 911 912
980   7 310 703 747   8 36 53 317 362 480 669
681 861   9 10 58 147 297 653 1108 1165
  10 254 484 498 784 1142 1146   11 50 602 742
831 907 908 961 986 1002 1098 1291   12 1086
1658   13 540 1028   14 559 785 1318 1563
  15 266 658 822 1301 1720 2007 2417 3055 3098
3398 3606 3613 4515 4862 4938   16 572 601
1297 1679 1708   17 833 1292
One (1) 12 1332
One (2) 15 1143 4339
ONE (2) 15 1144 1148
one (590)   1 160 166 294 375 444 483 595 614
657 666 674   2 10 100 209 230 255 256 257 262
310 359 381 395 406 434   3 32 40 145 146 246
256 291 351 427 470 495 496 499   4 97 162 169
392 401 503   5 107 113 270 295 309 347 348 349
353 354 362 373 374 375 391 498 510 513   6 66
218 247 264 298 382 464 467 474 505 539 604
682 701 717 722 728 787 820 829 837 856 874 924
990   7 35 51 68 90 138 167 311 465 479 539 543
549 644 792 815 907 934 939 945 1025   8 37 39
109 121 171 241 304 330 347 364 366 409 410 476
520 545 625 714 728 761 814 831 872 929 969 971
973 985 1061   9 4 27 37 58 113 132 233 298 299
308 452 561 782 803 812 895 963 998 1020 1059
1184 1197   10 11 38 71 116 119 138 152 158 371
392 410 444 445 476 525 526 530 555 571 581 639
641 704 819 825 840 1144   11 50 192 295 383
573 596 611 632 733 779 802 807 831 879 882 961
986 993 1015 1167 1170 1181 1220 1225 1226
12 41 50 65 127 412 414 438 439 455 487 505 508
509 513 666 686 687 694 753 765 793 809 835 958
969 971 1008 1017 1029 1125 1137 1168 1177 1192
1219 1226 1259 1319 1323 1324 1394 1442 1512
1522 1564 1585 1651 1669 1761 1778 1864 1878
13 58 81 103 115 167 196 203 214 278 279 300
506 554 583 593 597 645 649 650 757 777 798 819
825 869 898 909 931 967 977 989 1061 1145 1168
1200   14 2 3 4 27 55 61 105 169 174 185 191 214

224 257 304 358 421 431 439 486 492 622 641 783
787 829 882 965 985 1002 1013 1101 1136 1147
1182 1237 1238 1264 1271 1305 1320 1325 1333
1353 1362 1365 1386 1443 1449 1529 1530 1559
  15 91 94 95 556 596 754 763 779 867 886 952 970
1030 1250 1357 1807 1911 2193 2271 2449 2517
2553 2645 2848 2936 2939 3029 3074 3202 3211
3264 3296 3411 3613 3718 3966 3968 3970 3972
3973 4392 4402 4484 4602 4814   16 36 96 98 102
125 144 161 196 197 222 223 261 298 325 337 442
460 500 570 600 629 660 680 694 766 786 794 799
812 880 904 923 926 950 1008 1064 1085 1186 1206
1230 1299 1341 1357 1493 1513 1536 1538 1556
1580 1592 1593 1598 1603 1615 1768 1856 1860
1877 1886 1887   17 43 67 76 95 97 125 126 130
135 153 212 305 310 315 375 380 442 692 867 958
1098 1142 1220 1322 1444 1445 1481 1755 1770
1897 2102 2127 2129 2201 2209   18 24 36 42 59
65 74 119 122 143 150 162 164 212 225 253 262
292 405 438 443 444 446 447 471 483 522 523 536
541 548 568 594 618 640 658 660 675 700 777 802
835 847 858 908 962 970 1090 1093 1110 1141 1161
1169 1176 1183 1201 1245 1246 1249 1271 1292
1308 1381 1413 1436 1445 1497 1498 1577
one (8)   1 362   7 59 60   9 1144   10 572
  11 740 741 781
one (14)   15 158 160 271 500 668 808 914 960
1208 1495 3844 4081
Onehandled (2) 7 1019 1072
onehandled (2) 7 1018   11 762
onehandled (1) 15 4144
O'Neill (2) 9 311   12 178
O'Neill (1) 16 1255
O'Neill's (4) 5 13   10 96 509   12 364
onelegged (3) 10 7 228 1063
onelensed (1) 17 492
onepiece (1) 15 471
one's (1) 16 1383
ones (18)   6 394 778   7 1074   8 829
  10 595   11 244   12 1670   13 503
  14 1468   15 2717   16 161   18 27 86 456
850 1155 1416 1555
ongot (1) 14 93
onion (3) 8 761   13 936   15 3484
Onions (2) 10 596   15 3478
onions (10)   7 329   8 490 721   12 94 627
  14 1535   16 436 1415   17 309   18 189
onions (2) 15 808 3992
oniony (1) 10 622
Onlookers (1) 13 903
ONLY (1) 7 221
Only (34)   4 284 386   6 123 171 244 333 473
809 819   7 708   8 115 268 366 534   9 1156
  10 170 389   11 580 697   12 315 810 1639
1669   13 132 1102 1194   15 272 2562 2566
3437 3770 4285 4849   18 1038
only (214)   1 144 157 160 192 205 209 614
  2 52 143 438   3 191   4 117 236 452   5 95
351 390 483 498   6 548   7 153 493 603 705 744
  8 141 948   9 109 184 480 542 814 838 839 843
989 1037 1081   11 124 244 310 448 649 738 849
1086 1161 1192   12 5 251 253 327 369 464 472
776 801 855 921 955 1033 1168 1233 1347 1432
1478 1536 1539 1555 1556   13 100 204 215 290
329 367 417 455 507 528 643 659 672 697 750 794
900 953 1016 1087 1109 1192   14 238 266 420
611 794 914 954 1024 1051 1136 1262 1281 1320
  15 360 433 585 644 646 1095 2374 2375 2522
2885 2986 3049 3104 3296 3449 4383 4847

oral (1) 17 732
Orange (1) 15 4717
ORANGE (1) 15 3984
orange (6) 2 270 312 13 1076 15 4427 17 1701 18 308
orange (4) 15 989 1604 2253 3981
orangeblossoms (1) 3 242
orangeblossoms (1) 15 4158
orangefiery (2) 12 343 14 1170
Orangeflower (1) 15 3793
orangeflower (4) 5 491 501 15 332 2599
Orangegroves (2) 4 194 8 862
Orangekeyed (1) 17 2103
orangekeyed (2) 4 330 15 3295
Orangeman (1) 12 1634
orangeman (1) 12 1590
orangepeels (1) 8 516
Oranges (1) 4 204
oranges (4) 4 196 12 691 18 553
orangetainted (1) 15 2748
Orate (1) 14 366
oration (1) 12 904
orator (1) 7 804
Oratorians (1) 12 1680
oratory (2) 7 792 879
orb (2) 11 745 14 66
orb (1) 7 327
orb (1) 15 1443
orbit (1) 17 2014
orbits (1) 17 1113
orchard (1) 17 1559
orchestra (1) 12 1827
Orchestral (1) 9 32
orchidised (1) 14 1486
ordeal (2) 14 878 15 2380
Order (5) 11 638 12 879 15 896 17 1468
order (50) 2 192 3 185 8 596 962 966 1132 9 167 10 673 719 1008 1009 11 209 909 12 535 579 709 837 902 1108 1109 13 551 14 403 427 1132 1196 1517 15 2192 2456 2806 3040 16 334 512 1282 1322 1389 17 3 162 295 901 1021 1077 1086 1359 1410 1422 1608 1624 1936 2059 18 1078
order (1) 15 1419
orderbook (1) 14 1051
ordered (2) 12 1018 18 249
ordering (1) 18 358
orderly (2) 9 136 14 320
orders (12) 4 132 8 807 11 444 12 862 869 1025 1358 14 618 895 15 2833 16 796 18 930
ordinal (1) 17 739
ordinance (1) 14 1008
ordinaries (1) 12 1885
ordinarily (1) 17 365
Ordinary (1) 6 981
ordinary (7) 7 761 8 115 9 70 14 540 1288 16 818 18 101
ordnance (2) 12 528 17 1971
ore (3) 11 42 1006 17 1753
O'Reilly (4) 8 160 12 869 15 570 17 2136
OReilly (1) 18 1465
O'Reillys (1) 12 1304
Orelli (1) 12 869
ORGAN (1) 7 84
Organ (1) 11 1197
organ (12) 5 395 6 610 11 537 1199 12 219 476 1288 13 282 16 709 17 1200 2279 2284
organ (1) 15 1955
organgrinder (1) 17 2137
organgrinders (1) 8 721
organic (1) 17 1059
organisation (1) 5 424
organise (2) 12 995 1002
organised (1) 15 1145
organiser (1) 8 797
organism (5) 14 664 17 1086 2157 2161 2192
organisms (1) 14 1279
organs (8) 4 1 11 520 14 1177 15 642 1810 1983 16 788 17 1187
organs (1) 15 1787
organtoned (1) 15 920
orgasms (1) 9 1174
orgulous (1) 14 241
orgy (1) 16 1175
oriafiamma (1) 7 722
Orient (2) 10 816 14 382
orient (2) 3 43 14 938
orient (1) 15 1326
Oriental (1) 5 18
oriental (3) 17 338 1332 1524
oriental (3) 15 960 1318 1409
orifice (2) 10 940 17 2077
orifices (1) 6 425
oriflamme (1) 7 722
Origin (1) 17 1645
origin (5) 17 685 1114 1124 1127 1853
original (20) 1 80 9 366 779 1006 1008 10 412 11 602 12 734 13 373 14 15 793 16 778 910 1213 1452 1708 1848 17 392 1966
originality (2) 17 247 606
originally (4) 17 316 346 1289 1302
originals (1) 14 389
originating (1) 17 2130
Orion (1) 17 1049
ormolu (1) 17 1528
Ormond (16) 10 395 484 963 1198 1199 11 65 288 304 354 357 1142 1273 13 1064 16 712 1105 17 2050
Ormond (1) 15 3729
ornament (3) 12 1824 14 11 16 1524
ornamented (1) 15 1384
ornaments (1) 12 77
orotund (1) 17 1631
O'Rourke (6) 2 393 4 116 119 122 7 537 10 230
O'Rourke (1) 15 4338
O'ROURKE (1) 15 1672
O'Rourke's (2) 4 105 11 952
ORourkes (1) 18 451
orphan (1) 14 1123
ORPHANS (1) 15 1889
orphans (1) 12 1622
orphans (1) 15 1887
orreries (1) 17 574
orthodox (4) 16 3 1126 1564 17 24
ORTHOGRAPHICAL (1) 7 164
orts (1) 9 1094
O'Ryan (1) 12 280
Osborne (1) 12 916
Oscar (1) 12 1127
oscillation (1) 17 428
osculation (1) 17 2243

OShea (1) 18 479
O'Shiels (1) 14 37
osier (1) 16 478
Osiris (1) 7 856
Osmond (1) 17 794
osprey (1) 15 1016
Ossian (1) 12 1129
ossifrage (1) 14 396
ostensibly (2) 14 69 16 1432
ostentatiously (2) 16 1189 1429
osteopathic (1) 17 295
ostiarii (1) 12 1677
ostler (3) 9 664 747 1050
ostlers (1) 14 537
Ostrolopsky (2) 15 1859
O'Sullivan (1) 12 199
Osvalt's (1) 3 449
oth (1) 11 862
Othello (1) 15 409
Othello (2) 9 401 1021
Other (13) 3 182 4 325 6 26 8 481 482 487 691 9 205 1079 11 871 1012 12 1879 13 982
other (290) 1 157 2 46 3 175 182 4 350 364 424 5 119 245 295 306 374 377 390 418 446 468 6 172 218 382 446 496 546 591 615 726 856 947 984 1002 7 99 210 259 453 752 944 945 8 212 318 323 328 330 471 484 513 521 582 590 1118 9 162 205 236 434 647 663 851 988 1014 1135 10 43 117 129 556 597 606 708 722 834 851 863 1155 1158 1171 1205 11 34 148 159 160 487 577 803 856 871 901 936 969 1199 12 51 73 77 367 371 467 484 719 772 791 925 1023 1052 1101 1234 1323 1500 1684 1794 1851 13 396 436 634 666 709 714 724 725 820 875 928 1029 1035 1193 1219 1262 1275 14 12 106 127 190 203 212 225 228 234 285 299 426 432 444 517 538 544 595 738 793 920 966 1003 1013 1175 1189 1191 1239 1240 1268 1276 1403 1544 15 210 556 1053 1358 1631 2320 2429 3033 3210 3487 3883 4202 16 54 147 172 217 231 264 304 305 328 387 505 568 639 641 643 759 797 841 847 944 972 1045 1048 1063 1078 1081 1092 1123 1152 1175 1187 1199 1200 1213 1274 1296 1389 1393 1415 1458 1529 1610 1656 1746 1830 1860 1864 1890 17 126 135 175 310 657 720 864 893 961 1008 1065 1126 1131 1183 1200 1220 1295 1333 1417 1493 1503 1873 1903 1926 2190 2209 2307 18 45 89 104 235 242 253 260 322 351 395 438 472 543 545 551 614 630 655 693 845 849 947 964 969 1060 1090 1114 1132 1139 1211 1266 1269 1308 1317 1345 1357 1363 1395 1461 1483 1525 1555
other (2) 7 321 12 515
other (7) 15 159 808 1109 3047 4062 4622 4764
othermaninthestreet (1) 15 4347
other's (7) 3 32 13 810 818 16 1467 1568 1778 17 696
other's (1) 15 4764
Others (2) 9 360 13 1150
others (57) 1 136 258 2 167 178 3 296 6 581 656 699 786 7 97 395 1001 1037 8 411 662 874 1022 9 256 494 984 10 865 11 792 13 692 773 809 970 1058 1210 14 326 625 913 1183 1233 15 682 2420 3199 16 94 174 380 650 837 870 900 1047 1117 1118 1213 1542 1695 1747 1760 17 135 353 642 1648 18 785 895
others (1) 16 1261

P

P (5) 7 667 12 938 1539 17 601 1612
P (1) 16 1260
P (1) 15 3223
p 5 (1) 17 1364
p 24 (1) 17 1384
p 217 (1) 17 1371
P A (1) 17 1429
P C (2) 12 1894 17 1612
p c (1) 18 614
P C N (1) 3 176
P J (2) 12 928 930
P L G (1) 12 1895
p m (1) 15 1022
P O (7) 5 63 11 898 13 1105 17 1797
   1798 1805 1813
p o (1) 11 868
P P (4) 5 435 12 929 936 937
P P S (1) 11 894
p p's (1) 16 1131
P S (4) 4 413 5 258 11 32 890
Pa (3) 10 1165 1170 14 1487
pa (13) 10 1167 1172 13 387 394 15 2495
pabulum (1) 7 623
pace (17) 2 375 3 61 280 473 6 28 367
   7 967 14 699 15 2848 2947 16 532
   17 2 4 6 8
pace (2) 7 717 13 927
pace (2) 15 4429 4481
paced (1) 16 1771
pacem (1) 15 3640
paces (4) 5 229 6 873 1028 11 588
paces (1) 15 4045
pachyderm (1) 14 1095
Pacific (1) 17 187
pacifica (1) 7 721
Pacificus (1) 12 1707
pack (5) 6 638 10 682 15 968 17 1806
   18 37
pack (2) 15 3954 4328
packed (6) 4 142 202 204 12 1575
   16 1374 1654
Packer (1) 12 190
Packet (5) 17 1466 1733 1734 1735
packet (2) 11 682 17 307
packets (2) 5 18 10 1143
packing (1) 7 74
pad (8) 10 275 11 30 822 823 847 848 864
   895
padded (2) 3 103 6 386
padded (2) 15 2609 3316
Padding (1) 13 1201
padding (1) 18 56
paddock (1) 14 1515
Paddy (30) 6 142 297 300 421 452 570
   7 456 687 8 989 994 996 998 1005 1018 1024
   1027 11 1205 12 314 318 321 334 395 404
   801 811 15 1218 4195 17 1241 18 1261
   1279
Paddy (5) 5 115 116 127 7 734
Paddy (3) 15 1142 1205 1251
PADDY (9) 15 1209 1217 1225 1229 1245 1253
   1633 1637 1728
Paddyrisky (1) 12 565
padlock (1) 17 1561
Padney (2) 14 1556 17 866
Paff (1) 3 113

Pagamimi (1) 12 586
pagan (1) 8 663
paganism (1) 1 176
paganry (1) 14 411
Page (1) 13 1248
page (29) 2 82 155 176 4 154 157 158 162
   230 280 5 472 7 95 410 654 10 190 203
   11 238 312 1087 13 110 14 1156
   16 1274 1276 1482 17 695 733 1309 1324
   18 494
page (1) 15 4960
pageants (1) 9 753
Pages (1) 15 3187
pages (23) 1 366 2 95 3 136 145 4 346
   374 500 5 528 7 302 382 425 653 694
   8 835 9 2 10 585 838 845 14 996
   17 442 1075 1414 1776
Paget (1) 10 1178
pagoda (1) 15 2250
Paid (1) 16 451
paid (30) 1 292 631 6 939 7 18 8 497
   9 202 804 10 917 11 317 775 12 42 48
   335 1359 13 500 1045 1046 15 2522 3405
   3560 16 82 177 797 852 992 17 1662 2004
   2078 18 84
paid (2) 2 251 253
paidup (1) 17 1859
Pailer (1) 17 2324
Pain (3) 1 102 3 444 8 722
Pain (1) 15 1580
pain (14) 1 102 546 5 368 6 365 8 237
   509 9 855 11 876 12 269 844 14 209
   884 1283 17 1312
pain (1) 15 516
pained (1) 15 939
painful (7) 11 1008 14 1165 15 4557
   16 797 17 997 1001 1277
painful (1) 12 419
Painless (1) 15 1709
painless (2) 8 383 17 1748
pains (7) 5 489 9 593 13 1202 14 531
   689 967 15 701
painstaking (1) 12 595
Paint (1) 11 913
Paint (1) 13 912
paint (1) 13 1003
painted (4) 6 944 955 16 952 18 57
painted (1) 9 354
painted (4) 15 501 1927 2016 3877
painter (1) 9 922
painters (1) 13 1000
painting (3) 8 893 9 50 51
paintings (1) 13 406
paintpot (1) 17 1565
paints (1) 13 628
paintspeckled (1) 15 590
pair (41) 1 117 2 255 4 150 7 985
   8 556 9 629 948 10 559 1151 12 369
   1069 1292 13 184 801 1236 14 509 519 1478
   15 1911 2094 16 229 375 774 1043 1064 1672
   17 153 590 1304 1878 2092 2093 18 305 442
   457 469 714 1095 1144 1494
pair (3) 15 581 2606 4330
pairing (3) 9 539 15 3354 18 1360
Pairs (1) 15 1024
pairs (3) 2 255 17 1444 18 186
Paisley (1) 13 920
Pal (1) 14 1523
pal (3) 14 1523 15 627 16 1347

Palabras (1) 12 563
palabras (1) 9 577
Palace (3) 8 461 13 961 16 792
palace (7) 11 486 12 87 1394 1865
   13 323 14 403 18 562
palaces (1) 2 171
palatable (1) 16 56
palate (3) 4 4 8 820 897
palates (1) 15 589
pale (16) 1 16 573 3 311 397 4 435
   5 567 9 615 11 784 931 1071 12 298
   13 175 415 16 14 18 99 392
pale (1) 7 524
pale (1) 15 993
paled (1) 11 191
palefaced (1) 15 814
Palefaces (2) 1 166 10 341
palely (1) 7 727
paleolithic (1) 12 204
paler (1) 1 573
paler (1) 15 414
Palestine (2) 7 1057 17 640
Palestrina (1) 5 405
paletinted (1) 12 1288
palfrey (1) 15 1500
palfreys (1) 12 1594
Palgrave (2) 16 959 17 1738
Pali (1) 9 279
Palice (1) 9 16
pall (2) 15 482 3232
Pallas (1) 9 876
Pallbearers (1) 6 499
Palles (1) 7 502
palliate (1) 14 950
palliative (1) 17 1891
pallid (1) 8 656
pallid (1) 15 2050
pallor (3) 13 87 14 1404 17 1135
Palm (1) 10 731
palm (8) 1 100 4 161 6 192 7 1038
   9 621 740 18 114 453
palm (7) 15 466 473 2012 3678 3695 3701 4913
palmam (1) 10 841
Palme (1) 12 1277
Palme (1) 16 909
Palmer (6) 5 195 6 185 15 496 1047
   17 2079 2256
palmer (1) 14 220
Palmerston (4) 7 5 13 668 1046
palmistry (1) 15 3661
palmnut (1) 10 434
palmoil (1) 16 967
palms (4) 2 23 9 132 12 1713 17 1553
palms (2) 15 1410 2659
palpable (1) 13 310
Palpably (1) 16 221
palpably (4) 16 705 1012 1505 1784
palpation (1) 15 2360
palps (1) 1 123
pals (1) 15 1011
palsied (2) 15 20 1608
Paltry (1) 6 498
paltry (3) 16 541 18 466 504
paly (1) 13 193
pampered (1) 14 609
pampered (1) 15 353
pamphlet (2) 15 3275 17 1380
pampooties (1) 9 570
Pan (1) 12 565

Phaeacians (1) 9 110
phaeton (1) 17 1577
phallic (1) 15 650
phallopyrotechnic (1) 15 1495
Phantasmal (1) 1 263
phantom (3) 13 1078 15 1370 16 863
phantom (1) 15 3974
phantoms (3) 14 1083 1085 1113
phantoms (1) 15 2045
Pharaoh (1) 15 947
pharmaceutical (1) 17 93
phartridges (1) 15 1396
phase (1) 14 955
phases (3) 14 1269 17 1161 1997
Phedo's (1) 9 1139
phenomena (8) 14 1227 1269 17 1009 1132
    1256 1259 1927
phenomenally (1) 16 1820
phenomenologist (1) 12 1822
Phenomenon (5) 12 502 518 14 436 439
    442
phenomenon (16) 9 943 12 465 466 467
    476 503 14 428 15 2796 3355 16 769
    17 255 257 858 925 1262
Phew (1) 8 374
Phial (2) 11 691 15 4541
phial (3) 14 1013 1023 17 301
phial (1) 15 289
Phibsborough (2) 6 436 10 1188
Phil (2) 7 94 8 157
Philip (12) 4 502 6 191 8 278 711
    12 199 1253 15 3002 16 1229 17 544
    650 1252 1254
Philip (3) 15 814 2512
Philip (6) 15 2515 2521 2536 2582 2584
Philippe (2) 15 2583 2585
philippic (1) 16 986
philirenists (1) 15 4435
Phillaphulla (1) 15 3429
philoprogenitive (1) 12 478
philosophaster (1) 9 752
philosopher (6) 14 795 1295 16 281
    17 718 722 1761
philosopher's (1) 5 473
philosophised (1) 9 795
Philosophy (1) 11 1062
Philosophy (1) 17 1380
philosophy (3) 14 1252 15 2205
    16 1158
philotheology (1) 15 109
Philpot (1) 7 740
phiz (1) 7 173
phlegm (4) 2 444 5 483 8 864 10 634
Phlegmy (1) 10 632
phlegmy (1) 15 3211
Phocas (1) 12 1690
Phoebe (1) 18 1294
Phoenix (6) 7 633 8 715 10 1180
    12 871 15 1061 17 496
phoenix (1) 15 1935
phone (4) 7 219 233 376 12 856
phoned (2) 7 62 411
phonetic (1) 12 720
phonetically (1) 17 685
phonic (1) 17 731
phosphorescence (1) 8 25
phosphorescent (2) 15 2601 4477
Phosphorus (1) 8 21
Photius (2) 1 656 9 492

Photo (2) 1 685 18 601
Photo (2) 4 370 15 3261
photo (16) 4 401 5 80 93 13 416
    15 3259 16 1425 1427 1440 1454 1465 1644
    1648 18 22 564 655 1303
photocard (1) 17 1880
photocards (1) 17 1809
photograph (4) 6 966 13 232 15 1065
    17 2317
photograph (1) 15 1588
photographer's (1) 8 209
photographic (2) 16 1435 17 878
photographs (5) 13 713 14 1254
    17 1779 18 1005 1365
photography (2) 8 173 17 1589
photophobe (1) 17 225
Photo's (1) 14 1535
Phoucaphouca (2) 15 3349
phrase (3) 2 8 15 68
phrased (1) 14 1307
phraseology (1) 15 4443
phrases (2) 11 401 17 1882
Phthailer (1) 17 2326
phthisical (1) 17 1518
Phthisis (1) 8 392
phthisis (2) 17 1252 1254
phthisis (1) 15 994
phthook (1) 12 1571
Phyllis (2) 14 1130 1133
physic (3) 5 478 14 256 577
Physical (2) 17 513 1397
physical (3) 12 900 15 953 17 850
physician (4) 6 943 14 729 1310 18 181
physicist (1) 17 1760
physics' (1) 17 145
physiologist (1) 17 1763
physique (1) 15 788
physiques (1) 3 176
physog (1) 12 381
piace (1) 7 718
pianissimo (1) 18 908
pianist (1) 11 466
piannyer (1) 18 723
Piano (3) 4 422 11 573 650
piano (17) 4 405 8 1139 11 276 292 443
    485 15 3529 16 1432 17 664 665 1303
    1307 18 382 876 907 1215 1553
piano (1) 9 907
piano (6) 15 1268 2055 2493 3500 3502 4013
pianoforte (1) 15 917
Pianola (5) 15 4051 4073 4105 4114 4129
pianola (1) 15 1991
pianola (7) 15 2072 3530 3562 3667 3674 4005
    4026
pianoplaying (1) 16 799
pianos (2) 8 1116 11 846
pianostool (1) 15 4020
piastres (2) 12 1369
piazzetta (1) 14 1376
Piazzi (1) 17 1110
pica (1) 17 1393
piccaninnies (1) 14 1555
Pick (2) 6 980 11 1226
pick (18) 6 758 8 37 38 402 559 630 856 1042
    9 276 10 737 16 1195 1293 1477 18 763
    894 1025 1388 1411
Pickaback (1) 14 463
pickaxe (1) 13 789
picked (15) 1 520 3 500 5 479 6 832

8 60 10 254 14 539 16 710 1346 1515
    1688 17 1488 1494 18 45 430
pickeystone (1) 5 232
Picking (2) 4 487 13 817
picking (11) 5 164 8 674 11 3 192
    12 808 1506 14 626 16 298 708 971
    18 693
picking (1) 15 4330
pickle (1) 14 534
pickled (2) 8 746 9 276
pickmeup (1) 3 430
pickpockets (2) 15 245 18 1454
picks (2) 1 211 8 955
picks (4) 15 729 3597 3641 4749
pickthank (1) 17 1942
Pickwick (1) 9 142
picnic (9) 4 81 281 394 404 6 98 8 166 167
    18 628 946
picnicmakers (1) 15 3245
Pico (1) 3 144
Pictorial (1) 13 151
pictorial (2) 17 21 1780
Picture (2) 12 1065 1322
picture (22) 5 37 289 6 851 7 55 8 675
    11 1024 12 1476 13 334 389 446 910
    14 754 16 422 472 568 1356 1479 18 326
    557 560 986 991
pictured (1) 11 1274
pictures (11) 4 68 5 405 6 360 7 97
    12 1168 1404 13 231 703 794 14 1253
    18 1241
picturesque (3) 12 554 13 628 16 550
Pidgeon (1) 15 2579
pie (7) 8 136 11 499 522 617 12 813
    13 613 15 2202
Piebald (1) 6 323
piebald (2) 10 451 14 701
Pièce (2) 9 121 123
pièce (1) 15 3909
piece (26) 4 295 424 429 5 235 7 372 631
    8 822 10 1088 12 1585 13 153 481 991
    1246 14 911 15 3042 16 96 427 785 910
    948 1578 1668 17 392 18 943 1278
piece (3) 15 2709 2714
pieces (8) 4 285 8 194 728 9 1081 1084
    12 528 13 596 15 2551
pieces (1) 15 1766
pied (1) 3 450
Pier (1) 4 440
pier (9) 1 700 2 26 31 32 33 39 3 196
    17 151 18 1585
pierce (3) 2 43 6 868 15 4933
piercer (1) 15 3105
piercing (2) 11 161 13 137
piercing (2) 15 2722 2852
piercingly (1) 12 602
pierglass (1) 17 1342
Pierrepaul (1) 12 558
Piers (1) 8 1065
piers (1) 16 933
pies (1) 10 549
pieta (1) 18 1507
Pieter (1) 16 1811
piety (1) 14 921
pif (1) 15 3894
Piffpaff (1) 15 2556
Pig (1) 15 2572
pig (7) 8 86 12 576 1845 15 1917 2900
    3397

populace (1) 15 967
popular (5) 8 339 12 364 14 979 1303
  15 3246
popular (1) 16 1251
populated (1) 17 1005
population (2) 14 1422 17 1707
populo (1) 17 1031
porcelain (1) 17 922
porch (9) 2 184 205 427 5 319 7 15
  9 466 10 342 1190 17 1506
porches (2) 7 881 9 465
porches (1) 7 750
porcos (1) 15 4509
porcospino (1) 3 385
Pore (1) 14 1555
pored (1) 16 1682
Pores (1) 11 707
pores (2) 5 483 12 473
poring (1) 14 485
Pork (1) 17 1458
pork (6) 4 46 277 8 336 746 16 990
  18 910
pork (3) 15 989 1549 1575
porkbutcher (2) 4 152 165
porkbutcher's (1) 10 99
porkbutcher's (1) 15 155
porkbutchers (1) 18 912
porker (1) 15 2439
porkers (1) 11 556
porkpie (1) 13 1234
porkshop (1) 11 884
porksteak (1) 10 1267
porksteaks (3) 10 535 1123 1154
porksteaks (1) 15 3844
pornographical (1) 17 2259
Pornosophical (1) 15 109
porous (1) 4 48
porpoise (1) 3 473
porringers (1) 8 705
porringers (1) 15 1573
Port (1) 17 1737
port (8) 8 161 10 547 558 12 293
  13 1153 17 306 18 132 341
portable (1) 17 107
portal (1) 9 232
Portals (1) 9 230
portals (1) 9 229
portcullis (1) 9 1215
Porte (1) 14 943
ported (1) 14 644
portending (1) 17 884
portent (1) 14 1098
portentous (1) 12 174
porter (20) 3 195 4 106 134 5 99 306 309
  310 314 388 7 42 8 47 49 12 803 809 1362
  1795 15 586 596 2896
porterbottle (1) 3 152
porter's (3) 5 555 9 754 12 312
portfolio (1) 14 1013
portfolio (1) 7 320
portfolio (2) 15 817 843
portholes (1) 16 1677
portico (1) 9 1205
Portinari (1) 16 887
portion (2) 16 338 1168
Portland (1) 10 80
portlier (1) 14 585
portly (3) 6 708 841 875
portly (1) 15 1236

Portobello (4) 8 801 10 1134 12 983
  15 620
Portrait (1) 9 523
portrait (1) 17 1876
portrait (1) 15 144
ports (1) 13 1155
Portsmouth (1) 12 1332
Portugal (3) 12 1258 14 153 17 1739
portwine (2) 14 985 15 2233
Pos (1) 14 1472
posadas (1) 18 1595
pose (3) 14 1369 17 1427 18 560
pose (1) 15 2809
posed (1) 16 1447
Poser (1) 16 1386
poses (1) 15 2992
posies (1) 14 1152
posing (1) 15 2729
posited (1) 17 1118
Positing (1) 17 1744
position (20) 4 108 6 429 8 206
  13 856 1084 14 1239 15 3020 3243
  16 218 579 1536 17 154 1287 1289 1302 1436
  1652 1810 1811
position (3) 3 161 14 307 15 2583
positions (4) 12 553 15 3907 17 915
  1106
positions (1) 15 1829
Positive (1) 17 2256
positive (5) 14 826 16 531 17 352 1934
Positively (1) 8 189
positively (2) 16 1072 17 2206
posse (1) 12 534
Possess (1) 5 106
possess (5) 15 714 2341 17 291 926 1500
possessed (11) 4 523 9 345 14 898
  15 3359 16 307 1734 1864 17 741 1411
  2035 18 718
possessed (1) 15 2017
possessing (4) 15 2414 16 91 17 1703
  1749
possession (10) 12 606 866 15 3137 3311
  16 62 1342 1589 17 1667 1864 1931
possessions (2) 12 1523 15 826
possessor (2) 14 1465 16 1825
possibilities (5) 2 51 9 349 12 350
  17 580 646
possibility (11) 9 383 14 45 1413
  16 757 827 1324 17 176 760 912 1849 1850
Possible (1) 16 1419
possible (41) 2 51 52 67 6 821 9 174 177
  350 1042 10 5 12 570 13 484 14 151
  15 1055 1222 2106 2111 16 386 1153 1272
  1464 1467 1558 17 346 453 563 787 844 892 984
  1084 1101 1138 1153 1509 1588 1621 2084
  18 204 205
Possibly (2) 16 574 634
possibly (21) 5 175 14 1291 15 2375
  2898 16 238 325 615 805 897 1318 1499 1541
  1542 1560 1605 1893 17 1144 2206 18 76 369
  1002
possibly (1) 6 814
possing (1) 13 395
possing (1) 15 2183
Post (3) 5 53 15 2633 17 2141
Post (1) 17 1362
post (13) 1 223 3 186 7 15 8 336
  10 48 51 12 1583 13 1250 15 1023
  16 524 17 1805 1813 18 715

post (1) 15 907
POST (2) 8 101
postage (1) 17 1680
postagestamps (1) 15 3987
Postal (2) 11 909 17 1468
Postal (1) 16 489
postal (3) 5 2 8 1132 15 3040
postcard (11) 7 703 8 255 322 12 258
  1071 13 596 844 16 472 482 1235 18 229
postcards (1) 7 18
postcenal (1) 17 2262
postcreation (1) 14 294
postdiluvian (1) 17 456
Postea (1) 9 848
posted (1) 18 699
poster (8) 5 57 551 10 380 496 1221
  11 300 17 1771 18 707
posterior (3) 17 1997 2077 2232
posterioria (1) 14 1534
posteriors (1) 14 593
posterity (1) 9 682
postern (1) 10 1264
posters (1) 14 1246
postexilic (1) 17 710
posthaste (2) 7 65 14 784
posthumity (1) 14 957
posthumous (1) 15 1808
posticipated (1) 17 430
postman (1) 13 1170
postman's (1) 17 283
postmark (1) 16 488
postmenstrual (1) 14 1232
postmistress (2) 5 56 60
postmistress (1) 15 4346
postmortem (1) 6 886
postmortem (1) 16 437
postmortemity (1) 14 387
postnuptial (1) 16 1065
Postoffice (3) 8 1132 11 909 1180
postoffice (4) 5 53 76 11 821 15 2780
Postprandial (1) 3 222
postprandial (2) 3 222 224
postsatisfaction (1) 17 2244
postscript (2) 4 421 11 889
postulants (1) 15 3450
postulating (1) 14 999
posture (5) 17 1300 1426 1430 2158 2311
pot (12) 1 337 370 5 552 8 511 715
  10 271 12 613 816 14 816 16 79
  17 304 18 469
pot (2) 1 362 15 2288
potation (1) 16 970
potations (1) 16 1635
Potato (3) 4 73 8 1189 15 1952
potato (7) 8 445 1072 15 1035 1357 3509
  16 868 18 199
potato (6) 15 289 1310 1316 1435 3525 4579
Potatoes (1) 8 42
potatoes (6) 8 42 11 553 12 94 18 63
  1016 1068
potatoes (2) 15 3992 4334
potatosoap (1) 15 243
potency (3) 14 243 892 17 1163
potent (5) 1 650 15 1472 2359 3116
  18 1333
potentate (1) 12 1519
potential (3) 17 131 393 638
potentiality (2) 17 223 1080
pothecaries (1) 14 207

prefaced (1) 7 759
Prefer (1) 5 327
prefer (3) 3 140 8 758 13 831
preferably (3) 16 376 1752 17 1956
preference (2) 15 2933 17 20
preferred (6) 12 1139 13 418 15 2641
   16 1740 17 21 637
preferring (3) 9 806 14 889 17 294
prefers (2) 4 82 18 507
preformed (1) 14 1413
pregnancies (1) 14 1265
pregnancy (2) 14 309 979
pregnant (2) 14 259 18 1123
preindicative (1) 17 323
prejudice (1) 13 842
prelate (2) 1 32 12 608
prelates (1) 2 271
preliminaries (1) 16 18
preliminary (3) 16 1564 17 243 1626
prelude (1) 11 663
prelude (2) 15 4026 4047
premature (4) 14 968 1207 16 1184
   17 1642
prematurely (1) 15 1780
premeditated (1) 17 2190
premeditatedly (1) 17 80
premeditative (1) 17 2045
premiated (1) 12 107
premier (1) 16 1435
premises (18) 7 157 8 827 9 178
   12 394 1731 15 885 1673 3034 4297 17 93
   329 330 333 1519 1914 2039 2051 2253
premium (2) 13 1230 17 1697
premonitions (1) 17 282
Premonstratensians (1) 12 1681
prenatal (1) 14 956
prenativity (1) 14 386
prentice (1) 15 1017
preoccupied (1) 15 2034
preordained (1) 17 2212
preparation (4) 2 332 14 41 17 89 2044
Preparatory (1) 16 1
preparatory (2) 17 551 648
Prepare (2) 8 413
Prepare (1) 16 581
prepare (1) 17 354
prepared (8) 7 815 9 369 12 630
   13 878 16 79 1788 17 1694 2113
preponderance (1) 17 193
preponderant (1) 14 1384
preposterous (1) 14 1174
prepuce (1) 17 1205
prepuces (2) 1 394 9 609
prerogative (2) 14 919 17 2175
pres (3) 11 714 865 868
presabbath (1) 17 17
presbyterian (2) 12 1634 13 630
presbyterian (1) 15 1424
presbytery (1) 10 2
Prescott's (4) 5 460 8 1058 1059 13 921
Prescotts (1) 18 1342
prescribe (1) 8 729
prescribed (5) 12 1289 14 946 17 357
   358 513
prescription (1) 18 576
prescriptions (1) 5 471
presence (17) 2 299 8 425 12 594 1279
   14 631 802 947 15 644 3402 16 1459
   17 288 696 747 1168 2077 2123 2265

Present (1) 10 437
present (46) 4 398 6 950 7 599 679 729
   794 8 1133 9 1075 11 825 12 368 555
   649 730 927 1826 1837 13 461 464 14 16 44
   277 835 1230 1361 15 458 476 493 981 1471
   1777 4474 16 51 256 301 794 1555 1870
   17 447 448 871 1144 1145 18 185 404 615
   1305
present (1) 16 1253
presentable (1) 17 376
presentation (2) 17 1810 1811
presented (10) 10 1243 12 663 1514 1524
   1821 15 3031 3039 17 362 921 1199
presented (1) 15 1519
presenting (2) 12 660 1443
presenting (1) 15 1909
presently (1) 14 471
presents (4) 8 363 9 693 15 1677 2551
presents (1) 15 145
Preservative (2) 14 465 15 1952
preservatives (1) 17 1804
preservatives (1) 15 1571
preserve (1) 14 1165
preserved (3) 6 772 15 1790 18 1289
preserver (1) 15 1179
preserving (1) 14 722
presided (3) 12 670 1288 16 1663
President (4) 15 2217 2219 2222 2223
president (1) 12 901
presidential (1) 12 585
PRESS (1) 7 20
Press (5) 6 848 7 706 10 623 13 871
   15 3374
Press (3) 7 44 17 336
press (19) 2 290 347 3 58 4 453 7 108
   607 688 733 12 236 925 14 1455 15 805
   2140 16 1238 1548 17 1801 1814 1866
   18 1207
press (1) 13 1174
press (1) 15 1585
pressed (9) 8 643 1001 11 201 292 395
   14 1150 16 39 18 79
presses (2) 15 134 160
pressgang (1) 7 625
pressing (1) 6 511
pressing (1) 15 2943
pressman (3) 7 630 693 15 837
pressmen (1) 9 536
presstable (1) 15 928
pressure (6) 14 967 16 372 17 1087 1198
   1431 1482
presto (3) 14 1045 1060 18 1508
presumably (6) 14 1305 16 310 925
   17 1126 1127 1453
presume (5) 12 786 13 597 15 835 2375
   16 251
presupposed (1) 17 2212
pretences (2) 16 1131 17 2183
Pretend (1) 13 883
pretend (4) 8 878 18 192 1020 1485
pretended (3) 18 183 1069 1331
Pretenders (1) 3 313
pretenders (1) 3 317
Pretending (1) 3 194
pretending (15) 13 522 16 1531 18 3 49
   60 98 491 509 541 547 810 834 1018 1193 1219
preterite (2) 17 2218 2220
pretermit (1) 14 874
preternatural (1) 14 1006

pretext (1) 16 1870
Pretoria (1) 18 388
prettier (1) 13 510
prettier (1) 15 2587
prettiest (1) 15 441
prettily (1) 14 759
Pretty (5) 9 708 13 836 15 2414 2477
   16 228
pretty (27) 6 246 784 7 461 10 910
   12 1171 13 118 125 174 361 14 451 678
   794 1180 1225 1317 1327 15 2477 2978
   16 894 1433 18 276 676 1065
pretty (2) 9 267 17 815
prevailed (1) 16 808
Prevent (1) 4 448
prevent (1) 18 991
prevented (2) 17 417 670
Prevention (1) 15 697
preventive (1) 17 670
previous (7) 12 965 14 1168 17 327 466
   1197 1389 2280
previously (12) 12 349 15 3426 16 322
   606 1582 1698 17 233 1071 1449 1689 1923
   1949
prey (9) 1 422 3 300 8 77 10 621
   11 363 13 299 517 14 674 16 1324
prey (1) 15 4665
preying (1) 16 223
Prfff (1) 15 3390
Přhklštř (1) 12 565
priapic (1) 15 2395
Price (3) 2 334 340 17 2104
price (13) 6 672 772 8 876 9 746
   10 507 1137 15 625 3103 16 1157 1824
   17 1582 1662 1791
priceless (2) 9 2 15 1053
pricelist (2) 15 3322 16 1699
prices (2) 2 365 4 209
pricing (1) 8 552
prick (1) 15 87
pricked (1) 14 235
pricked (1) 15 1246
prickles (1) 4 183
Prickly (1) 8 846
prickly (1) 12 157
pricks (1) 15 2705
Pride (2) 12 1003 16 1299
Pride (1) 4 346
pride (5) 2 243 4 347 15 716 16 261
   1089
pride (1) 7 839
pride (1) 15 2288
prided (1) 13 165
prides (1) 14 1297
Priest (2) 11 1034 15 2548
priest (38) 3 120 4 93 5 344 348 369 386
   413 417 419 437 442 448 6 590 593 597 614 631
   847 8 32 111 125 1113 11 1009 1022 1081
   13 1039 15 2541 2649 2740 4437 16 1127
   18 120 489 490 760 1374 1543 1567
priesteen (1) 9 1117
priesthood (1) 7 850
priestified (1) 9 555
priest's (5) 1 739 11 1016 13 1124 1292
Priests (1) 6 984
priests (11) 8 708 9 1156 1221 12 1402
   13 710 1036 14 345 1169 15 2091
   16 1306 1395
Priests' (1) 15 1803

proveniences (1) 17 318
proverb (2) 4 519 15 2415
proverbial (1) 16 846
proverbially (1) 16 790
proves (4) 1 555 2 151 9 523 16 1121
provide (2) 14 213 16 1220
Provided (1) 15 665
provided (8) 12 540 617 629 14 49
   16 985 17 923 1540 18 1528
providence (3) 10 104 14 820 16 640
Providential (2) 15 201 4858
providential (1) 16 69
providing (1) 16 528
province (2) 12 1309 16 1237
provinces (1) 8 334
provincial (7) 7 19 9 116 598 602 10 39
   53 17 2175
provisional (2) 17 940 2074
proviso (1) 16 1624
provocation (2) 15 4788 17 2254
provocative (2) 16 1136 17 2243
provoke (1) 4 216
provokes (1) 15 4513
provoking (2) 15 3120 18 973
provost (3) 8 706 707 17 790
provostmarshal (1) 12 669
Provost's (1) 8 496
provost's (1) 10 1241
provosts (1) 8 707
prowess (1) 12 911
prowl (1) 16 112
prowl (1) 15 100
prowled (1) 3 247
prowling (2) 10 888 12 300
prows (1) 3 301
proximate (3) 17 870 1248 2246
proximity (4) 12 79 15 1048 17 1731
   2031
Prr (2) 4 19 20
Prrprr (1) 11 1286
Prrrrrht (1) 15 2556
Prrwht (1) 8 1024
prude (1) 16 740
prudent (7) 1 573 6 667 12 211 217 437
   14 56 16 1349
prudenter (1) 14 278
prudently (4) 3 29 16 1644 1648
   17 2118
prune (2) 17 1281 1285
prune (1) 15 3760
prunes (1) 13 901
pruning (2) 4 202 17 1584
pruningknife (1) 15 3464
prurition (1) 17 1450
Prussia (3) 14 572 17 482 1727
prussic (1) 12 1582
prussic (1) 15 1746
pry (1) 13 693
prying (3) 9 181 187 16 1867
psalm (1) 17 1029
psalms (1) 15 2451
Pschatt (1) 15 3947
pseudo (2) 9 492 16 1070
pseudonym (1) 12 725
Pseudonymous (1) 12 1697
Psha (3) 7 706 708 740
Pshaw (1) 14 1420
pshent (1) 15 2309
Psst (1) 11 1255

psychophysicotherapeutics (1) 17 295
ptake (1) 8 887
ptarmigan (1) 8 887
Ptolemy (1) 12 1251
Pu (1) 12 1495
Pub (1) 8 790
pub (6) 4 130 6 429 8 732 12 753
   13 964 18 1282
pub (1) 15 579
Pubb (2) 14 1230 1300
puberty (3) 14 930 17 1000 2287
pubhunting (1) 16 96
pubic (2) 9 1132 15 1785
Public (1) 17 1376
public (41) 7 620 8 396 516 9 439
   12 730 986 1322 1793 14 40 1272 1300
   15 232 1116 1159 1361 1688 3034 3534 16 57
   309 537 644 1189 1362 1368 1443 1486 1851
   17 48 182 969 970 1512 1624 1942 1943 2000
   2184 2185 2252 18 314
public (1) 9 97
public (1) 15 1829
publican (2) 16 134 435
publicans (1) 18 882
publication (2) 12 1071 17 651
publichouse (4) 7 669 672 8 1140 10 93
Publicity (1) 15 1707
publicity (4) 2 343 14 1042 1246
   17 2207
publicly (4) 5 437 17 978 1646 18 1365
publico (1) 12 708
publish (1) 9 1085
Published (1) 7 90
published (3) 2 411 7 907 12 727
publishing (1) 12 1049
Pubs (1) 13 1050
pubs (1) 5 9
pubs' (1) 7 198
puce (2) 1 516 3 175
puce (1) 15 4167
Puck (2) 9 1125 1142
puck (2) 10 1146 12 958
pucker (2) 10 1145 1147
puckered (1) 9 718
puckers (2) 10 1131 1142
Pucking (1) 12 978
pucking (1) 10 1135
Puddeny (1) 13 613
pudding (4) 8 43 411 13 225 14 843
puddings (1) 10 100
puddle (1) 16 809
pudendal (1) 15 2414
pudor (1) 15 2549
puerperal (1) 14 898
Pue's (1) 7 734
Puff (1) 11 511
puff (7) 7 480 978 9 302 10 771 11 509
   511 12 1897
puffball (1) 8 44
puffed (3) 8 507 11 509 514
puffed (1) 15 2669
puffing (2) 7 971 12 1784
puffing (2) 15 157 2931
puffpuff (1) 13 401
puffs (1) 16 528
puffs (1) 15 2292
puffy (1) 1 676
pugilist (1) 17 723
pugilists (1) 15 3246

pugnacious (1) 16 1596
pugnose (1) 5 132
pugnosed (1) 8 349
pugnosed (2) 15 192 4347
puissant (3) 12 1184 14 295 15 1472
Puke (1) 15 3043
puke (2) 8 49 12 958
puked (1) 10 634
Puking (1) 13 1186
puking (1) 14 1566
Pulbrook (3) 10 719 17 1981 2075
pulchritudinous (1) 15 2413
Puling (1) 15 4284
puling (1) 18 23
Pull (4) 3 474 6 17 850 14 1476
pull (16) 1 70 2 229 3 70 6 429 1032
   7 1013 8 279 11 249 12 443 14 1498
   15 4882 16 529 18 155 958 1166
pulled (17) 1 320 529 549 2 292 4 74 538
   6 9 7 1000 8 1143 10 134 208 686
   13 988 14 1153 15 2271 17 902
   18 809
pulled (1) 15 4796
pullet (1) 10 327
pulley (2) 15 711 17 1817
pulling (10) 7 787 901 8 1141 12 1396
   13 988 14 631 16 684 17 1217
   18 852 1372
pulling (4) 15 2300 2953 4741 4793
Pullman (1) 6 409
pullpull (1) 15 2981
pulls (4) 15 2951 4284 4447 4469
pulmonary (1) 14 1244
pulp (1) 8 908
pulper (1) 17 1605
pulpit (1) 6 183
pulpy (2) 12 98 16 468
pulpy (1) 15 492
pulsatilla (1) 15 2395
pulse (2) 8 879 13 1197
Pulses (1) 1 225
pulses (1) 13 689
pulsing (1) 11 702
puma (1) 12 1445
pump (6) 6 674 15 3132 16 6 1559
   17 544 568
pump (2) 15 2265 2273
pumping (2) 6 674 18 932
pumpkin (1) 8 397
pumps (1) 6 676
pumps (2) 15 2483 4037
pumpship (1) 12 1562
pun (3) 11 891 979 16 1872
Punarjanam (1) 15 2270
Punch (7) 14 193 229 313 324 401 416 1444
Punch (1) 15 2151
PUNCH (1) 15 1795
punch (5) 6 791 8 411 12 970 14 1435
   1590
punched (1) 3 179
puncheon (1) 16 933
punctated (1) 17 1800
punctilio (1) 16 1113
punctual (1) 14 1392
punctually (1) 10 1278
punctuated (1) 12 528
pundit (1) 11 267
pundit (1) 7 578
Pungent (2) 4 384 8 271

pungent (3) 8 651 819 11 514
pungent (1) 15 1174
Punish (1) 5 426
punish (7) 5 244 252 264 273 11 891
   13 787 18 135
punished (2) 11 473 14 1017
punishing (1) 12 973
punishment (5) 10 1076 12 450 1333 1335
   15 2966
punk (1) 14 543
punks (1) 9 639
Punkt (1) 9 700
punnets (1) 12 95
punt (2) 14 520 15 3111
puny (3) 13 598 14 327 831
pup (2) 6 599 11 806
Pupil (1) 8 418
pupil (4) 9 621 13 908 17 718 1494
pupils (1) 15 2545
pupped (2) 12 1298 15 1115
purblind (1) 15 1396
Purcell (1) 12 937
purchase (12) 4 192 7 941 8 141
   14 682 15 2331 16 145 17 1216 1504
   1662 1665 1673 1960
purchase (1) 15 1574
purchased (8) 15 4538 17 626 628 630 1428
   1805 1813 1866
purchaser (6) 12 37 40 42 45 48 50
purchasers (1) 17 54
purchases (1) 17 923
purchasing (1) 16 1764
Purdon (1) 15 611
Pure (4) 5 501 6 1011 8 760 13 364
pure (24) 4 44 6 737 11 12 315 745
   13 7 15 775 1805 2229 3105 3393 3458 4600
   4735 16 297 566 848 1286 1407 1734 17 562
   711 716 18 870
Purefoy (16) 8 277 358 431 479 10 590
   11 903 1103 13 959 14 510 1333 1335 1410
   1434 15 641 17 2054
Purefoy (3) 15 4345 4692
Purefoy (1) 15 1740
Purefoys (1) 18 160
purely (1) 9 46
purely (2) 15 902 903
purer (1) 11 315
purest (3) 12 355 396 15 2988
Purgatory (1) 12 1459
purgatory (3) 6 859 9 133 10 1173
purge (1) 13 1194
purgefire (1) 14 225
puritan (1) 9 873
puritanisme (1) 16 1453
purity (1) 13 88
purlieu (1) 9 1143
purling (2) 3 459 14 581
purling (1) 7 243
purloined (1) 15 1035
purple (10) 2 202 6 828 7 721 8 901
   12 82 172 1250 13 681 14 1363 17 1487
purple (7) 15 465 1477 1480 2035 2857 3378
   4285
purply (2) 11 483 18 1128
purpose (14) 6 735 12 89 13 47 340 485
   14 695 704 15 552 16 937 1506 1830
   17 275 890 18 951
purposed (1) 16 1867
purposely (1) 18 1138

purposes (7) 16 7 214 345 932 1726 17 175
   1678
purr (1) 15 2524
purred (1) 9 1
purring (2) 15 2537 4017
Purse (1) 8 1189
purse (11) 10 11 117 238 1134 12 961
   14 542 15 246 3533 16 508 17 301
   18 317
purse (1) 2 239
purse (1) 15 2051
pursed (1) 8 954
pursepoke (1) 15 243
pursestrings (1) 11 715
pursily (1) 10 796
pursing (1) 10 714
pursuant (1) 7 92
pursue (1) 8 536
pursued (3) 8 641 16 155 409
pursues (1) 15 366
pursuing (1) 10 1004
pursuing (1) 9 616
pursuit (2) 10 1260 16 1158
pursuit (1) 15 4335
pursuits (1) 17 1588
Purty (1) 8 602
pus (1) 3 214
push (5) 12 1434 13 570 15 3985
   16 536 647
push (2) 15 2624 4028
pushcar (8) 13 13 21 76 218 384 571 684 935
pushed (10) 5 339 7 73 281 634 8 650
   10 321 11 333 14 645 15 3274
   16 473
pushedback (1) 3 274
pushes (2) 1 173 10 513
pushing (5) 7 638 971 10 593 16 360 366
Puss (1) 15 2465
puss (3) 15 2465
pussens (3) 4 24 31
pussful (1) 9 566
pussy (1) 4 471
pussy (1) 15 1602
pusyellow (1) 15 2631
Put (12) 3 39 399 4 130 6 964 7 621
   8 925 9 367 10 302 11 1257 12 886
   13 799 15 1916
Put (1) 2 239
put (198) 1 496 520 530 579 618 2 283 321
   339 3 8 95 321 324 4 272 331 371 390 393
   485 5 28 169 267 346 348 421 545 6 119 168
   336 491 551 569 616 727 799 873 875 882 909 942
   7 169 198 227 606 680 728 935 1024 8 18 167
   348 386 415 505 517 815 839 984 1191 9 257 494
   660 10 52 260 476 547 635 708 899 950 951 974
   975 11 248 438 861 939 12 263 949 1087
   1361 1364 1507 1534 1555 1574 1655 13 64 163
   185 426 491 514 559 604 621 658 674 677 779 845
   997 998 1225 1244 14 163 204 314 512 599 612
   630 643 646 697 821 857 885 1009 1187 1586
   15 71 947 1167 2333 2403 3294 16 32 60 78
   181 199 223 285 296 354 464 571 740 781 959 1041
   1173 1248 1269 1353 1494 1594 1619 1639 1669
   1709 1732 1761 17 600 1033 18 112 179 199
   233 240 255 304 348 379 381 417 425 436 506 521
   579 639 667 704 733 768 771 772 801 824 830 924
   979 991 1011 1013 1064 1124 1132 1164 1204 1388
   1508 1514 1549 1602 1606
put (1) 15 1492

putoff (1) 18 341
Putrápesthi (1) 12 561
putrefied (1) 6 999
putrid (1) 15 1205
Puts (1) 8 760
puts (7) 5 202 9 995 12 848 1192 1577
   18 1223 1387
puts (5) 15 437 1316 1490 2588 2883
Puttana (1) 16 314
puttees (1) 15 2858
puttiest (1) 14 1541
Putting (3) 4 285 7 227 8 460
putting (24) 1 513 2 224 261 422 6 656
   7 351 8 786 859 10 1132 12 502 682 882
   890 966 1193 1471 1663 16 1195 1747 1785
   18 206 207 381 1082
putting (1) 12 427
putty (3) 6 327 16 571 18 989
Puzzle (1) 8 750
puzzle (3) 4 129 11 1024 13 933
puzzled (3) 1 368 9 507 16 664
puzzling (2) 6 716 16 1233
Pwee (3) 11 55 1203 1241
Pwfungg (1) 15 4247
Pyatt (1) 7 688
pyemia (1) 17 1254
Pygmalion (1) 8 924
Pyjamas (1) 15 2402
pyjamas (1) 13 1242
Pyjaum (1) 15 2275
pyramidically (1) 17 1533
Pyramids (1) 8 489
pyre (1) 17 127
pyre (1) 15 3232
Pyrrhus (8) 2 18 19 21 26 48 7 568 575
pyx (1) 3 121

Q

Rice (2) 12 1688 17 181
rice (3) 8 745 15 2900 4202
ricepowdered (1) 15 2974
riceslop (1) 14 513
ricestraw (1) 18 797
Rich (4) 3 196 7 1040 9 639 11 632
rich (31) 1 397 451 2 261 307 3 97
  4 529 5 122 130 139 8 273 635 686 9 625
  710 748 10 1005 1204 12 1463 13 235 978
  1208 14 148 674 1438 17 1532 18 500 518
  561 721 1155 1554
rich (3) 15 1176 2432 4348
Richard (14) 3 247 9 894 898 903 904 911
  916 971 985 987 989 12 1693 17 141 539
Richard (2) 9 634 637
richer (3) 11 347 767 14 149
riches (3) 13 216 14 288 16 991
richest (1) 16 988
Richie (36) 3 76 86 89 90 91 6 56 8 320
  9 973 1039 10 471 1191 11 343 358 444 479
  521 610 623 630 643 647 666 678 718 768 778 786
  787 1000 1028 1070 1164 1283 13 846
  17 141
Richie (1) 15 499
RICHIE (4) 15 504 511 515 2788
Richie's (2) 11 625 886
richlooking (1) 18 128
richly (3) 7 1060 9 680 15 1071
richly (2) 15 1445 1462
Richmond (7) 1 206 8 460 10 76 1192
  14 1549 15 2933 17 143
Ricketts (1) 15 2219
Ricketts (4) 15 2050 2082 2302 2709
rictus (1) 15 2570
rid (7) 1 137 5 82 10 684 13 853
  15 1167 16 311 1076
Riddle (1) 2 88
riddle (7) 2 94 98 101 7 477 504 588
  15 3563
riddle (1) 2 88
riddlemakers (1) 15 1435
riddling (1) 2 87
Ride (1) 15 3804
ride (8) 2 283 9 453 12 1779 13 147
  15 1072 2944 18 956 1418
ride (2) 15 3978 4679
rider (1) 14 1137
riderless (1) 15 3974
rider's (1) 14 1127
riders (1) 2 303
riders (1) 15 4127
ridge (1) 12 1877
ridicule (1) 17 696
ridiculous (1) 15 2402
Riding (2) 8 343 15 1017
riding (9) 3 301 8 831 10 510 11 302
  13 131 15 1145 3115 18 838 1026
ridingboots (1) 13 999
Ridsdale (1) 12 229
Rien (1) 15 2163
Rienzi (1) 12 607
rifle (1) 17 1716
rifletta (2) 10 351 15 2504
rifletterò (1) 10 354
Rift (1) 11 789
rift (1) 11 1164
rifts (1) 15 1268
rigadoon (1) 15 2537
rigging (1) 16 647

Right (23) 4 12 5 175 7 10 36 111 413 652
  655 704 8 432 1103 10 1213 11 499 901
  12 1320 1475 1753 13 815 14 1533
  15 3115 16 960 1557
Right (1) 15 1414
right (194) 1 50 139 285 505 2 222 396
  3 190 191 418 4 11 76 174 328 510 5 22 24
  27 76 174 200 217 391 393 6 74 169 200 404 424
  427 459 587 756 921 1024 7 265 354 380 381 586
  651 902 903 8 115 159 414 554 564 817 880 946
  968 1100 1137 1169 1170 9 378 497 814 1028
  10 79 390 417 478 506 720 829 872 938 948 956
  975 1139 1140 11 578 839 1157 12 130 774
  861 873 973 1033 1152 1254 1433 1436 1471 1892
  13 43 100 128 354 381 484 545 555 779 901 942
  14 100 202 212 238 527 833 1145 1184 1216 1232
  1502 15 231 234 1301 1517 2193 2325 2780
  3077 3302 3340 3945 4401 4488 4762 4780 4813
  4821 4834 4845 4849 16 54 340 395 418 855 969
  1021 1087 1095 1107 1157 1179 1636 1715 1716
  1721 17 6 158 361 374 971 1217 1223 1275 1288
  1312 1323 1441 1442 1450 1485 1486 1487 1488
  1499 1537 1993 2201 2312 2315 18 111 292 363
  390 667 958 1017 1094 1145 1157 1212 1223 1375
  1483 1516 1521
right (2) 2 398 8 748
right (18) 15 226 481 482 759 1343 1484 1499
  2265 2668 2713 2724 4113 4218 4316 4323 4860
  4959
rightabout (2) 8 1158 12 833
rightaboutface (1) 15 49
rightangled (1) 17 1994
Rightaway-Thrale (1) 16 1278
righteousness (1) 14 203
rightful (1) 12 590
righting (1) 4 7
rightly (1) 16 552
Righto (3) 10 983 14 1447 1574
rights (9) 9 788 789 12 966 13 615
  14 907 960 16 1525 17 1630 2271
rights (1) 15 3550
rightwiseness (2) 12 1136 14 98
rigid (1) 17 217
rigid (3) 15 2574 2723 3822
rigidity (2) 17 517 1201
rigmarole (1) 16 174
rigmaroling (1) 18 1190
rigour (1) 17 1617
rigueur (1) 16 871
riled (2) 16 1312 1639
rill (1) 7 243
rill (1) 15 4189
rilling (1) 1 689
rim (3) 11 346 17 502 18 989
rimirar (1) 7 722
rims (2) 7 811 8 562
Rinbad (1) 17 2325
Rinderpest (2) 2 333 14 576
Ring (4) 4 346
ring (29) 1 42 107 437 2 326 5 336 428
  8 458 9 102 10 389 396 11 113 545 1117
  12 667 1778 13 548 1112 14 583 15 716
  805 3068 3334 17 977 1206 1683 18 261 313
  408 866
ring (4) 15 468 1490 1492 3067
Ringabella (4) 10 400 11 850 853
ringaring (1) 15 2471
ringcraft (1) 12 963
ringdove (1) 13 592

ringed (1) 15 1319
ringfinger (1) 7 811
ringhoof (2) 11 113 545
ringing (9) 4 488 7 10 10 156 11 65
  175 12 601 13 196 493 18 1542
ringkeepers (1) 15 2612
ringlets (1) 7 29
ringletted (1) 15 1122
ringocandies (1) 9 628
ringropes (1) 12 986
ringroundabout (1) 9 282
rings (1) 14 1339
rings (4) 15 1814 2746 2857 3094
Ringsend (7) 3 156 6 34 54 7 6 1045
  16 1144 17 1722
ringsteel (1) 11 113
ringweight (1) 17 520
ringwise (1) 4 279
ringworm (1) 14 1426
rinse (1) 15 3074
rinsed (1) 4 272
rinsing (2) 4 127 5 386
Rio (1) 12 1371
Riordan (6) 6 378 8 847 17 479 18 4
  13 14
Riordan (1) 15 4339
RIORDAN (1) 15 1714
rioters (1) 14 1435
riotously (1) 14 276
riots (1) 9 744
Rip (6) 13 1112 1113 15 3158 16 426
Rip (1) 15 1847
rip (4) 5 294 6 80 13 479 15 1975
ripe (5) 7 941 9 282 10 305 12 97
  14 1418
ripemeated (1) 4 161
Ripening (1) 4 430
ripening (1) 4 202
Ripon (1) 17 1656
ripped (1) 8 892
rippedup (1) 6 45
Ripper (1) 15 1153
ripping (2) 5 78 18 633
Rippingham (2) 13 418 712
ripplecloth (1) 15 875
rippled (1) 6 486
rippling (1) 1 679
riprippled (1) 5 569
rise (13) 1 595 3 396 8 258 12 136
  14 28 1349 1588 16 1692 17 100 269 272
  2059 18 1319
rise (3) 15 3334 3553 4689
risen (3) 5 415 17 855 2063
risers (1) 17 1538
rises (5) 3 211 12 69 87 879 1351
rises (10) 15 683 1163 1325 1410 2263 3439
  3674 3707 4157 4688
risible (1) 7 448
rising (25) 1 469 643 2 319 3 126 454 472
  4 102 104 513 7 595 8 474 9 316
  10 478 11 737 12 298 1772 14 81 862
  15 3025 17 1161 1509 1544 2042 2043
  18 1571
rising (5) 15 184 3812 4064 4666 4780
Risk (1) 11 305
risk (4) 5 541 14 253 1307 18 445
risked (2) 17 349 18 166
risky (2) 8 859 16 1605
risolve (1) 9 941

room (41) 1 138 196 713 2 50 233 3 271
5 207 6 360 764 7 265 394 8 170
9 1115 10 1021 12 368 1403 13 205 1144
1265 14 735 15 3803 16 721 1096 1301
1317 17 138 1272 18 47 68 182 260 353 695
905 906 1139 1461 1462 1483 1489
room (2) 17 398 823
room (7) 15 40 4020 4030 4113 4256 4261
roomkeepers' (1) 12 635
Rooms (1) 11 139
rooms (10) 1 165 6 180 7 412 12 815
15 3074 17 1521 18 71 351 721 899
rooms (1) 15 1549
roomy (1) 10 913
Rooney's (1) 11 1229
Rooshian (1) 14 1561
roost (2) 13 967 16 1328
rooster (1) 16 1796
rooster (1) 15 3707
root (2) 10 807
rooted (3) 3 361 6 1012 14 938
rooting (2) 14 617 18 1106
rooting (1) 15 2853
roots (4) 12 79 13 454 14 939
15 1754
Rope (1) 15 4554
rope (6) 6 443 10 501 765 12 445
17 150
rope (3) 15 25 1178 4543
roped (1) 10 833
ropenoose (1) 15 4532
ropepulling (1) 15 4142
ropes (4) 6 974 11 1013 12 972
14 1466
ropes (1) 15 2612 4056
Roque (1) 18 398
Rorke's (2) 15 781 4618
Rorkes (1) 18 690
Rory (2) 12 134 216
Rory's (1) 12 216
Rosa (2) 12 227 16 202
Rosaleen (1) 12 190
Rosales (1) 18 1465
Rosalie (1) 9 1090
ROSALIE (1) 9 1189
rosaries (1) 13 812
rosary (5) 5 270 375 13 283 490 18 1465
rosary (2) 15 918 2659
Roschaschana (1) 15 1624
Roscommon (1) 14 614
Rose (3) 12 185 1708 14 1510
Rose (3) 7 591 11 1176 16 1681
rose (58) 1 200 319 4 63 306 6 906 907
7 720 823 8 672 9 269 929 1096 10 134
790 11 8 14 54 181 329 331 332 348 398 603
660 693 920 1107 1109 1134 1159 1178 1271
12 632 1134 1286 13 374 499 520 582 760
14 291 818 15 740 17 101 161 1681
18 651 768 1554 1603
rose (2) 1 597 10 1256
rose (1) 15 4150
roseate (1) 11 1152
rosebloom (1) 13 120
rosebud (1) 13 88
rosegardens (1) 18 1601
roseleaves (1) 5 36
Rosemary (1) 15 2388
Rosenallis (1) 7 91
Rosenberg (1) 15 3223

rosepetals (1) 15 1446
rosepink (1) 13 175
rosepink (1) 15 996
rosery (2) 9 651 11 907
Roses (1) 13 1009
roses (8) 5 8 265 277 285 9 627 13 230
14 1326 18 1558
roses (3) 15 1329 1340
rosettes (1) 15 1546
Rosevean (2) 10 1098 16 450
rosewater (1) 15 1333
rosewood (3) 1 104 271 2 146
rosily (1) 9 436
rosiny (1) 11 1013
Ross (3) 11 1063 12 1247 16 134
Ross (1) 10 793
Rossa (1) 12 199
rossies (1) 13 688
Rossini (1) 5 398
Rossini's (1) 16 1744
Rossnaree (1) 17 36
Rostrevor (1) 11 197
rostrum (1) 15 2185
rosy (2) 13 266 14 479
rosy (1) 15 4050
Rot (1) 6 777
rotation (1) 17 1311
rote (1) 11 247
roteatingly (1) 15 3378
Rotha (1) 12 227
Rothschild (2) 17 1748 2023
Rothschild (1) 15 1848
Rothschild's (1) 8 838
rots (2) 9 834 835
rotten (11) 1 412 5 72 16 130 18 513
552 916 977 1084 1241 1425
rottenness (1) 15 842
rotter (2) 15 852 1977
rotting (1) 1 110
rotto (2) 1 700 16 1187
rotto (1) 16 314
Rotunda (5) 6 321 11 765 15 1367
17 601 976
Rouge (1) 3 197
rouge (2) 13 856 15 2320
Rough (1) 8 52
ROUGH (2) 15 4521 4594
rough (8) 4 47 5 524 9 821 13 832
15 4953 16 1012 1634 18 957
rough (1) 15 365
roughly (5) 4 382 9 793 12 170
16 606 1581
roughly (1) 15 2945
roughness (1) 18 1014
rouging (1) 15 3839
rougy (1) 7 57
roulette (1) 15 2162
rouletted (1) 17 1682
Roun (1) 14 1489
Round (9) 8 321 491 11 228 727 12 620
13 1268 15 13 2471 16 722
Round (4) 15 4 1325 2041 2659
round (199) 1 9 148 168 221 223 327 451 559
743 2 28 197 234 3 55 120 132 349 4 15 18
48 53 84 156 322 434 5 210 271 335 343 377 502
552 6 46 173 252 321 380 383 416 419 430 510
608 626 801 802 839 919 960 1029 7 26 130 145
183 405 430 431 455 817 8 135 262 268 374 450
458 658 678 716 922 1047 1111 9 324 10 228

341 350 405 501 654 720 833 991 1048 1166
11 240 241 244 345 554 683 684 727 1178 1181
12 12 127 151 238 249 257 267 268 271 408 440
485 486 516 1019 1031 1034 1061 1486 1509 1561
1756 1786 1796 1850 13 64 202 622 645 810 936
956 1005 1037 1094 1110 1153 1161 1219
14 658 661 839 888 891 1059 15 498 2091
2471 2868 2982 3091 3803 4832 16 24 94 207
223 310 395 681 705 711 723 725 899 1010 1077
1096 1098 1102 1188 1522 17 501 502 1833
2328 18 407 409 486 587 642 739 819 833 849
974 1009 1026 1082 1120 1155 1195 1229 1381
1390 1423 1471 1579 1585
round (2) 10 617 12 27
round (25) 15 184 653 752 918 1234 1280 1601
1887 1888 1928 2041 2160 2300 2743 2751 2857
3668 4024 4028 4030 4367 4532 4805 4916
roundabout (2) 15 4113 4153
rounded (2) 8 412 13 699
rounding (3) 12 1906 16 650 1330
roundly (1) 9 1064
Roundness (1) 8 860
roundness (1) 18 797
rounds (5) 6 264 978 12 509 13 630
18 1480
Roundtown (5) 6 697 7 668 14 1363
17 57 468
Roundwood (1) 17 164
Rourke's (2) 16 55 59
rouse (1) 9 560
rousing (2) 12 699 18 812
Rousseau (1) 15 1848
rout (1) 10 365
route (5) 7 640 667 16 512 533 567
route (1) 16 60
route (1) 15 1401
routes (1) 16 532
roved (2) 7 355 11 185
Rover (1) 8 156
Rover (1) 16 653
rover (3) 15 1397 16 615 654
rovina (1) 15 2504
roving (1) 18 1453
Row (6) 4 422 5 63 14 1027 16 250 263
17 1797
Row (1) 15 4345
row (27) 5 17 272 467 6 447 8 747
10 80 655 830 11 558 12 174 14 625
15 636 2181 2182 4310 16 146 1223
17 150 2049 18 175 219 444 709 955 966 1147
row (1) 15 4367
Rowan (1) 12 1271
rowboat (1) 8 88
rowel (1) 15 1116
rower's (1) 12 892
Rowe's (1) 8 369
Rows (3) 7 591 14 1511 15 1731
Rows (1) 15 3
rows (1) 8 713
rowy (1) 18 1444
Royal (17) 3 377 8 880 10 1273
11 624 12 778 1526 15 3321 4555 4607
16 412 17 177 432 436 1808 1944 2082 2135
Royal (1) 15 1020
Royal (1) 15 1402
royal (25) 5 68 6 438 7 17 503 991
9 680 12 656 777 1379 1394 1845 13 1066
14 623 1067 15 785 1011 1395 1506 1517 2141
2820 16 343 17 553 1977 18 1038

669 671 684 687 688 693 695 703 704 706 710 711
718 722 736 737 772 798 880 882 884 891 894 895
919 920 926 958 1016 1018 1024 1026   7 25 26 33
34 36 54 55 62 67 105 111 113 116 117 122 124 126
132 149 154 155 160 171 172 173 188 250 254 268
273 274 276 279 282 284 299 318 325 342 348 350
351 354 369 376 380 382 393 399 403 407 417 419
420 423 430 435 436 439 447 453 455 457 461 462
468 474 476 478 481 484 490 494 496 504 508 510
513 520 521 526 532 539 545 548 553 562 572 586
588 599 600 603 605 608 612 616 623 625 635 638
641 644 648 658 671 672 675 676 679 695 696 698
700 705 725 728 741 742 744 746 755 768 773 774
782 791 797 800 802 804 822 872 879 885 896 906
909 917 918 923 926 937 952 961 967 971 981 988
996 1008 1015 1023 1031 1035 1036 1055 1057
1059 1061 1066 1072 1074   8 148 206 211 214
217 219 225 229 245 251 254 256 258 260 277 283
284 286 289 299 303 304 306 308 394 517 584 596
694 737 784 786 797 813 817 824 828 833 836 842
937 940 942 943 945 947 949 953 960 961 962 966
971 975 978 982 983 987 988 997 1003 1006 1012
1013 1019 1021 1024 1027 1080 1086 1089 1187
9 9 56 58 76 79 91 112 127 130 141 147 154 186
226 228 232 240 245 263 289 316 320 327 330 334
376 387 391 393 397 418 421 450 503 508 510 513
515 522 527 548 569 581 585 621 663 671 710 715
721 727 733 735 741 778 793 828 879 886 944 962
971 1020 1028 1030 1056 1059 1064 1067 1071
1085 1087 1098 1101 1158 1167 1195 1204
10 37 48 51 183 219 220 225 **263** 272 278 280 283
286 289 302 303 304 318 322 **332** 338 344 348 350
354 355 358 360 362 395 401 **406** 407 415 417 418
420 426 428 442 457 458 467 476 479 481 484 486
487 490 492 493 494 503 506 510 511 517 522 523
524 525 530 536 541 545 550 552 566 581 593 595
638 641 656 657 662 666 669 671 676 679 680 681
687 695 696 697 701 703 705 706 711 734 740 837
857 863 872 874 882 886 887 889 890 897 900 906
916 923 924 925 927 934 939 944 946 948 950 953
956 959 964 967 973 975 977 982 983 995 999 1004
1006 1019 1023 1026 1029 1032 1049 1054 1055
1057 1061 1066 1068 1072 1076 1082 1089 1091
1094 1119 1159 1171 1280   11 67 68 69 72 84 91
103 116 121 136 141 181 188 198 204 224 232 260
263 272 282 329 345 352 370 372 374 375 389 418
426 430 432 448 459 470 472 476 485 519 536 543
548 569 584 587 605 610 642 645 667 758 761 763
769 772 814 824 828 829 835 849 887 905 928 990
992 997 1000 1070 1148 1150 1158 1160 1175 1204
1210 1219   12 16 40 42 44 45 46 47 48 49 50 386
436 463 511 782 786 795 894 918 1210 1432 1446
1466 1599 1602 1607   13 26 61 68 70 71 74 82
193 243 246 247 252 262 266 267 268 274 320 359
378 389 391 443 456 457 458 473 525 532 535 544
546 549 550 682 688 704 914 1216 1225   14 43
98 102 113 115 131 133 135 138 171 175 178 180
197 208 210 214 219 227 229 247 254 259 281 287
289 310 341 355 357 361 436 449 451 459 483 502
665 672 689 721 746 756 794 806 808 823 841 885
887 965 1027 1113 1117 1122 1136 1140 1143 1161
1249 1281 1501 1573   15 408 476 1012 1018
1021 1033 1053 1836 2271 2372 2381 2625 2970
3274 4439 4600   16 59 98 111 170 206 231 260
323 362 379 408 418 447 465 504 590 614 622 683
694 727 740 745 815 845 885 913 916 920 962 1008
1109 1146 1147 1270 1295 1296 1299 1336 1349
1411 1425 1447 1479 1574 1577 1708 1718 1723
1761 1768 1818 1885   17 1085   18 65 81 108

125 136 175 178 184 204 209 213 270 278 303 309
325 333 363 391 425 461 517 522 533 560 571 577
674 780 785 789 820 824 835 857 888 891 975 987
1076 1179 1180 1185 1186 1203 1517 1572 1576
1577 1608

said (1) 1 596
sail (10) 1 575 675   9 753   11 21 590 597
    12 1773 1774   13 1151   16 639
sail (1) 7 522
sail (1) 15 2164
sailed (7) 6 1011   9 157   10 63 753 1096
    16 653 844
sailing (5) 10 296 753   16 421 496 1648
Sailor (2) 17 2322 2328
Sailor (1) 17 423
sailor (33) 10 7 228 239 1063   11 1252
    13 14   16 338 367 375 387 408 410 415 418 441
    447 458 465 609 612 620 664 680 690 696 919 938
    969 1672   17 868 1941   18 346 1412
sailor (3) 15 959 2060 4141
sailorman (1) 10 809
sailors (6) 10 13   13 1148   14 1247
    18 756 1425 1583
sailors' (1) 5 3
sails (3) 3 397 504   13 1156
sails (1) 15 3383
Saint (32) 2 69   3 465   4 136 205   5 330
    8 666 832 837   9 577 772 778   10 79 437
    12 33 225 229 1291 1671 1863   13 140 453
    14 221 500   15 1125 1453 1840   16 1453
    17 144 543 1227 1580   18 791
Saint (1) 16 1161
Saint (5) 15 15 537 1443 1493 4689
saint (26) 2 215   3 128 259   5 323   6 183
    609   7 844 1012   8 178 973   9 521   10 107
    111 144 408 769 929   12 574   13 378 395 450
    14 189 236   15 3358 4576 4638
saint (1) 9 579
saint (1) 15 1439
sainted (1) 15 1662
saints (9) 3 128   11 181 557   12 1642 1689
    1705 1708   13 489   18 759
saints (1) 15 1419
saith (9) 12 448 1723   14 244 250 297 299 362
    384 1431
sake (21) 1 287   6 281   7 313   8 398 998
    9 904   10 1019   11 127   12 639 1793
    13 884   14 220   15 433 3186 4239   16 406
    1546 1842   18 324 935
sake' (1) 15 433
sakes (1) 1 288
salad (2) 8 759   13 314
Salanka (1) 10 851
salary (2) 9 624   17 1544
Sale (1) 5 194
sale (6) 8 826   12 1731   15 2331 2374
    17 1668   18 517
sales (4) 10 525   13 159 234   17 485
saleshop (1) 11 1261
salesman (1) 11 1265
salesmaster (1) 14 571
salesmasters (1) 15 1432
salient (3) 14 740   17 1481 2269
saling (1) 15 3883
Salisbury (1) 7 558
Salivation (1) 15 1793
sallied (1) 10 553
sallies (1) 14 804
Sallins (2) 10 438   17 137

sallow (1) 7 135
Sallust (1) 7 583
Sally (2) 3 64   6 51
Salmon (4) 8 496   12 1459   17 790 1978
Salmon (1) 15 4344
salmon (1) 8 496
salmon (1) 15 1265
salmongaffs (1) 15 3958
Saloon (1) 15 1687
saloon (5) 6 409   11 275 313 440 451
Salt (2) 13 1064   16 622
salt (17) 1 631   4 232   5 39   8 136 1018
    12 643   13 820 1161   14 131 1097   15 785
    16 630 1025 1223   17 250 303   18 979
salt (1) 16 980
saltblue (1) 3 482
salted (3) 2 333   12 172   14 1211
saltee (1) 14 1466
Saltgreen (1) 10 877
salts (2) 15 287 596
saltwater (2) 8 86   18 971
Saltwhite (1) 6 993
saltwhite (2) 1 677   3 472
Salty (1) 8 540
salty (4) 8 86 746   14 549   18 132
Salut (1) 15 4080
salutant (1) 15 1557
salutation (1) 17 470
Salute (3) 6 451   15 18 4752
salute (8) 4 215   6 193 198   10 401 1245
    1279 1281   12 1840
salute (1) 15 4623
saluted (16) 6 509   10 64 86 87 94 95 98 99
    153 154 1180 1235   12 1836   14 835
    16 111 113
salutes (2) 10 1266 1278
salutes (1) 15 960
Saluting (1) 6 715
saluting (4) 6 452   8 410   11 343 434
saluting (2) 15 721 4855
salvage (1) 12 1888
Salvation (1) 5 432
salvation (2) 14 788 1588
salvations (1) 18 1225
salve (1) 14 130
salve (1) 15 1333
Salvi (1) 15 98
Sam (1) 10 758
Sam (1) 15 412
SAM (1) 15 419
Samaritan (1) 16 3
Sambo (1) 12 1325
Sambo (1) 15 413
Same (17) 5 322   6 87 233 560 771   7 219
    8 265 582 1074   12 758 1536   13 831 1003
    1123 1222   14 1476   15 206
same (149) 1 312 373   2 190 233   3 120 365
    4 209 344   5 71 186 219 304 312 325 362 363
    377   6 20 498 626 663 752 822   7 103 309 716
    8 94 151 439 477 714 825 891   9 866 870
    10 892   11 292 1248   12 159 173 999 1285
    1360 1361 1422 1425 1535   13 227 269 419 625
    776 783 830 939 949 1031 1104 1182 1195 1277
    14 389 467 525 582 736 742 894 1049 1195 1240
    1242 1276   15 206 1028 1047 2645 2769 3535
    3887 4445   16 152 215 382 467 642 684 712 768
    958 993 1061 1079 1145 1228 1307 1331 1354 1379
    1400 1482 1518 1542 1585 1637 1714 1791 1804
    1890   17 284 484 917 966 1142 1221 1325 1663

1786 1787 2084 2150 2276 2278 **18** 31 84 333
460 539 649 685 696 814 833 868 1007 1045 1060
1168 1280 1363 1383 1404 1450
same (1) **9** 1147
same (1) **15** 1492
samee (1) **14** 1448
sample (2) **15** 3751 **16** 332
samples (2) **12** 518 **13** 322
Samuel (2) **14** 1017 **17** 2046
San (1) **12** 1275
san (2) **3** 319 **16** 887
sana (1) **17** 1504
sanatorium (1) **4** 156
Sancho (1) **9** 308
sanctam (1) **1** 651
Sancti (1) **1** 351
sanctificantur (1) **12** 1746
sanctimonious (1) **12** 1507
sanctissimi (1) **12** 1748
sanctity (2) **13** 1121 **17** 1901
sanctum (1) **7** 300
Sand (1) **16** 1678
sand (31) **3** 31 147 153 160 205 207 265 287 294
326 332 346 355 360 361 362 371 373 454 **8** 489
13 18 42 52 57 58 254 1256 1266 1270
16 1145 **17** 1787
sandal (1) **3** 487
sandals (3) **3** 411 **4** 241 **14** 1103
sandals (1) **15** 2655
sandbags (1) **12** 576
sandblind (1) **14** 1086
sanded (3) **10** 819 1275 **13** 1287
sandflats (1) **3** 150
sandfrog (1) **18** 871
sandglass (1) **17** 1787
sandman (1) **13** 607
Sandow (1) **17** 1397
Sandow-Whiteley's (1) **17** 1817
Sandow's (3) **4** 234 **15** 200 **17** 513
Sands (1) **3** 290
sands (4) **3** 288 391 **13** 1176 **15** 4953
sandstrewer (1) **16** 43
sandstrewer (1) **15** 185
Sandwich (1) **8** 741
sandwich (5) **8** 756 764 777 818 **15** 564
sandwichbell (3) **11** 241 660 1220
sandwichboard (1) **16** 200
sandwichboards (2) **15** 480 485
sandwiches (1) **18** 950
sandwichman (2) **16** 234 **17** 1940
sandwichmen (2) **8** 123 **10** 377
Sandy (1) **5** 472
sandy (4) **4** 192 **12** 1878 **13** 311
15 3074
Sandycove (7) **1** 342 **5** 171 **15** 4886 4890
16 249 1611 **17** 42
SANDYMOUNT (1) **7** 39
Sandymount (12) **3** 18 **7** 5 6 9 1045 1046
10 1153 **13** 5 306 **16** 1611 **17** 1236 1255
Sandymount (2) **3** 21 **16** 1250
sang (34) **1** 250 259 281 **10** 539 540
11 321 590 593 674 717 718 730 776 779 785 791
1040 1175 **12** 542 **13** 303 312 314 552 675
14 233 **15** 4189 **16** 1817 **18** 274 374
1190 1292 1293 1295 1298
sangfroid (1) **16** 334
sanguine (3) **16** 527 1398 **17** 2233
sanguineflowered (1) **3** 230
sanitariness (1) **17** 1202

sanitary (2) **14** 1243 **17** 1543
sanitatem (1) **12** 1749
sank (12) **4** 81 **5** 302 347 **8** 792 **10** 240
1086 **11** 398 1081 1107 **16** 984
Sankey (1) **16** 1742
Sanktus (1) **10** 849
sanno (1) **3** 7
sans (2) **14** 783 **15** 122
Santa (2) **18** 757 1464
santa (1) **15** 2385
Santiago (1) **16** 489
Santisima (1) **18** 306
Santry (2) **12** 127 985
Saphiro (1) **12** 1087
sapience (1) **14** 9
sapphire (1) **14** 1105
sapphire (3) **15** 1279 1326 2292
sappyhead (1) **6** 1029
Sara (3) **12** 500 **14** 1495 **17** 141
Saracen (1) **15** 1530
Sara's (2) **3** 61 158
sarcastically (1) **15** 3136
sardine (2) **11** 1219 1221
Sardines (1) **8** 741
sardines (2) **8** 855 **18** 973
sarebbe (1) **10** 346
Sargent (7) **2** 123 130 135 152 163 175 182
sarks (1) **15** 4679
Sarsfield (2) **12** 179 1382
sartin (1) **14** 1474
sartorial (1) **16** 1832
sas (1) **15** 2524
sash (2) **10** 251 1136
sash (1) **15** 728
sashed (1) **12** 1281
sashes (2) **8** 124 **18** 631
Sassenach (2) **1** 232 **12** 1369
Sassenachs (1) **12** 1191
sat (40) **1** 37 329 338 352 687 715 **2** 303
3 284 **4** 13 389 **5** 417 **6** 9 464 949
9 325 549 **10** 115 283 **11** 342 608 728 879
1164 **12** 1122 1124 **13** 1085 **14** 124 165
182 198 455 **15** 462 1019 3425 **16** 984 1464
1786 1893 **17** 498 **18** 1173
sat (1) **16** 1886
Satan (3) **5** 446 **9** 689 **15** 3459
Satan (2) **9** 19 32
Satanic (1) **12** 1403
satchel (5) **2** 22 62 90 **10** 268 **11** 692
satchelled (1) **10** 76
satchels (2) **2** 96 **10** 1157
sated (1) **8** 975
sated (1) **15** 3746
sateen (1) **15** 3426
satellite (1) **17** 1149
satellites (1) **17** 1084
satellitic (1) **17** 1160
satin (5) **11** 8 110 203 360 1039
satin (1) **15** 472
satinlined (1) **15** 2816
satiny (4) **11** 8 813 1106 1134
satirical (1) **12** 728
satirically (2) **15** 307 3065
Satisfaction (1) **17** 2229
satisfaction (14) **12** 373 **13** 906 **16** 55
1562 1584 **17** 668 938 1491 1492 1909 2159
2227 **18** 83 98
satisfied (8) **6** 209 **9** 935 **16** 1234
17 350 351 **18** 122 165 1445

satisfy (3) **15** 1234 **16** 1463 **18** 1513
satisfying (1) **15** 3365
saturation (1) **17** 211
Saturday (10) **4** 406 **6** 351 **7** 951 974
8 573 **10** 1174 **15** 1807 **16** 500
18 594 1107
Saturday (1) **9** 441
Saturdays (1) **11** 486
Saturn (1) **17** 1107
Saturnian (1) **17** 1095
saturnine (1) **15** 2097
Sauce (2) **11** 877 **15** 3178
sauce (5) **4** 278 **8** 195 472 **13** 1041
15 2901
Saucebox (1) **4** 423
saucepan (4) **6** 940 **12** 621 **17** 158 161
saucer (4) **3** 212 **4** 37 47 **17** 300
saucers (1) **17** 299
saucestained (2) **3** 225 **8** 658
Saucy (1) **12** 1596
saucy (1) **10** 677
Saul (2) **6** 374 **15** 3500
sauntered (3) **4** 174 **5** 47 **11** 81
Sauntering (1) **11** 82
sauntering (2) **5** 50 **11** 83
saunters (1) **15** 352
saurian's (1) **15** 2456
sausage (3) **4** 179 **9** 897 **18** 558
sausaged (1) **15** 2306
sausageeating (1) **12** 1391
sausagepink (1) **4** 153
sausages (6) **4** 140 148 152 166 **5** 48
9 157
sausages (1) **15** 1575
savage (5) **12** 201 **15** 2674 **16** 475
18 312 594
savagely (2) **15** 1117 2891
savages (1) **16** 1211
Save (9) **4** 130 **5** 326 **8** 4 **10** 875
12 1016 1262 1263 **13** 848 **15** 4233
save (28) **1** 574 **2** 236 **3** 250 329 **6** 933
7 71 932 **8** 386 **9** 459 1059 **11** 620
12 1015 1579 **13** 301 751 919 **14** 253 268
1307 **15** 645 1472 1475 2207 2222 2360 2987
4558 4630
saved (16) **1** 62 **2** 146 **3** 317 **7** 540
8 10 **9** 211 238 **11** 480 483 **12** 1900
14 394 811 **15** 4195 **16** 905 1069 **18** 447
saved (1) **15** 2149
Saves (1) **13** 955
savez (2) **3** 169 221
Saving (1) **7** 546
saving (3) **6** 287 **14** 824 **17** 1667
saving (1) **15** 2025
savingsbank (1) **7** 200
savingsbox (3) **2** 218 250 261
Saviour (6) **6** 727 **7** 49 52 56 **8** 19
12 1805
Saviour's (1) **15** 2483
saviours (1) **7** 68
Savorgnanovich (2) **15** 1866
savour (1) **8** 819
Savourneen (1) **12** 188
savoury (4) **8** 1033 **11** 509 511 **14** 693
Savoy (1) **12** 94
savvy (1) **14** 1470
Saw (5) **8** 352 363 **10** 738 **13** 833 1260
saw (154) **1** 106 205 570 634 **2** 269 303
3 139 248 256 461 **4** 31 256 **5** 37 111 289

369 413 568 570 6 39 129 300 362 875 889 894
7 42 87 134 679 683 720 986 8 51 88 855 882
976 977 1083 1084 9 217 589 674 10 101 136
912 936 1034 1077 1080 1141 1150 1171 1191 1228
1266 11 24 302 614 646 678 719 725 731 732
934 1210 1212 1253 1281 1282 12 207 213 304
311 314 326 381 827 1060 1783 1897 1906
13 304 307 424 537 604 652 680 717 719 726 937
1279 14 172 438 565 567 1163 1367 15 378
384 1061 1188 2621 3355 3359 3392 3498
16 198 270 304 326 851 927 1086 1128 1146 1299
1333 17 780 810 830 18 39 70 219 220 249
256 272 288 293 294 321 344 398 476 763 983 1044
1092 1144 1231 1233 1262 1305 1312 1557 1578

saw (1) 11 665
sawbones (1) 14 1443
sawdust (5) 8 670 727 11 415 15 3022
16 616
sawest (1) 14 1430
Sawhimbefore (1) 15 4340
sawing (1) 11 575
Saxe (1) 15 543
Saxon (6) 1 51 732 7 563 9 44 139
12 1157
Saxons (1) 12 1368
Say (25) 4 134 135 276 6 810 8 630 1016
1092 1129 9 657 10 467 848 11 867 1091
13 26 387 802 901 1135 15 625 2190 3042
3068 4410 4467
say (237) 1 197 202 214 353 496 542 566 606
2 238 437 3 178 4 26 54 118 364 365 491
5 44 240 307 396 497 537 6 121 245 341 345
432 530 546 630 663 666 751 796 838 860 898 923
968 983 988 7 107 200 261 263 628 642 648 654
789 790 792 805 890 1073 8 85 117 154 346 487
505 536 596 923 924 964 982 1029 1071 1117 1123
1124 9 289 420 445 457 814 903 955 957 971 983
995 1073 10 67 70 152 336 429 728 732 826 829
865 893 980 1172 11 210 221 306 369 545 1011
1086 1173 12 392 657 729 844 892 1105 1145
1487 1614 1751 13 49 128 262 266 348 386 388
394 788 827 854 865 868 881 882 1063 1145 1153
1236 14 136 302 367 381 496 515 523 529 826
1063 1422 1507 1535 15 93 970 1003 1359 1367
1645 1984 2129 2200 2323 2371 2388 2392 2402
3517 3613 3938 4186 4473 16 48 74 94 240 333
393 501 627 652 719 741 750 755 770 807 838 897
902 1026 1037 1086 1097 1120 1146 1175 1211
1231 1264 1265 1384 1479 1689 1746 1750
18 110 115 199 241 268 302 317 324 338 339 373
386 440 448 671 706 720 729 743 829 843 956 1019
1033 1299 1377 1502 1581 1584 1606
say (1) 9 733
say (2) 15 900 901
Sayers (2) 10 832 12 955
Sayest (1) 9 740
saying (56) 1 350 454 509 525 549 704
2 382 5 311 6 48 7 180 779 8 448
529 531 9 450 1177 10 255 750 914
11 949 12 435 697 1087 1574 1597 13 265
580 619 14 476 481 612 880 1481 15 2092
2218 2224 4447 4482 4486 4566 16 485 848
1403 1408 1411 1523 1544 1587 1712 1714 1800
18 380 526 1384 1564
saying (1) 15 1929
sayings (1) 1 480
SAYS (1) 7 1053
Says (3) 1 684 6 629 9 820
says (468) 1 127 290 361 424 4 399 440

6 539 598 731 7 47 583 973 8 263 1117
9 114 309 382 423 1042 1076 1098 10 446 571
572 11 135 1058 12 6 8 9 12 13 19 20 23 24
27 28 52 53 54 55 56 57 58 59 60 61 62 67 100 122
129 130 131 132 136 137 139 141 143 144 145 146
147 148 209 210 211 213 218 220 233 238 240 241
257 260 261 262 265 266 267 272 273 274 278 279
300 302 303 307 308 310 312 314 316 317 318 319
320 321 322 323 325 326 327 330 331 332 334 335
336 377 378 379 383 384 387 388 390 396 403 409
412 421 424 427 432 433 434 438 441 455 456 457
458 459 463 464 519 521 522 523 701 702 704 751
755 757 758 759 760 765 767 768 769 818 819 820
823 824 825 826 827 829 850 852 854 855 857 880
884 886 887 888 939 941 942 943 944 947 949 951
955 988 990 991 993 994 996 1015 1016 1017 1019
1020 1021 1028 1029 1031 1032 1033 1036 1038
1040 1041 1043 1045 1048 1050 1051 1052 1054
1055 1057 1058 1071 1076 1077 1078 1079 1084
1085 1094 1095 1096 1097 1100 1141 1147 1149
1150 1152 1154 1155 1156 1159 1163 1165 1167
1175 1176 1180 1190 1197 1202 1203 1206 1208
1215 1217 1218 1219 1221 1222 1224 1226 1227
1232 1233 1237 1239 1258 1262 1265 1296 1299
1300 1306 1317 1318 1319 1320 1329 1330 1338
1341 1346 1351 1352 1360 1364 1376 1377 1379
1385 1389 1390 1399 1400 1402 1406 1407 1409
1410 1411 1412 1413 1417 1419 1420 1421 1422
1424 1426 1429 1430 1431 1434 1436 1465 1466
1467 1470 1471 1473 1474 1475 1481 1484 1485
1489 1490 1491 1502 1503 1504 1506 1511 1534
1536 1538 1539 1540 1541 1542 1545 1546 1548
1549 1550 1552 1554 1558 1559 1560 1563 1570
1586 1622 1623 1625 1626 1627 1628 1630 1632
1633 1634 1635 1638 1639 1642 1644 1646 1649
1650 1653 1654 1655 1656 1657 1665 1666 1668
1669 1672 1673 1674 1675 1751 1752 1753 1756
1758 1762 1763 1764 1765 1767 1771 1788 1803
1806 1807 1808 1811 1813 1849 1852 1903
13 1146 1198 14 545 547 551 565 568 573 578
579 580 581 584 585 589 591 594 599 609 613 618
621 622 629 639 647 921 1561 15 91 93 94 1302
1561 2254 2255 2424 2542 2807 3609 3716 4402
4517 4597 4644 4868 16 582 18 141 385 951
1034 1220 1229 1301 1434
says (1) 15 2245
scab (2) 12 834 15 700
scabbards (1) 14 1394
scabby (1) 4 477
scabs (1) 12 486
scaffold (4) 8 440 12 592 14 1460
16 1072
scaffolding (1) 15 585
scaffolding (2) 15 4365 4861
Scaife (1) 10 1259
Scald (1) 4 270
scalded (1) 4 272
scalding (2) 15 474 18 1134
scale (2) 12 1860 17 1971
scaled (1) 15 3294
scales (2) 11 842 14 158
scaling (1) 3 305
scallop (1) 2 215
Scally (1) 12 936
Scalp (1) 5 525
scalp (1) 13 561
Scamp (1) 15 396
scamper (2) 14 487 1128
scampered (1) 7 395

scampering (1) 7 955
scamps (1) 7 440
scandal (4) 14 535 15 4300 4840 16 740
Scandalous (2) 12 1107 15 1168
scandalous (3) 9 453 10 728 12 1104
scandals (2) 9 767 18 1318
scanned (4) 3 270 8 835 10 315 521
scanning (4) 6 157 733 11 857 17 492
scans (1) 15 1027
scant (1) 14 214
scant (1) 15 4160
scantily (1) 10 636
scanty (2) 4 387 15 3115
scaped (1) 14 258
scapegoat (1) 15 776
scapular (2) 13 1156 15 2228
scapulars (1) 4 176
Scarborough (1) 16 520
scarce (6) 13 16 304 14 334 568 605 1144
scarcely (13) 2 147 11 711 14 48 1240
1296 15 1456 16 441 707 1203 1460 1695
1788
scare (1) 7 690
scared (3) 1 170 13 1121 15 2221
scared (2) 15 758 3311
scares (1) 15 101
scarf (4) 1 478 4 435 13 1188 14 1131
scarf (2) 15 1382 3167
scarfpin (1) 17 1796
scarftie (1) 15 537
scarified (1) 12 1356
Scaring (1) 11 1142
Scarlatina (1) 6 124
Scarlet (2) 4 476 15 1758
scarlet (12) 7 344 367 957 8 124 126 514
12 343 13 518 14 1164 1185 17 320
1555
scarlet (7) 15 299 412 413 807 1329 1379 1382
Scarli (1) 18 1118
scarred (1) 7 140
scars (2) 5 6 13 1261
scathing (2) 13 576 14 927
scatter (1) 2 370
scatter (1) 15 7
scattered (4) 3 360 5 301 7 881 8 409
scattering (2) 7 955 14 1082
scatty (1) 13 32
scavengers (1) 16 1226
Scavenging (1) 8 354
Scene (1) 15 636
scene (30) 3 442 5 200 9 672 880
12 530 548 1180 13 10 446 624 14 1011
1203 1315 1359 15 4858 16 69 263 422 475
984 1043 1382 1557 17 421 611 621 636 639 642
18 171
scenery (1) 17 424
scenes (5) 6 415 10 727 12 1447 1462
16 849
scenes (1) 15 913
scent (9) 12 1004 13 640 1009 14 614
1055 15 2980 3799 16 971 17 1585
scent (1) 15 4330
scented (7) 4 91 5 568 13 153
14 1051 15 3080 3407
scents (1) 15 2014
Scep (2) 14 1224 1286
sceptical (1) 16 1543
Sceptre (6) 7 388 8 830 11 374
14 1127 1131 1140

Sceptre (5) 12 1223 1228 16 1280 1281 1284
Sceptre (1) 15 3976
sceptre (1) 12 1444
sceptre (3) 15 1164 1443 1566
Sceptre's (1) 10 507
Schedule (1) 14 1553
schedule (1) 7 92
scheduled (1) 12 961
scheme (13) 2 326 12 1283 16 506 965
   17 569 1316 1694 1710 1714 1719 1720 1724 1726
schemer (2) 7 618 15 3671
schemes (3) 17 1709 1744 1754
schemes (1) 15 1702
Schiffe (1) 16 1884
schilling (1) 17 1680
schlepps (1) 3 392
Schluss (1) 3 173
scholar (4) 12 731 14 505 15 4490
   17 521
scholarly (1) 14 705
scholarment (1) 14 1415
scholars (4) 14 188 190 202 17 1196
scholars (1) 15 916
scholars' (1) 14 183
Scholastica (1) 12 1711
School (7) 8 602 15 3010 3308 3311 3336
   17 1195 1635
School (1) 15 3325
school (29) 1 293 466 3 303 4 136
   5 42 236 6 171 8 2 187 1153 9 780
   10 42 13 134 810 909 952 14 555 1047
   1111 15 3323 16 158 160 1754 17 521 550
   1495 18 344 1007
school (1) 15 1404
SCHOOLBOY (1) 15 1535
schoolboy (3) 9 57 59 76
schoolboys (8) 9 53 56 10 40 76 1157 1158
   1279
schoolcap (1) 15 3318
schoolfellow (1) 17 942
schoolfellows (2) 17 802 818
schoolhouse (1) 2 187
schooling (1) 16 775
schooling (1) 15 3989
schoolmen (1) 9 56
schoolpoem (1) 8 664
schoolprizes (1) 10 840
schools (1) 17 1803
schoolurchin (1) 9 720
schoolyears (1) 17 645
schooner (2) 10 1098 16 845
Schorach (1) 15 1333
schschschschschsch (1) 5 427
Schwanzenbad-Hodenthaler (1) 12 560
Schwarz (2) 15 1860
sciatica (1) 15 2782
Science (3) 8 1050 14 1226 15 3019
science (9) 10 1148 12 464 467 471
   14 1227 1229 1280 17 562 927
sciences (1) 15 1826
scientific (3) 14 1226 1296 17 560
scientifically (1) 13 113
scientist (1) 12 468
scillas (1) 17 1556
Scilly (1) 16 1416
scimitars (1) 12 575
scintillant (1) 14 1409
scintillating (2) 17 1044 1359
scion (2) 3 315 12 293

scions (1) 15 3867
scission (1) 12 470
Scissors (1) 7 32
scoff (1) 18 140
scoffer's (1) 2 84
Scoffing (1) 8 676
scoffingly (1) 15 3212
scolded (1) 15 699
scolding (1) 15 317
sconce (1) 3 6
scone (1) 10 1087
scone (2) 15 4168 4180
scones (3) 10 1055 18 621 637
scooped (1) 16 941
scoopfuls (1) 8 2
scooping (1) 10 885
scooping (1) 15 2421
Scoot (1) 14 1447
scootlootshoot (1) 15 4133
scope (2) 14 1198 17 1709
scorbutic (1) 14 1248
scorbutic (1) 15 1204
scorching (1) 13 179
score (7) 9 623 11 686 14 1043 16 477
   606 1581 1829
score (1) 9 416
scorn (7) 8 1024 10 907 11 790
   13 579 597 14 864 16 617
scorned (1) 1 407
scornful (2) 1 418 7 619
scornfully (1) 15 892
scorpion (1) 18 786
scorpion (1) 15 2601
scorpions (1) 14 1090
scortatory (1) 9 632
Scotch (8) 8 321 338 522 530 9 751
   10 675 12 1456 14 738
Scotch (1) 15 2181
scotch (1) 8 1
scotch (1) 15 1572
Scotchman (1) 14 1208
Scots (2) 10 65 14 506
Scott (1) 10 743
Scottish (2) 13 1227 17 1856
Scottish (2) 15 1402 3842
Scotus (1) 3 193
Scoundrel (1) 11 928
scoundrels (1) 15 3191
scour (1) 18 520
scourge (2) 15 1082 3778
scourger (1) 12 1354
scourges (1) 15 1806
scouringbrush (2) 14 924 15 892
scouringbrush (1) 15 863
scout (1) 18 1141
Scowl (1) 13 1073
scowled (1) 10 1002
scowling (1) 12 1161
scowls (1) 15 1176
scrag (1) 18 945
scraggy (1) 2 124
scraggy (1) 15 2571
scramble (1) 1 692
scramble (1) 15 1585
scrambled (1) 1 688
scrambles (2) 15 35 131
scrambling (1) 16 1376
scrap (2) 4 404 18 1515
Scrape (2) 8 627 11 1036

scrape (1) 16 610
scraped (7) 1 327 2 149 150 3 362
   13 1003
scraping (3) 6 998 11 574 12 494
scrapings (1) 8 714
scrappy (1) 2 185
scrapy (1) 15 2970
Scratch (2) 4 19 13 823
scratch (6) 7 131 8 787 13 785 15 943
   16 522 1380
scratched (6) 7 148 8 799 10 579
   16 667 17 1449 18 1213
scratches (2) 15 2677 4890
scratching (3) 7 147 10 903 12 486
scrawl (2) 6 127 12 433
scrawled (2) 7 222 8 986
scrawled (1) 15 649
scrawls (1) 7 397
scream (3) 3 328 15 2455 18 570
screaming (4) 11 160 557 13 1205
   18 832
screaming (3) 15 1040 4111 4667
Screams (1) 7 391
screams (5) 15 38 431 2908 4259 4288
screech (1) 7 232
screech (1) 15 4664
screeching (2) 12 809 18 361
screechowls (1) 14 1086
screen (5) 6 380 7 110 10 1052
   17 1174 1531
screen (2) 15 2047 2873
Screened (1) 8 912
screened (1) 6 581
screening (1) 11 660
screens (1) 13 1173
screens (1) 15 3233
screw (3) 15 2653 3487 16 177
Screwed (1) 11 621
screwed (5) 2 298 4 115 13 308
   16 396 18 1291
screwing (1) 10 1163
screws (2) 10 1163 17 1602
scribble (1) 9 1057
scribbled (5) 3 406 438 7 108 10 381 393
scribbling (4) 6 895 9 1086 18 47 1490
scribe (1) 11 268
scribes (1) 16 1503
scrimmage (1) 5 271
scrimmage (1) 15 2046
scrip (1) 17 1932
scripturae (1) 14 1577
scripture (2) 17 687 1900
scriptures (1) 12 1726
scriveners (1) 15 1428
scrivenery (1) 17 665
scrofulous (1) 15 41
scroll (2) 4 93 12 1820
scrolls (1) 12 247
scrooching (1) 18 415
scrotumtightening (1) 1 78
scrub (2) 1 481 8 903
scruff (2) 8 873 12 149
scruff (1) 15 693
Scrum (1) 14 1463
scrumptious (1) 18 621
scrunch (1) 10 1162
scruple (1) 14 922
scruples (1) 17 1891
scrupulously (2) 13 638 14 851

señorita (2) 15 1067 17 1810
señorita (3) 13 1209 1282 15 216
senorita (1) 18 1405
sensation (9) 13 560 15 2424 2562
  16 1746 1837 17 281 776 779 1277
sensational (1) 16 1369
sensations (5) 1 193 12 348 15 3888
  17 1278 1311
Sense (1) 8 1121
sense (26) 1 581 612 614 2 335 336 6 785
  8 899 1108 9 735 741 837 10 1083
  15 106 1801 2196 3204 16 31 173 1140 1153
  1332 17 289 2218 18 840 1277 1406
sense (1) 2 295
senses (7) 4 163 8 614 1118 12 588
  14 1351 16 730 1303
senses (1) 15 2044
sensibility (1) 17 1318
Sensible (1) 17 1480
sensible (3) 6 930 14 851 17 1276
sensibly (1) 16 86
Sensitive (2) 5 35 8 1098
sensitive (5) 11 323 13 1200 17 20 245
  18 176
Sent (1) 7 542
sent (39) 2 1 3 142 355 5 21 6 209 275
  372 7 1064 9 493 10 1124 12 258 268
  369 439 1369 1854 13 611 844 920 14 95 580
  582 783 15 220 435 1065 4542 16 471
  17 33 411 18 329 451 453 612 614 716 784
  1027 1415
sentence (1) 2 87
sentenced (1) 8 1154
sentiment (2) 12 788 17 1893
sentimentalist (1) 14 1030
sentimentalist (1) 9 550
sentiments (4) 14 841 17 2154 2211 2227
sentinel (1) 3 153
sentried (1) 10 208
sentries (1) 18 610
sentry (4) 4 87 16 109 18 857 1585
sentrybox (5) 16 102 106 213 942 1725
separate (4) 15 3557 17 998 1543 2107
separated (2) 15 2106 17 2209
separately (1) 17 56
separating (2) 17 88 402
Separatio (1) 9 716
Separation (1) 4 416
separation (2) 17 1220 2208
separator (1) 17 2209
sepoys (1) 12 671
sepsis (1) 14 969
sept (1) 3 247
September (6) 17 480 2170 2276 2278 2288
  18 475
septentrional (1) 17 1992
Septentrionalis (1) 17 1125
septuagenarian (1) 17 1892
septuagint (1) 14 381
sepulchre (1) 14 395
sepulchre (1) 15 1341
sepulchres (2) 6 639 728
sequel (1) 16 1383
sequence (1) 17 60
sequent (1) 17 1192
sequins (1) 15 1276
serene (5) 11 746 14 1102 1444 15 1472
  18 1597
serfdom (1) 7 856

serfs (1) 12 1350
serge (3) 8 265 10 1244 11 880
sergeant (4) 6 79 15 742 4802 4821
sergeantmajor (3) 10 1134 12 964
  15 625
series (10) 16 1029 17 964 1080 2128 2130
  2132 2133 2143 2150 2300
series (1) 15 2073
serio (1) 10 355
seriocomic (1) 15 447
serious (5) 6 295 7 200 9 543 18 18 671
Seriously (1) 1 466
seriously (6) 1 99 6 11 9 543 544
  10 581 17 369
seriousness (1) 9 544
Sermon (1) 5 322
sermon (3) 5 398 10 144 13 283
serpent (2) 15 2140 2446
serpented (1) 3 339
Serpentine (2) 3 130 15 3930
serpentine (1) 17 1332
serpenting (1) 15 3408
serpentplants (1) 3 443
serpent's (1) 1 422
Serpents (1) 15 2447
serpents (2) 14 157 159
serried (3) 8 70 12 637 14 1384
serried (2) 7 295 314
Serum (1) 2 332
serum (2) 17 313 1063
servant (11) 1 146 154 312 483 638 11 1016
  1017 14 1343 18 802 1080
servant (1) 15 862
servants (7) 1 139 6 620 8 439 9 186
  14 371 15 409 18 61
servants' (2) 17 1521 1543
Servasius (1) 12 1705
Serve (1) 14 1414
serve (6) 1 406 7 555 9 1094 12 763
  14 1162 18 1516
served (14) 7 353 8 760 774 11 217 288
  519 542 775 13 240 484 15 2806 16 837
  1025 17 363
served (2) 10 15
server (5) 1 312 6 589 619 631 8 687
serves (2) 3 219 10 416
servest (1) 12 1605
Servi (1) 12 1681
serviam (1) 15 4228
service (15) 6 317 659 665 8 444 12 1291
  14 185 15 296 789 16 20 77 140 647 1397
  17 1546 18 724
services (2) 14 686 16 291
services (1) 12 419
servile (2) 17 747 1205
serving (2) 1 405 12 805
servitude (1) 16 225
servo (1) 6 601
ses (1) 14 1526
Sesame (1) 15 2434
sesame (1) 15 2444
sesquipedalian (1) 17 785
sessions (1) 12 1874
Set (2) 11 273 12 1385
set (55) 1 328 331 2 388 4 13 37 84 273 300
  303 6 105 801 7 492 493 960 8 44 554 657
  796 1010 9 44 102 922 10 445 960 11 413
  670 847 12 49 668 1774 1780 13 108 175 514
  548 554 614 689 14 37 63 117 141 642 658 684

  15 3263 16 1272 1339 1524 17 105 229
  1033 1555 18 170 307
set (4) 15 2 1501 2491 3738
setdown (1) 5 224
setier (1) 3 219
sets (2) 2 248 13 174
sets (2) 15 1931 2586
settedst (1) 14 368
settees (1) 17 1530
setter (1) 12 715
setter (1) 15 667
settin (1) 14 1473
Setting (1) 6 350
setting (6) 9 7 13 2 856 1079 17 1161
Settle (1) 8 416
settle (5) 7 1017 13 509 953 15 2867
  18 639
settled (9) 4 60 5 148 416 8 637 13 238
  555 1177 16 1506 18 836
settlement (1) 2 207
settlements (1) 17 1907
settles (2) 15 2059 2486
Settling (1) 11 912
settling (3) 5 134 8 1139 10 562
seul (1) 15 4120
Seven (5) 8 776 9 27 11 772 867 1275
Seven (2) 12 741 16 1737
Seven (1) 15 2656
seven (32) 1 442 443 3 136 5 403 7 934
  8 831 9 28 802 10 387 392 11 111 832
  835 12 43 1069 13 160 445 14 620 773
  812 1477 15 546 1674 2027 3075 3606 3613
  4938 16 421 1104 17 958 18 672
seven (1) 12 742
sevenfigure (1) 5 304
sevenmonths' (1) 15 904
sevens (1) 5 155
seventeen (5) 6 696 12 604 13 172 173
  15 1249
seventeenth (3) 3 181 12 580 15 2423
Seventh (1) 5 342
Seventh (2) 15 4449 4464
SEVENTH (3) 15 4458 4475 4559
seventh (2) 6 902 15 4371
seventies (1) 16 1198
Seventy (1) 14 74
seventy (2) 13 978 18 722
seventyfive (1) 4 78
Seventyseven (1) 15 2206
seventyseven (1) 15 811
seventytwo (2) 16 1330 1729
seventyyear (1) 9 833
sever (2) 16 1539 1868
Several (4) 15 1078 1376 1554 1763
several (19) 12 155 583 589 1532 14 236
  15 1045 16 483 559 772 1218 1322 1542 1551
  1568 17 940 1235 1358 1482 1744
several (1) 16 1261
several (6) 15 1550 1705 1829 1842 1844 2306
severally (1) 15 2639
severe (6) 9 737 14 804 872 15 998
  16 1754 18 1173
severed (1) 15 2620
severely (3) 15 266 1111 2383
sew (1) 8 613
sewage (5) 3 151 8 53 865 10 1197
  13 1233
sewed (1) 18 1030
Sewell's (1) 10 1101

sewer (2) 10 500 17 1702
sewers (1) 7 489
sewing (1) 8 1119
sewn (1) 17 1380
Sex (2) 4 295 15 2547
sex (14) 8 269 12 659 1837 13 585 664 14 678 733 830 1231 15 1772 2445 16 1837 17 1427 18 232
Sexology (1) 15 2423
sexsmelling (1) 15 3322
Sexton (1) 6 159
Sexton's (1) 8 500
sexton's (1) 6 464
sextuple (1) 17 1049
sexual (3) 8 866 14 1306 17 647
sexus (1) 14 347
Seymour (7) 1 163 702 703 6 470 7 743 748 17 792
Seymour (1) 15 1000
Seymour's (1) 1 695
sgeul (1) 15 1771
sguardo (1) 11 595
Shabby (1) 8 267
shabby (1) 10 855
shackled (1) 12 1138
Shackleton's (1) 10 720
shade (17) 1 561 4 193 10 211 13 1074 15 3303 3306 3309 3342 4933 16 118 1212 1281 1614 1747 17 1174 2300 18 1591
shade (3) 15 2040 2476 4285
shaded (7) 3 102 6 257 275 10 1211 14 1145 15 3265 17 1569
Shades (1) 6 749
shades (1) 14 1456
Shadow (1) 10 866
shadow (38) 2 84 3 334 408 413 4 531 6 552 9 30 38 47 88 164 269 361 400 402 463 479 480 10 1034 11 49 465 516 660 734 12 1412 13 297 1144 14 1377 15 2429 3029 16 1075 1310 1852 17 1133 1190 2301 18 650 654
shadow (1) 15 606
shadowed (3) 1 31 7 356 14 278
shadowing (2) 1 248 8 476
shadows (7) 4 92 6 750 8 526 9 1168 1191 14 1067 15 4942
shadows (1) 7 246
shadows (1) 15 1325
shady (3) 13 630 14 1573 15 4950
shaft (2) 13 601 17 1045
shafts (2) 1 315 3 272
shafts (1) 15 4690
shagart (1) 9 367
shaggy (2) 2 296 7 816
shaggybearded (1) 12 153
shaggychested (1) 15 2605
Shah (1) 11 1050
shah (1) 11 1248
Shake (3) 3 190 12 785
shake (13) 1 273 3 191 318 4 45 7 933 9 370 11 428 13 1186 14 1326 1492 15 747 3660 18 707
shake (1) 15 1377
shakebags (1) 9 911
shaked (1) 14 325
shakedown (1) 16 1621
shaken (1) 11 177
shaken (1) 15 15

Shakes (1) 9 1108
shakes (1) 14 487
shakes (9) 15 1103 1876 3657 4178 4462 4647 4838 4912 4922
shakescene (1) 9 926
Shakespeare (33) 2 238 8 64 9 47 159 166 172 174 176 180 226 241 370 410 441 504 508 634 729 834 882 958 998 1029 10 1061 11 905 12 191 15 111 497 2118 16 784 17 386 794 1122
Shakespeare (3) 9 121 123 15 3909
Shakespeare (1) 15 3822
SHAKESPEARE (2) 15 3825 3852
Shakespearean (1) 17 793
Shakespeare's (8) 1 556 2 152 6 345 9 44 394 989 16 1762 17 1365
Shakespeare's (1) 15 3855
Shakespeares (1) 16 364
Shaking (1) 6 621
shaking (9) 1 13 14 6 74 622 623 12 784 13 923 18 315 850
shaking (3) 15 1600 1704 4821
Shakti (2) 15 2271 2272
Shaky (1) 8 189
shaky (4) 2 163 4 539 7 266 10 132
shalal (1) 15 4618
Shall (6) 9 273 15 528 2688 2689 2691 4642
Shall (2) 2 356 6 852
shall (58) 1 167 2 202 3 27 455 9 385 445 498 499 790 813 864 1024 1059 1060 1098 1118 11 658 12 42 44 45 47 720 792 863 1359 1608 1609 1884 14 25 33 35 109 293 367 397 445 446 523 1070 1141 1576 15 428 835 974 1543 1898 1900 2101 2375 2421 2463 2894 2898 3935 18 768 1553 1603
shallow (1) 9 78
shallowest (1) 14 1176
shallows (1) 3 304
shalt (1) 14 1418
Sham (1) 15 3314
sham (4) 4 283 7 348 10 789 18 400
shambles (1) 9 134
shambles (1) 15 666
Shame (4) 6 123 838 13 997 15 1037
shame (11) 2 165 5 431 8 258 9 850 10 293 13 52 14 319 1065 15 2868 3265 18 613
shame (2) 15 1330 2299
shameclosing (1) 4 33
Shameface (1) 14 463
shamefaced (1) 10 306
shameless (1) 8 1125
shamewounded (1) 3 422
shamming (1) 15 2853
shammy (2) 10 812 17 301
shampoo (1) 6 19
Shamrock (1) 17 395
shamrock (3) 5 330 12 668 14 586
Shanagolden (1) 12 1314
shanderadan (1) 15 548
Shandygaff (1) 8 736
Shane (1) 12 178
Shanganagh (1) 12 1539
shanks (2) 3 336 13 484
Shannon (3) 10 385 12 112 1256
shan't (1) 15 836
shanties (1) 16 478
shanty (2) 16 1649 1704
shape (18) 6 207 7 682 9 947 10 209

12 663 13 142 163 503 16 10 332 931 1056 1100 1375 1521 18 246 287
shape (2) 15 1206 1549
shaped (1) 13 698
shapeless (1) 15 14
Shapely (3) 7 97 8 173 920
shapely (4) 1 268 2 266 13 170 14 1084
shapers (1) 11 574
shapes (4) 6 460 461 487 18 1562
shaping (1) 15 4062
Shapland (1) 3 81
share (5) 6 763 13 654 14 1020 1321 16 456
shared (2) 15 2786 16 1373
shareholder (1) 9 712
shares (4) 5 163 8 338 784 15 2933
Shark (1) 13 847
shark (1) 15 4144
sharks (2) 13 1162 16 691
Sharons (1) 18 1590
Sharp (1) 13 913
sharp (17) 2 185 196 3 437 5 536 6 638 7 116 10 747 11 839 997 14 869 1400 15 4527 16 973 1778 1865 17 124 2061
sharpened (1) 15 3941
sharpening (1) 8 673
sharply (4) 4 537 9 655 13 578 14 1212
sharply (2) 15 294 4782
sharps (1) 11 996
sharpset (1) 14 551
Shatter (2) 10 824 825
Shattered (1) 3 249
shattered (1) 2 9
shattered (1) 15 4245
shattering (2) 3 213 9 1111
shattering (1) 15 99
shaughraun (1) 7 629
shave (7) 1 46 6 744 10 699 15 199 17 276 278 279
Shaved (1) 5 521
shaved (4) 1 56 99 8 507 11 1266
shaven (2) 1 50 131 14 1362
shaven (1) 15 2252 2857
shaving (5) 4 520 16 20 656 17 277 286
shavingbowl (2) 1 306 319
shavings (3) 15 586 4891 16 2
shavings (1) 15 4921
Shaw (1) 9 440
shawl (4) 3 376 7 928 13 920 18 758
shawl (2) 15 89 365
shawled (2) 15 597 3442
shawls (6) 12 803 804 807 809 18 619 1587
She (239) 1 80 196 211 252 257 398 400 418 461 2 142 144 146 446 3 41 219 221 253 392 424 426 429 4 11 27 33 46 50 58 74 95 150 168 173 259 260 303 318 333 359 372 378 418 419 456 531 5 99 109 236 298 376 6 79 483 544 548 696 705 7 784 8 117 149 165 193 255 261 264 267 292 305 589 609 837 853 910 915 9 216 217 218 257 686 800 805 1159 10 126 135 169 305 393 557 559 808 810 870 875 1233 11 74 78 108 140 235 237 246 331 334 346 405 413 416 462 506 542 546 563 596 640 732 754 771 816 875 921 931 956 1056 1059 1072 1092 12 642 646 846 13 64 81 117 123 127 155 161 173 179 222 338 339 365 406 415 422 425 435 474 478 513 514 560 584 634 653 661

667 668 670 687 690 695 733 741 757 759 760 762 764 769 806 849 883 884 936 960 1012 1102 1114 1153 1240 1244 **14** 98 115 297 1073 1082 1129 1130 1140 1152 1313 1424 **15** 70 408 554 566 890 1724 2327 2337 2355 2599 2877 3294 3302 3340 3357 3358 3540 4179 **16** 738 879 917 1353 1355 1446 **17** 613 614 615 678 680 699 706 876 921 922 925

She (6) **1** 383 **3** 203 **5** 282 **16** 1681 **17** 821 825

She (35) **15** 287 361 372 386 577 862 1310 1316 1339 2014 2031 2059 2084 2289 2292 2588 2710 2712 2714 2742 2746 2748 2751 3530 3553 3842 3846 3857 4016 4095 4110 4118 4160

she (796) **1** 88 103 109 208 251 257 266 270 361 379 390 399 409 417 419 428 442 459 701 **2** 166 330 391 442 **3** 36 86 200 235 372 426 430 469 **4** 19 27 29 30 38 39 48 51 59 61 82 146 171 241 260 261 263 267 276 284 285 295 302 303 306 312 314 326 327 331 335 337 343 355 380 416 418 425 428 451 520 **5** 14 47 113 189 195 240 269 430 **6** 13 67 78 80 201 248 353 480 551 553 649 650 697 704 743 1002 **7** 533 534 949 **8** 24 41 112 145 148 149 150 165 173 195 212 229 244 245 251 256 258 265 277 284 304 306 318 349 379 394 395 418 584 629 717 889 903 907 912 915 916 924 932 1187 **9** 216 217 219 257 331 634 666 674 680 803 805 807 **10** 63 64 65 66 137 138 158 167 169 170 263 269 271 332 333 380 382 511 541 570 572 605 656 859 865 1057 1208 **11** 36 82 83 84 100 121 131 132 152 169 173 188 197 **198** 204 215 217 246 288 309 333 352 363 369 410 **4**17 418 462 487 491 504 510 512 544 545 546 564 638 690 726 727 730 732 738 770 807 814 815 871 876 922 923 925 930 955 971 973 980 1056 1057 1085 1105 1114 1123 1170 1201 1212 1255 1259 1260 **12** 259 640 643 644 676 687 688 812 847 993 1004 1006 1064 1165 1174 1396 **13** 29 60 61 63 75 82 84 86 91 93 95 100 112 115 121 123 126 136 142 145 146 149 152 158 159 161 163 164 165 166 176 177 178 181 183 184 189 191 192 194 202 214 215 219 221 226 228 229 235 244 251 254 257 262 266 267 268 271 272 273 274 276 278 292 293 294 297 308 312 321 328 332 340 342 357 358 361 368 370 384 386 394 411 416 417 418 419 421 425 428 429 431 433 434 437 438 444 451 453 459 460 461 463 474 476 477 478 479 481 482 484 492 493 494 498 500 506 507 515 516 518 521 523 525 529 530 537 555 557 560 562 569 576 577 580 581 582 587 588 593 594 595 597 600 602 603 614 617 618 627 628 632 635 636 638 642 643 644 645 649 650 651 652 655 656 668 673 678 688 689 693 696 698 699 700 704 707 712 715 717 719 721 726 727 730 742 755 761 766 772 775 782 803 827 828 848 855 867 869 872 880 885 890 894 898 905 907 908 915 922 926 929 936 941 983 997 1007 1012 1022 1085 1109 1111 1146 1154 1195 1196 1202 1207 1226 1237 1241 1253 1275 1280 1283 1300 1301 **14** 58 59 82 84 93 94 95 97 103 115 117 121 135 176 177 208 219 231 240 245 268 298 299 302 303 319 320 345 348 359 449 450 451 452 461 512 758 787 788 794 807 817 822 875 884 886 918 1038 1065 1100 1101 1102 1134 1136 1141 1143 1149 1150 1151 1153 1159 1160 1278 1306 1313 1316 1319 1327 1403 1496 1552 1569 1573 **15** 45 70 71 409 552 565 973 1233 1995 2314 2320 2345 2357 2578 2769 2827 3162 4420 4588 **16** 136 272 433 724 736 877 878 1210 1393 1408 1412 1418 1420 1429 1470 1471 1480 1509 1545 1547 1802 1878 **17** 440 483 491

615 676 677 681 683 685 706 708 866 868 877 880 882 896 902 903 905 920 921 924 926 **18** 5 7 11 12 27 50 52 61 69 73 75 191 194 202 211 213 214 216 218 219 220 222 236 240 242 243 244 293 419 441 442 477 480 484 494 499 500 525 613 616 622 623 639 641 652 656 659 667 672 674 717 720 727 749 753 754 785 827 846 848 851 934 935 937 994 1013 1015 1018 1027 1030 1034 1047 1049 1050 1054 1069 1072 1075 1076 1077 1083 1098 1099 1167 1168 1209 1255 1269 1438 1454 1505 1539

she (5) **10** 617 **13** 948 **14** 317 **17** 814 823

she (55) **15** 55 316 352 365 375 384 437 461 466 487 1027 1060 1117 1744 1970 1984 1990 1998 2011 2057 2059 2063 2299 2708 2852 3393 3402 3436 3458 3460 3502 3503 3504 3524 3570 3655 3656 3657 3664 3687 3692 3698 3710 3737 3769 4005 4218 4230 4268 4304 4586 4587 4652 4738

sheaf (1) **9** 291

Sheares (1) **12** 499

shearling (1) **12** 103

shears (5) **1** 170 **6** 935 **7** 31 40 **12** 1716

sheathmail (1) **15** 3461

Sheba (2) **9** 631 **12** 198

shebeen (2) **12** 802 **16** 1352

SHEBEENKEEPER (1) **15** 610

shebeenkeeper (1) **15** 606

Shebronze (1) **11** 365

She'd (2) **12** 1233 **13** 1009

she'd (7) **7** 702 **13** 96 178 265 474 702 **15** 408

shed (10) **13** 739 1167 **14** 565 **15** 2966 **17** 293 **18** 1006 1021 1080 1081 1268

shedding (1) **14** 1081

shedolores (1) **11** 734

Sheds (1) **17** 1737

sheds (1) **17** 1738

sheds (1) **15** 1552

shee (1) **14** 1507

Sheehy (6) **8** 515 **10** 17 22 26 27 29

sheeny (3) **9** 605 750 **14** 1526

sheep (8) **4** 160 **6** 387 598 **8** 726 **12** 110 617 **16** 1640 **18** 151

sheep (1) **15** 901

sheepdip (1) **12** 833

sheepish (1) **15** 2762

Sheep's (1) **17** 1471

sheep's (1) **12** 1666

sheep's (3) **15** 159 1766 2297

sheeps (1) **18** 1259

sheepsface (1) **12** 1907

sheepskin (1) **15** 4671

sheepskins (1) **15** 1048

sheepsnouts (1) **8** 727

Sheer (1) **16** 1214

sheer (1) **16** 297

sheeses (1) **14** 1543

Sheet (3) **4** 348 **8** 186 **15** 3660

sheet (15) **2** 176 293 **5** 494 **7** 109 **10** 369 **11** 826 943 **13** 680 **14** 486 **15** 4540 **16** 708 **17** 676 **18** 1001 1512

sheeted (1) **9** 221

sheeting (1) **3** 326

sheets (14) **2** 320 399 408 422 **4** 154 165 **5** 540 543 **7** 516 585 904 **11** 295 **14** 643 **18** 1124

Sheffield (1) **12** 621

shefiend's (1) **3** 379

shegoat's (1) **4** 305

Sheila (1) **12** 640

shekels (1) **12** 1551

Shelbourne (2) **8** 351 **15** 2995

shelf (5) **13** 773 **17** 298 302 317 **18** 1022

She'll (1) **15** 2877

shell (14) **1** 621 **4** 422 **8** 583 **11** 120 422 922 934 938 941 954 1077 1237 **16** 271 **18** 1048

shellcocoacoloured (1) **3** 327

Shelley (2) **9** 51 382

shellfish (1) **7** 826

shellgrit (1) **3** 373

Shells (1) **3** 495

shells (11) **2** 213 214 216 226 241 **3** 11 157 472 **8** 856 864 **12** 1716

shells (2) **15** 1843 2265

Shelter (1) **8** 492

Shelter (1) **16** 1231

shelter (14) **5** 223 **7** 642 **9** 786 **14** 488 **16** 8 320 354 387 705 923 1299 1704 **17** 326 2057

sheltered (3) **2** 70 **7** 882 **17** 1569

sheltering (1) **13** 212

shelters (1) **16** 794

Shelton (1) **17** 423

shelves (4) **8** 741 855 **17** 296 **18** 520

shelving (1) **3** 30

Shema (2) **7** 209 **15** 3228

Shepherd (1) **11** 1241

shepherd (2) **3** 228 **9** 681

shepherd (1) **15** 1918

shepherd's (1) **13** 1168

shepherd's (1) **15** 537

shepherds (1) **14** 1382

shepherds (1) **2** 64

sherbet (1) **4** 91

Sheridan (1) **15** 3004

Sheriff (2) **16** 1629 **17** 1727

Sheriff (1) **12** 417

sheriff (2) **8** 880 **17** 444

sheriff's (1) **11** 353

Sherlock (1) **10** 1011

Sherlock (2) **15** 1380 1848

SHERLOCK (1) **15** 1387

Sherlockholmesing (1) **16** 831

sherry (3) **10** 547 1127 **15** 1233

sherry (1) **15** 3838

She's (28) **1** 671 **5** 151 **6** 649 694 **8** 114 116 281 282 531 771 952 **10** 382 566 **11** 715 1267 1289 **12** 994 **13** 771 842 **15** 747 769 1288 2057 2873 2875 4170 **16** 420 421

she's (14) **5** 384 **6** 88 **8** 135 589 **10** 383 **11** 1103 **12** 501 **13** 773 827 866 1214 **14** 733 **15** 1739 4130

she's (3) **10** 1251 **12** 1568

shes (17) **18** 22 80 192 217 476 526 563 935 1017 1023 1025 1063 1064 1065 1083 1099

shesaw (1) **11** 1255

Shesfaithfultheman (1) **15** 4385

shesoul (1) **9** 288

shesouls (1) **9** 285

shew (1) **5** 390

shewbread (1) **5** 359

shewed (1) **14** 692

shield (4) **11** 854 **12** 1608 **14** 465 467

shielded (1) **14** 698

shielding (1) **1** 216

shields (1) **1** 664

shieling (1) **16** 423

Sin (3) 15 1947 4354 18 968
Sin (5) 10 204 606 641 17 734 2260
sin (24) 2 70 390 395 3 44 45 7 536
 9 541 1006 1008 1009 11 87 156 157 190 1188
 13 373 456 14 226 15 395 655 1070 2653
 18 1129
sin (1) 15 243
Sinai's (1) 7 867
Sinbad (3) 16 858 17 2322 2328
Sinbad (1) 17 423
Since (5) 8 481 998 11 1040 12 1377
 16 1370
since (44) 1 661 2 269 3 25 5 268 422
 6 234 549 850 7 763 8 506 9 1072
 10 682 12 607 1245 1861 1871 13 250 885
 14 755 884 1557 15 399 1115 2740 2769 3153
 16 40 459 543 831 934 1370 1405 1438 17 282
 343 2003 2262 2286 18 2 85 720 1450 1483
since (3) 6 164 7 829 11 782
sincere (1) 17 475
sincerely (1) 18 1230
sincerity (4) 12 789 13 278 17 476
 18 1230
Sinclair (1) 8 553
sine (2) 16 813 1558
sinewless (1) 16 1724
sinews (1) 16 854
sinews (1) 15 2845
sinewyarmed (1) 12 155
sinful (1) 11 87
Sing (3) 11 1214 15 2506 3130
sing (34) 1 257 3 257 5 **151** 10 791 823
 11 325 611 659 688 698 699 **773** 787 807 914
 12 921 13 498 862 14 314 15 2172 2511
 3130 3459 4718 16 1761 18 380 617 887 899
 1189 1268 1286 1339
sing (1) 11 928
sing (2) 15 4162 4718
singed (1) 15 2973
singer (3) 11 652 774 16 1443
Singing (4) 5 13 11 696 730 945
singing (29) 1 298 654 4 313 440 6 145
 8 118 767 10 556 11 321 681 850 12 79
 994 1397 1800 15 2208 16 345 1882
 18 75 80 149 278 376 377 441 701 767 1291 1507
singing (1) 6 146
singing (2) 15 417 3996
single (7) 10 729 13 329 873 16 1008
 1556 17 166 1063
singled (1) 16 368
singledeck (1) 7 11
singlepane (1) 17 1541
singlet (1) 15 4673
singly (1) 16 1309
singly (1) 15 597
Sings (1) 11 616
sings (4) 4 408 9 648 11 697 16 633
sings (7) 15 42 55 1954 2209 2670 3860 4560
singsong (1) 15 1332
Singular (1) 14 896
singular (3) 9 664 13 374 17 660
sinhedrim (1) 12 1125
Sinico (2) 17 947 1454
Sinico's (1) 6 997
sinister (2) 1 94 17 879
sinister (3) 15 212 708 1182
sink (4) 3 268 5 39 10 664 17 162
sinkapace (2) 9 5 6
sinking (6) 3 31 270 273 6 771 849 9 773

sinking (1) 15 2166
sinks (3) 15 2852 3911 4048
Sinn (4) 8 458 9 239 12 1574 1624
Sinn (2) 12 523
Sinned (1) 14 1575
sinned (11) 2 361 5 373 8 125 9 210
 1009 10 169 13 432 749 14 370
 15 1783 3215
Sinner (2) 18 383 1227
sinner (3) 5 232 13 433 14 1589
sinner's (1) 6 851
sinners (1) 13 442
sinning (2) 13 432 15 1783
Sinope (1) 12 1690
SINS (1) 15 3027
sins (12) 2 390 3 422 8 1148 9 787
 11 1040 13 1183 14 83 1344 15 235
 1898 3025 3638
sins (1) 15 2656
sinuous (1) 15 2016
siocair (1) 17 727
Sion (1) 3 264
Siopold (1) 11 752
sip (4) 11 140 163 16 810 18 127
siphon (1) 17 567
sipped (3) 8 766 11 140
sippets (1) 8 676
sipping (3) 3 217 8 1000 10 1127
Sips (1) 8 819
sips (2) 10 809 17 380
Sir (14) 3 68 291 6 191 8 1151 1174 1180
 9 628 12 1455 14 169 1342 1480
 15 1012 1356 17 1373
Sir (1) 16 1243
sir (198) 1 211 387 390 395 409 415 425 429 437
 442 445 459 460 536 2 2 4 11 14 19 20 26 32 33
 41 54 55 59 81 92 93 98 99 100 109 110 113 132
 136 138 162 175 180 190 223 279 286 400 422 426
 435 441 3 68 72 85 87 94 4 63 64 124 185 189
 419 5 1 485 507 511 514 557 6 915 1016
 7 184 191 398 403 404 406 530 1067 8 110 711
 757 765 776 780 1004 1024 1101 9 585 596 601
 643 790 819 820 1118 10 50 256 303 317 320
 323 332 389 390 391 395 407 417 428 431 538 721
 725 736 750 752 782 829 11 306 499 648 762
 861 927 929 12 188 1028 1096 1108 1109 1121
 1320 1338 1410 1875 1893 13 872 1049
 14 182 195 197 198 238 252 264 271 330 356 662
 721 770 1141 1448 1468 1550 15 794 1011 1029
 1118 1383 1478 1538 1673 2878 3023 3761 3767
 3791 3792 3914 3994 4843 4845 16 1215 1666
 17 1557 18 690
sir (4) 9 416 12 419 428 16 1523
sir (2) 15 1162 4341
sirdars (1) 15 1417
sire (2) 8 837 9 818
sireland (1) 9 36
siren (1) 16 1382
Sirenen (1) 16 1815
sirens (2) 16 1813 1889
sire's (1) 15 3106
sires (1) 9 852
Sirius (1) 17 1046
Sirr (1) 10 786
sirrah (2) 9 192 12 1600
sirring (1) 3 67
Sirs (1) 15 1642
sirs (2) 14 223 227
Sister (11) 8 145 153 10 280 12 1711
 13 781 818 15 3238 3346 3432 3435

sister (23) 8 513 9 71 383 694 10 716
 11 347 464 12 814 1778 13 51 252 665
 1223 14 167 15 2228 3238 3302 3340
 16 270 1035 1182 17 140 146
sister (1) 15 2021
sister-in-law (1) 13 1221
sisterhood (2) 3 35 14 1368
sisterly (1) 15 903
sister's (3) 13 55 14 876 15 3011
Sisters (1) 12 550
sisters (10) 1 367 7 98 9 852 10 9
 12 1285 1781 14 76 392 15 2222 18 250
sisters (1) 17 1352
Sisyphus (1) 15 4387
Sit (9) 1 347 2 290 294 3 79 92 296
 5 559 8 343 11 357
sit (27) 2 170 3 94 390 9 384 10 1020
 12 79 1213 1792 1799 13 154 394 688 911
 1056 1081 1129 14 494 532 15 2322 2894
 3424 4434 18 110 1117 1138 1197 1594
sit (1) 9 770
sithen (1) 14 126
sitinems (1) 14 1492
sits (8) 3 410 11 573 14 1041 16 433
 434 17 613 614 18 937
sits (2) 15 2052 4020
sitteth (2) 9 497 12 1358
Sitting (6) 2 151 6 764 8 4 199
 11 1229 15 3422
sitting (46) 1 320 4 497 5 285 290 335
 6 22 604 7 800 802 8 132 540 995 9 248
 561 10 22 129 286 340 1125 11 67 600 1022
 1024 12 250 881 1115 1116 13 349 421 908
 1302 14 484 504 666 16 270 481 852 855
 17 1426 1430 18 91 172 931 1138 1196 1329
sittingroom (1) 17 1521
situa (1) 11 484
situate (2) 7 91 17 1514
situated (3) 14 1183 16 56 17 1767
situation (5) 11 480 14 955 15 868
 16 1691 17 1954
Six (9) 4 453 8 158 337 852 853 11 996
 1267 12 1074 15 3606
Six (1) 15 3957
six (46) 3 12 4 371 425 453 505 517 5 33
 381 560 6 61 560 672 775 7 410 8 554 852
 9 18 647 10 374 390 391 392 467 469
 11 832 868 1263 12 1652 13 1068
 15 671 868 1643 2911 3191 3613 16 205 509
 655 989 1196 1438 17 96 298 380 1444
 18 672
six (1) 15 1953
sixchamber (1) 16 1632
sixeyed (1) 10 49
sixfooter (2) 13 982 16 1326
sixpence (6) 5 545 8 241 10 116 837
 12 41 17 1863
sixpence (1) 15 3763
Sixpences (1) 2 220
sixpences (1) 7 933
sixpenceworth (1) 15 4291
sixpenny (1) 8 368
six's (1) 15 3131
sixshilling (1) 9 108
Sixteen (3) 15 3629 3718 3719
sixteen (9) 12 882 15 2933 2959 3334 3475
 3714 3720 16 1196 1444
sixteens (1) 10 381
Sixteenth (1) 8 1163

sixteenth (4) 12 1111 14 474 15 393
16 177
sixth (3) 7 632 17 421 1441
sixthly (1) 17 443
sixtyfive (4) 5 199 16 1766 1774 1782
sixtyfour (1) 17 96
sixtyninth (1) 15 2206
Sixtyseven (1) 15 371
sixtyseven (2) 9 217 12 481
sizar's (1) 9 31
size (10) 8 1109 12 116 684 13 145
15 559 2362 16 1791 17 1431 18 150
1196
size (3) 15 590 1206 2684
Sizeable (1) 15 669
sizeable (1) 4 178
sized (1) 16 1428
sizes (1) 17 318
Sizing (1) 8 1098
sizzling (2) 4 238 278
Sjambok (1) 15 1883
skates (1) 15 4034
skatingrink (1) 18 1028
skedaddled (1) 8 432
skeeting (1) 18 918
skeezing (2) 12 407 18 290
skein (1) 11 683
Skeleton (1) 15 3976
skeleton (2) 2 145 13 971
skeleton (2) 15 2 2277
skelter (1) 14 1571
skeowways (1) 6 511
Skerries (1) 16 293
Skerrys (1) 18 1006
sketch (1) 4 518
sketched (1) 2 277
sketches (1) 9 312
skewered (1) 15 2899
skeweyed (1) 3 67
Skibbereen (1) 16 666
Skibbereen (1) 7 735
skies (3) 9 939 12 1113 14 1107
skiff (3) 10 294 753 1096
skill (3) 12 963 14 1310 1312
skills (2) 9 805 15 129
skilly (1) 8 130
skimpy (1) 8 310
Skin (2) 5 307 11 939
skin (32) 1 124 2 165 5 111 492 498
6 206 8 129 1130 1136 11 118 125 669
13 725 1020 14 1370 15 2784 2975 3104
3836 16 684 692 1069 17 279 1451
18 459 464 581 650 762 816 922 1064
skin (1) 15 1296
Skin-the (1) 16 1066
Skin-the-etcetera (1) 16 1070
Skin-the-Goat (9) 7 640 641 667 703
16 323 596 688 985 1357
skindeep (1) 5 430
Skinfood (1) 5 497
Skinner's (1) 16 1105
Skinner's (1) 15 4452
skinny (2) 13 483 18 1267
skinny (1) 15 3453
skins (2) 5 5 11 1231
skins (1) 15 2623
skipped (2) 1 30 16 1714
skipper (2) 16 726 969
skipper's (1) 16 786

skipping (3) 7 918 14 489 15 3205
skipping (1) 15 4056
skippingrope (1) 17 876
skirt (31) 3 255 4 151 164 521 5 454
10 202 275 383 384 440 474 1221 11 216 410
891 13 154 169 355 362 479 14 633
15 2330 3115 17 1998 18 298 471 672 811
1039 1139 1259
skirt (5) 15 34 288 2058 2858 3840
skirtdancers (2) 13 704 732
skirties (1) 3 331
skirting (1) 10 229
skirts (5) 7 1013 8 192 603 9 1193
18 290
skirts (1) 15 4678
skit (1) 12 1509
skitting (1) 18 879
skittish (2) 14 502 15 2324
skivvies (1) 12 1090
skivvy's (1) 1 138
skulking (2) 3 354 18 300
skull (12) 5 473 6 565 681 8 427 9 29
242 12 445 663 1528 14 857 1085
15 2345
skull (1) 15 501
skullcap (1) 15 1173
skullneck (1) 15 2575
skullpiece (2) 8 297 316
skulls (7) 3 207 5 562 6 172 8 724
10 589 12 1323 13 957
skunk (1) 15 3059
Skunked (1) 14 1538
sky (13) 4 94 96 6 137 8 900 10 181
12 120 694 13 1166 14 1385 15 339
18 795 1582
sky (2) 2 103 6 165
sky (4) 15 1326 2174 4413 4749
skyblue (6) 10 1242 1243 11 394 978
18 421
Skye (2) 8 848 17 504
skykicking (1) 15 4124
skyline (2) 1 107 575
slab (2) 8 919 10 378
slabbed (1) 3 224
Slack (1) 5 9
slack (5) 6 283 8 1141 9 340 10 450
11 795
slack (1) 15 2150
slackened (1) 3 61
slacktethered (1) 6 441
slag (1) 15 3503
slain (2) 2 317 17 1987
slain (2) 15 4476 4665
slainte (1) 3 224
slake (1) 9 1149
Slaking (1) 8 1085
slammed (2) 3 186 6 10
Slan (2) 12 819 15 220
Slander (1) 15 1770
slanted (4) 2 153 10 836 11 346
17 1292
slanted (1) 15 286
slap (2) 3 458 14 593
Slapbang (1) 15 2366
slapped (8) 1 349 2 209 3 265 371
4 296 7 425 10 451 14 593
slapping (3) 4 161 18 122 1369
slaps (3) 15 316 2912 3666
slashed (1) 15 299

slate (4) 9 1160 10 56 13 1051 15 4826
slate (1) 15 4034
slats (1) 6 361
Slattery (1) 12 936
Slattery's (2) 12 1565 14 1450
Slaughter (1) 8 754
slaughter (3) 12 870 14 567 1423
slaughtered (3) 10 587 12 863 15 2899
slaughterhouses (1) 6 396
slaughtering (1) 18 1436
slaughters (1) 3 306
slave (5) 3 296 14 371 15 1167 2892 3476
slaver (1) 1 310
Slaves (1) 8 490
slaves (3) 9 721 12 1347 1472
slaveys (2) 6 319 8 446
slaving (1) 18 1079
slay (1) 15 4538
sledded (1) 9 131
sleek (3) 1 742 4 22 12 85
sleekcombed (1) 6 575
Sleep (3) 5 33 11 1242 15 3272
sleep (43) 1 740 3 276 395 439 6 314 621
627 754 769 848 1004 7 751 8 378 504
9 467 11 638 12 69 13 892 1277 1283
14 966 16 163 243 249 825 941 17 282 861
1761 1766 1826 2120 18 233 606 651 905 925
1074 1205 1252 1427 1478 1543
sleep (1) 15 4914
sleeper (2) 16 1892 17 2022
sleepily (1) 4 74
sleepily (1) 15 1239
sleepin (1) 14 1473
Sleeping (2) 5 36 482
sleeping (11) 1 182 8 900 9 467 959
16 477 17 853 855 857 933 18 1199 1208
sleepless (1) 14 77
sleeps (2) 3 251 15 1804
sleepwalking (1) 12 398
Sleepy (2) 13 1115 15 3154
Sleepy (1) 15 3156
SLEEPY (1) 15 3157
sleepy (2) 1 13 4 56
sleepy (2) 15 2077 3942
sleet (1) 17 217
sleety (1) 15 1030
sleeve (4) 6 954 7 305 8 1008 16 1779
sleeve (6) 15 357 385 4031 4423 4472 4651
sleeves (2) 13 341 18 303
sleeves (4) 15 284 2185 3981 4078
slender (11) 3 208 6 576 8 777 1075
10 1116 11 434 796 13 734 14 1364
17 1295 1314
slender (1) 15 313
slep (1) 14 1441
slept (9) 9 623 804 10 803 12 70
15 3154 16 215 18 641 1246 1460
Sletty (3) 8 664 17 36
sleuthhounds (1) 12 1137
slewed (1) 5 131
slews (1) 15 185
slice (10) 1 363 477 4 11 318 389 8 800
15 2899 16 1657 17 317 730
sliced (1) 7 31
slices (2) 1 355 7 939
slick (1) 15 2192
slicked (1) 14 753
slid (12) 2 90 4 181 183 231 328 8 1140
10 468 482 11 427 1115 14 1011 1026

smi (1) 11 309
Smile (3) 9 21 15 3087
smile (32) 1 33 96 732 2 441 4 103
6 243 7 69 356 560 993 1068 8 475 811
9 21 139 509 790 10 496 12 162 1780
13 527 765 1073 14 1055 1315 16 248 698
778 1360 1434 18 1186
smile (1) 10 616
smile (9) 15 428 708 715 1319 1962 2023 3878
4173 4322
Smiled (1) 3 368
smiled (44) 1 377 3 312 4 100 286 315 344
432 5 183 6 54 243 702 7 444 8 114
9 506 531 716 777 1070 10 30 31 33 54 63 127
176 496 578 734 1195 1212 1221 11 266 309 347
417 949 950 13 360 764 17 2126 18 533
1116
smiledyawnednodded (1) 8 969
smiles (6) 6 721 732 9 486 777 14 1053
16 1384
smiles (7) 15 832 1317 1988 2034 2095 3746
3831
smilesmirked (1) 11 416
Smiling (1) 17 810
smiling (30) 1 449 579 731 4 168 284 445
5 544 6 224 243 7 727 1072 8 248 303
9 60 365 547 778 10 176 335 348 474 676
11 960 13 162 522 14 1117 1396 16 687
1073 18 888
smiling (7) 15 388 2252 2301 3649 4490 4959
4964
sminute (1) 15 406
smirk (2) 9 1177 18 526
smirked (1) 11 770
smirking (1) 16 1563
smirking (1) 15 2511
smites (2) 15 2272 2618
Smith (1) 6 226
Smith (1) 12 425
Smith (1) 15 4683
smithereens (1) 13 1164
Smithfield (2) 10 1190 17 485
Smith's (1) 10 1103
smithwork (1) 12 292
smiting (1) 11 461
smitten (3) 11 461 14 130
smock (1) 14 632
Smoke (1) 11 300
smoke (16) 3 240 4 238 384 6 944 8 44
605 1124 9 1219 10 1013 11 537
13 604 1275 15 1349 2866 3644 18 508
smoke (2) 15 2561 3233
smokeblue (1) 1 126
smoked (3) 9 101 11 801
smokepalled (1) 15 4691
smokeplume (1) 1 575
smokes (3) 5 8 7 834 10 1143
smokes (2) 7 836 9 1224
smoking (13) 1 716 4 90 5 6 10 103
1088 11 277 300 13 277 14 488
16 1876 17 1598 18 912 1028
smoking (4) 15 652 1174 4168 4557
smokingcap (1) 15 249
smokinghot (1) 8 730
smoky (2) 2 199 14 586
smoky (1) 15 30
smooth (10) 1 124 615 2 46 8 1029 1137
10 1 11 1112 12 85 13 1163 15 3119
smoothed (1) 6 1022

smoother (2) 6 38 18 581
smoothest (2) 8 1138 18 1145
smoothing (1) 13 57
smoothly (1) 11 1115
smooths (1) 15 2303
smoothshaven (1) 15 2974
smoothsliding (1) 9 1124
smoothworn (1) 15 3016
smote (1) 14 731
smother (1) 18 411
smothered (5) 8 193 12 1025 13 616
15 2580 3177
smouldered (1) 3 151
smouldering (1) 15 4212
smudged (1) 4 346
smugging (1) 12 807
smuggled (1) 5 547
smugglers (1) 16 580
smuggling (1) 10 365
smut (2) 15 3053 3249
smuts (1) 18 913
Smutty (1) 14 1498
smutty (4) 4 355 12 1168 18 22 1531
Smythe-Smythe (1) 15 3002
snack (2) 8 697 15 495
snaggletusks (1) 15 78
snail (1) 2 142
snail's (2) 2 127 139
snails (1) 8 857
snake (3) 9 541 13 517 15 2673
Snakes (1) 15 138
snakes (2) 11 964 12 1717
snakes (2) 15 2084 4127
snakespiral (1) 17 2116
snaky (1) 5 31
snap (5) 13 826 14 790 15 1030 2335
18 1564
snap (1) 15 2714
snapped (6) 1 618 4 165 8 264 11 811
16 587 18 574
snappiest (1) 15 2203
snapping (1) 16 1074
snappy (1) 18 1460
snaps (2) 15 2467 3439
Snapshot (2) 1 686 17 1589
snapshot (3) 13 795 15 3792 17 2316
snares (2) 5 444 14 1537
snarled (1) 6 63
snarls (1) 15 1149
snatch (1) 15 245
snatched (3) 9 606 13 203 254
snatches (2) 15 4121 4278
sneak (1) 15 822
sneaking (1) 16 1584
sneaks (1) 9 818
sneer (1) 15 75
sneered (1) 9 16
sneeringly (1) 10 909
sneers (2) 15 1970 3218
Sneeze (1) 9 809
sneeze (1) 13 994
sneezed (2) 10 456 16 1841
sneezes (3) 15 248 2442 2556
sneezing (2) 12 485 18 1083
sniff (2) 13 1024 1029
sniffed (2) 3 348 11 100
sniffing (3) 3 332 10 309 12 485
sniffing (4) 15 247 356 2040 3955
sniffles (1) 10 1126

sniffling (1) 3 349
sniffling (1) 15 88
sniffs (3) 15 2702 2962 3477
snigger (1) 15 2399
Snip (1) 15 2396
snip (1) 8 1008
snipped (1) 4 152
Snivel (1) 11 808
snivelling (2) 8 727 12 396
snivelling (1) 15 659
snivels (1) 15 3363
snooze (1) 13 1274
snore (2) 9 713 11 575
snores (1) 5 367
snores (2) 15 27 28
snoring (3) 3 481 12 251 15 3274
snorted (2) 3 117 11 144
snot (1) 3 500
snot (1) 15 136
Snotgreen (1) 3 3
snotgreen (2) 1 73 78
snotrag (1) 1 512
snotty (1) 18 891
snottynosed (1) 13 529
snout (4) 1 182 3 338 11 145 12 1231
snout (2) 15 584 1204
snouter (1) 14 1094
snow (3) 15 1769 17 217 18 860
snow (1) 15 7
snowball (1) 7 482
snowballs (1) 15 3334
snowcake (1) 15 4148
snowy (1) 13 734
snubnose (1) 15 3837
snuff (4) 6 235 13 329 330 1151
Snuffbox (1) 9 808
snuffbox (1) 15 445
snuffled (2) 8 799 804
snuffling (4) 8 836 983 10 479 488
snuffling (1) 15 2853
Snuffy (1) 8 397
snuffy (1) 11 134
Snug (1) 8 170
snug (6) 2 202 4 262 12 250 13 239
14 504 777
snugly (1) 2 22
So (100) 1 310 3 97 280 4 510 5 27 92
252 6 470 521 885 938 7 143 158 364 1031
8 945 946 1021 9 343 383 582 10 479
11 32 284 533 671 869 894 947 12 64 118 137
206 305 309 311 410 435 450 479 487 679 697 703
748 766 780 817 831 889 942 1018 1143 1178 1192
1229 1333 1426 1512 1561 1573 1597 1605 1621
13 473 537 1058 1109 14 105 467 474 591
15 103 105 254 328 1484 1564 2455 3108 3230
3427 3583 4044 4863 16 14 33 39 906 1043 1075
1083 1246 1327 1420 1714 1733
So (4) 1 361 587 16 1348
so (508) 1 552 2 157 264 283 325 4 47 351
398 511 5 39 153 206 249 250 340 363 492 501
6 177 219 471 528 536 620 650 657 754 768 792
818 961 1028 7 299 645 648 1013 8 268 380
457 542 599 833 854 861 884 957 961 962 1135
9 11 58 72 123 316 318 360 362 377 380 394 529
663 725 740 781 788 850 10 21 27 120 126 140
418 570 603 677 829 865 11 32 54 182 206 357
361 463 558 711 781 814 816 817 827 894 901 955
979 1015 1093 1115 1128 1136 1212 1254
12 312 332 448 454 458 484 594 596 698 723 786

827 847 895 1021 1039 1062 1133 1145 1188 1424
1478 1536 1569 1625 1645 1662 1751 1780 1795
1812 1887 1899   **13** 30 60 109 112 121 146 186
233 243 262 296 306 319 356 361 363 415 423 428
450 459 478 483 515 530 582 583 595 604 618 627
644 648 669 685 688 697 709 712 713 718 727 728
732 740 752 837 843 869 907 1004 1017 1118 1142
1164 1197 1210 1220 1226 1232 1253 1273
14 20 21 45 53 75 90 97 98 109 116 152 204 218
232 250 253 256 268 275 278 382 392 412 413 422
452 482 502 503 568 587 595 603 604 605 609 673
690 734 743 759 762 763 798 808 827 857 873 877
887 918 955 965 1040 1049 1168 1193 1202 1203
1265 1294 1336 1340 1358 1360 1370 1389 1510
15 264 307 398 428 892 1088 1111 1121 1315
1817 2090 2322 2323 2392 2464 2740 2762 2778
2816 2862 2886 2973 3082 3231 3620 3698 4072
4474 4720 4824   **16** 15 42 62 183 195 203 204
223 236 272 295 346 351 356 358 507 513 520 553
556 564 603 616 643 648 674 692 711 721 778 855
868 871 876 884 891 895 974 1014 1027 1042 1067
1078 1103 1118 1125 1130 1184 1192 1197 1285
1306 1307 1323 1409 1416 1417 1449 1458 1460
1485 1530 1544 1561 1580 1594 1595 1598 1610
1611 1660 1692 1772 1783 1831 1857 1861 1874
17 275 516 734 1073 1566 1754 1995 2059 2141
2142 2180   **18** 23 36 49 52 55 64 76 92 103 123
146 155 176 179 186 193 201 211 239 246 263 264
271 273 279 281 283 287 292 302 310 311 312 320
325 363 393 397 412 419 431 456 507 535 541 554
568 577 581 591 609 637 655 664 699 719 724 727
808 819 861 889 891 914 924 938 **998** 1015 1051
1054 1066 1139 1157 1173 1196 123**0** 1248 1292
1296 1336 1337 1352 1353 1356 136**2** 1372 1378
1380 1382 1383 1400 1409 1427 1455 1460 1461
1477 1479 1520 1536 1548 1576 1582 1607
so (3) 6 814   12 29   17 399
so (2) 15 901 1844
SO₄ (1) 16 801
soak (1) 18 1524
soaked (1) 8 850
soaker (1) 14 837
SOAP (1) 7 221
Soap (2) 11 1127 15 1946
Soap (1) 15 337
soap (19) 5 501 518 525 544 568 6 22 396 494
495 7 227 228 8 172 1191 1192 13 1043
1045 17 232 1989 18 1194
soap (1) 15 336
soapdish (1) 17 2106
soaped (1) 8 173
soaps (2) 5 501 510
soapsuddy (1) 16 19
soapsun (1) 15 341
soapy (1) 15 822
soar (1) 11 745
soared (1) 11 745
soaring (2) 11 747 749
soaring (1) 15 69
sob (2) 11 457 13 582
sobbing (1) 15 765
Sober (2) 7 200 15 4883
Sober (1) 15 2512
SOBER (3) 15 2515 2536 2584
sober (8) 8 598 12 692 16 61 62 129 730
869 1176
soberly (1) 5 1
sobriquet (1) 12 715
sobs (1) 12 654

sobs (1) 15 3219
socalled (2) 16 366 17 1052
Sociable (1) 5 225
social (9) 13 285 17 24 646 669 914 991 1084
1606 1619
social (1) 15 1702
socialist (1) 18 178
Socialiste (1) 15 4505
socialiste (1) 3 169
societate (1) 9 770
societies (1) 8 465
Society (7) 8 1073 13 666 15 1803
17 137 1638 1659 1856
Society (1) 17 1802
Society (1) 15 4677
society (13) 6 327 7 793 9 643
12 1170 14 923 15 854 1010 16 540
1558 1704 17 664 1618 18 1319
society (1) 15 1426
Society's (1) 17 2135
society's (1) 16 1832
sock (4) 17 1485 1487 18 1089
sockets (1) 3 271
sockets (1) 15 61
Socks (1) 17 866
socks (8) 2 255 6 106 9 948 10 1241
11 977 13 800 14 1548 18 421
socks (4) 15 413 1521 2656 2924
Socrates (4) 9 233 665 1199 15 111
Socrates (1) 9 1042
Socratic (1) 14 1216
Socratididion's (1) 9 237
sod (2) 6 328 808
Soda (1) 17 1473
soda (4) 8 359 540 599 16 10
sodabread (1) 13 1294
Sodachapped (1) 4 175
sodality (2) 5 340 13 448
sodden (2) 15 582 2149
Sodom (1) 4 222
sodomite (1) 15 3209
soever (2) 14 687 874
sofa (5) 7 558 17 1281 1285 18 664 1461
sofa (8) 15 2871 3575 3589 3620 3640 3795
3880 3911
sofacorner (1) 15 2075
sofas (1) 8 643
Soft (9) 2 286 287 3 434 5 178 8 909
11 13 15 3994
soft (45) 1 315 491 725 2 126 217 3 324
434 4 56 163 304 447 468 5 298 6 225 642
828 8 198 10 404 575 1088 11 293 1136
1201 12 506 845 13 338 341 440 699 719 740
955 14 1362 15 434 2886 2976 3104
16 654 1085 1089 18 366 1146 1383
soft (3) 15 466 1902 4560
softcreakfooted (1) 9 231
soften (1) 10 846
softened (1) 8 850
softens (1) 9 402
softens (1) 15 1319
softer (6) 4 59 6 872 11 695 17 278 279
softlier (1) 11 316
Softly (3) 8 907 11 589 1284
softly (21) 1 186 2 23 3 489 4 6 52
5 339 568 6 556 7 235 237 396 612
8 1169 9 1220 11 315 589 13 752
16 1119 17 119 120 18 1335
softly (9) 15 347 473 668 876 1968 3240 3434
4182 4486

softlyfeatured (1) 13 105
softness (1) 9 1220
softnosed (1) 12 1476
Softsoaping (1) 5 186
softy (2) 6 205 18 50
Soggarth (2) 12 179 15 4591
Sohan (1) 10 43
soi-disant (2) 16 620 1354
Soil (1) 6 783
soil (9) 3 268 4 477 6 776 12 890
15 1071 16 995 17 1586 1699
soil (1) 15 4128
Soiled (2) 8 243 15 3288
soiled (10) 2 227 4 213 265 321 7 821
14 1218 16 717 1465 1469 17 231
soiling (1) 16 1468
soirée (1) 16 978
sojourn (1) 17 1961
solace (1) 14 1074
solar (5) 12 344 17 98 1050 1132 1258
sold (15) 6 392 8 142 350 11 1266
12 35 45 999 1242 1371 1471 14 300
15 1066 2599 2995 16 1687
Soldier (2) 12 193 15 4379
soldier (9) 3 257 5 67 8 801 11 1082
12 967 15 4390 4407 4756 4762
soldiers (13) 5 57 66 10 13 353 1137
13 663 14 1247 15 4381 4519 16 83
1042 18 686 881
soldiers (1) 15 4421
sole (7) 4 323 8 889 10 635 12 46
13 823 17 246 1770
soled (1) 12 369
solely (2) 14 47 1186
Solemn (2) 8 66 1151
solemn (8) 7 46 8 1039 9 6 11 1020
1021 12 1121 1187 16 155
solemnity (3) 6 669 10 119 14 949
solemnity (1) 15 993
Solemnly (1) 1 9
solemnly (5) 1 726 2 251 442 9 1167
15 1068
solemnly (5) 15 1623 1681 2731 4459 4560
soles (2) 3 150 6 849
solfa (1) 11 247
solicit (2) 13 870 16 730
solicitation (1) 17 1314
solicitations (1) 11 656
solicited (3) 11 567 12 661 15 949
soliciting (1) 15 381
Solicitor (1) 6 1007
solicitor (12) 5 427 6 233 1007 10 1193
11 562 924 15 1230 16 74 1494 17 181
18 44 1070
solicitorgeneral (1) 17 445
Solicitors (1) 15 730
solicitors (1) 11 1225
solicitous (2) 17 2238 2246
solicitude (3) 14 15 16 300 17 2116
solid (10) 3 17 6 561 8 583 10 354
16 333 811 814 17 1276 18 723
solidity (1) 17 220
solids (1) 10 549
solidungular (1) 17 1578
Solitary (3) 17 612 613 617
solitary (5) 17 614 616 978 1350 1351
solitude (2) 14 1036 17 2037
Soll (1) 17 1383
solly (1) 14 1504

15 2218 4002 16 172 526 617 635 641 698 745
863 901 922 987 1074 1107 1160 1179 1291 1461
1481 1625 1858 1865 18 9 1301 1329
sort (1) 10 1254
sort (1) 15 4149
sorted (2) 2 185 11 383
sortita (1) 3 100
sorts (4) 16 560 1145 18 588 1562
sot (1) 8 189
sotto (1) 16 822
sou (1) 14 785
soubrette (4) 10 381 496 1142 1220
soubrette (1) 15 2985
sought (7) 8 88 9 29 11 398 1009
14 1194 17 285 1746
soul (63) 1 21 273 2 75 147 159 3 132 279
450 4 352 353 5 436 6 163 857 931
7 621 8 394 1161 9 3 77 130 171 466 805
898 10 460 690 877 911 1026 11 669 1023
1149 12 217 289 13 189 413 746 14 104
248 1035 1038 1079 1165 1563 15 259 1172
1254 2610 3580 16 737 748 749 765 1047 1626
18 6 106 141 142 698 1107 1115
soul (3) 2 106 11 530 551
Soulfully (1) 11 1044
soul's (3) 1 282 9 39 14 283
Souls (1) 9 808
souls (22) 3 421 4 342 352 5 447 9 285
468 1191 10 138 143 146 149 150 12 1887
13 762 818 14 225 249 472 15 4197
16 857
souls (1) 7 316
souls' (1) 6 933
soulth (1) 14 1021
soultransfigured (1) 15 1002
soultransfigured (1) 7 771
soultransfiguring (1) 15 1003
soultransfiguring (1) 7 771
Sound (2) 4 153 11 757
sound (22) 1 428 4 473 8 115 900 937
10 484 11 457 632 12 1676 13 281
14 520 706 15 2374 16 1351 17 182
1224 1226 1228 1758 2034 18 133 688
sound (2) 15 1619 3297
sounded (3) 10 1031 16 1174 1766
sounding (1) 6 390
soundly (2) 14 593 15 1112
Sounds (4) 3 17 7 213 11 650 16 362
sounds (10) 3 102 7 478 485 8 64
9 1000 11 837 1052 17 219 747 854
sounds (2) 15 1268 4049
Soup (1) 8 717
soup (16) 4 2 7 534 8 161 408 413 659 886
1072 10 285 290 292 11 699 16 573
18 358 359 529
soup (1) 15 1571
souped (2) 8 426 14 1559
soupladles (1) 12 1717
soupplate (1) 15 2358
souppot (1) 8 715
Sour (1) 11 854
sour (5) 12 284 1795 13 957 1010 16 976
sour (1) 15 428
sourapple (1) 8 436
Source (1) 13 1040
source (3) 16 1584 17 262 265
soured (1) 17 312
sourly (3) 7 240 10 239 1119
sours (1) 8 45

sous (1) 9 641
Souse (1) 11 945
souse (1) 15 3065
soused (3) 3 343
soutane (1) 15 2655
South (14) 7 715 8 1088 14 1331
15 170 4606 16 460 1299 17 177 420 878
1821 1839 2080 2257
south (21) 3 206 270 5 456 7 714 723
8 515 1064 12 1651 13 969 16 1061 1406
1410 17 204 578 1236 1516 18 25 867 899
south (2) 7 523 8 183
south (2) 15 139 335
Southampton (1) 16 513
southeast (1) 13 1079
southerly (1) 17 1505
Southern (1) 17 1729
southern (1) 16 353
southing (1) 3 442
southward (3) 1 574 5 467 8 665
Southwark (2) 9 914 17 1402
southwest (1) 12 1881
souvenir (1) 12 663
sovereign (13) 2 217 5 470 10 744
11 620 12 208 1132 1883 14 280 15 789
2373 2518 2647 16 1453
sovereign (2) 15 3565 3583
sovereigns (5) 1 296 297 2 219 10 1135
12 961
sovrano (1) 16 315
sovs (3) 16 1277 1286
sow (2) 9 390 15 4582
sow (1) 2 89
sowcunt (1) 15 3489
sowing (2) 14 615 17 1584
sowish (1) 10 810
sown (1) 14 833
sowpigs (1) 12 105
sow's (1) 15 3533
Space (1) 9 86
Space (1) 15 1583
space (25) 2 9 324 3 12 417 6 841
9 1082 1200 12 1408 14 139 1079 1362
16 236 937 1843 17 88 116 1064 1143 1246
1716 2015 2026 2310
space (2) 15 2168 4245
spaces (1) 9 87
spaces (1) 15 3951
spacewards (1) 15 4152
spade (2) 6 903 14 624
spades (8) 6 864 908 910 8 253 254 13 19
606 18 1317
spades (1) 15 482
Spain (14) 4 211 8 24 12 1253 1297 1381
1383 16 878 1121 1128 1420 17 1739 1986
18 781 1486
Spain's (2) 15 4585 16 1414
spake (3) 1 727 14 123 241
Spallanzani (1) 14 1235
span (2) 14 859 17 1772
span (1) 15 125
spangles (1) 2 449
Spaniards (1) 16 873
spaniel (3) 15 100 690 2039
Spanish (25) 3 230 4 61 5 495 7 360
8 351 761 11 1093 12 1298 15 2432
16 877 878 879 1409 1412 1415 1426 17 310
1687 18 398 564 773 777 1471 1476 1586
Spanish (2) 15 808 4498

Spanishy (1) 11 732
spanishy (1) 11 808
spank (1) 15 3077
spanking (1) 15 1095
spanned (1) 10 1228
spans (1) 15 1400
Spare (1) 15 1881
spare (7) 7 85 9 152 16 443 1008 1449
1861 18 454
spare (1) 12 1290
spared (1) 9 138
Spark (1) 12 1087
spark (1) 16 1666
sparkled (1) 13 587
sparkles (1) 15 1499
Sparkling (1) 11 394
sparkling (3) 13 12 15 3902 17 1548
sparks (1) 14 848
sparring (1) 10 1136
sparrow (1) 15 2485
sparrowfarts (1) 18 879
Sparrow's (1) 13 500
sparrows' (1) 6 626
spars (1) 3 504
Spartan (1) 15 1805
SPARTANS (1) 7 1033
spas (1) 16 520
spasm (2) 7 268 8 674
spasm (2) 15 183 2603
spasmodic (1) 12 203
spasmodically (1) 17 1218
spasms (1) 15 132
spat (4) 6 129 9 1133 10 635 12 1433
spatchcocked (1) 9 991
spates (1) 17 206
Spaton (1) 8 670
spats (1) 15 537
spatted (1) 10 757
Spattered (1) 15 590
spattered (1) 3 188
spatting (1) 12 1786
spaugs (1) 7 448
spavined (1) 15 3983
spawn (1) 14 328
spawn (1) 15 2598
Speak (6) 7 725 9 1217 15 3059 3914 4647
4648
speak (50) 1 393 431 433 570 3 194 451
4 423 6 262 343 7 176 555 1024 8 250
9 311 659 853 945 10 70 570 11 136 438
789 1009 1073 12 481 680 13 96 125
14 35 187 1290 15 306 660 951 1191 1810
2778 3432 4426 16 565 801 877 1103 1457 1580
1610 1857 1874 18 1248
speakeasy (1) 14 1507
speaker (3) 12 879 1618 14 1358
speakers (3) 17 966 971
Speaking (3) 1 481 6 534 7 789
speaking (18) 1 488 2 16 7 782 889
8 923 9 175 487 826 10 993 12 723 1568
16 578 607 728 1150 1444 1680 1770
speaking (2) 15 939 1825
speaks (6) 1 419 7 177 8 521 9 168 171
11 1105
spear (5) 2 17 4 88 9 925 12 200
14 129
spearmint (1) 4 475
spearpoints (1) 15 4612
spearspikes (1) 2 318

spec (1) 13 808
Special (2) 12 539 15 345
special (20) 6 407 7 403 635 914 920 966
 8 878 12 361 578 1884 16 104 685 1237
 17 359 487 519 590 1157 1971 18 674
special (1) 12 427
specialist (2) 15 1772 16 1317
speciality (1) 15 4883
Specially (1) 4 79
specially (4) 12 620 17 647 672 2157
specials (1) 14 1561
specie (3) 16 1277 1287 17 1688
Species (1) 17 1645
species (4) 14 971 16 473 17 465 1084
specimen (8) 12 730 13 81 15 844
 16 356 835 983 1388 1665
specimens (1) 16 328
speck (5) 4 186 524 10 404 13 58
 14 1061
speckled (1) 3 347
specs (1) 10 805
specs (2) 5 334 13 522
spectacle (8) 12 531 13 285 16 514
 17 499 1036 1146 18 1255 1289
spectacled (1) 7 197
spectacles (7) 7 440 810 14 65 1059 1246
 15 279 17 1878
spectacles (1) 15 250
spectacular (1) 16 546
spectator (1) 17 1259
spectators (3) 12 649 14 1364 17 1145
spectre (2) 9 168 14 1024
speculating (1) 10 1069
speculation (2) 9 53 17 1007
sped (2) 5 542 10 221
Speech (2) 9 978 11 625
Speech (1) 15 1708
speech (26) 1 426 2 367 3 459 6 151
 277 7 277 793 804 815 823 835 860 9 255 471
 978 12 799 1189 1519 1799 14 374
 15 1353 1383 2124 16 340 18 729
speech (1) 7 832
speech (1) 15 899
speeches (1) 7 199
speechless (1) 15 4308
speed (4) 5 542 8 796 9 39 12 1779
speedily (1) 14 1180
speeding (2) 11 597 746
SPEEDPILLS (1) 7 1022
speeds (1) 2 303
speedy (1) 14 876
speeeed (1) 18 679
spell (2) 14 1501 15 3449
spellbound (1) 11 420
spellbound (1) 15 312
spelling (1) 7 165
spellingbee (1) 7 166
spells (2) 7 293 16 1127
spelt (2) 6 725 16 75
Spencer (1) 17 173
spend (8) 6 930 9 535 12 1295 15 266
 2412 18 263 586 1527
spendthrift (1) 10 83
spent (4) 3 459 6 308 9 195 10 699
spent (1) 10 608
spent (1) 15 3333
Speranza's (1) 12 539
Speriamo (1) 10 350
sperm (1) 15 4549

spermacetic (1) 14 601
spermatozoa (2) 14 1234 17 1061
Sperrin (1) 12 1832
spew (1) 16 616
spewed (1) 8 495
sphere (2) 13 602 17 1275
spherical (1) 12 93
sphincter (1) 6 426
Sphinx (1) 15 3631
sphinx (2) 5 234 7 589
Spice (1) 6 759
spice (2) 9 352 13 1018
spiced (2) 3 218 15 565
spicegardens (1) 17 1980
spicy (3) 4 144 8 635 12 1321
spider (1) 14 1036
spider (1) 15 543
spider's (1) 12 1161
spiffing (2) 1 118 12 689
spike (1) 14 430
spiked (3) 11 34 923 15 709
spiky (1) 11 422
spilikins (1) 17 661
spill (1) 14 472
spilling (2) 1 690 12 808
spilling (1) 15 4315
spillings (1) 14 472
spillspilling (1) 15 509
spilt (3) 3 193 8 671 1010
spin (2) 11 746 16 823
spinach (3) 8 464 1029 12 92
spinach (1) 15 933
spinal (1) 12 470
spindle (2) 2 278 7 57
spindlelegs (1) 15 2484
spine (3) 6 253 10 662 11 669
spine (1) 15 2146
spine's (1) 15 657
spinnaker (1) 12 1774
Spinning (1) 15 3969
spinning (5) 8 581 10 209 1229 13 1020
 18 191
spinning (1) 15 4034
Spinoza (4) 11 1058 12 1804 17 722
 18 1115
Spinoza (1) 17 1372
spins (1) 15 4033
Spion (1) 15 796
spiral (2) 17 566 1108
spirals (1) 4 366
spires (1) 12 1734
Spirit (1) 15 2531
spirit (24) 1 151 7 143 565 567 985 8 335
 9 395 396 10 761 12 338 353 610 736
 14 293 15 1218 1899 3940 4235 16 38 593
 1124 1456 17 30 18 7
spirit (3) 7 864 8 67 9 170
spirited (1) 16 1191
spirits (10) 5 447 8 826 12 630 1731
 13 1109 14 156 852 1544 15 1790 3358
spiritu (1) 12 1743
Spiritual (1) 9 808
spiritual (5) 9 49 61 12 1886 13 87 373
spirituality (1) 7 557
Spiritus (1) 1 351
Spiro (1) 12 1087
spirt (1) 16 616
Spit (1) 14 1485
spit (7) 3 323 355 6 459 12 1432
 15 3188 17 898 18 454

spit (1) 15 4764
spite (9) 7 264 8 349 13 666 14 1266
 15 1736 16 19 17 389 18 648 890
spitfire (1) 13 221
spits (1) 1 414
spits (2) 15 86 3144
spitting (6) 4 203 7 1026 8 659 9 131
 12 1786 13 876
spittle (3) 8 908 11 577 15 2786
spittle (1) 15 2303
Spittoon (1) 15 3144
splash (2) 15 3763 16 1482
splashed (1) 8 689
splashes (1) 11 1111
splashing (3) 16 939 17 244 18 359
splashing (1) 15 3769
splayed (1) 3 30
splayfoot (1) 17 1296
spleen (3) 7 592 8 1048 14 232
spleen (1) 15 2097
Splendid (2) 15 1611 2432
splendid (14) 2 274 4 370 399 5 403
 11 171 12 85 13 818 15 400 3005
 16 892 17 1178 18 307 650 1500
splendidly (1) 18 1298
splendiferous (1) 14 1529
splendour (4) 14 13 18 15 1507
 17 1169
splinter (1) 15 467
split (11) 4 133 6 239 800 8 409 723
 12 256 13 273 15 1922 2994 16 1730
 18 1032
split (1) 15 4168
splitting (1) 13 327
spluttered (2) 9 1128 11 166
spluttering (3) 3 308 8 604 13 933
spoil (5) 8 885 13 855 16 1606 17 662
 18 1542
spoiled (3) 13 16 154 15 2649
spoiling (1) 9 947
Spoils (1) 3 373
spoils (2) 8 188 18 208
spoilsport (1) 17 1942
spoilt (1) 13 35
Spoke (1) 15 3395
spoke (37) 1 185 426 479 513 646 2 345
 3 308 367 6 315 720 732 922 7 755 972
 8 313 9 780 10 539 1014 11 153 722
 13 66 548 578 862 867 14 111 175 424 553 852
 966 16 62 554 1117 1176 17 746 18 837
spoke (1) 10 614
spoken (15) 1 216 370 627 661 7 794
 9 1056 12 738 1611 1658 14 801 1112
 15 207 3060 16 142 18 775
spoken (1) 7 866
spokes (1) 5 553
Spoleto (1) 12 1679
sponge (1) 15 3771
sponger (1) 18 426
sponger's (1) 16 1628
sponges (2) 5 488 14 1263
spongy (1) 3 477
Spontaneous (1) 10 728
Spontaneously (1) 15 2456
spoof (1) 16 828
Spooks (1) 15 1226
spoon (8) 4 298 378 6 380 8 395 657
 10 1091 17 379 18 932
spooncase (1) 2 202

stormclouds (1) 14 1384
stormily (1) 15 1244
storms (3) 9 403 13 286 1147
stormtossed (1) 13 8
stormy (2) 13 1151 16 652
Story (1) 17 1373
story (29) 2 54 59 4 518 537 6 409 722 754 7 94 310 502 752 8 55 9 522 633 12 512 1192 13 337 422 1060 1250 15 521 16 491 1361 1691 18 37 485 694 725 990
Stout (1) 11 1256
stout (12) 8 45 700 10 238 364 11 542 544 14 465 15 611 1674 17 1292 18 126 450
stout (1) 3 258
stout (1) 15 3952
stouter (1) 16 1480
stoutest (2) 14 782 16 586
stoutly (1) 15 2959
stouts (1) 8 680
stow (2) 5 369 14 86
stowaway (1) 15 943
stowed (2) 7 228 16 587
Stowing (1) 6 21
stowing (2) 2 211 8 121
straddled (1) 6 833
straggling (1) 10 353
Straight (1) 13 928
straight (25) 4 378 5 194 384 7 982 8 250 416 829 9 1103 10 657 662 731 12 677 800 13 952 14 1131 15 980 3117 4461 16 1129 1712 17 2313 18 133 275 836 1142
straighten (2) 4 309 16 852
straightened (2) 6 175 13 605
straightforward (2) 14 928 1273
straightway (2) 12 280 1136
straightways (1) 14 315
strain (9) 1 209 7 742 11 325 614 13 212 14 458 17 1312 2118 18 589
strained (1) 13 188
straining (4) 10 1227 11 1130 13 723 16 932
strains (1) 12 1828
strains (1) 15 920
strainveined (1) 17 2062
straits (3) 17 1983 18 859 860
Strand (1) 10 85
Strand (1) 16 1255
strand (19) 3 19 283 4 86 7 98 11 198 13 3 307 353 505 570 683 766 768 905 1246 16 909 1404 1882 18 1346
stranded (1) 3 303
strandentwining (1) 3 37
strands (1) 4 445
Strange (7) 4 530 6 77 7 87 10 978 13 1203 1228 15 660
strange (19) 3 145 4 86 5 295 7 763 8 1127 9 950 10 1084 11 716 12 59 13 106 763 983 14 150 239 508 16 1723 17 795 836 18 1452
Strangeface (1) 15 4340
strangely (2) 13 203 369
strangely (1) 15 1330
stranger (14) 1 661 9 37 782 14 365 368 720 746 1164 1356 15 1195 17 323 18 92 1315 1316
Strangers (1) 15 4586
strangers (5) 2 392 12 1151 1156 15 4196 17 2010

strangest (1) 15 952
strangle (1) 14 981
strangled (1) 13 735
strangled (1) 15 4223
strangles (1) 15 2277
strangling (2) 3 372 15 711
strap (3) 13 394 15 381 18 1174
strapped (1) 2 96
strapping (3) 2 211 3 245 14 598
Strasburg (1) 3 63
strata (1) 14 923
stratagem (1) 17 84
strategy (1) 2 71
Stratford (7) 9 149 173 260 649 694 711 1075
stratifications (1) 17 1058
stratosphere (1) 17 1090
Stratton (4) 6 184 10 141 1273 15 410
stravaging (1) 12 400
Straw (1) 8 1168
straw (20) 6 199 451 7 469 638 8 1136 10 102 1244 11 346 882 1252 12 170 893 13 156 14 1484 15 1804 3449 16 704 17 629 2103 18 1573
straw (2) 12 894 895
straw (1) 15 807 3738
strawberries (6) 5 496 10 312 12 97 98 13 1025 15 3805
strawberry (2) 14 985 18 948
strawberry (1) 15 2075
strawcalling (1) 8 1159
straws (2) 14 489 18 53
stray (1) 15 1346
strayed (3) 11 283 407 17 2001
strays (2) 16 328 17 2015
streaked (1) 15 3242
streaks (1) 6 362
streaks (1) 15 251
Stream (1) 8 176
stream (9) 5 563 564 566 571 7 498 8 94 95 13 739
streamed (1) 13 6
streamer (1) 15 1399
streamers (1) 15 3846
streaming (3) 6 488 11 301 1235
Streams (1) 9 85
streams (5) 12 71 643 14 1105 17 203 1713
streamy (1) 12 111
streel (1) 13 506
STREET (1) 7 443
Street (9) 3 34 366 9 1207 12 1461 13 643 15 854 3930 17 1253 2076
Street (1) 12 415
street (270) 2 386 3 131 4 120 191 210 231 360 417 433 490 5 4 10 70 134 183 229 397 561 6 34 58 233 316 366 372 376 829 7 16 669 684 913 916 940 1041 8 129 142 155 157 282 368 406 425 430 551 568 594 609 614 640 702 706 891 951 1028 1080 1087 1088 1122 1138 1167 9 86 159 554 1089 1218 10 47 68 76 108 111 222 229 368 497 505 526 543 545 674 703 720 744 745 765 773 781 920 961 972 981 1035 1063 1098 1101 1114 1124 1150 1154 1187 1227 1247 1263 1270 1271 11 488 812 845 883 1181 1197 1239 12 18 214 218 235 271 314 399 516 536 802 815 1026 1068 1121 1720 1721 1730 1857 1890 1918 13 500 794 841 868 914 927 931 1000 14 408 490 491 572 1047 1064 1227 1302 1440 1570 15 109 200 364 585 611 648 777 1386 2120 2206

2519 2987 3031 3049 3134 3335 3998 4641 4866 16 21 23 24 35 50 79 166 169 199 224 343 540 709 717 851 890 1422 1435 1629 1748 1798 1856 1882 1894 17 5 6 50 59 72 94 130 139 142 143 170 329 330 339 421 436 482 578 580 591 602 627 632 860 880 967 968 969 1176 1254 1376 1559 1581 1727 1785 1869 1982 1985 2001 2055 2056 2080 2085 2089 2105 2254 2257 2259 18 139 228 256 266 336 479 524 550 561 704 1026 1202 1217 1245 1286 1390 1447 1466 1493 1546 1589
street (2) 2 355
street (10) 15 1 174 604 930 1400 1703 1764 1812 4359 4365
streetorgan (1) 6 372
streets (13) 1 413 3 121 209 4 88 90 8 485 13 1051 14 1246 15 1116 3176 17 3 18 1468 1600
streetsingers (1) 12 542
streetwalker (1) 16 704
streetwalkers (1) 8 597
Streetwalking (1) 15 381
Strength (1) 13 206
Strength (2) 17 513 1397
strength (15) 2 349 5 420 10 1146 12 911 13 213 859 14 1075 1520 15 3473 16 1034 17 38 217 520 1196 18 596
strengthy (1) 12 1210
stress (1) 17 2117
stresses (1) 1 245
stretch (4) 3 437 11 362 16 834 18 584
Stretched (1) 12 543
stretched (15) 1 447 6 645 749 7 434 8 913 10 652 684 11 683 802 810 13 670 930 16 689 17 150 18 1103
stretches (5) 15 1 2289 3708 4930 4944
stretching (2) 6 44 11 360
strewing (1) 15 4327
strewn (1) 7 73
striated (1) 17 1335
stricken (2) 9 466 14 268
strict (5) 12 52 15 3023 16 497 1514 17 1624
Strictly (2) 8 97 15 2633
strictly (5) 11 1194 16 255 595 829 1364
stride (4) 3 11 8 298 9 1054 13 155
stride (1) 15 4328
strident (1) 15 4717
strides (2) 10 241 13 479
strides (3) 15 366 806 3783
Striding (1) 10 1260
striding (2) 7 359 10 1118
striding (1) 15 3421
strife (2) 2 185 14 952
Strike (2) 14 806 1577
strike (7) 1 276 5 262 9 54 12 1754 14 1515 15 4756 4759
strike (1) 15 2830
strikes (3) 6 810 12 93 15 2555
strikes (5) 15 1060 1566 3461 3622 4747
striking (11) 3 138 7 764 12 175 1290 14 1204 15 762 3579 3609 16 579 1592 1775
striking (2) 2 105 12 722
string (2) 11 803 870
stringed (1) 15 283
stringendo (1) 9 921
Strings (1) 4 97

tailormade (1) 15 543
tailor's (1) 1 169
tailor's (1) 15 1908
tails (7) 6 386 8 827 10 528 530 13 1028 18 514 997
tails (1) 15 1766
tailtickler (1) 14 575
Taim (1) 9 366
Tainted (1) 8 868
tainted (1) 13 958
taittering (1) 18 673
Take (24) 3 279 5 82 524 7 654 8 605 761 9 194 539 1058 10 613 11 107 246 702 826 12 260 1436 13 1103 1234 15 1118 2516 2959 3493 4891 16 1012
take (119) 1 615 2 336 3 70 79 407 498 4 452 5 106 335 510 513 556 6 14 340 646 902 7 26 133 887 935 942 998 8 241 262 267 320 351 466 735 740 759 910 997 1024 1120 9 668 984 10 421 639 724 894 1054 1094 11 360 494 12 125 258 388 392 433 437 702 795 1002 1139 1661 13 31 76 91 164 212 404 468 529 537 799 975 1095 14 336 466 549 577 592 689 772 1478 15 130 199 381 660 830 1642 2350 3485 3515 3601 3792 4739 4788 4901 16 12 19 722 785 928 1556 1760 1790 17 877 1220 18 105 230 234 265 280 286 311 316 329 367 521 537 590 798 1005 1038 1071 1302 1492
Taken (2) 15 4486 16 1438
taken (37) 5 488 6 401 757 7 521 8 292 9 132 543 1040 12 1041 1187 13 318 664 14 207 427 700 726 1075 1280 **1395** 15 638 1068 1168 2975 3836 16 200 **809** 1229 1319 1694 17 238 1911 2279 2286 18 365 498 1303
taken (1) 15 1588
Takes (2) 12 1227 13 1228
takes (21) 1 606 3 260 4 114 6 335 7 950 9 803 12 90 848 1512 13 803 989 1022 14 518 15 3387 16 261 18 65 223 227 252 420 1493
takes (1) 11 1285
takes (14) 15 164 720 973 1027 1613 2699 2736 3545 3584 3655 4013 4122 4703 4799
takest (1) 15 3638
Taking (6) 5 328 7 448 11 633 12 1470 13 874 16 144
taking (50) 1 459 548 617 3 122 5 70 6 33 142 880 7 33 260 319 462 972 8 199 257 258 531 834 951 9 3 10 975 1205 12 53 508 514 519 832 1103 1434 1753 13 84 291 307 329 330 545 1023 1294 14 262 1152 16 815 830 874 1397 1755 17 378 18 360 635 1330 1352
taking (2) 15 2698 3530
tālāfānā (1) 12 354
Talbot (11) 2 58 60 77 81 90 10 156 14 683 16 53 135 136 17 591
Talbot (3) 15 174 2074 2127
Talboys (1) 15 1111
Talboys (1) 15 4551
TALBOYS (5) 15 1057 1080 1087 1097 1113
talc (1) 15 3079
Tale (1) 9 883
tale (13) 1 572 2 46 8 420 9 357 10 544 12 1097 14 545 1010 1404 15 952 16 139 17 839 1077
tale (1) 15 580
talent (1) 7 688
talents (1) 7 605

Tales (1) 8 1153
Tales (1) 10 591
tales (2) 13 634 15 701
talionis (2) 7 756 14 1030
Talis (1) 14 707
talisman (3) 10 848 15 1313 2794
Talith (1) 15 1625
Talk (6) 3 430 432 5 76 11 912 15 1958
talk (32) 2 43 5 197 396 6 853 8 568 692 707 10 695 11 1196 12 312 394 895 896 1313 13 220 1146 14 545 15 2395 2883 4281 4428 16 909 1366 1645 17 797 18 13 100 221 592 1342 1456 1494
talk (1) 9 1144
talk (3) 15 2705 4261 4316
talkative (1) 14 714
talked (6) 9 544 592 11 797 798 800 13 233
Talking (6) 5 113 7 698 12 303 397 484 939
talking (57) 1 425 518 5 124 201 290 6 527 1006 7 52 957 8 229 441 9 429 10 731 11 1194 1199 12 8 65 242 330 450 493 679 683 692 705 805 1082 1143 1227 1414 1473 1474 13 575 943 1295 15 3887 4052 4762 16 248 464 748 895 900 1755 18 130 182 201 246 384 690 696 879 1017 1115 1163 1330
talks (2) 8 7 11 973
talks (2) 15 937 3548
tall (25) 1 319 5 411 6 252 582 7 505 8 126 166 9 74 269 10 328 930 997 11 70 588 688 12 1313 1647 13 113 235 236 486 15 4281 18 976 1089 1587
tall (2) 15 37 4771
Tallaght (1) 12 1453
tallhatted (1) 10 1237
tallies (1) 12 94
Tallon (1) 17 444
Tallons (1) 4 128
tallow (1) 7 928
tallowy (1) 6 778
tallwhitehatted (2) 10 310 377
Tally (1) 14 1570
tally (1) 16 1347
tallyho (1) 10 1264
tallyho (2) 15 4125 4329
Talmud (1) 17 754
Talmud (1) 17 1380
talons (1) 11 998
talons (4) 15 260 2011 2266 3940
tam (2) 4 281 399
tambourined (1) 11 863
Tame (1) 9 532
tamely (2) 6 949 16 1313
Taming (1) 9 1063
tammy (1) 15 557
Tamoshant (1) 12 865
tampered (1) 15 972
Tan (2) 8 1168 15 1091
tan (7) 10 307 1241 11 337 761 977 13 77 17 1814
tandems (1) 17 494
Tanderagee (1) 15 2259
Tandy (2) 3 81 260
tandy (1) 16 438
tang (1) 4 4
tangent (2) 16 1290 17 1224
tangible (1) 14 1227

Tangier (2) 10 310 18 860
tangle (2) 3 224 16 1482
tangled (3) 5 570 8 643 9 225
tanist (1) 3 247
Tank (1) 11 1170
tank (5) 11 760 820 872 1171
Tankard (1) 11 1177
tankard (4) 8 688 11 817 1167 1169
Tankards (1) 11 1038
tankards (5) 11 542 662 759 770 954
Tanks (1) 14 1506
tanks (3) 11 1282 17 169 18 611
tanned (1) 11 939
tanner (3) 8 926 12 1216 16 167
tanneries (3) 6 396 12 1244 17 222
tanner's (1) 15 1178
Tansy (1) 15 2736
tansy (1) 12 1616
tanta (1) 14 707
Tantalising (1) 6 760
Tantalus (1) 6 1010
tantamount (2) 14 1237 16 84
Tante (1) 10 362
tantras (1) 12 339
Tantum (2) 13 498 552
tantumer (1) 13 499
tanyard (2) 3 380 12 1312
Tap (46) 3 16 11 933 951 989 1010 1037 1075 1084 1100 1119 1138 1166 1186 1190 1208 1218 1223 1234 1273
tap (9) 1 266 7 117 8 372 541 11 1190 17 162 230
Tape (1) 15 2974
tape (2) 16 431 535
tapering (1) 13 89
tapers (1) 14 346
tapes (1) 6 71
tapestried (1) 15 2046
tapis (1) 16 534
tapped (9) 2 250 5 50 6 306 8 1104 10 1105 11 50 215 986 12 964
tapping (9) 8 1075 1111 10 423 641 1116 11 707 1190 1234
tapping (3) 15 2770 2775 2792
taps (3) 15 2392 2847 4436
tapsters' (1) 9 340
taptaptapping (1) 11 1234
Taptun (1) 12 1605
Tar (1) 12 1355
Tara (4) 4 490 7 880 15 2385
Tara (1) 8 624
tara (3) 8 623
taratara (1) 13 862
taraxel (1) 15 1653
Tarbarrels (1) 12 1829
tarbarrels (1) 16 1308
Tare (1) 14 1018
Taree (1) 8 623
Tarentum (1) 2 2
targets (1) 12 115
Tarifa (1) 18 1337
Tarjeta (1) 16 489
Tarnally (1) 14 1541
tarnation (1) 9 54
tarns (1) 17 201
tarpaulin (2) 16 479 1021
tarred (1) 13 949
Tar's (1) 16 1456
tars (1) 12 1334

tart (3) 8 273 12 676 16 165
tart (1) 18 1296
tartan (2) 2 266 16 1676
tartan (1) 15 2178
Tartar (1) 15 2867
tartar (1) 7 533
tarts (1) 8 1069
task (4) 9 371 14 663 16 1527 17 1008
tasselled (1) 1 255
tasselled (2) 15 2744 4498
tassels (1) 3 230
tassels (1) 15 249
Taste (2) 1 409 8 851
taste (17) 1 74 4 204 6 994 8 174 235
741 1123 11 843 13 148 1224 14 932
15 2739 16 808 895 1847 18 132 1033
tasted (3) 10 1093 14 415 18 129
tasteful (2) 12 663 14 706
tastefully (1) 12 1823
tasteless (1) 8 542
Tastes (3) 8 820 1096 1123
tastes (3) 8 81 85 18 1390
tasting (2) 8 153 18 272
tasty (4) 4 50 8 267 18 431 1481
taters (1) 15 154
tattarrattat (1) 18 343
tatterdemalion (1) 15 2074
Tattered (1) 10 838
tattered (3) 3 197 14 1551 18 962
tattered (1) 15 3160
Tatters (1) 3 353
tatters (1) 4 176
Tattoo (1) 16 677
tattoo (2) 16 1197 1345
tattooed (1) 16 668
tatts (1) 15 40
taught (12) 3 257 258 5 333 10 676
13 925 1075 14 594 15 2376 3078 3661
17 748 18 779
Taunted (1) 11 410
taunts (1) 15 2710
Taurus (1) 14 1109
taut (2) 3 42 10 252
taut (1) 15 2176
Tavern (1) 16 50
tavern (3) 16 1077 17 758 967
taverns (2) 3 251 14 536
taw (2) 5 233 12 21
tawny (4) 3 444 10 1127 12 157 159
tawny (3) 15 538 1318 3838
tax (2) 9 783 15 871
taxes (4) 8 383 12 1575 15 1634
16 991
Taxil (1) 3 167
Taxil (1) 14 306
taxing (1) 10 471
taxpayers (1) 17 182
Tay (2) 7 687 12 1387
tay (1) 5 15
Taylor (6) 7 793 814 823 12 1171 1174 1499
Taylor (1) 15 995
Te (1) 5 477
Te (1) 12 1749
te (2) 15 4164 4165
te (7) 1 276 277 738 3 396 14 294
15 1557 17 1231
Tea (6) 4 370 5 18 19 8 371
tea (61) 1 194 347 352 354 357 359 370 436 450
2 37 4 14 238 263 272 283 306 333 359 366 389

392 426 5 19 6 124 7 143 8 235 333 354
367 11 108 126 129 140 167 250 12 15 38
628 13 272 1222 1294 15 572 1895 2363
17 308 1980 2075 18 240 258 436 468 578 910
930 1074 1243 1505
teabathed (1) 11 266
teabrown (1) 15 3234
Teach (1) 12 838
teach (8) 1 79 7 144 555 12 511
14 157 15 3023 16 160 18 1363
teacher (2) 2 402 407
teaching (2) 5 42 7 96
teacosy (1) 13 460
teacup (2) 11 108 237
teacups (2) 12 804 17 355
teadust (1) 4 107
teahouse (1) 14 637
tealess (1) 11 453
team (1) 6 507
teams (1) 2 185
teapot (12) 1 331 4 270 272 297 299
11 108 15 457 458 460 3130
Tear (1) 8 684
tear (17) 3 405 5 303 385 11 804 1101
1140 1248 12 161 397 673 1908 13 596 1112
14 1136 15 2889 18 619 1092
tear (2) 15 1617 1964
teardrops (1) 15 3363
tearful (1) 13 68
tearing (6) 7 83 11 972 16 438 18 323
424
Tearle (1) 17 794
tearlessly (1) 15 3216
tearoom (1) 8 464
Tears (1) 14 1028
Tears (1) 9 33
tears (18) 6 519 12 643 652 839 1098
13 54 59 74 190 399 586 649 765 14 565
15 3218 3890 16 1541 18 1518
tears (6) 15 772 1715 1880 2708 3838 4179
teartap (1) 18 1077
tearwashed (1) 8 975
teas (5) 11 91 110 111 18 249 620
teas (1) 12 31
tease (3) 1 150 13 24 14 814
teased (1) 11 383
teasing (1) 11 824
teat (2) 13 402 958
teatray (3) 11 92 164 381
teats (1) 15 2456
Teazle (1) 1 211
Technic (1) 15 2392
technically (2) 4 86 16 878
teco (1) 15 1886
teco (3) 8 1040 1051 1052
Tecum (1) 3 82
tedious (1) 6 162
Tee (1) 11 1026
tee (2) 4 115 11 1025
teem (1) 18 1016
teeming (1) 14 74
teens (1) 15 3319
teetee (1) 14 1508
Teeth (1) 8 719
teeth (38) 1 25 132 378 412 3 213 232 493
494 4 34 527 5 214 496 7 373 685
8 660 1029 10 32 335 474 1172 11 631
13 236 527 819 892 1195 14 557 1149
15 1782 4527 16 469 1431 18 159 307 430
569 888 1200

teeth (7) 15 28 806 1339 2339 3196 3506 4680
teetotal (1) 16 795
teetotum (1) 18 1281
Telegram (3) 9 548 553
telegram (6) 3 198 7 64 9 41 486 546
12 874
telegramboy (1) 14 1515
Telegraph (1) 2 412
Telegraph (14) 2 419 7 27 181 232 411 412
665 966 974 13 1174 15 1125 16 723 1232
17 325
telegraph (4) 5 2 13 1147 15 2497
17 1674
telegraph (1) 15 1405
telegraphic (1) 17 772
telephone (7) 6 868 7 384 656 671
10 336 388 17 1525
telephone (1) 15 809
telephoned (1) 15 3030
telescope (4) 12 1194 16 767 17 566
1564
telescopic (1) 17 2014
Tell (37) 1 47 154 2 30 54 3 256 4 343
409 5 7 169 294 298 6 754 7 672 982
8 329 633 1018 10 486 11 891 12 189
1097 1400 13 66 1019 14 1495 1517
15 438 1894 1896 2191 3052 3716 3795 4192
16 492 1018
Tell (2) 12 26 13 312
tell (134) 1 183 407 505 563 2 251 3 64 86
133 139 245 4 115 5 245 247 251 254 258 426
453 455 6 60 722 891 7 431 549 631 651 979
981 989 992 1036 8 55 328 329 452 769 844 952
961 1093 9 357 672 688 727 738 787 936
10 391 444 447 530 545 552 939 950 11 128
428 697 783 870 876 12 780 782 783 785 811
1068 1330 1362 1586 1762 1765 13 463 617 750
751 753 833 887 901 943 1076 1299 14 502 535
718 1055 1420 1525 15 81 404 523 524 554 766
1542 1996 2914 3140 3693 4575 16 58 144 149
756 780 784 1173 1218 1232 1657 18 94 95 137
215 279 352 409 468 614 694 725 772 1021 1030
1034 1237 1392 1476 1515 1523
tell (2) 1 597 3 202
tell (1) 15 311
telling (42) 5 96 488 6 609 7 785 8 691
787 800 803 899 9 54 558 10 1152 1165
12 208 439 443 831 839 1034 1091 1144 1333
1343 1566 1623 1659 1660 1797 13 400 544 711
900 14 528 1308 1555 15 1527 18 7 355
955 958 984 1484
tells (5) 13 991 14 592 782 15 2393
18 728
telltale (1) 13 120
tellurian (1) 17 1159
tem (1) 16 1150
temper (6) 6 746 13 249 16 1606
18 70 179 200
temperament (1) 17 638
temperamental (1) 16 1074
temperaments (3) 16 873 882 17 559
temperance (5) 5 388 6 317 12 690
13 282 16 792
temperance (1) 15 1570
temperate (2) 14 939 17 202
temperature (4) 16 40 17 268 269 272
temperatures (2) 8 1128 14 1270
tempered (3) 12 619 17 1620 2033
tempers (2) 14 691 955

Thank (22) 1 617 2 223 422 4 169 185 5 270 6 1026 1033 7 171 8 776 781 9 316 12 760 15 1638 1933 2702 3071 3767 3791 4838 4839 16 447

Thank (2) 16 1336 1523

thank (9) 1 437 5 242 9 375 12 222 13 1030 14 762 15 1516 18 62 591

thank (1) 15 3068

Thanked (1) 14 166

thanked (5) 4 186 5 61 11 732 14 722 16 1522

Thankful (1) 13 789

thankful (1) 18 436

thankibus (1) 7 780

Thanking (3) 2 336 3 405 6 13

thanking (1) 14 575

Thanks (22) 1 28 120 2 175 4 281 398 5 175 6 161 889 915 7 117 8 1101 9 320 10 916 11 299 1122 12 238 13 1272 15 1478 2731 3599 4870 16 197

thanks (22) 2 225 4 405 5 142 149 541 6 775 7 111 791 8 84 357 764 1032 10 239 12 1517 1521 1744 13 550 940 14 751 1034 15 2679 18 732

thanksgiving (3) 5 449 14 1318 17 1879

Thanky (1) 7 468

thankyou (1) 7 546

THAT (2) 7 221 483

That (196) 1 28 127 345 469 483 632 2 15 248 289 324 383 415 420 3 38 367 368 438 495 496 4 258 341 352 363 483 528 5 69 153 177 208 342 378 500 507 513 6 63 154 202 271 359 369 371 417 469 670 677 888 923 924 7 176 256 293 521 630 631 632 686 784 814 879 890 909 1072 8 64 96 144 200 347 423 465 466 527 574 663 682 833 836 871 973 1012 1043 1114 1125 9 76 249 307 391 450 471 523 572 903 927 993 1078 1200 10 39 42 147 394 447 593 788 1074 1172 11 138 153 154 201 272 313 314 369 481 569 671 793 817 1034 1128 1173 1183 1224 12 23 275 458 464 650 996 1058 1429 1491 1618 13 114 188 275 487 750 777 788 961 988 1039 1136 1143 1158 1228 14 85 259 747 1045 1075 1117 1550 15 129 207 210 829 1192 1234 1359 1383 1384 1561 2365 2426 2452 2740 2762 2827 2993 3090 3143 3231 3293 3595 3613 3706 3713 4530 16 486 530 590 677 681 909 971 1085 1332 1352 17 237 718 1019 1139 1140 18 879

That (6) 1 261 567 592 7 327 9 1149 10 572

That (1) 15 1580

that (2360) 1 15 102 105 150 152 154 161 181 202 318 334 411 417 419 420 422 434 468 469 489 496 555 556 602 606 623 624 630 634 647 648 660 662 673 675 698 702 721 2 24 45 51 52 75 83 108 143 152 229 249 253 270 315 338 362 379 401 421 438 3 1 3 13 14 49 59 64 123 129 130 132 134 145 148 222 245 258 307 312 322 379 399 430 435 448 451 495 496 4 63 65 74 80 103 116 125 131 134 208 211 215 219 235 263 315 324 328 337 360 362 363 373 393 434 478 482 486 488 492 508 523 526 528 531 5 3 31 37 42 48 77 101 103 118 133 149 153 174 178 182 186 187 188 195 198 199 212 219 236 244 245 246 279 287 289 332 333 358 363 366 378 381 382 385 393 396 397 400 403 404 408 438 462 468 479 520 526 536 538 544 558 6 22 23 42 49 53 60 67 77 80 93 105 149 159 177 197 201 203 205 234 240 241 244 246 268 301 346 349 352 353 381 391 395 397 409 414 415 456 483 494 506 522 524 567 571 597 599 606 612 620 621 622 629 673 681 690 693 705 717 722 736 742 748 758 792 805 817 827 828 829 830 851 866 889 891 895 916 923 926 941 946 954 956 959 968 982 983 987 991 997 998 1002 1010 1014 1029 1032 7 36 83 88 96 132 133 142 151 152 154 156 160 206 208 215 227 233 248 339 340 341 342 352 361 378 383 439 453 502 544 566 567 630 636 641 652 655 669 685 693 698 701 711 748 751 753 763 764 783 785 835 842 883 886 890 925 947 982 985 1019 1026 1036 1062 8 18 25 41 49 53 60 76 79 86 87 93 100 109 110 119 124 133 142 146 147 156 163 166 169 170 176 180 182 184 188 192 208 226 237 244 256 266 269 273 283 289 304 318 328 337 348 350 369 376 378 379 429 430 442 458 471 486 512 517 528 535 538 542 544 559 565 571 584 605 607 608 616 622 623 628 662 675 704 719 720 725 751 759 760 775 800 801 804 815 820 822 824 844 852 854 890 909 940 943 948 950 956 964 965 976 982 1007 1023 1025 1035 1052 1107 1112 1114 1146 1147 1154 1164 1188 9 11 63 141 151 173 174 177 186 192 210 226 253 297 298 303 331 341 348 354 360 370 382 383 384 386 393 399 421 432 443 468 470 510 517 519 522 523 576 611 624 625 657 659 667 672 676 685 714 720 749 763 780 781 800 801 802 811 812 813 814 815 827 829 830 833 835 839 844 850 852 863 913 919 928 942 956 959 988 1006 1024 1031 1051 1071 1074 1076 1123 1158 1164 1202 10 3 21 24 35 44 61 66 74 83 88 91 118 129 137 139 146 151 162 171 191 225 236 288 371 383 384 399 401 444 445 518 560 588 602 605 672 679 680 696 725 730 732 734 750 757 759 762 787 789 790 791 797 869 892 905 916 918 925 942 949 950 1017 1028 1032 1048 1062 1079 1084 1142 1143 1146 1162 1167 1170 11 66 104 124 144 169 187 268 279 282 298 310 314 315 357 361 378 385 398 438 448 450 466 476 549 555 581 611 623 628 635 645 668 681 719 738 778 779 781 802 805 816 817 825 833 846 854 857 865 871 883 904 910 924 935 940 968 980 1015 1036 1046 1050 1058 1059 1092 1094 1101 1107 1110 1122 1123 1131 1148 1170 1172 1173 1175 1177 1180 1183 1210 1225 1228 1247 1250 1253 1257 1275 12 6 9 60 61 66 78 88 89 102 119 125 127 149 152 160 185 201 209 226 233 236 237 239 242 251 253 272 273 278 288 300 302 315 345 348 349 352 353 354 359 363 366 367 368 370 371 372 373 388 393 394 399 400 405 407 436 441 456 459 469 475 482 483 486 513 530 586 594 626 633 643 644 657 676 680 682 695 707 709 732 736 737 772 776 782 785 793 827 829 844 859 862 867 876 880 881 887 888 891 939 947 998 1020 1031 1043 1045 1046 1058 1062 1075 1084 1114 1123 1131 1135 1144 1146 1152 1154 1165 1176 1184 1185 1208 1215 1224 1239 1240 1242 1245 1248 1301 1317 1329 1332 1338 1346 1347 1363 1370 1373 1377 1378 1379 1383 1393 1400 1401 1413 1436 1467 1481 1482 1483 1490 1494 1500 1507 1509 1510 1511 1522 1534 1536 1538 1543 1552 1555 1577 1579 1581 1623 1636 1640 1644 1650 1651 1654 1661 1672 1735 1736 1744 1811 1812 1834 1862 1866 1869 1879 1884 1897 1913 13 11 17 21 31 33 44 46 47 53 59 86 91 92 95 104 105 111 117 121 128 130 133 136 142 145 149 151 158 163 165 171 181 184 185 186 195 223 229 233 234 246 260 265 286 293 296 300 301 306 308 315 316 320 329 332 341 343 347 369 376 379 386 395 405 407 409 416 418 421 425 426 427 429 435 443 453 455 456 457 462 479 483 487 495 502 503 513 514 515 518 523 530 540 541 554 558 561 566 569 578 580 582 592 593 598 600 601 602 603 604 608 610 615 619 621 632 634 635 642 643 644 649 650 652 661 662 664 666 671 689 691 699 701 702 703 705 706 710 711 712 713 725 726 728 730 731 736 747 752 761 763 765 780 786 787 793 801 824 828 843 844 848 851 861 868 883 888 889 891 899 906 907 909 910 916 921 923 924 930 940 949 958 963 965 974 985 987 992 994 997 1001 1005 1009 1030 1036 1037 1044 1045 1046 1047 1050 1061 1065 1081 1085 1086 1089 1092 1099 1108 1117 1134 1138 1150 1188 1195 1198 1205 1215 1224 1229 1239 1243 1245 1253 1262 1271 1299 1300 1301 1302 14 7 9 10 12 15 18 20 26 27 28 29 31 34 46 55 57 58 61 71 72 73 74 75 80 82 84 87 90 94 95 96 99 102 107 108 111 112 113 114 115 116 118 119 120 124 126 131 132 133 135 141 142 144 145 146 148 149 150 151 153 154 156 161 165 170 171 172 173 174 175 177 179 182 183 184 185 187 189 191 192 193 194 196 199 200 204 205 209 211 216 218 219 225 230 233 236 237 240 241 249 250 251 255 257 261 262 266 269 271 273 275 277 279 283 287 293 297 298 299 302 305 314 321 329 330 338 350 361 362 364 372 383 389 391 410 412 413 415 418 423 424 426 434 435 438 443 444 447 448 451 452 455 464 465 466 470 471 481 482 491 493 494 495 496 498 510 513 516 517 524 530 531 533 543 544 546 549 552 553 554 566 571 575 576 582 587 589 590 593 595 596 603 605 610 611 613 615 620 621 622 625 627 629 633 640 647 657 659 667 718 723 724 733 734 754 757 767 772 779 781 782 787 792 809 816 820 826 831 840 843 847 851 854 857 860 863 868 877 880 882 885 891 892 894 898 899 903 904 908 910 913 928 929 933 940 945 950 954 957 965 972 983 994 998 1006 1042 1049 1053 1078 1080 1140 1145 1148 1150 1152 1159 1179 1191 1197 1202 1217 1220 1223 1228 1232 1265 1267 1268 1281 1286 1297 1304 1312 1316 1321 1326 1337 1347 1353 1357 1366 1373 1379 1382 1404 1429 1451 1491 1503 1517 1518 1526 1551 1558 1576 1586 15 94 103 105 167 199 206 221 232 272 332 355 375 385 405 411 435 441 477 547 549 557 586 593 640 642 643 645 651 660 699 740 744 766 804 823 834 947 949 952 954 975 983 1001 1018 1034 1054 1089 1222 1233 1289 1357 1385 1456 1464 1505 1534 1642 1723 1790 1804 1808 1985 2001 2091 2093 2119 2196 2198 2200 2206 2288 2314 2323 2357 2376 2401 2421 2453 2462 2490 2511 2578 2579 2616 2696 2772 2886 2934 2935 2937 2941 2942 2959 2990 2994 3011 3067 3088 3139 3162 3248 3272 3274 3285 3295 3323 3354 3405 3407 3509 3516 3522 3525 3528 3594 3601 3631 3663 3664 3666 3676 3751 3871 3907 4109 4189 4202 4275 4298 4424 4441 4447 4473 4482 4515 4576 4582 4607 4818 4836 4861 4881 4951 16 15 17 36 47 70 71 72 76 98 107 108 119 128 136 150 173 180 183 187 198 206 207 217 222 224 227 228 230 232 241 257 264 271 272 278 280 284 287 292 295 306 307 346 351 353 412 416 425 462 467 470 492 501 506 540 556 567 570 577 581 599 612 615 618 624 627 635 638 641 643 646 656 670 674 679 692 712 719 724 729 737 740 741 750 751 759 764 772 778 781 785 815 819 827 833 837 848 850 855 865 873 877 901 904 905 906 907 910 925 930 960 964 966 967 974 987 992 994 996 1012 1018 1025 1031 1032 1035 1036 1037 1046 1050 1054 1066 1069 1075 1081 1090 1106 1107 1110 1132 1138 1146 1160 1164 1178 1183 1215 1240 1268 1285 1290 1291 1295 1299 1352

1363 1369 1372 1390 1392 1398 1409 1419 1422
1426 1446 1450 1458 1481 1486 1488 1492 1499
1502 1506 1508 1511 1533 1544 1549 1559 1570
1595 1608 1611 1613 1624 1625 1630 1646 1650
1661 1662 1666 1667 1669 1679 1689 1693 1696
1703 1724 1730 1739 1742 1750 1755 1762 1772
1775 1783 1788 1790 1792 1806 1820 1833 1842
1848 1864 1872 17 63 78 293 363 383 453 458
459 484 497 530 531 555 561 606 713 735 761 839
884 979 993 1074 1086 1093 1099 1228 1235 1236
1403 1608 1617 1634 1755 1760 1761 1844 1871
1883 1884 1936 1938 2127 18 1 4 16 24 26 39
44 50 51 53 54 55 56 59 61 65 69 71 74 76 79 87 88
89 91 101 103 107 111 125 129 130 134 139 144
150 151 153 174 181 182 186 193 197 206 209 216
218 222 224 229 231 234 235 237 239 241 243 251
254 259 260 261 264 268 269 273 278 279 285 292
309 318 322 326 345 346 365 369 370 371 374 381
385 388 402 415 420 425 426 427 429 431 441 444
449 454 455 457 459 460 463 466 471 476 478 481
487 491 492 493 495 498 502 504 514 521 524 533
535 537 544 545 555 562 563 564 565 571 572 573
575 585 592 598 601 605 612 626 628 630 653 655
658 669 683 697 700 704 712 716 723 725 726 727
730 741 742 748 774 775 782 787 795 797 802 805
812 814 815 833 836 837 841 856 857 858 864 865
866 867 871 872 873 874 876 877 885 888 889 892
894 899 900 901 907 908 909 910 911 912 915 916
917 921 933 937 938 944 953 962 964 968 969 972
991 992 997 999 1007 1014 1015 **1019** 1035 1038
1040 1041 1043 1050 1052 1056 **1057** 1059 1060
1065 1066 1071 1072 1075 1077 **1078** 1081 1084
1087 1090 1092 1101 1105 1107 **1110** 1111 1113
1117 1118 1129 1137 1145 1150 1152 1153 1168
1169 1174 1175 1177 1179 1180 1188 1190 1195
1197 1201 1203 1214 1220 1225 1229 1234 1235
1239 1250 1255 1257 1264 1265 1270 1272 1288
1289 1303 1317 1320 1323 1328 1337 1339 1345
1348 1349 1369 1370 1373 1382 1402 1404 1406
1417 1420 1425 1426 1427 1430 1444 1445 1447
1448 1451 1454 1458 1460 1465 1474 1496 1503
1509 1510 1513 1524 1528 1530 1547 1556 1561
1570 1575 1577 1578 1598

that (31) 1 584 589 2 14 78 6 146
7 471 768 769 770 830 831 832 838 863 864
8 183 9 733 1147 1148 1150 10 571 735
11 665 12 894 1290 14 650 16 648
17 398 1353

that (9) 15 910 924 1521 1583 2017 4078 4913
4915 4919

thatch (1) 14 85
thatched (1) 17 1504
that'd (3) 10 1135 12 263 1585
thatd (4) 18 168 1263 1402 1412
That'll (12) 5 174 7 330 380 586 902
8 1057 10 304 927 12 1806 15 4821
that'll (3) 12 1001 1586 15 3205
thatll (1) 18 170
THAT'S (1) 7 1006
That's (96) 1 88 365 390 444 667 2 249 447
3 200 407 5 165 6 36 264 473 613 735 745
7 214 381 481 688 844 903 1008 8 31 289 512
685 1023 1100 9 956 10 218 417 641 735 910
924 948 1049 1138 11 641 701 874 969 1052
1090 1265 12 130 855 888 991 1001 1148 1346
1349 1466 1476 1481 1541 1554 1625 1642 1666
13 772 782 860 873 968 1007 1059 1138 15 93
1368 1459 2206 2910 3165 3945 4005 4312 4813
4845 16 418 419 463 585 778 880 1021 1130
1135 1154

That's (2) 6 731 12 895
that's (56) 2 222 3 189 190 191 418 4 361
5 382 526 6 264 7 146 210 8 159 226 320
395 502 525 773 10 1136 11 559 965
12 25 457 765 767 783 1055 1101 1163 1331 1392
1424 1510 1546 1646 13 822 824 989 1043 1100
1161 14 579 1536 1584 15 264 360 596 820
1538 1977 3487 3657 4382 16 1137 1650
that's (1) 10 573
thats (36) 18 43 152 271 289 386 448 457 521
560 629 660 662 793 893 967 1008 1115 1126 1128
1154 1164 1212 1232 1241 1254 1260 1307 1358
1368 1371 1442 1510 1517 1519 1537 1540
thaumaturgic (1) 17 1825
THE (22) 7 1 14 20 61 78 120 203 236 272 386
464 483 626 726 841 938 970 995
The (1026) 1 31 34 45 73 78 88 107 116 139
143 146 152 232 245 274 293 306 327 335 346 347
386 387 393 475 497 565 574 577 578 608 643 650
661 672 675 700 714 733 739 2 6 40 75 115 128
143 173 233 246 259 273 275 325 328 380 419 428
3 37 56 58 66 83 97 100 109 111 147 200 207 234
239 266 271 282 297 310 313 322 323 335 343 348
354 359 387 404 416 426 448 4 10 15 18 68 78
92 116 141 142 151 152 164 165 176 225 264 283
293 305 329 344 345 366 381 455 461 468 474 478
498 531 544 5 29 34 42 45 60 74 91 99 105 133
138 178 200 222 295 301 314 325 334 338 344 348
349 386 417 437 440 442 448 472 474 479 6 26
30 38 45 91 115 120 132 140 171 172 173 201 207
222 227 256 299 312 332 338 359 361 364 366 370
375 383 399 425 434 458 459 462 469 472 478 480
481 486 490 509 521 579 582 584 590 614 619 631
637 640 641 656 659 665 667 677 708 709 719 726
728 749 755 770 778 787 789 799 800 801 821 825
833 840 848 864 872 873 874 908 909 914 917 942
947 954 974 995 997 7 6 28 46 50 97 101 108
125 130 147 149 159 174 180 237 265 280 325 344
345 355 384 396 415 422 425 432 435 469 473 479
489 491 530 532 534 545 562 563 564 597 606 608
609 613 615 635 656 663 670 684 690 774 792 877
881 891 910 911 912 8 24 25 58 65 76 160 233
254 269 279 330 364 394 438 459 471 473 496 499
516 522 529 566 584 587 589 606 622 640 774 877
900 901 1022 1078 1082 1094 1104 1127 1137 1158
1163 1172 1176 9 28 49 50 51 56 68 69 100
104 107 113 123 125 133 139 155 161 164 203 221
226 258 281 321 323 326 344 387 394 396 407 408
425 433 436 443 459 466 469 510 516 522 530 542
552 554 569 604 605 610 630 643 671 693 729 735
738 742 752 755 757 784 795 811 824 826 827 833
854 863 876 886 887 897 952 957 958 961 988 999
1007 1018 1020 1033 1046 1056 1060 1115 1117
1122 1124 1138 1164 1168 1178 1195 1199 1205
1209 10 1 22 41 49 69 70 119 122 134 155 156
180 181 200 239 249 250 281 299 319 326 330 373
382 388 403 411 416 437 440 458 476 479 503
515 537 550 566 594 613 633 640 643 649 685 688
691 709 712 715 750 759 815 821 833 892 928 946
948 956 958 972 989 992 997 1040 1063 1073 1074
1083 1117 1145 1155 1162 1167 1180 1182 1213
1235 1268 11 14 20 34 89 138 156 189 190 267
277 280 342 379 390 470 485 581 603 663 670 690
707 717 790 791 844 872 890 945 958 1007 1009
1016 1017 1020 1030 1031 1040 1080 1081 1083
1109 1121 1132 1172 1209 1222 12 124 151 158
161 185 186 197 219 263 269 396 397 403 426 457
468 503 519 523 525 528 547 551 555 577 581 589
596 604 608 624 635 639 717 733 769 795 825 857
859 867 872 879 881 901 907 919 926 938 949 963
964 967 969 971 973 977 1001 1005 1006 1038 1156
1157 1197 1202 1266 1279 1284 1347 1352 1385
1404 1432 1438 1446 1497 1504 1509 1518 1526
1550 1608 1772 1819 1825 1855 1858 1862 1888
1900 13 1 9 42 87 125 193 200 249 337 345 352
355 381 430 466 614 669 689 856 859 886 1038
1064 1066 1092 1097 1104 1115 1156 1168 1205
1223 1233 1270 1292 14 100 111 113 118 385
392 479 544 689 717 735 784 794 802 809 818 848
884 935 942 953 977 984 988 996 1011 1017 1025
1028 1029 1030 1032 1033 1034 1035 1036 1055
1063 1078 1123 1128 1145 1156 1161 1169 1177
1198 1199 1201 1209 1227 1239 1356 1379 1398
1407 1446 1512 1514 1565 1585 15 46 47 58 59
72 94 201 207 408 455 467 474 492 495 630 688
714 740 750 760 769 785 787 825 854 859 883 896
944 969 972 1105 1121 1197 1220 1232 1350 1394
1451 1452 1629 1731 1759 1796 1922 1967 1995
2001 2027 2088 2105 2112 2115 2166 2202 2316
2345 2369 2389 2445 2511 2643 2696 2717 2718
2780 2891 2947 3022 3025 3115 3137 3162 3175
3191 3289 3353 3354 3356 3359 3402 3424 3435
3449 3464 3503 3556 3577 3578 3594 3629 3631
3650 3660 3664 3761 3820 4042 4044 4170 4178
4192 4200 4214 4227 4269 4378 4407 4501 4519
4582 4590 4591 4634 4638 4641 4756 4926 4950
16 75 229 300 335 354 367 375 390 399 429 437
441 444 450 474 509 610 612 666 704 727 739 799
882 892 929 1001 1002 1010 1019 1021 1149 1174
1232 1304 1356 1384 1414 1456 1476 1567 1577
1604 1640 1647 1662 1672 1716 1719 1866 1874
1885 17 36 44 116 247 257 293 343 374 463 467
470 504 512 560 577 603 622 690 691 747 770 783
786 957 975 979 1030 1039 1102 1104 1192 1226
1243 1246 1257 1275 1295 1331 1350 1358 1410
1419 1427 1678 1699 1701 1753 1766 1819 1844
1850 1897 1928 1931 1949 1957 1959 1960 1963
1969 1974 2029 2037 2044 2061 2082 2212 2237
2244 2300
The (64) 2 102 103 104 285 355 3 204 257
4 348 369 6 145 357 7 253 591 735 1057
1058 8 62 549 1055 9 19 246 550 616 808 883
1001 1013 1063 1147 10 368 585 615 618 734
838 11 320 327 991 1176 12 220 542 740
13 314 633 1060 14 317 15 1023 16 979
1250 1253 1255 1680 17 401 416 640 1366 1367
1368 1369 1373 1375 1394 1645
The (118) 15 1 7 32 78 133 134 140 165 187
190 191 247 320 340 356 513 531 532 633 652 659
663 672 693 929 986 1128 1136 1173 1184 1204
1236 1269 1340 1373 1407 1408 1410 1411 1446
1447 1491 1495 1508 1509 1519 1520 1552 1565
1566 1586 1619 1703 1938 2042 2046 2071 2163
2238 2277 2278 2512 2611 2685 2692 2742 2923
3220 3232 3297 3479 3641 3729 3821 3854 3855
3951 3954 3960 3975 4017 4026 4047 4048 4049
4056 4061 4075 4081 4151 4260 4314 4322 4328
4421 4543 4544 4578 4669 4670 4687 4688 4695
4722 4819 4877 4902 4908 4909 4911 4916 4919
THE (181) 15 10 12 17 19 21 23 52 80 85 176
180 188 194 217 337 358 368 379 533 583 588 595
599 608 610 612 621 628 654 676 685 749 860 1039
1057 1080 1087 1097 1113 1131 1137 1144 1146
1148 1150 1157 1166 1185 1271 1363 1374 1470
1497 1531 1556 1560 1590 1592 1616 1735 1743
1761 1882 1889 1892 1924 1932 1940 2008 2018
2096 2102 2108 2113 2139 2156 2170 2180 2210
2213 2241 2279 2468 2613 2632 2663 2693 2754

2758 2763 2767 2774 2791 2797 2802 2819 2823
3027 3095 3226 3237 3239 3244 3255 3262 3269
3278 3282 3284 3290 3298 3301 3307 3313 3330
3337 3339 3343 3345 3347 3350 3369 3380 3391
3401 3410 3412 3415 3417 3419 3428 3431 3433
3440 3443 3452 3455 3468 3732 3897 3919 3964
3984 3993 4051 4073 4085 4105 4114 4129 4163
4172 4181 4188 4194 4201 4211 4216 4231 4237
4246 4263 4362 4516 4518 4523 4531 4546 4608
4620 4700 4704 4707 4712 4753 4755 4761 4765
4854 4878 4898

the (12615) 1 1 3 4 6 9 10 12 14 15 17 18 21 27
28 30 31 32 35 37 38 42 43 44 54 55 60 64 67 71 72
75 77 79 82 83 86 97 100 101 102 106 107 109 113
115 121 123 125 127 129 130 131 135 138 141 148
152 154 158 160 167 168 169 171 172 174 181 182
189 193 194 195 205 206 209 211 212 214 216 217
218 220 223 224 225 227 231 233 234 235 237 238
242 243 244 245 246 248 250 256 258 265 266 267
268 269 274 281 282 283 297 298 306 307 310 311
312 313 314 315 316 319 320 321 322 324 326 327
328 329 330 331 333 336 337 338 340 344 345 347
348 349 352 355 366 367 371 373 374 381 388 392
393 395 397 400 401 402 403 406 412 413 415 420
421 422 425 428 433 437 441 450 454 457 459 467
473 476 477 478 479 483 485 491 492 494 497 505
507 511 516 520 523 529 530 531 532 535 540 541
543 544 547 549 556 561 562 565 570 573 574 575
576 578 582 594 595 600 601 606 607 611 612 614
618 620 621 628 629 630 631 634 643 650 652 653
654 655 656 658 659 660 661 662 663 664 667 669
672 674 675 676 678 681 682 683 688 695 696 700
701 708 709 713 714 715 722 725 727 730 735 741
742 743 **2** 6 7 9 11 12 15 18 24 25 29 30 32 34
38 43 44 46 50 53 59 61 62 67 68 69 70 73 74 75 82
83 84 85 87 101 111 118 121 128 129 133 136 141
144 145 149 151 153 154 155 157 158 159 161 163
164 170 176 178 179 181 184 187 190 193 195 197
199 200 201 203 205 206 210 212 213 215 217 223
226 233 241 243 244 246 248 260 265 266 269 270
271 274 275 278 279 283 288 290 291 292 293 296
297 298 299 300 301 302 304 308 309 310 311 313
315 317 320 321 323 326 327 328 330 336 337 338
342 345 346 347 348 350 357 361 362 364 366 368
370 372 375 378 380 381 382 386 387 390 391 392
395 396 399 406 408 416 417 422 424 427 428 429
431 435 437 438 440 445 447 448 **3** 1 3 4 7 12 13
15 17 26 27 29 30 31 32 33 34 36 45 47 49 51 56 58
59 65 66 70 77 80 92 97 98 101 102 105 106 107
108 109 110 115 117 118 120 124 126 129 130 131
133 137 138 142 148 149 153 154 155 158 159 160
163 164 165 166 174 175 178 181 185 186 195 205
206 208 210 211 214 219 224 226 229 232 235 241
243 247 249 250 251 252 259 260 265 267 268 270
271 272 273 274 276 277 278 279 280 283 286 289
290 291 294 297 298 300 302 304 307 308 313 318
324 326 334 337 339 342 346 350 356 359 360 361
362 363 368 370 371 372 379 391 392 395 398 405
406 407 408 409 410 416 420 423 424 425 426 427
428 437 440 441 442 443 447 448 452 453 455 461
465 468 473 474 477 480 481 486 489 491 492 493
496 500 501 504 **4** 1 6 7 8 12 13 15 17 18 21 22
23 24 25 30 31 32 42 46 47 49 50
51 52 53 59 60 62 64 66 68 69 70 72 73 74 75 76 77
78 80 84 85 89 90 92 93 94 99 100 101 102 104 105
106 107 108 109 110 111 113 117 118 120 126 127
129 130 132 133 134 140 143 145 146 150 152 154
155 157 158 159 160 161 162 165 172 173 174 179
181 183 184 197 198 201 203 206 207 208 209 211

212 216 218 219 220 222 223 224 225 227 230 233
234 237 238 241 242 243 247 249 253 255 256 257
259 260 261 265 266 267 270 271 272 273 274 275
277 278 279 280 285 286 292 293 294 296 297 299
300 301 303 304 306 308 309 310 312 317 319 320
321 322 328 329 334 335 341 342 345 347 350 355
356 361 364 367 369 372 373 374 375 378 380 382
383 384 385 386 387 389 390 391 392 394 395 398
399 401 402 403 405 406 408 415 416 418 419 421
422 423 424 427 430 432 433 434 436 440 444 445
449 452 455 456 457 458 459 461 463 464 467 468
469 472 473 474 475 477 479 480 482 485 486 487
490 494 495 496 498 500 503 504 506 507 521 524
525 526 528 536 537 539 540 541 542 543 544 545
549 **5** 2 3 4 5 10 11 12 13 14 17 18 23 25 29 30
32 34 36 37 38 39 40 41 44 45 46 47 48 52 54 56 57
60 61 66 69 71 76 78 79 80 86 89 98 99 100 103
104 106 111 117 124 128 133 134 137 138 139 140
143 149 151 152 169 171 172 181 185 186 192 198
200 201 203 204 205 207 210 213 214 219 221 223
230 232 233 237 243 246 248 260 263 267 268 269
270 275 276 277 280 290 291 295 296 297 300 301
302 304 305 306 311 316 318 319 320 322 323 325
326 328 330 332 334 338 339 341 342 344 347 349
350 351 352 353 362 363 365 367 369 370 371 374
375 376 377 378 379 382 384 385 386 390 392 393
394 395 396 397 401 413 414 415 416 417 418 419
421 422 433 434 435 436 438 439 440 443 444 445
447 448 450 453 455 457 458 459 462 463 465 467
470 471 473 476 478 483 487 494 495 496 498 502
504 505 507 509 514 517 518 520 523 524 527 528
529 533 539 543 549 550 551 553 554 555 556 560
562 563 565 570 571 **6** 1 9 11 12 13 14 17 19 20
21 27 30 31 32 38 45 46 47 51 52 53 54 56 57 58 59
65 69 75 78 79 80 82 97 100 101 108 109 113 119
126 130 134 136 137 141 149 153 154 157 159 160
161 168 169 177 178 183 184 186 188 190 198 200
206 207 208 212 216 217 218 229 232 239 243 244
245 248 249 251 252 255 256 257 258 264 265 266
269 270 272 276 278 279 280 283 284 285 286 292
308 310 316 318 319 321 323 329 332 333 334 335
338 347 348 350 351 352 353 354 359 360 361 363
366 367 368 372 373 377 379 380 381 382 385 390
394 396 397 399 400 401 402 403 406 407 416 417
418 421 422 424 425 427 429 430 433 437 438 439
440 441 442 445 446 448 451 459 464 465 473 474
478 487 489 490 491 495 496 498 500 501 504 505
508 513 514 515 516 517 519 521 522 523 524 529
534 536 537 539 541 543 544 546 549 551 552 553
554 559 561 563 564 565 567 568 571 574 575 576
577 578 579 581 582 584 585 591 592 593 596 603
604 605 606 608 609 610 611 614 615 616 619 622
626 631 632 633 634 635 636 637 638 640 642 643
652 657 659 661 663 665 672 673 676 677 679 680
693 699 700 709 713 717 720 722 723 724 725 727
728 730 733 738 739 742 743 744 745 746 747 748
749 750 752 756 758 759 760 761 762 766 769 771
772 776 780 786 787 789 790 791 792 793 797 799
800 801 802 805 810 815 819 820 821 822 824 825
826 830 833 839 840 841 843 845 849 850 856 857
858 860 861 862 865 868 875 876 877 878 880 884
885 887 891 892 900 906 907 909 910 911 913 914
919 921 923 930 931 934 937 939 942 945 946 947
949 952 953 957 958 963 964 966 967 973 974 975
977 980 983 984 985 988 989 990 993 995 998 1000
1009 1011 1012 1013 1015 1021 1022 1027 1028
1032 **7** 11 15 17 22 26 31 33 40 42 43 44 45 47
51 52 53 55 63 64 69 70 71 73 76 80 81 85 89 90 91
100 103 104 105 108 109 113 118 123 127 131 132

134 135 139 140 142 145 146 149 150 151 154 157
162 163 167 168 170 174 175 176 180 181 184 188
194 196 197 199 200 201 208 209 210 211 212 213
217 218 222 226 228 232 238 239 242 248 251 255
256 257 258 259 262 274 275 280 292 294 297 301
302 304 305 306 308 309 310 311 312 315 333 339
341 343 346 348 350 353 355 359 363 367 369 375
379 382 383 387 388 390 391 394 395 396 397 398
399 401 403 405 408 409 411 412 416 422 424 425
426 433 437 439 440 442 444 445 447 448 450 451
453 455 458 459 460 463 465 469 475 479 480 481
482 490 491 497 503 506 510 516 518 521 526 533
534 535 536 537 539 540 542 553 554 555 556 557
558 562 563 564 565 566 567 569 571 575 585 586
591 592 595 597 600 601 602 605 607 608 613 619
620 624 625 629 631 632 634 638 639 640 646 650
653 658 667 670 671 672 676 679 680 686 687 690
693 694 697 698 699 701 704 705 706 708 714 716
723 727 729 733 736 738 742 744 747 748 751 753
755 756 757 765 777 783 784 786 788 791 793 794
795 796 798 800 804 805 806 811 816 820 826 853
873 877 878 879 880 881 885 886 888 893 899 901
904 908 909 911 912 913 916 918 925 927 931 933
934 940 941 942 943 944 945 946 949 952 955 957
959 963 964 971 972 974 975 976 977 978 982 984
985 988 989 993 997 998 999 1001 1002 1003 1004
1005 1008 1010 1011 1015 1017 1019 1024 1025
1026 1027 1035 1036 1037 1038 1043 1051 1055
1059 1061 1064 1066 1068 1074 **8** 4 5 9 11 13 18
19 20 22 23 25 29 30 32 34 35 37 40 43 45 46 48 50
51 54 58 59 60 64 65 70 74 75 76 78 88 89 93 94 95
96 97 98 100 109 112 114 115 124 125 129 134 136
137 139 141 147 149 151 153 158 159 160 161 162
163 164 166 170 175 176 179 180 181 185 186 187
188 191 193 194 195 196 198 201 206 211 225 230
233 235 236 238 240 242 251 253 257 261 264 265
267 269 272 274 275 279 281 285 292 295 296 299
309 311 315 316 317 321 322 323 325 328 329 330
331 332 334 338 339 341 344 347 350 352 353 354
359 360 363 365 366 369 376 381 383 392 396 401
402 403 404 405 412 415 417 419 421 422 423 425
427 428 430 434 439 440 442 443 444 447 448 449
452 453 457 459 460 463 465 466 469 470 471 472
474 475 481 482 483 488 492 494 499 502 505 506
507 509 510 512 513 515 516 518 519 520 521 523
526 529 533 534 535 537 539 540 545 551 552 556
557 561 562 564 565 566 567 569 572 573 577 578
587 588 594 595 597 598 599 601 613 616 617 618
620 626 636 650 651 654 661 664 665 671 674 676
678 683 686 687 688 690 697 705 706 712 714 715
718 720 722 723 725 741 744 746 747 751 761 762
773 778 790 795 797 801 802 807 809 812 814 819
820 823 825 826 827 828 830 834 840 847 848 849
856 857 861 862 866 873 874 875 876 879 880 881
882 884 885 891 892 893 896 897 901 902 903 907
918 919 921 934 936 937 939 940 947 949 953 955
958 960 968 973 977 979 981 984 993 1000 1008
1010 1023 1027 1031 1033 1038 1039 1043 1045
1046 1047 1048 1049 1060 1064 1070 1072 1073
1075 1081 1082 1083 1088 1090 1092 1099 1103
1104 1106 1109 1111 1115 1118 1122 1124 1126
1129 1135 1136 1138 1142 1145 1148 1151 1153
1155 1156 1158 1160 1162 1166 1169 1170 1173
1178 1181 1191 **9** 1 6 7 11 12 13 27 30 37 38 44
48 51 52 53 60 61 62 63 64 65 67 68 69 77 82 84 85
89 95 102 103 104 105 106 107 108 109 110 130
131 134 139 142 150 151 155 156 157 159 160 161
164 165 166 167 168 169 171 172 174 178 179 181
184 185 187 188 214 218 225 229 230 236 238 243

247 248 249 250 251 252 253 254 255 257 258 259
268 271 282 289 292 301 302 310 311 317 326 329
330 331 338 342 344 345 349 350 353 356 359 361
365 366 373 375 377 378 380 381 383 388 390 391
393 394 396 400 402 407 409 411 413 418 423 424
427 432 436 438 441 442 443 458 459 460 462 463
464 465 466 467 469 471 475 477 478 479 480 481
482 486 487 493 497 498 499 503 504 508 513 515
518 519 523 525 528 529 542 549 552 559 565 566
573 581 583 585 586 588 589 592 598 600 602 606
609 610 615 616 621 622 625 626 633 635 636 637
639 640 650 657 658 664 666 667 669 672 673 674
676 680 682 684 692 713 722 732 740 741 743 746
749 750 751 753 756 758 760 766 779 780 781 784
785 796 800 802 804 806 807 815 817 818 825 829
832 833 834 836 837 839 840 841 842 843 844 846
850 851 862 863 864 865 866 867 868 869 870 873
877 879 880 881 882 896 899 911 912 921 923 924
927 928 929 930 931 932 933 939 940 942 944 947
949 957 958 959 963 965 966 970 972 981 983 984
987 989 990 995 997 998 999 1000 1002 1003 1004
1005 1006 1009 1012 1014 1018 1020 1022 1023
1024 1033 1037 1038 1039 1040 1041 1047 1048
1049 1051 1058 1069 1073 1074 1075 1076 1081
1082 1088 1089 1090 1091 1093 1101 1102 1108
1111 1115 1128 1129 1130 1131 1132 1134 1135
1138 1160 1161 1166 1167 1168 1189 1191 1192
1197 1206 1214 1218 1219 1221   **10**   1 2 4 8 9 10
16 17 20 26 30 31 37 40 43 47 48 52 53 59 63 68 73
81 85 86 87 89 93 97 99 101 104 **106** 107 110 114
115 116 118 119 120 122 125 128 **129** 131 132 133
135 136 138 141 143 144 145 146 **147** 149 153 157
158 160 162 164 165 166 172 177 **182** 185 186 187
190 195 201 210 211 212 213 217 **220** 224 225 237
239 240 250 251 253 254 258 260 261 268 270 271
275 283 285 290 295 296 297 299 300 303 307 315
317 320 321 325 326 327 328 334 341 342 350 352
354 364 365 368 373 375 378 380 381 383 385 395
398 402 403 406 407 409 411 415 416 418 420 421
423 424 426 432 433 436 438 443 444 447 448 454
461 465 468 470 471 472 473 476 478 484 488 491
497 498 499 501 502 504 506 507 513 514 515 520
521 527 531 532 533 542 545 546 550 552 553 554
555 556 558 562 567 568 569 570 574 575 580 582
588 591 594 596 597 598 599 601 602 604 606 625
626 627 628 629 630 632 634 643 644 645 646 651
653 657 658 662 666 673 675 676 681 691 698 699
703 708 713 718 719 723 728 729 730 733 742 744
745 746 748 749 750 754 758 759 765 771 773 774
775 776 777 779 781 785 790 800 801 802 805 806
813 815 818 821 823 825 826 830 833 836 837 842
848 850 856 859 863 867 886 888 895 899 902 905
916 920 924 928 930 932 933 934 935 937 938 942
945 946 947 949 951 957 960 963 965 968 970 973
975 980 985 987 991 993 997 1004 1005 1007 1008
1009 1010 1014 1015 1022 1023 1026 1027 1031
1034 1036 1038 1041 1043 1045 1046 1054 1061
1063 1071 1073 1074 1080 1082 1083 1086 1093
1098 1103 1105 1109 1110 1111 1115 1118 1123
1125 1126 1127 1128 1130 1131 1132 1134 1136
1138 1139 1141 1142 1143 1146 1147 1148 1151
1152 1154 1156 1159 1160 1163 1165 1166 1168
1171 1177 1178 1179 1180 1181 1183 1187 1190
1191 1192 1193 1195 1197 1200 1202 1205 1207
1208 1209 1210 1211 1212 1216 1217 1218 1219
1223 1224 1225 1226 1229 1231 1232 1233 1234
1235 1240 1242 1243 1245 1246 1247 1248 1250
1258 1262 1263 1265 1266 1268 1272 1273 1276
1279 1280 1281   **11**   1 6 10 13 21 34 64 65 70 72

74 75 84 86 89 90 92 108 116 117 118 122 139 156
164 173 178 198 206 208 213 214 216 217 219 220
223 231 240 242 244 254 257 260 263 264 265 269
275 276 277 286 291 292 293 294 299 304 306 310
313 324 325 328 330 337 340 341 353 354 378 382
383 384 389 392 397 407 418 420 421 432 433 438
440 443 451 453 454 458 460 461 462 463 466 467
471 472 477 478 480 483 485 486 487 488 489 498
507 508 515 516 520 527 531 532 536 538 544 546
547 549 556 558 559 564 569 574 575 576 577 580
582 589 591 592 600 601 602 612 614 615 617 619
624 633 635 637 639 641 646 652 660 670 671 672
674 679 682 686 690 692 693 697 698 701 707 708
711 715 721 722 723 726 748 749 761 764 765 766
767 784 787 789 790 793 796 804 819 820 821 824
826 828 835 837 839 841 845 849 851 856 866 869
870 877 883 901 902 903 904 905 913 915 921 923
926 927 928 931 934 936 938 942 943 946 949 954
956 958 959 963 971 973 975 976 981 982 998 1006
1014 1020 1022 1025 1028 1034 1035 1042 1044
1047 1050 1061 1062 1063 1064 1072 1074 1077
1078 1081 1093 1097 1105 1108 1112 1113 1122
1123 1130 1132 1134 1139 1140 1142 1143 1144
1151 1153 1164 1171 1172 1173 1177 1178 1183
1184 1187 1190 1192 1198 1199 1200 1206 1207
1210 1220 1228 1230 1231 1240 1243 1248 1250
1251 1252 1253 1254 1255 1257 1259 1260 1266
1267 1268 1281 1287 1291   **12**   1 3 8 9 10 13 14
16 17 20 21 23 24 25 26 30 34 35 36 37 40 44 45 46
47 48 49 50 51 57 58 60 62 63 64 67 68 69 71 72 73
74 75 76 77 79 83 84 85 86 88 91 95 102 105 111
112 113 116 117 118 119 120 121 123 124 125 126
133 134 135 136 137 138 140 144 147 149 151 156
158 159 160 162 164 166 167 169 172 173 175 177
181 184 185 186 189 190 192 193 194 196 198 201
206 207 210 211 214 216 217 218 219 221 222 223
226 227 229 231 234 237 238 239 241 242 243 245
246 249 250 251 252 254 263 264 269 270 281 282
283 285 286 287 288 289 290 292 293 294 295 296
297 298 299 300 303 309 312 316 328 332 335 338
339 340 341 342 343 344 345 346 347 348 351 352
354 355 357 358 360 361 363 365 366 367 368 369
370 372 375 377 379 384 385 393 395 396 398 399
400 401 403 405 408 409 410 412 426 432 433 435
441 444 445 446 449 451 452 459 460 461 465 467
469 470 471 472 473 474 475 476 477 479 480 481
482 484 485 488 489 490 491 492 494 495 497 498
500 501 504 506 507 508 509 510 511 512 513 514
515 516 517 518 519 523 524 525 526 527 528 529
530 531 532 533 535 536 537 538 540 542 545 547
548 549 550 553 554 556 557 558 559 569 570 573
574 580 583 585 586 587 588 592 593 596 597 598
601 602 606 607 608 609 611 612 615 617 618 619
620 621 623 624 629 630 631 632 633 634 636 637
638 641 643 646 647 648 649 650 652 653 654 655
656 659 661 662 663 665 666 667 668 669 670 671
679 680 683 684 685 686 693 694 695 696 697 701
703 706 708 709 710 712 713 714 715 717 719 721
722 724 725 727 728 729 730 732 733 734 735 736
737 748 754 758 762 763 764 766 767 770 771 772
773 774 775 781 784 787 789 790 791 792 793 794
796 801 802 804 805 806 807 808 809 812 813 814
815 816 817 818 821 823 828 829 830 831 832 833
834 837 839 843 844 845 851 852 854 858 860 861
862 866 867 868 870 872 873 874 880 882 884 885
889 891 893 897 898 899 901 902 903 905 906 907
909 910 913 916 917 918 920 921 923 925 927 928
929 930 931 932 933 934 935 936 937 945 947 948
949 952 955 956 957 958 961 965 966 968 969 970

972 974 975 976 978 980 981 983 985 986 989 993
996 997 998 999 1000 1001 1003 1004 1005 1006
1008 1010 1015 1018 1019 1022 1023 1027 1028
1033 1034 1038 1039 1048 1049 1051 1052 1055
1058 1061 1064 1065 1066 1067 1068 1070 1072
1080 1081 1086 1087 1089 1090 1092 1094 1096
1099 1100 1101 1103 1106 1107 1110 1111 1112
1113 1114 1116 1117 1118 1119 1121 1122 1123
1124 1125 1126 1127 1128 1129 1132 1133 1134
1135 1136 1137 1141 1142 1144 1146 1148 1150
1156 1157 1161 1162 1163 1165 1166 1168 1173
1180 1181 1183 1185 1186 1187 1189 1190 1192
1193 1194 1197 1198 1199 1203 1208 1211 1212
1213 1219 1227 1229 1230 1231 1233 1235 1237
1238 1239 1242 1243 1247 1248 1249 1250 1253
1254 1256 1259 1260 1262 1263 1264 1267 1268
1275 1278 1279 1280 1283 1285 1286 1287 1288
1289 1291 1292 1295 1296 1297 1298 1300 1302
1303 1304 1305 1306 1307 1308 1309 1311 1313
1314 1315 1318 1321 1322 1323 1327 1329 1330
1331 1333 1334 1336 1338 1339 1342 1343 1344
1346 1347 1348 1349 1351 1352 1354 1355 1356
1357 1358 1360 1361 1364 1365 1366 1367 1369
1370 1371 1372 1373 1374 1375 1377 1378 1379
1380 1381 1385 1390 1391 1392 1393 1394 1396
1398 1399 1400 1402 1404 1406 1417 1422 1425
1426 1430 1432 1433 1434 1437 1440 1441 1442
1443 1444 1445 1447 1449 1450 1451 1452 1453
1454 1455 1456 1458 1459 1460 1461 1462 1463
1465 1466 1469 1473 1477 1479 1482 1485 1486
1489 1491 1493 1494 1496 1497 1498 1499 1504
1507 1508 1509 1510 1512 1514 1515 1516 1517
1518 1519 1520 1521 1522 1523 1524 1525 1526
1527 1528 1529 1530 1531 1532 1535 1536 1539
1541 1542 1545 1546 1547 1551 1552 1555 1556
1559 1561 1562 1565 1566 1567 1568 1569 1571
1574 1575 1576 1577 1578 1579 1581 1582 1585
1586 1588 1589 1590 1591 1593 1595 1597 1598
1602 1604 1605 1606 1607 1611 1618 1619 1623
1624 1627 1628 1631 1634 1636 1637 1638 1639
1640 1642 1651 1652 1654 1657 1659 1661 1662
1665 1666 1672 1674 1676 1678 1679 1681 1682
1683 1685 1686 1687 1688 1690 1703 1705 1708
1710 1711 1714 1721 1722 1724 1726 1727 1728
1729 1730 1731 1732 1733 1734 1735 1736 1737
1738 1754 1756 1762 1765 1766 1769 1770 1771
1772 1773 1774 1775 1776 1777 1779 1781 1782
1783 1784 1785 1789 1792 1795 1796 1797 1798
1799 1805 1807 1810 1811 1815 1817 1820 1821
1822 1823 1824 1825 1827 1829 1830 1831 1832
1834 1835 1837 1838 1839 1840 1841 1843 1845
1848 1849 1850 1854 1855 1856 1857 1859 1861
1863 1865 1866 1868 1869 1871 1872 1873 1874
1876 1877 1878 1880 1882 1883 1885 1886 1891
1892 1897 1898 1899 1904 1906 1907 1909 1911
1912 1913 1916 1917   **13**   1 2 3 4 5 6 7 8 9 10 12
13 15 18 20 21 24 29 32 36 37 38 44 46 47 48 49 52
55 57 59 60 61 64 74 76 80 85 93 94 100 101 104
106 107 110 112 117 120 124 127 130 132 133 134
135 137 139 141 142 143 144 148 151 152 154 155
157 159 162 163 164 169 172 177 178 179 181 182
184 189 190 192 194 195 196 197 201 202 204 205
213 215 218 219 220 226 227 228 232 233 237 246
247 248 254 255 258 263 264 267 269 272 275 276
279 281 282 283 284 286 287 288 290 291 293 294
295 298 299 301 302 303 305 306 307 310 319 320
321 322 324 325 328 329 330 331 332 333 334 335
339 341 343 345 347 348 349 350 352 353 354 355
362 363 364 365 367 368 369 370 371 372 377 378

723 725 727 729 731 733 737 742 743 744 745 746
749 750 751 752 756 757 759 761 763 764 767 768
770 773 774 775 777 779 780 781 782 785 788 791
792 794 796 805 806 807 808 809 810 812 813 816
817 819 827 828 830 833 835 838 839 840 841 844
845 847 850 853 854 855 859 860 861 863 865 866
867 868 870 872 874 876 879 882 886 889 890 895
900 902 903 904 906 907 908 909 911 912 913 914
916 919 922 923 924 926 930 931 933 936 938 939
940 942 944 945 947 951 952 957 958 959 960 962
964 965 966 967 968 969 970 971 973 974 975 976
978 983 984 986 988 991 992 993 997 998 1000
1001 1002 1004 1006 1007 1010 1013 1014 1016
1017 1019 1021 1022 1023 1026 1027 1030 1032
1034 1035 1037 1038 1039 1040 1043 1044 1045
1046 1047 1048 1050 1052 1059 1060 1061 1062
1063 1066 1067 1068 1070 1072 1074 1075 1076
1077 1078 1079 1080 1081 1083 1089 1095 1097
1101 1102 1103 1106 1107 1109 1114 1117 1118
1121 1122 1124 1126 1127 1128 1129 1130 1131
1133 1135 1139 1144 1145 1146 1147 1149 1152
1153 1154 1155 1156 1158 1159 1161 1167 1171
1172 1175 1177 1178 1179 1181 1183 1184 1185
1186 1188 1190 1193 1197 1198 1199 1200 1201
1202 1204 1205 1207 1209 1210 1211 1212 1213
1214 1217 1218 1219 1222 1223 1224 1225 1227
1228 1230 1232 1234 1235 1236 1237 1242 1244
1245 1246 1258 1262 1267 1268 1270 1274 1276
1283 1285 1286 1292 1293 1296 1297 1305 1306
1307 1311 1319 1321 1323 1324 1328 1329 1331
1332 1333 1334 1337 1338 1339 1342 1343 1344
1345 1346 1347 1349 1350 1351 1352 1353 1354
1360 1361 1362 1363 1366 1368 1369 1371 1372
1373 1374 1376 1377 1378 1379 1380 1381 1382
1383 1384 1385 1389 1390 1391 1392 1395 1397
1400 1402 1403 1406 1407 1408 1410 1412 1416
1422 1423 1425 1426 1427 1429 1430 1432 1433
1436 1437 1440 1441 1443 1444 1446 1447 1448
1449 1451 1452 1457 1458 1459 1462 1464 1465
1466 1467 1468 1469 1470 1472 1474 1476 1477
1479 1480 1482 1483 1484 1485 1486 1487 1489
1490 1492 1494 1495 1496 1497 1498 1499 1500
1501 1503 1504 1507 1509 1510 1511 1512 1514
1515 1516 1517 1518 1519 1520 1521 1522 1524
1525 1526 1527 1529 1530 1531 1533 1534 1535
1537 1539 1540 1542 1543 1544 1545 1546 1549
1550 1552 1556 1557 1558 1559 1560 1561 1562
1564 1568 1570 1572 1580 1583 1585 1588 1590
1592 1594 1595 1596 1598 1599 1600 1602 1603
1604 1606 1607 1608 1610 1611 1612 1613 1616
1618 1620 1622 1624 1626 1627 1630 1631 1632
1633 1634 1635 1637 1638 1642 1645 1647 1648
1649 1650 1653 1655 1657 1659 1660 1661 1662
1663 1665 1667 1669 1671 1674 1676 1678 1679
1682 1683 1685 1691 1693 1694 1695 1696 1697
1698 1700 1702 1703 1704 1707 1708 1710 1711
1713 1714 1715 1718 1725 1727 1728 1729 1730
1731 1734 1736 1737 1739 1741 1747 1748 1749
1752 1754 1756 1758 1759 1760 1762 1763 1765
1767 1768 1770 1771 1772 1773 1774 1775 1777
1778 1780 1781 1782 1785 1786 1790 1791 1792
1793 1794 1795 1796 1797 1798 1799 1801 1803
1804 1809 1811 1813 1820 1821 1823 1825 1828
1830 1831 1835 1836 1838 1840 1842 1843 1845
1848 1850 1853 1854 1855 1856 1857 1858 1860
1863 1864 1867 1874 1875 1877 1881 1883 1886
1887 1890 1891 1892 1893   **17** 3 5 8 9 11 13 15
16 17 25 28 29 30 31 32 34 35 39 40 44 47 51 57 58
60 63 65 71 72 75 76 80 84 85 87 88 89 92 93 94 95

96 102 103 104 106 109 112 113 114 115 116 117
119 120 121 122 124 125 126 127 129 131 133 136
137 140 141 143 144 145 148 149 151 155 157 158
160 161 162 167 168 170 171 172 174 176 177 180
181 182 184 186 187 188 189 191 193 194 195 197
202 210 211 213 225 226 227 228 229 230 238 239
243 244 245 246 247 249 250 251 252 255 258 259
260 262 265 266 267 268 269 272 273 275 281 284
289 294 296 298 302 309 310 314 315 317 319 324
325 327 332 333 335 336 338 339 340 343 344 346
353 356 357 358 359 361 364 365 366 369 373 374
375 378 379 384 386 390 393 394 410 411 418 420
421 422 425 428 430 431 432 434 435 440 441 443
444 445 450 451 452 455 457 459 461 463 464 465
467 468 469 470 471 473 474 477 479 481 483 484
485 486 490 495 497 499 500 501 506 509 510 516
517 520 522 532 542 543 545 546 547 550 551 552
553 555 565 566 567 568 572 573 578 580 581 602
603 623 624 626 627 629 630 631 636 639 640 642
646 648 649 654 655 663 668 671 675 679 681 683
684 688 699 709 711 712 718 720 724 731 732 733
735 736 738 741 742 745 748 749 753 754 756 758
759 765 767 768 770 771 772 773 774 777 778 780
786 787 789 790 791 792 795 798 801 809 810 812
829 833 838 841 842 843 844 845 846 847 848 855
861 862 872 876 878 879 881 890 892 894 897 899
900 901 907 911 912 913 914 915 916 917 921 926
927 931 932 933 937 938 943 945 947 949 951 952
953 954 957 958 962 963 964 965 966 967 968 969
970 973 975 976 977 979 980 981 983 985 989 990
991 995 996 997 998 1000 1003 1004 1005 1009
1013 1014 1015 1019 1020 1021 1022 1032 1033
1034 1036 1037 1038 1042 1043 1045 1046 1048
1051 1052 1054 1058 1059 1060 1061 1063 1068
1071 1072 1074 1077 1079 1080 1081 1083 1084
1086 1088 1089 1097 1101 1102 1103 1106 1107
1108 1109 1110 1112 1113 1114 1115 1116 1117
1118 1120 1121 1122 1125 1126 1128 1129 1130
1131 1132 1137 1140 1141 1142 1146 1147 1148
1149 1151 1153 1155 1156 1157 1162 1165 1166
1167 1168 1173 1177 1183 1189 1193 1195 1196
1197 1199 1200 1201 1203 1205 1206 1207 1208
1211 1212 1213 1214 1215 1216 1220 1221 1222
1223 1224 1226 1227 1235 1236 1237 1241 1243
1244 1247 1257 1260 1261 1262 1263 1264 1266
1267 1268 1270 1271 1272 1275 1279 1281 1282
1283 1284 1285 1287 1288 1289 1293 1296 1302
1306 1309 1315 1316 1317 1318 1321 1323 1325
1326 1327 1328 1331 1333 1335 1336 1342 1343
1344 1347 1348 1357 1359 1375 1382 1400 1401
1402 1403 1404 1405 1406 1407 1408 1411 1413
1414 1415 1417 1421 1423 1424 1428 1432 1434
1436 1438 1439 1440 1441 1443 1447 1448 1452
1453 1454 1455 1479 1481 1482 1483 1484 1485
1486 1488 1489 1490 1491 1493 1495 1502 1506
1512 1515 1517 1518 1519 1523 1546 1551 1553
1557 1579 1585 1586 1590 1606 1609 1610 1612
1617 1620 1621 1622 1623 1624 1626 1627 1636
1637 1638 1639 1640 1642 1643 1644 1646 1648
1649 1650 1652 1653 1654 1656 1658 1662 1663
1666 1667 1668 1669 1670 1675 1677 1684 1685
1686 1689 1691 1692 1693 1695 1696 1699 1700
1703 1704 1707 1710 1711 1714 1715 1716 1719
1720 1721 1724 1726 1727 1728 1729 1731 1740
1741 1744 1746 1751 1755 1756 1757 1760 1762
1763 1766 1767 1772 1773 1774 1777 1781 1782
1784 1785 1789 1798 1799 1803 1808 1815 1819
1824 1827 1838 1839 1844 1845 1850 1851 1854
1855 1856 1861 1865 1868 1870 1872 1873 1876

1879 1880 1882 1891 1897 1899 1900 1901 1911
1913 1914 1916 1918 1919 1921 1924 1925 1931
1936 1937 1938 1939 1944 1945 1946 1949 1950
1951 1952 1957 1961 1964 1966 1974 1975 1976
1977 1978 1982 1983 1984 1985 1986 1987 1988
1989 1990 1992 1993 1994 1995 1997 1999 2000
2002 2010 2011 2012 2013 2014 2015 2017 2018
2019 2023 2029 2030 2031 2032 2034 2037 2038
2039 2040 2041 2045 2046 2047 2048 2049 2050
2053 2054 2055 2057 2061 2068 2070 2077 2079
2082 2084 2085 2088 2097 2105 2107 2109 2110
2111 2112 2113 2116 2117 2119 2123 2124 2127
2128 2133 2135 2138 2141 2143 2144 2147 2149
2150 2157 2159 2163 2167 2170 2181 2186 2188
2189 2192 2197 2198 2208 2209 2210 2212 2213
2214 2215 2216 2217 2220 2222 2223 2224 2225
2226 2229 2230 2231 2241 2250 2251 2252 2253
2254 2255 2257 2261 2262 2265 2267 2269 2272
2274 2275 2276 2278 2279 2280 2284 2286 2287
2290 2294 2295 2296 2298 2303 2304 2308 2309
2313 2315 2316 2317 2318 2322 2323 2324 2325
2326 2328 2329   **18** 2 8 9 18 21 22 25 26 27 30
31 32 33 34 37 42 43 45 46 47 48 49 53 55 57 58 59
63 68 71 72 73 75 77 78 79 80 82 84 86 88 89 91 92
95 100 101 108 109 112 114 115 116 119 121 123
126 129 130 131 132 133 134 136 139 140 143 144
145 146 148 150 151 155 156 157 161 162 163 169
171 172 174 178 180 182 184 185 188 189 194 196
197 198 199 201 205 207 208 211 212 213 216 219
220 223 225 226 228 233 234 236 238 241 242 243
246 247 250 254 255 257 258 260 261 263 264 265
266 267 268 270 271 272 274 275 277 281 285 286
287 289 290 291 292 294 295 296 301 304 305 307
308 309 310 313 316 317 319 323 328 329 330 333
334 335 336 340 341 343 344 345 346 350 351 352
353 354 357 358 359 360 361 362 364 368 370 372
374 377 378 380 381 382 385 387 388 390 391 393
394 395 398 399 400 401 402 403 406 409 410 411
414 415 417 418 420 421 422 423 424 426 427 428
430 435 437 440 442 445 446 447 449 450 451 452
455 456 457 458 459 460 461 464 465 466 469 470
471 472 474 477 481 482 483 485 486 487 488 494
496 497 499 501 502 504 506 507 508 512 513 514
516 517 520 522 523 524 528 530 531 533 537 539
540 545 546 548 550 552 553 555 556 557 559 561
562 563 566 567 568 569 571 572 573 574 576 578
579 580 581 582 583 586 589 590 592 593 594 596
597 598 599 600 602 603 605 607 608 609 610 611
613 614 617 619 620 625 626 629 630 631 632 633
635 636 637 639 640 641 642 643 644 645 647 648
649 650 651 653 654 657 658 662 663 664 665 669
670 671 675 676 680 681 683 684 685 686 687 688
689 692 695 696 697 698 700 702 703 704 705 708
711 712 713 717 718 719 723 724 729 731 732 739
741 742 744 747 748 749 750 751 754 755 756 759
760 761 763 764 766 767 768 769 772 773 776 778
779 780 781 782 783 784 785 786 788 790 791 792
793 794 795 797 798 803 808 809 811 812 813 814
816 817 819 826 827 829 830 831 832 833 834 837
838 839 842 847 848 849 851 852 853 854 856 857
858 859 860 861 862 863 868 871 872 874 876 878
880 884 885 895 898 899 900 907 910 911 913 915
917 918 919 921 922 923 924 927 931 932 933 934
937 941 942 945 948 949 951 953 954 955 956 957
958 959 962 963 965 969 971 973 974 975 976 980
982 983 984 985 989 990 991 995 997 999 1000
1002 1003 1004 1007 1008 1009 1010 1011 1012
1014 1016 1018 1019 1022 1028 1029 1030 1032
1034 1035 1036 1038 1039 1040 1041 1042 1045

1046 1047 1048 1049 1051 1052 1054 1058 1060
1061 1063 1067 1068 1069 1070 1071 1074 1077
1078 1079 1082 1083 1085 1086 1089 1090 1091
1093 1094 1096 1097 1098 1106 1107 1110 1112
1114 1116 1117 1118 1119 1120 1121 1123 1124
1126 1131 1132 1133 1135 1136 1138 1139 1144
1145 1148 1149 1151 1155 1158 1161 1164 1165
1166 1168 1170 1173 1182 1185 1186 1187 1188
1192 1193 1194 1198 1199 1201 1204 1205 1207
1211 1212 1218 1219 1220 1221 1226 1227 1228
1230 1231 1232 1233 1237 1238 1241 1243 1246
1247 1252 1254 1257 1258 1260 1261 1262 1263
1265 1266 1269 1274 1279 1285 1286 1289 1291
1292 1296 1299 1300 1306 1307 1308 1309 1310
1312 1314 1317 1318 1319 1330 1335 1336 1337
1341 1343 1346 1347 1348 1355 1357 1358 1359
1360 1361 1363 1365 1370 1372 1373 1375 1376
1380 1382 1384 1388 1395 1396 1397 1401 1404
1405 1409 1410 1411 1412 1414 1415 1417 1418
1419 1421 1422 1425 1426 1427 1428 1431 1435
1439 1444 1446 1447 1450 1451 1452 1453 1456
1458 1459 1460 1461 1462 1464 1465 1467 1468
1469 1471 1473 1475 1476 1477 1479 1480 1481
1482 1483 1484 1487 1488 1489 1490 1491 1493
1495 1497 1498 1499 1501 1502 1504 1505 1512
1516 1517 1520 1529 1532 1536 1539 1540 1541
1542 1543 1544 1545 1546 1549 1551 1553 1554
1555 1556 1558 1559 1560 1561 1563 1566 1567
1569 1571 1572 1573 1574 1576 1578 1580 1581
1583 1585 1586 1587 1588 1589 1590 1591 1592
1594 1595 1596 1597 1598 1599 1600 1601 1602
1603 1604

the (166) 1 241 258 260 362 568 584 586 590
592 597 598 2 66 78 79 284 294 3 22 24 202
261 384 4 346 369 513 514 5 281 6 147 165
187 355 670 730 7 243 244 246 247 253 295 314
320 323 327 427 582 617 750 768 770 829 832 833
838 848 856 857 859 862 864 865 866 867 868 869
8 63 68 183 222 550 748 749 778 1055 1070 1074
9 24 97 115 266 550 616 637 798 808 1043 1063
1143 1147 1150 1173 1223 10 161 446 524 557
591 608 612 793 838 11 226 322 552 617 1289
12 28 362 417 419 420 425 427 515 1397 1801
13 1060 1175 14 405 406 407 15 1024 1125
16 980 1248 1253 1738 17 400 423 641 644
804 805 806 807 813 821 822 828 1367 1373 1380
1385 1395 1416

the (731) 15 8 30 33 35 40 41 50 62 63 73 74 99
100 124 126 127 132 133 134 135 136 137 139 140
141 142 145 147 148 149 150 155 157 158 164 173
175 186 191 192 196 214 247 248 250 251 256 260
285 288 300 335 340 352 356 357 361 366 387 415
482 485 487 500 506 518 536 577 604 606 607 613
620 649 651 653 667 668 669 672 673 674 690 705
726 729 742 744 746 752 759 770 785 793 807 808
814 832 852 857 863 896 900 902 907 908 909 910
911 912 914 915 917 918 919 920 928 929 933 960
967 986 987 988 992 994 996 999 1026 1109 1117
1129 1139 1140 1143 1163 1164 1168 1178 1182
1191 1197 1204 1208 1247 1263 1265 1266 1267
1268 1281 1316 1318 1324 1326 1327 1332 1341
1373 1376 1399 1400 1401 1402 1403 1404 1405
1407 1408 1411 1413 1414 1415 1418 1419 1420
1422 1423 1424 1425 1426 1436 1437 1438 1439
1440 1443 1444 1448 1469 1477 1491 1492 1499
1508 1513 1519 1546 1547 1549 1550 1552 1554
1565 1572 1573 1576 1577 1578 1580 1585 1586
1595 1601 1606 1607 1609 1703 1704 1707 1710
1739 1748 1823 1842 1850 1871 1885 1887 1888

1902 1919 1929 1930 1954 1955 1960 1993 1994
2012 2015 2016 2017 2021 2027 2031 2032 2034
2039 2040 2041 2047 2048 2049 2052 2053 2055
2063 2066 2072 2073 2075 2076 2083 2085 2115
2148 2149 2150 2153 2159 2162 2168 2174 2175
2177 2178 2179 2183 2186 2211 2212 2216 2252
2261 2262 2273 2274 2277 2281 2286 2289 2290
2292 2300 2303 2305 2308 2405 2406 2436 2460
2467 2476 2483 2485 2489 2491 2492 2500 2513
2575 2602 2611 2612 2629 2630 2631 2655 2683
2684 2697 2698 2699 2705 2708 2712 2722 2724
2727 2734 2736 2743 2751 2770 2789 2809 2829
2847 2851 2854 2871 2926 2947 3046 3047 3128
3156 3161 3168 3219 3220 3221 3224 3225 3232
3242 3305 3328 3341 3361 3374 3377 3378 3382
3384 3397 3408 3411 3414 3416 3418 3442 3456
3460 3470 3475 3500 3502 3504 3506 3525 3530
3538 3542 3548 3549 3551 3553 3562 3565 3568
3570 3575 3583 3584 3589 3590 3619 3620 3621
3622 3628 3629 3640 3642 3649 3667 3668 3673
3674 3723 3729 3730 3738 3757 3769 3795 3809
3821 3823 3831 3846 3856 3876 3880 3905 3911
3945 3950 3951 3953 3954 3958 3974 3976 3977
3978 3980 3981 3982 3983 3988 3995 4005 4013
4015 4016 4020 4021 4026 4027 4028 4029 4030
4032 4033 4048 4054 4058 4078 4081 4091 4099
4112 4113 4122 4157 4166 4173 4180 4206 4210
4225 4238 4243 4244 4256 4257 4260 4261 4264
4271 4284 4285 4310 4312 4314 4315 4316 4317
4318 4319 4320 4322 4324 4325 4326 4327 4330
4335 4338 4339 4344 4345 4350 4354 4356 4358
4360 4365 4366 4367 4388 4405 4413 4418 4423
4449 4450 4464 4476 4486 4508 4532 4543 4548
4549 4550 4554 4556 4579 4606 4612 4615 4622
4628 4665 4666 4673 4674 4676 4679 4681 4682
4688 4690 4691 4694 4696 4697 4703 4705 4709
4714 4722 4748 4749 4771 4775 4782 4786 4801
4806 4813 4817 4819 4826 4838 4860 4861 4887
4888 4902 4905 4908 4910 4911 4912 4914 4916
4917 4922 4927 4936 4937 4945 4946 4949 4956
4960

THE (13) 15 846 1560 2180 3027 4438 4442 4458
4475 4514 4559 4635 4707 4712

Theatre (7) 9 1131 17 420 435 2080 2138
2257 18 1038
Theatre (1) 15 1019
theatre (8) 5 363 6 184 8 600 11 1057
12 1846 14 898 15 3322 17 145
theatre (1) 15 1575
theatres (2) 16 1655 18 1040
thee (25) 3 264 9 375 1210 1211 11 17 248
14 762 1074 1075 1076 1406 1410 1420 1429 1433
1482 15 375 2437 2626 2688 2689 2691 3068
18 1427
thee (7) 6 853 7 471 9 96 11 344 402
13 312 17 1783
Theeee (1) 15 2694
thees (1) 9 448
theft (1) 17 2182
Their (32) 2 37 111 196 367 371 3 306 332
5 214 215 378 464 6 25 313 442 7 305 948
8 35 402 1034 9 255 279 12 446 553 1197
1366 13 586 762 791 1125 15 3183
16 993 17 432
Their (1) 8 782
Their (3) 15 414 590 4676
their (622) 1 166 225 246 275 316 405 408 571
651 654 664 2 25 29 36 37 40 47 85 95 96 116
120 122 156 159 171 196 202 300 303 308 314 350

362 365 366 369 371 372 3 30 70 113 118 127
193 194 213 214 215 218 274 277 296 300 302 307
313 319 343 370 388 462 466 490 4 47 95 138
159 162 365 479 483 5 23 216 217 218 220 224
290 328 335 343 353 354 357 358 408 409 416 426
454 561 6 29 37 91 100 140 172 173 210 228 278
386 388 390 428 485 486 509 524 633 656 658 678
683 709 711 719 721 761 864 907 910 921 936 1004
7 11 17 163 305 432 466 489 526 689 778 834 912
935 956 1002 1013 1017 1023 1025 1026 1044
8 3 31 61 76 77 124 126 324 391 393 399 407 408
410 412 428 437 461 526 546 555 604 656 724 727
948 1108 1115 1157 9 36 66 155 157 239 256 281
283 357 377 400 447 465 468 486 531 674 683 777
786 853 1129 1193 10 14 72 146 187 188 245
311 340 341 404 412 450 589 651 652 688 795 802
806 818 1003 1004 1007 1062 1126 1132 11 109
110 111 119 160 162 177 186 192 380 528 582 639
676 686 695 850 852 874 934 942 961 974 1018
1054 1103 1116 1143 1269 12 76 99 114 160 244
282 285 353 442 461 537 543 544 546 550 588 590
598 643 652 653 656 680 687 694 713 864 1024
1132 1134 1136 1181 1191 1196 1204 1238 1278
1323 1328 1348 1366 1408 1450 1593 1646
1714 1720 1776 1781 1815 13 18 19 55 94 103
238 240 305 351 357 375 376 404 452 469 505 530
571 576 604 687 750 804 812 819 888 904 913 950
957 974 1003 1028 1031 1089 1183 1186 1187 1189
14 36 168 181 202 217 224 235 258 265 278 342
350 387 388 468 472 488 528 544 547 606 608 641
643 645 652 675 678 690 691 692 699 711 716 849
850 852 869 939 949 1095 1116 1146 1191 1280
1321 1328 1332 1346 1358 1361 1368 1380 1382
1387 1399 1416 1420 1436 15 1369 1391 1392
1395 1396 1397 1529 2362 2364 2412 2422 2447
2452 2456 2817 2862 3081 3122 3184 3322 3358
4052 4402 4479 16 7 16 103 122 240 265 311
336 475 480 544 562 574 583 776 852 874 1001
1006 1032 1034 1051 1091 1203 1213 1214 1264
1303 1307 1309 1319 1328 1370 1398 1486 1507
1508 1532 1536 1548 1563 1580 1631 1633 1688
1692 1705 1732 1767 1831 1835 1852 1889
17 11 18 24 27 43 61 70 142 154 155 178 180 204
262 294 388 446 449 466 477 525 527 532 548 739
748 751 755 756 758 769 797 893 907 971 1001
1083 1105 1106 1112 1150 1187 1188 1192 1222
1224 1359 1574 1876 2180 2228 2242 18 88 127
232 290 291 369 387 394 396 401 409 583 599 609
631 632 669 679 687 691 709 710 725 726 868 884
886 936 1028 1059 1159 1221 1236 1242 1271 1276
1278 1323 1334 1343 1371 1389 1392 1414 1419
1541 1543 1565 1568 1587 1594

their (7) 7 321 839 865 8 778 9 1224
16 1894 17 413
their (55) 15 37 48 50 60 61 86 179 413 580 590
604 684 916 919 926 1147 1151 1269 1325 1341
1415 1419 1446 1460 1492 1747 1749 1905 1939
2019 2020 2022 2214 2537 3238 3302 3453 3955
3979 4056 4058 4061 4062 4063 4064 4077 4331
4421 4551 4678 4920
theirhisnothis (1) 17 1184
Theirs (1) 15 4397
theirs (4) 2 367 6 723 13 751 16 1386
THEM (1) 7 1071
Them (3) 5 285 10 595 16 655
them (649) 1 79 98 117 118 120 121 149 151
205 331 434 506 513 514 520 528 533 543 572 580
600 602 662 2 22 23 46 50 120 131 134 136 137
210 230 234 303 314 369 388 410 442 446 3 5 6

20 45 107 110 143 152 206 248 264 292 299 307
343 344 345 347 404   4   26 27 40 98 142 178 182
203 204 212 213 244 250 351 405 433   5   31 69 70
225 235 301 328 335 344 350 359 383 390 422 564
6   15 122 126 204 226 253 373 387 393 435 484
502 504 515 524 565 602 626 627 635 675 678 685
717 733 764 779 784 816 842 870 879 933 937 943
981 986 991 992 1004 1016   7   22 102 264 343
346 437 438 466 555 571 621 634 640 676 720 811
824 870 919 953 956 961 1012 1023 1024   8   35 57
71 82 99 135 151 228 259 304 324 325 326 343 352
391 395 397 398 400 420 422 438 457 467 511 512
557 617 625 713 728 741 758 864 865 886 921 1093
1120 1126 1149 1155 1158   9   1 13 28 39 65 106
158 243 255 283 357 434 446 540 662 806 859 936
972 984 1113 1196 1203 1214   10   77 175 263 305
314 374 389 396 405 448 468 469 478 496 505 570
588 597 598 660 661 681 739 807 824 825 902 913
916 932 954 968 973 992 1001 1025 1142   11   84
89 411 450 467 488 578 634 674 677 684 803 849
910 1018 1020 1021 1022 1034 1087 1090 1225
1231   12   83 90 224 284 308 328 351 433 453 514
546 588 707 833 1090 1114 1130 1133 1156 1157
1186 1197 1204 1262 1372 1463 1517 1547 1768
1769 1770 1778 1780 1910   13   49 90 176 177 179
288 340 356 361 377 408 414 425 468 469 470 471
474 493 501 575 588 603 703 775 778 791 797 799
822 825 863 870 884 887 894 911 912 955 957 968
974 975 976 1004 1018 1021 1023 1086 1088 1122
1128 1131 1135 1185 1191 1192 1244 1249
14   10 42 53 58 124 132 148 165 167 194 198 218
280 283 285 318 319 324 343 348 358 402 443 461
462 464 465 473 485 544 567 583 618 631 679 750
808 829 841 862 866 898 903 1010 1011 1015 1089
1113 1122 1128 1142 1148 1228 1344 1347 1348
1370 1392 1396 1400 1429 1562   15   205 267 275
881 1528 1636 2220 2260 2364 2769 2987 3075
3115 3121 3176 3177 3187 3281 3411 3628 3804
3948 4497 4586 4593 4618 4760 4862 4864
16   17 39 84 191 196 266 478 481 484 571 590 591
609 610 622 645 671 737 781 783 853 854 896 967
1004 1033 1043 1051 1124 1150 1209 1298 1312
1363 1365 1381 1535 1639 1678 1688 1768 1794
17   234 368 369 372 478 746 797 1036 1291
18   10 18 55 60 68 71 118 158 164 191 239 252
259 308 312 383 395 406 410 417 420 421 434 435
440 441 443 444 535 536 538 541 549 554 577 581
591 597 598 602 603 604 627 629 636 658 665 691
699 707 746 750 756 777 792 796 817 834 844 851
853 892 901 907 962 998 1058 1086 1091 1097 1100
1126 1222 1237 1243 1247 1269 1275 1287 1348
1357 1359 1371 1381 1433 1441 1442 1482 1549
1555 1557 1564 1569
them (4)   1 362   7 581   9 190   17 414
them (16)   15 480 581 613 632 1426 1436 2034
2059 3733 3846 3956 3978 4063 4082 4323 4768
theme (4)   9 997   11 802   14 1200
17 796
themes (1)   17 648
themselves (48)   4 508   5 414   6 782 789
875   7 825   8 34 48 80 152 247 472 935
10 378 621 1275   11 697 1088   12 570
13 469 563 790 793 809 1196 1201 1218
14 158 641 865 1180   16 1185 1533 1598
17 1064 1199 1911 2272 2307   18 158 384 411
881 891 1323 1419 1566 1567
themselves (4)   15 1747 1749 1750 4678
Then (137)   1 11 72 179 330 380 474   3 4 304
4 35 127 128 182 280 322 390 392 427 538

5   28 254 262 271 299 347 362 364 416 419 425
430 553   6 16 24 362 380 424 513 615 616 679
778 779 780 845 847 855 910 932   7 142 145 188
210 687 798   8 365 398 447 629 718 754 852 1029
1122 1130 1136   9 545 1033 1081   10 158 380
390 908 945 1159   11 61 620 772 803 971 1018
1081   12 132 287 494 705 770 795 811 848 1343
1611 1662   13 113 220 439 552 741 883 943 965
971 975 989 1032 1113 1139 1163 1215   14 117
218 228 241 415 443 632 773 1404 1578   15 245
637 1838 1967 2389 2553   16 395 885 913 1025
1078 1146 1302 1340 1490 1665   17 2240
Then (7)   3 201   9 23 24 908   11 1289
17 400 813
Then (7)   15 160 959 2669 2723 2751 4148 4922
then (405)   1 17 24 219 311 499 517   2 8 10 43
58 67 143 319   3 49 283 317 347 359 360 418 467
4 47 58 206 273 284 295 296 373 460 483 527 530
534 535 536   5 14 171 240 302 386 407 413 415
474 490 505 539 547   6 24 25 82 152 178 200 297
350 394 467 523 705 811 957   7 153 173 210 212
218 311 457 459 576 712 807 820   8 64 76 86 163
170 181 245 392 582 583 597 608 611 640 675 686
733 764 792 853 874 1033 1038 1064 1090
9 201 243 265 331 385 485 681 708 832 977 1087
1110 1160 1199   10 418 432 508 586 676 784 887
1107   11 61 84 108 176 521 541 808 839 913 935
948 1110 1115 1200 1201 1232 1237   12 267 268
326 360 381 436 444 466 605 679 692 926 1113
1210 1424 1440 1475 1479 1526   13 40 126 140
162 204 227 238 244 281 335 353 367 385 386 490
496 559 620 659 676 681 727 736 737 755 759 761
765 783 785 806 815 825 865 884 891 935 1051
1082 1092 1133 1189 1220   14 50 87 91 93 100
111 145 163 252 271 289 303 348 431 434 435 516
552 559 560 599 819 918 1045 1152 1369
15   478 548 669 1349 2208 2343 2408 2409 2429
2769 3319 3323 3388 3395 3892   16 16 98 216
321 398 700 720 726 899 906 966 973 1038 1073
1126 1176 1189 1199 1210 1283 1309 1324 1330
1341 1347 1381 1402 1433 1439 1463 1472 1585
1719 1866   17 4 5 80 453 454 469 472 473 497
611 621 993 1036 1151 1182 1186 1189 1192 1293
1348 1483 1490 1903 2151   18 16 20 33 53 61 99
106 121 137 173 190 191 228 278 302 318 327 328
330 334 349 354 358 372 373 435 474 503 510 567
578 628 638 641 642 645 662 684 724 764 780 807
920 923 924 929 934 956 989 993 1012 1037 1055
1080 1117 1121 1163 1166 1191 1220 1221 1228
1237 1238 1243 1271 1276 1299 1311 1318 1327
1343 1347 1364 1366 1395 1424 1471 1477 1504
1507 1508 1520 1522 1524 1532 1538 1552 1559
1567 1605
then (3)   3 383   11 781 1290
then (21)   15 321 335 424 758 1241 1316 2034
2039 2059 2158 2300 2405 2709 2755 2759 2853
2958 3542 4039 4931
thenar (1)   17 246
Thence (1)   14 1450
thence (5)   1 397   14 490   16 23   17 169
1441
thenceforward (1)   14 50
Theobald (2)   11 763   12 184
Theodore (2)   14 1410 1416
Theodore (1)   15 4345
THEODORE (1)   15 1740
Theodore's (1)   8 361
Theodotus (1)   12 1693
theological (2)   1 577   14 1002

theology   (2)   5 440   8 32
theologicophilolological   (1)   9 762
Theoretical   (1)   17 743
theoretical   (1)   17 742
theories   (1)   17 1644
theorising   (1)   9 517
theory   (9)   9 438 504 755 1066 1074 1077
14 993   17 1151 1643
Theosophos   (2)   14 1168 1170
Theother   (1)   18 879
THERE   (1)   7 1042
There   (107)   1 94   2 4 322 416 420   3 27
222 473   4 112 405 406 549   5 67 68   6 169
196 240 269 546 972 1001 1020   7 25 685
8 245 306 323 454 502 567 569 971 982 1138
9 397 461 539 774   10 211 256 522 526 536 669
1045 1077   11 467 469 690 691 901   12 68 69
122 377 880 884 1004 1078 1115 1560   13 96 278
434 592 656 894 1026 1119 1286   14 188 504 618
747 1044 1076 1206 1229 1344 1569   15 950
1779 2344 2367 2489 2541 3323 3344 3520 4015
4266   16 166 268 433 490 547 601 653 670 679
683 962 1000 1273 1295 1749   17 995
There   (2)   8 416 748
There   (3)   15 905 4925 4928
there   (582)   1 26 228 307 347 420 427 641 673
684 685 724   2 169 341 410   3 107 143 159 208
276 283 290 321 361 409 410 470 485 502   4
17 72 87 108 131 153 226 327 451 452 482 490
5   10 24 55 90 95 108 173 188 263 293 357 465 556
6   125 171 173 180 181 201 207 219 226 246 259
284 354 376 377 559 577 585 604 645 651 675 770
805 862 892 926 951 977   7 102 148 156 224 225
227 431 456 543 642 645 665 685 692 814 815 930
8   28 144 184 199 209 229 323 325 448 497 510
525 561 563 572 585 588 723 742 817 823 868 934
980 1059 1086 1107 1137 1164 1177 1192   9 183
222 334 397 460 461 497 564 591 631 673 679 714
884 922 923 963 1032 1051 1072 1099 1102 1138
1141   10 74 75 186 274 307 402 460 499 514 518
538 539 540 547 550 759 764 769 771 862 980 1161
1168   11 220 230 357 415 491 590 633 739 893
912 938 1021 1046 1198 1207   12 2 17 68 87 108
118 246 250 311 328 351 361 379 395 401 411 439
505 541 657 676 688 695 778 783 811 881 886 1008
1027 1031 1060 1080 1091 1102 1121 1122 1124
1129 1186 1229 1232 1245 1368 1462 1486 1503
1656 1860 1910 1914   13 6 11 40 76 113 149 189
229 281 284 300 337 340 346 349 369 375 408 412
428 463 476 480 501 535 541 549 565 570 586 603
624 638 641 647 652 697 706 708 710 715 717 748
751 760 768 860 894 913 960 984 1044 1073 1077
1103 1120 1171 1176 1182 1216 1260 1276 1300
14   17 20 64 74 76 97 105 112 123 124 128 132
146 149 153 157 161 166 168 187 199 278 348 364
434 445 455 500 507 510 573 611 684 687 694 723
789 810 811 869 917 1035 1041 1064 1158 1204
1316 1320 1333 1346 1357 1361 1372 1381 1395
1402 1408 1419 1443 1452 1458 1492 1503 1589
15   231 493 498 586 712 786 947 955 1040 1170
2192 2217 2425 2539 2718 3022 3068 3137 3175
3274 3393 3449 3713 3886 3908 4024 4264 4378
4801 4832 4874 4881   16 6 11 17 25 27 32 124
126 135 182 200 207 251 261 312 325 328 352 393
400 419 420 425 434 477 481 509 536 551 614 636
638 684 725 726 780 801 828 832 864 868 892 894
904 923 952 960 995 996 1052 1096 1185 1213 1271
1310 1320 1345 1385 1419 1420 1457 1463 1542
1579 1610 1750 1751   17 43 74 371 509 713 837

856 1057 1098 1140 1453 1709 1834 2196 2282
2288 2328 **18** 14 21 36 79 105 163 203 206 258
278 280 281 297 309 347 387 396 405 409 458 465
484 501 511 527 540 556 559 603 607 610 619 683
695 703 749 758 775 796 797 805 806 808 864 921
924 949 950 951 965 966 967 1003 1005 1012 1021
1042 1043 1057 1073 1085 1134 1145 1149 1198
1222 1296 1318 1321 1338 1352 1372 1410 1411
1415 1423 1460 1464 1481 1490 1514 1519 1522
1537 1548 1569 1570

there (2) **9** 417 **17** 813
there (4) **15** 242 3822 4925
thereabout (1) **14** 476
thereabouts (4) **14** 1181 **16** 1198 **17** 35 923
thereafter (2) **12** 1536 1722
Thereat (2) **14** 237 343
thereby (6) **12** 473 **14** 397 1285 **16** 1399 **17** 131 181
there'd (1) **13** 247
thered (2) **18** 737 1348
therefor (2) **12** 291 **14** 93
Therefore (2) **14** 107 370
therefore (8) **7** 807 **9** 691 695 **14** 33 41 1172 **16** 140 756
therein (5) **12** 447 1737 **14** 153 755 **15** 1171
There'll (1) **16** 157
therell (1) **18** 368
thereof (3) **7** 736 **12** 298 1735
Thereon (1) **12** 292
There's (58) **1** 177 340 512 614 673 **4** 213 331 355 380 **5** 163 170 360 555 **6** 41 134 **7** 399 **8** 111 560 828 1081 1086 **9** 450 585 **10** 582 982 **11** 91 395 404 964 **12** 13 455 880 1176 1239 1400 1760 **14** 548 733 1484 1525 1562 **15** 359 420 421 422 878 1093 1534 1727 2884 3089 3231 4266 4290 4310 **16** 452 657 856
There's (1) **7** 578
there's (26) **1** 336 519 **4** 162 **5** 383 453 **6** 414 871 **8** 720 985 **9** 819 **10** 698 736 **11** 1207 **12** 209 443 751 1571 1586 1658 1793 **13** 973 1014 1124 **15** 438 3136
theres (26) **18** 105 120 137 199 495 569 723 745 775 808 908 960 1066 1100 1102 1108 1158 1166 1231 1351 1355 1405 1488 1512 1558 1564
Theresia (1) **17** 1909
Thereto (1) **14** 401
thereto (4) **14** 70 115 161 **17** 2254
thereunto (1) **15** 1482
thereupon (1) **16** 1781
thereward (1) **14** 54
therewith (2) **12** 284 1682
thermal (1) **17** 270
thermometer (1) **17** 1520
These (7) **2** 219 **3** 288 **5** 355 **14** 1245 **15** 1390 **16** 1797 1817
These (1) **9** 267
these (92) **1** 52 160 335 443 567 **2** 84 168 230 349 367 409 **3** 145 289 415 **4** 79 495 **5** 501 510 **6** 106 960 **7** 82 824 **8** 304 **9** 46 111 497 787 978 **10** 302 410 **12** 175 625 632 862 1461 **13** 1261 **14** 152 159 211 223 289 462 694 752 757 765 812 900 992 1056 1062 1172 1249 1254 1257 **15** 715 1095 2421 2422 2911 3104 4576 **16** 100 335 1011 **17** 366 462 477 510 569 688 741 745 850 940 973 993 1070 1299 1311 1340 1361 1888 1902 1912 1916 1930 1934 2097 2227 **18** 627

these (1) **17** 398
theta (1) **17** 1049
thewless (1) **10** 1117
They (214) **1** 114 181 402 481 541 630 678 **2** 17 35 49 95 120 185 341 361 365 **3** 29 47 55 70 263 297 322 339 342 **4** 26 41 178 183 209 363 364 375 400 545 **5** 45 138 261 351 356 363 406 547 559 **6** 29 183 202 249 272 341 345 346 378 394 404 453 476 479 574 593 658 719 722 723 816 834 838 860 867 921 993 1004 1017 1027 **7** 50 63 431 459 499 568 572 916 931 932 935 939 941 942 947 1000 1010 1024 1041 **8** 56 61 78 83 84 119 130 152 377 382 389 409 414 488 505 523 536 540 596 878 922 930 963 966 993 1046 1071 1092 1123 **9** 116 289 308 356 465 491 544 850 890 978 1206 1216 **10** 71 94 263 342 356 385 495 520 532 790 791 884 915 981 991 1046 1072 **11** 108 110 159 474 516 544 806 893 973 1038 1047 1082 1090 1279 **12** 332 1354 1365 1386 1406 **13** 18 138 284 665 807 808 853 967 1088 1095 1118 1168 **14** 287 639 698 1069 1085 1092 1397 1398 **15** 274 277 593 1527 1966 2129 2396 2415 3181 3186 3279 3366 3486 4186 **16** 45 350 756 1116 1124 1781 **17** 572
They (1) **9** 1152
They (22) **15** 6 25 131 424 675 899 1275 1380 1413 1822 1828 1905 2022 2929 3722 4077 4082 4261 4321 4681 4764 4856
they (762) **1** 116 120 163 166 403 505 529 566 622 **2** 28 45 50 51 52 96 121 339 347 348 352 362 418 437 **3** 16 135 180 274 346 370 409 455 464 **4** 40 68 109 126 128 130 138 175 195 221 276 351 365 377 480 491 **5** 31 73 216 217 219 226 277 307 324 326 346 388 396 399 410 411 434 435 440 497 510 552 **6** 14 19 29 61 121 176 201 239 245 270 348 372 382 406 436 471 512 608 610 622 725 728 764 771 780 783 796 818 838 846 855 886 936 938 945 958 988 **7** 81 106 128 223 261 263 309 339 496 572 642 650 843 903 1002 1003 1010 1013 1023 1031 1051 **8** 42 49 71 79 125 150 154 241 330 393 405 421 422 487 488 497 498 517 538 543 544 558 569 729 744 752 758 846 847 865 875 935 968 972 1034 1071 1115 1116 1120 1124 1147 1159 **9** 67 85 87 286 408 628 708 740 891 1037 1048 1060 1062 1195 1207 **10** 20 38 41 42 70 82 139 140 150 151 379 412 448 504 715 716 728 732 789 824 834 865 953 956 1006 1033 1035 1038 1043 1058 1126 1128 1158 1162 1163 1247 **11** 152 174 177 206 221 522 609 668 678 769 877 935 937 942 945 993 1004 1049 1083 1101 1157 1168 1245 1269 **12** 70 80 238 244 283 284 297 393 435 444 446 447 450 460 461 504 571 643 647 649 651 707 889 1082 1131 1134 1135 1138 1188 1200 1237 1256 1325 1326 1336 1349 1352 1371 1374 1380 1386 1388 1543 1547 1566 1573 1625 1646 1720 1723 1745 1776 1779 1780 1781 1789 1879 1910 1911 1913 1915 **13** 11 145 171 176 186 201 220 231 234 237 238 239 313 318 329 335 344 367 391 440 413 414 419 437 461 467 470 473 490 533 552 592 602 604 680 683 685 688 692 717 720 739 760 765 784 790 792 793 795 797 807 813 822 827 829 847 855 864 870 874 879 895 903 913 916 925 945 953 954 971 1004 1019 1031 1034 1063 1066 1069 1078 1126 1127 1145 1146 1153 1155 1157 1168 1189 1193 1196 1236 1262 **14** 12 52 57 75 77 78 105 119 123 125 126 142 145 152 155 156 157 159 161 174 188 196 200 202 207 208 209 216 222 235 237 252 325 326 340 343 355 356 358 393 412 456 458 459 460 464 465 467

481 514 527 547 567 596 599 604 609 676 781 809 851 928 1066 1083 1087 1091 1096 1110 1112 1200 1265 1315 1346 1347 1349 1365 1450 1503 **15** 266 287 444 476 635 660 661 1301 1390 1391 1395 1900 2371 2440 2441 2445 2453 2672 2680 2738 2973 3082 3185 3188 3321 3861 3887 3889 3903 4109 4381 4868 4892 **16** 9 20 23 33 34 41 56 66 81 85 100 124 125 151 195 240 267 273 293 298 309 329 336 471 480 542 544 571 584 590 672 673 675 719 774 794 797 822 851 852 875 895 906 1025 1027 1033 1097 1102 1118 1124 1129 1130 1145 1205 1295 1298 1302 1304 1319 1327 1334 1339 1485 1488 1492 1493 1507 1526 1546 1579 1641 1703 1709 1725 1733 1734 1770 1805 1888 1893 **17** 2 8 369 548 559 1036 1185 1220 1830 1903 **18** 21 23 34 46 127 137 145 152 157 162 165 171 206 207 238 239 241 245 297 298 299 315 369 373 376 384 394 409 448 451 452 470 473 505 541 544 548 564 570 575 577 582 609 610 664 666 676 692 706 710 711 712 716 746 784 789 792 794 796 804 806 807 826 827 829 849 854 855 868 880 884 885 887 894 928 929 936 974 975 996 1026 1033 1036 1066 1078 1081 1100 1125 1131 1145 1170 1196 1237 1243 1261 1262 1270 1271 1313 1322 1333 1374 1378 1379 1380 1382 1385 1388 1389 1394 1415 1419 1434 1437 1439 1440 1441 1456 1458 1459 1464 1502 1518 1545 1565 1566 1567 1570 1571 1584
they (2) **6** 355 **9** 1152
they (17) **15** 7 49 416 425 591 924 1557 3224 3227 3331 3735 4056 4058 4083 4091 4132 4675
they'd (11) **4** 117 **5** 391 **6** 756 **7** 102 **8** 235 **11** 914 **13** 529 **15** 2680 4053 **16** 1129 1130
theyd (5) **18** 158 311 365 410 883
they'll (2) **4** 360 **10** 1160
theyll (2) **18** 887 1210
They're (10) **5** 333 383 **6** 818 **7** 455 705 **12** 441 1203 **13** 1128 **15** 4632 **16** 589
they're (8) **8** 878 967 **12** 1542 1644 **13** 797 1020 1143 **16** 201
theyre (35) **18** 23 117 244 246 311 402 483 515 540 549 558 591 636 806 807 816 840 891 977 1040 1061 1127 1143 1157 1242 1275 1283 1339 1391 1445 1501 1540 1568
theyve (3) **18** 405 1157 1542
Thibet (1) **17** 1989
Thick (1) **8** 616
thick (24) **1** 355 363 450 **2** 124 139 **4** 2 168 **5** 39 408 **8** 730 **10** 141 285 1043 **11** 365 **13** 1256 **14** 1438 **15** 3465 3780 4392 **16** 228 825 **18** 147 206 706
thick (1) **15** 3750
thickens (1) **9** 886
thickens (1) **15** 2831
thicker (2) **18** 577 638
thicket (3) **15** 3411 3416 3418
thicklugged (1) **12** 1198
thickly (3) **1** 66 447 **14** 1019
thickly (1) **15** 4931
thicknesses (1) **11** 293
thickplotting (1) **2** 366
thickveiled (1) **15** 752
Thief (1) **17** 644
thief (4) **9** 101 **10** 147 **12** 13 **15** 1040
thievery (1) **16** 1453
Thieves (1) **15** 4665
thieves' (1) **15** 245
Thigh (1) **11** 18

thigh (6) 5 155 6 105 11 414 12 1301 15 2316 17 1818

thigh (4) 15 1297 2618 3524 4125

thighcasing (1) 15 2982

thighplates (1) 15 1854

thighs (7) 6 96 100 15 2992 3120 3425 16 1355 18 1145

thighs (1) 15 2159

thimbleful (1) 10 724

thimbleriggers (1) 2 310

thimbleriggers (1) 15 3961

Thin (1) 4 50

thin (9) 2 176 7 809 8 1090 9 1178 10 203 14 1435 17 1326 2096 18 456

thin (1) 15 2484

Thine (1) 15 2620

thine (1) 14 1417

Thing (3) 5 364 8 187 9 651

thing (194) 1 206 684 2 32 143 3 237 238 4 118 172 481 5 113 287 345 377 418 6 87 108 331 395 405 549 622 626 668 676 738 810 7 104 792 802 8 289 365 383 447 538 980 985 9 303 432 843 877 10 498 727 776 1139 11 183 1121 1180 12 65 455 1104 13 165 265 300 329 562 706 709 792 923 989 1005 1015 1123 1246 1301 14 56 135 151 237 426 483 881 1031 1052 1192 1518 1587 15 333 359 559 983 1114 2254 2297 2469 2473 2538 2965 3001 3127 3268 3484 3511 3515 4534 4951 16 18 38 82 87 153 172 180 298 443 516 635 743 766 898 901 904 959 995 1060 1108 1153 1204 1291 1368 1402 1408 1481 1489 1496 1519 1615 1708 1719 1833 17 1751 2213 2214 2215 18 1 20 33 65 88 92 122 144 224 229 237 348 364 438 446 479 486 487 537 543 567 619 629 634 661 731 751 907 957 1007 1067 1090 1102 1105 1150 1152 1161 1173 1177 1206 1210 1242 1246 1267 1308 1360 1382 1383 1385 1387 1473 1516 1530 1532 1534 1537 1577 1585

thing (2) 5 115 9 551

thingamerry (1) 13 476

thing's (1) 3 255

Things (1) 8 477

things (104) 2 219 272 3 2 65 4 7 260 7 138 842 8 50 55 115 240 452 557 720 739 856 868 1108 1115 9 348 350 1048 10 90 715 722 740 882 1171 11 124 186 491 1102 12 1141 1672 13 179 185 280 300 449 580 641 724 823 868 940 1251 14 388 526 752 785 1265 1296 1359 15 878 2445 2647 2792 2979 2986 3883 3888 3891 16 248 466 639 826 1142 1312 1403 1409 1567 1614 1645 1656 17 689 18 146 180 290 405 407 421 474 491 539 580 588 601 619 631 729 776 983 1018 1020 1063 1082 1185 1415 1487 1536 1560 1582

things (1) 3 203

things (2) 15 311 2175

Think (9) 5 187 8 108 348 1134 11 310 1095 13 1110 15 477 4137

think (134) 1 93 160 379 498 505 636 647 2 222 268 402 3 418 421 4 128 320 5 79 239 248 249 503 6 103 367 659 662 815 860 1007 7 49 135 146 485 747 783 989 8 118 137 149 388 503 571 685 860 893 1063 1116 9 251 303 343 542 719 761 10 38 66 1023 11 138 150 204 210 358 480 790 830 834 945 1049 12 136 859 954 994 1402 1646 13 843 878 949 1005 1008 1009 1069 1200 14 773 832 1113 1154 1155 1167 1284 1518 15 398 593 786 833 1891

4950 16 52 202 764 822 907 1130 1478 1565 17 134 18 24 96 102 112 148 170 272 288 334 410 439 535 609 620 693 738 750 806 818 889 902 939 1044 1097 1133 1134 1362 1451 1551

thinker (1) 15 1468

Thinking (2) 8 24 11 1194

thinking (42) 1 218 488 4 488 5 211 380 6 197 204 533 7 603 8 116 278 355 558 9 560 11 533 12 1030 13 186 219 296 427 867 885 14 1262 15 713 1671 2081 2219 16 182 263 614 18 35 49 94 124 169 342 861 1175 1249 1410 1582

thinking (1) 15 1251

Thinks (3) 6 61 11 1023 13 1117

thinks (22) 1 51 88 155 431 3 200 7 787 8 279 9 1165 11 903 12 677 13 1237 14 1063 15 3630 17 614 615 18 50 281 519 1022 1214 1236 1363

thinks (2) 1 589 4 513

thinsocked (2) 10 185 264

Third (3) 7 119 11 303 15 203

third (26) 1 450 641 4 550 7 730 9 958 987 10 591 12 1112 1303 1357 1876 13 998 14 465 1032 1334 15 637 3398 4590 16 265 276 696 1276 17 54 155 477 1704

thirdly (1) 17 433

thirds (1) 16 973

thirst (7) 3 154 485 4 129 7 942 12 141 14 1530 17 215

thirsted (1) 12 288

thirstily (2) 1 340 2 312

Thirsty (1) 15 3610

thirsty (2) 8 851 18 536

thirteen (8) 4 505 517 6 775 825 827 17 139 232

thirty (2) 6 513 8 870

thirtyfive (2) 9 831 11 836

thirtyfour (1) 9 673

thirtyone (1) 15 1457

Thirtytwo (2) 5 44 15 3374

Thirtytwo (1) 15 1546

thirtytwo (4) 8 57 360 12 587 15 2781

THIS (1) 7 1063

This (62) 1 137 2 101 219 3 104 496 5 380 566 6 657 7 80 122 8 486 494 9 63 595 601 1097 10 329 409 506 610 1094 11 883 12 1104 1468 13 979 1211 14 167 214 294 380 455 734 1018 1236 15 116 334 738 940 967 1064 1679 1757 1768 2379 2393 2738 2957 3104 3243 3528 3533 3592 3597 4281 4470 4735 16 31 140 1358 18 878

This (1) 16 1248

this (373) 1 21 49 136 292 339 468 473 538 566 2 56 168 214 234 363 367 376 401 3 236 259 276 385 409 412 442 456 482 4 44 478 490 523 5 102 182 199 368 463 468 513 6 97 114 125 153 248 301 316 483 604 751 788 936 956 996 1004 1033 7 62 166 264 279 313 378 407 430 738 910 971 8 71 125 220 256 294 347 349 495 570 578 594 675 677 771 787 820 866 877 939 9 45 88 154 181 194 222 294 600 775 849 1047 1065 1085 10 276 462 588 613 639 704 844 847 850 1076 11 263 329 439 446 502 733 825 833 863 1120 1205 12 49 169 170 219 220 332 356 370 373 412 467 483 548 640 761 788 793 1146 1266 1362 1471 1500 1543 13 42 104 214 217 286 456 706 786 787 940 988 1008 1018 1046 1053 1079 1134 1157 1207 1252 14 51 63 127 143 151 165 167 198 206 209 235 282 284 290 334 338 361 372 402

420 456 467 478 483 503 526 529 545 548 554 567 595 604 668 678 679 681 696 714 748 797 816 835 883 906 910 912 921 936 1020 1021 1034 1053 1120 1141 1162 1178 1294 1332 1374 1379 1412 1438 1465 1466 1541 1542 1563 1572 1579 1585 15 205 259 306 392 400 405 445 468 635 657 836 837 880 942 968 1010 1109 1160 1167 1285 1472 1485 1505 1517 1525 1631 1755 2129 2189 2191 2199 2408 2419 2473 2496 2498 2782 2893 2999 3068 3104 3557 3783 4176 4427 4471 4568 4775 16 51 107 131 172 235 354 422 450 451 593 688 697 736 761 774 918 1141 1149 1172 1237 1578 1646 1664 1800 17 272 557 589 633 693 765 767 801 809 829 858 1016 1092 1330 1404 1579 1657 1824 1840 1843 1868 2143 2247 2250 2273 18 89 97 349 379 408 416 443 467 472 536 568 614 640 660 661 717 734 925 954 978 1050 1129 1130 1134 1146 1196 1206 1207 1210 1260 1310 1314 1420 1429 1493 1517 1534 1547 1557

this (8) 2 106 305 7 831 8 416 9 288 423 17 1783

Thistle (1) 15 4451

thistledown (1) 15 3372

Thither (2) 10 1258 12 91

thither (3) 12 89 13 626 14 26

thnthnthn (2) 11 2 100

tho' (1) 7 244

thole (1) 14 75

tholice (1) 14 1566

Tholsel (1) 10 930

tholsel (1) 12 1186

Thomas (25) 1 546 3 314 6 941 8 620 1070 1174 1181 9 772 778 10 408 416 1183 12 181 188 193 916 1702 1862 14 1524 16 558 17 426 444 1980 2075 18 650

Thomas (1) 16 1259

Thomond (2) 12 111 1309

Thom's (4) 7 224 8 157 12 1817 13 1126

Thom's (1) 17 1362

Thoms (1) 18 1223

thon (1) 14 1523

thong (3) 2 208 11 796 15 710

Thor (1) 14 409

thoracic (1) 17 244

Thornley (1) 15 1030

thorns (2) 5 278 330

Thornton (2) 4 417 8 394

THORNTON (1) 15 1818

Thornton's (1) 10 299

thorntree (1) 14 291

thorough (3) 13 339 16 189 1589

thoroughbred (1) 12 493

thoroughfare (7) 6 403 10 75 12 10 15 199 1385 17 500 1512

thoroughfares (3) 17 49 970 2030

thoroughly (9) 8 472 12 78 15 772 16 38 511 746 761 998 1106

Thos (1) 6 462

THOSE (1) 7 1014

Those (27) 4 159 5 31 279 382 404 496 6 784 8 73 156 478 543 1065 9 1059 10 148 159 646 723 11 124 152 1069 1077 12 1141 13 906 14 1314 15 2438 3525 16 194

Those (2) 4 442 443

those (282) 1 23 252 663 2 51 264 3 431 4 60 97 220 234 409 480 5 103 358 367 434 446 452 6 66 200 401 501 771 832 980 7 223 224

308 706 795 842 900 8 37 143 185 194 204 240
318 330 345 366 428 445 451 473 545 554 561 568
767 872 1030 1061 1146 1159 9 2 18 112 178 467
616 648 674 738 744 801 813 973 983 1008
10 90 138 389 421 458 498 748 767 782 784 894
11 154 186 190 481 831 852 912 983 1035 1078
12 12 286 313 349 452 602 674 712 723 1022
1029 1114 1123 1134 1181 1297 1373 1391 1506
1542 1571 1626 1658 1780 1826 1840 1887
13 84 86 109 144 178 185 291 327 342 379 410
436 500 625 704 725 732 745 748 795 906 970 1018
1057 1077 1087 1159 1182 1215 1227 1248 1261
14 225 228 276 338 349 360 510 523 710 720 756
823 835 865 986 1117 1148 1293 1327 1361 1434
1435 1544 15 822 2315 2329 2403 2448 2452
2680 3947 4508 4809 16 76 672 767 781 823 843
851 866 867 875 892 893 903 1055 1061 1111 1143
1194 1450 1509 1585 1742 17 175 1259 1882
2023 18 36 57 127 128 136 290 318 400 405 407
432 446 470 488 518 538 539 540 552 583 589 596
599 600 604 611 618 633 670 710 740 791 844 853
867 892 918 926 940 942 952 1024 1090 1141 1155
1159 1170 1207 1227 1238 1240 1259 1340 1345
1356 1374 1384 1390 1398 1413 1425 1444 1463
1495 1545 1554 1556 1593

those (2) 4 442 9 733

those (2) 15 1702 2485

thot (1) 14 1555

Thoth (1) 9 353

Thou (7) 6 597 11 802 14 1411 1415 1430
15 3827 18 382

thou (38) 5 445 9 183 194 483 740 1211
12 1605 14 327 328 329 362 365 368 370 372
377 378 379 380 1101 1343 1410 1413 1418
15 130 375 753 1489 2246 2497 3827

thou (9) 7 59 60 8 1053 9 146 11 740
741 13 646 647 16 1322

Though (15) 6 457 15 2440 2498 4130
16 119 172 391 491 831 1290 1386 1461 1505
1579 17 520

though (154) 3 474 4 480 5 20 6 809
7 602 818 8 537 9 44 244 379 801 1035
10 447 1024 11 721 723 1111 12 732 793
863 13 23 82 88 91 192 191 228 328 413 539
548 600 637 749 1034 1277 14 62 135 151 441
703 722 733 773 789 852 893 1174 1275 1283 1347
15 558 565 645 1801 3425 4383 4470 4569
16 37 64 89 118 129 136 141 170 173 178 189 217
282 307 324 337 341 502 555 561 640 710 739 761
767 825 827 849 863 866 943 1040 1055 1060 1085
1096 1186 1204 1217 1270 1291 1327 1368 1369
1370 1418 1453 1478 1479 1506 1523 1541 1558
1573 1586 1595 1598 1608 1717 1735 1752 1754
1765 1847 17 101 170 285 607 628 630 873 1096
1450 1625 18 30 54 82 123 140 145 167 196 209
211 915 1053 1058 1113 1255 1274 1284 1298 1307
1367

though (2) 2 66 10 1251

though (1) 15 901

Thought (7) 2 74 5 188 6 362 8 599
10 603 13 773 14 1549

thought (109) 1 428 626 2 49 74 3 1 75
123 221 4 156 6 131 300 405 619 7 159 702
763 8 380 471 1066 9 255 507 619 731 807
858 1112 10 12 33 83 137 143 161 171 442 702
733 11 971 980 1025 1098 12 256 827 1754
13 80 146 183 304 319 330 342 460 481 494 518
547 596 668 915 1207 14 460 510 668 832 857
1008 1048 1361 1401 15 873 1151 1336 1338

3049 3698 16 52 590 790 1205 1311 1581 1723
17 240 285 530 18 4 67 73 134 144 340 463
498 606 764 840 883 1055 1163 1248 1315 1324
1325 1396 1405 1472 1604

thought (1) 10 446

thoughtest (1) 15 3827

thoughtful (3) 2 268 11 517 14 1367

thoughtful (1) 15 4955

thoughtfully (7) 5 162 7 762 10 1068
1091 13 425 16 1425 1466

thoughtfully (2) 15 2313 2420

thoughtout (1) 12 718

thoughtreading (1) 15 445

Thoughts (1) 17 1372

thoughts (21) 1 652 6 921 8 65 717 1046
9 162 235 352 13 526 636 642 654 888
15 1972 16 1517 1786 17 527 528 529 2299

thoughts (1) 9 1145

Thou'll (1) 14 1555

thous (1) 9 448

Thousand (3) 12 1752 15 3882 16 1244

thousand (28) 3 143 7 91 138 8 263 858
895 10 726 11 836 1014 12 261 275 534
1036 1372 1712 13 750 1024 14 776 860
15 1154 1249 2416 3107 3545 16 1553
17 95 96 97

thousand (1) 15 1549

Thousands (1) 6 515

thousands (10) 4 364 5 571 6 674
12 1815 16 1309 17 1078 1246 18 1592

thousandth (1) 17 928

Thr (1) 15 3055

thrall (1) 14 768

Thrash (1) 15 1104

thread (3) 10 941 18 640 1029

thread (1) 15 1571

threadbare (1) 1 106

threads (3) 6 746 832 13 739

threat (1) 14 1220

threatened (1) 11 101

threatening (3) 7 946 8 625 11 220

threateningly (1) 10 681

Three (45) 1 610 2 218 222 233 234
4 371 504 505 5 499 6 869 7 119 192
8 128 289 363 373 435 482 602 1058 9 533 890
11 1089 12 147 1670 1791 1830 13 499 925
1049 1220 1221 15 343 1040 1372 1687 2517
2596 3105 3584 17 546 547 711

Three (3) 9 416 15 1024 17 1374

Three (1) 15 2179

Three (1) 15 2213

three (115) 1 349 441 443 444 551 2 255 258
269 3 251 4 11 40 131 182 504 517 5 513
6 498 578 774 830 7 160 720 932 934 8 266
282 482 629 684 1020 9 214 292 561 894 957 998
10 3 40 393 510 745 848 1245 11 141 474 878
962 1041 12 16 38 39 43 206 512 817 1309 1310
1460 1703 1878 13 9 174 238 1046 1077 1135
1221 1235 14 103 114 517 526 643 645 1137
1189 15 546 1192 1372 2233 2343 2667 2934
2959 3055 3259 3543 3557 3657 16 201 303 563
628 1276 1488 1876 1877 17 97 130 154 380 381
394 542 655 867 981 1257 1340 1531 1537
18 186 595

three (2) 9 1174 14 317

three (8) 15 499 1279 1612 1880 2405 3726
3831 4045

threecornered (1) 13 335

threefour (1) 7 101

threemasted (1) 10 1098

threemaster (2) 3 504 16 450

Threepence (1) 4 180

threepence (5) 3 195 4 169 5 546
12 40 15 669

threepenny (2) 7 933 943

threequarter (1) 13 154

threequarter (1) 15 2743

threescore (1) 17 1055

threnes (1) 14 1427

threshold (2) 4 76 11 434

threshold (2) 15 2027 2031

Threw (1) 11 556

threw (23) 1 725 3 498 5 276 7 64 534
8 52 57 60 75 10 268 912 11 159 12 984
13 254 353 467 14 735 15 497 16 215
1872 17 1491 18 346 602

threw (1) 10 615

Thrice (1) 14 763

thrice (2) 1 10 14 77

thrice (1) 15 1378

thrift (1) 15 2988

thrifty (1) 16 869

Thrill (1) 11 1101

thrill (4) 5 401 6 748 11 1083 16 1374

Thrilled (1) 11 1085

thrilling (2) 8 403 16 1664

throat (15) 1 12 2 114 443 8 795
10 634 11 143 589 731 928 12 685
13 519 546 582 15 4540 18 436

throat (4) 15 1280 2366 2624 3812

throats (1) 15 4528

Throb (1) 10 822 11 702

throb (3) 10 823 11 25 702

throbbed (3) 11 315 701

throbbing (2) 10 834 11 12

throbs (1) 7 162

throes (2) 8 398 14 114

throne (9) 3 53 8 4 9 751 12 611 1391
15 2861 3017 16 1199 18 506

thrones (3) 9 280 284 12 1213

throng (2) 12 536 15 3320

throng (2) 15 1586 3044

thronged (3) 6 487 12 547 16 1748

thronged (1) 15 1401

Throstle (1) 11 22

throstle (3) 6 240 241 11 631

throttled (1) 12 150

Through (8) 3 271 4 106 7 74 9 86
10 519 11 674 13 371 14 1527

Through (2) 2 78 79

Through (3) 15 184 2168 3377

through (196) 1 27 242 349 714 2 125 153
322 327 429 446 448 3 2 8 11 12 15 216 397 428
441 477 503 4 88 120 161 247 278 366 379 454
472 498 515 549 5 4 52 54 60 316 447 457
6 10 33 37 130 136 347 360 387 399 439 508 517
521 589 699 816 876 7 33 70 196 198 217 439
701 971 997 1068 8 46 296 309 326 449 536 577
9 89 148 380 515 873 1045 1197 10 264 366
415 770 800 818 842 1086 1182 1189 1261
11 217 440 537 840 931 934 1053 1116 1232
12 215 342 397 517 614 637 986 1248 1315 1880
13 336 413 626 719 736 752 1040 1072 1083 1171
14 99 102 438 491 511 782 860 884 889 1059
1072 1288 1545 15 647 1023 2193 2439 2447
3028 3356 3503 3789 4117 4183 16 79 151 304
494 505 506 903 992 1374 1652 1881 17 104 109
115 165 169 179 263 266 492 498 550 551 552 943

944 1005 1006 1020 1318 1485 1513 1698 1997
2025 2026 2309 18 159 257 340 574 636 646 959
984 1028
through (1) 8 222
through (38) 15 8 62 136 173 416 604 694 912
1027 1244 1255 1267 1558 1586 1842 2153 2159
2178 2305 2561 2611 2715 2727 2871 3161 3344
3361 3367 3414 3421 3945 4142 4143 4157 4314
4423 4549 4679
throughout (2) 15 827 17 1550
throve (1) 14 938
Throw (4) 1 724 5 421 7 399 11 686
throw (26) 3 412 5 534 537 8 83 875
12 882 1662 13 52 352 478 590 792 951 1251
15 4479 16 299 302 1182 17 337 18 21
468 747 787 1359 1402 1504
throw (3) 15 1446 1717 1764
Throwaway (1) 14 1132
Throwaway (11) 12 1219 1226 1551 1563
15 2936 4814 16 1242 1278 1280 1281 1282
throwaway (5) 8 6 10 294 753 1096
17 332
throwaways (1) 17 1940
Throwing (1) 13 1191
throwing (9) 7 981 12 316 13 577 1130
1185 18 72 680 852 1259
throwing (1) 15 4331
thrown (5) 10 119 13 1250 14 1267
17 332 337
thrown (2) 15 192 4255
throws (6) 15 1763 2943 3642 4027 4312 4568
thrue (1) 14 1567
thrush (3) 6 240 11 631 773
Thrust (1) 14 1543
thrust (10) 1 149 5 446 539 7 345 664 904
8 312 1186 9 556 14 855
thrust (2) 15 481 4611
thrusting (2) 1 67 3 226
thrusts (5) 15 124 2158 2942 3360 4737
thu (1) 8 692
thùd (1) 2 8
thumb (10) 1 616 2 382 4 299 7 114
810 10 1069 11 1114 12 139 17 2315
18 80
thumb (6) 15 466 960 3202 3733 4860 4913
Thumbed (1) 10 845
thumbnail (4) 1 693 2 250 4 338 11 3
thumbnails (1) 11 193
thumbprint (1) 15 3681
thumbs (3) 6 720 10 1219 15 2384
thumbs (4) 15 1208 2302 2658 2660
Thummim (1) 17 2047
Thump (2) 7 76 101
thump (2) 7 101
Thumping (3) 7 72 76
thumping (4) 12 508 15 2895 2897
18 382
thumps (1) 15 2186
Thunder (1) 4 458
thunder (8) 9 616 11 963 12 529
13 600 14 487 1088 1388 18 134
thunder (1) 7 857
Thunderation (1) 14 1462
thunderbolts (1) 18 136
thundered (3) 12 165 14 409 422
thunderhead (1) 14 427
thunders (1) 14 776
Thunderstorm (1) 3 486
thunderstorm (1) 8 837

thunk (1) 15 2384
thurible (2) 13 491 496
thurifers (1) 12 1677
Thursday (13) 2 93 4 44 5 128 6 392
812 9 277 13 119 14 474 15 333 1022
3685 17 931 18 594
Thursdaymornun (1) 15 3829
Thursday's (1) 15 3687
Thursdays (1) 12 742
Thus (4) 1 727 14 362 16 754 808
thus (4) 9 684 15 3277 16 529 1671
thwarted (1) 6 277
Thy (5) 6 126 13 459 14 766 767 1437
thy (32) 1 335 3 470 9 449 817 12 1227
14 107 365 367 371 374 842 1075 1076 1414 1416
1418 1419 1430 15 2437 3277 3655 4655 4656
16 1269 17 729 730 18 29
thy (10) 2 239 3 381 382 386 7 472
8 67 9 170 612 16 1743
thyme (1) 8 468
thyself (2) 9 1153 12 1600
Ti (1) 15 351
ti (1) 7 718
Tibble's (1) 16 805
Tiberias (1) 4 155
ticed (1) 14 461
Tichborne (2) 16 1343
tick (1) 6 172
ticker (1) 14 1469
ticket (8) 10 115 118 119 12 1898 15 637
16 524 17 1378 1791
tickets (7) 3 180 8 185 12 777 14 462
17 320 18 424 1225
tickets (1) 15 1575
ticketwriters (1) 15 1433
Ticking (1) 13 1197
ticking (2) 4 212 18 1309
tickle (2) 6 67 16 1795
Tickled (1) 7 1074
tickled (6) 3 124 8 233 10 185 265
13 257 16 1263
tickled (1) 9 22
tickles (3) 7 1072 12 1173 15 1295
tickling (4) 15 2136 2999 18 586 812
ticklish (1) 13 778
Ticktacktwo (1) 15 1603
tidal (2) 14 1269 17 219
tiddledy (1) 3 492
tiddledywinks (1) 17 661
Tide (2) 9 1084 13 1259
tide (15) 1 247 674 3 3 288 297 326 337 393
461 5 460 9 753 13 471 15 4954
17 1712 18 958
tide (2) 15 996 1850
Tides (1) 3 393
tides (2) 17 191 224
tidied (1) 13 571
tidings (5) 1 130 5 181 10 1234 14 95
16 1011
tidy (1) 8 387
tidying (1) 6 590
tidysized (1) 16 1134
Tie (1) 15 2081
tie (11) 1 513 679 3 182 5 89 10 57 330
1244 12 1336 13 800 831 18 421
tie (2) 15 1355 1379
tied (2) 15 3067 18 1113
tied (3) 15 1237 1571 2253
Tiens (2) 3 450 14 1558

tiens (1) 14 1558
tierod (1) 17 1541
ties (4) 2 255 7 598 14 922 16 1383
tiffs (1) 13 94
tiger (1) 16 1796
tigers (1) 12 977
Tighe (1) 16 208
Tight (6) 5 529 8 296 11 484 13 771
14 1507 15 1820
tight (19) 3 296 6 10 511 8 316 10 57
514 564 833 870 985 11 357 481 555 13 480
15 1819 2822 3320 16 1464 18 260
tight (5) 15 48 2668 2854 4036 4039
tighten (1) 18 1531
tightened (1) 11 614
tightened (1) 15 2606
tightening (1) 8 678
tightens (1) 15 4946
tightly (3) 9 788 789 15 2322
tightly (1) 15 1821
tightpacked (1) 15 503
tightrope (1) 15 2176
tigress (1) 15 1100
tilbury (1) 14 795
tilebooks (1) 9 355
tiled (1) 17 1521
Till (4) 9 619 13 367 814 15 1970
till (127) 1 212 487 547 2 191 396 3 408
4 35 75 76 184 261 335 429 462 5 104 6 10
29 144 308 565 636 7 213 310 8 49 112 199
231 454 806 9 1001 1105 10 195 386 411 545
552 1019 1158 11 61 73 128 372 383 488 814
838 971 12 30 274 510 685 774 837 1144 1192
1345 1358 1647 1843 1847 13 52 216 220 346
383 519 761 870 888 953 1023 1154 1162 14 73
348 500 539 1099 1107 1387 1514 15 81 405 510
603 1593 1958 2711 2916 3388 16 406 908 1271
1317 1364 1365 1366 1395 1494 1507 1575 1878
17 453 1068 1327 18 21 98 134 165 283 302
305 362 381 575 595 771 779 808 963 995 1051
1070 1132 1360 1364 1580
till (2) 7 327 11 1289
till (1) 15 125
tilly (1) 1 399
Tilsit (1) 12 422
tilt (1) 13 268
tilt (1) 15 237
tilted (4) 3 438 8 621 10 211 11 377
tilted (3) 15 452 509 4315
tilting (1) 4 272
Tim (2) 7 639 800
timber (4) 12 835 14 573 17 1276 2062
timbers (1) 14 1525
timberyard (2) 5 230 232
timbrel (1) 14 1350
Time (23) 1 459 2 49 316 370 4 519
5 12 462 502 6 985 7 187 8 380 791 853
11 188 841 1073 12 504 13 108 897
14 1544 1561 15 4184
Time (1) 17 644
time (343) 2 10 269 420 3 11 12 27 245 256
4 74 185 187 302 319 356 452 490 542 5 59 73
92 211 224 273 274 297 349 368 373 382 406 436
453 462 463 488 505 6 330 350 578 695 763 788
866 919 933 996 7 101 198 264 360 436 544 556
632 636 763 986 992 8 71 109 318 332 392 411
438 444 525 570 571 581 603 610 625 719 1036
1049 1072 9 247 278 380 401 518 539 559 624
640 895 1164 1200 10 3 6 217 411 418 427 507

562 656 828 894 912 1129 1144 1152 11 303 385
389 439 540 650 921 959 1098 1193 12 1 127
203 452 509 537 652 763 776 787 803 835 884 948
1173 1243 1377 1450 1464 1668 1866 13 10 94
138 189 453 463 474 499 532 533 535 545 557 558
562 568 575 606 625 783 784 831 864 885 901 917
985 988 989 1003 1013 1016 1023 1050 1070 1074
1077 1087 1300 14 118 169 200 277 292 559 596
604 742 812 900 1111 1196 1326 1336 1341 1453
1457 1553 1574 15 95 204 400 442 539 1022
1118 1199 1321 1807 1970 1985 2144 2191 2207
2419 2550 2795 2806 2893 3054 3354 3481 3559
3580 4445 4555 4563 16 39 84 86 152 198 215
270 339 362 371 570 623 649 689 697 768 799 937
939 950 974 1036 1221 1222 1300 1362 1449 1517
1542 1554 1574 1593 1604 1637 1679 1685 1715
1730 1839 1843 1860 17 357 484 492 854 1484
1515 1677 1678 1916 2025 2027 2052 2295
18 42 55 77 101 131 148 156 163 187 209 219 266
273 305 317 333 345 357 379 398 401 415 502 528
532 549 586 611 649 652 731 769 775 808 809 862
921 1013 1042 1064 1077 1110 1135 1141 1208
1218 1222 1239 1249 1299 1311 1375 1376 1383
1399 1452 1484
time (5) 1 300 304 2 106 8 68 778
time (5) 15 74 1492 2049 4026 4049
Timeball (1) 8 109
timedulled (1) 10 801
timehonoured (4) 12 666 921 16 37 674
timekeeper (2) 7 7 17 1529
timely (2) 12 664 16 1797
TIMEPIECE (1) 15 1131
timepiece (2) 14 1471 17 1335
timepiece (1) 15 1129
Time's (1) 15 4244
Times (2) 10 781 15 752
Times (5) 6 945 8 323 10 161 12 1367
16 911
time's (2) 14 289 331
times (71) 1 404 610 2 234 3 12 466
4 40 210 5 307 8 204 311 454 455 503 767
10 159 174 767 848 11 84 459 836 1041
12 133 313 517 632 840 13 6 342 750 774 902
14 563 645 1367 15 1372 1913 2027 2144 3584
3789 3907 16 198 533 902 1403 1488 1510 1877
1888 17 135 542 1048 1111 1162 1872
18 143 231 255 284 673 760 772 895 1127 1179
1408 1415 1512 1526
times (1) 17 414
times (1) 15 920
timid (1) 15 2884
Timidity (1) 12 1276
Timing (1) 4 521
timorous (1) 16 1088
Timothy (2) 12 937 14 1441
Timothy (1) 15 1377
tin (12) 1 156 7 932 12 495 497 697 1229
1651 1843 14 548 15 2900 17 1323
18 486
Tinahely (1) 9 38
Tinbad (1) 17 2322
tinbox (1) 12 1857
Tinct (1) 15 1652
tincture (1) 5 490
tinderbox (1) 1 619
tingating (1) 18 419
Tinge (1) 6 828
tingled (1) 8 355
tingling (4) 9 147 13 514 690 15 1095

tinily (1) 10 127
tinily (1) 15 4020
Tink (2) 11 11 286
tinkers (1) 12 1181
tinkle (2) 11 456 17 1570
tinkle (1) 15 4125
Tinkling (1) 11 981
tinkling (2) 11 960 14 797
tinkling (1) 15 4919
Tinnahinch (1) 7 92
Tinned (1) 15 4344
tinned (2) 8 496 497
tinny (2) 18 276
tins (1) 8 855
tins (1) 15 1765
tinsel (1) 15 3263
tinsel (1) 15 471
tintacks (1) 17 1602
Tiny (3) 11 45 13 1107 14 1368
Tiny (1) 15 2161
tiny (22) 5 23 6 322 7 95 8 297
9 117 10 125 398 491 11 420 791 1108
13 23 58 257 626 1017 1131 14 1061
15 2469 18 284
tiny (1) 15 958
Tip (3) 11 1281 13 992 995
tip (10) 5 57 8 566 11 1003 1047
12 1002 1223 1555 15 1149 2092 18 426
tipped (6) 4 39 11 1029 12 393 14 796
1514 18 764
Tipperary (4) 10 776 12 1252 15 1018
17 1976
tippet (1) 14 600
Tipping (1) 11 706
tipping (2) 18 368 1043
tipple (1) 14 1491
Tips (1) 8 887
tips (2) 4 41 6 239
tipstaff (1) 14 539
tipster (1) 15 1289
tipsycake (1) 15 3324
tiptapping (1) 10 126
tiptoe (1) 7 595
tiptoed (1) 9 887
tiptoeing (1) 15 3160
tiptoing (1) 9 329
Tiptop (4) 5 142 6 429 8 740 11 196
tiptop (2) 13 324 18 783
tiptouch (1) 15 2970
tipup (1) 17 1541
Tir (1) 9 413
tir (1) 9 366
Tirconnell (1) 7 542
Tired (2) 13 1101 16 624
tired (19) 1 562 5 35 7 1023 8 1099
9 516 981 10 819 11 807 13 87 1177
1248 15 210 16 622 1547 1572 18 93 133
789 1478
Tiresome (2) 6 630 11 574
tiresome (2) 6 947 8 385
tiroirs (1) 15 4090
'Tis (10) 4 125 7 888 11 1178 12 1342
1620 14 515 666 1507 15 3580 3826
'Tis (1) 2 106
'tis (4) 14 546 568 573 733
Tisdall (7) 8 302 9 1116 10 919 1102 1106
1261 11 1124
Tisdall (1) 15 2308
Tisntdall (1) 11 1125

tissue (7) 2 24 4 204 7 416 10 300
11 1161 17 307 508
tissuepaper (1) 11 1238
tissuepaper (1) 15 2041
tissues (8) 7 387 390 396 401 437 451 596
15 2389
titbit (4) 3 477 4 502 11 901 13 1060
Titbits (1) 15 934
Titbits (1) 4 467
titbits (1) 16 1653
tithefarmer (1) 9 712
TITILLATING (1) 7 1069
titillationes (1) 14 708
titivate (1) 11 1047
title (7) 4 158 7 516 10 606 16 1333
17 1374 1379 1395
titled (1) 16 1827
titledeeds (1) 17 1666
titlepage (2) 4 100 17 1395
titles (5) 1 650 3 139 10 601 14 900
17 1359
tittered (1) 11 76
tittering (1) 2 38
titties (1) 18 536
Tittlemouse (1) 15 1985
Tivy (2) 6 560 563
tlee (3) 15 2007 17 867
tlone (1) 15 2007
tloo (1) 17 867
tlwo (1) 15 2007
Tnetopinmo (1) 15 4708
TO (1) 7 272
To (118) 1 176 210 391 406 420 505 506 540
2 86 330 406 3 228 466 488 4 47 171 192
216 237 5 92 521 6 161 449 737 821 7 92
299 412 891 8 399 531 539 1169 9 171 510
595 684 10 869 11 47 229 243 244 286 564
708 754 862 871 872 905 923 932 995 1064 1096
1101 12 1190 1197 1596 13 835 14 50 222
334 535 605 679 845 865 875 1438 1454 15 57
1115 1911 1965 2546 2675 2814 3019 3151 3446
3447 3456 3522 3581 4290 4479 4528 4701 4937
16 109 253 350 793 1014 1227 1332 1565 1667
1691 1711 1713 17 82 231 276 352 931 945 962
963 964 1201 1203 1635 1640 2127
To (15) 2 107 5 283 284 288 292 6 165
7 581 8 1054 9 97 909 11 751 12 417
745 14 351 17 1881
to (4546) 1 19 35 36 43 46 49 61 65 67 69 70 75
82 86 89 92 93 97 103 125 130 135 137 144 150 154
156 160 167 170 183 189 194 200 207 214 218 220
248 251 270 273 274 276 297 309 314 320 329 330
331 339 352 368 390 391 393 406 407 411 418 419
422 425 426 431 433 438 439 447 449 465 466 469
472 474 480 481 488 494 497 511 513 514 516 520
529 546 547 549 558 560 562 563 566 572 578 582
583 594 595 602 605 606 614 615 618 627 636 637
649 661 667 676 678 680 687 692 697 698 704 710
721 727 741 2 16 17 23 42 43 49 52 86 87 116
131 134 135 147 157 169 172 177 178 187 203 219
226 241 247 283 288 291 292 297 298 307 310 316
320 330 338 340 341 342 352 362 369 376 377 392
402 415 417 420 424 426 437 441 445 3 2 10 31
39 43 50 61 94 95 110 113 115 122 129 130 133 137
139 142 143 150 153 158 166 168 179 180 183 184
188 192 194 198 223 243 256 257 267 268 275 283
295 299 300 303 323 328 344 351 354 362 375 392
398 399 400 401 406 407 415 422 428 430 435 464
481 483 495 4 4 21 23 27 28 29 35 38 43 49 64

75 77 86 92 110 115 123 134 172 174 177 207 215
218 225 241 251 265 266 273 277 292 309 331 334
350 360 376 378 387 390 391 395 403 404 405 417
426 428 433 449 451 455 456 457 459 461 463 465
468 469 472 473 475 476 481 494 504 508 519 523
530 536 549 **5** 9 26 30 33 36 40 41 45 51 69 71
76 84 95 105 109 117 120 124 151 153 166 167 170
172 174 182 195 197 198 204 207 225 234 235 236
242 250 252 253 256 258 262 265 297 305 306 320
321 325 326 334 335 341 348 351 352 355 356 357
371 372 379 388 394 395 400 409 419 421 425 427
428 429 435 436 446 464 473 478 479 480 494 499
502 504 512 526 534 537 543 545 546 547 554 561
6 9 14 15 18 25 36 38 47 60 66 72 74 79 82 95 98
114 125 127 143 161 185 188 192 198 216 217 237
239 262 269 270 272 273 274 279 283 322 338 342
343 345 347 352 363 380 381 382 395 401 402 404
405 407 412 416 420 421 424 425 430 435 445 447
450 457 474 475 477 481 483 495 505 506 519 530
533 537 539 541 553 564 565 570 579 584 593 602
604 610 611 615 617 620 629 630 634 637 642 647
653 673 695 712 721 723 735 739 743 747 751 753
754 760 761 768 779 781 788 789 790 795 799 800
803 806 808 811 812 818 830 832 842 845 847 852
854 867 870 872 879 883 888 889 899 902 906 911
918 921 927 930 933 941 944 945 951 954 956 958
986 989 995 998 1000 1003 1004 1008 1012 1028
7 11 26 51 53 55 81 83 92 102 109 113 130 131
147 152 161 165 166 172 176 177 181 187 192 204
207 213 215 218 226 231 233 237 255 256 259 264
279 292 297 301 304 305 310 313 329 338 340 359
365 376 379 390 397 401 405 408 424 430 431 442
450 451 455 462 465 492 497 513 516 526 531 542
543 553 554 563 569 572 574 595 616 624 628 634
667 670 672 676 682 687 695 701 702 709 734 746
747 777 782 786 809 810 811 820 823 824 826 834
842 881 894 906 907 915 916 918 931 936 942 943
946 947 960 974 976 993 996 997 1003 1004 1012
1023 1024 1039 1041 1055 1062 **8** 3 7 22 23 34
35 46 55 80 82 83 93 96 99 100 117 119 131 134
141 146 147 168 184 199 215 225 229 234 237 239
247 262 267 272 281 283 289 298 306 311 312 321
324 325 327 331 332 336 344 348 355 356 360 361
365 372 376 377 378 382 384 386 387 396 410 413
414 415 417 419 425 427 429 440 441 443 446 467
480 487 506 511 521 555 559 560 561 565 571 573
574 575 578 580 596 611 613 618 625 633 639 660
661 666 673 683 684 694 704 705 722 723 747 768
786 795 831 839 864 872 874 875 878 880 884 888
898 922 923 930 933 934 936 942 951 966 967 968
971 980 981 983 984 1001 1006 1016 1018 1019
1023 1029 1036 1037 1049 1057 1071 1072 1073
1076 1077 1081 1082 1087 1090 1092 1097 1103
1112 1115 1119 1127 1139 1142 1143 1149 1154
1158 1165 1166 1167 1170 1192 **9** 1 9 10 13 19
27 29 36 38 43 48 66 67 69 72 80 86 89 94 95 100
109 111 113 122 133 142 150 152 160 163 167 168
172 175 177 184 185 189 195 197 214 219 230 235
241 242 243 246 248 253 256 257 259 280 289 305
306 309 317 322 329 331 339 349 357 370 377 383
391 400 401 408 422 429 432 435 439 445 451 452
454 461 467 469 474 475 495 498 508 512 514 519
553 564 565 569 570 572 573 586 602 610 611 613
618 619 623 624 630 633 663 665 676 678 680 681
682 686 696 709 713 722 723 735 748 751 773 781
782 784 788 789 795 796 805 806 811 819 825 834
838 839 840 849 903 916 924 938 945 955 962 971
973 979 985 991 998 1007 1011 1016 1031 1037
1040 1056 1057 1064 1065 1068 1075 1076 1077

1078 1079 1081 1101 1128 1129 1156 1160 1177
1190 1192 1193 1197 1201 1208 1210 1221 **10** 2
3 4 12 19 21 22 24 26 27 39 44 46 47 53 62 65 70
72 75 81 85 91 105 106 108 111 114 120 133 134
135 139 148 149 151 158 177 181 196 209 210 211
217 239 254 269 270 274 286 289 321 336 342 384
386 410 418 430 432 436 444 445 453 471 473 504
506 513 515 518 532 547 566 568 570 589 597 651
658 677 684 695 697 708 713 737 745 762 776 782
785 817 822 834 846 847 851 874 888 893 894 908
916 924 926 934 942 952 960 964 1005 1006 1007
1008 1014 1023 1026 1044 1051 1054 1065 1069
1081 1089 1094 1131 1135 1136 1139 1151 1154
1157 1162 1166 1168 1170 1172 1173 1194 1210
1220 1234 1236 1242 1243 1245 1248 1266 1268
1274 1276 1280 **11** 11 74 89 92 98 110 111 118
121 136 152 160 169 171 173 175 176 180 219 250
284 286 293 294 297 304 306 310 324 325 346 356
360 369 384 419 428 430 431 438 478 483 488 531
540 554 562 564 571 573 578 590 596 600 617 620
621 638 640 659 661 669 670 671 674 677 689 697
699 705 706 707 713 717 718 719 737 746 754 798
823 830 833 835 839 842 845 849 871 892 905 910
923 930 931 938 954 971 975 978 982 1011 1014
1018 1022 1041 1047 1049 1057 1071 1073 1076
1077 1085 1092 1098 1102 1113 1121 1132 1144
1159 1167 1172 1173 1182 1196 1199 1200 1210
1213 1232 1249 1258 1260 1264 1266 1267 **12** 3
8 9 15 21 30 35 40 42 46 48 54 58 62 74 79 83 134
140 148 155 158 167 169 203 216 221 227 238 243
251 258 263 268 269 271 272 285 287 288 289 290
298 311 312 335 338 341 345 346 347 348 350
351 358 363 367 369 372 388 390 392 393 398 400
402 412 433 436 443 447 469 471 474 475 481 484
486 491 495 506 507 511 513 531 538 549 553 557
571 573 577 582 588 590 592 595 609 611 623 625
626 627 631 632 633 638 642 644 645 646 653 657
661 674 675 680 694 705 706 708 721 722 729 732
748 751 753 760 762 778 780 782 783 785 788 791
792 795 796 797 798 800 802 815 822 833 837 838
839 842 844 850 851 852 857 864 867 870 877 884
891 893 894 895 905 910 911 914 917 919 920 924
947 956 957 961 967 968 969 971 976 979 982 985
995 996 999 1004 1033 1034 1036 1046 1048 1061
1062 1065 1067 1068 1070 1071 1082 1088 1096
1103 1109 1114 1121 1122 1123 1133 1141 1145
1160 1162 1174 1183 1184 1187 1194 1195 1207
1212 1215 1219 1226 1229 1231 1250 1252 1253
1254 1257 1259 1289 1292 1307 1313 1315 1317
1318 1322 1326 1327 1335 1359 1363 1370 1373
1381 1383 1386 1392 1393 1396 1400 1406 1412
1426 1434 1439 1441 1443 1450 1466 1467 1471
1475 1477 1486 1489 1493 1505 1508 1515 1516
1521 1524 1527 1535 1547 1551 1554 1556 1561
1562 1563 1565 1571 1574 1576 1577 1600 1603
1612 1614 1636 1661 1665 1671 1672 1724 1737
1754 1755 1761 1769 1771 1774 1775 1778 1779
1784 1787 1797 1798 1799 1815 1816 1817 1821
1834 1844 1862 1868 1871 1877 1883 1886 1889
1904 1908 1909 1911 1916 **13** 1 7 11 14 21 23
24 31 33 42 44 46 47 48 49 52 58 76 77 81 84 86 91
92 94 95 96 99 103 104 106 111 112 113 124 125
132 133 134 137 138 152 155 158 162 163 173 177
180 182 190 192 199 202 208 209 212 215 217 220
224 241 244 245 250 251 253 257 262 266 269 270
274 278 280 286 288 289 292 299 301 302 303 318
319 320 321 322 335 336 343 348 350 351 352 356
357 361 364 369 386 388 390 393 395 404 405 407
408 409 419 423 426 430 437 440 443 452 454 455

456 458 459 463 464 465 466 468 469 470 477 482
486 487 491 493 496 498 499 504 506 509 512 519
522 525 529 530 533 538 544 545 554 555 556 559
566 568 570 571 573 581 582 585 588 593 597 599
605 608 611 612 615 617 628 629 632 634 636 641
644 651 654 655 656 658 659 664 668 677 683 692
693 694 696 697 699 705 707 710 715 716 717 718
719 721 722 730 733 734 746 751 752 754 759 760
762 766 767 780 788 799 804 807 809 814 817 824
825 835 838 840 843 844 845 847 852 853 854 861
862 863 867 869 875 881 882 883 886 896 900 913
914 917 918 919 921 923 930 931 934 950 953 954
958 959 960 966 967 971 972 974 982 994 995 1008
1022 1024 1037 1038 1039 1047 1059 1068 1071
1074 1081 1084 1086 1095 1104 1109 1122 1133
1145 1146 1150 1158 1160 1169 1186 1190 1191
1197 1199 1200 1206 1213 1217 1218 1220 1223
1224 1227 1228 1231 1232 1234 1238 1239 1242
1244 1248 1251 1271 1276 1299 **14** 9 20 22 23
26 27 28 29 35 44 50 52 53 55 58 63 64 67 70 75 76
81 86 89 96 98 99 100 103 107 109 111 115 117 118
120 121 126 128 132 137 139 148 150 154 156 157
159 162 166 168 175 178 180 181 185 187 189 196
197 198 201 204 210 215 217 221 227 229 232 236
237 243 246 250 253 254 261 283 287 291 298 320
329 332 336 341 342 343 345 351 354 358 359 362
363 364 368 369 371 373 374 381 397 398 410 412
416 420 421 424 425 432 433 435 440 443 445 448
451 473 478 479 485 491 494 498 501 503 504 510
512 515 518 525 529 530 532 546 549 552 555 556
561 564 566 567 577 582 594 595 603 605 608 610
611 623 625 626 633 634 636 643 654 656 658
661 663 670 672 673 674 678 680 681 684 685 686
688 703 704 705 706 711 714 718 725 726 729 741
744 748 750 751 752 760 761 764 766 772 773 775
784 790 795 801 802 811 819 821 822 823 824 825
827 832 834 835 842 843 845 854 857 862 866 867
869 873 878 879 880 881 883 886 887 889 893 900
902 906 910 915 916 918 919 922 928 932 935 939
943 944 945 946 953 957 958 963 969 979 980 982
991 995 999 1004 1005 1007 1008 1010 1016 1022
1023 1029 1034 1039 1047 1057 1061 1071 1076
1091 1096 1098 1114 1118 1120 1121 1124 1156
1157 1164 1165 1166 1167 1176 1178 1183 1184
1186 1191 1192 1193 1196 1203 1206 1208 1216
1222 1224 1225 1227 1235 1237 1255 1257 1258
1259 1263 1264 1271 1272 1279 1281 1283 1284
1290 1293 1305 1307 1317 1318 1320 1321 1324
1341 1342 1346 1349 1352 1353 1358 1401 1402
1414 1427 1431 1444 1457 1463 1466 1469 1471
1477 1478 1479 1491 1493 1494 1496 1502 1509
1512 1516 1517 1520 1523 1530 1532 1539 1543
1559 1576 1578 1584 1585 1586 1588 1589
15 44 55 56 93 116 122 204 231 233 234 274 277
287 306 381 385 408 429 431 457 478 488 523 541
550 558 594 638 660 682 697 711 756 766 772 780
821 830 837 852 854 869 880 943 944 947 970 974
975 977 978 980 981 1001 1003 1011 1021 1022
1028 1048 1052 1054 1055 1066 1069 1070 1071
1072 1096 1116 1149 1159 1167 1191 1211 1263
1323 1359 1368 1480 1481 1485 1498 1513 1517
1528 1530 1538 1542 1544 1634 1658 1688 1712
1741 1754 1772 1783 1784 1785 1802 1810 1817
1899 1916 1965 1968 1991 2088 2092 2101 2117
2121 2193 2194 2196 2201 2204 2218 2220 2259
2288 2321 2323 2324 2330 2332 2343 2344 2357
2358 2360 2365 2388 2393 2395 2397 2399 2400
2401 2408 2425 2446 2448 2455 2456 2496 2522
2541 2542 2550 2590 2645 2679 2688 2689 2691

toolbox (1) 17 1601
tooled (1) 17 1367
toooo (1) 18 678
Tooraloo (1) 10 490
tooralooloo (1) 15 4920
tooraloom (16) 5 15 16 6 686 15 1725 4827 4828
tooraloom (2) 15 4916 4917
tooth (4) 8 663 701 15 3484 17 1564
toothache (2) 3 186 11 575
toothed (1) 14 856
Toothless (2) 1 708 3 496
toothless (1) 2 429
toothless (1) 15 4161
toothsome (1) 4 391
tootle (1) 12 997
tootles (1) 8 674
Tootling (1) 11 1053
tootsies (1) 14 1464
Top (1) 8 728
top (26) 1 14 233 3 133 4 479 6 627 7 127 132 145 931 1005 8 233 10 303 465 12 20 766 13 56 15 2233 16 524 674 1214 17 1297 1536 2097 18 133 937 1258
top (7) 15 132 1748 1842 2216 3525 3565 4166
topboots (3) 2 283 286 287
Topers (1) 8 363
topers (2) 8 1160 10 767
Tophet (1) 14 398
topiary (1) 17 1514
topic (2) 16 425 911
topical (2) 12 733 17 417
topics (2) 16 100 1890
topknot (1) 15 2253
topnobbers (1) 6 222
toponomastic (1) 17 752
topper (2) 7 171 10 1266
Topping (1) 15 3773
topping (1) 11 707
toppling (3) 2 9 3 249 16 1003
toppling (2) 15 689 4245
tops (2) 13 171 17 154
tops (1) 15 3318
Topsyturvy (1) 14 463
toque (2) 8 266 15 557
toques (1) 12 1287
Torah (2) 17 753 2049
torch (1) 10 398
TORCHBEARERS (1) 15 1374
torchbearers (1) 17 1655
torches (1) 17 1656
torches (1) 15 3960
torchlight (2) 6 978 17 1654
torchlight (1) 15 1373
torcs (1) 3 301
tordant (1) 3 169
tore (8) 4 537 5 260 300 6 168 7 521 15 4273 16 666 18 558
toreadors (1) 15 3960
torero (2) 15 1069 17 1810
tormented (1) 18 812
Torn (2) 4 439 5 156
torn (6) 1 109 4 308 7 519 9 4 14 1551 15 3187
torn (3) 15 935 4158 4327
toro (1) 18 632
Toros (1) 17 1986
torpor (1) 15 2166
torrent (3) 12 652 14 1389 18 1598

torrent (1) 15 3991
torrential (1) 12 531
torrents (1) 17 206
torrid (1) 17 202
Torry (1) 8 17
tortoise (1) 11 166
tortoiseshell (2) 13 639 1136
tortoiseshell (1) 15 1027
torts (1) 15 1642
tortured (1) 1 274
tortured (1) 15 2574
Tory (1) 14 683
tory (1) 2 268
Toss (1) 8 346
toss (3) 1 498 8 904 13 268
toss (1) 15 4677
Tossed (1) 11 419
tossed (10) 1 330 4 265 387 5 386 7 333 390 8 916 12 1772 18 337 972
tosses (3) 15 2714 3619 3763
tossing (2) 13 475 18 478
tossing (1) 15 2286
TOSTOFF (1) 9 1181
tot (1) 4 134
total (10) 8 570 15 1804 16 1264 1696 17 237 315 346 1329 1706 1707
totally (3) 16 1747 17 850 2102
tother (1) 14 173
toto (1) 16 780
tot's (1) 13 257
tots (1) 7 95
totted (1) 10 97
Tottenham (1) 12 235
totters (3) 15 4019 4152 4748
totting (1) 15 28
totty (1) 12 1660
Touch (9) 1 290 3 434 436 7 293 8 591 9 296 10 967 11 640 15 3103
touch (36) 1 155 3 434 436 4 103 511 5 104 178 6 18 80 7 135 8 898 9 433 530 1161 10 582 11 560 12 500 13 708 1158 1198 14 1463 15 1278 2389 3458 4066 4068 16 167 865 1179 17 289 18 73 158 190 800 811 1383
touch (1) 15 1585
Touched (1) 8 899
touched (24) 2 133 6 709 7 40 8 293 513 905 1090 9 531 826 970 10 958 1264 11 346 580 601 668 12 653 14 657 762 15 359 16 371 614 18 107 312
Touches (1) 15 3144
touches (2) 6 670 8 1128
touches (1) 15 2500
touching (14) 6 673 7 811 11 676 1115 13 625 14 203 961 1315 15 3558 16 89 331 1127 18 1039 1040
touching (2) 15 2489 4064
touchingly (1) 10 791
touchmenot (1) 18 1037
touchy (1) 6 754
tough (3) 3 388 8 747 14 1437
tougher (1) 6 778
toughness (1) 12 158
toupee (1) 15 2253
Tour (1) 8 1064
tour (12) 5 162 6 212 217 445 8 771 1047 12 989 991 998 16 513 518 17 2176
Touraine (1) 18 1189
toured (1) 16 412

Touring (1) 15 231
touring (1) 6 221
tourist (1) 16 265 564 17 1720
Tourists (2) 7 150 194
tourists (1) 10 340
tourists' (1) 13 1139
Tours (1) 12 1694
tours (1) 16 1654
tous (1) 3 235
tousled (1) 4 248
Tout (2) 15 4045 4046
tout (1) 5 14
tout (1) 3 234
touts (1) 15 3962
tow (2) 13 1234 14 739
toward (1) 14 640
Towards (1) 10 230
towards (102) 1 12 181 224 230 363 454 523 569 600 620 672 2 179 184 381 382 3 160 310 339 346 4 248 383 473 5 138 183 301 394 542 549 6 136 534 862 910 1027 7 74 118 125 297 356 480 571 797 819 971 1029 1064 8 123 309 313 410 565 690 697 702 834 902 1028 9 90 161 407 476 486 10 9 17 247 311 357 488 718 899 902 930 932 961 991 1027 1212 1270 11 214 275 343 1151 1253 12 659 13 348 354 363 406 467 14 391 874 1376 16 596 1882 1887 17 149 338 561 562 617 1046 1051 1213
towards (17) 15 141 164 578 604 653 2015 2257 2300 2722 2752 3254 3384 4029 4218 4737 4747 4786
towel (3) 1 559 12 985 18 574
Tower (2) 7 6 1046
tower (22) 1 10 49 148 227 281 313 538 541 566 3 271 297 4 29 6 987 12 151 166 1455 13 45 1205 14 365 1539 16 515 18 783
tower (2) 15 4166 4690
towering (1) 13 600
towering (1) 7 316
Towers (1) 4 236
towers (1) 8 491
towhorse (1) 10 102
Town (1) 11 887
town (26) 1 695 4 132 6 284 558 8 873 9 116 409 412 804 10 106 989 1005 1015 13 322 1223 14 498 654 663 780 1495 15 3119 16 909 953 1366 18 409
town (1) 15 1626
townbred (1) 14 1212
townclerk (3) 16 661 1354 1674
Towncrier (1) 11 1243
townhithe (1) 14 88
townland (1) 7 91
townlands (1) 10 159
towns (1) 6 217
Townsend (1) 5 10
township (1) 10 1274
townsmen (1) 15 4717
towpath (1) 6 440
Towser (1) 15 692
towser (2) 12 149 706
toxicum (1) 14 1534
toxin (2) 17 631 1919
toyable (1) 9 1139
toys (3) 1 265 3 291 16 1769
trace (5) 5 564 8 95 10 1082 12 1204 15 3024
traceable (1) 17 770
tracery (1) 17 1509

Trees (1) 13 1078
trees (24) 2 428   3 208   4 94 193   6 488
    7 701   8 404 857   10 101   12 75 79 1260
    1263 1715   13 681 720 1172   14 1158
    15 3306   17 14 45 898 1570   18 852
trees (1) 15 3328
treeshade (1) 10 16
treestems (1) 15 3409
trefoil (1) 17 1389
trekking (1) 3 392
trellis (1) 17 1527
trema (2) 6 239   15 351
tremble (3) 12 167   14 23   15 2869
trembled (2) 11 1108   14 911
trembles (1) 3 230
trembles (1) 7 859
trembles (1) 15 4670
trembling (8) 1 282   2 145   7 810   8 651
    724 1082   13 728   14 39
trembling (2) 15 1121 2854
tremendous (2) 18 144 154
Tremendously (1) 15 460
tremendously (1) 14 1563
tremour (1) 13 695
tremulous (3) 11 45 1031   17 2117
trench (1) 17 187
trenchancy (1) 15 4445
Trenchant (1) 15 496
Trenchant (1) 6 149
trenchant (1) 11 1148
trenchant (1) 6 147
trencherman (1) 12 1611
trend (1) 16 1590
trentals (1) 14 1427
trente (1) 9 1135
trespass (4) 2 324   10 426   17 1629 2187
trespassed (1) 14 206
trespassers (2) 17 1560 1628
trespasses (1) 15 1929
Tress (1) 17 1212
tresses (1) 13 510
trews (2) 9 337   12 170
trial (4) 2 335   3 484   12 346   17 1517
triangle (3) 9 1065   16 887   17 1995
triangled (1) 14 1108
triangular (2) 17 1438 1778
tribal (3) 12 175 1211   15 2321
tribe (15) 6 251   12 201 1125 1126 1127 1128
    1129
tribe (1) 7 846
tribes (2) 12 1125 1241
tribune (1) 12 555
tribune's (2) 7 881   16 1504
tributaries (1) 17 204
tribute (5) 2 85   9 722   12 1837   14 14
    286
tributes (1) 17 2009
trice (1) 14 697
trice (1) 15 2636
trick (15) 3 420   10 697   11 392
    12 1174   13 886 1238   14 595 1357
    15 195 204 4176 4434 4590   16 502 1046
trick (1) 15 2692
trickies (1) 7 1009
trickies (1) 15 4144
trickle (2) 1 477   4 388
trickleaps (1) 15 196
trickling (1) 8 643
trickling (1) 15 4189

tricks (1) 7 785
tricks (1) 15 1604
tricky (1) 12 978
Tried (2) 8 537   9 403
tried (22) 5 39 320   6 272   9 280 754
    12 595 1094 1370   13 161 651   14 1022
    15 2986 3473   16 186 189 634   18 453 557
    569 803 1259 1474
tries (1) 16 1491
tries (2) 15 4575 4873
Trieste (1) 16 576
Trieste-Zurich-Paris (1) 18 1610
trifle (3) 6 806   14 1322   16 832
trifled (1) 13 593
trifling (1) 11 486
Trik (1) 12 565
Trilby (2) 18 1042 1043
trilingual (1) 17 1724
triliteral (1) 17 581
trilled (1) 11 378
Trilling (1) 11 9
trilling (3) 9 1142   11 9 225
trillions (1) 17 1061
trim (1) 6 767
trimmed (3) 13 156 199 237
trimmed (1) 15 1442
Trinacria (1) 14 1232
Trinidad (1) 16 271
Trinitarians (1) 12 1682
Trinity (19) 7 801   8 412 424 428 706 707
    9 31   10 342 366   12 1112   13 133 135
    15 86 3005 4297 4302 4591   17 791
    18 1331
Trinity (1) 15 4329
trinity (1) 9 911
Trinity's (2) 8 476   10 1264
trinketed (1) 15 328
trinketware (1) 14 1052
trinkst (1) 14 1432
trio (1) 11 474
trip (3) 4 452   13 1185   16 510
tripe (1) 5 37
tripes (3) 1 206   8 750   14 541
triple (6) 10 1189   11 292 293   12 1282
    14 1583   15 3487
triplets (1) 14 961
trippant (1) 3 337
tripped (3) 9 1157   13 485   16 1858
Tripping (1) 1 42
tripping (3) 11 960   12 1063   14 778
tripping (1) 15 4045
Trips (1) 17 1374
trips (3) 15 1281 1608 2023
tripudium (1) 3 448
tripudium (1) 15 4013
trireme (1) 7 847
Trismegistos (1) 15 2269
Tristan (1) 12 192
tritely (1) 1 705
Tritonville (3) 6 30   13 277 631
triumph (3) 1 650   11 363   17 2224
triumph (2) 15 1216 1441
triumphaliter (1) 15 98
trivet (1) 16 1623
trivial (2) 7 764   16 1690
triviality (1) 9 287
triweekly (1) 16 1563
troath (1) 11 249
trod (3) 3 147   5 338   10 1043

troglodyte (1) 17 2051
Troilus (1) 9 401
trolley (1) 7 3
trolley (1) 15 186
trolleys (1) 7 1044
trolling (2) 9 1125   16 978
trollop (1) 14 733
trombetta (1) 9 34
Trombone (1) 11 576
troop (2) 7 877   14 1114
trooping (1) 14 1091
Troops (1) 15 4662
troops (2) 15 4606   16 1016
trop (1) 16 1454
trophies (1) 15 4623
trophy (1) 7 778
tropic (1) 17 195
tropical (2) 16 1632   17 1553
troposphere (1) 17 1090
troppo (1) 11 541
trot (6) 6 622   10 794   11 698   13 971
    15 2948
troth (1) 14 357
trots (1) 15 3728
trotted (6) 3 336 358   6 437   10 364
    11 884
Trotter (1) 17 1471
trotter (4) 15 159 256 669 672
trotting (5) 3 332   6 172   8 704   12 255
    18 1290
trottingmatches (2) 5 298   18 1069
trou (1) 11 484
troublants (1) 15 3893
Trouble (2) 8 389 943
trouble (32) 1 23   4 463   5 90   6 15 916
    7 543   8 220 420 429 942 948 1003   10 454
    989   11 210 437 546 548 649   12 781 1060
    1144   13 351 877   15 1649 4415 4511
    16 93   17 1826   18 34 526
trouble (1) 7 581
trouble (1) 15 930
troubled (7) 2 40   4 432   8 108   10 638
    11 684   13 455   15 3547
troubles (9) 9 4   10 781   12 390   13 58
    381 1194   16 606   18 726 1459
troubling (2) 6 93   18 1126
trough (1) 5 565
troughs (1) 8 413
trounced (1) 15 1112
trouser (3) 1 65 448   17 1444
trouser (2) 15 201 1309
trouserbutton (1) 15 3439
trouserfly (1) 3 477
trouserleg (2) 5 50   10 354
Trousers (4) 8 1189   11 555   13 831
    17 586
Trousers (1) 8 92
trousers (35) 1 122 169 704   2 224   3 371
    4 73 461 495 538 542   5 468   7 229   8 1141
    1168   10 57 364 905 1282   11 481   13 201
    801   15 1118 1911 2094   16 36 655   17 73
    75 1437 2040   18 313 961 1093 1231 1372
trousers (8) 15 299 816 875 957 2035 3841
    4037 4330
trousers' (3) 4 182 439   10 324
trovarmi (1) 10 358
trove (1) 13 639
trowed (1) 14 135
trowel (1) 8 577

trowel (1) 15 4455
trowlers (1) 18 1290
Troy (8) 2 392 6 682 7 910 8 1152
  9 622 12 1 9 14
Troy (1) 15 4358
truant (1) 9 245
truce (1) 14 1427
trucks (1) 6 402
truculent (1) 17 2050
truculent (2) 15 147 2491
trudged (3) 3 370 9 246 10 818
trudges (1) 3 392
trudging (1) 4 161
True (9) 8 828 9 11 11 56 873 1276
  12 778 951 14 584 15 207
true (51) 2 143 275 4 40 536 5 326
  6 244 811 9 11 36 709 811 843 10 828 851
  978 11 992 1009 12 207 358 395 991 1130
  1131 1133 1362 1376 1658 13 46 91 1136
  14 450 840 848 1017 1229 1262 1333 15 1210
  2805 3009 16 421 554 1656 17 691 692
  18 487 492 737 775 776 1577
true (1) 10 735
Trübsal (1) 14 1432
truedup (1) 15 3250
Truelock's (1) 15 645
truepenny (1) 9 183
truer (2) 12 783 14 1423
truerhearted (1) 13 35
Truest (1) 14 78
truest (3) 12 403 13 279 14 184
Truffles (1) 15 2851
truffles (3) 8 722 15 2439 2741
truism (1) 16 1013
trulls (1) 14 620
truly (8) 10 546 11 815 12 1131
  13 434 16 45 948 1388 18 513
truly (1) 17 401
truly (1) 15 913
trumming (1) 15 425
trumped (1) 15 944
Trumpery (1) 14 1550
trumpet (1) 12 1497
trumpeted (1) 14 1093
trumping (1) 11 1156
Trumplee (1) 17 604
Trumps (1) 12 565
truncated (1) 17 1331
truncheon (1) 15 1203
truncheons (1) 8 408
trundle (1) 6 800
trundled (1) 6 638
trundling (1) 17 1584
trunk (6) 1 133 515 5 568 15 2191
  17 1778 2098
trunk (1) 15 606
trunkhose (1) 11 495
trunkleg (1) 15 2994
trunks (3) 6 91 140 14 509
truss (2) 12 688 15 3251
trussmakers (1) 15 1429
Trust (2) 8 250 13 1251
trust (7) 1 161 12 772 13 178 414
  16 279 17 2185 18 1171
trust (1) 15 1829
trusted (1) 13 693
trustees (2) 12 50 51
trusts (1) 3 424
trusty (2) 16 1330 1498

truth (27) 1 505 3 323 7 1075 9 1018
  10 166 12 459 1038 1039 1048 13 80
  14 210 259 535 1204 15 2259 16 325 431
  781 1120 1311 17 323 711 716 18 737 1237
truthfully (2) 16 218 744
Try (12) 3 290 5 274 6 845 7 192
  8 861 1188 10 610 11 122 15 2741 3969
  16 158 787
try (40) 2 342 413 3 50 323 4 519 5 95
  6 114 539 945 7 836 8 565 1142 9 979
  10 266 704 966 11 116 739 12 1131 1363
  1409 13 111 359 668 14 1591 15 2542
  16 755 791 1039 1130 18 473 484 511 551
  1360 1382 1414 1547 1571
Trying (1) 15 594
trying (42) 2 342 377 3 184 5 36 6 537
  8 376 967 10 658 888 1172 12 390 491 506
  800 1082 1195 1322 1386 1426 1787 1799
  13 1238 1271 15 943 16 266 348 427 517
  1208 18 28 96 209 248 342 549 551 570 693 713
  1041 1044 1268
tryon (1) 16 580
tryst (1) 13 1169
tsar (1) 15 4435
Tschink (1) 11 1280
tschink (1) 11 57
Tschunk (1) 11 1280
tschunk (1) 11 57
tsong (1) 18 908
Ttob (1) 15 1400
Tu (1) 9 642
tu (2) 14 1540
tua (1) 7 717
tuae (1) 10 198
Tuam (1) 12 1706
Tuam (1) 12 1748
tuam (1) 12 1746
tub (3) 1 481 4 435 15 3073
tubbing (1) 8 171
tube (5) 12 1568 14 437 438 15 86
  18 970
tubercles (1) 14 693
Tuberculosis (1) 15 1689
tubers (1) 15 2439
tubes (2) 10 100 11 884
tublumber (1) 15 4150
Tuck (1) 14 1553
tuck (3) 4 257 13 1055 18 189
tucked (8) 3 298 5 319 8 200 658
  10 115 12 254 13 606 18 1238
tucker (1) 14 758
tuckin (1) 16 871
tucking (1) 10 562
tuckstitched (1) 8 809
Tudor (1) 9 630
Tudor's (1) 12 1308
Tuesday (6) 3 491 6 887 8 292 13 158
  501 17 655
tuft (1) 6 912
tufts (1) 15 2290
Tugela (1) 18 403
tugged (5) 1 593 8 480 10 667 1155
  11 388
tugging (2) 10 654 13 507
tugging (2) 15 4597 4770
tugs (1) 4 256
tugs (1) 15 31
Tui (1) 12 1749
tuis (1) 10 205

tuition (1) 16 1841
tuk (1) 14 1539
tulips (2) 5 264 17 1556
Tullamore (1) 12 1457
tulle (1) 15 4035
Tully (1) 14 384
tum (4) 3 492 11 890
tum (1) 13 499
Tumble (1) 15 2342
tumble (3) 13 486 832 16 1634
tumbled (2) 3 213 15 3719
tumbler (6) 8 657 840 11 225 317 12 821
  17 1412
tumbler (1) 15 4315
tumblerful (1) 17 905
tumbles (1) 9 260
tumbles (1) 15 2152
tumbling (3) 12 492 17 1565 18 593
tumbling (1) 7 244
tumescence (3) 14 67 17 1201 1313
tumescent (1) 15 2360
tummies (1) 8 3
tummy (1) 13 610
tumultuary (1) 14 849
tumultuously (1) 14 1398
tumulus (1) 14 397
Tun (1) 16 1816
tunbelly (1) 3 385
Tune (1) 8 1116
tune (7) 1 299 11 841 1014 1062 1238
  12 694 15 1720
Tuned (1) 11 650
tuneful (1) 3 102
tuner (3) 11 277 314 1210
tunic (1) 8 419
tunics (1) 15 61
Tuning (1) 11 1050
tuning (1) 11 277
tuningfork (3) 11 313 600 1207
tunket's (1) 14 1546
tunnels (1) 18 372
Tunney (1) 13 333
Tunney's (2) 10 1128 1168
Tunney's (1) 15 3838
tuo (3) 6 601 12 1743 14 303
tuorum (1) 10 197
Tup (3) 11 707 708
tup (1) 11 25
Tupper (3) 12 1170 1173 1499
tupthrob (1) 11 709
turban (1) 2 214
turban (1) 15 314
Turbaned (1) 4 88
turbans (1) 18 1593
turbary (1) 17 1501
turbines (1) 17 221
turds (1) 16 1877
turf (10) 6 328 440 451 911 7 606 10 105
  13 1135 14 476 1188 15 3084
turfbarge (1) 10 101
turgidity (1) 17 190
turgidly (1) 14 1385
Turk (1) 12 1369
Turkey (1) 14 509
turkey (3) 5 546 8 85 15 3746
turkey (1) 15 2434
turkeys (1) 8 753
Turkish (6) 4 192 5 502 6 757 13 1241
  17 338 2094

Turkish (1) 15 298
Turko (1) 4 89
Turko (1) 1 258
Turko (1) 15 4612
Turks (3) 11 942 16 1128 18 1495
turlhide (1) 3 303
Turma (2) 1 737 17 1230
turma (1) 1 277
turmoil (1) 14 321
Turn (8) 2 80 3 269 5 375 8 216
  10 467 483 15 1364 3178
turn (47) 1 363 4 392 524 5 33 171 556
  6 109 7 301 466 8 905 1103 1154 9 261
  752 10 154 467 480 485 771 898 12 1443
  1795 13 390 632 977 1054 14 451 602 669
  726 944 1553 15 657 943 1263 16 1777
  17 111 188 261 737 1103 18 87 116 1009 1267
  1530 1533
turn (3) 1 239 264 3 445
turn (10) 15 60 906 1850 4075 4101 4153 4322
  4421 4838 4909
Turnbull (1) 17 48
Turnbull (1) 15 3326
Turncoat (1) 15 791
TURNED (1) 7 84
turned (129) 1 86 125 230 368 465 472 549 569
  634 719 2 82 188 444 3 159 278 336 503
  4 12 59 74 231 345 374 386 5 3 47 76 150 229
  378 472 6 29 140 372 427 708 831 865 921
  7 42 130 409 527 547 647 702 746 797 819 916
  954 1029 8 228 641 702 1022 1046 1069
  9 111 472 512 613 670 1177 10 73 203 312 357
  398 453 585 773 813 836 926 1033 1107 1117 1138
  1139 1140 11 215 250 460 476 602 634 666 730
  953 12 3 118 13 143 331 1246 14 1157
  15 1290 1724 2988 3137 16 50 193 195 336
  387 395 441 487 568 608 707 1036 1088 1117 1196
  1238 1292 1522 1733 1846 17 116 880 1262
  18 40 1077 1135 1317 1423
turned (1) 10 617
turned (3) 15 126 958 1147
turnedin (1) 12 1497
Turnedup (1) 8 1168
turnedup (2) 3 371 13 800
turnedup (1) 15 3841
Turning (5) 1 742 3 270 406 4 120
  6 777
turning (38) 1 286 317 730 2 218 435
  4 17 258 500 6 24 412 733 898 914 7 455
  545 635 10 378 690 908 11 188 436 472 637
  15 978 16 54 71 597 1053 1423 1655
  17 105 121 162 1216 18 257 408 1291
turning (2) 15 2902 4061
turningpoint (1) 17 990
turnip (1) 17 1605
turnip (1) 15 1610
turnips (2) 6 994 8 927
turnips (1) 15 3992
Turnkey's (1) 8 459
turnover (1) 15 3318
turnovers (1) 4 83
Turns (2) 10 476 13 826
turns (7) 5 481 6 308 807 10 480 1014
  16 1085 18 1387
turns (23) 15 67 744 785 1191 1849 2031 2063
  2142 2492 2692 2709 3500 3663 3698 4015 4017
  4096 4112 4126 4426 4460 4817 4934
turnscrew (1) 17 1602
turnstile (2) 7 943 9 1122

turpentine (1) 13 1002
Turpin (1) 12 194
turpitude (1) 15 3904
turreting (1) 15 314
turtle (1) 4 386
turtle (3) 15 1257 2902 3254
turtledove (1) 9 540
turves (1) 17 1599
tusk (1) 9 459
tusked (1) 14 1093
tusks (1) 15 416
Tut (1) 14 778
tut (1) 14 778
tutelam (1) 12 1749
tutelary (1) 14 924
tutt'amor (1) 11 594
TUTTI (1) 15 4134
tutto (1) 15 2504
Tutu (1) 3 197
twain (2) 9 413 14 78
Twang (1) 11 811
twang (1) 3 127
twanged (3) 4 96 7 372 11 796
twanging (1) 15 425
Twankey's (1) 15 283
'Twas (5) 9 559 10 829 12 211 15 435
  3276
'*Twas* (5) 7 471 472 11 779 785 787
'twas (2) 11 780 14 1071
'*twas* (2) 9 98 11 694
tway (1) 14 76
tweaked (1) 2 388
tweed (6) 6 828 7 505 8 1107 14 1211
  17 1582 18 1573
tweeds (1) 12 1246
Tweedy (19) 4 63 6 233 693 11 503
  12 1003 15 779 3767 16 798 1437 1442
  1745 17 56 411 1420 1984 2082 2100 18 723
Tweedy (2) 15 4612 4622
TWEEDY (2) 15 4617 4751
Tweedy-Flower (1) 16 525
Tweedy's (2) 4 87 5 66
tweezers (1) 17 1602
tweezers (1) 15 4352
Twelfth (1) 16 1738
twelfth (3) 1 708 5 404 17 94
Twelve (5) 1 539 4 425 6 682 825
  12 1452
Twelve (1) 15 1577
twelve (17) 1 733 2 203 222 3 59 5 33
  6 756 7 210 9 38 12 1125 1130 1134
  14 77 121 2517 16 1576 17 143 572
twelve (2) 15 1843 2274
twelvefold (1) 15 921
twelvemonth (1) 14 516
Twelvetrees (1) 12 1271
Twenty (10) 6 237 834 7 385 9 623 631
  12 1226 1372 13 1115 14 1428 15 4814
twenty (19) 1 43 2 270 5 310 6 513
  7 941 1002 8 135 385 9 649 11 281
  12 1088 1219 1240 1563 15 1525 2936 3154
  16 636 1310
Twentyeight (5) 7 220 385 8 608
  13 1126
twentyeight (1) 4 236
twentyeight (2) 15 1416 1492
twentyfifth (1) 5 152
twentyfive (1) 17 662
Twentyfour (1) 11 1225

twentyfour (1) 11 878
twentyfour (1) 15 3726
twentyone (3) 8 384 387 17 129
twentysecond (1) 10 1139
Twentyseven (1) 10 391
twentyseven (1) 6 393
Twentyseventh (1) 6 933
twentysix (1) 9 258
twentythree (1) 8 609
Twentytwo (1) 15 3719
twentytwo (6) 13 222 15 3714 3718 3719
  17 97
'*twere* (1) 7 320
Twice (2) 13 977 17 860
Twice (1) 15 3667
twice (38) 1 327 2 292 3 407 4 427
  6 10 655 7 62 402 952 9 657 669 1013
  10 139 262 644 11 445 582 831 1061
  12 977 999 13 353 15 2986 3833 16 30
  161 401 1700 17 79 834 18 11 58 328 493
  512 707 942 1547
twice (1) 15 3666
Twicreakingly (1) 9 12
twict (1) 15 887
Twig (1) 14 1493
twig (5) 2 145 8 446 10 202 441
  15 2223
Twigg (2) 8 331 527
twigged (1) 13 915
twikindled (1) 14 974
Twilight (5) 8 378 14 1083 17 612 614
  617
twilight (7) 4 248 13 369 624 751 14 966
  1080 18 898
twilight (2) 7 324 13 647
twilight (2) 15 4075 4082
twill (1) 4 253
twin (3) 9 177 12 281 14 1003
twine (1) 3 125
twined (3) 11 82 83 634
twinge (1) 15 2782
twinging (1) 15 417
twingtwang (1) 15 415
Twining (1) 15 4099
twining (4) 1 245 246 11 81 14 351
twinkle (1) 15 3773
twinkled (2) 1 615 13 1181
twinkling (5) 3 336 9 102 11 324 958
  13 1066
twins (19) 13 16 17 41 55 305 345 355 363 381
  406 466 492 505 529 895 14 961 15 1669
  18 161 539
twins (3) 15 133 1603 2512
twins' (1) 13 571
twirl (1) 15 4122
twirled (1) 6 141
twirling (3) 6 109 10 1014 15 2383
twirling (6) 15 2289 2302 3858 4056 4088 4092
twirls (2) 15 4024 4038
twist (1) 18 743
twisted (9) 1 451 4 322 8 894 1010
  9 611 809 873 11 82 821
twisted (2) 15 584 1239
twisting (4) 6 101 10 1048 12 1479
  18 849
twisting (1) 15 2906
twists (3) 15 1346 2300 2901
twitch (1) 7 709
twitch (1) 15 2334

unsullied (1) 13 746
unsunned (1) 15 1769
unsurpassed (1) 15 2440
unsympathetic (1) 17 1949
untastable (1) 16 1141
untaught (1) 9 477
untidy (3) 5 456 8 264 10 77
untied (2) 13 186 16 1211
Until (1) 17 823
until (6) 12 47 15 1170 16 1065 1301
  17 459 1664
untimely (1) 9 456
unto (5) 9 1052 13 458 14 377 391
  16 1556
untold (1) 15 932
untonsured (1) 1 15
untrammelled (1) 13 673
unturned (1) 12 721
Unusual (1) 17 685
unusual (3) 16 119 17 1683 1684
unusually (1) 15 2380
Unveiled (1) 9 279
unveiled (2) 9 269 14 1032
unveiled (1) 15 3469
unwashed (2) 7 373 16 662
unwearied (1) 11 717
unweave (2) 9 376 378
unweaving (1) 15 4092
Unwed (1) 9 1062
unweeded (1) 6 477
unwelcome (1) 14 853
Unwell (1) 14 1566
unwell (1) 15 3066
Unwholesome (1) 3 150
unwilling (1) 14 98
unwound (1) 11 681
unwrapped (1) 4 275
unwrinkled (1) 16 1573
Up (18) 6 237 620 8 347 434 597 11 604
  1187 13 895 14 1502 15 791 3129 3399
  3750 4473 4519 4618

up (749) 1 8 24 36 70 82 109 128 161 179 206
  228 235 281 298 324 334 345 346 449 451 498 508
  520 547 588 673 676 687 688 701 704 730 2 113
  116 125 149 174 298 320 342 348 388 3 66 123
  152 242 278 331 344 345 362 462 498 504 4 33
  49 85 93 102 104 105 110 114 115 126 154 165 171
  173 182 212 233 255 256 263 297 321 378 384 417
  430 460 463 468 469 486 487 498 503 544 5 74
  98 99 114 124 127 153 154 171 188 303 336 375
  385 401 414 415 448 452 463 469 471 488 494 503
  509 551 6 75 79 109 122 133 168 218 219 283
  350 394 403 423 425 426 428 429 519 564 566 577
  606 607 622 642 675 678 679 726 727 728 730 737
  757 758 765 780 807 834 842 864 902 998 7 22
  45 103 134 137 187 219 233 389 396 401 416 431
  600 664 687 699 725 727 878 932 944 996 1001
  1013 1017 1024 8 19 30 44 60 71 96 99 153 166
  191 192 194 200 215 216 228 251 253 258 274 320
  369 375 384 397 404 409 415 417 446 460 468 474
  488 489 512 559 560 569 574 617 630 676 688 718
  730 744 750 773 784 787 805 834 856 876 948 955
  963 983 1008 1031 1042 1083 1098 1154 9 155
  164 329 475 478 496 606 761 785 803 847 872 896
  1017 1054 1074 1086 10 229 254 330 363 383
  389 396 439 502 520 547 559 620 657 662 666 721
  737 887 895 1009 1022 1023 1038 1051 1132 1140
  1155 1162 1207 1268 11 30 605 765 842 871 872
  903 1050 1076 1127 1198 1249 12 60 119 214

250 252 258 259 264 269 273 279 300 309 312 350
379 445 461 487 504 519 529 611 688 749 754 770
802 812 816 827 835 891 893 947 957 962 989 1031
1044 1096 1109 1162 1194 1195 1215 1231 1233
1319 1326 1334 1396 1403 1404 1406 1471 1475
1477 1495 1512 1570 1571 1578 1588 1636 1659
1663 1753 1766 1770 1784 1794 1827 13 60 126
131 147 161 184 244 253 276 278 332 353 385 394
423 447 454 474 479 484 485 497 505 531 539 546
553 555 570 572 573 590 598 605 609 611 621 664
696 697 720 722 729 756 762 787 804 812 857 883
901 916 923 959 970 982 993 1005 1050 1082 1101
1120 1166 1186 1191 1213 1239 1267 1279
14 44 70 156 158 162 273 300 329 421 437 472
485 490 491 513 529 539 594 607 612 617 626 644
684 842 1010 1129 1280 1349 1402 1418 1473 1477
1570 1577 15 91 199 485 573 786 805 928 944
975 1052 1054 1116 1233 1263 1609 1803 1971
2196 2207 2217 2398 2542 2815 2944 2987 2994
3066 3075 3107 3115 3118 3143 3176 3288 3446
3447 3820 3948 4266 4379 4382 4522 4756 4864
4874 4882 16 3 19 40 71 98 183 201 376 395
396 450 505 532 541 543 581 582 610 634 654 708
710 809 831 856 925 933 943 971 992 1073 1111
1121 1146 1225 1334 1342 1346 1347 1365 1380
1385 1397 1485 1492 1501 1515 1537 1552 1565
1603 1617 1620 1625 1639 1653 1750 1772 1789
1808 1859 1876 17 600 1106 1652 18 3 15 37
42 45 49 70 74 97 109 110 127 134 150 152 160 180
187 204 227 229 233 250 291 325 381 404 405 420
424 444 460 472 475 484 494 495 506 511 522 529
537 538 540 543 548 558 574 594 602 608 628 639
645 663 664 665 684 694 707 711 733 738 758 763
766 772 782 804 805 807 811 824 851 855 856 872
913 914 917 919 931 932 933 934 977 979 996 1035
1041 1056 1060 1064 1088 1096 1102 1104 1106
1120 1122 1129 1135 1146 1147 1156 1180 1206 1211
1238 1259 1281 1291 1322 1347 1350 1382 1391
1411 1413 1418 1420 1432 1446 1498 1504 1511
1522 1527 1539 1541 1548 1551 1563 1584

up (7) 1 384 5 283 284 288 292 6 165
  12 28
up (53) 15 35 288 297 404 729 904 926 988 1026
  1059 1078 1246 1399 1494 1499 1558 1589 1608
  1715 2058 2164 2174 2289 2291 2964 3463 3524
  3550 3565 3584 3597 3641 3669 3698 3750 3916
  3982 4000 4109 4121 4148 4278 4284 4330 4413
  4449 4548 4552 4648 4661 4681 4750 4860
Upanishads (1) 1 371
upbraid (1) 1 406
upcast (2) 6 929 17 2300
upcurled (1) 15 832
upcurling (1) 15 2355
updraught (1) 17 257
upended (1) 1 329
upfloor (1) 14 170
upheavals (1) 17 1004
upheld (1) 14 142
upheld (1) 15 2037
uphold (1) 15 2657
Upholding (1) 11 291
upholding (1) 17 1627
upholstered (5) 12 539 15 1391
  17 1281 1294 1530
upland (1) 17 1604
uplift (1) 14 413
uplifted (3) 7 367 10 403 15 3426
uplifted (2) 15 322 2217
Upon (2) 9 80 842

Upon (1) 1 240
upon (121) 1 105 658 2 17 85 3 51 53
  6 587 7 254 449 806 8 520 811 843 905
  9 63 494 615 836 842 1088 1210 10 658 1053
  1221 1222 1223 11 21 238 267 538 591 1033
  1149 12 532 571 616 637 786 1117 1330 1354
  1597 1744 1773 1912 1914 13 6 47 193 281 689
  691 14 216 272 291 309 313 352 375 424 494
  636 667 673 693 706 713 715 716 722 727 750 756
  825 847 874 876 917 926 971 981 1054 1092 1109
  1163 1315 1358 1377 1390 15 1394 1506 1810
  2437 4427 16 7 10 12 431 458 1361 1368 1508
  1538 1594 1603 1682 1839 17 124 281 410 1014
  1152 1509 1670 1871 1920 1928
upon (7) 15 37 185 1173 1275 2854 3227 4182
upp (1) 11 249
Upper (1) 7 1046
upper (17) 1 68 3 78 5 521 7 5 669
  8 1034 9 1088 10 108 972 12 980
  16 82 1200 1748 17 170 296 317 1559
upper (2) 15 1764 2478
Uppercross (1) 17 53
upright (9) 6 175 8 514 689 915 10 667
  15 4427 16 1881 17 619 1343
upright (3) 15 160 1935 3987
uprightness (1) 9 745
Uproar (1) 15 935
uproar (1) 2 317
ups (2) 12 1505 16 466
Upsala (1) 3 235
Upset (1) 6 421
upset (4) 6 368 416 14 1196 18 445
upsets (1) 7 261
upsetting (1) 16 1407
upshot (1) 16 1549
upside (3) 16 1709 18 1475
upstairs (9) 4 298 469 10 685 1019
  11 236 15 2025 16 1376 1857 18 1489
upstanding (1) 15 778
upstarched (1) 15 413
upstart (1) 15 1091
upstiffed (1) 3 54
upstream (1) 3 505
upswelling (1) 3 461
uptodate (1) 16 564
uptrunks (1) 11 1053
upturned (5) 9 645 11 93 109 17 1293
  1315
upturned (3) 15 2851 2931 3799
upturning (1) 3 463
upturns (1) 15 4171
upupa (1) 14 1086
upward (6) 3 150 248 480 5 569 8 792
  10 1227
upward (1) 15 2624
upwardcurving (1) 1 735
upwards (2) 12 477 15 2667
uram (1) 12 1816
Uranian (1) 17 1095
urban (1) 15 913
Urbane (1) 9 1
Urbe (1) 17 1503
Urbright (1) 6 160
urchin (1) 7 395
Urchins (1) 15 175
Urchins (1) 15 176
urchins (2) 10 244 254
urge (3) 9 357 14 953 15 1054
urged (9) 9 470 695 10 822 11 174 404
  652 15 1054 1069 16 811

V

W

washing (14) 1 475 4 458 8 482 13 956 16 715 716 17 1565 18 574 904 1011 1095 1357 1584
washingsoda (1) 4 147
washkitchen (2) 16 140 150
washstand (3) 17 2106 2107 18 923
washy (1) 18 413
Wasn't (1) 6 700
wasn't (25) 5 333 456 6 347 826 978 7 339 398 8 217 418 10 573 12 775 13 186 418 477 501 677 730 806 15 3293 16 153 1048 1090 1304 1454
wasnt (19) 18 156 197 216 236 240 259 265 278 321 325 656 735 892 966 1093 1095 1187 1284 1446
waspwaisted (1) 15 4055
wassailing (1) 14 168
wastage (1) 17 179
Waste (2) 8 581 15 658
waste (9) 4 192 219 6 816 10 151 14 1086 15 253 16 1554 17 1699 1702
wasted (2) 1 103 270
wastepipe (1) 15 1031
wastest (1) 15 3827
Wasting (1) 8 1036
wasting (1) 3 263
wastrels (1) 14 276
Wat (1) 9 248
Wat (1) 15 1846
wātāklāsāt (1) 12 354
Watch (12) 5 130 8 299 300 303 317 10 695 13 936 15 4044 18 400
WATCH (38) 15 676 679 696 717 724 732 735 755 771 782 799 858 864 870 882 1042 1152 1155 1196 1198 1202 1221 1223 4772 4783 4790 4798 4803 4810 4816 4823 4829 4833 4842 4844 4846 4850 4854
watch (30) 3 282 6 86 336 7 204 8 560 735 747 979 981 1046 9 270 10 2 312 507 1231 12 979 1026 13 545 547 556 558 847 983 14 1067 1382 1452 15 275 18 182 345 422
watch (13) 15 36 270 674 743 744 746 793 4336 4771 4786 4813 4826 4838
watchchain (3) 1 514 6 720 13 539
watchchains (1) 15 1814
watched (28) 1 397 2 36 184 3 441 4 21 34 39 274 5 234 6 37 442 7 63 8 309 9 662 932 1206 10 184 482 800 1199 1205 1217 11 406 454 13 772 15 1062 16 1064 1886
watcher (3) 1 30 14 80 16 942
Watchers (1) 14 76
watches (6) 3 414 4 95 10 988 1215 12 590 14 1376
watchfob (1) 15 242
watchful (4) 2 303 7 735 8 5 10 1080
Watching (2) 6 849 8 39
watching (19) 1 37 174 669 4 113 359 5 353 6 78 7 162 9 67 13 494 1114 14 1403 15 733 2520 18 303 611 643 921 1446
watching (2) 15 168 3625
Watchman (1) 15 3223
watchman (3) 7 646 16 106 18 1597
watchman's (1) 16 213
watchpocket (1) 13 982
watchtower (1) 12 69
Water (3) 3 324 5 504 6 439
water (111) 1 83 182 195 244 266 358 370 681 689 714 743 2 32 3 90 342 453 462 471 4 44 91 273 516 5 40 296 346 460 491 501 504 565 6 449 621 627 987 7 211 258 949 1048 8 39 94 611 1003 1007 1010 9 203 10 146 295 11 117 211 619 640 772 982 983 12 57 748 974 1000 1001 1735 13 26 1129 1161 14 83 152 475 491 523 632 644 700 749 1367 15 332 3793 4230 16 6 377 571 626 917 975 1191 1588 17 172 175 176 183 234 238 269 271 273 275 313 567 799 1540 1594 1706 1713 1831 18 60 216 597 780 826 929
water (3) 1 591 592 12 744
water (4) 15 3374 3770 4293 4315
Waterbury (1) 15 270
waterbutt (1) 17 1571
watercarrier (3) 9 1186 15 3467 17 183
Watercloset (1) 15 3916
watercloset (1) 3 52
watercloset (1) 7 495
watercourses (1) 17 224
watercress (1) 18 1481
watered (1) 6 87
wateredsilk (1) 15 450
WATERFALL (3) 15 3298 3347 3428
waterfall (1) 15 3303
waterfall (1) 15 3297
Waterford (2) 6 234 14 1332
Waterford (1) 15 1416
Watering (1) 4 216
watering (1) 16 1654
wateringcan (1) 17 1583
wateringplaces (1) 8 1064
waterjug (1) 13 163
waterjugjar (1) 15 2037
Waterlilies (1) 5 35
waterlily (1) 15 898
Waterloo (2) 15 745 3915
waterlover (1) 17 183
watermarked (1) 17 1807
watermelon (1) 15 3922
waterpartings (1) 17 207
waterproof (1) 4 67
waterproof (2) 15 2033 2698
waterrings (1) 17 899
Waters (3) 3 330 12 929 1819
waters (26) 1 249 2 327 3 444 457 469 4 221 5 365 7 894 8 415 9 807 10 20 11 963 12 71 1254 1462 13 4 1251 14 394 742 1114 15 3438 17 213 983 1135 1164 18 1148
waters (5) 7 244 848 8 63 550 9 190
waters (2) 15 2149 3379
watersheds (1) 17 206
waterspouts (1) 17 205
waterspray (1) 17 1554
watertight (1) 12 1718
waterway (2) 6 442 12 1298
waterways (2) 6 447 17 1725
waterworks (3) 13 551 17 173 174
Watery (1) 6 39
watery (3) 2 142 3 474 18 554
watery (1) 2 66
Watling (1) 10 773
wattles (2) 7 663 14 395
wattles (2) 15 811 2434
wave (5) 7 772 11 1106 12 75 13 117 16 1387
wave (1) 15 2661
waved (6) 1 742 11 546 596 13 758 1007 14 1130

wavenoise (1) 3 339
wavering (1) 1 629
Waves (1) 8 550
waves (25) 2 83 3 56 307 341 465 4 221 8 545 11 21 300 936 949 1078 12 355 1213 1307 1782 1869 13 12 286 15 3437 16 629 17 188 18 669 1559
waves (2) 2 78 9 190
waves (3) 15 2268 4414 4418
wavespeech (1) 3 457
Wavewhite (1) 1 246
waving (5) 2 445 7 791 959 9 1162 12 598
waving (2) 15 1409 3960
wavyavyeavyheavyeavyevyevyhair (1) 11 809
wax (13) 1 104 271 5 492 493 512 6 425 10 1215 12 1719 13 451 14 369 15 2817 17 1539 1784
waxed (3) 14 216 412 16 1026
waxedup (1) 8 182
waxen (2) 4 207 13 87
waxies' (1) 7 1008
waxing (3) 9 79 14 341 17 1162
waxing (1) 15 2546
waxwork (1) 17 579
waxworks (1) 16 851
Way (7) 7 51 11 549 573 1049 15 65 18 1038
Way (1) 15 1584
way (264) 1 209 673 692 2 7 325 3 59 158 342 491 4 51 60 151 211 292 350 485 5 78 82 149 185 187 219 304 385 412 6 33 243 270 272 279 430 483 606 792 817 876 1032 7 74 112 176 177 218 308 597 751 893 8 54 149 237 281 317 330 370 376 555 823 948 1020 1046 1073 1081 1104 1111 1146 9 202 257 529 565 601 602 781 993 1065 10 37 114 383 411 506 570 758 1001 1091 1105 1182 1200 1268 11 329 380 477 515 611 943 1094 1192 12 102 121 474 517 637 666 678 759 821 1393 1720 1851 13 143 190 260 301 308 396 570 580 607 714 730 824 825 867 921 922 955 1030 1050 1059 1082 1110 1111 1219 1231 14 218 398 448 808 817 1019 1242 1570 1572 15 232 743 2220 2221 2288 2447 2497 2499 2522 4876 16 37 152 304 312 382 427 428 473 499 511 562 594 612 660 665 707 785 850 855 867 894 917 955 1090 1176 1203 1213 1296 1393 1394 1398 1400 1433 1507 1619 1627 1660 1677 1701 1736 1792 1806 1826 1827 1831 17 167 728 880 909 943 1044 1107 1827 18 54 83 103 112 225 233 277 313 328 329 338 417 420 437 483 533 539 567 590 629 772 793 807 815 833 982 991 1008 1037 1049 1057 1060 1066 1164 1165 1180 1198 1246 1258 1260 1269 1280 1317 1318 1368 1373 1376 1420 1458 1483 1504 1520 1540
way (3) 2 251 253 7 244
way (1) 15 903
wayawayawayawayaway (1) 3 404
wayfarer (1) 17 1266
wayfaring (1) 14 71
waylaid (1) 10 984
waylaying (1) 16 121
Ways (1) 13 927
ways (20) 2 380 4 176 10 172 173 13 18 331 897 14 379 1242 15 3078 16 13 959 1289 1565 17 66 1441 18 189 1120 1475
wayside (1) 6 429

wd (1) 18 616
WE (2) 7 77 120
We (133) 1 42 340 440 554 605 648 2 110 113
262 279 389 3 75 98 319 474 484 4 402 403
5 355 6 126 259 295 339 367 657 662 803 809
857 919 991 7 37 154 160 359 481 484 485 553
554 555 565 603 623 807 894 1061 8 157 1130
9 101 188 277 291 312 318 360 596 618 619 794
993 1044 1098 1129 10 407 552 556 874 878
1058 11 443 488 582 726 727 789 1024
12 723 730 949 1150 1156 1296 1364 1377 1379
1381 1399 1506 1634 1636 1665 1669 13 756
14 227 1462 1505 1573 15 111 623 741 761
836 843 941 1504 1516 1528 2350 2419 2775 2800
3151 3254 3302 3303 3392 3393 3535 4460 4495
4606 4775 4822 4839 16 450 460 1171
We (3) 7 427 12 362 17 1370
we (273) 1 158 411 412 431 433 440 524 648
2 263 310 349 3 174 4 26 206 294 352 362
363 365 5 108 249 265 355 445 453 499 562 564
6 8 14 85 118 415 656 759 829 836 961 1033
7 35 497 499 732 894 8 50 95 125 158 162 169
194 402 568 587 609 640 926 929 1116 1117 9 2
184 185 240 247 273 280 289 322 323 376 439 440
558 559 561 564 565 611 619 754 775 776 812 814
883 884 927 928 956 1094 1108 10 288 547 548
553 733 749 11 442 576 687 789 814 843 979
1064 1246 1257 12 64 118 148 523 524 732 736
1075 1245 1300 1384 1390 1601 1645 1906
13 455 801 840 891 926 1087 1097 1108 1112
1184 1189 1237 1280 14 33 225 **228** 281 300 311
392 397 398 721 774 1141 1153 **1154** 1231 1241
1242 1262 1277 1550 15 120 **392** 400 428 462
540 571 743 802 835 836 1505 1525 1527 1683 2195
2197 2372 2403 2419 2434 2580 2719 2833 2946
2987 3019 3066 3129 3149 3173 4461 4563 4830
4870 4875 4881 16 677 752 886 1138 1225
18 56 86 131 174 181 210 217 242 248 259 264
275 281 283 320 354 355 391 436 481 620 627 638
640 642 668 677 789 809 833 848 904 937 946 960
980 984 1055 1068 1070 1110 1122 1182 1183 1215
1216 1237 1239 1297 1344 1392 1398 1403 1446
1450 1459 1485 1517 1552 1572 1576 1596
we (13) 1 300 304 2 14 7 295 313 846 849
8 1074 9 138 417 733 1223 11 781
Weak (3) 3 263 5 268 8 177
Weak (1) 15 367
weak (16) 2 125 142 166 4 39 177 6 327
650 7 807 10 577 13 973 15 954 2226
2531 16 271 1717 18 23
weak (1) 7 857
weak (1) 15 241
weakened (1) 9 1007
weaker (1) 11 717
weaker (1) 15 367
weakly (3) 5 535 8 83 1078
weakly (1) 15 277
weakness (5) 7 594 15 3473 16 842 1382
18 1181
weal (1) 15 3713
weals (1) 15 3779
Wealth (1) 8 636
Wealth (1) 15 1584
wealth (6) 13 116 119 16 515 17 505
1698 1752
wealth (1) 7 847
wealthy (1) 12 1170
wealthy (1) 15 1811
weaned (1) 15 540

weaning (2) 15 3294 18 575
weapon (8) 5 426 6 480 913 9 461
12 615 15 3116 3139 16 587
weapons (1) 17 1524
Wear (2) 6 351 8 1165
wear (23) 1 120 121 122 5 355 8 452
13 91 324 335 14 787 15 2333 3079 3251
16 1465 18 10 443 486 627 768 1374 1536
1553 1603
wear (1) 7 581
wearables (1) 14 1547
WEARER (1) 7 14
wearily (1) 1 36
wearily (1) 15 4091
wearing (16) 2 156 9 1155 11 882
12 593 13 179 198 1013 15 1049 2315
16 221 17 2004 2072 2090 18 84 378 839
wearing (8) 15 270 465 728 1014 1521 1546
1904 4018
wears (4) 3 431 13 827 15 1805 4131
wears (2) 7 579 10 1252
wears (7) 15 2249 2306 2479 2482 2657 4034
4449
Weary (2) 3 468 17 2319
Weary (1) 15 4083
weary (10) 2 171 3 464 7 1064 9 475
10 778 11 937 13 287 14 1311
17 2317
weasel (1) 3 289
weasel (1) 15 2339
weaseleyed (1) 14 1582
weather (16) 4 124 5 558 6 132 8 52
820 10 23 723 11 197 543 13 1211
15 400 1121 16 367 652 915
weather (1) 15 1469
Weathercocks (1) 7 309
weathered (1) 16 902
weathereye (1) 11 1077
weathers (1) 5 224
weatherwise (1) 14 485
Weave (1) 2 52
weave (4) 1 662 9 376 378 15 4642
weave (1) 2 356
weave (1) 15 4091
weaver (1) 2 53
weavers (1) 15 1430
weaving (1) 15 4091
web (3) 12 1161 13 1019 14 1036
webbed (2) 10 800 801
webs (1) 7 136
we'd (1) 11 1258
wed (7) 9 679 11 474 18 20 33 392 948
1476
wed (1) 9 1127
Weda (1) 15 3853
wedded (2) 1 246 16 1547
wedding (5) 6 950 11 473 474 12 1267
15 3083
wedding (2) 15 1814 2745
weddingbells (1) 13 196
weddingcake (1) 18 522
wedged (1) 15 6
wedges (1) 15 4039
wedlock (2) 14 344 855
Wednesday (1) 16 500
wee (9) 11 55 1202 1203 1241 13 29 610
14 1532
weed (3) 15 1351 1357 18 1073
weed (1) 15 653

weedbeds (1) 17 1726
weedgrown (1) 13 5
weedladen (1) 17 1584
weedless (1) 4 220
weeds (5) 3 461 5 461 6 934 14 93
18 1283
weeds (2) 15 2264 3839
weedy (1) 6 442
week (27) 1 698 4 425 6 187 300 328
7 998 10 429 1147 11 1077 12 16 517
1069 1112 13 158 181 1144 1271 14 1151
1467 15 4875 16 1488 17 1883 18 253
349 477 572 1150
weeklies (1) 16 1378
Weekly (2) 13 292 18 992
Weekly (3) 7 43 652 15 812
weekly (6) 7 89 94 12 42 15 1690
17 395 1802
weeks (16) 4 453 7 119 8 356 12 1652
13 238 15 2911 3107 3259 16 201
17 1449 2280 18 70 863 1109 1151
weeks' (1) 2 259
ween (1) 9 98
Weeny (1) 13 1131
weeny (1) 10 571
Weep (1) 15 1936
Weep (2) 2 57 64
weep (3) 6 647 14 679 773
weep (2) 2 64 9 33
weepers (1) 6 603
weepers (1) 15 4805
weepest (1) 15 3240
Weeping (1) 13 1119
weeping (7) 3 65 6 240 456 7 685
12 1029 1092 18 874
weeping (1) 9 32
weeps (1) 12 395
weeps (1) 6 166
weeps (1) 15 3216
Weeshwashtkissinapooisthnapoohuck
(1) 15 3812–13
weeshy (1) 10 571
weggebobbles (1) 8 535
weighed (5) 12 1116 13 1156 14 644
17 844 1137
Weighing (2) 6 842 15 2667
weighing (2) 7 993 16 1603
Weighs (1) 13 846
Weight (3) 8 393 1109 15 1145
weight (19) 5 39 40 41 43 44 46 6 522
11 982 12 4 13 326 823 15 2356 2820
2861 3293 17 91 200 18 957
Weightcarrying (1) 8 343
weighted (1) 15 500
weir (1) 17 172
weird (2) 1 367 15 833
weirdlooking (1) 16 835
weirs (1) 17 1596
Weiss (2) 15 1860
weiss (1) 15 257
Welch's (1) 13 85
Welcome (1) 3 440
welcome (13) 1 328 8 16 1166 9 491
10 428 1274 11 194 1016 15 1517
16 1071 1367 1671 1692
welcome (1) 17 1783
welcome (2) 15 1441 4457
welcomes (1) 3 74
welkin (2) 12 1834 14 82

We'll (11) 1 296 318 458 730 7 628 8 436 11 438 12 1364 13 1272 15 3207 3212
we'll (10) 1 163 515 4 133 350 6 221 429 8 1024 10 852 12 1258 15 4481
Well (99) 1 202 442 488 497 2 3 234 400 3 224 4 92 232 419 5 135 167 176 208 6 177 178 216 261 414 755 768 772 811 843 899 943 962 982 7 68 105 156 289 741 742 803 988 8 50 142 179 496 688 784 996 9 200 864 1071 10 51 66 454 687 732 736 744 767 771 11 206 210 559 599 754 927 946 1066 1126 1128 12 767 854 1076 1180 1399 1490 1502 1542 1586 1644 1656 1673 1808 13 442 830 855 979 1157 1231 14 355 664 1343 1482 15 802 1098 2135 2329 2343 2466 2957 3138 4896 4936
well (173) 1 114 119 517 3 292 400 4 428 529 5 99 141 165 296 369 469 6 204 213 331 604 857 870 888 992 7 213 312 340 461 824 8 39 169 218 361 763 764 884 942 952 964 9 86 370 827 10 18 19 20 27 439 557 767 771 936 1056 11 642 644 691 1039 1242 1258 1260 12 78 238 390 437 736 888 925 1117 1131 1618 1908 13 60 128 228 977 989 1030 14 135 670 749 879 1120 1265 1268 1302 1558 1560 15 488 556 772 1091 2357 2466 2516 2626 3075 3077 3207 3426 4896 16 81 138 187 206 539 549 605 635 790 958 1139 1546 1660 1678 1700 1892 17 210 1793 18 23 42 46 76 170 191 225 264 332 349 355 368 386 404 476 548 578 621 723 727 747 843 868 931 1022 1023 1027 1037 1048 1076 1083 1103 1199 1226 1228 1232 1275 1277 1334 1376 1378 1379 1394 1427 1444 1449 1469 1511 1524 1531 1541 1569 1571 1604
well (1) 14 317
well (1) 15 3738
wellbeloved (1) 12 297
wellbuilt (1) 14 68
wellchosen (2) 7 759 15 999
wellconducted (1) 15 1824
wellcreamed (1) 15 3078
Wellcut (1) 6 842
welled (1) 11 701
welleducated (2) 18 13 1494
Wellesley (1) 12 196
wellfed (1) 1 107
wellfilled (1) 13 793
Wellington (3) 10 532 12 1460 17 2049
Wellington (1) 15 148
wellkempt (1) 9 1111
wellknit (1) 1 132
WELLKNOWN (1) 7 529
wellknown (10) 12 552 907 1289 1827 15 1117 1158 4840 16 1407 1489 17 1835
wellknown (1) 15 1376
wellmade (1) 15 1824
Wellmannered (1) 8 553
Wellmeaning (1) 8 1156
wellnigh (1) 1 525
Welloff (1) 2 24
welloff (1) 18 422
wellpleased (2) 3 215 9 268
wellpraised (1) 7 321
wellpreserved (1) 16 832
Wellread (1) 7 307
wellremembered (1) 14 1363
wells (1) 17 205
wellset (1) 9 165
wellshaped (1) 1 580
welltailored (1) 16 1208

Wellturned (1) 5 118
wellturned (1) 13 168
wellused (1) 15 3038
wellwhipped (1) 18 1287
Welly (1) 15 306
Welsh (3) 10 38 12 235 735
Welsh (1) 15 1403
welshcombed (1) 7 332
welsher (2) 14 559 1392
Welt (1) 11 1231
welt (1) 4 525
welt (1) 15 1060
welted (1) 10 1143
weltering (3) 9 954 18 611 662
welterweight (1) 12 964
Welts (1) 7 48
wench (2) 9 260 14 314
wenching (1) 14 665
wend (3) 12 102 14 109 16 1627
wended (1) 12 1720
wending (1) 3 467
wenowach (1) 15 1333
Went (2) 5 59 10 771
Went (1) 17 803
went (179) 1 35 40 82 189 194 251 309 320 360 461 529 622 2 82 226 292 427 3 349 449 4 35 49 172 267 468 472 495 5 27 77 210 214 236 344 6 183 303 467 631 642 684 788 838 7 222 316 377 424 567 568 572 904 908 1010 8 22 184 586 834 1073 1104 1183 9 242 610 676 1125 1129 1162 1214 10 93 209 249 270 500 520 532 830 981 1035 1038 1051 1124 1173 11 86 151 156 318 341 420 421 556 638 765 822 823 848 1136 1187 1189 1224 12 64 267 644 686 975 1082 1086 1229 1231 1561 1819 13 202 220 241 340 363 411 430 463 537 662 695 721 727 766 844 882 1045 1053 1170 1174 1184 14 57 85 138 533 636 661 15 540 647 2117 3028 3365 16 139 172 575 582 640 654 930 1036 1224 1236 1344 1345 1374 1402 1406 1481 1507 1799 1882 17 880 2070 18 59 158 215 258 351 486 520 554 676 692 787 819 833 853 856 1000 1051 1119 1355
wept (5) 3 68 7 574 9 224 11 79 416
Werburgh's (1) 6 609
We're (13) 1 562 6 117 139 7 1015 10 938 12 1222 13 756 1031 14 1505 1565 15 171 338 3584
we're (4) 10 723 12 1490 1758 13 1228
Were (17) 1 59 5 452 10 675 12 210 1019 13 1077 15 3579 3743 17 27 371 509 569 720 1057 1185 1709 1834
Were (2) 2 105 17 1370
were (483) 1 144 194 225 543 2 52 111 121 129 185 402 3 75 128 135 139 175 184 192 319 390 428 449 4 6 7 10 35 183 302 403 5 108 356 562 6 24 29 131 270 272 278 617 724 836 938 961 7 497 499 553 554 603 608 633 699 701 807 824 843 1036 8 150 157 568 587 618 910 9 56 167 192 348 393 441 470 487 524 558 615 714 802 860 983 1141 1220 10 20 38 41 42 82 90 95 148 150 156 159 172 178 185 413 434 442 448 502 526 546 555 733 767 789 791 826 915 953 1006 1162 1163 1178 1185 11 345 576 1123 1147 12 8 156 160 162 171 175 338 353 355 357 359 361 369 372 482 504 541 548 577 583 590 605 618 636 645 651 656 798 886 920 924 927 939 960 1022 1292 1297 1365 1366 1378 1386 1388 1566 1573 1656 1714 1826 1829 1837 1839 1840 1866

1867 1870 13 9 11 16 18 41 57 59 89 107 109 138 145 164 171 202 229 284 318 337 341 345 375 380 381 414 415 434 451 455 471 533 551 574 587 641 649 669 689 692 695 696 716 720 739 768 784 841 890 1000 1210 1271 1293 14 63 132 143 146 161 174 202 204 209 211 222 231 289 355 356 461 462 467 470 591 625 638 639 641 652 669 678 691 719 774 785 800 826 836 848 849 850 851 886 928 978 985 1014 1112 1130 1132 1133 1144 1145 1172 1178 1190 1200 1216 1249 1255 1348 1361 1423 15 290 444 447 448 548 570 878 973 1032 1336 1674 2419 2440 2672 2680 2706 2987 2999 3211 3323 3449 3683 3835 4052 4196 4268 4306 4775 4822 4830 4861 4863 16 39 56 77 81 82 151 185 192 265 281 310 336 350 352 364 425 547 636 642 673 677 719 742 775 781 794 825 855 868 882 957 960 962 1001 1002 1033 1050 1113 1149 1205 1206 1213 1226 1229 1264 1314 1319 1321 1329 1339 1362 1367 1370 1485 1486 1493 1509 1517 1542 1544 1569 1580 1598 1608 1652 1688 1695 1770 1824 1831 1838 1856 1893 17 20 43 80 452 515 527 532 609 677 725 781 871 893 908 917 960 966 972 1068 1103 1182 1192 1207 1228 1235 1573 1769 1873 1921 1927 1965 2035 2084 2090 2101 2143 2154 2271 18 9 86 117 135 171 217 239 242 260 283 291 299 303 349 351 396 410 433 470 526 534 548 577 632 640 642 646 664 668 673 677 712 789 831 850 868 883 924 974 1111 1216 1218 1222 1261 1378 1380 1390 1398 1450 1486 1535 1572
were (8) 1 463 591 7 317 9 1152 10 608 16 1249 1253 1254
were (1) 15 912
weren't (4) 3 129 175 8 980 16 1327
werent (3) 18 556 960 1070
Werf (1) 15 4508
Werner (1) 6 221
Werner's (1) 10 1107
west (21) 1 428 3 392 6 829 8 157 568 609 9 413 10 1187 11 269 384 1239 12 75 1881 13 2 927 1001 14 484 15 2206 17 4 59 18 266
westend (1) 7 558
westering (1) 3 393
Western (3) 17 1729 1730 1736
western (1) 17 2229
Westland (9) 5 17 63 467 14 1027 15 636 16 250 263 17 1797 18 709
Westland (1) 15 4345
Westmeath (2) 1 683 17 882
Westminster's (1) 2 302
Westminster's (1) 15 3977
Westmoreland (3) 8 155 371 16 1435
westward (3) 10 753 14 82 17 2308
Wet (6) 6 187 8 435 11 1254 15 649 4522 16 1305
Wet (1) 13 912
wet (26) 3 131 265 395 5 110 6 299 9 536 11 72 76 182 269 12 1480 1505 13 77 376 395 851 929 979 14 781 15 3020 3091 18 226 310 572 1201 1228
wetbob (1) 15 3004
wethen (1) 18 1251
wether (1) 14 570
WETHERUP (1) 7 337
Wetherup (2) 7 342 16 1701
Wetherup (1) 15 4356
wetted (4) 1 105 272 2 146 8 656
wetted (1) 15 4182

wetting (4) 14 778 16 1316 17 243
18 252
Wettstein (1) 12 984
we've (1) 16 1018
weve (1) 18 1457
Wexford (5) 10 435 11 1064 12 1250
15 623
Wexford (1) 7 427
Wha (1) 14 1523
Whack (1) 5 478
whack (6) 4 151 164 11 891
Whacking (1) 4 150
whacking (1) 14 1136
Whale (1) 16 1795
whale (2) 1 182 3 144
whalebone (1) 15 2976
whalemeat (1) 3 306
Whaler (1) 17 2323
whales (1) 3 303
Wha'll (1) 15 2181
WHAT (3) 7 337 1006 1050
What (404) 1 161 180 192 193 197 202 231 339
496 545 558 607 642 2 18 43 81 108 109 113 189
195 374 379 385 418 3 36 134 135 426 435
4 100 131 190 269 302 313 319 337 376 393 522
542 5 14 43 92 118 199 240 286 311 350 408 500
6 33 97 103 205 218 248 268 271 528 606 622 684
688 700 880 899 7 137 230 247 269 347 378 489
514 588 650 753 783 789 967 978 987 8 24 140
176 244 249 257 529 558 735 742 743 939 1052
1064 1144 1164 9 147 233 236 402 411 419 422
583 728 814 846 859 942 945 1113 1123 10 3
447 454 727 729 758 797 844 854 857 862 869 925
943 1017 1038 11 94 354 356 385 494 495 512
688 691 889 949 996 1049 1095 1209 1255
12 12 54 61 148 327 328 330 522 859 882 945
1088 1089 1180 1254 1317 1421 1430 1484 1507
1614 1901 13 33 473 527 745 816 842 862 878
885 1008 1034 1035 1117 1128 1140 1196 1231
1257 1262 14 290 565 589 808 829 1038 1137
1497 1507 15 67 167 259 267 438 618 625 639
642 647 871 1634 1656 1701 1731 1873 1998 2066
2117 2124 2155 2345 2409 2964 3042 3054 3087
3090 3109 3127 3129 3285 3286 3334 3464 3474
3562 3683 3725 3743 3775 3795 4176 4225 4271
4312 4416 4482 4566 4759 4822 4828 4939
16 618 660 964 1158 1166 1168 17 1 60 70 80
108 123 148 157 160 183 236 241 248 255 272 277
291 296 319 322 342 351 359 382 392 404 410 417
446 462 503 527 532 559 561 576 597 611 618 621
659 660 674 688 703 715 724 745 761 776 779 781
787 864 871 875 886 929 935 949 956 960 973 1018
1032 1036 1157 1171 1199 1210 1224 1228 1256
1274 1299 1302 1330 1333 1340 1348 1357 1408
1417 1426 1430 1446 1551 1567 1573 1579 1588
1592 1606 1616 1672 1752 1765 1769 1774 1838
1839 1840 1843 1849 1854 1873 1882 1887 1905
1921 1927 1930 1958 1962 1968 2000 2006 2009
2024 2028 2035 2042 2059 2063 2067 2071 2081
2084 2090 2101 2122 2132 2143 2200 2247 2271
2298
What (4) 5 115 144 9 798 10 734
what (479) 1 77 117 161 179 184 204 219 424
2 1 30 86 237 238 242 243 244 251 404 3 113
135 175 190 192 231 320 4 26 28 61 98 115 116
149 294 336 375 478 492 515 519 5 41 107 135
169 245 248 252 258 371 388 424 6 158 203 408
512 572 623 672 704 820 886 901 938 7 96 129
145 214 1009 1020 1051 8 81 116 134 162 215

246 328 329 354 381 527 547 577 665 749 751 863
884 922 924 972 981 1006 1093 1159 9 86 185
348 349 350 369 400 429 445 451 473 479 558 649
727 731 738 788 789 927 957 971 999 1027 1035
1041 1158 10 42 66 462 480 523 563 635 663
687 1069 1151 1209 11 135 208 432 559 611 731
838 865 1025 1058 1087 1232 1245 1265 12 120
252 253 260 316 337 434 454 487 766 777 811 949
958 1000 1022 1058 1163 1168 1177 1240 1329
1330 1338 1384 1385 1402 1419 1470 1490 1556
1603 1623 1631 1660 1666 1903 13 75 128 136
141 159 161 267 344 377 423 437 464 502 524 544
585 617 659 673 755 795 802 813 828 829 833 873
879 881 908 972 1019 1020 1033 1059 1143 1145
1160 1188 1216 1249 14 23 64 170 216 217 225
229 327 335 397 399 436 455 500 534 637 687 800
843 870 905 966 1009 1019 1022 1076 1104 1368
1394 1437 15 287 445 477 551 585 779 1338
1391 1538 1974 2091 2217 2226 2333 2376 2566
2703 3037 3125 3177 3445 3607 3903 4299 4428
4439 4486 4817 4822 4870 4884 4886 16 4 192
250 283 293 296 298 360 370 386 600 628 732 766
787 894 897 1058 1099 1137 1173 1298 1411 1479
1521 1529 1572 1616 1639 1683 17 11 66 134
275 291 698 769 787 909 920 945 1021 1029 1034
1040 1242 1245 1249 1256 1311 1497 1744 1754
1954 1991 2154 2210 2227 2250 2302 2306 2311
18 33 41 67 87 92 97 108 111 113 138 142 158
166 170 181 208 214 215 217 221 224 231 235 238
244 250 268 269 270 275 297 311 318 324 373 404
439 442 448 475 476 484 485 491 510 526 538 542
571 613 635 641 643 705 706 713 718 733 735 770
772 796 818 827 832 835 870 928 938 962 968 990
1025 1032 1051 1106 1121 1122 1130 1147 1160
1161 1163 1172 1181 1250 1280 1284 1300 1302
1307 1308 1317 1322 1327 1355 1358 1366 1371
1376 1389 1393 1397 1406 1419 1430 1434 1440
1442 1457 1463 1466 1477 1506 1510 1519 1540
1545 1579
what (3) 5 282 10 571 573
what (5) 15 899 919 4367 4914 4916
whatdoyoucallhim (1) 4 214
whatdoyoucallhim's (1) 12 328
whatdoyoucallthem (1) 11 675
Whatever (3) 12 1041 14 60 15 398
whatever (31) 6 67 780 956 11 210 561
12 1769 13 95 559 14 46 617 1278
15 3210 16 125 336 648 854 1170 1205 1871
18 112 145 225 298 384 792 987 1091 1240 1395
1438 1566
What'll (1) 12 1016
what'll (1) 8 996
whatll (1) 18 1553
whatness (2) 9 84 14 399
whatnot (2) 14 543 15 3173
What's (48) 2 10 4 116 5 520 536
6 116 384 7 233 293 453 953 8 998 9 607
901 927 10 224 271 325 454 507 886 1032
11 350 448 502 12 133 145 300 302 456 704
842 1028 1215 1511 13 65 1244 1252
14 1453 1547 15 651 3474 3505 4378 4447
4773 4799 16 364 1800
What's (3) 1 598 5 121 126
what's (24) 6 423 790 982 7 182 8 578
9 986 10 276 11 703 12 678 1058 1180
1543 13 535 912 991 1138 1157 14 817
15 2866 3505 3693 16 695 1338 1520
whats (5) 18 151 471 507 614 640
whatsoever (5) 12 447 14 8 16 99 1863
18 961

whatten (1) 14 1546
Whatwhat (1) 12 1000
whatwhat (1) 12 1001
whatyoucallit (3) 18 820 872
whatyoumaycall (1) 5 16
whear (1) 14 1540
wheat (4) 3 119 10 816 14 1418
18 1560
wheatbellied (1) 9 541
wheaten (1) 14 1048
Wheatenmeal (2) 15 2376 2379
wheatkidneys (1) 14 155
Wheatley (1) 12 181
Wheatley's (1) 5 389
wheedle (2) 13 1231 18 52
wheedling (3) 1 356 360 11 186
wheel (6) 5 553 6 177 353 10 776
12 1777 15 203
wheel (1) 15 4122
Wheelbarrow (1) 9 1213
wheelbarrow (2) 17 1585 18 883
wheeled (5) 6 637 8 56 61 83 10 972
wheelgear (1) 17 914
wheeling (2) 6 228 8 51
wheeling (1) 15 3945
wheelmen (2) 10 651 16 553
Wheels (2) 8 431 17 615
wheels (10) 6 24 26 30 47 69 140 637 8 431
17 490 18 1592
wheels (2) 15 1602 4121
wheelspokes (1) 10 1228
wheelwright (2) 6 938 12 1776
wheeze (4) 5 178 7 591 11 487 12 212
wheezy (2) 3 70 10 544
Whelan (3) 8 353 15 2234 17 425
whelks (1) 2 213
Whelps (1) 9 137
When (60) 1 357 2 187 237 3 144 324 375
5 469 6 815 7 823 1002 8 609 937
9 199 201 261 865 1028 10 487 783 1057 1138
11 20 24 69 678 687 1253 12 272 847 1910
13 828 914 941 992 1077 1189 14 945 1159
1461 15 378 384 476 975 1001 1662 1669 1683
2348 2361 2525 2610 2621 2987 3015 3387 3831
4604 17 1574 1575 2327
When (4) 11 530 665 1284 17 1370
when (486) 1 91 119 208 257 258 266 327 333
357 489 543 673 3 179 276 302 449 491 4 54
340 402 480 525 5 43 83 127 236 249 265 324
495 514 562 6 206 270 300 415 577 585 743 745
750 829 861 969 1031 7 171 225 267 308 628 888
8 30 155 177 194 215 353 487 517 568 966 979
998 1084 1128 9 73 185 192 219 350 379 381 402
499 543 628 636 663 676 680 695 721 928 936 1004
1005 1192 10 119 133 146 166 360 553 765 1066
1162 1163 1280 11 36 295 463 556 621 624 678
722 725 830 973 980 1049 1057 1071 1105 1170
1196 1211 12 4 65 207 312 338 385 444 460 609
622 626 630 636 647 658 665 677 806 960 974 984
1027 1162 1305 1306 1449 1566 1573 1630 1728
1755 1776 1783 1827 13 93 109 129 134 161 163
176 183 201 219 229 238 271 272 273 312 314 327
340 394 453 531 537 562 576 635 641 698 775 797
805 807 822 832 840 848 870 871 879 881 891 905
920 924 954 961 1000 1008 1031 1111 1125 1151
1159 1198 1202 1225 14 11 16 53 69 217 262
318 334 398 623 676 678 826 875 938 1110 1118
1132 1150 1264 1338 1352 1372 1405 1470 1576
15 306 392 540 584 877 885 978 1017 1031 1049

1211 1673 2229 2234 2805 2978 3000 3010 3059
3066 3082 3365 3835 4196 4204 4239 4756 4866
16 28 70 75 80 128 218 263 386 430 480 540 546
561 605 607 608 648 677 717 721 803 809 845 859
860 925 932 954 965 1026 1062 1115 1121 1122
1130 1187 1243 1303 1313 1316 1334 1336 1347
1362 1373 1443 1470 1489 1496 1497 1498 1526
1547 1557 1581 1582 1585 1695 1847 1861 1870
17 126 281 294 331 334 376 447 448 449 453 454
455 563 589 695 834 917 923 1036 1071 1087 1091
1169 1170 1326 1423 1725 1757 1830 2004 2070
2115 2122 18 2 23 25 31 41 47 58 59 70 77 91
103 105 107 113 117 118 135 143 154 171 175 182
204 206 207 223 226 227 247 250 258 259 265 272
273 288 291 293 320 329 343 344 346 347 363 375
378 413 429 434 467 477 493 499 510 529 533 546
555 560 561 586 625 626 630 639 644 647 663 664
673 681 694 704 708 742 748 749 754 758 760 763 770
781 794 815 830 841 851 862 877 887 902 916 923
937 979 1011 1029 1036 1049 1054 1067 1103 1139
1150 1152 1167 1172 1182 1214 1245 1247 1257
1277 1293 1312 1314 1324 1366 1383 1400 1423
1436 1446 1504 1530 1602
when (3) 1 590 592 12 423
when (1) 15 906
whenas (1) 12 1779
Whence (1) 17 2018
whence (3) 10 105 12 1359 13 6
whenceness (1) 14 400
whenever (10) 6 646 990 10 420 428
13 481 14 909 1473 18 184 203 643
WHERE (1) 7 1050
Where (97) 1 57 192 254 2 5 56 307 3 50
86 432 488 4 126 485 5 37 84 463 527
6 44 118 152 168 378 506 826 894 899 987
7 361 442 453 557 639 640 693 706 739 900 902
925 1051 8 18 600 606 1083 1145 1184 1189
9 334 551 977 1199 10 266 279 669 806 824
1007 1231 11 59 71 188 356 739 12 1079
1240 1248 1622 1847 13 779 793 916 1097 1099
14 907 1112 1441 1442 15 120 1647 1980 2434
3054 3437 4293 4303 4312 4313 4884 16 256
996 1139 17 327 1235 2070 2331
Where (1) 17 824
where (205) 1 148 243 320 478 710 739
2 69 185 3 108 376 424 443 4 451 5 201
484 6 434 469 533 649 724 7 412 661 1011
8 140 431 567 575 1037 1191 9 248 292 378
453 460 523 610 662 923 1031 1040 10 96 295
343 378 408 434 495 607 698 736 808 824 951 997
1033 11 119 337 422 464 544 739 857 1036 1235
12 71 209 360 699 974 1004 1026 1314 1398 1548
1554 1621 1665 13 76 96 190 262 274 332 334
384 401 421 570 631 632 689 696 729 968 1015
1025 1091 1120 1292 14 127 439 445 499 832
833 1080 1184 1366 1376 1380 1573 15 290 635
1169 1663 1983 3173 3208 3405 3424 3450 3516
3525 3885 4575 4954 16 9 23 41 47 56 58 93
101 149 191 217 248 321 416 418 419 509 514 554
596 644 658 803 940 1145 1258 1371 1629 1725
1811 1824 1827 1854 17 482 491 540 622 797
978 1276 1986 2295 18 19 108 110 250 297 299
314 356 374 388 465 494 501 505 546 569 677 709
806 867 966 1006 1027 1140 1170 1335 1403 1411
1439 1441 1486 1539 1602
where (3) 16 593 1322 1868
where (3) 15 2021 3876 4316
whereabouts (4) 12 345 16 1321 1630
18 109

Whereas (4) 15 1158 16 181 1379 1454
whereas (9) 12 1111 14 249 299 15 1160
16 1211 1327 17 530 2128 2130
Whereat (2) 14 232 657
whereat (1) 10 1051
whereby (4) 12 1188 14 45 222 1339
wherefore (3) 12 451 14 209 16 1532
Wherein (1) 14 470
wherein (5) 3 49 447 9 682 12 1442 1911
whereof (2) 12 1777 14 216
whereon (3) 3 80 10 1226 12 1714
Where's (21) 1 335 5 66 7 181 182 185
457 8 242 9 939 10 288 11 476 1122
14 1444 1451 1537 15 22 609 2937 3129 3931
4012 4590
wheres (6) 18 604 1050 1136 1207 1557
wheresoever (1) 14 240
Whereto (1) 9 952
whereupon (1) 16 239
Wherever (2) 2 348 15 71
wherever (4) 7 883 12 157 18 909 932
wherewith (2) 14 129 235
wherewithal (1) 16 179
wherry (2) 14 641 17 1595
whet (1) 11 393
Whether (3) 8 440 9 787 14 1460
whether (34) 1 406 9 47 10 1188
12 351 360 573 862 13 420 14 39 42 171
398 669 671 727 1005 15 458 2087 2398
16 187 303 407 567 1228 1315 1561 1773
17 557 647 1205 18 413 461 1168 1537
Whetstone (1) 15 2101
whetstone (1) 9 977
Whew (3) 6 866 13 867 15 3416
wheysour (1) 2 166
whh (2) 5 454
Which (26) 4 519 5 113 6 580 7 412
496 9 82 794 11 628 12 1465 14 260
382 646 1012 15 129 2095 2109 2112 2114 3500
17 252 606 657 1103 1415 1956 2269
which (462) 1 2 109 200 217 310 580 615 634
2 52 116 160 264 325 326 358 377 438 4 4
5 563 6 508 842 7 310 492 678 842 843 891
949 1038 8 95 500 520 9 44 88 89 104 167
298 382 383 384 394 400 422 450 582 785 804 839
931 962 983 990 1010 1015 1200 10 63 89 94
172 548 820 914 993 1248 1276 11 879
12 42 78 159 161 174 203 281 367 476 529 533
552 571 572 589 594 601 602 606 614 617 641 664
717 724 728 731 734 786 791 797 918 922 924 965
968 980 988 1185 1351 1463 1465 1518 1529 1531
1630 1721 1723 1725 1819 1824 1863 1866 1868
13 10 42 97 111 127 152 162 296 417 428 445 475
637 743 14 9 15 30 38 40 43 64 67 101 130 150
163 226 238 239 245 249 251 267 281 282 287 299
315 340 386 389 391 416 430 438 442 444 446 453
457 462 467 473 497 509 533 549 550 606 629 635
658 664 679 696 698 701 705 727 744 755 767 792
797 822 824 827 837 842 846 847 856 864 866 871
901 908 911 934 937 950 954 959 976 983 995 998
1006 1016 1135 1136 1149 1175 1183 1184 1187
1189 1194 1198 1221 1224 1239 1243 1245 1266
1272 1279 1283 1287 1300 1302 1309 1345 1413
15 803 812 825 826 977 982 1053 1384 1544 1803
1899 2107 2111 2120 2315 2331 2360 2424 2625
2772 3275 3296 3398 3890 3891 4539 4542 4554
4701 16 3 14 16 33 34 64 74 84 87 92 169 177
235 267 282 292 294 301 310 325 343 356 358 453
472 493 498 504 521 533 551 586 598 642 644 651

667 707 709 715 805 896 914 937 950 958 974 983
987 1004 1014 1068 1114 1131 1154 1174 1177
1195 1196 1197 1216 1222 1237 1246 1271 1321
1323 1325 1361 1373 1393 1394 1421 1426 1432
1433 1445 1446 1459 1470 1473 1479 1507 1509
1583 1588 1590 1593 1612 1659 1667 1673 1685
1686 1711 1733 1745 1757 1760 1770 1777 1804
1813 1819 1821 1829 1837 1840 1858 1871 1876
1889 17 9 37 43 75 106 152 172 232 242 261
286 287 299 314 325 337 371 379 510 514 563 609
638 643 677 709 850 873 905 1003 1004 1049 1054
1066 1093 1124 1127 1144 1235 1283 1286 1293
1444 1485 1636 1662 1674 1776 1777 1787 1803
1824 1878 1933 1948 1963 1965 1966 1985 1987
1989 1990 2103 2125 2283 2289 2295 2296
18 276 1535
which (3) 4 514 7 769 16 1253
which (27) 15 1 6 466 501 580 694 705 1027
1060 1499 1704 1984 2060 2072 2147 2148 2186
2252 2307 2436 3843 3905 4033 4450 4456 4538
4706
whiff (5) 6 611 10 818 11 301 1236
13 965
whiffs (2) 4 107 11 1236
Whig (1) 9 598
While (12) 4 46 275 5 20 56 7 993
10 512 11 796 799 918 16 924 1023 1274
While (2) 6 166 8 222
while (104) 1 275 515 541 4 173 516
5 100 406 459 7 168 8 346 521 9 678 750
913 10 97 116 222 373 469 986 1015 1238
11 40 236 247 520 786 797 906 916 917 918 919
1004 12 80 164 200 526 553 598 1370 1562 1838
13 21 218 411 617 1137 14 161 235 347 479
503 710 716 800 868 875 911 940 1014 1020 1177
1208 1216 1311 1350 15 444 1047 1395 2358
2892 2897 2977 3031 3789 4394 16 45 54 64 215
359 557 975 1057 1467 1643 1648 1785 1798 1891
17 29 284 440 455 458 1346 1826 18 766 855
1432 1551
while (1) 10 611
while (3) 15 911 918 3548
whiled (2) 12 536 16 1275
whiles (7) 2 23 6 918 13 105 14 123
326 423 1376
Whilst (1) 16 578
whilst (1) 16 1770
whim (1) 14 1127
whimpering (1) 15 3845
whimpers (1) 15 2914
whimsy (1) 14 715
Whinbad (1) 17 2322
whined (1) 7 421
whinge (1) 1 213
whining (2) 15 532 577
whinny (1) 15 2123
whip (3) 6 564 11 525 14 1136
whip (1) 15 4908
whipped (3) 9 495 10 1086 12 1350
whipping (2) 1 168 9 1134
whipping (1) 15 907
whips (1) 15 2588
whirl (1) 7 963
whirl (1) 15 4122
whirled (2) 9 286 10 432
whirligig (1) 14 1323
whirligig (1) 15 4112
whirling (1) 9 286
whirlpool (1) 9 464

whores (12) 15 597 2021 2405 2705 2973 3831 3905 4256 4260 4314 4316 4321
whores' (1) 12 1199
whoreson (2) 9 985 986
whorled (1) 2 214
Whorusalaminyourhighhohhhh (1) 15 2211
Who's (23) 3 325 4 340 5 153 7 665 8 215 773 994 10 399 510 11 10 242 12 8 325 330 1488 14 1465 15 2461 2462 3504 3529 4275 16 198 1016
Who's (1) 15 1582
who's (4) 11 560 14 1579 15 3557 4762
Whose (5) 7 273 583 8 811 12 768 1807
whose (39) 6 162 941 7 275 556 8 520 717 9 66 778 1009 10 13 1047 1203 1225 12 87 201 731 797 973 14 169 449 1090 1177 1206 1219 15 1360 2321 2425 3866 16 135 137 338 511 1187 1296 1517 1524 17 904 18 882 1412
whose (1) 1 198
whose (1) 15 2016
whoso (2) 14 231 240
whosoever (1) 13 443
whowhat (1) 15 4367
Whrrwhee (1) 2 384
Whusky (1) 3 90
Why (111) 1 161 193 208 307 506 2 45 441 3 7 408 494 496 4 41 47 235 529 5 196 243 352 455 475 6 318 412 956 1012 7 339 712 731 735 8 432 445 538 943 1116 1171 9 332 452 455 712 984 990 997 1200 10 887 911 11 149 364 721 732 869 893 942 969 12 319 1630 13 107 799 841 842 899 1007 1010 1015 1209 14 372 436 815 1113 15 163 208 487 670 853 1361 1660 2445 2547 3175 3601 3609 4407 4426 16 259 345 410 458 465 664 1124 1404 1676 1709 17 77 288 497 555 765 838 841 843 889 940 989 1007 1070 1351 1354 1421 1492 1893 2147 2195
Why (5) 5 121 7 845 8 1070 1074 9 1127
why (74) 1 88 2 362 439 447 3 38 200 5 69 273 428 6 232 400 888 8 86 9 471 673 1071 1135 10 731 11 463 641 943 1090 12 451 1628 13 146 230 523 530 772 783 1127 14 33 335 1274 15 3250 3406 4397 16 140 252 590 633 710 715 880 964 1043 1217 1480 1491 1531 1668 1864 17 229 889 2126 18 102 174 241 629 914 1008 1237 1254 1305 1348 1386 1392 1442 1451 1488 1565 1567 1568 1578
why (2) 3 202 7 581
wi (1) 14 1489
wibbly (1) 14 815
wicked (5) 5 446 9 912 13 433 14 458 466
wicked (1) 15 3015
wickedness (1) 5 444
wicker (3) 10 299 17 304 1577
wicket (2) 14 1491 16 1684
wickets (1) 5 560
Wicklow (6) 5 181 10 1124 1130 16 552 17 164 1406
Wicklowmen (1) 9 36
Wide (1) 13 838
wide (19) 2 357 3 444 6 40 67 7 1055 8 247 9 295 1222 10 515 573 979 12 1248 1303 13 170 14 81 1081 15 330 16 412 938
wide (2) 7 327 8 417

wide (2) 15 299 3351
widebrimmed (1) 10 1244
wideleaved (2) 5 317 13 156
wideleaved (1) 15 214
widely (1) 3 459
widemouthed (1) 12 153
widening (1) 15 2873
wideopen (1) 6 313
wideopen (1) 15 388
wider (2) 16 1209 17 1709
widespread (1) 16 1318
widest (2) 16 1152 17 1620
widewinged (1) 12 159
widgeon (1) 12 1615
Widow (2) 12 1534 13 85
widow (17) 3 131 5 460 6 727 758 9 796 986 10 158 12 773 13 1228 14 595 15 3231 3931 16 134 17 479 489 18 1127 1389
widow (4) 15 283 1606 3837 3857
widowed (2) 3 54 9 985
Widower (1) 13 1232
widower (8) 3 53 7 538 9 824 13 657 15 2783 3833 17 1889 18 1300
Widowhood (1) 6 549
Widows (1) 13 1227
Widows' (1) 17 1856
Widows' (1) 15 3842
widow's (2) 9 686 13 1230
widows (4) 6 548 9 1046 12 1622 18 1283
wielding (1) 9 131
Wife (9) 4 149 5 141 381 6 60 7 200 8 398 763 13 970 1153
Wife (1) 9 1171
wife (122) 2 391 392 393 3 211 5 151 190 258 266 286 6 245 349 541 694 746 831 7 230 532 536 8 17 329 399 949 951 9 236 633 665 722 790 814 1052 10 17 26 123 125 158 546 556 765 779 11 485 689 697 972 1003 1209 1231 12 226 234 247 254 513 766 772 773 812 839 994 1051 1061 1081 1098 1106 1107 1163 1171 1568 1652 13 220 657 788 875 911 973 1223 1232 1281 14 87 204 215 231 361 595 15 345 777 1067 1232 3765 3926 4539 16 421 424 429 544 797 876 1437 1441 1546 1557 1657 1745 1800 17 141 142 365 674 1177 1846 18 532 994 1117 1273 1279 1280 1396 1397 1425 1485 1510
wife (2) 9 423 1127
wifeless (1) 3 253
wife's (5) 3 211 6 568 12 767 769 16 716
wife's (1) 16 980
wifes (1) 18 1206
wifey (2) 13 241 982
wig (2) 15 939 3761
wigged (1) 15 2973
wiggle (1) 18 1041
wight (2) 12 448 14 149
wigs (3) 7 305 8 1160 13 247
wigwams (1) 3 156
wil (1) 14 1539
Wild (2) 3 19 7 543
Wild (1) 15 1445
wild (26) 1 731 2 43 3 164 244 266 4 208 429 7 963 8 900 9 307 410 10 200 11 269 949 12 720 1381 13 673 1223 14 261 15 3144 4841 18 790 830 1442 1559

wild (1) 9 304
wild (4) 15 1915 2629 4507 4675
Wilde (5) 1 143 554 9 530 532 1069
wilderness (4) 7 490 15 1899 17 1022 2053
Wilde's (4) 3 83 451 9 522 10 1109
wildfire (1) 13 1194
Wildgoose (1) 15 635
wilding (1) 9 823
wildlooking (1) 18 1413
Wildly (1) 8 913
wildly (2) 15 3357 18 103
wildly (1) 15 3815
wilds (3) 14 614 16 554 17 1974
wildwood (1) 18 1297
wile (1) 14 165
wiles (1) 9 1062
wilful (2) 11 411 17 2189
Wilhelm (1) 9 2
Wilhelmina (1) 14 890
Wilkie (1) 18 653
Wilkins (1) 13 909
Wilkinson (1) 6 774
Will (36) 1 43 45 2 191 3 38 4 402 447 448 6 752 7 357 981 8 844 1067 9 423 427 599 740 793 924 10 320 11 56 146 248 1096 1278 12 1409 13 936 1101 1253 1255 14 506 1529 15 1480 2463 2499 4575 4883
Will (1) 9 417
will (298) 1 28 29 291 318 420 468 480 630 632 739 2 28 235 244 251 338 339 395 401 404 413 415 420 430 3 25 26 47 48 128 276 295 369 399 414 452 454 455 488 490 491 501 4 163 457 5 79 113 170 173 176 177 224 249 252 254 425 433 438 6 18 67 126 369 371 449 482 598 842 924 926 1000 1001 7 26 71 256 565 678 805 894 895 907 918 978 998 1010 8 17 304 308 402 536 552 569 735 853 1035 9 44 141 237 256 302 316 318 324 358 433 434 438 452 457 459 479 684 787 789 794 795 796 938 983 1007 1073 1076 1094 1097 1202 1208 10 69 302 322 323 383 418 695 703 875 937 956 1072 1133 11 374 438 442 658 671 687 825 870 888 890 918 12 47 240 413 434 448 507 546 733 736 751 796 994 1041 1118 1152 1295 1299 1300 1301 1306 1317 1347 1374 1410 1649 1675 1812 13 41 275 787 872 943 953 986 1039 14 85 176 201 284 285 311 365 452 499 522 567 763 764 775 781 911 1035 1068 1114 1118 1154 1334 1341 1348 1349 1352 1372 1429 1435 1573 15 711 897 967 979 982 983 1081 1167 1358 1629 1683 1840 2376 2385 2409 2417 2437 2496 2553 2848 2901 2918 2920 2966 2973 2975 2978 2981 2983 3065 3073 3076 3079 3081 3153 3183 3185 3186 3187 3188 3191 3206 3474 3509 3606 3791 3831 3940 4184 4304 4402 4420 4636 4738 4832 4951 16 248 1195 1718 17 1883 2004 18 97 367 475 620 940 987 988 1077 1229 1338 1432 1608
will (10) 2 397 398 7 845 863 9 798 1043 1044 12 29 16 405 1743
will (2) 15 1715 4914
will-o'-the-wisps (1) 15 3
willed (3) 3 48 13 99 14 1070
willer (1) 14 1069
WILLIAM (1) 7 38
William (34) 5 325 6 774 8 1045 9 443 526 643 729 899 921 987 10 86 87 111 1176 1214 1221 12 189 226 827 927 933 16 492 910 1242 1767 17 306 386 1122 1370 1388 1556 1651 1789

William (2) 9 583 637
William (2) 15 1422 3821
Wᴵᴸᴸᴵᴀᴹ (1) 15 1479
Williamite (1) 14 497
Williamites (1) 12 1380
Williams (1) 18 942
Williams's (1) 10 654
Willie (3) 9 524 525 527
willing (6) 2 172 8 910 9 1023 12 1780
   15 2531 3450
Williss (1) 18 848
Willow (1) 16 1683
willow (2) 12 1293 13 1119
willowpatterned (1) 4 145
willowy (1) 12 639
willpower (2) 15 2388 3215
Will's (2) 9 795 993
Wills (2) 9 526 911
wills (1) 9 722
Willun (1) 9 676
Willy (7) 12 313 327 388 392 403 783
   13 954
Willy's (1) 13 795
wilt (1) 14 365
wilt (1) 13 647
wily (1) 16 625
WIMBLES (1) 7 1070
Wimple (1) 8 144
wimple (1) 15 3434
win (13) 3 166 8 827 10 847 11 374
   1023 12 148 13 207 15 780 1063 1840
   2401 3947 16 1854
wince (1) 13 1217
winced (1) 13 578
winces (3) 15 1246 2787 3720
winch (1) 17 568
wincing (1) 15 2772
WIND (1) 7 995
Wind (1) 15 2447
wind (58) 1 185 367 573 602 662 2 53
   3 104 266 288 4 94 220 242 436 6 318 796
   993 1029 7 51 192 294 309 880 999 8 191 193
   9 479 10 182 1146 11 55 591 592 597 963
   1178 1202 1203 12 376 958 1311 1773
   13 959 1140 14 243 290 482 484 523 643 644
   1106 16 437 903 1131 17 1133 1826
   18 903 909 918
wind (2) 15 2752 3408
Windandwatery (1) 8 537
windbag (1) 7 315
Windfall (1) 7 266
Winding (1) 14 1469
winding (9) 1 6 678 5 316 7 944 11 34
   923 13 556 558 14 1106
winding (1) 15 1441
windingsheet (2) 6 18 15 4642
windingsheet (1) 2 356
Windmill (2) 5 2 18 856
window (62) 1 172 257 2 6 292 382
   3 427 4 140 317 432 5 17 560 6 78 119
   176 257 762 7 255 256 442 571 8 500 551 626
   834 1045 1069 10 94 222 247 250 800 801 831
   1046 1130 1223 1263 11 341 454 1235 1261
   1274 13 131 295 337 371 632 15 645 2780
   16 430 17 126 614 811 1175 1541 18 372
   574 703 705 764 1045 1086
window (6) 15 144 605 652 2513 4210 4225
windowpane (1) 7 238

Windows (1) 4 136
windows (21) 4 237 498 6 33 37 385
   8 114 620 9 249 10 240 421 1107 1115 1195
   12 548 1732 13 447 1173 18 645 681 995
   1594\
windows (1) 17 807
windows (4) 15 912 1400 1751 3996
windowsash (1) 10 542
windowsill (2) 18 692 1035
windowsills (1) 15 1405
windpipe (2) 12 173 15 4721
windpipes (1) 8 750
windraw (1) 3 374
Winds (1) 18 899
Winds (1) 8 183
winds (4) 7 882 13 1151 16 1410
   18 1427
windscreen (1) 10 759
Windsor (1) 10 947
Windsor (1) 9 759
Windy (2) 7 668 8 184
windy (4) 7 910 8 1173 17 1974
   18 264
Wine (6) 5 387 8 794 850 1171 12 144
   1251
wine (22) 5 390 7 143 8 819 826 851 854
   897 1155 10 547 847 12 1730 1731
   14 502 1352 1532 15 117 1790 3205 3274 3868
   4564 16 90
wine (4) 1 301 590 592 17 415
wine (1) 15 1330
winebark (1) 12 1298
winebig (1) 10 1230
winebin (1) 17 1548
winebottle (1) 9 579
winecoloured (1) 17 1532
wined (1) 3 224
winedark (4) 3 394 10 804 12 1298
   17 785
winefizzling (1) 14 1581
wineglass (1) 8 796
winegrapes (1) 15 1329
winejar (1) 14 1163
winejug (1) 7 888
winelodge (1) 14 553
winepress (1) 8 898
winerooms (2) 10 992 1212
Wine's (1) 11 87
wines (1) 8 1123
wineshops (1) 18 1596
Winetavern (1) 16 168
wing (4) 14 1503 15 557 2474
wing (1) 15 135
winged (2) 12 1189 17 1134
winging (2) 15 1269 4666
winglike (1) 1 601
wings (4) 1 595 2 8 387 8 678
wings (4) 15 250 3414 3708 3946
wingshoulders (1) 15 2460
Wink (1) 15 3158
wink (5) 12 393 479 14 547 18 651 1260
winked (6) 8 959 1016 10 762 13 1181
   16 402 485
winkers (1) 12 1394
winking (2) 2 148 11 375
winking (3) 15 186 2383 4832
Winkle (6) 13 1112 1113 1114 1282
   15 3158 16 426
Winkle (1) 15 1847

winks (2) 13 608 16 214
winks (3) 15 1739 2223 3750
WINNER (1) 7 386
Winner (1) 16 1285
winner (1) 14 1513
winner (1) 15 4673
winners (3) 2 307 14 1137 15 1289
winning (4) 2 44 14 92 624 18 1421
winningly (1) 13 64
winningpost (1) 15 3974
winnows (1) 15 2752
Winny (2) 13 418 712
wins (3) 9 959 986 14 1131
winsome (1) 13 81
winsome (1) 15 2587
Winsomely (1) 11 309
winter (6) 4 155 14 271 15 1806 2785
   18 915 916
Winter's (1) 9 883
winter's (1) 10 554
wintertime (2) 1 542 16 649
wipe (6) 1 69 11 1101 15 3091 3493 4826
   18 1538
Wiped (2) 11 1051 15 848
wiped (9) 1 71 111 4 334 537 7 1002
   10 262 941 13 393 14 765
wipes (2) 8 810 18 226
Wiping (1) 13 950
wiping (4) 6 299 7 1025 8 656 10 635
Wire (1) 11 351
wire (8) 8 154 572 13 813 14 1486 1515
   15 551 3465 18 625
wire (1) 15 186
wirefences (1) 11 841
Wireless (1) 15 1500
wireless (1) 17 1674
wires (3) 11 292 13 1147 16 529
wires (1) 15 415
wirily (1) 4 39
wirst (1) 9 491
Wisdom (8) 6 703 969 8 126 158 11 296
   906 15 1008 17 2139
Wisdom (2) 15 479 4337
wisdom (7) 2 233 376 9 52 477 14 402
   1207 17 1586
wisdom (1) 7 769
Wise (4) 6 546 7 937 11 299 644
wise (15) 2 448 5 234 6 53 9 780
   11 296 13 223 1138 14 63 1063 15 2596
   3606 16 131 1694 17 1345 18 242
wisely (1) 16 1787
Wish (7) 5 211 11 721 914 1181 1224
   13 872 1091
wish (24) 1 183 212 5 244 247 6 106 126
   274 7 711 9 451 827 12 140 633 13 81
   14 1119 1121 1142 15 4461 4473 18 104
   433 508 734 905 1121
wish (2) 1 591 9 98
wishcard (1) 18 1360
wished (11) 9 713 11 181 373 13 357 404
   529 16 1031 17 839 18 430 584 1381
wishes (2) 8 336 14 1320
wishing (1) 15 970
wishly (1) 14 550
wishswish (1) 8 348
wisp (1) 6 752
Wispish (1) 8 266
wisps (2) 2 186 12 305
wist (1) 14 229

wistful (1) 13 194
Wit (1) 9 537
wit (11) 8 119 9 245 12 1184 14 189
298 381 710 786 823 15 3656 17 94
witch (4) 1 401 11 903 15 830 2001
witch (1) 4 514
witchery (1) 13 107
witches (1) 15 4679
witching (1) 15 467
witchroasting (1) 9 752
WITH (3) 7 77 737 970
With (88) 1 167 683 2 36 166 3 52 185 329
372 5 16 231 6 425 451 598 686 775 921
7 274 999 8 526 594 638 749 1135 9 310
10 433 455 891 1025 1111 11 38 80 169 213
214 215 273 289 557 653 956 1009 1017 1091 1097
1118 12 316 317 673 1023 13 215 311
14 311 529 752 1025 1326 1429 1510 15 375
1725 2353 2441 2666 3054 3068 3399 4227 4527
4827 16 438 1179 1215 17 599 698 810 830
1029 1040 1179 1270 1271 1311 1312 1948 2115
2154 2250 2321
With (2) 1 586 5 147
With (14) 15 365 513 672 2011 2049 2072 2127
2714 2852 3224 4033 4125 4913 4915
with (2059) 1 26 44 46 52 60 61 89 93 99 117
123 125 127 128 145 147 155 166 169 170 171 173
177 180 213 234 251 255 258 265 267 272 296 299
332 345 377 385 413 422 446 485 495 500 506 525
526 534 578 581 616 625 656 658 664 672 682 693
700 726 2 30 34 37 62 72 130 149 176 186 199
200 223 261 274 286 290 304 318 342 425 3 16
36 46 53 54 59 63 97 102 118 125 139 146 156 163
165 188 213 214 217 232 247 252 279 305 316 338
345 362 410 417 429 432 489 493 495 4 1 3 15
35 43 45 82 91 93 114 115 132 133 142 153 193 195
205 232 237 242 262 263 300 306 314 335 347 355
369 371 384 391 403 410 422 432 436 440 458 534
537 5 6 13 14 22 38 39 48 57 60 72 89 101 102
107 117 128 150 216 232 233 239 244 264 272 298
328 334 336 343 357 376 377 437 446 450 504 561
6 3 27 47 49 51 58 61 63 65 80 100 111 123 173
180 262 280 299 310 321 354 360 379 485 492 507
510 518 523 527 533 547 560 568 573 575 589 590
591 594 614 622 625 638 650 660 669 673 690 696
732 735 740 749 766 769 776 784 801 817 840 887
912 923 929 932 935 939 957 998 999 1022 7 29
36 40 57 65 114 168 175 200 206 207 215 223 271
293 300 307 332 333 341 361 387 388 407 416 453
456 476 567 574 593 595 616 621 664 688 730 752
756 772 800 802 810 835 875 880 896 933 958 972
1025 1043 1048 1061 8 21 45 54 72 101 132 138
146 147 164 167 170 182 195 230 235 273 295 318
325 331 333 341 347 353 360 363 373 378 408 422
428 465 468 470 488 512 514 521 527 530 553 576
597 601 614 657 658 676 684 686 691 705 711 712
713 745 761 810 811 818 820 838 847 857 858 879
880 885 893 904 925 935 951 958 975 981 1024
1029 1032 1035 1050 1075 1115 1123 1125 1128
1157 1160 1173 9 18 52 59 68 74 81 147 154 157
165 265 284 285 296 372 388 427 432 436 442 444
448 453 468 469 471 473 474 481 489 501 533 547
560 578 593 618 630 644 671 672 710 725 743 749
751 752 756 783 786 803 818 821 822 830 831 837
851 852 853 854 863 872 875 878 880 888 963 994
999 1035 1117 1119 1162 1169 1184 1209 10 32
58 102 116 122 125 131 135 141 168 176 181
200 201 207 225 237 245 262 270 299 330 334 371
423 434 440 474 486 500 501 512 525 528 556 557

566 575 588 640 673 679 713 719 752 767 778 789
802 808 812 819 820 832 848 859 876 885 887 895
905 907 908 932 934 986 988 1005 1009 1069 1094
1099 1102 1125 1136 1157 1187 1191 1192 1212
1220 1242 1266 1267 1269 1276 1281 11 38 50
57 67 92 116 122 129 130 153 158 167 174 189 263
289 318 367 391 398 411 423 426 434 450 459 462
518 520 523 525 537 542 570 624 626 632 648 652
668 676 737 759 760 790 795 800 807 819 832 847
852 863 941 942 957 986 987 1027 1034 1060 1118
1187 1188 1191 1192 1198 1204 1234 1240 1252
1256 1266 1278 12 1 7 10 78 80 107 114 117
119 122 127 149 157 171 172 173 175 214 243 247
250 254 257 258 291 314 328 353 375 376 384 405
410 440 451 466 481 488 501 502 503 505 514 544
548 579 602 613 632 645 651 663 667 682 686 689
690 695 724 753 774 784 800 803 806 808 811 813
827 833 836 840 912 955 968 970 972 974 986 1010
1024 1027 1047 1063 1064 1066 1070 1080 1081
1092 1107 1124 1142 1143 1165 1173 1174 1178
1190 1197 1203 1215 1231 1235 1249 1253 1256
1258 1263 1268 1281 1282 1288 1296 1297 1300
1303 1305 1307 1314 1321 1323 1326 1335 1343
1347 1374 1387 1393 1394 1395 1414 1415 1434
1469 1475 1496 1497 1505 1508 1525 1569 1580
1582 1585 1588 1589 1597 1598 1599 1615 1616
1660 1663 1676 1712 1735 1745 1759 1770 1771
1774 1778 1784 1800 1819 1844 1848 1851 1873
1907 1915 13 13 14 17 18 19 22 30 32 36 54 55
59 71 89 93 102 103 105 116 123 140 144 148 151
153 157 167 170 174 175 199 205 210 211 213 218
222 231 235 236 245 246 250 268 270 273 310 314
315 326 335 336 341 351 366 372 376 382 383 393
400 407 425 435 438 443 449 460 462 476 478 485
505 507 522 524 527 538 550 572 576 587 593 594
619 621 622 626 628 636 648 655 658 663 666 669
670 684 703 721 723 740 745 769 770 777 783 795
798 802 810 811 817 825 834 845 851 854 858 873
875 894 898 910 935 949 959 976 982 1011 1036
1084 1093 1123 1131 1135 1136 1138 1144 1156
1191 1195 1197 1200 1208 1215 1249 1256 1261
1266 1287 1294 14 9 24 30 41 51 62 66 81 83 87
89 95 99 106 112 119 127 132 147 165 169 186 189
198 201 205 214 216 235 245 256 276 300 304 305
311 313 325 326 346 351 359 360 374 377 378 379
388 392 442 448 456 462 476 487 489 494 498 499
503 504 509 516 519 520 527 531 536 538 542 547
558 561 564 566 572 577 579 583 593 598 600 601
602 612 617 621 625 632 636 652 656 674 680 684
685 688 695 697 698 703 714 729 731 739 741 745
748 756 757 764 796 802 803 808 813 822 823 829
839 844 846 862 866 870 889 891 894 897 905 909
920 922 924 925 933 942 957 969 976 978 992 1006
1010 1015 1016 1020 1039 1040 1051 1057 1070
1082 1093 1096 1104 1116 1129 1140 1146 1148
1149 1155 1161 1195 1212 1226 1288 1294 1300
1316 1320 1333 1340 1352 1361 1364 1366 1368
1375 1377 1384 1388 1393 1396 1401 1407 1414
1416 1419 1429 1502 1513 1544 1590 15 11 91
94 95 206 253 420 422 447 448 457 521 549 557
559 572 637 643 665 700 709 710 715 762 787 794
804 820 823 826 869 871 886 888 893 950 972 1045
1069 1070 1125 1199 1235 1283 1288 1350 1384
1485 1526 1690 1691 1734 1756 1757 1917 1971
2112 2190 2199 2202 2234 2324 2351 2355 2363
2364 2371 2377 2379 2393 2396 2452 2495 2516
2541 2546 2549 2551 2552 2578 2580 2600 2616
2717 2718 2778 2786 2794 2882 2899 2900 2953
2970 2974 2975 2976 2979 3016 3029 3066 3077

3079 3085 3117 3120 3139 3165 3178 3184 3208
3209 3251 3259 3265 3288 3308 3356 3358 3425
3426 3465 3634 3692 3765 3789 3801 3865 3868
3883 3889 3893 3947 4042 4195 4239 4268 4381
4390 4405 4443 4445 4501 4539 4587 4636 4651
4732 4762 4775 4863 4868 4891 16 53 55 83 88
89 118 125 142 146 147 161 165 174 182 198 199
208 210 225 229 242 248 270 273 274 276 334 341
352 359 387 397 412 424 439 442 448 451 506 516
519 522 525 529 530 532 534 557 560 579 602 610
617 651 653 664 667 684 697 700 706 714 718 724
725 729 775 778 780 791 798 818 825 835 849 860
866 871 875 882 887 901 912 915 922 928 949 972
985 989 998 1027 1034 1045 1051 1059 1063 1089
1098 1124 1128 1131 1160 1176 1178 1180 1187
1195 1228 1254 1271 1276 1277 1287 1300 1301
1320 1329 1331 1347 1348 1363 1376 1380 1387
1389 1403 1408 1411 1428 1430 1432 1466 1469
1473 1474 1481 1483 1486 1502 1506 1507 1516
1518 1522 1525 1541 1549 1553 1554 1555 1564
1567 1589 1592 1607 1624 1631 1634 1639 1645
1654 1655 1664 1676 1725 1749 1754 1766 1772
1786 1795 1827 1829 1841 1853 1857 1862 1869
1870 1880 1890 17 6 48 51 53 55 58 68 117 125
130 133 153 203 212 231 243 247 284 285 286 291
305 310 339 363 443 475 489 493 497 499 515 567
574 594 642 646 659 670 677 699 700 701 702 706
707 708 716 725 728 735 736 774 785 787 810 830
842 863 866 904 955 981 1021 1039 1049 1054 1064
1065 1071 1089 1097 1117 1165 1174 1179 1180
1211 1235 1261 1276 1292 1303 1309 1312 1313
1314 1315 1317 1344 1346 1359 1379 1385 1400
1435 1450 1490 1492 1502 1506 1508 1509 1510
1520 1521 1522 1526 1527 1529 1531 1532 1534
1535 1538 1539 1540 1543 1545 1548 1553 1555
1561 1571 1572 1576 1577 1582 1583 1595 1597
1601 1604 1610 1620 1621 1640 1667 1688 1690
1717 1727 1728 1751 1771 1773 1777 1778 1794
1804 1822 1838 1857 1859 1860 1884 1889 1894
1908 1910 1939 1974 1980 1982 1988 2022 2033
2050 2067 2071 2086 2087 2096 2098 2116 2149
2151 2152 2165 2166 2180 2182 2188 2204 2219
2222 2242 2266 2276 2278 2296 2314 18 2 3 18
28 30 32 40 45 49 54 65 67 70 74 79 86 87 89 90 93
100 111 120 122 127 129 130 144 146 151 153 159
160 161 162 172 177 183 187 190 192 195 200 207
212 213 218 220 222 224 233 235 242 248 249 251
253 261 263 271 290 291 295 298 309 311 313 318
321 325 326 337 342 352 353 357 359 365 366 369
374 383 392 396 400 406 407 415 416 419 421 423
427 428 430 434 447 463 474 482 491 494 504 507
513 514 525 538 541 542 544 545 547 553 563 565
566 571 573 585 586 587 590 593 609 623 625 631
640 642 644 655 657 662 664 669 686 689 692 699
700 702 707 713 721 730 743 744 749 751 752 753
755 758 759 761 792 797 800 802 803 805 807 828
835 844 856 860 868 889 894 902 906 910 913 917
919 921 926 934 940 949 954 964 970 971 972 976
979 981 985 988 990 1000 1004 1009 1012 1013
1014 1021 1023 1024 1039 1049 1053 1059 1066
1067 1069 1087 1088 1089 1096 1100 1109 1113
1114 1132 1149 1162 1171 1176 1185 1194 1198
1200 1203 1206 1219 1226 1240 1241 1242 1252
1253 1254 1256 1257 1267 1269 1271 1277 1293
1306 1315 1330 1348 1354 1356 1359 1365 1376
1377 1382 1400 1417 1425 1475 1479 1480 1486
1488 1494 1495 1553 1555 1560 1585 1594 1597
1605
with (16) 3 383 4 290 349 5 121 126

7 _{244 428 848 866 867} 9 _{190 354} 10 ₆₁₄
13 ₉₄₈ 15 ₁₀₂₄

with (335) 15 2 3 4 14 30 33 35 73 88 101 137
159 164 178 197 213 214 242 249 259 264 269 271
279 284 299 314 316 322 366 387 417 428 441 450
461 465 472 479 509 514 516 531 581 589 590 606
613 632 664 666 673 684 703 705 708 715 728 797
808 815 829 914 916 917 919 921 935 939 960 986
993 994 1005 1059 1060 1107 1122 1176 1180 1182
1190 1237 1241 1246 1251 1263 1279 1310 1317
1319 1332 1333 1339 1343 1355 1377 1379 1382
1401 1409 1427 1443 1444 1445 1447 1448 1477
1494 1548 1553 1555 1565 1571 1600 1602 1607
1614 1617 1703 1722 1822 1823 1841 1883 1885
1915 1927 1938 1960 1962 1964 1990 1993 2005
2006 2036 2042 2046 2057 2058 2060 2079 2085
2097 2111 2123 2152 2158 2160 2181 2185 2253
2257 2264 2268 2269 2271 2272 2274 2290 2299
2303 2334 2339 2399 2420 2433 2441 2466 2478
2483 2486 2492 2501 2513 2514 2537 2602 2612
2627 2631 2661 2670 2678 2682 2705 2715 2721
2722 2723 2743 2752 2762 2770 2805 2811
2835 2845 2847 2853 2857 2859 2877 2925 2931
2943 2985 3015 3102 3124 3128 3160 3234 3242
3285 3318 3333 3351 3360 3365 3372 3406 3420
3434 3469 3503 3506 3513 3533 3590 3623 3664
3726 3733 3828 3838 3843 3845 3846 3853 3877
3882 3900 3904 3911 3956 3958 3959 3960 3987
3991 4022 4026 4029 4035 4036 4055 4063 4075
4077 4078 4082 4096 4099 4100 4123 4124 4126
4132 4147 4158 4159 4167 4173 4186 4206 4212
4219 4220 4223 4243 4275 4293 4319 4322 4325
4326 4333 4351 4359 4370 4450 4455 4462 4476
4507 4524 4532 4537 4551 4557 4560 4586 4613
4614 4623 4672 4676 4682 4720 4778 4813 4838
4856 4870 4918 4920 4921 4931 4938 4949 4958
4966

withal (4) 9 ₂₅₄ 12 _{595 1009} 14 ₄₃₄
withdraw (1) 14 ₆₆₁
withdrawing (1) 17 ₁₂₁₇
withdrawn (2) 1 ₅₈₁ 14 ₁₁₂₅
withdrew (3) 4 ₁₈₆ 8 ₁₁₄₃ 11 ₈₁₃
withered (1) 9 ₁₀₁₁
withered (1) 15 ₄₂₁₈
withering (4) 6 ₉₄₈ 7 ₈₂₁ 13 ₈₂₆
14 ₃₉
withers (1) 13 ₈₂₇
withheld (3) 9 ₇₈₂ 11 ₆₆₁ 14 ₁₁₆₃
Within (1) 14 ₆₀
within (38) 1 _{103 227 270 281} 2 ₆₈ 3 ₃₉₄
4 _{177 305} 5 _{237 361} 7 ₈₈₂ 8 _{431 792}
9 ₁₀₄₂ 10 _{249 646 823} 11 ₃₂₁ 12 ₁₆₀
14 _{228 365 414 457 488 863 1044 1061}
15 _{1104 2198 3106 3948} 16 _{827 1324}
17 _{87 1515 1665 2279 4320}
within (2) 15 _{807 4320}
Without (3) 10 _{732 977} 17 ₅₄₃
Without (1) 17 ₈₁₈
without (127) 1 ₃₂₄ 2 _{189 204} 3 _{27 28 42}
253 490 4 _{130 210 478} 5 ₂₇₈ 6 _{449 484 875}
917 1019 1029 7 _{108 438 872 873} 8 _{312 743}
9 _{635 1041} 10 _{775 823 1277} 11 _{288 1092}
12 _{67 401 546 569 672 918 1116 1570 1663}
13 _{142 285 294 372 495 611 665 692 710 759 766}
845 1021 1163 14 _{152 309 310 478 479 526 823}
837 1030 1407 1421 1422 15 _{495 777 970 1096}
1118 1948 2236 2348 3935 4788 16 _{42 225 230}
283 409 487 531 637 779 953 1083 1360 1402 1447
1563 1586 1711 1789 1838 1862 1867 17 ₁₁₇

500 597 927 957 1067 1585 1923 2034 2283
18 _{59 71 76 102 240 282 385 467 531 656 784 788}
1010 1199 1239 1373 1418 1486
without (4) 4 ₂₈₉ 5 ₁₄₄ 9 ₅₅₀ 12 ₂₉
without (3) 15 _{926 2045 2168}
withouten (1) 14 ₁₅₁
withsay (2) 14 _{98 312}
withstand (1) 14 ₃₁₂
withstood (1) 9 ₃₇₃
Witless (1) 7 ₈₂₆
witness (11) 2 ₁₂₄ 9 ₁₀₃₂ 12 _{571 1335}
13 ₄₈₈ 15 _{3791 4276 4461 4788} 16 ₅₂₃
17 ₂₂₆₅
witnessbox (3) 5 ₄₃₈ 12 ₁₀₉₂ 16 ₁₃₇₃
witnessbox (1) 15 ₈₁₄
witnessed (2) 13 ₂₉₈ 16 ₁₃₇₅
witnesses (4) 3 ₁₈₂ 14 ₈₂₇ 16 ₁₃₇₅
17 ₂₂₀₃
witnesses' (1) 15 ₈₃₆
witnessing (2) 14 ₂₃₆ 16 ₁₅₁₅
wits (7) 3 ₄₃₃ 8 ₆₁ 9 ₅₃₇ 10 ₁₀₇₂
14 _{780 865} 18 ₁₀₀₂
Wittenberg (1) 9 ₈₃₂
witty (6) 8 _{116 119 685} 9 ₅₃₃ 14 _{202 1156}
witwanton (1) 14 ₄₁₁
Wives (2) 9 _{758 806}
wives (8) 8 ₇₄₇ 9 _{340 1046} 11 ₈₇₅
14 ₄₄₂ 17 ₆₅₉ 18 _{599 1271}
wives (1) 8 ₇₇₈
wives' (1) 9 ₆₄₇
wiving (1) 14 ₄₄₆
wizard (1) 15 ₃₉₆₂
Woa (2) 9 ₇₀₇ 10 ₄₅₂
wobble (1) 10 ₄₈₂
wobble (1) 15 ₁₂₆₆
wobbled (2) 10 _{373 468}
wobblers (1) 14 ₁₅₆₂
wobbly (3) 8 ₇₂₅ 14 ₈₁₅ 16 ₁₇₂₄
Woe (1) 6 ₅₉₆
woe (7) 11 _{437 632} 12 ₁₀₉₇ 14 _{119 186}
725 15 ₄₀₆
woe (1) 15 ₄₅₈₇
woebegone (1) 8 ₅₀₈
Woffington (1) 12 ₁₈₁
woful (1) 1 ₅₉
woful (1) 2 ₆₄
wogger (4) 18 _{616 624 668}
Woke (1) 8 ₂₅₁
woke (3) 3 ₃₆₅ 12 ₁₇₆₆ 18 ₁₃₄
wold (1) 15 ₃₁₅₆
wolf (3) 12 ₁₆₆₆ 14 ₇₃₀ 16 ₁₆₃₉
wolfdog (1) 12 ₇₁₅
wolfdog (1) 15 ₆₆₃
Wolfe (4) 10 ₃₇₈ 12 _{184 499} 15 ₄₅₁₇
Wolfe (1) 15 ₄₆₈₂
wolfeyes (1) 15 ₃₆₉
wolfing (1) 8 ₆₅₅
wolf's (1) 3 ₃₄₆
Wolseley (1) 18 ₆₉₁
Wolsey's (1) 10 ₁₄
Wolstan (1) 12 ₁₆₈₇
wom (1) 11 ₉₂₉
Woman (15) 5 ₄₂₇ 6 ₂₂₇ 7 ₆₈₄
11 _{641 877} 12 ₁₈₆ 13 _{110 992} 15 ₄₇₈
1758 2548 2549 2551 2554 2962
Woman (1) 10 ₃₆₈
woman (162) 1 _{345 389 395 403 415 425 433}
437 454 2 _{312 329 390 394} 3 _{233 331 372 422}
468 4 ₄₁₈ 5 _{196 342 348} 6 _{12 89 245 517}

518 696 851 7 _{536 784} 8 _{32 146 177 269 379}
524 534 616 618 634 846 971 1125 9 _{237 519 639}
1030 10 _{134 200 201 440} 11 _{171 976 1061}
1088 1104 12 _{218 255 1051 1052 1378 1525}
1534 13 _{301 435 457 775 802 874 975 1234 1237}
14 _{46 108 112 113 171 205 208 231 245 786 803}
918 980 1304 1312 15 _{206 594 611 769 859 1962}
1974 2551 2553 3029 3425 3458 3779 3905 4271
4648 16 _{139 1354 1393} 17 _{12 613 706 707}
1158 18 _{13 23 34 60 98 117 176 232 245 255}
319 329 472 477 495 498 559 583 655 697 746 805
827 839 855 935 947 970 993 998 1079 1119 1120
1147 1197 1254 1334 1349 1389 1397 1407 1423
1438 1440 1457 1480 1519 1579
woman (2) 10 _{615 618}
woman (6) 15 _{25 38 297 578 3046 3837}
Womanbody (1) 14 ₁₄₈₃
womancity (1) 15 ₁₃₂₇
womaneyes (1) 8 ₂₂₅
womanhood (1) 16 ₁₄₂₉
womanish (2) 14 ₈₁₃ 15 ₃₀₁₆
womanly (5) 13 _{223 435} 14 ₆₇₆
15 _{1799 3427}
Woman's (3) 14 ₁₈₆ 15 _{2097 3678}
woman's (26) 1 _{356 421} 4 _{227 450} 6 ₅₁₉
939 8 ₉₁₄ 9 ₄₆₁ 10 _{252 604 847}
11 ₄₁₄ 13 _{200 517 920} 14 _{117 292 725}
15 _{2444 2447 2554 2555 3153} 16 _{419 896}
17 ₄₂
woman's (1) 15 ₄₃₃₄
womans (7) 15 ₃₈₉₁ 18 _{326 519 838 1380}
1402 1577
Womb (2) 3 ₄₄ 17 ₂₃₁₉
womb (11) 5 ₅₆₇ 7 ₇₂₄ 11 ₁₁₀₄ 14 ₆₀
109 292 337 729 970 15 ₄₂₀₄ 17 ₂₃₁₈
Wombed (1) 3 ₄₅
wombfruit (3) 14 _{2 3 4}
wombs (3) 9 ₆₆₄ 10 ₅₈₇ 11 ₁₁₀₃
Women (12) 5 _{78 104 342 453} 6 ₇₅₃
8 _{136 558 630} 9 ₃₃₈ 13 _{909 1037 1071}
Women (3) 15 _{1460 1585 1811}
Women (1) 15 ₁₅₉₀
women (84) 1 ₇₀₆ 3 ₁₆₆ 5 _{69 449}
6 _{379 484 546 624 790 1014} 7 ₁₀₀₅ 8 ₃₄₅
416 707 928 968 1071 1146 9 _{255 351 674}
10 _{170 340 727 818 1275} 11 _{558 686 1035}
1089 12 _{512 1406 1482 1507 1546} 13 _{107 662}
710 781 783 1031 1058 1187 14 _{116 265 534 587}
640 993 1258 15 _{402 661 2398 2772 3176 3699}
4183 16 _{63 87 476 717 741 893 1206 1550 1555}
18 _{9 16 36 57 157 205 473 632 736 1130 1358}
1363 1435 1436 1437 1458 1525
women (2) 3 ₁₃₄
women (3) 15 _{5 1745 4123}
womenfolk (1) 14 ₄₈₉
women's (4) 13 ₉₆₈ 14 _{119 946} 15 ₂₇₃₈
women's (1) 15 ₄₅₇₈
womens (1) 18 ₁₁₅₄
womoonless (1) 11 ₁₀₁₂
Womwom (1) 15 ₁₂₇₃
Won (1) 15 ₄₈₁₃
won (20) 7 ₃₅₉ 8 _{801 830 837} 9 _{339 938}
11 ₇₂₀ 12 _{1218 1233 1569} 13 _{225 255}
14 _{60 299 702} 15 ₅₄₆ 17 ₁₆₇₆ 18 ₄₀₂
425 1091
won (1) 4 ₅₁₄
Wonder (41) 4 _{28 40 61 149 205 215 327 489}
5 _{31 191 268 326} 6 _{232 397 747 786 990}
7 ₉₈₄ 8 _{81 93 665 1035 1098 1109} 10 ₃₈₃

523　11 560 1036 1229 1250　12 1534
13 759 825 833 960 984 997 1025 1120 1127
15 3621
wonder (56)　3 68 315 494 495 497　5 395
6 185 454 563　7 294　8 904　9 421 802
10 74 695 1092 1276　11 380　12 1655
13 479　14 33 119 186 1099 1264　17 830
1770　18 12 115 121 124 208 217 235 240 367
455 527 544 558 935 936 953 967 1092 1133 1137
1252 1300 1304 1326 1399 1451 1458 1463 1471
wondered (6)　9 1207　13 230　14 120 170
16 191 1227
Wonderful (8)　1 435　5 424　9 548
11 627 931 947　13 414 865
wonderful (14)　1 572　3 140　8 47
9 112　10 25 828　11 791　12 59
13 116 238　14 626　15 1462 3258　18 808
wonderfully (4)　10 19　12 1449　14 897
16 1461
wondering (4)　1 423　11 490　13 528
16 633
wonders (3)　3 192　12 1723　18 552
wonderstruck (1)　15 4962
wonderwide (1)　15 3169
Wonderworker (4)　17 1819 1820 1830 1833
wonderworker (2)　11 1224　18 716
wonderworkers (1)　17 1838
wondrous (4)　13 210 731　14 222 268
wondrous (1)　10 609
wondrously (1)　14 157
Won't (5)　5 563　8 1171　13 1277
14 1503　15 3067
Won't (1)　3 21
won't (36)　1 88　3 200 256　4 276　5 8 9
6 70　8 32 307 630 931 964　10 386 426
11 132 437　12 409 758 826 1075 1239 1256
13 262 814 1276　14 476　15 369 404 2270
2511 2880 3693 4563 4727　16 250
won't (4)　1 300 304　9 1127　17 817
wont (15)　13 11　14 75 255 1139　18 472
1066 1117 1191 1282 1283 1334 1362 1457 1524
1527
woo (4)　9 454 938　12 83　13 207
woo (1)　13 312
Wood (4)　10 1196　12 34　17 137
18 654
wood (11)　3 110 149　4 179　6 347 816
7 460　8 822　13 768 1191　15 4950
17 1547
wood (1)　15 3341
woodbine (1)　15 536
woodcocks (1)　18 832
woodcocks (1)　15 4668
wooden (5)　9 622　13 1270　16 321
17 155 235
wooden (1)　9 1147
woodland (1)　15 3408
Woodman (1)　12 1290
wood's (1)　15 4933
Woods (2)　4 148　18 942
woods (3)　9 578　15 4942　16 632
Woodshadows (1)　1 242
woodshavings (1)　15 4937
Woodwind (1)　11 1055
Woodwinds (1)　11 1054
woodwork (1)　7 140
wooed (3)　7 776　9 938　13 1092
wooer (2)　9 669
wool (7)　3 37 432　10 852 853　12 1242
14 269 570

woolgathering (1)　16 626
woollen (3)　4 532　17 2041　18 92
woolly (1)　18 1448
woos (1)　9 986
woozy (1)　14 1562
Worcester (1)　12 230
Word (3)　9 61 429　13 459
word (110)　1 334 612 614　2 128 164 244 336
3 222 435　4 118 331 335 361 367　5 206 246
263　6 240 345　7 65 479 562　8 40 424 531
9 80 375 864 904 1025　10 183 336 893 977
1114　11 13 680 720 1009　12 60 63 479 549
1145 1192 1236 1523 1658　13 37 55 385 582 749
14 91 96 230 259 264 292 293 309 368 417 473
599 634 792 853 889 975 1348 1360 1390 1401 1456
15 207 827 1543 1561 1809 2194 2236 2325 2750
2882 3032 4192 4597 4600 4645　16 63 170 199
764 1086 1455 1602 1617 1693 1885　18 238 326
490 565 618 750 775 1248 1418
word (1)　15 4161
Words (3)　1 660　11 703　15 1948
Words (1)　16 1738
words (110)　1 217 246 252 272 283 525
2 40 247 264 293 331 346 368　3 407 415 420
4 343　5 217 273 404 421　7 139 485 729 759
767 824 836 881　8 115 477　9 13 51 111 168
175 353 462 577 679 738 1007 1010　10 14 71
816 826　11 87 676 696 839 926 1081 1092 1275
1284　12 796 1437　13 24 120 124 289 330 591
14 104 119 223 289 362 425 429 430 462 745 752
765 790 801 849 876 996 1277 1358 1509
15 833 999 3279　16 904 971 1026 1062 1109
1143 1147 1667 1798　17 637 1307 1317 1882
18 319 740 743 1170 1340 1531
words (1)　7 839
words (1)　15 666
Wordsworth (2)　6 941　9 820
Wore (2)　11 696　13 1241
wore (22)　3 302　6 303　7 817　8 165
11 726 1056　12 168 170 1285　13 155 181
800 801 900　15 1662　18 26 440 457 836 858
1125 1547
WORK (1)　7 120
Work (3)　9 158　13 1243　15 2516
work (57)　1 157　2 161 342 350 402　4 453
5 320 332 434　6 188 980　7 306　8 327 356
387 532　9 49 70 104 438　10 489　12 125
966 1821 1824 1888　13 460 911　14 40 1120
1414　15 699 844 1023 3086 3748　16 213 504
598 694 793 813 968 1007 1140 1147 1148 1151
1152 1155 1744　17 487 1205 1417 1421 1424
workaday (1)　7 88
Workbasket (1)　8 1119
worked (7)　7 687　8 572　12 1286 1541
15 979 2806　16 1703
worker (2)　7 88　12 907
workers (1)　14 1258
Workhouse (1)　12 1457
Working (3)　7 83　8 663　15 1290
working (9)　7 201　9 1074　10 1053
12 123　13 695　15 2228　17 221 1092
1578
working (1)　15 3009
workingman's (1)　12 221
workman (1)　18 370
workman's (1)　15 1355
workmen (1)　15 1546
Works (2)　17 1363 1365
works (16)　6 397　7 224　8 122　9 529

778 899　13 556 1047　15 3036　16 1126
1451 1500　17 386 753　18 488 580
workshop (2)　14 1258 1271
World (1)　15 3935
World (2)　7 635 638
World (1)　15 2177
WORLD (1)　15 2180
world (140)　1 399　2 15 141 158 159 203 390
3 27 142 391　4 228 418　5 30 245 447
6 108 514 516 547 571 995 1001 1002　7 81 435
536 911　8 47 147 317 328 329 472 521 529 583
636 921　9 44 52 88 105 151 218 222 226 236 254
841 851 990 1012 1041 1042 1047　10 588
11 871 1184　12 78 251 726 802 1070 1242
1248 1266 1303 1417 1576　13 1 85 287 330 655
672 897 928 1094 1263　14 184 206 212 481 620
756 784 856 1070 1344 1545 1577　15 236 330
786 977 1357 2117 2166 2236 2457 3136 3638 3891
3926 4183 4202　16 412 424 456 542 607 794
1107 1225 1546 1657 1790 1850　17 464 1407
18 8 9 100 137 238 268 437 467 552 739 755 829
854 876 880 963 1158 1211 1435 1439
world (3)　7 859　8 417　17 416
world (2)　15 100 2575
worldfamous (1)　12 620
worldish (1)　10 159
worldly (1)　15 375
worldrenowned (1)　12 596
World's (1)　7 98
World's (1)　15 1577
world's (3)　15 1459　17 579 1820
worlds (6)　3 410　10 824　13 189 423
15 526 1686
worm (1)　16 1831
wormfingers (1)　15 3733
worms (1)　18 1168
worms (1)　15 1255
wormwood (1)　3 210
wormy (1)　10 805
worn (5)　5 338　8 489　13 151　15 2818
17 75
worn (1)　15 4159
worried (1)　16 1616
worries (1)　10 140
worries (1)　15 2556
worry (2)　5 410　7 294
Worse (1)　15 3291
worse (30)　1 163　3 387　4 425　5 189 392
499　7 1031　8 719　12 1542　13 774 942
14 774 1561　15 1287 1985 2444 3291 4732
4822　16 1362 1465 1566　18 94 284 314 996
1100 1220
worship (8)　9 85 744　12 1106　14 60 311
15 1498　16 1751　17 970
worshipful (2)　12 1874　15 760
worshipper (1)　15 1758
worshippers (1)　5 459
worshipping (1)　13 564
worships (1)　15 1415
Worst (3)　6 202　13 879 963
Worst (1)　15 1578
worst (9)　6 335 571　8 494　9 812
13 1084　15 3272　16 1402　18 27 238
worsted (1)　9 461
worsting (1)　1 663
worth (29)　6 371　7 89 989　8 895 1018
10 527 744 936 945　11 616 1060　12 1313
1386 1908　13 326 842　14 286 595 681 786
1421　16 138 990 1138 1700 1782　17 1689
1829 1953

worth (1) 9 1152
worthful (1) 14 85
Worthington (1) 16 966
worthless (1) 7 808
worthy (10) 12 1199 14 57 332 571 651 989
  16 681 971 1025 17 1401
wotted (1) 14 443
wotting (1) 14 85
Wought (1) 12 1087
Would (23) 1 436 490 3 96 320 321 4 146
  317 6 432 579 846 957 7 711 8 611 612
  1003 13 659 900 1241 14 772 15 429 2297
  3149 17 2012
would (355) 2 141 232 370 3 320 321 323
  413 4 110 129 134 367 372 420 5 77 171 186
  188 291 335 6 77 131 177 178 205 246 433 435
  548 619 776 789 866 980 7 744 8 133 150 377
  518 574 599 713 745 876 924 1007 1029 1049 1110
  1145 9 27 76 82 127 176 348 393 444 473 537
  560 995 1050 10 19 24 28 38 169 669 670 729
  1069 1147 11 539 545 623 769 1009 1064
  12 26 120 124 125 256 372 441 470 643 644 685
  699 749 798 896 1026 1043 1135 1139 1145 1368
  1478 1535 1662 1664 1671 1754 1795 1850 1898
  1899 13 43 60 115 142 151 160 164 167 172 189
  197 200 207 208 212 214 219 221 222 231 235 237
  240 241 262 271 308 319 390 404 413 422 439 484
  487 512 523 544 580 585 595 598 603 628 629 652
  653 654 655 665 668 670 673 710 733 760 761 974
  990 14 27 83 84 114 115 136 221 231 239 241
  252 254 314 327 399 417 419 432 440 441 458 471
  481 502 544 559 560 596 607 610 689 692 749 786
  787 788 837 838 866 891 950 1019 1030 1125 1171
  1180 1224 1237 1251 1255 1360 1429 15 105
  646 821 950 976 1723 1995 2641 3365 3450 3476
  3484 3625 4410 16 4 16 176 179 226 504 510
  515 618 717 746 752 757 814 843 916 996 1000
  1003 1036 1060 1120 1136 1163 1220 1233 1269
  1295 1297 1302 1324 1351 1403 1456 1478 1540
  1556 1561 1618 1619 1623 1630 1660 1693 1705
  1791 1801 1829 1840 1849 1860 1876 17 69 448
  449 450 454 455 457 458 459 460 549 551 873 935
  989 1076 1098 1356 1606 1623 1674 1744 1752
  1839 2000 2006 2013 2017 2019 2024 2126
  18 11 85 89 90 104 115 159 190 192 310 373 406
  562 734 824 841 997 999 1060 1128 1152 1208 1354
  1378 1410 1441 1561 1606
would (6) 1 464 7 864 866 9 267 550
  10 15
would (1) 15 899
wouldbe (2) 13 47 16 972
Wouldn't (12) 4 423 6 412 991 7 310
  8 136 497 887 10 684 11 649 13 819 905
  15 3947
wouldn't (49) 1 207 412 3 237 4 419 533
  5 189 371 410 6 297 415 433 993 7 241
  8 106 544 824 10 263 605 715 716 11 470
  494 679 892 12 142 435 700 1204 1360 1534
  1843 13 61 178 685 776 972 1004 15 641
  2297 3006 3136 3366 16 155 279 284 1409 1478
  1588
wouldnt (37) 18 68 114 193 229 350 362 379
  397 491 503 651 777 800 810 845 1016 1105 1107
  1113 1135 1146 1157 1171 1245 1247 1329 1352
  1435 1439 1452 1454 1485 1513 1519 1534 1564
  1581
wouldyousetashoe (1) 15 1603
wound (7) 4 366 11 241 683 1178 13 580
  16 1620

wounded (2) 9 460 14 129
wounds (3) 1 217 13 435 15 1608
wounds (1) 15 4623
wove (2) 11 926 929
woven (6) 2 87 9 379 12 1246 1714
  15 4933
Wow (3) 13 931 14 1463 15 4766
wow (2) 15 4766
wrack (1) 3 10
Wrangle (1) 13 845
wrangle (1) 18 44
wrangle (1) 15 4367
wrap (2) 7 137 18 674
wrap (1) 10 615
wrapped (4) 4 165 7 1003 16 1492 1727
wrapped (1) 15 1026
wrappers (1) 17 1369
wraps (1) 8 350
wrastling (1) 9 897
wrath (3) 7 806 14 1353 16 1086
Wreaker (1) 14 83
wreaker (1) 17 2021
wreath (5) 6 575 583 634 840 908
wreath (2) 15 4158 4805
WREATHS (1) 15 654
wreaths (4) 6 21 505 524 946
wreaths (1) 15 653
Wreck (1) 11 1018
wreck (4) 13 1250 15 953 16 906
wrecked (1) 16 432
Wreckers (1) 13 1069
wreckers (1) 16 962
wrecks (1) 16 962
Wren (2) 6 446 17 1429
wren (2) 15 1451
wrenbushes (1) 15 1449
wrenching (1) 6 491
Wren's (1) 15 3184
wrest (3) 9 740 10 807 815
wrestling (1) 15 581
wretch (8) 6 235 11 138 12 433
  13 746 1102 14 854 15 3052 18 545
Wretched (1) 8 723
wretched (5) 1 252 12 255 14 470
  16 729 1111
Wriggle (1) 15 1615
wriggled (1) 6 975
wriggles (2) 15 1246 2549
wriggling (1) 11 805
wriggling (2) 15 664 3733
Wright (1) 12 226
wring (4) 11 105 15 4597 4644 4721
wrings (1) 15 4232
wrinkle (1) 12 15
wrinkled (4) 1 402 6 326 9 374
  14 323
wrinkled (1) 15 2923
wrinkles (2) 15 3657 18 753
wrinkles (1) 15 2451
wrinkling (1) 15 75
wrinkly (1) 18 1162
Wrist (1) 3 428
wrist (2) 4 168 15 2554
wrist (1) 15 441
wristbangles (1) 15 317
wristlet (1) 15 2051
wrists (1) 14 600
Wristwatches (1) 13 984

Writ (1) 16 773
Writ (1) 9 98
writ (5) 3 82 10 945 951 14 287 350
Write (5) 8 613 11 868 1086 13 1256
  15 1091
Write (1) 1 596
write (52) 2 131 3 139 428 4 360 5 251
  255 6 66 742 7 616 712 8 64 884 893
  9 19 928 1068 10 320 410 1085 1089
  11 230 713 714 821 860 862 12 708 13 636
  643 813 814 843 14 636 15 2499 3778
  16 345 18 490 580 622 719 731 734 735 739
  741 765 841 853 1173 1333 1364 1526
Writer (1) 14 872
writer (3) 4 504 9 252 12 724
writer's (1) 14 496
writes (7) 2 340 7 266 9 510 12 1332
  15 813 17 615
writes (2) 15 1871 3723
writhe (1) 15 2264
writhing (2) 3 461 14 1107
Writing (2) 15 380 16 1154
writing (23) 4 400 408 413 421 6 449 743
  884 8 132 134 135 9 779 1123 10 438
  11 874 14 1107 1487 16 1229 17 610
  679 773 18 327 1053 1490
writingtable (2) 4 19 15 3173
writs (1) 12 1025
Written (1) 4 502
Written (1) 11 1291
written (30) 2 128 3 141 415 4 517
  6 617 7 263 9 112 309 455 478 524 756 913
  1010 10 162 11 610 969 13 422 642
  14 517 15 1801 3199 3388 17 392 424 1398
  1788 18 325 1525
written (1) 15 1005
Wrong (1) 15 3704
wrong (37) 1 177 209 2 402 4 233
  6 116 384 9 390 10 790 11 696
  12 358 1033 13 43 774 868 984 14 1180
  15 978 1971 2826 2827 3288 3706 3871 4773
  16 1088 1096 18 713 729 817 932 1021 1051
  1100 1109 1249 1343 1401
wrong (2) 5 121 126
wrongdoing (1) 16 1055
wronged (1) 16 1495
Wrongfully (1) 6 477
wrongfully (5) 6 475 14 960 15 762 763
  1771
wrongs (1) 17 2201
wrongways (1) 14 450
Wrote (1) 8 321
wrote (41) 2 415 5 253 269 6 1002
  7 738 1038 9 117 829 867 1047 1069 1076 1158
  10 321 850 964 11 825 861 871 888 896
  12 806 14 755 15 766 1016 3034 3173
  16 783 881 910 1254 17 736 738 882
  18 318 330 613 717 720 737
wroth (1) 9 79
wrought (2) 14 146 243
wrought (1) 7 770
wrung (1) 13 736
wry (1) 7 1068
wrynecked (1) 15 1238
wud (1) 9 897
Wull (1) 9 896
wus (1) 14 1473
wusser (1) 15 2220
Wy (1) 10 35

wy (1) 6 374
Wylie (7) 10 652 13 135 196 197 198 427 632
Wylie's (1) 13 206
Wyndham (1) 17 793
Wynn's (1) 17 2258
Wyse (32) 8 950 10 968 973 979 986 989 995 1015 1025 1033 1040 1212 12 1178 1206 1258 1267 1294 1317 1319 1341 1379 1414 1419 1421 1475 1486 1490 1538 1573 1586 1623 1628
Wyse (2) 15 4352 4353
WYSE (2) 15 1533 3304

X

X (4) 7 669 672 951 16 753
x (2) 11 836 16 1636
x x x x (1) 5 259
x x x x x (1) 18 623
Xanthippe (1) 9 234
Xavier (1) 17 144
Xavier's (1) 10 108
Xenophon (1) 7 254
Xinbad (1) 17 2326
XL (1) 4 422
Xmas (2) 17 1781 18 453

Y

Y (2) 8 126 12 561
y (5) 7 168 12 563 18 1465 1472
y (1) 14 792
Y M C A (2) 8 5 359
yacht (1) 13 1208
yachting (1) 7 984
yachtingcap (1) 10 579
yachtsman's (1) 15 3739
yadgana (1) 15 2555
yahoos (1) 12 1353
Yailer (1) 17 2326
yak (1) 14 1090
yale (1) 14 416
yanked (1) 14 1584
yankee (4) 7 785 9 54 139 12 1168
yapping (1) 15 2189
yaps (1) 15 2851
Yard (1) 16 1192
yard (15) 6 171 459 8 936 9 565 711 10 1101 11 105 111 12 497 835 1562 14 572 17 129 148 167
yards (5) 8 61 14 642 16 389 393 18 659
yarn (1) 16 685
yarns (1) 16 823
Yashmak (1) 11 943
yashmak (1) 11 1233
yashmak (1) 15 300
yawn (7) 6 750 8 975 10 125 16 348 1266 1664 18 342
yawn (1) 15 4672
yawned (2) 10 126 16 14
yawning (1) 6 466
yawning (1) 15 1697
yawns (2) 15 1241 2624
yawp (1) 9 139
yclept (2) 14 125 189
Ye (3) 6 88 7 889 13 1093
ye (12) 14 282 283 285 318 470 1446 1523 1538 1562 15 643 1543 1607
Yea (2) 9 540 15 1543
yea (4) 12 447 15 1900 16 793 1844
Year (3) 5 198 8 156 13 1108
year (69) 1 367 3 492 4 197 209 5 181 368 396 465 6 395 626 7 90 207 702 8 17 31 71 158 268 365 558 570 598 1155 9 587 599 10 550 11 905 1197 12 1752 1861 13 208 590 1092 1284 14 103 205 482 1049

15 401 546 868 1632 2399 2416 2424 16 618 910 950 960 990 17 34 95 239 457 459 461 883 1194 1803 1876 2278 18 161 375 501 603 782
yearly (1) 4 199
yearned (3) 8 792 13 437
yearning (2) 13 106 14 982
yearns (2) 13 194 214
Years (1) 15 4203
years (126) 2 271 349 371 391 3 143 4 364 6 697 794 968 7 537 924 8 158 179 265 387 704 858 869 1047 1154 9 167 217 394 497 623 631 649 673 680 831 936 10 1089 1090 12 717 1425 13 16 649 925 953 1028 1115 1152 1283 14 88 121 570 770 859 1043 1110 1323 1328 1428 15 539 1359 1525 1755 3154 3476 3629 3714 3718 3719 4203 16 411 421 606 838 1029 1035 1203 1310 1405 1438 1443 1568 1582 17 418 447 448 451 456 457 458 460 472 481 483 503 749 861 1054 1071 1130 1131 1519 1665 1671 1689 1760 1761 1857 1858 1918 1919 2068 2282 18 396 474 624 698 719 774 805 823 992 1115 1216 1307 1357 1575 1592
years (1) 9 288
years' (3) 8 438 17 1546 1662
Yeates (1) 8 552
Yeats (3) 9 304 1161 15 2254
yell (2) 11 171
yelled (2) 11 173 12 1357
yelling (4) 7 913 919 956 8 437
yelling (2) 15 2138 3442
Yellow (2) 11 725 728
Yellow (1) 15 250
yellow (36) 1 2 315 3 232 431 493 4 248 5 239 523 6 362 582 850 8 689 782 838 1142 10 143 146 285 290 292 1209 12 96 13 1076 14 1144 1579 15 120 2672 17 1104 1304 1395 2241 2242 18 128 1202 1495 1600
yellow (11) 15 299 738 1604 1821 1927 2249 2339 2415 2598 4126 4167
yellowed (1) 3 214
Yellowgreen (1) 8 901
yellowish (1) 13 1133
yellowjohns (1) 12 1255
yellowkitefaced (1) 15 3386
yellowly (1) 15 3831
yellowslobbered (1) 10 245
yells (1) 12 1345
yells (1) 15 192
yelped (1) 3 343
yelping (1) 3 318
yelps (1) 15 2575
Yelverton (1) 15 4550
YELVERTON (5) 15 1013 1036 1076 1092 1110
Yeoman (1) 11 1083
yeoman (6) 11 1082 1097 1249 14 686 16 20 1397
yeomanry (1) 12 1318
yer (1) 14 1538
yerd (1) 14 1527
Yes (195) 1 48 184 197 622 699 713 2 14 35 39 92 162 175 180 410 435 3 60 68 85 140 179 490 4 63 138 233 239 298 340 355 358 5 123 136 168 310 360 385 486 503 507 514 6 7 89 111 168 194 247 267 272 285 371 405 425 567 568 703 808 894 1010 7 55 191 219 318 411 412 568 665 666 692 894 918 961 8 209 279 280 284 565 591 599 757 765 797 863 889 1088 1164 1172 1188 9 127 240 303 336 343 387 503 583 10 4 5 23

28 41 303 323 332 389 391 392 395 407 430 602 610 613 723 725 758 828 964 1049 **11** 112 221 222 224 229 338 424 447 504 508 564 611 638 641 692 824 870 887 970 1000 1129 1175 1254 1291 **12** 274 319 888 991 1020 1032 1048 1106 1320 1410 1420 1546 1646 **13** 194 411 779 985 1007 1017 1030 1124 **14** 447 1016 **15** 345 349 570 576 1028 2500 2539 2757 2918 2959 3230 3272 3405 3767 4390 4744 4873 **16** 365 1106 1452 1650 1723 1852 **17** 119 164 571 **18** 1 1609

Yes (1) **5** 128

Yes (1) **15** 932

yes (161) **2** 242 **3** 140 418 **4** 62 239 448 **5** 11 38 75 136 142 380 463 499 **6** 7 89 201 221 542 567 963 **7** 385 543 568 700 742 **8** 159 349 872 1189 1192 **9** 198 311 318 429 679 **10** 25 318 395 430 **11** 67 870 1174 **12** 991 994 **13** 243 579 794 **14** 1518 1558 **15** 576 720 2524 2539 3230 3231 3272 3346 3915 4445 4609 **16** 612 894 1800 **18** 20 22 34 38 46 66 76 90 95 109 110 132 143 168 214 222 233 236 239 302 338 383 440 442 470 487 521 527 535 536 555 563 580 634 673 781 795 808 809 818 822 873 899 901 907 916 939 943 949 956 1047 1105 1151 1180 1207 1256 1261 1284 1307 1313 1314 1319 1321 1406 1438 1511 1532 1568 1574 1575 1576 1577 1578 1581 1592 1599 1602 1603 1605 1606 1607 1608

yes (1) **15** 930

Yessex (1) **11** 229

yester (2) **13** 761 **15** 2410

Yesterday (1) **16** 1575

yesterday (18) **4** 402 415 509 **8** 341 950 **10** 747 **12** 1515 **14** 1137 **15** 3629 **16** 256 605 1574 1577 1758 **18** 46 459 821 1327

yesterday's (1) **4** 83

YET (1) **7** 1071

Yet (15) **1** 482 **2** 140 **6** 245 348 548 **11** 802 810 **13** 137 882 1155 **14** 1348 **15** 2445 4002 **16** 825 1055

Yet (2) **10** 1254 **17** 1353

yet (64) **1** 102 213 311 **2** 7 237 **3** 422 **4** 522 **5** 148 154 462 **6** 789 845 1003 **7** 842 873 **8** 248 791 **9** 43 309 461 498 750 **10** 31 826 917 **11** 184 188 190 243 351 352 737 1027 **12** 175 595 1009 **13** 188 1076 **14** 121 500 522 527 726 873 1083 1222 1273 1323 1542 1587 **15** 2441 2953 3758 **16** 60 556 564 1288 1461 1478 **17** 521 2197 2203 **18** 1050

yet (1) **17** 1398

yewfronds (1) **15** 2047

YEWS (8) **15** 3237 3282 3301 3307 3339 3345 3431 3452

yews (1) **15** 3235

yield (2) **5** 105 **15** 1528

yielded (4) **8** 638 642 **10** 619 **16** 1743

yielding (3) **4** 506 507 **8** 915

yilo (1) **10** 849

Yo (1) **15** 2766

yodels (1) **15** 2609

yodled (1) **11** 442

yoghin (1) **15** 2269

Yogibogeybox (1) **9** 279

yoke (4) **3** 228 **6** 92 **12** 1282 **15** 2966

yoke (1) **15** 3990

yokefellow (1) **3** 228

yokel (1) **9** 667

Yom (3) **8** 36 752 **15** 1623

yon (2) **14** 1546 **15** 4636

yonder (2) **11** 1105 **14** 1366

yoni (2) **15** 2550 2552

Yook (1) **14** 1567

Yooka (1) **14** 1567

YORE (1) **7** 737

yore (2) **10** 174 1204

York (7) **8** 1147 **10** 90 **12** 94 536 **15** 3804 **16** 1244 **17** 432

York (2) **7** 635 638

York's (1) **3** 314

Yorkshire (6) **15** 1983 4003 4027 4115 4117 **17** 1733

Yorkshire (3) **10** 1242 1255 1256

Yorkshire (1) **15** 4677

YOU (2) **7** 614 1071

You (265) **1** 53 62 73 79 91 118 194 198 204 207 212 496 524 551 553 624 625 636 698 **2** 1 18 21 178 225 230 236 268 272 289 315 338 402 410 417 **3** 11 105 128 129 130 137 175 183 192 290 295 369 420 **4** 55 194 **5** 96 169 172 185 303 514 531 **6** 217 246 530 757 791 1000 **7** 145 146 149 157 474 481 599 602 617 627 630 643 648 775 798 887 998 1035 **8** 139 213 462 771 955 **9** 72 195 203 487 537 632 684 738 949 952 972 983 1064 1068 1081 1094 1208 **10** 413 421 445 671 696 731 828 950 966 1066 **11** 37 183 208 315 481 869 872 888 891 1041 1096 1139 1194 **12** 275 316 326 522 762 886 1000 1001 1204 1215 1411 1499 1670 1897 **13** 192 270 307 337 512 **14** 1112 1341 1464 1468 1503 1528 1570 1574 **15** 93 275 369 375 395 431 434 447 448 488 620 721 736 740 761 772 812 832 852 1100 1192 1195 1216 1287 1295 1523 1673 1677 1681 1715 1717 1836 1890 1891 1980 1996 2100 2109 2198 2200 2201 2206 2297 2399 2421 2542 2641 2775 2798 2803 2848 2866 2951 2966 2975 2999 3073 3076 3198 3199 3245 3261 3263 3272 3281 3449 3458 3474 3601 3625 3644 3788 3804 4066 4183 4189 4299 4370 4471 4587 4647 4744 4788 4858 **16** 85 158 199 262 378 432 443 456 464 748 814 893 995 1022 1109 1157 1158 1160 1331 1339 1646

You (7) **4** 288 **7** 846 849 855 **9** 1013 **10** 614

You (1) **17** 416

you (1591) **1** 8 29 43 53 54 59 74 79 88 89 92 93 94 112 128 134 144 150 151 157 161 171 180 183 189 196 208 209 213 228 291 295 318 322 342 346 353 354 370 373 379 415 424 425 427 428 436 437 440 480 487 496 499 505 506 522 532 536 538 542 551 609 611 617 622 636 642 648 682 712 717 730 **2** 21 56 132 134 137 161 183 191 223 236 237 243 244 251 253 254 262 270 337 361 374 379 389 401 404 410 413 417 423 425 438 439 **3** 8 23 27 38 62 75 92 95 96 106 108 128 129 139 140 142 175 176 180 184 195 196 200 221 222 238 246 256 291 298 312 318 320 321 326 353 399 405 421 427 428 449 484 **4** 17 40 83 98 99 115 116 123 133 169 185 195 197 214 251 252 255 302 313 317 332 354 357 370 376 380 522 **5** 39 43 83 84 87 91 104 108 135 162 167 169 170 173 185 186 242 243 244 246 247 248 249 250 251 252 253 254 264 287 294 305 361 365 424 426 428 453 455 456 474 478 481 484 499 507 514 524 537 549 556 557 **6** 5 18 68 94 103 144 151 192 194 214 215 218 220 406 408 485 527 556 557 616 617 659 675 677 712 717 755 765 796 797 807 812 815 843 846 847 853 854 860 861 862 871 882 891 938 961 962 966 967 996 999 1000 1001 1003 1026 1033 **7** 26 49 113 115 122 126 146 150 151 154 156 171 213 241 288

310 350 357 380 407 419 435 502 504 510 527 541 544 549 601 602 616 625 630 631 633 651 652 655 678 692 693 698 706 711 712 728 731 739 740 782 783 786 787 798 804 814 836 844 907 945 977 981 1004 1020 1051 **8** 10 21 33 37 85 94 135 140 202 203 207 231 242 243 245 250 276 307 327 330 367 388 452 454 459 469 503 535 536 537 539 540 544 546 562 563 578 611 612 693 710 716 756 764 776 781 784 813 827 828 858 860 884 888 925 952 961 966 977 979 980 1003 1018 1019 1030 1077 1081 1086 1087 1093 1123 1148 1149 **9** 18 27 72 86 93 112 114 116 123 158 178 192 197 214 251 273 303 306 316 321 323 343 363 364 370 371 386 400 429 451 479 513 528 530 533 542 551 552 554 558 564 569 570 571 575 599 600 614 649 656 660 671 681 725 727 801 820 829 832 846 847 849 891 903 904 938 954 956 957 958 962 971 972 979 1038 1065 1068 1069 1071 1072 1084 1085 1094 1098 1102 1158 1159 1160 1193 1209 1210 **10** 18 35 48 51 260 266 279 302 314 320 322 394 413 418 420 428 429 430 442 457 462 487 490 493 530 537 545 552 582 656 657 662 663 666 668 672 675 677 679 680 682 684 697 701 711 721 783 815 823 825 854 857 862 869 872 912 934 936 938 949 959 1024 1058 1119 1120 1147 **11** 34 40 56 98 116 128 146 184 201 210 248 257 261 276 280 296 345 358 364 375 428 435 437 472 487 526 527 561 575 586 605 612 658 659 690 714 715 755 783 794 810 826 830 832 834 835 838 839 851 868 869 870 891 906 916 917 918 919 968 970 1024 1061 1080 1126 1146 1196 1232 1238 1240 1245 1257 1265 1276 **12** 6 8 12 52 101 124 208 210 213 220 222 263 274 278 287 288 303 304 307 310 320 331 337 409 413 434 465 494 685 701 704 707 748 756 758 760 761 777 788 792 796 811 852 859 888 893 894 939 951 954 992 1002 1015 1016 1019 1031 1038 1039 1041 1042 1045 1046 1054 1058 1088 1096 1105 1108 1147 1153 1155 1193 1197 1215 1240 1265 1317 1319 1330 1361 1362 1363 1385 1402 1409 1412 1419 1434 1436 1473 1476 1488 1504 1509 1543 1556 1560 1586 1599 1607 1608 1614 1650 1654 1660 1661 1668 1756 1761 1769 1771 1909 **13** 51 53 114 160 185 186 230 248 271 273 274 275 359 414 512 532 566 567 705 709 787 792 814 816 817 819 828 829 836 853 861 863 864 865 866 869 873 880 881 900 901 924 929 944 971 991 992 993 994 995 1008 1015 1019 1020 1026 1029 1030 1031 1032 1035 1039 1049 1057 1071 1072 1073 1081 1085 1093 1105 1118 1132 1135 1150 1160 1163 1192 1198 1210 1211 1226 1231 1249 1263 1271 **14** 319 427 451 452 573 581 584 592 721 747 757 760 807 808 814 816 843 886 891 1058 1104 1118 1119 1120 1121 1142 1154 1167 1322 1338 1339 1342 1367 1441 1453 1477 1480 1492 1497 1502 1506 1507 1510 1520 1525 1532 1535 1559 1580 1581 1583 1586 1587 1589 1590 1591 **15** 11 53 81 91 92 93 195 253 254 259 260 261 266 267 274 290 306 325 326 328 329 355 376 378 380 381 382 384 385 395 398 399 406 408 428 429 431 434 435 437 438 442 447 452 476 477 478 488 490 493 523 539 548 550 551 556 557 558 573 600 602 603 613 645 742 745 746 767 779 787 794 805 819 832 833 852 865 871 876 878 947 983 1088 1098 1191 1192 1283 1291 1336 1338 1344 1347 1480 1516 1538 1542 1561 1638 1642 1658 1660 1674 1715 1834 1873 1890 1891 1893 1895 1971 1981 1985 1990 1996 2027 2081 2105 2126 2189 2192 2194 2196 2199 2200 2205 2217 2218 2221 2222 2254 2292 2297 2315 2316 2324 2333 2334

Z

Zarathustra (3) 1 728 14 363 1431
Zaretsky (1) 12 1091
zeal (3) 2 144 369 9 593
zealous (2) 9 12 10 36
zebra (1) 3 255
zenith (2) 17 1212 1609
zenith (1) 15 2176
zephyrs (1) 7 245
Zermatt (1) 14 1394
zero (1) 17 1247
zest (1) 8 1032
zigzag (2) 15 2686 4335
zigzagging (1) 7 445
zigzags (1) 15 4332
Zinfandel (2) 8 1009 1015
Zinfandel (5) 12 1224 16 1279 1280 1281
    1282
Zinfandel (1) 15 3977
Zinfandel's (1) 8 830
Zingari (1) 18 296
Zion (3) 8 14 17 333 759
Zion (2) 15 249 1619
zivio (1) 12 600
zmellz (1) 3 293
zodiac (1) 17 573
zodiac (1) 15 2274
zodiacal (2) 14 1092 17 1213
Zoe (5) 15 1315 2070 2195 4304
Zoe (1) 15 2524
Zoe (21) 15 1279 2021 2040 2123 2281 2641
    2700 2729 3507 3542 3549 3644 3661 3722 3776
    4028 4029 4049 4075 4260 4323
ZOE (76) 15 1282 1286 1294 1298 1303 1307
    1314 1320 1331 1337 1345 1352 1957 1969 1976
    1982 1989 1997 2002 2010 2024 2029 2062 2069
    2080 2125 2132 2283 2287 2296 2540 2560 2565
    2593 2695 2701 2707 2732 2872 2917 2952 3417
    3501 3510 3514 3523 3555 3564 3587 3633 3646
    3654 3662 3677 3682 3686 3691 3700 3705 3715
    3736 3754 3817 3832 3874 3923 3999 4004 4014
    4023 4087 4093 4116 4205 4265 4309
ZOE-FANNY (1) 15 2230
Zoe's (2) 15 2492 3550
zones (1) 17 202
Zoo (1) 15 1189
zoo (1) 13 1185
zoological (1) 17 575
Zouave (1) 12 1067
zouave's (1) 15 1853
Zrads (1) 13 933
zrads (3) 13 934
Zulu (1) 12 1510
Zulus (1) 1 156
Zut (1) 1 665